Chinese Society
under Communism:
A Reader

Chinese Society under Communism: A Reader

Edited by **WILLIAM T. LIU**

University of Notre Dame

John Wiley and Sons, Inc. NEW YORK LONDON SYDNEY

To My Father

Preface

Current literature on modern Chinese studies is still scattered in scholarly journals. Those studies found in monographic publications are primarily devoted to one or a few specific dimensions of Chinese society. This book represents an effort to give comprehensive coverage to a range of topics. Most of the selections are analytical and descriptive papers free of cumbersome technical terms and can easily be understood by intelligent laymen and undergraduate students. There are a number of selections taken from Chinese Communist' publications that may not be readily accessible except to students working at major libraries.

As a whole, the framework guiding selection hinges on the editor's approach to the problem as a sociologist. Communist China may be viewed as a social system. Like any other social system, its smooth functioning depends on how consistently each component is related to the other, how clearly the polity man define its goals, and how effectively various institutions can perform their functions without impairing such goals. In the last fifty years, the huge complex of control apparatus, subjected to various internal pressures, has undergone some drastic changes. The system itself experienced a painful period of adjustment and readjustment until a new and more efficient and centralized political machine was established by the Communist party. The traditional and age-old problem of control over an enormous population by the imperial government was by no means less significant when the party achieved a military triumph in 1949. Similar problems must now be solved by using different means guided by the Communist ideology. Like the old imperial regime, the Communist government has a high degree of centralization in respect to fundamental policies and values. The new regime differs fundamentally from the traditional empire, however, in that the high degree of *centralization* goes along with a great deal of *decentralization* in implementation of policy. Its power is extended to every level of the entire system and is manifested in the behavior and thought of every man, woman, and child. No longer is the old adage true: "the sky is high, the emperor is far away," for the new political power is channeled through every social group and its impact on the individual is proximate.

A substantial portion of the book, therefore, describes the stabilizing factors of traditional society, how it collapsed and how reintegration took place and finally provided the basis for a Communist victory in China. To introduce the reader to the past history of China does not mean that the minute details of the contemporary scene in China can always be explained by the past, but that an understanding of the present without some knowledge of the past is impossible.

In making selections, the major disappointment is that, while perhaps some social survey materials are available on various aspects of social life in China, little effort has been made to systematically and comprehensively study the attitudes and behavior of the Chinese people under the Communist regime. Under the present travel regulations imposed by the Chinese government, this is not possible. Efforts to make inferences on the behavior of the Chinese people, with some control of social class and regional differences, by interviewing refugees in Hong Kong are underway, chiefly the work of American scholars, but they are not yet available. Most research materials on China rely heavily, if not exclusively, upon published or unpublished documents and newspaper accounts. We know, for instance, more about the political and economic systems of China than we do about the lives, motivations, hopes, and despairs of the Chinese people. Material on interpersonal relationships, aspirations, and the details of child-rearing are conspicuously lacking. The selections presented on the health and mental lives of the people today may only suggest what has happened in China since 1949; more systematic materials are needed.

Many people have assisted in these selections. To the authors and publishers, the editor owes gratitude for permission to use their material. I am grateful to Morris Janowitz of the University of Chicago for his encouragement and suggestions, to Stephen Kertesz of the East European and Soviet Union Program of the University of Notre Dame for the generous allowance which made it possible for me to use several major libraries. I also wish to thank Henry J. Lethbridge and Mrs. Anita Li of the University of Hong Kong for making it possible for me to use the facilities and library materials at the University of Hong Kong during the summer of 1962. Mary O'Hara Ryan spent many hours of her valuable time in the library, for which I am most grateful. Last, I must acknowledge the contribution of my wife, May Lee, for her patience with me when my schedule necessitated frequent absences from home.

William T. Liu

October, 1966

Contents

Chinese Society
under Communism:
A Reader

Chapter I
Introduction

The subject of China under Communism is highly complex and little understood in spite of research efforts, published or unpublished, on various aspects of the meaning of the Communist victory in China. There are two basic problems with which a person must be confronted in order to understand the multiple aspects of Communist society in China. The first problem is to acquaint oneself with the historical background of China's long past. The second problem is to choose a perspective through which facts and events can be examined and explained. A number of experts argue that unless one understands the historical background of China's problems, particularly the period known as the "recent past," it is virtually impossible to know the meaning of various programs promulgated by the Communist government in Peking, or to know the significance of the changes wrought in China during the fifteen years since the defeat of the Nationalist government. This argument sounds reasonable enough, but one rarely knows just how recent is the "recent past." For example, it would be difficult to understand the power relations within the Communist party without going as far back as the beginning of the Nationalist regime of the 1920's and the 1930's. The Republican Revolution (1911), which was followed by a period of over thirty years of war-lordism and consolidation of power by the Nationalist party, like the Communist victory (1949), did not happen suddenly. Domestic problems and foreign pressures over the seven decades since the First Opium War (1840) and the ensuing years of intense nationalism merit careful study. Some believe that the social structure of the old China and the huge bureaucratic system of the empire are the keys for understanding the sociopolitical problems of China. Hence, for some, the "immediate past" encompasses historical material going back to the seventeenth century or beyond, and the value basis of the new Confucian ideology had its origin in the writings of Chu Hsi. The present concern, however, is primarily focused on transitions within the social system in recent decades. Historical facts are introduced only where relevant contrasts can be made, particularly with respect to the institutional patterns of control and their consequences.

Those investigators whose conceptual framework lies essentially in the structure of political and social institutions tend to look at *change* in China in terms of the structural characteristics of the *control apparatus* in the traditional society. Karl Wittfogel maintains that the control of certain irrigation systems and agricultural centers and the subsequent development of huge bureaucratic systems to maintain effective control were characteristic of *Oriental society* and fundamentally different from the modern European and American nation-states.[1] "Oriental society" shared the characteristics of other ancient and medieval empires: Egypt, Mesopotamia, India, and possibly the Incas and Aztecs as well. These ancient empires were dominated by vast bureaucracies under monolithic governments. S. N. Eisenstadt, after having carefully surveyed the organizational characteristics of ancient empires, identifies several elements that existed in all centralized bureaucratic states. One common feature was the ruler's "autonomous political goals;" another was the "limited differentiation of political activities and roles."[3] Imperial China is a prime example of such an imperial bureaurcracy. There was no opportunity, for example, for various groups—occupational or kinship organizations—to express political interests. All the bureaucratic units were designed specifically to serve as vehicles for the imperial power. The rigidity of the political machinery allowed no evolution or flexibility. When external pressures compelled change, the old system collapsed.

The idea of closely associating ideological development and the institutionalization of political processes in society was the basis of Max Weber's work on China.[4] In traditional China, the elite were what Weber called the "literati," or scholar-officials—from a broader stratum, the "gentry." "The Chinese Mandarin," observed Weber, ". . . has determined the whole destiny of China. . . ."[5] Hence, the works of Hsiao-tung Fei and others are particularly significant for understanding the basis of social control in traditional China.[6] Fei contends that the dual function of the gentry was to uphold the ideal goal of Confucian society on the one hand and, on the other, to represent local interests and protect the larger kin from being exploited by the imperial power.[7] Perhaps the institution of the gentry was so stabilized and self-contained that local government was never allowed to develop, except as an extension of the administrative arm of the imperial government. Fei's analysis, therefore, gives ideological substance to the role of institutional control in the classical society of China.

Closely related to this interpretation of the gentry at the pivotal institution in traditional China is the view wherein the *family* and kinship are considered as the hub of social control. Hsiao Kung-Chuan's careful description of the patterns of rural society and its control[8] may help the reader to understand the function of the clan and its role in the economic development of China in the recent past, as analyzed by Marion Levy.[9] More significant is Hsiao's own thesis that in imperial China the main problem always centered around the ways and means of maintaining firm control over the populace. The solution, as it was worked out in China during the successive dynasties from Ch'in to Ch'ing, consisted essentially in the development of an administrative apparatus designed to provide material needs, dispense intergroup justice, and inculcate the precepts of the Confucian classics in order to assure acceptance of, or acquiescence to, the existing political-social order. Clan rule, therefore, was designed to help the imperial government conserve rather than innovate. The Nationalist government, particularly in the two decades following 1928, faced the problems of maintaining an even balance between strong centralized control over regional, clan and local powers and advancement at the same time toward a constitutional government based on support from the peasants and villagers. Situational difficulties, such as the lack of effective local self-government, illiteracy, and political apathy, were too complex to be overcome within a short period of time. Government officials failed to develop a thorough and effective program for concrete action on a scale which would have broad, penetrating impact. Different factions of the Kuomintang party, motivated by the drive to seize more power within the ranks of the party, failed to implement the specific programs for social and economic reconstruction outlined by Dr. Sun Yet-sen. Movement toward a constitutional system was further blocked by both the internal power struggle and external political and military pressures, exerted chiefly by the military government of Japan. The result was a total societal failure which to a great extent paved the way for the Communist victory. The Communist party based its fundamental philosophy of government on what may be called a more sophisticated form of centralized control from the top— the Leninist concept of "democratic centralism."

A few years after the Communist victory, the large mass of mainland China's population was brought under a tight totalitarian control it had never before experienced. The strength of the Communist "organizational weapon," in contrast to that of the ancient monarchy, lay in the efficiency of its powerful monolithic political machinery, which extended deeply into every stratum of Chinese society. Aside from the ideological passion that compelled the Communists to translate ideas into concrete social action, the failure of the old system, which followed the Confucian blueprint separating the ruling elites from the mass of people, made it a practical necessity for the Communists to use the "people" as the basic weapon for a new political order. They were defined as anyone except the old landlords, reactionary bureaucrats, warlords, and urban capitalists, who are the enemies of the people. For

Marxist-Leninists, the gaps among groups—be they aristocracy, peasantry or the old middle class of the preindustrial societies, the new intellectual, the capitalists and the proletariat of the industrial countries—must be fully exploited for political purposes.

Mao's strategy stems essentially from the political wisdom of Marx. He grasped that the underlying factor in political control is the conflict of interests among groups. The ideological dynamism of a group must be sustained by continuous, visible conflicts of interest with other groups. The fact that government represents certain group interests, rather than a mythical public interest, can only be accepted if it is presented to the mass as the will of the majority. Although the means employed—terrorism, coercive persuasion, or positive incentives—may be contrary to the principles of democracy, the net effort of uniting the party with the mass is achieved.

Certain factors ordinarily identified as the "woes" of China may have been more responsible than the decline of institutional control for shaping the destiny of modern China. The urban economy in China depended mainly on the light handicraft of farm households. During the World War I years of 1917–1918, the nonagricultural sector of the farm economy actually expanded. This short-lived prosperity was soon followed by a large postwar influx to the urban markets of imported consumer goods from European countries. The Chinese countryside, already harassed by natural calamities and crop failures, suffered the death of its supplementary nonagricultural industries, so essential to the household economy. As a result, the cities were inundated by large waves of migration from the rural areas. Unemployment and unrest grew, sweeping the nation. On the political front, the ineffectiveness of the central government permitted the rise of sectional military powers during the first two decades of the Nationalist regime. The proliferation of regional powers not only severely impeded unification of the nation, but also made a constitutional democracy virtually impossible even if other sectors of the social system were ripe for its development. For military leaders, the only effective solution to any problem was to apply a combination of military and political strategy in dealing with each other. Ambitious to seize political power, but possessing only meager political means, the leaders of both the Chinese Communists and the Kuomintang recognized the necessity of relying on military force.[10]

There were, in fact, some similarities between the early political tactics of Mao and those of the Nationalists. Both the Communist party and the Kuomintang consisted of professional revolutionaries and new intellectual elements whose slogans of anti-imperialism had given them a common bond and their identity. They were, above all, nationalistic. These similarities are reflected in the Communist attitudes toward the traditional Chinese culture, attitudes best described as selectively critical.

But from superficial similarities of aim, i.e., to build a modern China, there soon emerged sharp disagreement on specific means of attaining the goal. The Kuomintang plan was essentially a modification of the bureaucratic government with an orientation toward modern Western democracy. The Nationalists were a small minority of new intellectuals who were supported by industrialists and landlords. The Communists, however, was able not only to attract the progressive bourgeoisie and new intellectuals, but to gain support from the proletariat and the peasants who constitute the people and who, under the determined leadership of the Chinese Communist party, could achieve ultimate success by seizing power through the inherent "law of contradictions."

The Communist party is the monolithic party of professional revolutionaries. Its strength lies in the homogeneity of its leaders' career backgrounds. During the years since the Party's victorious seizure of the political power in China, there have been only two threats to the unity of the top leadership. The first was the abortive attempt of Kao Kang and Jao Shu-Shih during 1954–1955 to overturn the rigid structure of power relations. The second, occurring during the fall of 1965, shows clear signs of large-scale power struggle and presumably represented a powerful effort of Mao's part to return to the revolutionary idealism. This purge involves some top ranking party members as well as nonparty intellectuals in the name of "The Great Proletarian Cultural Revolution." The long-range effect of the purge is yet to be carefully assessed by experts. The immediate effects, however, are reflected in the reorganization of cultural, educational, and propaganda machinery, including the disruption of selective college students for the fall of 1966.

For researchers and government strategists, the major difficulty is to detect, from whatever relevant material is available, evidence of internal cleavages among top leaders of the Communist party in China. Confronted by the tremendous task of building of viable political machinery, of improving the economic lot of the people, and of gaining international recognition among the members of the family of nations, there are undoubtedly continual debates and differences of opinions among the top leaders. In the future, the party hierarchy will inevitably change, chiefly because of the age structure of its members. Whether such change will make internal cleavages visible to the outside probably will depend on the background of the successors as well as on internal crises of international tensions. When members of the Central Committee's Politburo can no longer recall shared life experiences, as do the present members, whose bonds of unity were forged during the famous long march of the mid-thirties, divergence of opinion will be harder to contain and resolve. In spite of these possibilities, it is expected that the future leadership will continue Mao's strategy of using both political and military means to deal with domestic and international tensions. Changes in this basic strategy would require fundamental shifts in the social organization of the military, industry, and government. These shifts will evolve rather than occur drastically.

Above all, the party follows the Leninist tradition of "democratic centralism." It is directed by the 7 members of the Standing Committee of the Politburo along with 20 other members. The Central Committee of 193 regular and alternate members provides resources from which top leadership will be recruited; its function is to supervise the more than 17 million members and the hundreds of provincial and local party branches.

The rapid growth in party membership since the Communist victory in 1949 notwithstanding, the party and the Young Communist League total only about 5 per cent of the entire population. The success of the party in controlling the population results from a combination of several tactics commonly known as Maoism. For example, the technique of the "mass line method," employed to organize every individual into various groups for political purposes, has been communication innovation. The person is de-individualized through a series of successive or concurrent memberships according to sex, age, occupational and religious status. Rather than generating new political ideas and participating in political communities in order to articulate the self-interest of the group, "mass groups" are designed to disseminate information and to work out the ways and means of implementing policies within the specific framework of the group. Groups are organized, therefore, to serve as intermediaries between the decision makers of the centralized government and the mass of the populace. They are the vehicles through which the party realizes one-way control. Mao describes the mass line method as "from the masses, to the masses," and "the linking of the general to the specific."[11] Secondly, the principles of "democratic centralism" gave the party complete control over the administrative structure at all levels. The distinction between the party and the government, therefore, is blurred by the dominance of the party over the government and, concurrently, the occupancy by key party members of all important positions in the administration and the armed forces. Other minor parties exist, but only to give the impression of "democracy," without its substance.

The control apparatus does not limit its functions to the party alone, although it is "led" by the party. The principle of the mass line method is implemented by a careful and deliberate effort to create mass organizations which, together with other minor parties and "study groups," form the familiar "united front," supplying the links in a chain of control extending over the entire population of 700 million.

Perhaps an important distinction between the Kuomintang and the Communist government in implementing changes and exercising political power over the huge population of China is that the former made only expedient changes in the system of government to meet the demand for a democratized system, while leaving intact the essential features of the old society in all but several urban centers. Whether by the poor design of Kuomintang architects or because of internal and external pressures, the course of historical development that resulted in a total defeat on the mainland reflected the lack of an effective central government as well as the absence of mass support. The Nationalist government's plans were not designed to motivate political enthusiasm among the masses, even if they did stimulate small groups of intellectuals and urban workers who would otherwise have remained politically apathetic. A number of important legal and social reforms had taken place since and before the 1911 revolution. The changes that took place during the Nationalist regime were limited to a few urban centers, and their impact has been exaggerated, perhaps because they were highly visible. The Communists, on the other hand, aimed to bring about a basic change in the entire social system. The Communist party and the government, with the support of mass organizations, could provide the vehicle for organized and planned change. The party leaders in China deeply believe that the moving force lies in the motivations and attitudes of men, and that external persuasion must be supported by the "faith" of men. It is the doctrine and the logic of Marxism-Leninism that unite and activate the control apparatus, but it is the process of interpersonal encounters—including mutual support, antagonistic suspicion, collective decision making, and the like—that gives a unique dynamism to the total process of change.

But social change does not depend upon the structure of the polity alone. How political machinery exercises its power and how a set of ideological principles is interpreted depends on the conditions underlying use of the power or the application of the ideology. In this perspective there is more to the problem than control apparatus alone. Other aspects of the social system must be mobilized for the implementation of the goals set forth by the party. Economic problems of capital investment, production, transportation, and marketing, for example, involve simultaneously the shifting of activities in foreign policy and the adjustment of the educational calendar and the content of trade and academic programs. Educational problems in turn require comprehensive planning of the training and research resources, with meticulous attention to the labor supply in various sectors of the economy. The organization of the military must be consistently geared to the party's international stance. It is not enough to speak of planned change without being concerned for the substance of, and the preconditions for, change.

Following the Soviet example of primary emphasis on heavy industry and efficient political control of labor force allocation and manpower training, the Chinese Communists are building up their economy at a rate that could be an important model for other developing countries in southeast Asia and elsewhere. When the Communists took over the mainland in 1949, they were confronted with an almost complete lack of industrial expertise. In addition, the regime inherited a war-torn, highly inflationary economy. The party worked out a strategy that tolerated a period of co-existence between the state and private enterprise. Although Communist ideology required a curtailment of private enterprise in China, the actual rate of reduction and the forms of control by the party over private business depended upon the strength of the economy itself. During this period (1949–1952), the main objectives were to rehabilitate the economy, to repair and to build transportation systems, and to initiate a number of large-scale public works. On the agricultural front, between 1949 and 1952, the Chinese Communists implemented a thorough land reform and prepared to replace the traditional rural clan organizations with collectivization of the land and work force after 1952. This initial three-year phase served as a transitional period toward the ultimate communization.

In spite of the economic strains of the Korean War, the Communists were successful in implementing their initial economic rehabilitation objectives. Thus, in 1951, they commenced long-range economic planning in the form of several successive Five-Year Plans to be inaugurated in 1953. Clearly, with Soviet assistance, Communist China piled up an impressive five-year record of overall economic growth. It was on the basis of these early economic successes that the Communists were to push forward their efforts to build a socialist society. By 1958, however, the "Great Leap Forward" had resulted in a disastrous failure. The Second Five-Year Plan, which was to follow at the conclusion of the First Five-Year Plan, was in fact five year-to-year plans. The lesson of the 1958–1961 economic failure led the Chinese Communists to rely almost totally on their own technical and material resources. In capturing the spirit of "self-reliance," the mass control and propaganda machineries had to be mobilized to promote the economic goals of the party-government leadership. The political organizations directed mass movements for nationwide reeducation on understanding the class struggle, training new technical experts, experimenting with new agricultural methods, and establishing half-study and half-work schools.

By 1963, the evidence showed a gradual economic recovery in China. With an annual increase of 2 per cent in population, the per capita yield, however, had been less encouraging. The progress made between 1961 and 1963 must not be exaggerated. It must be noted that the recovery did not exceed the 1958 level in several areas of the economy. In the long run, China will continue to suffer from the accelerated educational processes operative during these "hunger years." Despite massive government efforts aimed at short-term development of scientific manpower to meet current demands, the long-term problem of filling the gap between top-level minds in science and engineering and the growing number of professional technicians on a lower level has become more serious in the past ten years. Too preoccupied by immediate crises and demands, the Chinese Communists have not been able to resolve the conflict between their ambition to increase the number of top scientists and the narrow demands of politics. Peking's policies of self-imposed isolation virtually cut off able young men from the vital sources of knowledge usually found in the West. Ideological passion may enhance the spirit of self-reliance, but it also limits the scope of China's total scientific training program. China will suffer from the high cost of her pride.

The economic future of Communist China depends on a very delicate balance of economic pragmatism and ideological commitment. This has been shown by the retreat from the ultimate goals of communization of the rural population outlined in the Central Committee's resolution of August, 1958. Private plots, which symbolize the party's concession to material incentives, still exist, but new trends toward a more rigorous political activism among the poor peasants are again appearing on the horizon. After nearly four years of economic recuperation, a promised new upsurge is outlined in the Third Five-Year Plan scheduled to begin in 1966,[12] coinciding with the new official policy of returning to collectivization on a larger scale and to local economic projects with the slogan "flying leap." Whether such new moves will prove to be an ideological triumph remains to be seen. The situation as it has been developing in Communist China demonstrates that the relationship between the polity and the economy has a "double-bind" effect; each contributes to the other in the process of the planned social change.

Economic problems, like educational problems, are in large measure related to the enormous population growth in Communist China. Illiteracy has always been a major problem in underdeveloped countries. In spite of the government's energetic efforts to reduce the illiteracy rate, there is still a huge gap between the full-time enrollment in primary schools and the number of children of school age toward the end of the fifties. As a part of the Great Leap Forward in 1958, the Communists had become committed to the rapid expansion of educational facilities. To implement the projected plan, the regime faced a persistent dilemma in allocating scarce capital: the requirements for economic investment vied with growing expenditures for education. A resolution was worked out whereby the responsibilities for school expansion were to be undertaken by local social groups. The outcome was the introduction of half-time study and half-time work schools.

These schools, which first received national publicity in early 1958, soon became the pivotal educational undertaking in rural communes.

The same experiment took place in the early sixties on more advanced educational levels in Kiangsi Province and, beginning in 1965, new types of half-time study and half-time work projects appeared in the urban scene on a noticeable scale.[13] The significance of the experiment lies not only in its crucial role of solving basic educational problems in a country with an enormous population increment, but also in the fact the experiment embodied the political concept of study closely integrated with productive labor.

Planned social change depends on the government's accurate estimate of the vital statistics of the country. The first census, conducted in 1953, revealed a reported total figure of close to 600 million on the mainland. The tremendous size of the population induced leaders of the party to endorse birth control programs in spite of their ideological commitment of Marxism. Detailed studies of some areas based on the 1953 report showed an average annual crude birth rate of 37 per one thousand population and a death rate of only 17 per one thousand.[14] According to the official report given by the Chinese government, an increase of 65 million was reported between 1952 and 1957. Meanwhile, the rural population continued to increase in spite of large-scale rural migration to urban areas.[15] As a result, the state was forced to wage continuous campaigns to persuade people to return to the countryside in order to ease the surplus of urban workers. Improved sanitation and health services in rural areas eventually will further reduce the death rate. The net increase, according to the present trend, will bring the total Chinese population to 1 billion within the next fifteen years. What is certain, however, is that the efficient political machinery will inaugurate a much more effective birth control campaign if the Communist leaders find it convenient to follow the Malthusian rather than the Marxist interpretation of population growth and economic development.[16]

In reality, however, the system as it worked out in Communist China had already shown a direct conflict between *rationally efficient* and ideologically correct methods of solving problems. A monolithic power center by no means prescribes a rigid structure of the system itself. In the early days of economic rehabilitation, for instance, the Communists had to borrow the Soviet experience with factory management together with the technical know-how of factory directors who might be party secretaries. The early tendency toward "parallelization" of authority, that is, the separation of political and economic power, ran contrary to the basic organizational principles of the Chinese Communists. It was later corrected by the system of collective responsibility of the party committee, which combines both the political and technical elites of the organization. Franz Schurman's analytical description of the process of finding a "satisfactory solution" by trial and error in his paper on industrial management in Communist China shows tremendous flexibility in the system.[17] Communist society in China is, therefore, distinctly marked by its maintenance of tight control over the vast majority of individuals as well as flexibility in adapting to the new demands of a changing environment.

The duality of a powerful centralized control machine and a remarkable capacity for change through a high degree of flexibility in the political system of Communist China is noteworthy. The imperial government of China was centralized in decision making; however, its power was undercut by the distance of the capital from the vast remote land area of the country. The old political system was so marked by rigidity that the advent of new forces would inevitably destroy the system rather than allow for alteration through trial and error. Between the imperial era and the Communist regime a period of close to half a century of incipient change, marked, especially during the twenties, by tremendous intellectual vigor, introduced new patterns of thinking which had an enormous impact for change in major institutions. The Communist leaders were able to take advantage of the momentum. The changes that have taken place in China since the Communist victory of 1949 surprise no one, whereas the innovations of the Nationalists had caused considerable astonishment. These changes are expected, even though many of them are accomplished through the use of terror. With an unusual degree of top-level stability, the individuals in positions of authority could readily adapt to change without threat to themselves. The tight control apparatus, therefore, facilitates rapid and comprehensive change rather than prevents it.

The alteration of the political and economic systems invariably will require the change of institutional values in other sectors. Undoubtedly, the Chinese Communists did not anticipate that all citizens would welcome the new regime with equal degrees of enthusiasm, or react to change with blind hostility. The older segment of the population can be reeducated, but their potential contributions to the new polity are limited. It is the new generation of Chinese citizens whose thoughts and behavior are of greater importance to the leaders of Communist China. Since no single institution can have a greater impact on the socialization of the younger generation than the family, the design for family change was made with particular care and with extreme caution. Contrary to what might be the general impression about family life in Communist China, laws with regard to family behavior, including marriage, divorce, and the care of the young, have been enacted and executed with tighter institutional control than ever before. To complement the objectives and functions of the family, the Communist party explicitly promulgated new programs and new objectives for all institutions that could be mobilized to transform the old society into a new one. The transformation of institutional objectives in education, the arts, literature, work and leisure, and the family, all helped to reidentify their participants as new social realities, with new missions and new hopes, reflecting and implementing the social change to which they owe their existence.

The current laws on marriage and family life are designed to break the grip of the old on the young. The objective here is to promote value change through intergenerational conflict never experienced in the traditional Chinese society. The new structure of the family itself promotes a different kind of morality and interpersonal ethics. The age gap between generations in terms of authority-obedience relationships disappears. All men, all women, are therefore, treated as equals with regard to duties and responsibilities, rewards and punishments. All are, in fact, contributing units to the economy and the polity.

A number of contemporary writers, surveying the trends discussed above, have characterized modern China under Communism as a "society controlled by mass media."[20] If one interprets such a concept as different from a "mass society," it may be both intriguing and deserving of more systematic analysis. The two views of a *mass society* are not applicable to Communist China. The first model of mass society is that of a so-ciety—presumably most western industrial nations—made up of masses of segregated, isolated individuals, interdependent yet lacking in any central unifying value or purpose. In this sense, mass society refers to a condition of personal existence.[21] The second model refers to a kind of institutional participation—a mass involvement. It means that the centers of economic, political, and leisure life have to take account of and adapt to the interests and desires of large numbers of people. It, in a sense, means that a large number of people take part in political activities. Neither one of the two views of mass society can be used to analyze the conditions now existing in China. The freedom from traditional bonds in China is merely the result of an organized and methodically controlled removal of China's past from the present. It does not leave a moral vacuum. It has, in fact, imposed a sense of direction and purpose on every individual in the society. The individual's thoughts and behavior are supported by many well-organized and closely knit groups with which he can identify his existence. Mass participation in the political and economic life of the country, on the other hand, is well designed by a central authority, to which few individuals have access and where important decisions are made.

The nature of Chinese society under Communism, its impact on the personality development of the new generation of Chinese citizens, its direction and its pace of change, and other pertinent data are still little known. Extensive research must be done and the cumulative results must be coordinated and cross-referenced for meaningful explanations. Our original task, in its simplest form, was to introduce the reader to the historical continuity of, as well as the revolutionary changes in, Chinese ideas. To do this it was thought necessary to give details of the various institutional frameworks and the processes of their control apparatus in the social system itself. Our objective is to point out that the present government in China is both Communist and Chinese. Many of the research materials introduced here will enable the reader to find out which *orthodox* Marxist and Leninist ideological precepts have been put into effect in the course of socio-political development in the last twenty years, which have been modified or abandoned, and for what reasons. To a great extent, the changes that have taken place occurred within the limits and possibilities of directed social change from a predominantly agrarian society to an industrially oriented society. These limits themselves are set by the resources and ideological baseline of the Communist society.

Communist China has learned a great deal from its past experience, as well as that of the Soviet Union, about the need for authority and discipline. The original prerevolutionary theory of the Bolsheviks was modified after 1917 when the Communist party assumed political responsibilities in the Soviet Union. Effective political control over the masses was then achieved by a curious amalgam of polite terror and primitive "grass-roots" democracy.[22] These two coexisting elements have long marked the characteristic rigidity of the Soviet political bureaucracy. The result was a progressive weakening of political enthusiasm from the central hierarchy to the local level of the bureaucracy and ultimately among the population at large. The successes and failures of orthodox Leninism in the Soviet Union must be also evaluated against the changing nature of the economy itself. Some authors strongly believe that Bolshevik doctrine must be reformulated, and adapted to the problems that are common to any industrial society.[23] Hence it may also be true that a modification of Maoism in Communist China is inevitable as industrialization develops further and that certain features inherent in a modern industrial society cannot be eliminated without destroying the entire system. Communist China will provide an excellent opportunity for testing this hypothesis.

Notes

1. Karl A. Wittfogel, *Oriental Despotism: A Comparative Study of Total Power*, New Haven: Yale University Press, 1957.

2. S. N. Eisenstadt, *The Political Systems of Empires*, New York: The Free Press of Glencoe, 1962.

3. *Ibid.*, p. 19.

4. Max Weber, *Essays in Sociology*, translated and edited by H. H. Gerth and C. Wright Mills, New York: Oxford University Press, 1946.

5. *Ibid.*

6. Fei Hsiao-tung *China's Gentry*, Chicago: University of Chicago Press, 1953, Chung-li chang. *The Chinese Gentry*, Seattle: University of Washington Press, 1955.

7. Fei, *op. cit.*

8. Hsiao Kung-Chuan, *Rural China: Imperial Control in the Nineteenth Century*, Seattle: University of Washington Press, 1960.

9. Marion Levy, "Contrasting Factors in the Modernization of China and Japan," *Economic Development and Cultural Change*, 1954, pp. 162–177.

10. Cf. Tang Tsou and Morton H. Halperin, "Mao Tse-tung's Revolutionary Strategy and Peking's International Behavior," *American Political Science Review*, LI (March, 1965), pp. 80–99.

11. Mao Tse-tung, "On Methods of Leadership," June 1, 1943, in *Selected Works*, Vol. 4, New York: International Publishers, 1954–56, pp. 111–113.

12. *Current Scene*, "Decision for an 'Upsurge,' " III (April 15, 1965), 17.

13. Paul Harper, "Closing the Education Gap," *Current Scene*, III (March 15, 1965) 15.

14. A. Doak Barnett, *Communist China and Asia*, New York: Vintage Books, 1960, p. 54.

15. *Peking Daily Worker*, December 30, 1957, SCMP, 1963.

16. See Ma Yin-ch'u, "A New Theory of Population," *Current Background*, No. 469 (March 27, 1958).

17. See Franz Schurmann, "Organizational Contrast Between Communist China and Soviet Union," in Kurt London (ed.), *Unity and Contradiction*, New York: Frederick Praeger, 1962, pp. 65–81.

18. Cf. N. S. Esendadt, "Transformation of Social, Political, and Cultural Orders in Modernization," *American Sociological Review*, 30 (October, 1965), pp. 659–673.

19. K. C. Yang, *The Chinese Family in the Communist Revolution*, Cambridge, Mass.: The M.I.T. Press, 1959.

20. Cf. Frederick Yu, *Mass Persuasion in Communist China*, Frederick Praeger, 1964.

21. Including more recent works on alienation and *anomie*.

22. Cf. Barrington Moore, Jr., *Soviet Politics: The Dilemma of Power*, New York: Harper and Row, 1965 edition.

23. Notably the works of Alex Inkeles.

Chapter II
Backgrounds of Communist China's Social Structure

Students of American society may find that to understand its social institutions it is necessary to trace their development from the medieval concepts of property and property rights and the normative foundation of feudalism. When industrialization in England was beginning, the traditional value orientation that dominated the quality of social relationships could be characterized by what John Stuart Mill called the "theory of dependence." Authority and power were associated with property and property rights. A man's virtue was proven by his obedience; the structure of authority was both the expression of the prevailing value of *lineality* and its sustaining force. The rise of social Darwinism toward the end of the nineteenth century led to an affirmation of the struggle for existence, which, added to the classic economic argument of "scarcity," helped to shape a new type of motivational force conducive to competition as a style of life, with its consequences of innovation, reason, and freedom.

Within the cultural and historical framework of a competitive society, the dominant note is insistence on the individual's rights. The society that places dominant value in its economic institutions, as Parsons and Shils argue, determines social relations mainly by private property. The state exists, therefore, for the maintenance and protection of individual rights and, in R. H. Tawney's words, "the fundamental of all rights was private property—property absolute and unconditioned."

Philosophers in the Western societies would argue, therefore, that the fundamental concept of civil and business organizations lay in the medieval foundations of property rights. Western individualism thus has come to *reflect* and *express* its own experience of reality, as it has been affected by the "struggle for power," which has given a culturally shaped meaning to authority.

The Confucian society of traditional China had a different set of experiences. The need for social power is a universal human phenomenon, as is economic scarcity. The specific mode of regulating interpersonal struggles for power, however, depends by and large upon the institutional framework of the society. In the classical Chinese society, the solution was largely patterned by Confucian ethics. It was the all-embracing concept of interpersonal ethics that provided a basis for the political, familial, and legal institutions in old China and that gave remarkable stability to the society throughout many dynastic periods.

Just as the student who wishes to understand Western social institutions must examine the normative structure of feudalism, a student would find it immensely helpful to study the institution of family and clan to gain insight into the fabric of Chinese society. Hsiao's work on the social structure of rural China is an exhaustive attempt to describe the mechanism of political control through the clan organization. Similarly, Fei's earlier analysis of the role of the gentry unveils the subtle political role played by scholars and learned men in an era when local political organizations were weak or nonexistent and when representatives of local interests in the capital were needed. The bureaucrat-scholar and the elaborate system of clan rules fulfilled many of the functions of a complicated legal system; consequently, the latter one was not allowed to develop. Franz Michael's paper presents background for understanding the functional relationships among the imperial bureaucracies, the clan, and the local administrative units.

The official-scholar, as a social institution, monopolized the function of role allocation in the traditional Chinese society. Confucius believed that all occupations are trivial except that of the scholar, who was the theologian of the society. Social ascendence and mobility patterns, therefore, were determined *rationally* by civil examination. Illegitimate means of social mobility did exist, but these were ignored. The abandonment of the civil service examination, therefore, created a vacuum in the institutional structure of role allocation. The collapse of the stable control apparatus led to a new phase of Chinese history carefully documented in Marion Levy's paper. Attempts to find more adequate answers to new problems faced by the society are ably analyzed by Chow and by Ch'ien. The reader may be surprised to learn of the remarkable developments that occurred during the transitional period of the Republican government; their significance has not always been noticed by students of modern Chinese history.

Natural and Human Resources

1. GEOGRAPHY, PEOPLE, AND NATURAL RESOURCES

CHANG-TU HU ET AL.

Geography and Population

An area of four million square miles and a population of well over six hundred fifty million people make China one of the largest and most populous countries in the world today. It compares favorably with the other Pacific nations in natural resources and geographical location. Though possessing an extensive coast line with many good harbors on the eastern seaboard, China developed as a land power rather than as a sea power, the fertile plains of North China being the historic center of Chinese expansion and influence.

Besides a certain resemblance in size and contour (see Outline Map of China Superimposed on the United States), China and the United States, lying largely in the same latitudes (25° N. to 45° N.), share a comparable, continental-type climate and vegetation. There is, however, a marked difference in topography. Whereas the United States, bounded by two oceans, tends toward an equal development of east and west, China expands from the loess highland and the central plains eastward and southward to the sea. In the northwest, China has a vast hinterland of deserts and plateaus screened off from Soviet Central Asia by high mountain ranges. The borders between southwestern China and India and Burma are as yet undelimited.

A majority of Chinese cities are found in the central, eastern, and southeastern areas favored by a temperate climate and gentle terrain. The west, though known to abound in natural resources, has remained only partially explored because of its adverse terrain and climate. Improved transportation and communications will doubtless change this development pattern. Exploration, irrigation, and reclamation projects in the northwest and southwest have been incorporated in the Communist government's five-year plans and the

SOURCE: Selected from Chang-tu Hu et al., *China: Its People, Its Society, Its Culture*, New Haven: HRAF Press, 1960, pp. 40, 42–47, 49, 55–57, 65–68, 95–96, and 100–101. Reprinted by permission of HRAF Press.

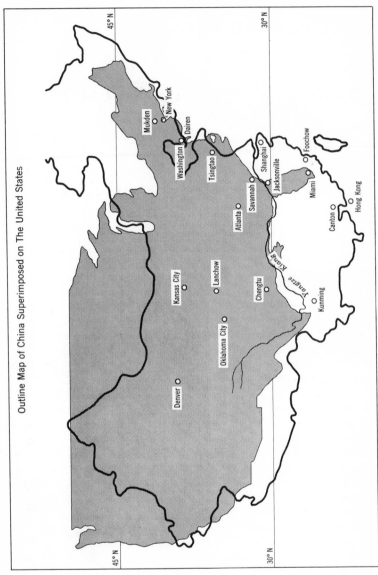

Outline Map of China Superimposed on The United States

Winfield, Gerald F., *China: The Land and the People* (New York: William Sloane Associates, 1948), p. 20.

industrialization of Manchuria is fast transforming it into an area comparable to the northern New Jersey-New York complex.

PHYSICAL SETTING

Extending over 2,500 miles from its Pacific coast to the Pamir plateau in Central Asia, China exhibits great variety in topographical relief. Surrounding the plateau of Tibet in the southwest are mountains the loftiest of which rise over 25,000 feet while some despressions in the Turfan basin in Sinkiang are 141 feet below sea level. The Mongolian plateau, the world's widest, stretches for a distance of over 2,000 miles. The desolate high plateaus in Tibet and Tsinghai (Kokonor), enclosed by mountain ranges, contrast with such rich lowlands as the Red Basin of Szechwan and the lake basins along the middle and lower Yangtze valley. Great fertile plains, particularly in the coastal delta area of the great rivers, are located amidst large masses of hills and uplands.

Mountains, Rivers, and Harbors. From the Pamirs, a central mountain knot of all the mountains of Asia, four major limbs of the Central Asia ramparts extend toward China. The Altai, T'ien Shan, Kunlun, and Himalayan mountain systems each consist of several parallel chains and form the chief watersheds of all the principal rivers in China. Their passes afford natural land routes between China and its neighbors in Mongolia and Central Asia.

The Altai and Himalayan systems form the natural boundaries of China in the northwest and southwest; the T'ien Shan divides Sinkiang; the Kunlun system branches all over the country, forming the backbone or skeleton of its topography. Running eastward from the Pamirs, the Kunlun system divides the Tarim basin of Sinkiang from the high plateaus of Tibet, then branches off into three separate chains: (1) the Altin Tagh–Nan Shan ranges in the north, which divide the inland drainage of the Mongolian plateau from the Yellow River; (2) the Tsinling–Ta-pieh ranges in the center, which form the major watershed between the Yellow River and the Yangtze; and (3) the Thanglha Ri range in the south, which meets the eastern end of the Himalayan system in Sikang and northwestern Yunnan.

In addition to these four major systems are two mountain groups in the northeast and southeast, the so-called Sinic mountains, which seem to have no direct relation to any of the major systems in the west. In between the mountains of the northern group are valley plains, such as the Chiao valley plain between T'ai Shan and Lao Shan in the peninsula of Shantung; and the Sungari-Liao plain surrounded by Hsing-an Ling (Khingan), Ch'ang-pai Shan, and the Jehol hills in Manchuria. The southern ranges, the Nan Ling, form a major geographical divide between the lower Yangtze and the various short independent streams which flow separately into the southwestern China Sea.

Since the general topography of China orientates toward the east, all the great rivers flow eastward to the Pacific. In the northeast, the Amur (Hei-lung Chiang) drains a great part of the Manchurian basin as it winds along its 2,500-mile course. Though navigation is limited to small steamers and native craft, these can go as far as the confluence of its two upper reaches and even beyond during the flood season. Other Manchurian rivers include the

Liao Ho, the chief river in southern Manchuria, as well as the Tumen and the Yalu, which form the boundary between China and Korea. Carrying very little ordinary shipping, the importance of the Yalu lies primarily in hydro-electric power development and in its timber traffic.

The main river of North China, and the second largest in the country, is the Yellow River (Huang Ho), which acquires its characteristic yellowish muddy color from the tributary rivers of the loess plateau of Kansu. From Kansu it winds 2,980 miles through the northern provinces eastward to Shantung where it empties into the Gulf of Chihli (Po Hai). The Yellow River valley includes an area of 600,000 square miles. Abundant silt and an almost unvarying water level limit its transportation capacity, creating as well a control problem. To keep the flow channeled, the Chinese have been continuously building up its embankments with the result that the present river bed is 16 feet or more above the general level of the surrounding plain, held to its course by man-made levees. Along its lower course, the Yellow River floods regularly, particularly in late summer and early autumn, and no important towns have grown up along its banks.

Central China is drained mainly by the Yangtze and its numerous tributaries. The Yangtze (Ch'ang Chiang) is by far the largest river in China. From sources only 50 miles (as the crow flies) from those of the Yellow River, it travels 3,237 miles, draining over 700,000 square miles. From the confluence of its two headwaters in the upland of southern Tsinghai, it flows southward to western Szechwan as the Chin-sha Chiang; then, beyond the great bend in northwestern Yunnan it turns sharply to the east and traverses the whole length of Central China to the East China Sea.

The Yangtze can be divided into three parts: a torrential upper course that includes many rapids and falls; a middle course of 960 miles, on parts of which (such as the Yangtze gorges) navigation is limited to junks and river streamers of no more than 200 tons; and a lower course of 1,062 miles navigable by both coastal and ocean-going vessels. On its way to the sea, the Yangtze is divided by the Ch-ung-ming Island into two channels. The southern channel, known as Wu-sung, has a deeper entrance closer to Shanghai, from which ocean-going vessels can sail up to Hankow, 630 miles inland.

In Central China, the Huai Ho and the Fu-ch'un Chiang are next to the Yangtze in importance. The Fu-ch'un Chiang is one of the main rivers along the Chekiang coast. The Huai, the largest river between the Yangtze and the Yellow, is unique in that it is the only long river without a natural outlet, and consequently it frequently floods.

Important rivers that drain the southeastern coastal regions are the Min Chiang and the Chu Chiang (Pearl River). The Min is navigable over most of its course although upstream navigation is rather difficult in the flood season. The Pearl, the chief river in Kwangtung and Kwangsi, is the fourth largest river in China and its valley covers a drainage area of 150,000 square miles. The Pearl is a general name for a network of three waterways, which meet south of Canton to form a big estuary consisting of many channels separated by a number of islets. The main eastern channel, Hu Men (Boca Tigris), enters the sea near Hong Kong, while the main western channel flows close to Macao.

Farther southwest are two independent rivers, the Mekong (Lan-ts'ang Chiang) and the Red River (Yüan Chiang), of which only the upper courses are in Chinese territory. Both flow southward through a large part of Indochina before entering the sea, but are unnavigable in China.

Pacific drainage accounts for 50 per cent of China's total drainage area; inland drainage, 39 per cent; and the Indian Ocean and the Arctic, the remaining 6 and 5 per cents respectively. Today, with Outer Mongolia and Tannu Tuva independent, none of the Arctic drainage except a small portion of the upper Irtysh (one of the upper reaches of the Ob River) via the Zaisan Nor is in China Proper. Fairly long stretches of the upper reaches of the principal rivers of the Indian Ocean drainage are in China, but these rivers enter the sea through other nations' territories. The Salween (Nu Chiang), the Irrawaddy, and the Tsangpo (Ya-lu-ts'ang-pu) all have their sources in the mountainous regions of Tibet and western Szechwan. The Tsangpo flows eastward from its Himalayan home to drain southern Tibet, then bends abruptly south to India, where under the name of Brahmaputra it merges with the Ganges to empty into the Bay of Bengal. The upper courses of both the Salween and Irrawaddy drain a large portion of western Yunnan before they reach the sea by way of Burma.

Inland drainage covers a number of upland basins in the vast dry interior of North and Northwest China. Due to meager rainfall and difficult terrain, the inland rivers are as a whole rather small and lack outlets to the sea. They generally flow into lakes or die in the desert, most of them entirely inside China. The Tarim, the longest inland river in the country, consists of numerous streams coming down from the mountains in southern Sinkiang.

While the inland rivers are valuable for irrigation in the dry interior of northern and northwestern China, their water supply from the snow-clad mountains is rather limited. On the other hand, the upper courses of the Red River, Mekong, Salween, and Irrawaddy provide potential sources for the development of waterpower in the plateaus of Southwest China. There are too many torrents and rapids, especially in the summer monsoon season, to make navigation possible. No transportation is available along their courses except on some parts of the upper Red River, the upper Irrawaddy, and the east-west stretch of the Tsangpo, where small native craft are sometimes seen. At 12,000 feet the Tsangpo or upper Brahmaputra is the highest navigable river in the world.

The coast line of China extends from the mouth of the Yalu River in the northeast to the mouth of the Pei-lun River in the south. It forms a great arc with the peninsulas of Liaotung and Shantung in the north and that of Luichow in the south protruding respectively into the Yellow Sea and the South China Sea. The coast is separated from the Pacific Ocean by a chain of islands and archipelagos, such as Liu-ch'iu, Taiwan, Pescadores (P'eng-hu), Hainan, and the Pratas (Tung-sha), Paracel (Hsi-sha), and Spratly (Nan-sha) groups, which not only gives China a continuous series of partially enclosed coastal seas like the Gulf of Chihli, the Yellow Sea, the East China Sea, and the South China Sea, but also forms the two great gulfs of Liaotung in the north and Tonkin in the south.

The general configuration of the coast line comes to a length of 2,500 miles. If the minor inlets are included, the distance amounts to nearly 7,000 miles. Of this total, some 3,000 miles are sandy and the rest, rocky. The sandy coast is characterized by wide, relatively flat beaches on a shore line of long straight stretches coupled with sweeping curves. The adjoining country is often low and flat with marshes or lakes. Shoals and generally shallow water are usual along these sandy coastal areas although good natural harbors, as at Shanghai, can be found at the mouths of the larger rivers. In contrast, the rocky parts of the coast of China are often highly indented. Fairly deep seas broken by numerous islands and islets are characteristic of these coastal areas. Such conditions create many good natural harbors but the characteristics of the hinterlands, hilly to mountainous, limit the exploitation of these coastal features. Thus no port of importance has been developed except at or near the mouth of a large river, as at Canton. The big port planned for South China is to be situated at Huang-pu (Whampoa) on the estuary of the Pearl River.

Other ports of importance are An-tung at the mouth of the Yalu River, Port Arthur (Lü-shun), and Dairen (Ta-lien) on the Liaotung Peninsula. Port Arthur is the leading naval base and Dairen the chief commercial port of Manchuria. There are also three developed ports along the Shantung coast; Chefoo (Yen-t'ai) on the north; Wei-hai-wei, not far from the tip of the peninsula; and Tsingtao, lying on its southernmost part at the entrance to the bay. Farther south, numerous good harbors can be found all along the coast. Some of the moderately developed ports are Yin-hsien (Ningpo), Foochow, Amoy, Swatow, and Chan-chiang.

Climate. Although most of China lies inside the temperature belt, it has an extreme continental climate with a summer temperature (especially in Central and South China) higher than that of the tropics and a winter cold which in the far north is more severe than in the frigid zone. In winter the temperature decreases rapidly from south to north, ranging from an average of 60° F. south of the Nan Ling range to about 40° F. along the middle and lower Yangtze valley, to just below freezing or about 30° F. in the North China plain and southern Manchuria, and to well below freezing at about 0° F. and −17° F. in central and northern Manchuria respectively. In summer the temperature is more nearly uniform over the whole country, with a July mean of 80° F., but northern China has much cooler nights and a shorter hot period than southern China.

Rainfall is essentially seasonal, most of it occurring in the summer. The amount of precipitation decreases from south to north, with an annual average of 60–80 inches in the Pearl River valley and the hilly land along the southeastern coast, 40–60 inches in the Yangtze valley, about 25 inches over the North China plain, and less than 10 inches in the interior. To the northeast, in the Manchurian basin, the rainfall varies from about 30 inches in southeastern areas to less than 10 inches in the Barga district and the eastern Gobi.

Most of the later summer rain along the southeastern coast is due to typhoon influence. Typhoons bring some cooling, a temporary relief from the prolonged summer heat, but also cause damage to crops and to a considerable degree determine the type planted. The crops grown along the southeastern coast of China are therefore predominantly low standing—peanuts and sweet potatoes are common—in preference to higher standing crops that would be more easily damaged by typhoons.

Soils. The soils of China can be classified into three main groups: nonacid or sweet soil in the north, acid soil in the south, and neutral soil in the central area. The leaching effect of the nonacid soil is weakened by flat topography, low annual rainfall, and limited irrigation whereas the acid soil of the south is subjected to leaching by hilly terrain and abundant rainfall. For climatic reasons more crops are raised in the southern regions where the soil is poor than in the northern areas where the soil is rich. The nonacid soil region represents the wheat area, and the acid soil region, the rice area.

The transitional belt of neutral, slightly acid soil includes western Hupeh, southern Shantung, the Yangtze delta, and northern Szechwan. The deltaic plains, both north and south, such as the lower Yangtze valley plain and the Pearl River delta, are all only slightly leached, contain a fair percentage of calcium and other soluble minerals, and are quite fertile.

Broadly speaking, the productivity of the land in China corresponds to the distribution of the population. The populous areas are the valley plains of the winter wheat and millet area (the loess plateau of Northwest China), the winter wheat and kaoliang area (the North China plain and Shantung highland), the Szechwan rice-growing area (Red Basin), the rice and wheat area (the lower Yangtze valley plain), and the double-cropping rice area of the Pearl River delta. The Yangtze delta and the Red Basin of Szechwan, which have slightly leached and weak acid soils, are the most densely populated areas. . . .

POPULATION

Well over 650 million people live in China today if the estimates made on the basis of the 1953 census—a population of approximately 583 million and a 2 per cent annual increase—are correct. These millions form an immense reservoir of manpower vitally important to the rapid industrialization of China but also generate pressures and problems for the Communist regime as well as the other nations of the world.

The Communists began their preparations for a nationwide census, the first since 1909, shortly after assuming power in 1949. In June 1953, as part of the registration for the general elections at the primary level, each voter was directed to fill out a census questionnaire, giving his name, domicile, sex, age, and nationality. The total population figure of 601,938,035 published in November 1954 by the State Statistical Bureau (see Table 1) included, however, more than 7.5 million Chinese on Taiwan and approximately 12 million Chinese abroad, reducing to about 583 million the population actually living in mainland China at the time of the census. Those who were directly surveyed and registered amounted to 574 million.

Study of population statistics for China over the past three hundred years reveals a steady growth from 70 million in 1650 to 583 million in 1953—a more than eightfold increase. (If a population of 150 million in 1650, given in another source, were used, the increase would still be almost fourfold in three hundred years.) The present 2 per cent annual rate of increase, if main-

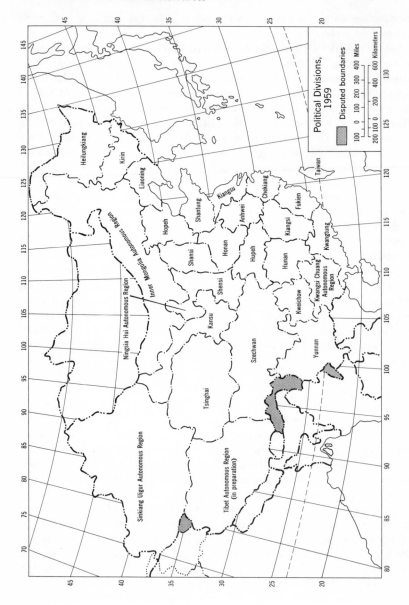

Political Divisions, 1959

Disputed boundaries

tained, will result in a population by 2000 of at least 1.5 billion, or more than half the present world population.

The phenomenal growth of the Chinese population is largely due to a high birth rate. In the past this was countered by a similarly high death rate resulting from a low standard of living and poor sanitation as well as frequent calamities such as famines, floods, and wars. But during the twenty-two years of the Nationalist rule (1927–49) the birth rate was estimated to be thirty-five per thousand and the death rate twenty-five per thousand, representing a yearly net gain of ten persons per thousand. This rate of increase is already quite high when compared with that in such countries as Sweden, Switzerland, Belgium, and England. In one of its studies the Communist government has set the present average birth rate at thirty-seven and the death rate at seventeen, for a natural increase of twenty per thousand. The lower death rate has been attributed to the government's successful public health work, the improvement in living conditions, and the decrease in the infant death rate.

It has been commonly presumed that India, Japan, and China, generally speaking, have more males than females, and past Chinese population estimates often indicated an unusual preponderance of males over females. As recently as 1927 the Chinese government in a population report of twelve provinces, showed the sex ratio to be 124:100. Previous investigations revealed an even greater excess of males. This may be due in part to the traditionally low position of women in society, which used to lead to the abandonment of baby girls, but may also reflect the tendency not to report females, especially young ones, in past years. The nearly equal sex ratio of recent years is therefore one indication of the new social status enjoyed by women. The 1953 census, covering a directly registered population of 574 million, reports 297,553,518 males and 276,652,422 females, a sex ratio of 107:100, much lower than any previous ratio. It agrees, however, with the normal distribution of sexes among many other peoples and there seems to be little doubt of its validity.

Of the 574 million Chinese, 338,400,000 persons belonged to the age group of eighteen and over, constituting 59 percent of the total registered population. Of this group 1,850,000 persons were eighty to ninety-nine years old; 3,384 had reached the age of one hundred or more, the oldest recorded age being one hundred fifty-five (sex not given). On the other hand, 235,200,000 persons belonged to the age group of seventeen and under, constituting 41 per cent of the total registered population. Of this group 89,500,000 were children up to four years of age, 63,100,000 were between five and nine, and 82,600,000 were from nine to seventeen. With forty-one persons out of every one hundred in the seventeen-and-under group, the source of China's manpower in the next few decades will be very large indeed.

The life expectancy of the Chinese has never been very high. Judging from the results of recent sample studies, the life expectancy of the present-day Chinese at birth is 31.9 for males and 34.2 for females; at the age of 20 the figures are 35.6 and 39.3 respectively; at 40 they are 23.5 and 25.6; at 60 they are 11.5 and 12.1. Compared with other Asian nations, life expectancy in China is slightly higher than in India, but less than in Japan

A comparison of the age compositions of the populations in China and in the United States reveals a general similarity in age distribution for the group between five and fifty-four, and life expectancy figures within this group seem to be much the same in both countries. There are important differences, however, in the four or under and fifty-five or over categories. A higher Chinese birth rate, even though offset to a certain extent by a higher infant mortality rate, results in a much higher proportion of infants four years old or younger in the Chinese population. The United States population, on the other hand, reflects a longer life expectancy at fifty-five and over in a higher percentage of people in this age group. . . .

Ethnic Minorities

The Chinese Communists use the term "minority nationalities" to designate ethnic minorities within the People's Republic of China. A minority nationality is defined as a community of common origin, bound together by a common language, a continuous area of residence, and a sense of group identity in economic and social matters as well as in standards of behavior and other distinctive traits. Physiological elements are considered secondary although marked physical differences exist between the various nationalities in China.

In the past the Han-Chinese attitude toward the non-Han ethnic groups was that of the bearers of a high civilization toward primitive tribal peoples. Steeped in age-old prejudice, the Han-Chinese had formed misconceptions based largely upon incorrect and improbable tales rather than on their own observations and personal contact.

In recent years, however, a significant change has taken place in the Chinese attitude toward the minority peoples. During the Nationalist administration a minimal effort was made to allay the traditional Han-Chinese prejudice toward these groups, to discourage categorization of them as "barbarians" and "aborigines," as well as to assimilate them into the national norm.

While also trying to minimize group divergences, the Chinese Communists have recognized that at the present stage the millions of minority peoples can achieve social and cultural progress only in their own accustomed patterns and habits of living. Present efforts are therefore concentrated on bringing the leaders of the ethnic groups into closer association with the government and on training the minority youths in Chinese schools and universities to undertake the task of social and economic transformation among their own people. In economic, cultural, political, educational, and public health activities, the Communist government endeavors to diminish the differences among the groups without trying actually to absorb them into Han-Chinese culture. The goal of Communist nationalities policy is to remove the factors that had for centuries caused them to defy the central government and, through better communications and direct contact, to bring them under effective control. The government has, however, shown by its recent suppression of the Tibetans that it will not tolerate more than a mild degree of resistance among these groups.

CLASSIFICATION AND DISTRIBUTION

There are probably few areas in the world where so many ethnic groups have lived together for so many centuries as in China. These groups, distributed over a wide area both in the hinterlands and the border regions, have undergone a complicated historical process of migration, assimilation, and transformation. Moreover, designations for these people have changed from time to time, making it difficult sometimes to trace the origin of particular groups or to keep track of their movements from one region to another.

The minority nationalities, constituting about 6 per cent of China's 650 million population, are concentrated mainly in seven border regions: ( ) Manchuria; (2) Inner Mongolia; (3) Sinkiang, Tsinghai, and Kansu; (4) Tibet; (5) Szechwan, Yunnan, and Kweichow; (6) Kwangtung and Kwangsi; and (7) Taiwan (see the map, Minority Nationality Areas). Ten of the non-Han ethnic groups have a population from one million to over six million (see the plate, Larger Minority Nationalities in China). Among them, the Koreans in Manchuria are immigrants from Korea; the Manchus, who were of Tungus origin, have become completely Sinicized; and the Hui, descendants of the Turkic-Uigur soldiers and merchants who moved to China more than a thousand years ago, have lost much of their racial identity through intermarriage with the Han-Chinese. Aside from these, the more important and distinctive non-Han ethnic groups in China are the Mongols, the Uigurs, the Tibetans, the Miao-Yao, the Chuang, the Yi, and the Puyi.

The Mongols constitute the major ethnic groups on the Mongolian steppes and are divisible into three groups: the Eastern Mongols, the largest group in Inner Mongolia, related to the Khalka of Outer Mongolia; the Western Mongols, or Oirat; and the Northern Mongols, or Buryat. Small numbers of Mongols are found in Sinkiang, Manchuria, and Kansu. Other ethnic groups in Inner Mongolia include the Daur, Orochon, Yakut, Solon, and Tungusic immigrants from Manchuria. All are relatively unimportant numerically.

The Uigurs (Nev Uigurs, or Eastern Turks) live mainly in the southern part of Sinkiang and generally call themselves after the names of their adopted cities. Other groups in Northwest China include the Hui, Kazak, Kirghiz, Monguor, Tadjik, Tatar, and Uzbek.

The Tibetans are distributed principally in Tibet and in the Chamdo region of Szechwan; some are found in Tsinghai and Kansu, where their neighbors include the Monguor, Salar, and Turki.

The Miao and Yao, though not closely related, are often classified together. They constitute one of the most important groups in South and Southwest China. The Miao are distributed widely over the mountainous areas of Kweichow and Yunnan in the west to Hunan, Kwangtung, and Kwangsi in the central south. The Kwangtung group, located on Hainan Island, is descended from Miao soldiers brought there centuries ago by the Chinese government to quell the rebellious Li. The Miao are subdivided into such groups as the Red, Black, Blue, White, and Flowery Miao. The Yao inhabit the mountainous regions of Kwangtung and Kwangsi.

The Chuang, numbering over six and one half million, constitute the largest of the ethnic minorities in China. This Thai-speaking group is located principally on the plains and in the valleys of western Kwangsi.

The Yi (Lolo) are located principally in the Liang Shan area on the borders of Szechwan and Yunnan.

The Puyi (Chungchia) are distributed in low marshy areas around Kuei-yang and in southwestern Kweichow province.

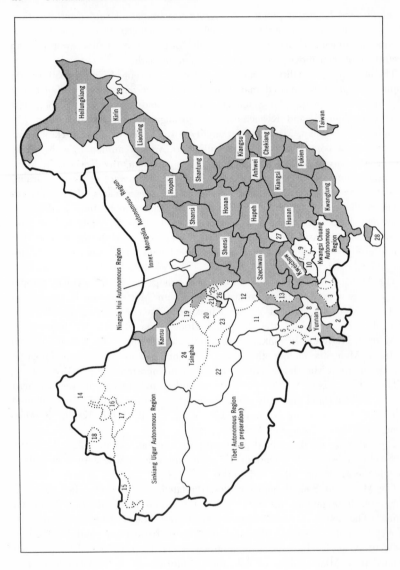

Many of these minority nationalities are indigenous groups that settled in their homes in ancient times; others moved to their present locality only in recent centuries. Although their migratory routes were different, they seem to have followed a general southward movement from the deserts and plateaus of the north to the Yellow River plains, or from the central south and southwest regions toward the tropics. While northern groups like the Mongols, Manchus, and Tungus have repeatedly pressed southward and have just as often been pushed back to their original abode by the Han-Chinese, southern groups such as the Thai and Miao penetrated beyond the Chinese national boundary into Burma, Indochina, and Thailand.

Nationality Autonomous Districts (Chou)*

Yunnan

1. Te-hung (Thai and Chingpo)
2. Hsi-shuang-pa-na (Thai)
3. Hung-ho (Hani and Yi)
4. Nu-chiang (Lisu)
5. Ti-ch'ing (Tibetan)
6. Ta-li (Pai)
7. Wen-shan (Chuang and Miao)
8. Ch'u-hsiung (Yi)

Kweichow

9. Southeastern Kweichow (Miao and Tung)
10. Southern Kweichow (Puyi and Miao)

Szechwan

11. Kan-tzu (Tibetan)
12. A-pa (Tibetan)
13. Liang-shan (Yi)

Sinkiang Uigur Autonomous Region

14. I-li (Kazak)
15. K'e-tzu-le-su (Khalka)
16. Ch'ang-chi (Hui)

17. Pa-yin-kuo-leng (Mongol)
18. Po-erh-ta-la (Mongol)

Tsinghai

19. Hai-pei (Tibetan)
20. Hai-nan (Tibetan)
21. Huang-nan (Tibetan)
22. Yü-shu (Tibetan)
23. Kuo-lo (Tibetan)
24. Hai-hsi (Mongol, Tibetan, and Kazah)

Kansu

25. Lin-hsia (Hui)
26. Southern Kansu (Tibetan)

Hunan

27. Western Hunan (Tuchia and Miao)

Kwangtung

28. Hainan (Li and Miao)

Kirin

29. Yen-pien (Korean)

* *Peking Review,* Vol. II, No. 21, May 26, 1959, p. 9.

LANGUAGES AND DIALECTS

There is a multiplicity of languages and dialects in China. In addition to the many dialects of Chinese are the languages of the numerous minority nationalities in the border regions. Some of these languages are related to Chinese, which is the most important branch of the Sino-Tibetan language family, while others belong to other language families such as Altaic and Austroasiatic (for classification and distribution, see the plate, Languages of China). These speech communities intermingle and often overlap, some extending beyond national boundaries (see Chapter 4, Ethnic Minorities).

The Sino-Tibetan languages are spoken by a larger population than any other minority languages. Presumably they originated in the Pamirs and then branched out over the eastern half of the Asian continent from the Tibetan plateau eastward to the coastal regions of China, and from the Indochina peninsula northward to Sinkiang, Mongolia, and Manchuria.

Like most Sino-Tibetan languages, Chinese has a basically monosyllabic structure, which means that the basic constituents of Chinese words and phrases are single syllables. While most Chinese words consist of one syllable each, there are a number of polysyllabic words.

The Chinese language contains a system of tones: the relative pitch levels used in pronouncing the syllables. Chinese, Tibetan, Burmese, and Thai all have tones, and similar developments of the tonal systems in these languages have been traced. In ancient times, there were four tones in the Chinese language; these developed into eight tones, not all of which are present in modern dialects. Mandarin, the standard Chinese dialect, has four tones: two even tones, *p'ing-sheng* (the upper even, *yin-p'ing*, and lower even, *yang-p'ing*); one rising tone, *shang-sheng;* and one falling tone, *ch'ü-sheng.* For the sake of convenience, these are designated respectively by western scholars as the first, second, third, and fourth tones. In a language that abounds in homonyms, tones are essential in distinguishing words that sound the same but have different meaning. In Chinese, tense, number, and case are not distinguished by inflection as in some European languages.

Dialects. Mandarin, by a wide margin the most extensively used Chinese dialect, is followed in importance by Wu, Hsiang, Hui, Kan, Hakka, Min, Yüeh, and a number of more local dialects. Although derived from a common base, quite different pronunciation and linguistic structure from dialect to dialect make most of them mutually unintelligible.

Formerly the language of the officials, Mandarin spread from North China to the Central-East and Southwest and is today the mother tongue of some 380 million people in many parts of China. Three main groups of Mandarin dialects have been distinguished. (1) Northern Mandarin, of which Peking Mandarin is the representative, is spoken in an area that encompasses the entire Yellow River basin and extends to Manchuria in the northeast and Sinkiang in the northwest. (2) Southwestern Mandarin, a fairly homogeneous group of dialects, occurs in a large part of China's southwestern hinterland, including the Szechwan Red Basin, the Yunnan-Kweichow plateau, and the central Yangtze plains. (3) Southern Mandarin, basically similar to the northern group, is spoken in the lower Yangtze valley from Hankow eastward to Nanking.

The Wu dialect, spoken by approximately thirty-five million people, had its origin in Soochow, one of the cultural centers of the imperial period. From there it spread to regions south of the lower Yangtze and gained great importance with the rise of Shanghai as a metropolitan center in East China. There are generally six to eight tones in the Wu dialect.

A group of minor dialects occurring south of the Yangtze valley consists of Hsiang, spoken by fifteen million people in central Hunan; Hui, spoken by three million people in southern Anhwei; and Kan, spoken by eight million people in northern Kiangsi. The Hsiang or Hunan group resembles to some extent Southwestern Mandarin. The number of tones varies from six to seven.

The Hakka dialect is found over an area extending on an east-west axis from Fukien to Kwangsi, including southern Kiang-si and northern Kwangtung, with offshoots in Taiwan and Hainan; it also spreads to the Chinese settlements in the Philippines, Indochina, Burma, Thailand, Malaya, and Sumatra. In China itself speakers of Hakka number approximately ten million.

There is a great resemblance between Hakka and Kan, and they are sometimes grouped together. In northern Kiangsi, the Hakka and the non-Hakka speech communities have intermingled to such an extent that it is difficult to ascertain whether the dialects they speak are Hakka, Kan, or a mixture of both. When the two dialects are not mixed they are distinguishable. Hakka differs from Kan mainly in tonal system and final consonants.

The Min or Fukien dialect can be divided into two groups: Northern Min and Southern Min. The former, spoken by six million people in northern Fukien, is represented by the Foochow dialect; the latter, spoken by fifteen million people, is represented by the Amoy dialect in southern Fukien and by the Swatow dialect in northeastern Kwangtung and on Hainan Island. The original Chinese population in Taiwan speaks the dialect of Chang-chou (Lung-ch'i), a city some twenty miles from Amoy. In their variant forms, the Southern Min dialects have been taken by Chinese emigrants to Indonesia, Malaya, and the Philippines. The tonal system resembles that of the Wu and Hakka groups.

Yüeh or Cantonese is spoken by some forty million people in China and abroad. Its speakers include not only those in the provinces of Kwangtung and Kwangsi, but also many overseas Chinese in various parts of the world. For instance, the dialect of Chung-shan is popular among the Chinese people in Hawaii, and the dialects of T'ai-shan (Toishan), K'ai-p'ing (Hoiping), and others are used by Chinese residents in Chinatowns of the United States. Cantonese is also the dialect of a number of Chinese communities in Indochina, Thailand, Malaya, and Indonesia.

Written Language. The earliest written records of the Chinese people were the Shell and Bone inscriptions, *chia-ku-wen.* This form was superseded by the Seal Script, *chuan-shu,* and the Scribe Script, *li-shu.* With the use of the writing brush and paper in the early Christian ear, Chinese writing gradually assumed its present form known as the Regular Script, *k'ai-shu.* In the evolution of the Chinese written language, there clearly has been a tendency toward the simplification of the written forms (see the plate, Evolution of Chinese Writing).

The structure of the Chinese characters is very complicated. They are divided into six main categories: pictographs, ideographs, compound ideographs, phonetic loan characters, phonetic compounds, and derivative characters. Among these, the pictographs and the simple ideographs are the basic forms from which the others are derived, but the phonetic compounds constitute the largest class of Chinese words, and many new forms are currently being coined.

The creation of new words and expressions is, however, characteristic mainly of vernacular Chinese, *pai-hua,* in contradistinction to literary Chinese, *wen-yen* or *wen-li,* based on the language of the Chinese classics and preserved by scholars in an inflexible and conservative style for the last twenty centuries. The literary language, which lends itself to a remarkably concise style through the omission of the particles ordinarily used in daily speech, has been the medium for many masterpieces of Chinese literature but differs so greatly in syntax and grammar from vernacular Chinese as almost to constitute a separate language. This disparity reduces any confusion between the two, and a Chinese scholar fluent in the classical language considers it quite natural to turn to his dialect for everyday purposes.

Pronunciation of literary Chinese depends upon the dialect of the reader: a Mandarin speaker will ready the literary language with Mandarin pronunciations and a Wu speaker with Wu pronunciations. Sometimes, because of its terseness, literary Chinese cannot be fully understood when read aloud. Certain written characters have no colloquial rendering, and some colloquial words have no written equivalents. In the latter case, a character of the same meaning may be used as a substitute, or a "vulgar character" may be invented.

Despite its shortcomings, literary Chinese has exerted a tenacious influence on Chinese intellectuals, who are still able to read with ease the classical literature of ancient China as no other people can read their ancient language and literature. The ability to read and write in literary Chinese is the hallmark of a Chinese scholar of the old type just as the ability to use a foreign language is an asset to a modern Chinese scholar.

Imperial Control and Stability of Old China

2. THE ROLE OF THE CLAN AND KINSHIP FAMILY

HSIAO KUNG CHUAN

The presence of the clan in a village introduced a principle of cohesion which would not otherwise have been present. For this reason the clan was useful to the imperial government as an instrument of rural control, but at the same time the control of the clan itself presented some baffling problems. The main purpose of this chapter is to ascertain the place of the clan organization in the system of rural control, but we must first examine the structure and functions of the clan itself.

The *tsu* or clan was primarily a kinship group;[1] but since ancient times it had had its roots in some territorial location.[2] As a recent investigator pointed out, "The *tsu* is a group descended from one ancestor who settled in a certain locality or neighborhood."[3]

The locality in which a clan originally settled might be a city or town, but more often it was a spot in the country from which a full-fledged village might spring. In fact, it was in rural areas that the clan usually attained its fullest development,[4] and the village often owed much to the clan. While rural communities were not always the outgrowth of clan settlement, the presence of the clan tended to give them a higher degree of cohesion than would otherwise have been possible. In many instances, as a modern writer said, "All the village organizations, except possibly those based on economic status, are determined directly or indirectly by clan relationships. . . . Neighborhoods are largely made up of families of the same clan."[5] In such cases, it is justifiable to regard the clan as "the solidary unit of the village."[6]

SOURCE: Selected from Hsiao Kung Chuan, *Rural China,* Seattle: University of Washington Press, 1960, pp. 323, 327–328, 331–332, 335–337, 339, and 341–343. Reprinted by permission of the University of Washington Press.

The reason for the strong affinity between the clan and village is obvious. The predominantly agricultural population of the village tended to be less mobile than city dwellers, and kinship ties were therefore better preserved in the villages than in the cities.[7] Hence different patterns of social organization obtained in cities and villages, guilds and "civic" associations being typical of the former as clans were characteristic of the latter. . . .[8]

It may also be noted that just as several clans might live in one village, one clan might dwell in several villages when the brood had outgrown the original homestead.[9] The Wang clan of Hsing-lin Ts'un in T'ung-kuan (Shensi) was a very good instance. At the downfall of the Yüan dynasty (1367), a certain Prince I found refuge in this village. His descendants became peasants and remained so during the Ming and Ch'ing dynasties, although some of them entered the brotherhood of scholars at the end of the Ch'ing dynasty. The clan kept no written genealogy, but the clan relationship among the more than eighty households that dwelt in six different villages were preserved unimpaired for centuries.[10]

The differences in composition between monoclan and multiclan villages was reflected in some difference in organization. In the former, where kinship group and rural community were virtually identical, village leadership was none other than clan leadership. For example, a village in Ningpo (Chekiang), inhabited by a single clan, "elected" an "elder" who "presided over the administration of community affairs" and at the same time served as clan head who took charge of clan matters.[11] Similar arrangements were found in other parts of the empire.[12] In multiclan villages the situation was somewhat different. Clan heads did not necessarily serve as village heads, although they often exerted noticeable influence on village affairs.[13] The presence of more than one kinship group in one community might give rise to interclan rivalry or to open conflict, as we shall see later. For the moment it may be noted that there was no more social equality between different clans dwelling in one village than between individuals belonging to one clan. As gentry members of a clan dominated its commoner members, so some clans in a given community might be in a position to discriminate against others. Their discrimination might be based on seniority in residence, numerical strength, or the superior status of some of their own members. This was observed even in North China where the clan organization was comparatively weak. As a Western writer indicated, "There is . . . an emphasis on the status of the members of the old accepted families and a tendency to disregard the more recent immigrants into the community and to consider them as outsiders. . . ."[14]

It should be noted, however, that while intraclan social differentiation resulted in intraclan social inequality, especially in clans with considerable wealth,[15] gentry members were usually satisfied with enjoying ceremonial privileges and control over the group. Their superior positions and prestige rendered them not only natural leaders of their group but often benefactors of their less fortunate fellow clansmen.[16] They were generally disposed to be charitable and helpful to the latter, not merely because a helping hand extended to kinsmen served to strengthen the solidarity of the group but also because charity, being traditionally regarded as a mark of virtue, was an effective method to enhance their own prestige.

Details of clan organization varied in different instances, but normally each kinship group recognized a suitable member as its head and set up a sort of clan government for managing or administering its affairs. The clan head often bore the name *tsung-tzu* or *tsu-chang;* he might be the ceremonial head, the chief executive, or both.[17] Sometimes a number of "executive members" might be selected to assist the clan head to discharge his duties, particularly the management of the clan property and ancestral hall.[18] In the larger clans subheads were instituted, each to lead one of their branches (*fang*), and were usually given the title *fang-chang* (heads of branches). In such cases affairs concerning individual branches might be managed by the several *fang-chang*, but those involving the whole clan were managed or decided upon by the consent or with the cooperation of all these heads.[19] Occasionally, the clan resolved itself into a sort of "direct democracy," when all its members under the leadership of *tsu-chang* and *fang-chang* met in the ancestral hall to settle important matters. The heads led the discussion and junior members voiced their assent.[20]

Age, seniority in generation, and personal ability were as a rule the primary qualifications for clan leadership, but social and economic status were often equally decisive. In some clans the choice of the *tsu-chang* was limited to members of the oldest living generation, although the person chosen did not have to belong to the oldest line.[21] In others the choice was made on the basis of "merit," provided that the candidates were sufficiently advanced in age.[22] In most cases gentry members were given preference, and the possession of adequate property was sometimes regarded as a condition for holding certain offices. . . .

In the last analysis the criterion of "ability and virtue" tended to merge into that of rank and wealth, for the simple reason that unlettered peasants had little opportunity to demonstrate whatever personal capacities they may have possessed, and scholarly degrees, official ranks, or substantial estates were easily taken to be ample proof that those who had them were men of parts. Moreover, personal power often came with social superiority and financial influence, and it was inevitable that clan members of lesser consequence should acknowledge the leadership of their gentry kinsmen.

Social status did not play a uniformly important role in all clans. This was true because the material and financial resources of clans invariably came from contributions made by their eminent and wealthy members. The wealth of the kinship group therefore depended upon the prosperity of its most successful members. In this sense it would be even more pertinent to say that the less social differentiation appeared in a clan, the poorer it would remain. But since clan organization could not develop to any great extent unless there was a certain degree of local prosperity and since wealth was unevenly distributed in imperial China, gentry domination of the clan must have been the normal state of affairs, at least during the Ch'ing dynasty.

Clan Activities

While different clans stressed different types of activities, all clan activities of any importance presupposed gentry leadership. The following were the most frequently undertaken:[23] (1) compilation and revision of genealogical records; (2) "ancestor worship" and the institution of ancestral halls, ritual land, and ancestral graveyards; (3) material assistance to clan members; (4) education of young clansmen; (5) punishment of misconduct and settlement of disputes; and (6) self-defense.

GENEALOGICAL RECORDS

From its inception, probably in the third century of the Christian era, the compilation of genealogical records was essentially a gentry institution.[24] The *tsu-p'u* or *tsung-p'u* of more recent times differed from the *p'u-tieh* of the Wei and Chin dynasties in more than one respect, but they served substantially the same basic purpose of tracing and recording genealogical ties, and like the earlier genealogies, they were very largely the work of the gentry.

Not all clans possessed genealogical records. Those that did almost always had among their members a fairly large number of scholar-officials. Clans in more modest circumstances often were without such records, especially those in nothern provinces where the clan phenomenon was less pronounced than in the south.[25] For instance, of the 208 clans that were found in T'ung-kuan (Shensi), only two had *tsu-p'u;* the rest either never had one or failed to preserve any that had been previously compiled.[26] Of the 168 clans in Lo-ch'uan (Shensi), only eight had genealogical records. Even in the south, some clans had no genealogical records; in Ching Chou (Hunan) only thirty-eight among a fairly large number of clans kept them.[27] . . .

"ANCESTOR WORSHIP"

"Ancestor worship" probably had a wider appeal than genealogical records, but it was not free from gentry domination or control. A distinction should be made between worship by the clan as a whole and worship by individual families which might or might not belong ιo a clan. The latter was quite often practiced even by commoner households in the village, but the former was definitely a gentry affair.

The reason is obvious. Clan worship involved the possession of an ancestral hall,[28] some ritual or sacrificial land, and perhaps also an ancestral graveyard.[29] These in turn presupposed the existence of some well-to-do clansmen who deemed it desirable to cotribute money or land to make them possible. The *tsu-tz'u* or *tsung-tz'u* (ancestral hall, literally, clan hall) and *chi-t'ien* (ritual or sacrificial land) in particular were the chief objects of gentry attention. Officials, retired or otherwise, and titled scholars often willingly gave money or land to their own clans. Contributors naturally had a decisive voice in the management of ancestral halls and ritual land which were made possible by their generosity. The institution or augmentation of clan property was often regarded by successful men as the crowning achievement of their careers. . . .

The ritual land constituted the economic basis of clan organization. The possession of such property enabled the clan to display a variety of activities which might go beyond the maintenance of sacrificial rites. The amount of ritual land at the command of some kinship groups in South China, where their activities covered the widest scope, was quite considerable. A modern investigator was of the opinion that land owned by clans in a given locality might amount to as much as 75 per cent of all land under cultivation there, and ordinarily the proportion was between 23 per cent and 40 per cent.[30] We have no estimates for the nineteenth century, but a few figures from various sources, incomplete and presumably inaccurate as they are, may serve to give some idea of the situation. The ritual land might be used also to extend material assistance to members of the clans; in fact, some of the clans chose to designate their land as *i-chuang* (welfare form).[31]

The total amounts of land owned by these clans, assuming that these were the only ones that owned land in the localities mentioned, were quite small compared with the figures given by this modern investigator. But to the individual clans the possession of land amounting to 1,000 or more *mow* was certainly a considerable asset; even ritual land of a few hundred *mow* would enable the kinship group to perform some of the basic functions which would otherwise have been impossible.

The theory of the ritual land, as understood by earlier writers, was that the land remained as the permanent property of the clan and that the proceeds from the land were to be used for maintaining the sacrifices and for the benefit of the clansmen. The view as expressed in the following passage is representative:

> The ritual land is popularly known as *chen-ch'ang t'ien*. Not only big clans and households but even the smaller families and branches often possess it. . . . I happened to read in the gazetteer of Hsin-ning [Kwangtung] that the local custom sets great store by the construction of ancestral halls, for which ritual land is generally provided. Three uses are made of the annual proceeds [from the land], namely, [1] on the first day of each month sons and younger brothers of the clansmen are summoned to the hall where exercises in literary composition are held for them; those who take part in the local elementary examinations are given "examination paper fees"; those who become government students are given subsidies and expenses in connection with the regular annual examinations; and those who go to take the examinations at the provincial or imperial capital are given travel expenses; [2] clan members who are sixty or over are given sacrificial meat and an annual rice subsidy; [3] those clansmen who are destitute, sick, or disabled are given grain, the amount varying with the size of their respective families; those who lack money to finance weddings or funerals are also given suitable assistance; and in case of famine, rice certificates are distributed to the needy members. . . . Similar practices prevail generally in Kwangtung province, although the amount of activities varies porportionally with the amount of land possessed [by the clans]. I think this institution accounts for the fact that inhabitants of this province are willing to study and attach importance to scholarly degrees.[32]

Other writers echoed this view.[33] While it was possible that persons who instituted the ritual land were prompted by the desire to perform duties toward their ancestors and to look after the welfare of their clansmen, there was nothing to prevent them from attaching a hidden utilitarian value to their action. According to a modern Chinese writer:

A piece of land is usually contributed to the [clan] organization by a member who is a governmental official, the pretext being that the products of the land may cover the expenses necessary in the keeping up of the ancestors' tombs and regular sacrifices. But, in fact, this common property is a common security with which the position of the clan may be maintained in the wider power structure of the community. It finances the education of the young members so that they may be able to enter the scholar class and attain high official position and protect the interest of their kinsmen.[34]

This is a plausible interpretation of the matter, although the writer seems to have oversimplified it. At any rate, two things are clear: first, ritual land was invariably instituted by members of a clan who enjoyed gentry status and possessed some wealth; second, the control or management of the clan property was usually placed in the hands of propertied and privileged clansmen.[35] It was the ritual land that gave many a clan its financial foundation, and its was ritual land also that rendered gentry domination a natural and perhaps inevitable consequence.

MATERIAL WELFARE

Material welfare of the clan was promoted in a variety of ways. The most common practice was to give subsidies or relief to aged and needy clansmen, with proceeds accrued from clan property or grain stored in clan granaries. A good instance of the former was afforded by the Yang clan of Chiang-yin (Kiangsu). Part of the revenue from the ritual land (a little over 1,000 *mow*) was used to set up a rice and clothing allowance, to a share of which every descendant who was sufficiently old or destitute was entitled, the amount each received varying with the age of the recipient. Widows who did not remarry, orphans, and disabled clansmen were placed on the allowance list also. Special subsidies were granted to pupils who studied in the schools, apprentices in the trades or crafts, and persons who had funerals or weddings in their families.[36] In some clans preference was shown to members of the branch to which the founder of the ritual land or welfare farm belonged. In the Chao clan of Ch'ang-shu (Kiangsu), for example, members of the "elder" branch were to receive more substantial aid from the *i-chuang* (welfare farm) than members of the "younger" branch.[37] In the Hua clan of Chin-kuei (Kiangsu), one hundred *mow* of land was set aside in 1876 for the exclusive benefit of the progeny of the ancestor from whom the founder of the *i-chuang* himself was descended.[38] Clan granaries were less common than welfare farms, but a few instances were noticed in Hsiang-shan (Kwang-tung). The Fang, Yang, and Miu clans each established in the mid-nineteenth century an *i-ts'ang* granary for their own members, situated in the rural areas where they resided. The Yang clan granary had an endowment of 950 *mow* which was calculated to insure a constant supply of grain for the storehouses.[39]

Clan aid was sometimes rendered to members in the form of loans. It was an established practice in the Ch'en clan of Nan-hai (Kwang-tung) that clansmen who desired it could borrow money from the funds realized from the ritual land. If the borrower could not repay he might lose his own land in order to make good his debt.[40] The Yang clan of Wusih (Kiangsu) was so generous to its members that during the Taiping uprising in the 1850's the clan mortgaged the ritual land and lent the money thus raised to members in need.[41] . . .

EDUCATION OF CLANSMEN

Clans were normally interested in educating their younger members, thus enabling them to participate in the state examinations which opened the path to academic degrees and official ranks. This interest was displayed in various methods of encouraging literary studies and in providing facilities for such studies.

Quite often financial assistance was given to budding scholars who had demonstrated aptitude or zeal in their studies. Such practices prevailed in some clans of Fang-kuo Hsiang (Chi-an, Kiangsi), Ch'a-k'eng (Hsin-hui, Kwangtung), and Hsiang-t'an (Hunan),[42] where scholarly distinction was put at a premium. The benefits given to clansmen were in proportion to the degree of scholarly advancement which they severally attained. . . .

Many clans also made efforts to promote education by providing school facilities for their youthful members, especially those who belonged to families of modest means. They established *tsu-hsüeh* (clan schools) which were also known in different cases as *chia-shu* (family schools), *tz'u-hsüeh* (shrine schools), or simply *i-hsüeh* (welfare schools). A few examples will suffice to illustrate. The Chang clan of Lu-chiang (Anhwei) established a *chia-shu* "to instruct the sons and grandsons of the *tsu*," which was maintained with part of the revenue from 3,300 *mow* of "welfare land" donated in 1823 by a clansman who once served as provincial director of education in Hupeh. The Ko clan of Ho-fei established an *i-hsüeh* for the exclusive benefit of its children and youths, with an endowment of 300 *mow* of land contributed in the early nineteenth century by a clansman holding the *chien-sheng* title.[43] The Li clan of Huang-ts'un village in Hsing-an (Kiangsi) had the distinction of having maintained a clan school during a long period. This school, known as *Huang-ts'un i-shu,* was first established sometime in the Chih-cheng reign (1341–67) of the Yüan dynasty; its endowment in the form of land was increased in the Hung-chih reign (1488–1505) of the Ming dynasty. It was destroyed as a result of war at the end of the Ming dynasty but was rebuilt by the clan in the fifty-third year of K'ang-hsi (1714). Unfortunately, the local historian was silent concerning the subsequent story of this school.[44] Sometimes different branches of a clan established separate schools for their own members. An instance of this sort was found by a Western writer in Phenix village (Kwangtung), a monoclan community: "There are four buildings of a semipublic nature: the chief ancestral hall of the entire village . . . the ancestral halls and schools belonging to two different branches of the village group . . . and the small temple . . . south of the market center."[45] In fact, the clans of Kwangtung took so much interest in education that, according to a native writer, "everywhere ancestral halls were used for classrooms"[46]

Large and well-organized clans often took pains to keep order and uphold morals in their own communities. Written codes of conduct echoing the basic principles of Confucianism (often known as *tsung-kuei,* "clan regulations") were sometimes formulated. The precepts were either repeated orally on suitable occasions[47] or posted in writing at appropriate places in the ancestral halls.[48] Sons were urged to be filial to their parents, wives dutiful to their husbands, brothers affectionate one to another. All were warned against laziness, extravagance, gambling, quarrels, violence, and other offensive conduct.[49] Adultery and failure to perform filial duties were pronounced grave offenses, often punishable by expulsion or even death.[50] In some instances infanticide and opium smoking were sternly forbidden.[51] One of the well-known clans of Hunan set forth a number of regulations, many of which echoed the maxims of the Sacred Edict, and reprinted in its genealogical records some forty articles of the Imperial Code, thus making clear to its members what was right and lawful in personal conduct, family relationships, and economic matters.[52]

Clan regulations were enforced by rewards and punishments, which were in some instances quite well defined and rigidly applied. For example, meritorious deeds performed by clansmen might be recorded in special "books of virtuous clansmen,"[53] or commemorated by petitioning the government for honorary plaques or arches.[54] Violations of clan regulations were dealt with by the heads of the clans. When the transgression was serious, the case might be heard in the ancestral hall, in the presence of clansmen, old and young. The purpose was not so much to elicit the verdict of public opinion as to pillory the victims and deter future offenders. The punishment inflicted on the erring clansmen might be open censure, flogging, fine, suspension of privileges, ostracism, or even death.[55] Such corporal and capital punishments were, of course, unauthorized by the government and therefore illegal. But seldom did they come to the attention of local officials.

In spite of clan regulations, disputes and quarrels frequently arose among clansmen. The settlement of disputes thus became also an important activity of the clans. Naturally, the leaders or heads of the kinship groups were charged with this task, and in some clans written rules were formulated to guide their leaders in exercising their authority.

Notes

1. Another translation for the term *tsu* is "sib." See Robert H. Lowie, *Social Organization* (1948), pp. 58, 236, and 237, for discussion of terminology. Hu Hsien Chin, *The Common Descent Group in China* (1948), prefers the phrase "common descent group."

2. Ku Yen-wu, *Jih-chih lu,* 10/22b, quoting Ch'en Mei's comment on a passage in the *Chou-li.*

3. Hu Hsien Chin, *The Common Descent Group* (1948), p. 9. She gives another definition on p. 18. "The *tsu* is a group descended from one ancestor who settles in a certain locality or neighborhood." James D. Ball, *Things Chinese* (1904), pp. 172–73, roughly equates the Chinese with the Scottish clan. This is hardly an accurate view.

4. Ch'ü Ta-chün, *Kuang-tung hsin-yü* (1700), 17/5a-6b. This passage is

quoted also in *Kuang-chou* (1878), 15/8a-b. Olga Lang, *Chinese Family* (1946), p. 180, supports the view that the clan was essentially a rural phenomenon: "Clans exist only in villages or small towns. There are practically no clan ancestor temples and no clan heads in the cities." This, however, is an overstatement. Ancestral halls existed in such large cities as Peking, Tientsin, Nanking, and Chengtu, as late as the twentieth century. See note 7.

5. Martin C. Yang, *A Chinese Village* (1945), p. 241.

6. Daniel H. Kulp, *Country Life* (1925), p. 135.

7. Hu Hsien Chin, *The Common Descent Group* (1948), p. 10: "The *tsu* is of the greatest importance in rural neighborhoods, in large villages and small towns, although at times its main ancestral hall is located at the county [*hsien* or *chou*] seat or even in the provincial capital. But in the large cities, with their sharp differentiation of the professions and of social classes, it becomes lost." The relatively high degree of mobility among city inhabitants also exerted an adverse influence on the clan. However, the cities, being centers of social and political influence, were often chosen by clans of relatively large size and strong organization as sites for their *ta tsung-tz'u,* that is, common or central clan temples shared and supported by branch halls located in the surrounding countryside. *Chia-ying* (1898), 8/2b, affords an excellent example of such an arrangement: "The local custom attaches importance to the kinship tie. All clans, large and small, have ancestral halls. Inhabitants of villages who dwell together by clans invariably have *chia-miao* [family shrines], which are really ancestral halls. In addition to these halls, there are *ta tsung-tz'u* in the prefectural city. These are built jointly by the branches of] the clans that dwell in the several districts that compose the prefecture."

8. The affinity that existed between the clan and the village was observed in India. For example, B. H. Baden-Powell, *Village Communities in India* (1899), p. 23, describes one type of "tribe" in the following words:". . . the existing group remembers only its descent from some one ancestor, and is not numerous enough to be called a 'tribe.' In all probability one man (or two or three brothers) obtained a settlement in some region that was vacant, and the families multiplied into a 'clan,' keeping up the memory of their common descent and acknowledging a certain solidarity. . . . We find a large extent of country containing several hundred square miles, now divided up into 'village' groups, all composed of landowners whose families have a common designation and are reputed descendants of one ancestor; or of two or three families, not more." Cf. the same author's earlier book, *The Indian Village Community* (1896), chapter 6, sec. 3. Radhakamal Mukerjee, *Democracies of the East* (1923), p. 255, indicates an even closer affinity: "In India, since the clans lived in separate villages, and were exogamous and reckoned descent along the male line, they took a special course because their members lived in one or more villages. In the Central Provinces one of the names of the clan is *khera,* which also means a village, and a large number of the clan names are derived from, or the same as, those of villages. Among the Khonds all the members of one clan live in the same locality about some central village." Professor Murkerjee goes on (p. 299) to describe what he believes to have been the Chinese system: "In China the economic association of the village community is obscured by the clan system. The clan jointly possesses property, and indeed the property of the ancestral hall is divided among the poorer members at a very low rental. . . . The ancestral clan fields are inalienable, into whose possession or use it is a sacrilege to bring an intruder."

9. *Nan-ch'ang* (1919), 27/1b: "One *hsing* [surname] may embrace as many as one hundred clans or several dozen of them. Those that dwell in the *tu*

and *t'u* [rural divisions] are so distributed that sometimes one *tu* contains several clans and sometimes one clan is found in several *tu* or *t'u*." *Tu* and *t'u* were rural divisions made for revenue collection purposes but had become territorial units in some parts of the empire.

10. *T'ung-kuan* (1944), 25/1b. See Hu Hsien Chin, *Common Descent Group*, p. 107, for an instance in which a clan dwelt in two villages.

11. L. Donnat, *Paysans en communauté* (1862), p. 85: "Comme celui de Tching-fou, celui de Si-fou-et les autres, le village d'Ouang-fou est habité par les descendants d'un même nom. Il a été fondé, il y a plusieurs générations, par une famille de la souches des Ouang, qui abandonna le lieu qu'elle occupait au-dessus de Hang-tcheou pour venir s'établir aux environs de Ning-po. Le livre des ancêtres (Tsong-tching-bou), où sont inscrits depuis plusieurs siècles les naissances et les décès, est déposé entre les mains du Tchong-tchiang, l'ancien du village, élu par tous les chefs de maison dan la pagode de Oueï-tung-sze, afin de présider à l'administration des affaires communes."

12. Robert K. Douglas, *Society in China* (1894), p. 115: "It often happens that one family becomes the possessor of an entire village, and then we have such names as *Chang-chia chwang*, 'the village of the Chang family' . . . and so on. In such cases the seniors of the clan act as the village elders." See Marion J. Levy, *The Family Revolution in Modern China* (1949), p. 239: "Sometimes the neighborhood consisted of members of only one *tsu*, in which case the neighborhood and the *tsu* organizations were usually conterminous."

13. Burgess, *Guilds,* (1928), p. 25.

14. *Ibid.*

15. Hu Hsien Chin, *Common Descent Group*, p. 29: "The material on hand thus indicates that the poorer the *tsu,* the less the social differentiation." Lang, *Chinese Family* (1946), p. 180, draws a similar conclusion: "The well to do are more clan conscious," We can hardly regard as accurate the following statement in Leong and Tao, *Village and Town Life* (1915), p. 25: "The whole clan then being but a huge family, it follows that all the members of the clan have equal rights and duties towards the ancestral hall."

16. For example, the Fang clan of Nanking (Kiangsu) and the Yang clan of Wusih. See Hu Hsien Chin, *Common Descent Group,* pp. 166–67, quoting from Fang Pao (1668–1749), *Wang-ch'i hsien-sheng wen-chi* (1881), 14/3a, and *Anyang Yang-shih tsu-p'u,* Vol. XVI, *chüan* 23, p. 47a.

17. *Ibid.,* pp. 120–28, quoting from Lu Chiu-kao (1732–94), *Shan-mu chü-shih wen-chi* (1834), 2/1a-4b; T'ung-ch'eng (Anhwei), *Wang-shih tsu-p'u* (1847), Vol. I., *chüan* 1, pp. 34a–35a; Nan-feng (Kiangsi), *T'an-shih hsü-hsiu tsu-p'u,* Vol. I, pp. 1b–2a; and Hunan, *Tseng-shih ssu-hsiu tsu-p'u,* Vol. I, "Wen-i," part 4, pp. 1b–4a.

18. Leong and Tao, *Village and Town Life* (1915), p. 28. Cf. Lang, *Chinese Family* (1946), p. 175: "The clans of Kwangtung and Fukien had two sets of leaders: (1) the clan elders, and (2) the clan executives. The first group, led by the clan head, consisted—theoretically at least—of the eldest men of the eldest generation of the clan. Exceptions, however, were not uncommon. . . . But the clan elders are only venerable figureheads. Real power is in the hands of the clan executives: managers, treasurers, committee members. These men have, of course, to belong to the socially prominent and wealthy families if merely because the well to do alone can afford the degree of education required of them. Most of them were over 50 years of age, but advanced age was not of first importance."

19. Hu Hsien Chin, *Common Descent Group,* pp. 119–20, quoting from *Tseng-*

shih ssu-hsiu tsu-p'u, Vol. I, "Wen-i," part 4, pp. 1b–4a.

20. *Ibid.,* p. 131, quoting from *Lu-chiang chün Ho-shih ta-t'ung tsu-p'u, chüan* 13, p. 1b.

21. *Ibid.,* p. 127, quoting from T'ung-ch'eng (Anhwei), *Wang-shih tsu-p'u,* Vol. I, *chüan* 1, p. 34b.

22. *Ibid.,* p. 119. Clan heads who had actual charge of practical matters were often chosen primarily for their managerial abilities. See, for example, *Tzu-yang Chu-shih ch'ung-hsiu tsung-p'u* (1867), *chüan mo, shang,* p. 44b.

23. Some clans engaged in rather extensive activities. Those in Ning-yüan (Hunan), for example, were said to have performed sacrificial rites at the ancestral graveyards on the fifteenth day after the vernal equinox; after these rites they distributed rice and food to the several hundred clansmen who usually attended, gave subsidies to clansmen who married or to whom sons were born, invited to feasts in their honor all clansmen who were fifty *sui* and over, punished erring clansmen by whipping or suspending the privilege of receiving the sacrificial meat, and gave encouragement to scholars who obtained the *sheng-yüan* degree or who taught in the clan schools. *Yung-chou* (1867), *chüan 5, shang,* 42a–b.

24. Chao I, *Ts'ung-k'ao,* 17/6a–9a. This well-known historian, writing late in the eighteenth century, traced the origin of genealogical records to the ancient Three Dynasties, but held that such records acquired practical importance only with the adoption in the Wei dynasty (third century, A.D.) of the *chiu-p'in chung-cheng* system of official appointment (i.e., the system of classifying candidates into nine grades, very largely on the basis of family status, and recommending them for appointment by the *chung-cheng,* special functionaries in charge of the matter). During the Six Dynasties (fourth to sixth centuries), when the line between "high" families and commoners became quite rigidly drawn, acquaintance with the *p'u-tieh* (genealogical records) attained the dignity of an independent branch of "learning."

25. Wu Ju-lun (1840–1903), *Jih-chi,* 15/48a.

26. *T'ung-kuan* (1944), 25/9a.

27. *Ch'ing chou* (1908), 2/12a–21b.

28. Justus Doolittle, *Social Life,* (1876), I, 225, clarifies the matter thus: "Ancestral halls may be divided into two classes; those in which all the ancestors of families having the same ancestral name and claiming relationship are worshipped, and those in which the ancestors of a particular branch of the families having the same ancestral name and claiming near relationship are worshiped." This explains why in many instances one clan possessed a number of ancestral halls.

29. Edwin D. Harvey, *The Mind of China* (1933), pp. 244–46, quotes from the *Chinese Repository,* I (1832–33), 449 ff., the following description of the sacrificial rites performed in ancestral halls and graveyards: "When there are large clans, which have descended from the same ancestors, living in the same neighborhood, they repair in great numbers for the performance of the sacrificial rites. Rich and poor, all assemble. Even beggars repair to the tombs, to kneel down and worship. This usage is known by the phrase, *sao-fen-mo,* 'sweeping the tombs,' and *pai-shan,* 'worshipping the tumuli. . . .' On some of these occasions . . . even where there are two or three thousand members of a clan, some possessing great wealth, and others holding high ranks in the state—all, old and young, rich and poor are summoned to meet at the *'tsu-tsung-tze-tang.'* or the ancestral hall. Pigs are slaughtered; sheep are slain; and all sorts of offerings and sacrifices are provided in abundance. The processions from the hall to the tombs, on these occasions, are performed in the grandest style which

the official rank of the principal persons will admit. . . . Such is the sum of a grand sacrifice at the tombs of ancestors. But to many the best part of the ceremony is to come, which is the feast upon the sacrifice. The roast pigs, rice, fowls, fish, fruits, and liquors are carried back to the ancestral hall; where, according to age and dignity, the whole party sit down to eat and drink and play."

30. Chen Han-seng, *Landlord and Peasant* (1936), pp. 31–32. Lang, *Chinese Family* (1946), p. 174, states that in Kwangtung, ". . . the proportion of land belonging to the clan varies; among the 24 clans of Kwangtung investigated in 1937 the variation extended from 10 to 90%. These extremes are rather rare. In the majority of cases the clan claimed 50%–70% of the land cultivated by its members, the rest being their private property. This ratio seemed to be typical of Kwangtung. The clans of Fukien possessed less land." Until we have access to adequate data for making a more accurate survey of the situation, all estimates, including those made by Chen and Lang, must be regarded as merely tentative.

31. Theoretically, *i-chuang* or *i-t'ien* was clearly distinguishable from *chüt'ien* (sacrificial or ritual land) by the purposes which these were each supposed to serve. The ritual land of a clan was designed to maintain the sacrificial rites, whereas welfare farms were used to give aid to needy clansmen. The purpose of the latter is explained in *Wang-shih chia-p'u* (Wu Hsien, 1911), *chüan* 2, *hsia*, p. 35a, in these words. "When *i-t'ien* is instituted, talented ones will not be compelled by the necessity of making a living to neglect their [scholarly] pursuits; those who do not study will not be compelled by hunger and cold to become unworthy; widows, widowers, and orphans will receive support, and all will have the wherewithal for financing weddings and funerals." In actual practice, however, this distinction was not always maintained; the same land might be used for both purposes mentioned above. See, for example, Chang Hsin-t'ai, *Yüeh-yu hsiao-chih,* cited in note 81. Li Tz'u-ming, *Jih-chi,* vi, 82a, gives an instance in Hunan (1870's) where a high-ranking military officer donated 3,600 *mow* of land. Chang Chung-li, The Gentry in Nineteenth-Century China (Ph. D. dissertation, University of Washington, 1953), pp. 167–169, has a table showing large welfare farms in Wu Hsien, Ch'ang-chou, and Yüan-ho Hsien, based on data given in *Wu hsien chih* (1933), 31/11ff. The largest of these, totaling 5,300 *mow,* was established by the Fan clan (Wu Hsien); the smallest, barely over 1,000 *mow,* by a member of another clan. The amount of land varied in direct proportion to the size and prosperity of the clan owning it. The following statement from *Chang-shih tsu-p'u* (Kuang-chi, Chekiang, 1841), illustrates this point: "Most of the eminent and great clans institute welfare farms. . . . None is more prosperous than the Tu clan of Shan-yin; the land which it owns amounts to one thousand *mow.* . . . Our clan has a small number of members . . . as a rule, the amount of land it owns does not exceed one hundred *mow.*" It is untrue that all or most of the clans in South China had ritual or welfare land. It was said of Wu Hsien (Kiangsu), the place where welfare land was supposed to have originated and where the local economy was fairly affluent, that "wealthy and powerful clans number no less than one hundred, but only about a dozen of them [have welfare farms] as a matter of record." *Wang-shih chih-p'u* (1897), *chüan shou,* "Keng-yin i-chuang chi."

32. Chang Hsin-t'ai, "Yüeh-yu hsiao-chi" (n. d.), in Wang Hsi-ch'i, *Ts'ung-ch'ao,* 4/305a. See *Chia-ying* (1898), 8/7b, for a similar statement.

33. *Kuang-chou* (1878), 15/26b–27a; *Hua hsien* (1924), 9/26b; Kulp, *Country Life* (1925), pp. 86–87.

34. Fei Hsiao-t'ung, *Peasantry and Gentry,* p. 5.

35. For example, "Regulations of the Ancestral Hall," in *T'an-shih hsü-hsiu tsu-p'u*, 1/1b–2a, quoted in Hu Hsien Chin, *Common Descent Group*, Appendix 14, pp. 124–25: ". . . formerly representatives of each branch used to take turn in holding the office of manager of the ancestral hall. Often this person happened to be one who was not wealthy, so that the ancestral rites were neglected and the taxes were unpaid. . . . After deliberations in public, it has been decided that from now on the manager of the ancestral hall must be a wealthy person chosen publicly by the whole *tsu*. . . . The manager of the common granary must be a wealthy man, chosen publicly by the members of the *tsu*. . . . The rice stored at the common granary is to guard against famine, and the post of manager should be filled by a wealthy man."

36. Hu Hsien Chin, *Common Descent Group*, Appendix 58.

37. *Ibid.*, pp. 143–44.

38. Wang Hsien-ch'ien (1842–1918), *Wen-chi*, 13/1a–2b.

39. *Hsiang-shan* (1923), 4/3a–b.

40. *Nan-hai* (1910), 17/8a–b.

41. Hu Hsien Chin, *Common Descent Group*, p. 67, quoting from *An-yang Yang-shih tsu-p'u*, Vol. XVI, *chüan* 23, pp. 47a–48a.

42. *Fang-kuo* (1937), *chüan shou;* Liang Ch'i-ch'ao, *Wen-hau shih*, p. 60; and Hu Hsien, *Common Descent Group*, p. 120.

43. *Lu-chou* (1885), 34/29b and 53/10a.

44. *Hsing-an* (1871), 7/27a.

45. Kulp, *Country Life*, p. 14.

46. *Ju-lin* (1883), 21/18b. The statement quoted is the last line of a little rhymed piece written by a local poetaster to depict the blissful prosperity of his home community. The piece runs something like this:

> "In all directions as far as the eye can see kitchen
>   smokes rise;
> Amidst every grove of tall bamboo and ancient banyan
>   trees a village looms.
> Reading and singing, scholars self-confidently thrive:
> Everywhere are ancestral halls used for classrooms."

47. Hu Hsien Chin, *Common Descent Group*, pp. 54–55, quoting from Cheng T'ai-ho (*ca.* 1277–1367), "Cheng-shih kuei-fan," in *Ts'ung-shu chi-ch'eng*, gives a pertinent instance: "On the first and fifteenth of the month after the head of the family has led the members in paying their respects in the ancestral hall, they come out and he sits in the elevated part of the hall. The male and female members of the family stand below (that is, at the bottom of the steps). Twenty-four beats are sounded on the drum. Then a young boy chants: 'Listen, listen, listen! All who are sons must be filial to their parents. Those who are wives must respect their husbands. Those who are elder brothers must love their younger brothers. Those who are younger brothers must respect their elder brothers. Listen, listen, listen! Do not attend to your private benefit so as to harm the duty of all! Do not be lazy so as to neglect your affairs! Do not live luxuriously so as to deserve the punishment of Heaven! Do not listen to the words of women, so as to confuse harmonious relations. Do not commit wrongs by violence so as to disturb the peace of the home! Do not become drunk, so as to pervert your nature. . . . Look back at the instructions of the ancestors! To them is tied decay and prosperity.' " Hu Hsien Chin, *Common Descent Group*, p. 186, gives another instance of oral instruction.

48. Leong and Tao, *Village and Town Life*, p. 25.

49. For example, Hu Hsien Chin, *Common Descent Group*, pp 133–36, quoting

from *P'i-ling Ch'eng-shih tsung-p'u,* 1/88b–89a; *Wang-shih tsung-p'u,* Vol. II, *chüan* 1, p. 1b; *I-shih tsung-p'u,* Vol. I, *chüan* 1, pp. 33b–34b; and *T'anshih hsü hsiu tsu-p'u,* Vol. I, "Regulations," p. 3a–b.

50. *Nan-hai* (1910), 20/19a, gives an instance occurring in the nineteenth century, in which a young man who indulged in gambling, and beat his mother when he was enraged by her scolding, was put to death by order of a gentry clansman. Hu Hsien Chin, *Common Descent Group,* p. 123, describes the practice known as "opening the ancestral hall," that is, convening the clansmen to deal with wayward members.

51. *Tung-kuan* (1911), 98/9b, gives a very interesting instance. "In the Ch'en *ts'un* of Tung-kuan Hsien, Kwangtung, the clansmen number less than five hundred, but the clan regulations are strictly enforced. The villagers regard opium as an enemy. Any person who is addicted to it is severely punished by the *tsu-chang* [clan head] and then ordered to get rid of [the habit]. If the offender proves incorrigible after repeated warning, he is then ostracized from the clan." According to *Chih-hsin pao* (1898), 59/9a–10a, the Chang clan of Sha-wei Hsiang (Hsiang-shan Hsien, Kwangtung), formulated a set of rules prohibiting the use of opium by its members. All addicts were compelled to stop smoking opium within a year. Those who failed to do so were punished by suspension of the privilege of receiving the sacrificial meat (a sort of excommunication). Hu Hsien chin, *Common Descent Group,* p. 121, quoting from *tsu-p'u* of the Tseng clan of Hunan: "The whole *tsu* [clan] is forbidden to drown girl infants. No matter whether the family be rich or poor, within one month of the birth of a girl it should be reported to the head of the *fang* [branch]." Those who practiced infanticide were punished by fine and flogging.

52. *Tseng-shih ssu-hsiu tsu-p'u* (1900), Vol. I, "Wen-i," part 3, pp. 1a-1lb, reprinted forty provisions from the *Ta-ch'ing lü* (the Ch'ing code) governing family relationships, marriage, graves, and payment of taxes. In addition to these, the work gives the clan regulations (a total of twenty-two articles, each with a short note of explanation) which enjoin its members to perform filial duties toward their parents, to revere their superiors and elders, to maintain harmonious relationships with their kinsmen and neighbors, to instruct their offspring, to carry on their own occupations peacefully, to value frugality, to make early payments of their taxes, to do no wrong, etc.

53. Hu Hsien Chin, *Common Descent Group,* p. 133, quoting from *Hsü-shih tsung-p'u,* Vol. I, *chüan* 1, p. 7a–b.

54. *Fu-shan* (1924), 10/10b-12a.

55. In addition to sources cited in notes 109 and 110 above, see *Hua hsien* (1924), 9/23a; Kulp, *Country Life,* pp. 321–22; William Martin, *Cycle of Cathay* (1896), p. 335; and Hu Hsien Chin, *Common Descent Group,* pp. 55–63.

3. THE ROLE OF THE GENTRY

Fei Hsiao-tung

The term "gentry," *shen-shih,* refers to a class of persons with a definite position and definite functions in the traditional society of China. Here, by "traditional society," is meant the period after the breakdown of feudalism and the unification of the empire under a centralized monarchical power not long before 200 B.C. The development of the gentry class has a history; only through this history can we understand its characteristics.

The class that is here called gentry is also sometimes referred to as *shih ta fu,* "scholar-official." Actually the gentry class, although closely linked with the group of scholar-officials, should be distinguished from it. To be born into a gentry family did not necessarily insure that one became a scholar or an official in traditional China. Under feudalism the situation was different. At that time the gap between the nobles and the commoners was great. *Shih*[1] and *ta fu,*[2] although they were the bottom of the hierarchy of the ruling class, were still a part of that class and as such possessed real political power. But after the breakdown of feudalism political power was no longer portioned out but became concentrated in the person of one man, the monarch. In order to carry out his administrative functions, the monarch required assistance. This was given him by the officials. The officials then were no longer relatives or members of the ruler's own family but rather employees—the servants, or tools, of the monarch.

After the breakdown of feudalism there was another important change. The throne became the object of capture by the strong, by the hunters after power. Under feudalism, in which political power was distributed to relatives and kin, anyone not born into a noble family was a common man who had no chance of reaching the throne, of touching or even of seeing the divine paraphernalia of monarchy. No more than a woman can change into a man could a common man become royal. But, when feudalism went, anyone could become emperor. Thus political power became an object of struggle. This is illustrated by the story told by the historian Ch'ien Ssu-ma of Huang Yu, who during the Ch'in dynasty (255–207 B.C.), in watching an imperial procession, said to his friend, "This I can seize." Since that time the struggle for political power has never ceased. Political power in the eyes of the people has become something precious to be sought after, an enterprise for large-scale entrepreneurs.

Unfortunately, since the breakdown of the feudal structure in China, political power has no longer been transmitted permanently in certain families, and

SOURCE. Selected from Fei Hsiao-tung, *China's Gentry,* Chicago: University of Chicago Press, 1953, pp. 17–20, 24–36, 39–44, 49–52. and 58. Reprinted by permission of The University of Chicago Press.

up to the present no peaceful means of attaining it has ever been found. We continue to be convinced that the way to gain political power is through "taking up the stick" and fighting civil wars. Those few who emerge victorious in this struggle become emperors; the defeated become bandits. So we have had a succession of tyrants. A few people rule the mass. The nature of this despotic monarchy is not changed by the handing-on or relaying of power. In England, when a monarch was killed, monarchical power itself received a blow. Changes of monarchy led in time to a growth in the power of the people and to a government monarchic in name only. But, in China, blood flows from the people's veins, while those who attain the throne are but a few fortunate adventurers, like Liu Pang, the first emperor of the Han, who was born a lowly peasant, or Chu Yuan-chang, the founder of the Ming dynasty. When we study official versions of Chinese history, we find presented to us a continuous line of dynastic descent; but we should not forget that the authority of these rulers was continuously challenged by civil wars and unscrupulous adventures.

To struggle for political power by violence is dangerous. If a man succeeds, he may become emperor; but, if he loses, he will be killed, and not only he himself but his whole family and clan. When he is challenging the established emperor, he is called a bandit and rebel, and the might of the army is directed against him. Moreover the empire gained by violence may be lost by violence also. Twice in history, according to tradition, emperors tried to give up their power to other men who they thought would make better rulers. But those to whom the power was offered did not want it. They preferred to run away rather than to take on the responsibility. We do not know how far these two emperors were sincere in their desire to give up their power and to what extent this action was no more than a gesture or a piece of complicated political intrigue. There is no question of the fact, however, that in all of Chinese recorded history there is not a single case of voluntary abdication from the throne. Those abdications which did take place were forced. "The empire that was won on horseback will be lost only on horseback," as the popular saying goes.[3] . . .

There was a weak point, however, in this centralized monarchical system. He who held power, the emperor, as I have said, could not administer the country by himself. Even though he might not wish to share his authority, he still required help in ruling and must therefore employ officials. These officials, with whom the ruling house had no ties of kinship, functioned merely as servants with administrative power but no power of policy-making. It was within the inefficiencies of this system that the ordinary man found his opportunity to carry on his private concerns.

It is true that previous to the unification of Ch'in (221 B.C.) there were attempts to establish an efficient administrative system. This was done under the influence of the *Fa Chia,* or Legalist, school of thought. Theoretically, the system proposed by this school of thought was a good one. In order to have an efficient administration of the country, a legal basis must be established, with everyone controlled by the same law. Shang Yang, as prime minister of Ch'in, attempted to put this theory into practice. But the theory unfortunately neglected one small point. One man, the emperor, was left outside the law. And this omission destroyed the whole system of the *Fa Chia.*[5]

If the highest authority were bound by law, then administrative authority would be able to cage the tiger. But in Chinese history this has never happened. As a result, the ruled, including the officials themselves, have never sought for efficiency in administration. Rather the opposite has been true. Inefficiency and parasitism, on the one hand, remoteness of imperial control and a do-nothing policy by the emperor, on the other—this has always been the ideal. Yet this ideal of government, of a "good emperor" as one who presided but did not rule, has rarely been attained. As far as the officials were concerned, the next best thing, then, could only be to protect themselves, to keep a back door open for their relatives, and to be able to use their position as a shield against the emperor's whims. To protect not only themselves but their relatives and their whole clan from the unchecked power of the monarch, and to do this not by constitutional or by legal means but by personal influence—this is what they sought. Not by challenging the emperor's authority but by coming close to him, by serving him and from this service gaining an advantage in being enabled to shift the burden of the emperor's demands onto the backs of those lower down, did the propertied class attempt to neutralize the emperor's power over them and to avoid the attack of the tiger. Groups of officials, with their relatives, formed, thus, in Chinese society a special class not affected by the laws, exempt from taxation and conscription. Nevertheless, they had no real political power.

To escape domination while approaching the source of power takes a highly developed skill. The position of the officials was not easy. As the old sayings go, "When the emperor orders your death, you must die" and "All the blame is mine; the emperor can do no wrong." . . . The officials must be two-faced: severe toward the people and compliant toward the emperor. They must know the art of going just so far and no further in order that they might not be caught either by the fury of the emperor or by the wrath of the people. Chinese officials' life has been described as the art of maneuvering on a stormy sea. Experience through the ages was the teacher. It may be noted that in Chinese the expression, "Do not speak to me officially," does not mean the same thing as in English but rather, "Speak to me sincerely."

In normal times to be an official was no direct economic advantage. Why, then, should people want to be officials? The poem of T'ao Yuan-ming expresses the feelings of one such man:

> "Why should I be an official?
> I bend my back
> For only three piculs of rice.
> Why should I not go back to till the land?[6]"

T'ao Yuan-ming was a typical unwordly poet. Yet, in spite of his talent and his interest in the things of the mind, even he had to "bend his back" and occupy an official position and withal receive only a small financial reward. Why did such a one accept this position instead of staying home where he was happy? The fact is that, if he had shown his scorn of officialdom by leaving office, he would probably by now be "a man without an arm." The choice lay between "bending the back" or being disabled. The necessity for becoming an official was a little like the need for being inoculated. Just as one runs the risk of having a bad reaction to an inoculation, so in becoming an official one may risk having one's property confiscated or even one's head cut off. But, once the inoculation is over, one has gained protection. This analogy is not too apt, since from an inoculation one person becomes immune, whereas if one has been an official one can protect a whole group of people. As a result, it happened that sometimes a group would join to aid in the education of one man so as to enable him to reach officialdom. "One man rises to officialdom, then all his dogs and chickens will be promoted," is the saying.

In Chinese traditional society the clan or big family naturally constituted a group which could take action of this sort, supporting one of their members until the time when he should become a scholar and be eligible for the official examinations. Once this individual attained official honors, the whole clan could rely upon him. Without any strong person at court, it was difficult to protect one's property. Ku T'ing-lin was an official during the Ming dynasty, but, when the rule passed to the Manchus, he refused to continue in an official position, gave up traveling abroad, and shut himself up at home with his books. Yet for his own protection he was obliged to send his two nephews to the Ch'ing court to serve his enemies. This was made possible by the fact that, as we have said, Chinese officials did not share in the political power of the emperor but served their monarch by neutralizing and softening down his power rather than by supporting it. With his nephews in court, the uncle was protected even in secret rebellious activities. According to Chinese tradition, officials did not work seriously for the government, nor did they like to continue as officials for a longer period. Their purpose in entering the government was to gain both immunity and wealth in this order. The Chinese officials when in office protected their relatives, but, when this duty to the family had been performed, they retired. Retirement and even a hermit's life were the ideal. In retirement there was no longer any authority to be served with watchful care, while the relatives who had gained protection from their kinsman official owed him a debt of gratitude. Now he need only enjoy his social prestige and grow fat and happy. As we say in China, "To come back to one's native soil, beautifully robed and loaded with honors, is the best thing in life."[8] Such a man will not attempt to seize power; his children will not play at being emperor. Nor will he have any idea of reforming the social system, for that system will do him no harm. Once out of the way of imperial influences, he may enjoy the economic power of a landowner.

This is the sort of man I mean by gentry. The gentry may be returned officials or the relatives of officials or simply educated landowners. In any case, they have no real political power in shaping policies and may have no direct connection with politics whatsoever, yet they do tend to have influence at court and to be immune from political exploitation. And the more fearful the ruler and the more tiger-like, the more valuable is the gentry's protective covering. In such circumstances it is difficult to survive except by attaching one's self to some big family.

. . . Since the establishment of a central unified political power in the third century B.C., the gentry as a class have never attempted to control political power. That is, although occupying official positions, they have not exercised any decisive powers as to policy. Under the feudal system sovereignty belonged to the aristocracy; under the monarchy, to the king-emperor. The question which arises, then, is this: Why in Chinese history has there been no period in which the power of the aristocracy revived or in which a bourgeois middle class took over political power? The answer to this question leads us to a study of the political consciousness of the gentry and their attitude toward their own position. Why did they not struggle with the monarch to gain control? Why was there no movement similar to Magna Carta in England? The class who were landowners in the economic structure were gentry in the social structure. Why did they become so neutral, so negative in politics? . . . What was the attitude of the gentry class toward their political position? It is true that their attitude was not cause but rather effect of the political system upon them. Nevertheless, it may be said that the attitudes of acquiescence which developed within the political system tended to reinforce the system.

Every social structure has a system of attitudes which define proper behavior and support the structure. What I am going to discuss in this chapter is the attitude of the gentry toward the monarchical power after they had come to be controlled by that power.

In the political philosophy of the traditional gentry class there was an important idea called *tao-t'ung*.[9] This idea took shape before the firm establishment of monarchical power and was probably necessary for its development. In my analysis I am concerned particularly with the period before the firm establishment of monarchical power when feudalism was in process of breaking down.

I am not inclined to think that this social philosophy originated in the minds of a few scholars. On the contrary, I believe that the scholars' elaboration of the system was accepted by society because it reflected a point of view which was generally shared. The function of the scholar was to formulate, to clarify, and to crystallize this point of view into a doctrine. In the period of transition between feudalism and imperialism the school of thought which reflected the philosophic trend of the times best was that of Confucius and his followers. But the Confucian school was only one of many in this period of the "hundred schools." It was only later, after the stabilization of the imperial power, that Confucianism came to be so popular and dominating. This shows, I think, that the ideology of the Confucian school represented the point of view best adapted to the Chinese imperial system. . . .

It appears to me that the development of the idea of *tao-t'ung* took place in Chinese traditional society because there had appeared a new type of person, the scholar-intellectual, one excluded from political authority but still possessing social prestige. Since he did not have political power, such a man could not decide political issues. Yet he might, through making known his opinions and formulating his principles, exercise a real influence. Such men did not try to control political power in their own interest but endeavored rather to put forward a set of ethical principles which should restrict the force of political power. The system of *tao-t'ung* which they developed came to be accepted by the gentry as the norm for their activity in politics. Eventually it came to serve the gentry not only as an ethical system but also as a protection for economic interests.

As the gentry attempted to restrict political power by ethical means, they put forward the teachings of Confucius, calling the latter the creator of *tao,* and a "king without a throne." And his spiritual descendants are those whom we now call master-scholars. . . .

The separation of political power from ethical power is one of the fundamental ideas in Confucian philosophy and is also an important factor in the Chinese power structure. It may be compared to the separation of church and state in the West but is not exactly the same. . . . In European medieval history worldly power submitted to divine power, monarchical power submitted to religious power. When, in a later period, these two powers became separate as the powers of church and state, the civil rights of the people came to be recognized. In Western political thinking it came to be accepted that the power which does not come from heaven could come only from the people, the common man. So long as the monarch derived his authority from his divine origin, he might slight the popular will. But once the throne was separated from the church, and it was recognized that the king's power was secular, it was quite natural that the people should be allowed to have their say and to share in government. It seems to me that in the Western political system power was never entirely independent and self-justified but was always based on an authority derived from either divine or popular sources. The situation in China was somewhat different.

In China, Confucius also recognized a duality of power, but for him the two systems were not in the same order. One was not necessarily subordinate to the other; rather they were seen to be parallel. In China political power was like Caesar's, but the other type of power, in contrast to the West, was not viewed as having a divine origin. Some people think that Confucianism is a system of religion, yet it recognizes no supernatural force. This is not the only way, however, in which it may be distinguished from Western religions. Another aspect of Confucianism in which it differs from the West is its relation to action. Jesus Christ was using his power in the same domain to control human affairs. As a result of this conflict, one power became subordinate to the other. But the Confucian *tao-t'ung* stands not for action but for the upholding of a standard or norm which defines the Way of a good emperor (and a good citizen). It is one thing whether the monarch acts according to the Way or not. It is another whether we have made clear the Way to be a good ruler. Christ made clear the good and wanted action toward that good. But Confucianism is divided into two parts: (1) the knowing what is good and (2) the doing what is good. Thus the man who knows what is good does not necessarily have an obligation to carry it out. In fact, he may not be able to do so, since what he is able to do depends upon his social position. So we have the differentiation into separate categories of the scholar who knows and the monarch who does. . . . For the *tao,* or Way, is detached from worldly events. The Way can be perfected irrespective of actual happenings in the world. To make this Way effective, to practice it, is not the duty of a man who is not in a position to do so; in other words, of the man without political power. The man who has control of political power may administer his affairs according to the Way or may utterly disregard it. Those who are not in his position of authority may themselves maintain the Way, and they may "push it and try to make it work," so that the Way will be followed by the man who controls the country. But they must not try to usurp the position of the man in power. What Confucius means when he speaks of "push it and make it work" is simply the use of persuasion. Confucius never assumes the authority assumed by Christ. As a result, in the Chinese scheme, the political line is active, the ethical line passive. . . . To employ and to discharge belongs to the man who has power; to work or to hide is the role of the man who has the Way. According to this system, there will be no conflict. From the point of view of the person who upholds the norms, practical politics may sometimes coincide with the norm and sometimes not. One may distinguish those nations which have *tao* and those which have not. Yao and Shun are examples of those who ruled the nation according to the *tao*.[10] Yü and T'ang are other examples. So also monarchical power may lose its Way, and, when this occurs, the man who knows it, and through this knowledge possesses it, should guard it and keep it safe from harm. Such a man must work hard to cultivate himself so that the norms will not disappear entirely. But he will have no idea of trying to correct the conduct of the monarch. This, then, is the Confucian view: the one who knows should be ready to present his views when asked but when not asked should keep them hidden. These scholar-masters do not desert the Way in time of difficulty, but only when the monarch in his behavior approaches the Way will they come forth and act as officials. . . .

The real problem, then, is the link between the political and the ethical lines. The ideal of the Confucian school was that of the kingly Way—*wang-tao*—in which both political and ethical lines coincided. But how could that ideal be realized? Here we find the conflict in Confucius' ideas. Since he had been brought up under a feudal system, he valued a social order of this sort, one in which a stable society was ruled according to well-established traditions. The feudal tradition prevented him from breaking the connection between the political line and kinship; the static ideal made him abhor social changes. This is the first point to be noted with regard to Confucius' attitude. He took for granted the political system and did not wish it to be changed. At the same time, he was living when the system was actually disintegrating; men in a certain position no longer behaved according to the norm set up for them. To meet this difficulty, Confucius detached the norms from actual practice and set them up as an ideal type of behavior which was not to be deviated from. . . .

If the ethical line cannot control the political line, though scholars may repeatedly criticize the government as not acting according to the *tao,* in actual everyday politics the emperor, or the man who possesses political power, will not feel shame and will disregard them. In a state which is misgoverned, in which the scholar folds up his norm and hides it in his bosom, what happens to the people? Scholars may say, as Confucius once did, "If Heaven will not destroy this work what harm can my enemy do to me?" But Confucius also said, "Heaven may destroy this work, and those who come later will never again have a chance to learn the Way." Scholars may die, for they are men of this world, not of another. How can they hide when the imperial power rules the entire land? The imperial power may burn the books and bury the scholars alive.[11] It may kill students because of some writing which injures the emperor. It may block the ethical line entirely for a time. Confucius was not able to solve this difficulty, namely, that, living together in the same world, the two lines, ethical and political, cannot let each other alone. Although the ethical line of the scholars may be willing not to struggle against the political line, the political line can, and often does, suppress the ethical. When this happens, what can scholars do? The positive way to meet this dilemma is, as was done in the West, to conquer the imperial power and subordinate practical politics to the socially accepted norms. But positive measures of this sort are not in accordance with the feudal tradition, and we find very little in Chinese history of this sort of positive resistance. Another line was taken.

When Confucius appealed to Heaven, that Heaven was an indifferent abstraction which would not interfere with worldly events.[12] But when the ethical line of the scholars was suppressed by the emperors to such a degree that there was no possibility of their gaining any power in politics, they tried to convert Heaven into a really active force. Confucian *tao* has no inherent power. It cannot *do* things, for doing things is the emperor's task. In the Han dynasty, however, the conception of a realistic God who would interfere in human affairs gradually took shape. Tung Chung-shu (179?–104? B.C.), a scholar of the Han dynasty, interpreted the *Spring and Autumn Annals* in such a way as to threaten the royal power with heavenly anger. In a statement addressed to the emperor Wu he said: "Your servant, in reading the *Spring and Autumn Annals*, has come to see that, in this work done by previous generations, there is presented a relation between Heaven and Man. I realize the awfulness of this relation. When a nation loses its *tao*, Heaven will first warn the people by famines and disasters. If the emperor does not look back upon himself to criticize himself, then Heaven will warn him by portents. If he still does not change his way, then he will court real disaster. This shows the benevolence of Heaven, which wishes to stop disturbances in the world."

In Tung's formula Heaven comes first, the emperor second, the scholars third, and, at the bottom, the people. Following this formula, the emperor should no longer be repressive but should be awed and restrained by the behavior of Heaven. But the question is: Since Heaven expresses approval or disapproval through natural phenomena, who knows the meaning of the heavenly signs? Who is able to interpret these signs but the scholar? Thus Tung really emphasizes the importance of the scholar, in that he alone could interpret Heaven. The first part of this conception was different from the usual Confucian point of view and especially that developed by Mencius, according to which the will of Heaven is to be expressed in the will of the people. According to this new idea, scholars should interpret the will of Heaven as expressed in natural phenomena. It was not an attempt to control political power democratically but rather, indirectly, through religion. The role of the scholar was simply to help the monarch to meet Heaven's demands; and the punishment of the emperor, if it came, would be through natural disasters and not by the people. Theoretically, monarchical power was thus subordinated to religious power, and the scholar given a position of some independence. In other words, the scholar's ethical line was no longer to be held down by the political line of the emperor. . . .

Thus the relation between the scholar and political power changed in the course of history. In the beginning they were separated from practical politics; they were regarded as maintainers of the ethical way but not as positively effective in government. In the process of concentration of monarchical power this same class was unable to protect its own interest; its members turned to religious sanctions in the hope that divine authority, in controlling the monarch, would at the same time offer them protection. But the divine sanctions were not effective, and thus the only alternatives came to be either to rebel or to surrender. Since the scholar class were never in any sense revolutionary, they chose the latter course, becoming officials. And they even degraded themselves by becoming utterly subservient to the emperor. This is the historical process which determined the later position of the gentry in the social structure. They did not themselves attempt to take over political power but found security by subordinating themselves to the mercy of the imperial court. In the power structure of traditional China the gentry were a distinctly noncombative element.

Notes

1. *Shih:* "This word is often translated 'scholar,' but this is only a derived, metaphorical sense and the whole force of many passages in the *Analects* is lost if we do not understand that the term is a military one and means 'knight.' A *shih* was a person entitled to go to battle in a war-chariot, in contrast with the common soldiers who followed on foot. Confucius, by a metaphor similar to those embodied in the phraseology of the Salvation Army, calls the stout-hearted defenders of his Way 'Knights'; and hence in later Chinese the term came to be applied to upholders of Confucianism and finally to scholars and literary people in general. The burden of most of the references to *shih* in the *Analects* is that the Knight of the Way needs just the same qualities of endurance and resolution as the Soldier Knight" (Arthur Waley, *The Analects of Confucius* [London: George Allen & Unwin, 1938], pp. 33–34).

2. *Ta fu:* lower-ranking official under feudalism.

3. [This phrase seems to refer back to the story told of Kao-tsu, the first emperor of Han, and the Confucian scholar Lu Chia. "After his [Lu Chia's] return in 196 or 195 B.C., he is said to have quoted the *Book of Odes* and the *Book of History* to Kao-tsu, whereat the latter scolded him and said, 'I got the empire on horseback; why should I bother with the *Book of Odes* or the *Book of History?*' Lu Chia replied, 'You got it on horseback, but can you rule it from horseback?' Then he proceeded to quote cases, from ancient history, of kings who had lost their thrones through their wickedness, concluding with the Ch'in dynasty, which Kao-tsu had himself overthrown" (Pan Ku, *The History of the Former Han Dynasty*, trans. Homer H. Dubs [Baltimore: Waverly Press, 1938], I, 21).]

4. [Waley discusses the social situation in which the Legalist school rose to power under the title "The Realists," in *The Way and Its Power* (London: George Allen & Unwin, 1934), pp. 68–86. The *Fa Chia* system, in spite of its recognition of the importance of a "rule of law," and its effort toward

greater efficiency in government, does not appeal to the Western liberal mind. *The Book of Lord Shang,* trans. J. J. Duyvendak (London: A. Probsthain, 1928), supposedly the writing of Shang Yang, otherwise known as Wei Yang or Lord Shang, expresses the extreme position of the Legalists. Duyvendak comments: "Law, having been applied theoretically only in order to enforce the observance of the standards set by natural moral law, now became the instrument for enforcing the standard set up by the state. Here came a clash between the law and moral traditions. Never had this idea of law anything to do with the codification of the conceptions of justice living in the hearts of the people; it was merely penal laws and institutions, deemed expedient for the government's centralising and imperialistic purposes; it was the expression of the state's own growing self-consciousness. It is very remarkable that, when we find the necessity for publishing the laws urged, it is not, as elsewhere, an expression of the popular wish to safeguard the people's rights and privileges for the future; on the contrary, it is government itself that desires their publication as a safeguard of its own power, as it expects that the laws will be better observed if people know exactly what punishments and non-observances will entail. Consequently, to have a deterrent effect, the laws have to be severe" (p. 81).]

5. [But, according to Fung Yu-lan, the highest ideal of the Legalist school actually was that "ruler and minister, superior and inferior, noble and humble, all obey the law." Fung quotes from Han Fei-tzu, a leading Legalist: "Therefore, the intelligent ruler carries out his regulations as would Heaven and employs men as if he were a spirit. Being like Heaven, he commits no wrong, and being like a spirit, he falls into no difficulties. His *shih* (power) enforces his strict teachings, and nothing that he encounters resists him." Fung interprets this passage as follows: "By comparing the ruler with Heaven, Han Fei-tzu means that he acts only according to the law, fairly and impartially. That he employs men 'as if he were a spirit' means that he makes use of them according to this 'method' or *shu,* secretly and unfathomably." The gulf between this conception of law and the conception held in the West may be one reason why the ideal of "Great Good Government" has, as Fung says, "never yet actually been attained in China" (Fung Yu-lan, *A History of Chinese Philosophy,* trans. Derk Bodde [Peiping: H. Vetch, 1937], I, 320–22).]

6. "T'ao, who lived in the fourth and fifth centuries A.D., was our poet of nature *par excellence.* Once he served as a district magistrate. When he could not longer stand the ordeal of formality he burst out upon the occasion of the arrival of the provincial inspector, his superior, 'I cannot bow to a mean fellow from the street just for five pecks of rice.' So saying, he left his official hat hanging on the wall and went right home" (C. W. Luh, *On Chinese Poetry* [Peiping, 1935], p. 16).

7. In "The Old Man with the Broken Arm (A Satire on Militarism)," *ca.* A.D. 809, by Po Chü-i.

8. Po Chü-i thus congratulates himself on the comforts of his life after his retirement from office:
"Lined coat, warm cap and easy felt slippers,
In the little tower, at the low window, sitting over the sunken brazier.
Body at rest, heart at peace; no need to rise early.
I wonder if the courtiers at the Western Capital know of these things or not?"
(From *A Hundred and Seventy Chinese Poems,* trans. Arthur Waley [New York: Alfred A. Knopf, 1919], p. 239.)

9. [*Tao-t'ung,* literally "*tao*-series," "*tao*-succession," "*tao*-transmission," in usage something like "the orthodox transmission of the *tao* or Way." The *Chung Yung,* or Doctrine of the Mean, defines the Confucian *tao* as follows: " 'The

Universal Way for all under Heaven is five-fold, and the (virtues) by means of which it is practiced, are three. There are the relations of ruler and subject, father and son, husband and wife, elder and younger brother, and of friend and friend: these five constitute the universal Way for all. Wisdom (chih), human-heartedness (*jen*) and fortitude (*yung*): these three are universal virtues for all. That whereby they are practiced is one. Some are born and know it; some study and so know it; some through painful difficulties come to know it. But the result of their knowing is one' " (quoted by Fung Yu-lan, *A History of Chinese Philosophy*, trans. Derk Bodde [Peiping: H. Vetch, 1937], I, 373).

Han Yu of the T'ang dynasty (768–824), in his essay *On the Nature of the Tao*, wrote: "What I will call the *Tao* is not what has hitherto been called the *tao* by the Taoists and the Buddhists. Yao transmitted the *tao* to Shun. Shun transmitted it to Yü. Yü transmitted it to Wen, Wu, and the Duke of Chou. Wen, Wu, and the Duke of Chou transmitted it to Confucius, and Confucius transmitted it to Mencius. After Mencius, it was no longer transmitted."]

10. See note 1.

11. [These events took place under the harsh Ch'in empire, in 212–13, as a means of enforcing intellectual conformity. All books throughout the empire, with certain important exceptions, were collected by the government and burned, and over 460 scholars were allegedly buried alive.]

12. [The substance of this and the following paragraphs as set out here by Fei would be disputed by many scholars in certain respects. That Heaven to Confucius was an indifferent abstraction is not the view of others (cf. Fung Yu-lan, *op. cit.*, I, 58: "For Confucius, Heaven was a purposeful supreme being"). Second, it is more widely thought that the theory of the Will of Heaven here attributed to Tung Chung-shu antedates him by almost a thousand years (see the chapter on this subject in Herrlee G. Creel, *The Birth of China* [New York:Reynall & Hitchcock, 1937]).]

4. THE ROLE OF THE LAW

Franz Michael

Any treatment of such a basic topic as the role of law in China, old or new, becomes meaningful only if it is related to a discussion of the philosophy of law in our own tradition. In order to make an evaluation that brings the Chinese situation into relief, one has to compare, contrast, or relate the role of law at the different stages of China's development with its role in the Western tradition. Since the basic philosophical assumptions, on which all definition and discussion of law are based, are themselves controversial

SOURCE: Selected from Franz Michael, "The Role of Law in Traditional China," in *The China Quarterly*, No. 9, pp. 124–132. Reprinted by permission of *The China Quarterly*.

in our own tradition, this is a very hazardous undertaking; but it is crucial to any understanding of China, past and present.

Under whatever school of thought, the positivist school or any form of belief in natural law, Western law is regarded as something of a special system that maintains the moral order of human life in society. This law either contains the moral code itself as an expression, albeit incomplete, of divine or natural absolute, or agreed upon, values; or it guarantees a realm of freedom in which ethical principles are at least a part of the substance of human existence thus guaranteed. This latter concept is held by philosophers as well as practical jurists, who have come to it from widely divergent theoretical and practical approaches. The German philosopher Kant excluded his great concept of ethics—of *Sittlichkeit*—from his concept of law. Law was only the "sum total of the conditions under which the arbitrariness of one person can be related to the arbitrariness of another under a general rule of freedom." And this in a way was the beginning of the positivist school of law in Germany. In the United States this concept has, as recently as February of last year, been defined by an American legal scholar in an essay on "The Challenge of the Rule of Law."[1] To him law is "a specific technique of social ordering deriving its character from reliance upon prestige, authority, and force of politically organised society." This law is meant to include "no moral or ethical coloration." Ethics, however, remain a recognised factor of human life, outside the law but protected by it.

The positivist view can, of course, go to the extreme of omitting all ethics or subsuming them under utility—a view indicated, for instance, by an American lawyer who wrote an essay in a collection produced in the United States twenty years ago under the title *My Philosophy of Law*.[2] In this essay the law is described simply as the system of state action which the lawyer has to understand in order to gain the greatest advantage in the protection of the interests of his clients. But when put to the test, I believe that the positivists will almost always bring in ethics in one form or another, and the attack made against these ethics by the Communist system today may clarify the issue. The definition of the rule of law given by the International Commission of Jurists shows something of this realisation in its cautious, positivist language. The rule of law is the "complex of value acceptances and of practical institutions and procedures which experience and tradition in the different countries of the world, often having themselves varying political structures and economic backgrounds, have shown to be essential to protect the individual from arbitrary government and to enable him to enjoy the dignity of man"[3]

Whether defined by the positivist or the naturalist, law is regarded as something vital to the existence of a moral order, something which—though created by man—stands and is regarded as a force in itself. The Greek legal philosopher and statesman Solon, who introduced the laws that settled a growing social conflict between the nobility and the *demos* in Athens and laid the foundation for Greek democracy, prided himself that he had been fair and impartial to both sides in the conflict by elevating and maintaining law as the supreme arbiter. He said, "Thus I stood with a mighty shield and protected them both; but still prior to them I protected the sacrosanct law."

This concept of law as something superior to the conflicts, even to the lawgiver himself, who is bound by it, at least until the law is changed, is a basic Western concept of Graeco-Roman origin. It is the law that is the guarantor of the freedoms and the social order. Whether in the monistic constitutional tradition, to which belong such diverse figures as Hobbes and Rousseau, Hegel and the French Jacobins, and from which derive the continental European legal systems, or the pluralistic tradition, in which one may count Aristotle, Augustinus, Thomas Aquinas, Grotius, John Locke, Montesquieu, and Alexis de Tocqueville, and the whole Anglo-Saxon legal system, or whether in the tradition of state law which represents the will of the lawgiver, or the growth of law out of the customs and the practice of the courts, the resulting law is something above the quarrels of the day, the most highly respected guarantor of the social order. This is the great tradition of law in the West.

Law in Imperial China

In China—Imperial China, the China of the period from the third century B.C. until the revolution of 1911—law never assumed that role. It has often been said that in this traditional China there was not government by law but government by man. This, in my view, is only another platitude that is as common as it is wrong.

Certainly, law in Imperial China was not the chief guarantor of the moral order, although it did help to enforce it. There was in China state law that dealt with the structure and functioning of government; and there was also a general code enforced by the Imperial Government that regulated the subjects' behaviour. This legal code, which was issued in new form by each successive dynasty on the basis of the code of its predecessor and enforced by the officials of the Imperial Government, was, however, in form and concept a criminal code only. Its principal purpose was intimidation and assertion of the power of the state against attack and against disturbance of the social order. There was no code for an impartial adjustment of human conflicts.

In time, it is true, some rules of what we would call civil law were introduced, or perhaps crept into, this penal code. To give just a few examples, there were stipulations that dealt with violations of contracts of sale of land and houses or of agreements on pawned goods or on division of inheritance. In such cases the articles of the law provided not only rather severe punishment for offences against the rules of contract or inheritance but also secured the protection of the personal interests of the offended party. The development of such concepts of the protection of private rights in the codes of imperial times is a fascinating topic which can still be explored much further. Even in the code of the last dynasty, however, the *Ta-Ch'ing lü-li* and its added stipulations, these rules were few and scattered and remained entirely unsystematised. They read almost like a grudging concession to the demand for final government sanction of developing concepts of protection of rights in social and economic relations. They did not establish a system of law in the Western sense.

This absence of a general system of law sanctioned by government still did not mean that there existed that alleged "government by man," which we referred to before. For much more important than the penal code sanctioned by the government was the moral code enforced by society. This moral code has been given a position of respect which can certainly be compared with that of the law in the West. In Chinese the moral code is called *li*—a term treated with the utmost respect and very difficult to translate. It has usually been rendered as etiquette, a code of behaviour, or "rites," and it covers the whole scope of proper human behaviour, in family, social, economic, and official dealings. It covers this behaviour from the point of view of ethical standards that are believed to be absolute norms that dictate human behaviour. It is the ethical content of these norms that really makes up the *li*. *Li* has therefore been translated by the late Dr. Hu Shih, the Chinese scholar in the field of history of philosophy, by the German term *Sittlichkeit*, the concept of ethics of Kantian and Hegelian philosophy. I consider this to be an excellent rendering of the term.

In traditional China this *li* took over much of the function filled by law in Western tradition. Because an ethical rule, rather than law, was the main standard and directive force for human behaviour, this system has been given the aforementioned label, "government by man." But *li* was still a code, a system of norms that were generally accepted, applied, and enforced, though they were enforced by society rather than by the government. *Li* was therefore a system of enforced norms—the term that I was given as a student as the positivist definition of law. It does not fulfil Austin's definition of law as "the command of the sovereign," but command it was.

In Western tradition the enforcement of moral rules by society has not only covered much less ground because of the prevalence of law but has also been so much less effective that we do not think in terms of enforcement when we speak of the moral code. I believe that the tradition of *li* in Chinese society was much stricter; and it was therefore a system of moral norms under which people lived—a rule of moral norms, not an arbitrary rule by men.

How did this system come into being?

Confucianists and Legalists

The Chinese imperial order had its beginnings in the last centuries before our Christian era, when in China an older feudal order broke down, and in the resulting anarchy and confusion of political and social transition there was an intellectual groping for new rules for the emerging social order. At this time China experienced its greatest intellectual growth. It has often been pointed out that these centuries of the founding of all the major philosophical schools in China were also the period of the greatness of philosophy and religion in Greece and India; and one may wonder about this coincidence. In China this has been called the period of the Hundred Schools of Thought that were contending for acceptance in the minds of thinking men and of the rulers of the contending states of that time. Of these many schools two are of crucial importance for our argument. These are the *Fa Chia* and the *Ju Chia*—the Legalists and the Confucianists. These two schools, of which the Confucianists appeared the earlier, developed in sharp conflict with each other.

The school of Confucius, holding to the premise that man is good by nature[4] and that his good qualities can be brought out through education and that those who had cultivated their moral qualities should through example and direction manage society, aimed at the introduction and acceptance of a new code of behaviour at a time of breakdown of feudal loyalties and of trickery and moral chaos. Confucius and his followers started with the moral rules of family relations, still valid at the time, and expanded these rules into a system that could be applied in society and state. These rules were to be formed into a new code of behaviour for the "noble men" who were to be the new leaders of society. These "noble men"—in Chinese *chün-tzu*—were at first mainly of aristocratic birth, but their qualification for their new role was not inherited; it was the result of their education in the rules of ethics and moral behaviour that qualified them to be examples for others and to understand the problems of human behaviour and social relations well enough to direct human affairs. These rules of behaviour were given in the examples of the teachings of a morally interpreted history and in many of the well-known Confucian sayings which directed the noble man as to what to do and what not to do, and formed a code which eventually was to pervade all social life.

For this way of thinking, law enforced by authority was a bad thing. Law was regarded only as punishment for violations of the social and political order. The need of such punishment was an admission of the inadequacy of the moral code and a sign that education and the example of virtue had failed. This attitude has remained throughout imperial history. When law was accepted as necessary, it was an unpleasant admission, and the dislike of law by the educated was applied even to the codes. "One does not read the codes" became a known quotation, indicating the view that the law was vulgar, and for vulgar people only.

The opposite view was held by the Legalists, a view expressed best by their greatest theoretical writer Han Fei-tzu.[5] According to this school, man was bad, and had to be kept in order by a strict rule of law and punishment. Han Fei-tzu ridiculed the views of the Confucianists. It was fine if a good man ruled, but only one out of ten was good; and rule by bad men without an enforced code was terrible. Law was better even for the sages, who had in it a standard to apply, let alone for a situation where there were no sages. Law was a good guarantee against a rule serving personal interests, which would be inevitable without it. The state was not like a family; and family loyalties and social loyalties could well be in conflict. The examples were given of the son who was punished under the moral code because he denounced his father who conspired against the government; and the soldier who could not be punished because his flight from the enemy was meant to preserve his life for reasons of filial piety.

Neither did Han Fei-tzu believe in the moral character of the Confucian scholars themselves. These intellectuals were to him lazy and corrupt men who lived on others by clever talk. Instead of their order of social rules and examples, he wanted strict laws applied equally to all. These laws must be "clear, easy to know, and strictly applied." They were to be written down and kept under the closest protection, so that no one could secretly change them. He provided for an office that would give to anyone clear answers on the meaning of the law. The law of the Legalists, as described most impressively by Han Fei-tzu, was based on the principles of objectivity and universality, mainstays of a system of laws in our own tradition. If this law was limited in scope, with its concentration on punishments and rewards, and harsh in its regulations, it contained the main concepts of a legal tradition, being clear and definite, equal to all, and binding on the lawgiver himself, the opposite of the present Communist concept of law, to which it has been sometimes compared.

In the political battles of that time, the Legalists won the day. The first emperor Ch'in Shih Huang Ti, who brought about unification and centralised government of China by military force, used Legalism as the basis of his political and social structure. The equal application of laws was of the greatest importance for abolishing the remnants of the feudal order; but in victory the Emperor's Legalist adviser also induced him to destroy the Confucian opposition. This policy led to the infamous "burning of the books," that is, the books that dealt with the political and historical thought of the opposition—not the books that dealt with practical matters; and the Confucian scholars themselves were persecuted—put to death or driven from positions of influence.

The political structure built on this system did not, however, outlast for long the strong man who was its founder. The new dynasty, the Han, that emerged from the chaos of the resulting civil war, reintroduced eventually the principle of a bureaucratic structure and adopted a code of law for the punishment of crimes against the state and the social order. But in the realisation that it needed the services of the educated, the dynastic government made its peace with the Confucian scholars, and secured their services for the state. With the services of this group the government had to accept its political philosophy and moral code. In fact, it was their beliefs and teachings that eventually became the ideological foundation of the new Chinese society and of the dynastic governments that ruled it.

Importance of the Moral Code

This philosophy, however, belittled government-enforced laws and stressed the force of moral persuasion. The moral code that was now to sustain government and society was laid down in the teachings of the Confucian school; and the Confucian scholars themselves were the guardians and arbiters for the interpretation of the rules of this code. Since the moral code itself, by its very nature, could not be incorporated into government law, it remained outside the direct control of the dynasty and its officials. This moral code remained a supreme norm of social and political action to which the Confucian scholars could refer as an objective system of rules valid for the emperor and his officials as well as for the scholars and society at large. This code of behaviour was preserved by the teachings of the Confucian scholars themselves, who therefore regarded themselves as the guardians of this moral system. Since the government was not the lawgiver for these rules, they could be used even in any move of defiance against a government that was believed to act in contradiction to them. It goes without saying that if *li* is to be compared with the Western norms, it comes closer to customary law and court decisions of pluralist origin than to monist law of Western systems of condification.

There was thus a double source of authority: that of the government power, based on force and enabling it to carry out political action and enforce punishment according to the law; and that of the moral code, which gave the moral sanction to government authority but only to the authority that was exercised within the rules of this moral code. This moral source of authority was believed to be a natural law, and though not under the control of any social or political group, it was interpreted and handed down from generation to generation by the Confucian scholars. This dualism of two sources of authority supported a system that on the whole proved to be eminently workable, and, as shown by the long history of Chinese culture, extraordinarily durable.

It could and did lead to conflict. Indeed, in my view, the whole course of imperial Chinese history, in which dynasties rose and fell but the social order continued, can be interpreted on the basis of this dualism, under which the authority of the moral code continued to be valid and effective while the authority of each dynastic government grew and declined. At the time of the collapse of any dynastic government, and of its laws no longer sustained by a working administration and military force, the social and ideological system not only continued but from it there was rebuilt the political structure of the new dynasty that had been set up by military force. The basis of this dualism was the double role played by the educated stratum, the Confucian scholars, in state and society.

The role of this educated Confucian group, of course, did not remain static. From more limited beginnings it grew in time and went through several stages of development. There was competition for the monopoly of this role of the Confucian scholars, especially from Buddhism in the early centuries of our era; but eventually their monopoly was secured and their role became formalised. The mark of the Confucian scholar was already in Han time an examination degree bestowed by the government after a test of his qualifications based mainly on knowledge of the Confucian classics. In Sung time, when the Confucian scholars' complete monopoly of government service was established, the examination system was expanded and formalised. From then on, only degree-holders were regarded as recognised scholars qualified to enter government service or to possess the authority for leadership and management of public affairs in society.

The Role of the Gentry

This important educational stratum that assumed the management of affairs in state and society has been referred to by a number of names, both in Chinese and Western languages. The term most common in English has been "scholar-gentry" or simply "gentry," a term which has some unfortunate connotations. In England the term meant a hereditary, landed group. In China the qualification for belonging to this group was not hereditary but the result of educational accomplishment, and membership had no relation to land. But since the term "gentry" has been generally accepted, I still continue to use it to describe this privileged, educated, upper group, of whom I have been speaking.

The arduous education of this group in the Confucian classics, as certified in the state examinations, was not only the basis for a monopoly of government service; it also enabled the gentry to exercise functions of social leadership in areas in which the state administration remained inactive. These functions were carried on by the gentry on their own initiative, autonomously, not under any orders or discipline of the government but simply in accordance with their interpretation of their responsibilities as persons educated in the moral code and able to apply it. Only the most crucial matters of state affairs were handled by the officials of the government; and even many of those were taken over by the gentry in times of government decline or crisis. All the other day-to-day affairs of communal life, including the protection of the principles of the moral order in family life and social relations and the arbitration of conflicts between families and individuals, were handled mainly by the gentry. The settlement of local conflicts included almost all the realm of business transactions in sales and rent of land, pawnshop and mortgage business, and commercial transactions. Indeed, since there was no commercial code and very little legal guarantee, commercial transactions depended on the good faith of the parties involved and on the code of behaviour applied to business affairs. In case of disagreement on interpretation or execution of a contract there were also the guilds, whose secretaries, often members of the gentry, would arbitrate in many cases. The special guarantee regularly given for many business transactions by shop owners demonstrated the strength of a development of practices that had something like legal force but remained outside the realm of state enforcement.

The much greater realm of the rule of *li* as compared to that of law corresponded to the larger sphere of the gentry's autonomous management of the public affairs of society as compared to the official action of the government's administrators. The prevalence of *li* over law thus corresponds to that of the gentry's functions over the acts of the officials. Law was the final force that maintained and guaranteed peace and order, and officials could enforce the government's will and the law, but when the government fell and the law was no longer valid, local leadership and the rule of *li* continued until a new structure of government and of law was established. One may well speculate that the special position of the educated stratum, the gentry, which served the government but maintained its autonomous position as guardian of the political philosophy and its moral code, explains the strength of the *li* and the limitations of law in imperial China.

Notes

1. W. Burnett Harvey, *Michigan Law Review*, Vol. 59, No. 4, February, 1961, p. 605.

2. *My Philosophy of Law, Credos of Sixteen American Scholars,* published under the direction of the Julius Rosenthal Foundation, Northwestern University (Boston; Boston Law Book Co., 1941). The essays in this collection cover the whole range of views on law in Western tradition.

3. *Journal of the International Commission of Jurists,* Vol. 2, No. 1, pp. 7–18, Spring–Summer, 1959, as quoted in W. Burnett Harvey, "The Challenge of the Rule of Law," *Michigan Law Review,* Vol. 59, No. 4, p. 612.

4. This is the Mencian tradition. Confucius himself did not clearly indicate whether he regarded human nature as good or bad but held that it had the quality of being educable to goodness. Hsün-tzu regarded human nature as bad but came to the same conclusion that man could be educated. Whatever the assumption as to human nature, education was believed to develop the good in man.

5. For a discussion of the work of Han Fei-tzu, see Jean Escarra, *Le Droit Chinois* (Peking: Henry Vetch, and Paris: Libraire du Recueil Sirey, 1936), pp. 31 *et seq.*

The Transition—A Collapse of Control and the Process of Reintegration

5. THE ROLE OF THE FAMILY

Marion J. Levy

Any problem of social change is a problem in comparative social analysis. Three stages must be distinguished either explicitly or implicitly. First one must distinguish the basis from which change takes place, *the initial stage.* Second, one must distinguish the stage during which the change takes place, *the transitional stage.* Third one must distinguish the stage of the system when the change studied is considered completed for the purposes of the problem in hand, *the resultant stage.* It should go without saying that there is always an arbitrary element in the distinction of these stages since the process of change in some respects is ubiquitous in all empirical systems. The test of whether or not one has chosen one's stages well rests on whether or not these distinguished have been useful in the generation of tenable hypotheses relevant to the problem attacked.[1]

For any problem of social change one must either explicitly or implicitly have data or hypotheses of some sort on at least two of these stages. Given knowledge of the initial stage and the transitional one, predictions can be made about the resultant one. Given knowledge about the initial one and the resultant one, hypotheses can be erected about the transitional stage and so forth.

SOURCE: Selected from Marion J. Levy, "Contrasting Factors in the Modernization of China and Japan," in *Economic Development and Cultural Change,* 2 (1954), pp. 163–177. Reprinted by permission of The University of Chicago Press. Copyright 1954 by The University of Chicago Press.

In the case of China and Japan the initial stages distinguished are both relatively little industrialized. A system for present purposes will be considered more or less industrialized to the extent that its system of allocation of goods and services (including in that allocation both consumption and production) involves tools that multiply or magnify in whatever complex way the effect of the human energy involved in their use and to the extent that inanimate sources of power are applied. In this sense of the term there are elements of industrialization in the initial stages of both China and Japan as those stages are distinguished here—and probably in any society. But these elements are certainly small by comparison with those involved in "modern Western" nations such as the United States, Great Britain and Germany. They are also small by comparison with the elements involved in Japan of the 1930 period. It is in this sense that the initial stages of China and Japan distinguished here are spoken of as non-industrialized or relatively little industrialized.

The period of Chinese society that will be considered its initial stage is that period of the Ch'ing Dynasty in the middle and latter part of the eighteenth century. The period of Japanese society that will be considered its initial stage is that of the reign of the Shogun Iyemitsu (1623–1651). These stages will be referred to respectively as "traditional" China and "traditional" Japan. In both cases there are no doubt many elements of social structure for which an authentic pedigree can be traced further back in the history of the societies concerned. Here, however, we are concerned with the character of the initial stages and not with their origins.

These two particular stages have been chosen for present purposes in order to accent two sources of change in the societies. The first has to do with sources that were indigenous to the societies concerned. The second has to do with the sources of change that came from social systems outside the two societies considered. In the two countries the internal sources of change were markedly different, but the external sources of change were identical. In the case of China the internal sources had to do with the breakdown of the Imperial Bureaucracy. This was a breakdown of a sort that had been seen in many of its facets in the history of previous Chinese dynasties. In the case of Japan the internal sources of change had to do with the breakdown of a feudal[2] social system—a breakdown in which a major role was played by the changing actual role of the merchants in the society. In both China and Japan the external sources were virtually identical. They were the factors involved in modern industrialization. Neither China nor Japan was responsible for the development of the highly industrialized social systems that provided the factors that were the external sources of change in both cases. If the changes described in both cases as internal sources are in fact internal sources of change, then it follows that these internal sources are themselves products of the operation of the systems that have been referred to as the initial stages of the societies concerned. This in turn argues that whatever differences we may find between China and Japan with respect to their resultant stages must be primarily a result of their differences in their initial stages. This would follow in so far as it is in fact true that their external sources of change were identical and their internal sources of change were different. Their resultant stages can only be a result of the impact of their internal and external sources of change on the social bases from which change took place. The internal sources of change can only be a result of the developments of that same initial stage. In this particular case therefore the differences in the resultant stage would seem to be primarily a result of the different initial stages into which the external factors were introduced.

The Problem of Change in China

THE INITIAL STAGE

Perhaps the most significant feature of "traditional" China for present purposes is the fact that it was "family oriented" to an overwhelming degree.[3] This society was overwhelmingly "family oriented" in the sense that ideally speaking it was expected that decisions be made primarily with reference to family interests. In the ordinary course of events the crucial question for decisions was, "How will this affect my family?" When family interests were in conflict with those of other groups in which individuals participated, family interests were to take precedence. The individual owed loyalty first, last, and always to his family. This was true even in a conflict between an individual and the Imperial Bureaucracy. Crimes of violence against the Imperial Family itself were sometimes forgiven if they were committed to avenge wrongs to one's family. Conversely, of course, in recognition of the virtual obligation of such vendettas, the entire family of a man was sometimes wiped out to prevent attempts at revenge by family members other than the person directly guilty of the act calling for punishment. The whole Confucian theory of order rested in considerable part on the theory that, if family members were so well imbued with filial piety that they would never consider informing on one another, the individual members could not possibly be the sort of people who would, as individuals, commit improper acts.

There were several organizations that brought pressure to bear on family groups and limited the extremes to which the individual might go in sacrificing the interests of others to the interests of his family. Especially noteworthy in these respects were such organizations as the neighborhood councils and the guides. Even in these, however, pressure was often brought in family terms. The individual was constrained in effect by the threat that he would achieve only the short run interest of his family—that in the long run his acts would so unite other families against his as to bring about its downfall. In such organizations families were represented by family heads, and pressure on individuals was usually brought to bear through the family head, rather than directly.

The family in "traditional" China was not only the overriding focus for individual loyalties in the ideal case. It was also the basic unit in terms of which the economic aspects of life were carried out. The average Chinese family, and that means the ordinary peasant family in "traditional" China, was self-sufficient in both production and consumption to a degree that it is difficult for persons from highly industrialized societies to understand. They produced most of what they consumed and consumed most of what they produced, ideally speaking. When substantial goods and services had to be purchased from the outside, the situation was considered unfortunate, and when substantial payments in the form of rent, taxes, interest, and payment for consumption had to be made, that too was considered unfortunate. Even in gentry families in which such self-sufficiency obviously did not exist, their dependency on non-family members as producers was minimized, at least ostensibly, by the use of servants who were often quasi-family members and by cutting to a minimum the number of family members through whom these outside contacts were made.

Finally, the family was the basic unit in terms of which the allocation of power and responsibility took place. It has already been suggested above that the individual was controlled primarily through pressure brought to bear on him by the family head. The average Chinese had most of his contacts with family members. The hierarchy of power and responsibility with which he was most familiar was that of his own family. In so far as he participated in groups outside his family group, these were likely to be organized on a pseudofamily basis, or he was likely to be controlled, in so far as he was controlled, on the basis of the implications of his deviance for the fortunes of his family.

There were, of course, organizations of considerable importance for Chinese society apart from the family organization. These often required decisions that were not in accordance with those that might have been made by unbridled family "self-interest." Most notable among these was perhaps the Imperial Bureaucracy. "Traditional" Chinese society was dependent in many respects upon some highly organized administrative machinery. This dependence was particularly marked with regard to problems centering about irrigation, but in most of the dynasties, whatever were the reasons, the production of certain strategic goods and services (e.g., certain metals, salt, communications, etc.) were also handled on this basis. The equipment and organization involved required considerable talent to devise, but they were also subject to extremely low rates of obsolescence, and apparently also to relatively slow rates of decay. This is true at least by comparison with the situation in a highly industrialized system in which the attention to equipment and organization must be unremitting in a sense and to a degree unnecessary in the Chinese case.

When the bureaucracy was working as it was "supposed to," individual family interests were rigidly ruled out. Nepotism in recruitment was banished by a most carefully worked out examination system. During one's service in the organization every attempt was made to remove temptation for putting one's family interests above one's duties to the state. But no attempt was made to teach the members that such family interferences were bad. It was the responsibility of the system to insulate the individual from such pressures by properly conducted examinations, by refusing permission to serve in one's home area, and the like. The attempts to insulate the individual always broke down in many cases through the years, and no long run attempt was made to convert the individuals recruited for the service to a point of view that subordinated the family. The dynastic cycle in China for some two thousand years was a continual breakdown and renovation of the Imperial Bureaucracy. Any attempt at conversion as opposed to insulation would probably have been extremely difficult. It would have involved a radical departure from the tenets held good and true throughout the rest of the society and would have undercut many of the other aspects of the bureaucracy itself. Whatever the alternatives may have been, as it existed, the Imperial Bureaucracy did not provide an organization that took precedence over the family, ideally speaking, for the individual member of the society. The underlying theory of government was that a proper government could not be unjust to any family, that no filial son could have reason therefore for not obeying the government. A good family man could not be other than a good citizen.

Friendship groups of various kinds and degrees tempered family relationships, but here again in case of clear contradiction between the interests of one's family and one's friends, the family interests, at least ideally speaking, took precedence. The overwhelming significance of the family as a center of attention in the society was demonstrated in other ways than this matter of precedence, however. In membership groups outside the family the terminology of kinship was likely to be applied, particularly if the relationships involved were considered to be extremely close and binding. Close friends were likely to be referred to as "older brother," teachers assumed a role likened to that of "father" or "father's elder brother" relative to their students. Thus quite apart from the precedence taken by the family in case of conflicts, in the ordinary course of these relationships outside the family, family solidarities were continually being called to mind, simulated, and reinforced.

Organizations like the neighborhood ruling councils, the guilds, etc. have already been mentioned above. They often operated in such a way as to limit the pursuit of family self-interest, but as has been pointed out above, they operated frequently through the use of family pressures. The strong emphasis on continued family residence in a single locale enhanced this possibility in the case of the neighborhood groups, and the tendency of apprenticeships, particularly in the more lucrative fields dominated by the guilds, to be given on highly nepotistic bases enhanced this possibility in that field. The use of the family as the vehicle of governmental control as exemplified in the pao-chia system is too obvious to require further mention. But in these respects again the family priority was made clear in other ways. Here too there was the transfer of kinship terms to non-kinship relations. But the matter was highlighted by what happened when the patterns in these areas did not work out as they would have under conditions generally considered ideal in that society. When, for example, a given family in a neighborhood became so powerful that pressure could not be successfully exerted on it by the threat of its long run disadvantage, family "self-interest" did take precedence over the neighborhood council, or more properly the neighborhood council came to be completely dominated by the members of that powerful family. When this happened, the interests of other families in the area were preserved only if their abrogation served no useful purpose for the family in power or if the family head of the family in power were a benevolent despot in the area and took an essentially paternal attitude toward those over whom he could in fact have exerted power.

The comparison of China and Japan in these and in other respects has often been confused by the use of the term "feudal" to denote both of these social systems. This can, of course, be done legitimately depending on one's definition of the term. But its use in this connection has, perhaps, on the whole been more misleading than any other single term used in discussions of the industrialization of non-industrialized areas. If the term is used to mean that from the point of view of the observer, the peasant had a difficult time of it in both societies, that individuals were not treated "democratically," that there was a great gulf between the "haves" and the "have nots," that most people made their livelihood from agrarian pursuits, that many of the "haves" lived on income secured by virtue of ownership of land, etc., then both cases may be described as "feudal." But the connotations of the term "feudal" include as a minimum the factors listed above[4] as the defining elements in the term. Unless the term is redefined by the user, these connotations go along with it, and the term is not usually redefined. In the sense of the term "feudal" as defined explicitly above, "traditional" China was decidedly not-feudal; in this sense China has not been truly feudal for the last two thousand years. In this sense Tokugawa Japan was feudal. It is the hypothesis here that the structural differences involved in this distinction are of primary importance in understanding the different experiences that these two systems have had with industrialization. This is not logomachy. It has very practical implications. If in fact the basis from which change is taking place today in China were feudal in the sense of that term as defined here, then China would present very different possibilities and probabilities of change than in fact seem to be present.

"Traditional" China did not contain a closed class system. It is true that the paths of social mobility were frequently badly clogged, but it is doubtful that they were actually ever completely closed during the last two thousand years of Chinese history, and certainly they were never ideally closed during that time. It is true that some groups were at least in theory excluded from social mobility by excluding their members from admission to the examinations, i.e., to the path par excellence of mobility upwards in that society. But the vast mass of the population was never so excluded. Ideally speaking a peasant family could always climb to the top of the tree if it could produce and educate a son of great talent.

The ideal type family in "traditional" China was the gentry type family. There was in fact mobility upwards, and there was also mobility downwards. Peasant sons did rise to the top of the bureaucracy. Wealthy gentry families not only lost their wealth and power in many instances, but they often returned to the status of peasant families or worse. In societies like those of medieval Europe and Tokugawa Japan, peasants were expected to remain peasants and nobles to remain nobles. Wealthy peasants were not nobles, and poor nobles were not peasants. The expectations, both ideal and actual, of every member of those societies were that one and one's family would retain forever the class status into which one was born. However much the actual expectation may have been of a similar sort in China, the ideal expectation was not of this order. It is extremely doubtful that the actual closure of class membership in "traditional" China ever approached that of Tokugawa Japan, but even if it did, their differences in ideal patterns in these respects mark them as animals of a different species. There are few points about which we may feel certain in the social sciences, but the importance for understanding social phenomena of the distinction between ideal and actual patterns is one of them. In comparing social systems, the presence of similar actual patterns but different ideal patterns in a given sphere cannot be without structural implications, of either a static or a dynamic sort. To the extent that this is so, even if one were to grant that the actual class closure in "traditional" China approached that of Tokugawa Japan, an admission by no means certainly justified on empirical grounds, the differences in their ideal patterns in these respects might still be of strategic importance in their respective problems of industrialization.

The allocation of power and responsibility in "traditional" China was also quite different from that involved in a feudal society. It is true that there existed only in so far as each individual responded to the expected family controls and the relations among different families remained in equilibrium. In time of upset, change, or crisis one owed loyalty first to one's family and only secondarily to the power-responsibility hierarchy outside the family. When new situations arose, the family head decided whether he and the other members of the family would go along with orders from outside the family or not. When the individual was not in a position to decide such a question on the basis of family interests (either because of separation from or loss of his family members), he was in a position of "individualism by default." He would under such conditions go along with the rules of magistrates or princes or whatever if he felt his interests coincided with theirs or if he felt that the force at their command was such that he had no alternative.

Within the family the hierarchy of power and responsibility was clearcut ideally speaking, but the position of a given family relative to other families and to organizations other than families was subject to considerable shifts. Hence the third condition of the definition of feudal given above (i.e., the identification, at least individually speaking, of each individual as responsible to some particular individual higher than himself in the hierarchy and related to others outside of that direct line by virtue of his overlord's relation to them. . .) was not met. The orientation of the family head was not first, last, and always to someone over him in the general social hierarchy of power and responsibility, but rather was owed to the organization of which he was the head. His loyalty and submission to others outside that organization was ideally speaking primarily instrumental for the welfare of the organization that he headed. It was generally to be expected that he be ruthlessly rational in seeking to maximize that welfare. Last, but not least, if he could maximize the welfare of his own family at the expense of others in the society, the responsibility was not considered his but rather that of the sovereign. The right to transfer allegiance from the reigning sovereign was built into the Chinese social system in an interesting fashion. As long as everything went well in terms of the value of that society, the sovereign was conceived to have and to rule in the name of the Will of Heaven, but when this was not so, he no longer held the Will of Heaven, and correspondingly he no longer had the right to rule or the right to the loyalty of his subjects. Revolts were *prima facie* evidence that something was wrong and something for which the sovereign was responsible. A successful revolt was final proof of the fact. This concern was focused on what, from an outsider's point of view, often seem minute details. Suicide was considered a terrible thing by the Chinese as by many people, but in China a suicide was indicative of the fact that something was radically wrong in the realm. Local officials had to look into the matter, and at least in theory a report of the full investigation had to be presented directly to the Emperor himself. The matter had its positive side as well. Acts that indicated that things were going well had also to be recognized by the sovereign, and so, for example, the countryside was studded with memorial arches set up by the Emperor to commemorate a particularly well preserved widowhood or the like.

It would be beside the point here to go into detail about the many ways in which these factors were interrelated with other aspects of the social system, or the roles they played both in adapting the system to its setting and in maladapting it to that setting. Actually under the circumstances it made for a system of control which was characterized by relatively long periods of stability and of gradual disintegration and which tended to be restored after a period of decay in a renovated rather than a revolutionized form. What is important from the present point of view is that it was a system of control that was peculiarly vulnerable to certain types of changes, that these changes, if introduced rapidly, could result in rather dramatic disintegration of control. The keystone of social structure in these respects was the family structure. For roughly two thousand years family structure does not seem to have been radically altered in these respects, and no genuine alternative was offered for it. But in the nineteenth and twentieth centuries there were forces elsewhere in the world that impinged on China and undercut the "traditional" family structure.

Turning for a moment from these problems of control, the special situation of the merchants in "traditional" China must be considered. Ideally speaking the merchants held roles of extremely low prestige in "traditional" China. They were ranked well below the peasants who were, of course, ranked well below the gentry. There were even periods in which attempts were made to make a closed class of the merchants by forbidding them or their sons or grandsons from taking the Imperial Examinations. For reasons that need not detain us here, these attempts were never successful in the long run. In actuality the merchants who were successful as merchants frequently became powerful politically and prestigious socially despite the ideal patterns of the society to the contrary. This sort of violation of the ideal patterns of a society should not seem strange to Westerners who are really quite familiar with the phenomena in the form of racketeers and the like controlling local and even state governments, amassing fortunes through corruption, escaping the punishment ideally decreed for such activities, and eventually in some cases becoming highly respected members of their communities. If one reads the documents expressing the ideals of the members of "traditional" Chinese society, or questions extremely conservative members of the area even today, one comes away with a picture of merchants as the lowest of the low, a picture quite at variance with their obvious affluence and power at many times in Chinese history. But again this discrepancy between ideal and actual patterns is of great importance for understanding the social phenomena of modern Chinese history.

It is probably true that the merchants in "traditional" China tended to be rather more emancipated from the traditional features of their social environment than were Chinese in the roles of gentry, peasants, artisans, etc. This is probably one of the reasons that attempts were made to restrict their power and influence. By and large the merchants made their fortunes by trading rather than production. As such, unlike the other members of the society, the self-sufficiency of their families was minimal. They produced neither what they sold nor what they consumed. Their contacts with persons outside their own family groups were therefore broader than those of most of the members of their society. They saw more of China and of other lands, as well as of people drawn from wider backgrounds. One would expect that these people with their greater perspective, their commercialism, and the like would have been the ideal people to break new ground when industrial influences were first felt, that they would convert easily to the roles played by members of the "middle class" in modern Western societies such as England and the United States. But this does not turn out to have been the case, and at least some of the explanation of this would seem to lie in the factors already mentioned.

Often when there are discrepancies between the ideal and actual roles of individuals, the pressure placed on those actually holding high positions to acquire the ideal ones as well is enormous. Many of the rising bourgeois in England sought to become landed gentry there. Many racketeers and political bosses in the United States seek to become businessmen. Often the transition is spread out over several generations. In "traditional" China prestige par excellence lay in the roles of the gentry. The gentry were expected to depend for income on the perquisites of political office and the absentee ownership of land. The most aristocratic circles in the Western world have not for many, many decades denigrated the stain of participating in "trade" to the extent common even to the present day in China. The successful merchant, like all other Chinese was under great pressure to secure the future of his family. This called for an education of some directed to their entry into the bureaucracy, and hence a classical Chinese education, and the investment of capital in land rather than its continued reinvestment in the business. This investment of profits in land was further reinforced by the almost shady status of trade and hence its vulnerability to exploitation by the scholar officials who held political office. This exploitation could be prevented only by being able to buy and control officials or by having in positions of power officials with whom one had strong personal relations, preferably kinship ones in that society. Land ownership, the major economic basis of the gentry was also vulnerable to the pressures of the officials, but by virtue of its eminently respectable status and by virtue of the fact that an official threatening the income from absentee ownership of land simultaneously threatened all of the gentry in his area, income from land was not nearly so vulnerable in these respects as were both the income from and capital invested in commercial pursuits.

There were other factors than these involved, but these alone will suffice to indicate that there was a considerable source of motivation for a flight of both talent and capital from the merchant role. A merchant who got his sons a classical education, invested in land, and terminated his involvement in trade laid a firm foundation for gentry status for his family in the future.

If he got a son or another relative into the bureaucracy, he established thereby connections that increased his security from exploitation. The emphasis on talent in the bureaucracy, even at its most corrupt, increased the motivation for sending the ablest of one's sons or male relatives into these roles rather than into merchant roles. These factors, combined with the open class structure of "traditional" Chinese society even as regards the merchants, made of the merchant role a transitory social status both ideally and actually. Merchant roles, if successful in a monetary sense, enabled one to accumulate the economic base necessary to guarantee, or make possible, gentry status for one's family in the future. The more a given merchant in fact followed such a path, the more successful he was adjudged by others in the society. A merchant was most fully successful to the extent that he and his ceased to be merchants and were enabled to do so by virtue of his commercial successes.

In this general background of "traditional" China, for which only some of the more strategic features for the present problem have been touched upon, there were several sources of stress and containment of stress that must be noted here. The facts of stress in this society have often been overlooked by the more romantic writings in this field. The writers are not altogether to blame in this regard. The errors here have arisen largely from a presentation of the ideal rather than the actual picture of the facts of social life in China and from focusing attention on some phases of the life history of individuals to the exclusion of others. For example, the picture generally given of the "traditional" Chinese family is a picture of the ideal gentry type of family. This ideal type was often approximated among the gentry, but the same type of family was also the ideal type for the peasants and others in the society. These latter, however, did not approximate the family type they held to be an ideal. The misunderstanding is not hard to acquire for Chinese not approximating this ideal type will nevertheless unhesitatingly describe it as the type characteristic of all Chinese. When the discrepancy between their picture and the facts is pointed out, they will usually reply that of course they and their neighbors are poor and hence are unable to live in the "true Chinese style."

An example of the second source of error mentioned above is to be found in the frequent treatment of the role of women as "secure" by contrast with the uncertainties facing women in modern Western societies. However tenable this may be as a comparative statement, it gives a misleading view of the position of Chinese women. At some stages of their lives they have indeed a large measure of security, but at others they are to a rather remarkable degree in positions of considerable stress. One of the most intriguing aspects about "traditional" Chinese social structure is that virtually every individual in the society went through periods of great social stress, but could in terms of the ideal patterns at least, and to a high degree in terms of the actual patterns as well, look forward to stages of greatly reduced stress. Males, for example, had a rather strenuous time of it as youths being prepared by their fathers to be able to fulfill the roles essential for the perpetuation of the family. When they reached the stage of family heads, which they frequently did when they were married and had children of their own, these stresses were removed, if they had not been either removed or adjusted to prior to that time. Women were highly insecure as youngsters growing up in their parental families if economic conditions were difficult, because relative to their brothers they were marginal members of the family, especially as regards the future of the family. In good times or bad, however, a woman was subjected to very considerable stress when she married and assumed the role of daughter-in-law in her husband's family. When whe attained the role of mother-in-law relative to her sons' wives, she was as much relieved from stress as was possible for a woman in that society, assuming of course that her husband's family as a whole was not in a particularly bad way when she reached that role.

Some of the most fundamental sources of stress in "traditional" Chinese society were concentrated within the strongest unit of solidarity of that society, i.e., the family. There is not time to go into these sources in detail, but short of a theory holding the Chinese to be inherently masochistic, notable stresses must be granted as the result of relations between fathers and sons, mothers-in-law and daughters-in-law, and men and women. Less notable ones perhaps resulted from certain relations among brothers, brothers and sisters, women in the family apart from the specific roles already mentioned, etc. Suffice it to say that there is good reason to believe that there were sources enough for motivation to defy, desert, or modify the family patterns if opportunities to do so presented themselves.

There were many other notable sources of stress in the society. General economic conditions were close to a subsistence minimum for a large proportion of the members of the society in the best of times. In times of crop failures, despotic officials, and the like, whatever margin existed could easily be and was often wiped out. Relations between the townsmen and the villagers were an important source of difficulty. Those whom the peasants often regarded as exploiters (i.e., landlords, usurers, officials, merchants, etc.) were typically town dwellers. The economic structure of "traditional" China was one in which the townsmen were supported by goods and services from both the towns and the villages, but the villagers were supported almost entirely by what they produced alone. The village economy was the keystone of the whole economy, but as far as most of the villagers were concerned the flow of foods and services was a one-way affair. When times were difficult, the townsmen were likely to be regarded as the source of difficulties by the villagers whether this was in fact justified or not.

Another source of stress in the society was, of course, the breakdown of the bureaucratic system. The insulation of that system from the family pressures on which the society was based was not in fact effective for long. Graft and corruption grew as the dynasties went their course, and this was no less true of the Ch'ing than of the others. As the system decayed, the irrigation and communications systems also decayed. This had its implications in lowered productivity. More and more of a premium was placed on the officials squeezing all they could from whomever they could get hold of. Taxes were often collected years in advance. Combinations of officials and merchants preyed on the peasants in many ways. In regions in which official power declined powerful families were often able to become the effective governing force in the area and exploit the rest of the population there. A popular saying in China held that it was better to live in a tiger infested area than in one ruled by a bad government, and it is not without significance that the district magistrate's yamen was known frequently as a "tiger's mouth."

Despite these sources of stress and strain, the structure of "traditional"

Chinese society seems to have been a remarkably stable arrangement for a non-industrial society of the scale encompassed. Most of the patterns here referred to as "traditional" seem to have a pedigree of nearly two thousand years. During this long period a typical dynastic cycle of decay, chaos, refurbishment of the system, and then decay again went on. The cycle generally took about three hundred years. But even at its best the system contained many strains. It is an hypothesis of the present paper that the structure had built into it a very potent method of containing these strains. The family stresses in particular were contained by the fact that the possibilities for alternative employment for rebels were so restricted. As noted above, people were hired primarily on the basis of who they were, and the primary criterion of who a person was depended on his family status. A rebel from the family cut himself or herself off from this source of identification, and in doing so he or she was virtually certain to break the major ethical tenet of the society and to sin against filial piety. No respectable employer wanted such a person. The jobs open were those of extremely low status and jobs in which life was very likely to be "poor, nasty, brutish, and short." There were rebels, of course, but they were rather effectively disposed of by the opportunities open to them, and those who avoided these fates and who prospered were usually at some pains to disguise the fact that they had ever been rebels.

There were more positive sources of containment too. Each family head was emancipated from direct responsibility to other members of his family, but he was responsible to the ancestors for the welfare of the family. In so far as he continued sincere in these devotions, he was likely to try to prevent such stresses from getting out of hand. Nevertheless, it is hardly likely that this positive obligation did more than modify the extremity of these stresses.

Relative to the more general stresses in the society mentioned above, the overwhelming tendency for redress was via a refurbishment of the system rather than by revolutionary change. In the first place, the system, when relatively devoid of graft and corruption, was probably as effective and well-balanced a system of organizing and controlling a large scale highly decentralized system as the world has ever seen. This was particularly so since the units of the system were capable of such a high degree of economic self-sufficiency and hence, with the technologies available, so difficult to control in detail by a highly centralized governmental organization. In the second place, the relatively slow disintegration of the dynasties, gave the people a relatively prosperous period to look back on. The lack of basic structural changes either from within or without the system tended in this context to focus attention on reform of the system and return thereby to things as "they should be" rather than on radical change of the system. This tendency was further reinforced by virtue of the fact that the intellectual and ethical authorities revered by the members of the system were well aware of such breakdowns and had counseled dealing with them via renovation.

THE TRANSITIONAL STAGE

There were two sources of change in the transitional period of modern China, and indeed they continue to operate today. The resultant stage of China is phrased negatively for present purposes—China has not made much headway with industrialization. Those sources were on the one hand the disintegration of the typical patterns of "traditional" China, particularly those having to do with the Imperial Bureaucracy, and on the other those new forces that were introduced to China with the introduction from the West of social patterns pertaining to modern industrialization. The factors involved in the first have already been touched on above and are in general too familiar to require extended comment here. They involve the tremendous increase in graft and corruption in government to the point of virtual governmental impotence. In China the Ch'ing rulers fell and were replaced by a republic in name. This latter made a start in the direction of reform, but it had more to cope with than had past reformers. It had to cope with the sources of disintegration added by the new forces, and it did not succeed. The new forces precluded at least temporarily the return to the old situation, and the heritage of the old situation made the successful establishment of the new especially difficult—at least sufficiently so that none of the modern rulers of China had succeeded in coping with the situation in terms of the new forces. Certainly the Nationalist regime did not, and the Communist regime has not yet shown that it can do so.

There is not space here to detail all of the special features of the new forces that were imported into these two societies. For present purposes brief mention of two will have to suffice. In the first place, the new forces placed a tremendous emphasis on an entirely different sort of social relationship than had been common in either China or Japan. In the second place, the development of industrialization when it became available to China and Japan, given their respective economic bases, had of necessity to be carried out on a large scale or none, at least with regard to many crucial areas.

In the sphere of relationships industrialization carried with it an emphasis hitherto unequalled in social history on what the sociologists speak of as highly rational, highly universalistic, and highly functionally specific relationships. For present purposes these terms may be explained as follows. In a highly industrialized situation a tremendous amount of action has to be based on what would amount to tenable engineering criteria of efficiency and the like, rather than on traditional arguments about the right and wrong way to do things. The individual has to think critically and in scientifically tenable terms about how to do things, what to buy, when to sell, where to locate, and the like. In this sense his actions in many spheres have to be highly rational rather than traditional. In regard to choosing people for jobs and the like he has to place great emphasis on what a person can do that is germane to the reasons for which he is chosen—on his abilities rather than on who he is. In this sense great emphasis must be placed on highly universalistic rather than on particularistic criteria. Under highly industrialized conditions relatively small differences in skill may have tremendous implications both in terms of what is accomplished and in terms of accidents prevented. This is true even when mechanical aids have reduced the task performed to button-pushing. Finally, in many of the relationships in a highly industrialized situation the obligations, etc. involved in a relationship must be precisely defined and delimited regardless of how complex they may be. At least a tendency in this direction is extremely important. The machines of modern industry are so inordinately productive and the interrelationships of even a single operation with others in the system are so complex that one cannot rely on vaguely defined relationships to handle these matters. The craftsman who makes carriages may perhaps have a personal relationship with all his customers and all his workmen and all his suppliers, but this is not possible for a modern manufacturer of automobiles or steel. In this sense an emphasis is placed by modern industry on functionally specific relationships rather than on functionally diffuse ones.

With regard to the special problems of scale involved in the industrialization of China and Japan, or of any late-comers to industrialization for that matter, the basic problem involved is, perhaps, the implication of these scale requirements for the problem of planning and control. Given the discrepancy between the basis of industrialization in these two countries and the stages of development it had reached in the West, it was necessary for these countries to import en masse what had been developed gradually elsewhere. Railroad systems and communications in general had to be undertaken on a large scale if they were to be of maximum usefulness or even to be useful at all. The lack of ready convertibility of the capital in private hands to uses of this sort virtually forced governmental involvement in these projects; certainly this was true if, as in the case of Japan, the members of the system were anxious to carry out such a program without permitting control of the program or of the country to fall into the hands of foreign individuals or foreign governments. It is perfectly true that industrialization grew up in countries like England and the United States with relatively little centralized planning, and it may even be true that it could not have developed had such planning been present, but China and Japan were not developing industrialization. They were taking it over after it had become rather highly developed. The gradual passing from a system of highly decentralized highly self-sufficient units to a system of highly interdependent units could not be repeated in these countries. If they were to industrialize at all, they had to institute systems of highly interdependent units and radical departures from their prevailing highly self-sufficient ones. They were faced at the very outset with large-scale problems of coordination if they were to take advantage of their special situation as late-comers to industrialization. They could not even modernize methods of agricultural production without raising a whole host of other problems such as systems of roads, repair depots for equipment, agricultural stations for testing and growing special seeds, etc.

This problem of coordination involves a problem of control, by force if necessary, in cases in which deviance develops or threatens. More importantly it requires that there be patterns in operation that tend to minimize the development of deviance. In the last analysis it is the latter rather than the former that is crucial because of the limited effectiveness of the use of force and the fact that every effective use of force on a large scale implies the presence of patterns that motivate conformity without the actual invocation of force. Pure force or threat of force can never explain the whole of such control, because the use of force always raises the problem of "Who guards the guards themselves."

In the transitional period in China the internal sources of change provided motivation aplenty for individuals to try the new patterns introduced from the West. The family strains alone were capable of motivating many individuals to seek alternative roles if those were available. By the latter part of the Ch'ing dynasty the disintegration of the Imperial Bureaucracy was far advanced. This disintegration itself put pressures of many sorts on individuals. Tenancy rates were high, usury was extreme, graft and corruption were such as to subject individuals to the most capricious types of exploitation, irrigation systems were in bad repair—conditions had reached a state at which many were willing to try anything.

Into this situation which had been seen in China at the end of dynasties before, the new forces were injected. There was plenty of motivation for the injection of these forces by Westerners either on a peaceful or a forceful basis. China represented vast potential markets and also a vast potential source of production. The fact that the Chinese had little with which to buy foreign goods went along with the extremely cheap labor force, and the latter meant that China could be used by others as the scene of low cost production for sale outside of China. The West had, of course, had contacts with China for some hundreds of years prior to this time, but the patterns that were now introduced had only just developed in the West; they were no more a part of eighteenth century Western Europe and the United States than they were of eighteenth century China. Now they were cast into the picture of dynastic decay, and they immediately began to disintegrate the most effective form of control in the society.

For the first time in modern Chinese history at least the strength of the family system was seriously undercut in those areas affected by the new forces. These new patterns wherever introduced offered the possibility of alternative employment on relatively objective grounds, and consequently they offered those subjected to strains by the prevailing system the possibility of a way out that did not depend upon a refurbishment of the old. The absolute amount of industry introduced was never great, but the effects of it spread far beyond the limits of the new ventures themselves. Jobs offered on the new basis attracted reservoirs of unemployed to the areas concerned, and these offered a radical price competition for the more traditional forms of employment and so threw open these in turn to a greater degree of relatively objective employment opportunities. Family controls disintegrated in and around the most populous centers of China at the very time that the controls of the Imperial Bureaucracy were in a state of disintegration. The individuals who either willingly or unwillingly were separated from their families as the major orientation of their decisions became radically "individualistic by default," and thereby they compounded the difficulty of controlling and co-ordinating their activities. The introduction of extremely cheap goods, meanwhile, competed with handicraft labor, lessened the self-sufficiency of the peasant families, and increased their vulnerability to exploitation by the townsmen.

At the same time the scale on which industrialization had to be carried out, if it was to be carried out at all, was such that a great deal of co-ordination and control was necessary. The groups from whose ranks officials had been drawn in the past were completely incapacitated by their training to do the sort of planning necessary in this situation, for they were above all trained to seek solutions in precedents (and there were no indigenous precedents for these requirements), to operate on the basis of extremely vaguely defined and delimited relations, and to select people on the basis of who they were rather than on the basis of what they could do. The merchants were only to a slight degree convertible for the new requirements. They were used to thinking primarily in commercial rather than in industrial terms and to taking their capital out of such pursuits and putting it into land as soon as possible. They were as little oriented to the reinvestment of talent as they were to the reinvestment of capital. Furthermore in a situation of extremely unstable governmental control, they had more to lose if they tried to set up plants and factories than if they depended primarily upon trading. In the former case a turn of the political wheel could cost them not only their inventories but their capital investments as well, and these capital investments were more difficult to conceal or move than were inventories. The international settlements offered some protection in these respects, but nevertheless there was a tremendous motivation to seek profits on a commercial basis rather than on an industrial basis.

The industrial development, however, was essential to solve certain other problems, if China could not return to a refurbished form of the "traditional" patterns. One of the great sources of strain between the towns and the villages lay in the fact that the towns were supported almost entirely by income that had its origins in the villages. They produced for export to the villages almost nothing that was capable of increasing net or general productivity there and hence bettering the lot of the peasants. Modern industry could have produced goods and services cheaply enough to compete with handicraft labor and could have made available new tools and techniques, but only the former got anywhere for the profit in them was immediate and obvious. The net result of this was a further impoverishment of the peasants that increased their alienation and played a vital role in their at least passive support of a new change in government that overthrew the Republic which had replaced the dynasty.

In those few areas in which modernization did make some headway the same sort of changes seen elsewhere in the world in company with modernization began. Again family change was prominent. The family changed in composition, type, role in the life of the individual, and all the rest, but what is important here is that it could no longer be used as the main basis for control of individuals. And yet Chinese society had developed no other forms of control that would operate effectively and stably in the absence of family controls. For the last five decades or more China has been a sort of no man's land with regard to modernization. It has bits and parts of it, but it has not achieved any considerable level of industrialization. It also has not been able to regain a stable version of the "traditional" society it once had. The present rulers of China offer a picture of momentary stability, but so far they have not accomplished anything that indicates any basic alteration in the picture of Chinese social structure. They have not accomplished the changes necessary for industrialization. They have eliminated, at least for the time being, the usual forms of graft and corruption, but the prognosis is for their replacement on the basis of party membership rather than the more usual nepotistic basis. If the present regime is not able to modernize, its general prognosis would seem to be much the same as that of its predecessor.

THE RESULTANT STAGE

In the case of China the resultant stage is not different from the transitional one in respects relevant here. The most relevant characteristic of it for present purposes is that industrialization was unable to make any dramatic headway in China. It is true that many of the "traditional" patterns seem doomed, but the stage reached, at least prior to the communist hegemony, was one in which there was an uneasy balance between the new and the old. The inheritance of the past, stands out as a major obstacle to the firmer establishment of the new, and what in effect has been established of the new by its direct and indirect effects undercuts the possibility of the stable re-establishment of the "traditional" patterns.

Notes

1. For a more extended treatment of social change from which these concepts are taken see: Marion J. Levy, Jr., *The Structure of Society,* Princeton University Press; Princeton, 1952, esp. pp. 71–76, 140–148.
2. The term feudal is here applied to social systems with the following characteristics: (a) closed social classes, (b) a well-defined hierarchy of power-holders, (c) identification, at least ideally speaking, of each individual as responsible to some particular individual higher than himself in the hierarchy and related to others outside of that direct line by virtue of his overlord's relations to them, and (d) a distribution of goods and services, most especially land ownership and control, primarily on the basis of the ranks distinguished in the hierarchy of power and responsibility.
3. Only the sketchiest outline of points about "traditional" China will be given here.
4. See Note 2.

6. THE ROLE OF THE GENTRY

Chow Tse-tsung

The year 1918 may be regarded as the natal year of the new Chinese literature. New poetry in the vernacular was widely experimented with by the new intellectuals and was the first fruit of the vernacular movement. Most of the poems

SOURCE: Selected from Chow Tse-tsung, *The May Fourth Movement,* Cambridge, Mass.: Harvard University Press, 1960, pp. 278–279, 283–284, 287–289, and 293–299. Reprinted by permission of the publishers. Copyright 1960 by the President and Fellows of Harvard College.

in Hu's *A Book of Experiments,* which was published in March 1920, were composed in 1918. Leading reformers in Peking, men such as Liu Fu, Lu Hsün, Shen Yin-mo, Yü P'ing-po, Chou Tso-jen, Chu Tzu-ch'ing, K'ang Pai-ch'ing, Ch'en Tu-hsiu, Li Ta-chao, Liu Ta-pai, Fu Ssu-nien, and Lo Chia-lun, joined in writing vernacular poems. A second development was the introduction of modern European literature in a new translation technique. Works of Ibsen, Strindberg, Andersen (Northern Europe); or Dostoyevsky, Kuprin, Tolstoy (Eastern Europe), as well as the modern Greek Ephtaliotis and the Pole Sienkiewicz, were translated into a written Chinese influenced by the grammar and style of the original European languages.[1] A third innovation was a new essay form. The column, "Random Thoughts" *(Sui-kan lu)*—consisting of a number of acute satiric short essays by various contributors—was established in *New Youth* starting with the April 1918 issue and in *Weekly Critic* a little later. Pieces by Ch'en Tu-hsiu, Liu Fu, Ch'ien Hsüan-t'ung, and later Lu Hsün and Chou Tso-jen appeared in *New Youth.* It marked the beginning of a new kind of Chinese short essay which, usually with a sarcastic tone, became a devastating political weapon in later years. Fourthly, the modern Chinese short story was created in 1918. Lu Hsün, joining *New Youth* at Ch'ien Hsüan-t'ung's insistence, first published his short story, "The Diary of a Madman" *(K'uang-jen jih-chi)* in the May issue of the monthly.[2] His collected short stories, the first collection of this type in Chinese, *Cries (Na-han,* published in September 1923) were all composed in the period between 1918 and 1922. Fifthly, the new drama movement was started in 1918. *New Youth* published a special issue on Ibsen in June and a special issue on the reform of the traditional Chinese opera and drama in October. Early essays on the new drama showed the great current influence of Ibsen.

But the spread of the new literary movement to wider circles did not start until 1919. By the spring of that year the literary revolution was arousing both more support and more opposition. After the May Fourth Incident, the vernacular language was widely used in the majority of student publications. Almost all magazines, newspapers, and literary writings began to change to the new literary medium. Hu Shih described in 1922 the incident's influence upon the literary revolution as follows:

> The student movement of 1919 was of great significance for the new literary movement in popularizing the use of the vernacular in writing all over the country; though the student movement and the new literary movement were two different things. Moreover, after the May Fourth Incident, the enlightened Chinese, gradually, awakening to the significance of the 'intellectual reform,' either took an attitude of welcome, or of study, or of toleration, toward this new tide. Their previous hostile attitude toward it gradually decreased. As a result, the literary revolution was able to develop freely. After 1919, vernacular literature spread as though it wore seven-league boots.[3]

In October of 1919, the National Alliance of Educational Associations resolved to ask the government to promote the vernacular officially.[4] On January 12, 1920, the Ministry of Education issued an ordinance providing for the substitution of the vernacular for the classical literary language, from the fall of that year, in the Chinese language instruction in the first and second grades of the primary schools.[5] In March, it ordered the abandonment of text books in the classical language in all grades of these schools.[6] This adoption of the vernacular quickly spread to the middle and higher schools. In 1920 and 1921, the vernacular was officially and popularly recognized as the "national langauge." Meanwhile, a Chinese "national phonetic alphabet" was established in the years 1918 and 1919. . . .

Humanitarianism, Naturalism, and Romanticism:
The Society for Literary Studies and the Creation Society

After the success of the literary revolution through their joint efforts during 1919 and 1920, the new intellectual leaders began to separate into natural groupings according to their special interests. A number of early leaders of the literary revolution actually dropped out of the drive to develop a new literature. Ch'en Tu-hsiu interested himself in social and political movements; Hu Shih gradually turned his attention to the study of the Chinese classics and the old vernacular novels; Ch'ien Hsüan-t'ung and Liu Fu concentrated on the study of linguistics; Fu Ssu-nien and Lo Chia-lun went abroad to study history; Shen Yin-mo and some others turned again to write poems in the classical language. On the other hand, Chou Tso-jen and Lu Hsün and many other young writers began the task of introducing more Western literary theories and works, and of producing creative literature in the spoken language. In this development, the literary revolution, just like the cultural and political movements, branched out in different directions. . . .

Under the influence of Chou Tso-jen and Mao Tun, the Society of Literary Studies at the beginning advocated a "literature of humanity." The theory had first been developed by Chou in 1918 when he published his article "Literature of Humanity" in *New Youth,* by which he meant a literature based on individualistic humanitarianism[7]; in 1920 he stated that literature should be for mankind's sake instead of for "literature's sake."[8] Later when the Society for Literary Studies was established, Chou embodied the theory in its manifesto, which he drafted. The manifesto declared: "Literature is a form of labor, and a form of labor very significant for humanity."[9]

The idea "literature for humanity's sake" was never adequately explained. At the beginning it was supposed to oppose both the traditional, orthodox theory that "literature is meant to convey the tao" and the light attitude taken toward literature by the contemporary Saturday Group (*Li-pai-liu p'ai*). The society rejected both the ideas that literature is merely a tool of morality and that it is independent of humanity, i.e., the concept "art for art's sake." But in further interpretations of the literature of humanity, the members of the society did not seem to take a uniform stand. Their views are vague and ambiguous. Chou Tso-jen simply identified the idea of humanity with idealism.[10] On the other hand, Mao Tun showed a tendency towards realism and naturalism. In his opinion, "genuine literature" should be the "literature of humanity." "Literature at present," he said, "has become a kind of science whose subject matter for study is humanity—contemporary humanity—and whose tools of study are poetry, drama, and fiction. With artistic skill, the writer's revelation of humanity must be the life of all mankind, without an iota of selfishness or the least particle of subjectivity. Of course, the people described in literary works will have thoughts and feelings, but these thoughts and feelings must surely be common to the masses, common to the whole of mankind, and not just to the writer himself."[11] Mao Tun emphasized the objectivity of literature, accepting the Western idea that "literature is the reflection of life," or the mirror of society, the nation, the circumstances, the times, and the writer's personality.[12] (Mao Tun, whose name was originally intended to mean in Chinese "contradiction," did not see a contradiction between the claim he made at times that literature is a "science" in which the subjective bias should be completely suppressed and the personal view play no part, and the claim at other times that the writer's personality must after all be reflected in literature.) He also rejected both the ideas that "literature is meant to convey the tao" and "literature is for literature's sake."[13] . . .

From Literary Revolution to Revolutionary Literature

As a whole the new literary revolution, in the period of the May Fourth Movement, was a manifestation of the trend against the idea that "literature is meant to convey the tao," and of the trend to establish the vernacular as a national language. Whether art was held to be for humanity's sake or for art's sake, for the most part literature remained in practice independent of all aims beside human interests and revelations or self-expression. The Society for Literary Studies and the Creation Society represented the main currents of the new literature in this period. The former emphasized the revelation of human and social realities; the latter emphasized unrestricted expression of personal feelings. In their works few of these writers suggested concrete solutions for the problems of society and life. Their spirit was one of protest and self-consolation.

In later years the two societies were deeply affected by changing circumstances. After the May Thirtieth Incident of 1925 in connection with the Shang-hai anti-British and anti-Japanese strikes, the Creation Society, as a result of the worsened political situation, moved into its second period, giving up its individualism, pessimism, and the idea of "art for art's sake." It adopted "revolutionary literature" as its battle cry and fought against imperialism and warlordism. The same incident also caused the split and collapse of the Society for Literary Studies. Lu Hsün and Chou Tso-jen went on to establish a new literary group, the Thread-of-Talk Society (*Yü-ssu she*), insisting on realism and humanitarianism; while Hsü Chih-mo, Hu Shih, Wen I-to, and Liang Shih-ch'iu organized the Crescent Moon Society (*Hsin-yüeh she*), advocating symbolism. After 1928, the Creation Society entered a third period, propagating "proletarian literature." Then in 1930 the League of Leftist Writers (*Tso-i tso-chia lien-meng*) was organized under the leadership of Lu Hsün; against it stood a group advocating "nationalist literature" (*min-tsu-chu-i wen-hsüeh*) led by Huang Chen-hsia, Wang P'ing-ling, Shao Hsün-mei, and others. Later controversies in literary circles involved such problems as whether or not literature should be independent of politics and whether or not literature had a class character. From the thirties on, leftist writings dominated China's new literature.

The practical aspects of the new literature movement, developed from 1917, were successful; as a consequence the archaic literary language and the old stereotyped literature declined rapidly. The vernacular came to be widely employed in writing and teaching. As the written language tended to become one with the spoken, knowledge and education became more easily popularized. Moreover, poetry, essays, short stories, novels, and the drama all took new directions. Literary criticism and literary theory also made great advances. Literature was thus brought closer to the realities of life and society. It also came to enjoy a greater popularity. Trends of the new literature toward naturalism and socialism in later years exercised a considerable influence upon the intellectual and psychological development in Chinese youth. It is in such senses as these that the literary revolution should be recognized as having played a significant role in modern China's intellectual and sociopolitical transformation.

. . . It is no exaggeration to say that, of all the activities of the new intellectuals, the new thought tide was the most significant. The main aim of the reformers in the May Fourth Movement was the creation of a new China; one method was to be the substitution of new thought for the old and traditional. From the time *New Youth* was established, this had become the major idea of the new reform movement. In a sense, the May Fourth Incident was a result and manifestation of this idea.

Most of the leading new intellectuals during the early period adopted an uncompromising attitude on ideological reform. This attitude is well exemplified in Ch'en Tu-hsiu's and Hu Shih's joint answer to a reader of *New Youth* in 1918: "The old literature, old politics, and old ethics have always belonged to one family; we cannot abandon one and preserve the others. It is Oriental to compromise and only go half way when reforming, for fear of opposition. This was the most important factor behind the failures of reform movements during the last several decades."[14] . . .

New Thought: Realism, Utilitarianism, Liberalism, Individualism, Socialism, and Darwinism

While the older generation and the conservatives clung to traditional thought and ethics, the new intellectuals, influenced by Western ideas, were rallying to the support of "Mr. *Te*" (Democracy) and "Mr. *Saï*" (Science), as they conveniently dubbed the new currents. It was in the names of these two gentlemen that Confucianism and its followers were attacked. An examination of the ideas of the new intellectuals during the early period of the May Fourth Movement reveals that they were a mélange of postseventeenth-century Western ones; especially highly regarded were ideas stemming from the American and French Revolutions.

During the two decades before 1919, various Western philosophic ideas had been popularized in China. Utilitarianism, the theory of evolution, and empiricism were introduced by Yen Fu's translations. These included Thomas Huxley's *Evolution and Ethics* (translated in 1894–1895, published in 1895 and April 1898); Adam Smith's *The Wealth of Nations* (translated from late 1897 to the fall of 1900, published late in 1901); John Stuart Mill's *On Liberty* (translated in 1899, published in October 1903) and *System of Logic* (only first half, translated in 1900–1902, published in 1902); Herbert Spencer's *Study of Sociology* (translated in 1898–1902, published in May 1903); Edward Jenks' *A Short History of Politics* (translated in 1903, published in February 1904); Montesquieu's *L'Esprit des lois* (translated in 1900–1905, published in September 1904–1909); and William Stanley Jevons' *Primer of Logic* (translated in the fall of 1908, published in the same year). Those intellectual leaders who were middle-aged at the time of the May Fourth Movement had been influenced mainly by these works. French revolutionary ideas were first introduced by Liang Ch'i-ch'ao at the beginning of this century. Rousseau was popularized by Liang's lucid essays. After 1906, Lamarck's *Philosophie Zoologique*, Kropotkin's *Mutual Assistance,* and other French philosophic works were introduced by Wu Chih-hui, Li Shih-tseng, Ts'ai Yüan-p'ei, Chang Chi, and Wang Ching-wei. Schopenhauer, Nietzsche, and Kant were introduced by Wang Kuo-wei and others. Some of Bertrand Russell's works were translated into Chinese before the May Fourth Incident. They reinforced the influence of British empiricism introduced earlier. Russell's work, with John Dewey's introduction of the Cartesian method later, laid a foundation for the study of mathematical logic in China.

At the beginning of the May Fourth period, all these ideas affected in various degrees the critical thinking of the new Chinese intellectual leaders, but realism and utilitarianism were the most widely prevailing principles. In the opening article of the first issue of *New Youth,* Ch'en Tu-hsiu suggested a utilitarian and realistic approach to the problems of life. He expressed his admiration of John Mill and Comte.[15] In Ch'en's opinion, one of the fundamental differences between East and West was that the latter paid more attention to practical matters while the former paid more to ceremony.[16] Therefore, for the rejuvenation of the Chinese people, he advocated the adoption of realism as one of the principles of Chinese education.[17] Utilitarianism was propagated also by many other writers.[18] These ideas were later merged with pragmatism. After the May Fourth Incident, though the young were gripped by fantasy, they still based, or at least pretended to base, their activities on practicality.

Liberalism was a catchword among the intellectuals in those early years. Individual freedom had been propounded by Liang Ch'i-ch'ao and the Kuomintang leaders at the beginning of the twentieth century. In the first issue of *New Youth,* Ch'en Tu-hsiu emphasized individual freedom, and came out in opposition to any kind of slavery.[19] In the second issue, he published his Chinese translation of Samuel F. Smith's "America" (American national hymn).[20] Edmund Burke's speech in the House of Commons supporting the resistance of the American colonists was also translated and published in the monthly.[21] In the main, the concept of freedom current among these Chinese intellectuals was derived from Rousseau's theory of general will and from British utilitarianism.[22] They talked of freedom in terms of human rights, and freedom of speech and the press.[23]

At a time when most people had become aware of the need for national unity and the importance of statehood, some new intellectuals tended to emphasize individualism. They maintained that the defense of a sovereign and independent republic should not be at the expense of individual freedom.[24] Most of the new intellectual leaders rejected the idea that statehood and nationalism should be ultimate ideals. They conceded only that these were temporarily necessary for the betterment of the welfare of the individual.[25] Ch'en Tu-hsiu realized that the most significant difference between East and West was that Western civilization, be it British, American, French, or German, was based on a thoroughgoing individualism, whereas the Eastern variety was based on family or clan units. As he understood them, Western ethics, moral principles, political theories, and law all tended to advocate individual rights and welfare, freedom of thought and speech, as well as the development of individuality. Under the Eastern system, a man was a member of his family or clan, and not an independent individual. This system destroyed individual dignity and self-respect, choked free will and independent thought, deprived a person of equal rights under the law, and encouraged people to rely on others. Consequently, he suggested the substitution of individualism for the family system.[26] Hu Shih also stimulated the spread of individualism by introducing Ibsen to China. He explained Ibsen's opposition to the conformity imposed by law, religion, and moral principles. Ibsen asserted, so Hu said, that society "destroyed individuality by force and suppressed the spirit of individual freedom and independence."[27] Ibsen's ideal was a life in which an "individual might develop to the full his talent and individuality."[28] Hu, influenced by Ibsen's plays, such as *A Doll's House, An Enemy of the People,* and *Ghosts,* drew attention to the inferior status of women in Chinese society, and encouraged Chinese women to protest and secure emancipation, as well as exalted independent thinking.

Among the pre-1919 intellectuals there were some who toyed with ideas of socialism or anarchism on the ground that only thus could the freedom of the individual be balanced by the equality of others. These ideas were derived mainly from the early French socialists and anarchists, but also owed something to traditional Chinese ideas. However, most of the vanguard intellectuals were not completely committed to socialism, perhaps because they felt that the same liberal program which would achieve individual freedom would also achieve equality. Therefore, they preferred to advocate the equality of every individual's right, and to propound the ideas of universal love and mutual assistance.[29] In discussing the French contribution to modern civilization, Ch'en Tu-hsiu hailed the socialist idea of economic and social equality as the latest tendency of modern European culture. Private property could not be abandoned immediately; the rich and the poor would be leveled by social policies.[30] These ideas had been promoted previously by Sun Yat-sen and by many socialists and anarchists. After 1919, they had increasing appeal for the youth of China.

Turning to science, we find that most of the new intellectuals emphasized Darwin's theory of evolution. It was on the basis of this theory that they attacked religion and tradition. Some of them, for example Tai Chi-t'ao, while accepting this theory, advocated mutual assistance. They thought that whereas life was maintained by struggle, mutual assistance was the best way to advance humanity in this struggle. In any case, Darwinism was the first scientific theory to exert a strong influence upon Chinese social thought.

Technology and the control of nature were also recognized as significant aspects of the scientific civilization of the West. The new intellectual leaders discarded the old idea that the spiritual civilization of the East was superior to the materialistic civilization of the West. Wu Chih-hui in particular was the champion of the beneficence of a material welfare achieved by the control and improvement of tools, although he himself lived a very simple, stoical life.[31] Wu believed in the "omnipotence of science."[32]

New Methods: Pragmatic, Skeptical, and Agnostic Approaches and the Beginning of Marxist Influence

The fact that the new intellectual leaders had a better training in logical thinking made their arguments against the old gentry more effective. This was true especially in the case of Hu Shih who gave more emphasis to methodology than did other writers. In the re-evaluation of the Chinese tradition, Hu insisted that all inferences must be based on evidence and anything without proof should be held doubtful. As a means of verification, historical evolution or, in Dewey's phrase, the "genetic method," i.e., concentrating attention on the origin and evolution of the subject, was emphasized. This method owed a debt to Huxley's agnosticism, but stemmed immediately from Dewey's pragmatism. As Hu himself said:

> My thought is influenced mainly by two persons: one is Huxley and the other is Mr. Dewey. Huxley teaches me how to doubt and teaches me to believe in nothing without sufficient evidence. Mr. Dewey teaches me how to think and teaches me to consider the immediate problems in all cases, to regard all theories and ideals as hypotheses which are in need of verification, and to take into account the effect of thoughts. These two persons make me understand the character and function of scientific methods.[33]

In the prevalent climate of agnosticism, an iconoclastic spirit arose among the new intelligentsia. Ch'en Tu-hsiu, Hu Shih, Wu Chih-hui, and Lu Hsün were "laughing lions" who "annihilated with laughter," as Nietzsche said of Voltaire in Europe, and with all their strength called for the destruction of idols.[34] Ch'en said: "Destroy! Destroy idols! Our beliefs must be based on reality and reasonableness. All the fantasies handed down from ancient times, religious, political, and ethical, and other false and unreasonable beliefs are idols which should be destroyed! If these false idols are not destroyed, universal truth cannot be restored to the profound beliefs in our minds."[35] This was the call of the time.

On the whole, it is fair to say that, in the early period of the May Fourth

Movement, pragmatism, skepticism, and agnosticism were the principal critical approaches found in the reformers' attack on traditional ethics and ideas. There was no strong competition from either materialism or dialectical materialism until the middle of the twenties.

However, as early as 1915, Ch'en Tu-hsiu had developed some interest in the economic interpretation of history and society.[36] Materialism in a vague sense was also advocated to some extent by a few writers.[37] In 1916 and 1918, Li Ta-chao's writings showed some embryonic traces of dialectics in opposition to the "genetic method."[38] But no genuine Marxist theories could be found in Li's writings in this early stage. Beside Chu Chih-hsin's translation of a part of *The Communist Manifesto* in 1906 as we have mentioned, the earliest Chinese translation of Marx's major work published within China was his *Wage, Labor and Capital,* which appeared with the title "Labor and Capital" (*Lao-tung yü tzu-pen*) in the Chinputang newspaper, *The Morning Post,* from May 9 to June 1, 1919. In the summer of 1919, following the vogue of pragmatism, dialectical materialism came to the attention of the Chinese intellectual leaders, but they took a more or less critical and skeptical attitude toward it, and did not accept it as a whole. The Society for the Study of Socialism established in about December of 1919 was not dedicated primarily to Marxism, but in the main to guild socialism, syndicalism, and anarchism. Organized study of Marxism did not begin until the spring of 1920.[39]

A notable critical introduction to Marxism was published in May 1919 by Li Ta-chao, who was in fact basically sympathetic to it. He said: "Recently there has appeared in philosophy a neoidealism which may rectify Marx's materialism and remedy its defects."[40] Li actually took a revisionist view of Marx's historical materialism: (1) He followed Eugenio Rignano's criticism of Marx that historical materialism was contradictory to the theory of class struggle. He imagined Marx might have replied that class struggle would ultimately be part of the process of economic change; "but," Li remarked, "even though this reply would be true, it would be a forced interpretation, and somehow self-contradictory."[41] (2) To Li, historical materialism had the defect of determinism or fatalism; but this was offset by the rallying cry of *The Communist Manifesto* which called upon the working classes to unite and struggle[42] (3) Marx overlooked the function of ethics and the humanitarian movement in the course of history. It was here that Li prescribed the remedy of neoidealism. (4) Li remarked: "Marx's theory was a product of his time; in his time it was indeed a great discovery. However, history should not be interpreted forever by this theory which was formulated at a specific time and under specific circumstances, nor should Marxist theory be accepted as a whole and applied uncritically to modern society. On the other hand, we should not disregard its historical value and specific findings."[43]

It is striking that Li's criticism of Marx's materialistic interpretation of history was rejected by one of the Kuomintang leaders, Hu Han-min. His long article "A Criticism of Criticism of Historical Materialism" was almost a direct rebuttal, point by point, of Li's article. Hu Han-min also seems to have been the first to study Chinese history, philosophy, ethics, and institutions in the light of historical materialism. His "A Materialistic Study of the History of Chinese Philosophy" was published in October 1919.⁴⁴ The Chinese translation of Karl Kautsky's *Karl Marx's ökonomische lehren* (1887) published in *Ch'en pao* from June 2 and that by Tai Chi-t'ao from November were the first major, systematic introduction of *Das Kapital* into China.⁴⁵ Following these, Li Ta-chao published his "Material Change and Ethical Change" in December 1919 and "An Economic Interpretation of the Cause of Changes in Modern Chinese Thought" in January 1920.⁴⁶ The latter was the first attempt to explain the new thought movement in terms of materialism. But it must be noted that Tai and Hu approached Marxism differently from Li. The two former emphasized the nationalist implications of the theory, while Li followed the line of class struggle. This factor led to their later split.⁴⁷

Meanwhile, a Chinese translation of the first section of *The Communist Manifesto* was published in the students' monthly, *The Citizens,* on November 1, 1919 (Vol. II, No. 1), and that of Marx's preface to *Das Kapital* on October 1, 1920 in the same magazine (Vol. II, No. 3). The manifesto was translated in full into Chinese by Ch'en Wang-tao and published in April 1920. After these translations, Part III of Engels' *Anti-Dühring* (1877) was translated in *The Construction* in December 1920 (Vol. III, No. 1). Marx's preface to *The Critique of Political Economy* (1859) was translated in *The Eastern Miscellany* in January 1921 (Vol. XVIII, No. 1), and Engels' *Socialism: Utopian and Scientific* was first rendered into Chinese by Shih Jen-yung and published in the *New World* (*Hsin shih-chieh*) fortnightly after 1912. A translation of the latter by Cheng Tz'u-ch'uan was published in book form by the Shanghai Ch'ün-i shu-chü in 1921.   The above includes the list of almost all major works of Marx and Engels which Chinese students of Marxism could read in their own language in the years before 1921. It is notable that most of the works were translated by those who were not finally converted into Marxism.⁴⁸

After 1923 dialectical materialism began to be accepted by some Chinese writers and from the latter part of the twenties onwards it had increasing influence on Chinese thinking. However, to pursue it further here would be a diversion from our immediate concern with the May Fourth period.

Notes

1. Hu Shih *225,* "The Chinese Literature of the Last Fifty Years," p. 200.
2. See Lu Hsün *349,* Complete Works of Lu Hsün (Shanghai, 1938), I, 277–91. Lu Hsün also recalled that Ch'en Tu-hsiu was most enthusiastic in encouraging him to write stories. See his "Wo tsen-mo tso-ch'i hsiao-shuo lai" ("How Did I Start to Write Stories?"), written on March 5, 1933, in *Nan-ch'iang pei-tiao chi* (Collected Gibberish) (Shanghai, 1934), in *349,* Complete Works, V, 107.
3. Hu Shih *225,* "The Chinese Literature of the Last Fifty Years," p. 207.
4. "Records of Current Affairs," The Chinese Educational Review, XI, 2 (Nov. 20, 1919), p. 108.
5. For text of the ordinance see "Records of Current Affairs," *ibid.,* XII, 2 (Feb. 20, 1920), p. 1.
6. For text of the ordinance see "Record of Current Affairs," *ibid.,* 4 (April 20, 1920), pp. 5–6.

7. Chou Tso-jen *119*, "Literature of Humanity," New Youth, V, 6 (Dec. 1918); see also his *122*, "Intellectual Revolution," Weekly Critic, No. 11 (Peking, Feb. 2, 1919); and his *121*, "Plain People's Literature," reprinted in Hu Shih, ed., *Chien-she li-lün chi* (Anthology of Essays on Constructive Theories of the New Literature) (Shanghai, 1935), pp. 210–13.

8. Chou Tso-jen *118*, "Requisites for the New Literature," a speech delivered at the Young China Association in Peking, Jan. 6, 1920, in Cheng Chen-to, ed., *Wen-hsüeh lun-cheng chi* (Anthology of Essays Concerning the Literary Controversy) (Shanghai, 1935), pp. 141–44.

9. [The Society for Literary Studies] *501*, "Wen-hsüeh yen-chiu hui hsüan-yen" (The Manifesto of the Society for Literary Studies), The Short Story Monthly, XII, 1 (Shanghai, Jan. 10, 1921), Appendix, p. 1.

10. Chou Tso-jen *118*, "Requisites for the New Literature," p. 144.

11. Shen Yen-ping [Mao Tun] *364*, "The Relations of Literature to Man and Ancient China's Mistaken Ideas on the Position of Men of Letters," The Short Story Monthly, XII, 1 (Jan. 10, 1921), p. 10. Cf. Ayer's English translation *568*, "The Society for Literary Studies," p. 51.

12. Shen Yen-ping [Mao Tun] *362*, "The Responsibility and Efforts of the Researchers of the New Literature," reprinted in Cheng Chen-to, ed., Anthology of Essays Concerning the Literary Controversy, pp. 145–49; also Mao Tun *365*, "Literature and Life," *ibid.*, pp. 149–53.

13. Shen Yen-ping [Mao Tun] *363*, "What Is Literature?," *ibid.*, pp. 153–59.

14. Hu Shih and Ch'en Tu-hsiu, "Lun *Hsin ch'ing-nien* chih chu-chang" ("A Discussion on the Advocacies of *New Youth*"), letter in reply to Yi Chung-k'uei, New York, V, 4 (Oct. 15, 1918), p. 433.

15. Ch'en Tu-hsiu *49*, "Call to Youth," New Youth, I, 1 (Sept. 15, 1915), p. 5.

16. Ch'en-Tu-hsiu *63*, "Differences of Basic Thought between the Eastern and Western Peoples," *ibid.*, 4 (Dec. 15, 1915), pp. 2–4.

17. Ch'en Tu-hsiu *48*, "The Principles of Education of Today," *ibid.*, 2 (Oct. 15, 1915), pp. 3–4.

18. See Li I-min, "Jen-sheng wei-i chih mu-ti" ("The Sole Aim of Life"), *ibid.;* and Kao I-han *225*, "Utilitarianism and Life," *ibid.*, II, 1 (Sept. 1, 1916).

19. Chen Tu-hsiu *49*, "Call to Youth," p. 2.

20. Chen Tu-hsiu, trans., "Ya-mei-li-chia (Mei-kuo kuo-ko)" ("America—the American National Hymn"), *ibid.*, I, 2 (Oct. 15, 1915).

21. Liu Shu-ya, trans., "Mei-kuo-jen chih tzu-yu ching-shen" ("The Spirit of Liberty in the American Colonies") (from Burke's speech "Conciliation with America"), *ibid.*, 6 (Feb. 15, 1916).

22. See Kao I-han *253*, "The Republic and the Self-awakening of Youth," *ibid.*, 1 (Sept. 15, 1915); and his *257*, "Self-government and Freedom," *ibid.*, 5 (Jan. 15, 1916).

23. Ch'en Tu-hsiu, "Fa-lan-hsi-jen yü chin-tai wen-ming" ("The French and Modern Civilization"), *ibid.*, I, 1 (Sept. 15, 1915); Kao I-han, trans., "Tai-hsüeh Yin-kuo yen-lun tzu-yu chih ch'üan-li lun" ("A. V. Dicey's Discussion on the Right of Freedom of Speech in Great Britain") [from Chap. VI of his *The Law of the Constitution*], *ibid.*, 6 (Feb. 15, 1916).

24. Kao I-han *253*, "The Republic and the Self-awakening of Youth," p. 7.

25. Kao I-han *254*, "State Is Not the Final Goal of Life," New Youth, I, 4 (Dec. 15, 1915); also Ch'en Tu-hsiu *48*, "The Principles of Education Today," *ibid.*, I, 2 (Oct. 15, 1915), pp. 4–5; and his *54*, "The Year 1916," *ibid.*, I, 5 (Jan. 1916), p. 3.

26. Ch'en Tu-hsiu *63*, "Differences of Basic Thought between Eastern and Western Peoples," pp. 1–2.

27. Hu Shih *209*, "Ibsenism," New Youth, IV, 6 (June 15, 1918), p. 497. Hu conceded that Ibsen's individualism was one of the most fundamental principles of his (Hu's) view of life and his religion. See his *200*, "An Introduction to My Own Thought," preface (written on Nov. 27, 1930) to Selected Essays of Hu Shih, pp. 8–10.

28. *Ibid.*, p. 502.

29. See Wang Shu-ch'ien *494*, "The Problem of the New and the Old," New Youth, I, 1 (Sept. 1, 1915), p. 3; I Pai-sha, "Shu Mo" ("A Study of Motzu"), *ibid.*, 2 (Oct. 15, 1915) and 5 (Jan. 15, 1916).

30. Ch'en Tu-hsiu, "The French and Modern Civilization," pp. 2–3.

31. Wu Chih-hui, "Ch'ing-nien yü kung-chü" ("Youth and Tools"), New Youth, II, 2 (Oct. 1, 1916); "Tsai lun kung-chü" ("Second Essay on Tools"), *ibid.*, 3 (Nov. 1, 1916).

32. Wu Chih-hui *510*, "A New Conception of the Universe and of Life, Based Upon a New Belief," in Wu Chih-hui's Academic Works and Other Essays (Shanghai, 1925, 1926), p. 118.

33. Hu Shih *200*, "An Introduction to My Own Thought," p. 3.

34. Georg Brandes, *Main Currents in Nineteenth Century Literature* (New York, 1905), III, 57.

35. Ch'en Tu-hsiu *58*, "On Iconoclasm," New Youth, V, 2 (Aug. 15, 1918), p. 91; see also [Chu] Chih-hsin *128*, "Inviolable Sacredness and Iconoclasm," *Chien-she* (The Construction), I, 1 (Shanghai, Aug. 1, 1919), pp. 169–72.

36. Ch'en Tu-hsiu *48*, "The Principles of Education Today," p. 5.

37. Li I-min, "The Sole Aim of Life," pp. 2–3.

38. Li Ta-chao *298*, "Youth," New Youth, II, 1 (Sept. 1, 1916); "Chin" ("The Present"), *ibid.*, IV, 4 (April 15, 1918), pp. 307–10.

39. Hu Shih's article *219*, "Experimentalism [or Pragmatism]," New Youth, VI, 4 (April 1, 1919); the next issue (May 1) was the special one on Marxism; see also above, Chap. IX.

40. Li Ta-chao *303*, "My View on Marxism," New Youth, VI, 5 (May 1919), p. 536.

41. *Ibid.*, p. 533.

42. *Ibid.*, p. 534.

43. *Ibid.*, p. 537.

44. Hu Han-min *188*, "A Criticism of Criticism of Historical Materialism," The Construction, I, 5 (Dec. 1919), reprinted in Hu Han-min, A Study of the Historical Conception of Materialism and Ethics, ed. Huang Ch'ang-ku (Shanghai, 1927), pp. 1–61.

45. Hu Han-min *187*, "A Materialistic Study of the History of Chinese Philosophy," The Construction, I, 3 (Oct. 1919) and the following issues; also in Hu Han-min *188*, A Study of the Historical Conception of Materialism and Ethics, pp. 63–153. Tai Chi-t'ao's retranslation from Japanese of most of Kautsky's book, which was given the Chinese title "Ma-k'e-ssu Tzu-pen-lun chieh-shao" ("Introduction to Marx's *Capital*") appeared in The Construction, I, 4 (Nov. 1, 1919), pp. 811–21, and the following issues. The translation was later completed by Hu Han-min and published in book form in Shanghai in 1927. (Kautsky's book was written before his split with the orthodox Communists).

46. Li Ta-chao *304*, "Material Change and Ethical Change," New Tide, II, 2 (Dec. 1919), pp. 207–24; and his *305*, "An Economic Interpretation of the Cause of Changes in Modern Chinese Thought," New Youth, VII, 2 (Jan. 1, 1920), pp. 47–53. See also Benjamin Schwartz *735*, *Chinese Communism*

and the Rise of Mao (Cambridge, Mass., 1951), Chap. I, pp. 17, 23–24. Ho Kan-chih considered Li Ta-chao's latter article as the first by a Chinese to survey intellectual history in the light of Materialism. He did not mention Hu Han-min. See Ho's *170*, History of the Chinese Enlightenment (Shanghai, 1947), Chap. IV, p. 117.

47. Benjamin Schwartz *735, Chinese Communism and the Rise of Mao,* Chap. II, pp. 32–33.

48. See above, Chap. IX, n. k.

7. THE ROLE OF THE LAW: CONSTITUTIONAL MOVEMENTS AND THEIR FAILURES

Ch'ien Tuan-seng

Like revolutionary France, the Chinese Republic had many constitutions and draft constitutions, some provisional and others definitive. Not counting the Constitutional Principles of 1908 and the Constitution of Nineteen Articles of 1911 of the Manchus, there were five such constitutions or draft constitutions: (1) the Provisional Constitution of March 12, 1912; (2) Yuan Shih-k'ai's Provisional Constitution of May 1, 1914; (3) the Draft Constitution of the Anfu Parliament of August 12, 1919; (4) the Ts'ao K'un Constitution of October 10, 1923, and (5) the Draft Constitution of Tuan Ch'i-jui's regime of December 12, 1926. All were government-sponsored. There were many more drafted by private persons or semipublic bodies.

Of the five instruments, the Constitution of 1923 was perhaps the best drafted and the Provisional Constitution of 1912 the most respected. In 1912 the Republic was new, the hopes for the future were high, and the revolutionary spirit was not yet ebbing. The Provisional Constitution, representing the spirit of the times, was a symbol of a change and a promise of modernization. It was due to this quality that it was resurrected time and again and was always held in some measure of affection by those who were genuinely republican.

The Constitution of 1923 had a long and a checkered history. Its first draft made in seclusion by the Constitutional Commission of the old Parliament at the Temple of Heaven in Peking was not contaminated by the evil influence of Yuan Shih-k'ai. It was on the whole a carefully conceived instrument, impracticable for China at that time perhaps, but certainly no more so than any other constitution attempted by China before or since. The draft received careful consideration by the old Parliament and was the subject of many

SOURCE: Selected from Ch'ien Tuan-seng, *The Government and Politics of China,* Cambridge, Mass.: Harvard University Press, 1950, pp. 70, 73–74, and 77–78. Reprinted by permission of the publishers. Copyright 1950 by the President and Fellows of Harvard College.

heated debates in 1916–1917 at Peking and also by the same Parliament in 1918–1920 at Canton. It was finally enacted by the same Parliament in Peking in 1923. Because of the fact that the Parliament of 1912 was perhaps more representative of the people, at least of the politically articulate, the constitution which had undergone thorough deliberations by it could not fail to attract more favorable attention from the public than the ones which were made by less representative bodies.

But neither of these two constitutions, to say nothing of the others, was able to bring China any nearer to real constitutionalism. The Constitution of 1923 was utterly discredited, for it resulted in the election of Ts'ao K'un as President. The Constitution of 1912 was too often honored in the breach and too often suspended.

The experience of constitution-making during the entire period of the Peking regime had therefore meant nothing to the people of China. As far as the common people were concerned, it had not provided for them political stability nor improved their material well-being. It had only enabled the politically unscrupulous to take advantage of the constitutions to promote their selfish and personal interests, almost invariably to the detriment of the national interest. . . .

In the early years of the Republic it was a moot question whether presidential or cabinet government would be better for China. Some favored the former, claiming that it was better suited to China; others favored the latter in their anxiety to guard against the personal dictatorship of an ambitious and unscrupulous man. There were repeated experiments with both. Sun Yat-sen's government at Nanking was admittedly presidential. Then the Kuomintang tried to impose a responsible cabinet on Yuan Shih-k'ai. But Yuan Shih-k'ai had no patience with any cabinet which even claimed to derive its authority from the Parliament. He bolted and resorted to personal government long before the promulgation of the Constitution of May 1, 1914 which made him the undisputed ruler in theory as well as in fact.

When Li Yuan-hung and Feng Kuo-chang were presidents, Tuan Ch'i-jui's cabinets enjoyed the powers of a responsible cabinet. The president was weaker than the premier both in personality and in military following. Tuan Ch'i-jui was in no danger of being interfered with effectively by the President, but his inability to recognize the limitations of the executive power, added to the disrupted state of the legislature and the incompetence of the individual legislators, also rendered impossible the normal workings of a responsible cabinet. From Tuan Ch'i-jui's own point of view the cabinet system must have seemed unsuitable for China, for when he had a chance to be a dictator he readily chose dictatorship rather than any other system. That was why he styled himself Chief Provisional Executive in 1924.

The alternation of the presidential and the cabinet systems and the failures of both resulted in a readiness to experiment during the first years of the new regime following the reorganization of the Kuomintang in 1923, with a third alternative—the collegiate executive which was also subsequently discarded. The important thing to remember is that the American presidential system, the British cabinet system, and the Swiss collegiate system all require for their successful operation the existence of a powerful assembly representing the people and strong enough to compel the executive to stay within the constitutional limits allowed him. Since there had never existed such an assembly in China, hope for the success of any of the three systems of the executive was vain. . . .

The decade and a half of the early Republican regime witnessed many an issue of legitimacy. In many controversies of a constitutional and political nature the question of legitimacy was brought up, and figured prominently or even predominantly. When Li Yuan-hung succeeded after Yuan Shih-k'ai's death, there was this controversy; under which constitution, the one of 1912 or that of 1914, was he succeeding? After Chang Hsün's fiasco of the Manchu restoration in 1917, Feng Kuo-chang stepped into the presidency but there arose, first, the issue of reviving the Constitution of 1912 and second, the issue of restoring the old Parliament previously dissolved on the Chang Hsün's demand. Feng Kuo-chang was elected vice-president by the old Parliament under the old Constitution. If the Constitution were not revived and Parliament not restored, by what right could Feng Kuo-chang claim to be the president? That was exactly the stand taken by the Canton regime, which was set up in 1917 and which in fact styled itself the "Constitution-Protecting Government." The peace negotiations of 1919 between the North and South failed, partly because the two sides could not agree on the question of reinstating the Constitution and the Parliament.

When the old Parliament was again restored in Peking in 1922 there was new controversy as to whether the new members who had substituted for the old members absent from the sessions when that Parliament met in Canton, in 1918–1920, were to continue or the old members, disqualified by the Parliament in Canton for their absence, were to be seated. This controversy in turn arose from the controversy over the legitimacy of the Canton sessions of that Parliament. It was decided by the members who met in 1922 at Peking that those sessions were illegal and therefore the new substitute members could not be members of the Parliament in 1922.

These are only a few instances in which the question of legitimacy or illegitimacy was argued at great length and with vehemence. There are many more, some of which involved the legitimacy of particular leaders to be at the head of the separatist regime in Canton.

It may seem strange that legitimacy should become an issue, in a period of chaos and civil wars when the observance of law was not a marked virtue among politicians. But let us not forget that China in her long past had seen in connection with imperial successions many legitimist wrangles, compared with which the Papal Successions in the Middle Ages appeared quite simple. The wrangles might be unreal, but they nevertheless absorbed the interest of the literati-official class. It is conceivable that the question of legitimacy may loom up again in connection with a disputed choice of laws or men, in party or in government. . . .

China in its monarchical days had always been a universal empire. It was an accepted institution; no alternative was ever conceived, still less tried. Intermittently the empire might be badly disrupted, but that was an abnormal situation. Normally the emperor reigned supreme throughout the empire not checked by any device of decentralization.

With the coming of a Western form of state, the comparative merits of a unitary versus a federal state also came to be discussed by the Chinese. The idea that a large country like China might do well to adopt the federal structure received attention in both the revolutionist and reformist publications in the first decade of the century. As early as 1911, when the Revolution was still in progress, the Provisional Assembly of Shantung had expressed its preference for federation. At the zenith of Yuan Shih-k'ai's autocratic reign in 1914–1915, some publicists again advocated federalism. They hoped that an increase in provincial powers might serve as a check to the despotism of the central government. For similar reasons, the Kuomintang members of Parliament in 1916–1917 were also inclined to stress local autonomy at the expense of the central government, which was, at that time, in the hands of Tuan Ch'i-jui and was therefore not to be entrusted with too much power.

In the years between 1919 and 1922 the movement for federalism gained some momentum. The civil wars not only between the Northern and the Southern regimes but among the military factions almost everywhere were creating a general pessimism as regards national reconstruction. Thinking people were led to ask themselves this question: If the country as a whole could not be saved by one stroke within a short space of time, would it not be more advisable to concentrate their efforts for the time being on the saving of their own provinces? When the peace negotiations between the North and the South were going on in 1919, the demand for some sort of local autonomy became fairly general. A gathering of eight civic bodies in Shanghai in 1921 which called itself the Conference on the State of the Nation even went so far as to draft a model federal constitution and urged both the central and the provincial governments to go federalist accordingly.

Unfortunately, this demand for an institutional change was readily utilized by the militarists of the provinces who were more interested in their own personal power than in real provincial autonomy. They advocated or accepted federalism for their provinces, not to give the people provincial self-government but to assure themselves of something like a permanent control, free from the interference of the central government. This was so in Hunan where the provincial military governor made full use of the Provincial Constitution of January 1, 1922 to make himself virtually independent of both the Peking and Canton regimes. That apparently democratic constitution was voted on by the people and was supposed to have been in force from 1922 to 1924. But certainly the people of Hunan never had any real self-government in those years. The Province of Chekiang also had a democratic constitution prepared in 1921, and its military governor also pledged to abide by it wholeheartedly. But he too never relinquished any part of his control and the constitution was not even nominally enforced. A number of other provinces also went in for constitution-making, but the result was the same. In no province was autonomous government brought nearer to the people.

The Ts'ao K'un Constitution of 1923 was federalist in nature. But by that time the movement for federalism had already evaporated. No thinking man would still be naive enough to contend that federalism could be protection against the despotism of the central government or the civil wars among the militarists. Something else was needed to effect the eradication of both. Federalism might be a good thing for China but it would not work until despotism and militarism were first gone. No wonder the Manifesto of the rejuvenated Kuomintang of 1924 declared against federalism. Thereafter for a long time there was no further consideration of it.

However, the problem of an equitable division of governmental powers between the central and the provincial governments still remains. In China the tendency for a strong central government to absorb all powers and for recalcitrant provincial governors to be de facto autonomists has always been pronounced. A stable regime in order to remain stable has to devise means of distributing powers equitably between the two tiers of government. The failure of the federalist movement in the early 1920's only meant that it could not solve the pressing problems of despotism, militarism, and lawlessness and disorder in general. It did not mean that it might not be a good means to effect the desirable distribution of powers.

Chapter III
The Control Apparatus

In answer to persistent outcries from various moralists and parents on the weakening decline of family bonds in the United States, Talcott Parsons points out that the modern American family represents a necessary transitional stage. In its net effect during this period of change, however, it is no less important than the family of an earlier era. Political organization in earlier twentieth century China was no less an institution undergoing metamorphosis than is the American urban family. Since the change from an old, ineffective huge bureaucracy to a modern nation-state was more dramatic,—often being brought about by physical force and intense political struggle, the changes that took place were more obvious, and their proximate impact caused more emotional reactions among the general population. Although it was clear that the government in China during the first two decades of this century was characteristically a decaying ancient society, the situation was not always well understood. The vast rural area suffered from a disastrous economic failure at a time when the pressures for a strong centralized government were greatest. Leaders of the Kuomintang were concerned over the rural problem; so were leaders of the Communist party. The Nationalists had an enormously ambitious and elaborate reform plan, but were not able to bring it to reality. Perhaps the reason was not so much the Nationalists' support of landlords as the Communists' ability to agitate the landless peasants. Mao's tactics—as well as his theories—were as Marxian as they were immensely pragmatic. The Communists' experiments in rural land reform were greatly enhanced when the Kuomintang–Communist United Front broke up and the Communists were driven to the countryside.

Having the support of the peasants, the Communist party was, and still is, primarily a revolutionary party. It has at its base a fraternal concept of comradeship, with the discipline of the military guided by ideology. The aim of the party is as unmistakably clear as its method of changing the minds of men is effective.

In this section the reader is first introduced to Mao's own words on the goals of the Communist Party in China. This is followed by Lewis's overview of the party structure and Gingsburgs and Stahnke's sketch of the basic legal structure—which departs significantly from the clan rule of the imperial era.

The philosophic system of Communism is basically "legalistic" as it is psychological. Instead of removing "misfits" from existence, the Chinese Communists believe in changing them, in thoughts as well as in deeds. Frederick Yu and Franz Michael each present the elaborate plans that have been devised to achieve such goals.

Whatever cannot be achieved politically or by police force, can, Mao believes, be achieved by violence. In three separate articles the ideology of military control and the social structure of the military are clearly analyzed by Kashin, Powell, and Mao himself.

The Structure of Control Organizations

8. THE ROLE OF IDEOLOGY

MAO TSE-TUNG

Twenty-four years have elapsed since Sun Yat-sen's death, and under the leadership of the CCP, Chinese revolutionary theory and practice have made big forward strides, fundamentally changing the realities of China. Up to the present, the Chinese people have gained the following two major and basic lessons of experience: (1) We must awaken the masses in the country. This is to unite the working class, the peasant class, the petty bourgeoisie, the national bourgeoisie into a national united front under the leadership of the working class, and develop it into a state of the people's democratic dictatorship led by the working class with the alliance of workers and peasants as its basis. (2) We must unite in a common struggle with those nations of the world who treat us on the basis of equality and with the people of all countries. This is to ally ourselves with the Soviet Union, to ally ourselves with all the New Democratic countries, and to ally ourselves with the proletariat and the broad masses of the people in other countries, to form an international united front.

"You lean to one side." Precisely so. The forty years' experience of Sun Yat-sen and the twenty-eight years' experience of the CCP have taught us to believe that in order to win and to consolidate the victory we must lean to one side. The experiences of forty years and twenty-eight years, respectively, show that, without exception, the Chinese people either lean to the side of imperialism or to the side of socialism. To sit on the fence is impossible; a third road does not exist. We oppose the Chiang Kai-shek reactionary clique who lean to the side of imperialism; we also oppose the illusion of a third road. Not only in China but also in the world, without exception, one either

SOURCE: Selected from Mao Tse-tung, *On People's Democratic Dictatorship.*

leans to the side of imperialsim or to the side of socialism. Neutrality is mere camouflage and a third road does not exist. . . .

"You are dictatorial." Dear sirs, you are right; that is exactly what we are. The experience of several decades, amassed by the Chinese people, tells us to carry out the people's democratic dictatorship. That is, the right of reactionaries to voice their opinions must be abolished and only the people are allowed to have the right of voicing their opinions.

Who are the "people"? At the present stage in China, they are the working class, the peasant class, the petty bourgeoisie, and national bourgeoisie. Under the leadership of the working class and the CP, these classes unite together to form their own state and elect their own government so as to carry out a dictatorship over the lackeys of imperialism—the landlord class, the bureaucratic capitalist class, and the KMT reactionaries and their henchmen representing these classes—to suppress them, allowing them only to behave properly and not to talk and act wildly. If they talk and act wildly their action will be prohibited and punished immediately. The democratic system is to be carried out within the ranks of the people, giving them freedom of speech, assembly, and association. The right to vote is given only to the people and not to the reactionaries. These two aspects, namely, democracy among the people and dictatorship over the reactionaries, combine to form the people's democratic dictatorship.

Why should it be done this way? Everybody clearly knows that otherwise the revolution would fail, and the people would meet with woe and the State would perish.

"Don't you want to eliminate state authority?" Yes, but we do not want it at present, we cannot want it at present. Why? Because imperialism still exists, the domestic reactionaries still exist, and classes in the country still exist. Our present task is to strengthen the apparatus of the people's state, which refers mainly to the people's army, people's police, and people's courts, for the defence of the country and the protection of the people's interests; and with this as a condition, to enable China to advance steadily, under the leadership of the working class and the CP, from an agricultural to an industrial country, and from a new Democratic to a Socialist and Communist society, to eliminate classes and to realize the state of universal fraternity. The army, police, and courts of the state are instruments by which classes oppress classes. To the hostile classes the state apparatus is the instrument of oppression. It is violent, and not "benevolent." "You are not benevolent." Just so. We decidedly will not exercise benevolence towards the reactionary acts of the reactionaries and reactionary classes. Our benevolence applies only to the people, and not to the reactionary acts of the reactionaries and reactionary classes outside the people.

The function of the people's state is to protect the people. Only when there is the people's state, is it possible for the people to use democratic methods on a nation-wide and all-around scale to educate and reform themselves, to free themselves from the influence of reactionaries at home and abroad (this influence is at present still very great and will exist for a long time and cannot be eliminated quickly), to unlearn the bad habits and ideas acquired from the old society and not to let themselves travel on the erroneous path pointed out by the reactionaries, but to continue to advance and develop towards a Socialist and Communist society accomplishing the historic mission of completely eliminating classes and advancing towards a universal fraternity.

The methods we use in this field are democratic; that is, methods of persuasion and not coercion. When people break the law they will be punished, imprisoned, or even sentenced to death. But these are individual cases and are different in principle from the dictatorship over the reactionary class as a class.

After their political regime is overthrown the reactionary classes and the reactionary clique will also be given land and work and a means of living; they will be allowed to re-educate themselves into new persons through work, provided they do not rebel, disrupt, or sabotage. If they are unwilling to work, the people's state will compel them to work. Propaganda and educational work will also be carried out among them, and, moreover, with care and adequacy, as we did among captured officers. This can also be called "benevolent administration," but we shall never forgive their reactionary acts and will never let their reactionary activity have the possibility of a free development.

Such re-education of the reactionary classes can only be carried out in the state of the people's democratic dictatorship. If this work is well done the main exploiting classes of China—the landlord and bureaucratic capitalist classes—will be finally eliminated. Of the exploiting classes there remain the national bourgeoisie among many of whom appropriate educational work can be carried out at the present stage. When socialism is realized, that is, when the nationalization of private enterprises has been carried out, they can be further educated and reformed. The people have in their hands a powerful state apparatus and are not afraid of the rebellion of the national bourgeois class.

The grave problem is that of educating the peasants. The peasants' economy is scattered. Judging by the experience of the Soviet Union, it requires a very long time and careful work to attain the socialization of agriculture. Without the socialization of agriculture, there will be no complete and consolidated socialism. And to carry out the socialization of agriculture a powerful industry with state-owned enterprises as the main component must be developed. . . .

The basis of the people's democratic dictatorship is the alliance of the working class, peasant class, and the urban petty-bourgeois class, and is mainly the alliance of the working class and the peasant class because they constitute eighty to ninety per cent of the Chinese population. It is mainly through the strength of these two classes that imperialism and the KMT reactionary clique were overthrown. The passing from New Democracy to Socialism mainly depends on the alliance of these two classes.

The people's democratic dictatorship needs the leadership of the working class, because only the working class is most far-sighted, just and unselfish and endowed with revolutionary thoroughness. The history of the entire revolution proves that without the leadership of the working class, the revolution is bound to fail, and with the leadership of the working class, the revolution is victorious. In the era of imperialism no other class in any country can lead any genuine revolution to victory. This is clearly proved by the fact that the Chinese national bourgeoisie has led the revolution many times and each time had failed.

The national bourgeoisie is of great importance at the present stage. Imperialism is still standing near us and this enemy is very fierce. A long time is required for China to realize true economic independence and become free from reliance on imperialist nations. Only when China's industries are developed, and she no longer depends economically on powerful nations, can there be real independence. The proportion of China's modern industry in the entire national economy is still very small. There are still no reliable figures at present, but according to certain data it is estimated that modern industry only occupies about ten per cent of the total productive output in the national economy of the whole country. To cope with imperialist oppression, and to raise our backward economic status one step higher, China must utilize all urban and rural factors of capitalism which are beneficial and not detrimental to the national economy and the people's livelihood, and unite with the national bourgeoisie in a common struggle. Our present policy is to restrict capitalism and not to eliminate it. But the national bourgeoisie cannot be the leader of the revolutionary united front and should not occupy the main position of state power. This is because the social and economic status of the national bourgeoisie has determined its feebleness; it lacks foresight, lacks courage, and in large part fears the masses. . . .

We must overcome difficulties, and must master what we do not know. We must learn economic work from all who know the ropes no matter who they are. We must acknowledge them as our teachers, and learn from them respectfully and earnestly. We must acknowledge our ignorance, and not pretend to know what we do not know, nor put on bureaucratic airs. Stick to it, and eventually it will be mastered in a few months, one or two years, or three or five years. At first some of the Communists in the U.S.S.R. also did not know how to do economic work, and the imperialists also waited for their failure. But the CP of the Soviet Union won. Under the leadership of Lenin and Stalin they not only could do revolutionary work but also reconstruction work. They have already built up a great and brilliant socialist state. The CP of the U.S.S.R. is our best teacher from whom we must learn. . . . We can rely wholly on the weapon of the people's democratic dictatorship to unite all people throughout the country, except the reactionaries, and advance steadily towards the goal.

9. THE ROLE OF THE PARTY

John Wilson Lewis

The constitution of the Communist Party of China formalizes the elite's concept of its mission, internal relationships, methods of operation, and hierarchy of authority. Based on the Constitution of 1945, the present Constitution was passed at the Eighth Party Congress in 1956. It provides the most important outline used by the elite in China to guide the Party's work and to indoctrinate those recruited to Party membership, although since 1956 Party leaders have emphasized the human dimension of the leadership structure rather than the formalistic details of bureaucratic charts and procedures.

Above its local level, the Party branch, which may be formed on the basis of residence or place of work, the Party is structured along geographical lines. The essential chain of command runs from the primary Party committee to committees at the county (or municipality), provincial (or autonomous regional), and national levels. For convenience, these levels or their equivalents may also establish subordinate bureaus or committees to coordinate local areas under their command, but only committees at the principal command levels are responsible to counterpart Party congresses. These congresses elect representatives to the next higher congress—that is, the individual Party member in the branch does not elect "his" representatives to provincial and national congresses—and elect the crucial committees at their respective levels composed of cadres, the committees constitutes the real line of political authority. . . .

As the prototype for all "working-class" organizations in China, the Communist Party structure follows the principle of democratic centralism. In addition to the well-known requirements that inferior levels and the "minority" obey senior levels and the "majority," the theory of democratic centralism adapts organization to process and action. It stipulates that members must participate actively within limits set by the central leadership and that in the process of decision-making cadres must encourage the sharing of ideas and information before the policy is set as well as the active implementation of the policy after decision. To achieve genuine participation within guided limits, the Party leaders emphasize effective inner-group communications, especially regular meetings, reports, and follow-up supervision. The organizational use of such a process of decision-making presumably obviates the need for coercion, although the Party has established and recently strengthened its apparatus of discipline.

The key concept in the formulation of the Party's structure is membership solidarity. The Party highlights this concept for two reasons: Party members

source: Selected from John Wilson Lewis, ed., *Major Doctrines of Communist China,* Chapter Four, "The Party Structure," New York: W. W. Norton, 1964, pp. 111–115. Copyright 1964 by W. W. Norton & Company, Inc.

Numerical Growth of the Chinese Communist Party, 1921–1961

	Number of members	Years covered	Average annual increase
First Revolutionary Civil War 1921–1927			
1921 (1st Congress)	57	–	–
1922 (2d Congress)	123	1	66
1923 (3d Congress)	432	1	309
1925 (4th Congress)	950	2	259
1927 (5th Congress)	57,967	2	28,508
1927 (after "April 12")	10,000	–	–
Second Revolutionary Civil War 1927–1937			
1928 (6th Congress)	40,000	1	30,000
1930	122,318	2	41,159
1933	300,000	3	59,227
1937	40,000	4	−65,000
War of Resistance to Japanese Aggression 1937–1945			
1940	800,000	3	253,333
1941	763,447	1	−36,553
1942	736,151	1	−27,296
1944	853,420	2	58,635
1945 (7th Congress)	1,211,128	1	357,708
Third Revolutionary Civil War 1945–1949			
1946	1,348,320	1	137,192
1947	2,759,456	1	1,411,136
1948	3,065,533	1	306,077
1949	4,488,080	1	1,422,547
People's Republic of China 1949–			
1950	5,821,604	1	1,333,524
1951	5,762,293	1	−59,311
1952	6,001,698	1	239,405
1953	6,612,254	1	610,556
1954	7,859,473	1	1,247,219
1955	9,393,394	1	1,533,921
1956 (8th Congress)	10,734,384	1	1,340,990
1957	12,720,000	1	1,985,616
1959	13,960,000	2	620,000
1961	17,000,000	2	1,520,000

Reprinted by permission from John W. Lewis, *Leadership in Communist China* (Ithaca: Cornell University Press, 1963), pp. 110–111.

with different backgrounds and experiences have tended to form exclusive, independent groups; and in the very formation of unified group relationships Party members have often adopted the traditional "familylike" habits. Solidarity thus has meant both a Party-wide consensus or "comradeship" and individual commitment to the "collective" rather than to personal associates.

In addition to their attacks on localism, departmentalism, careerism, individualism, and other common deviations from Party solidarity, the Communist leaders have confronted the task of integrating the major "generations" that comprise the Party's membership. The table given above shows the growth of Party membership since 1921. According to Liu Shao-ch'i, more than 80 per cent of the more than 17 million members in 1961 joined the Party after 1949, and thus failed to share the critical revolutionary tradition with the senior membership. The division into revolutionary and postrevolutionary generations must be further subdivided to appreciate the pressures for disunity and diversity within the Party. From 1921–1927, the typical new Party member was an intellectual student; from 1928–1949, a peasant soldier; from 1950–1958, a young worker; and from 1958–1961, a village peasant. Viewed from the standpoint of major experiences, these Party members are also labeled as "Long March," "Yenan," and "new" members. By age divisions in 1956, the latest figures available, 24.83 per cent were 25 or younger, 67.54 per cent were between the ages of 26 and 45, and 7.63 per cent were above 46, but official reports indicate that only a small percentage of the first two age groups fought in the revolution. Despite the fact that the Party has conceived the development of genuine solidarity in terms of "education and persuasion," the obvious sources of disunity have required even greater emphasis on rigorous discipline and careful supervision.

Although the apparatus of the Chinese Communist Party may be depicted in the form of a pyramid rising from the base of Party members to the apex of the Standing Committee of the Political Bureau under Mao Tse-tung, certain elements in the Party apparatus make the pyramidal concept somewhat inaccurate. Certainly a small number of leading cadres controls a great many Party members who, in turn, regulate an even greater number of non-Party Chinese, but the actual form of organizational control emphasizes the "small group" rather than the large meeting, where decisions are announced without warning from the podium. Composed of fewer than 15 members, the small group personalizes the leadership apparatus at all levels of the "pyramid" and provides the framework for membership initiative and participation. In the Communist system an important element of reciprocity thus exists between the leaders and the led, and this binds the individual to the organizational life of the Party. Consequently, it has become almost impossible for a member simply to merge with the crowd and masquerade as an enthusiast without continuous participation and verbal commitment.

To achieve this level of organizational involvement, the Party requires that every Party member join a branch and participate in its activities and in the activities of one of the Party groups within the branch. Naturally, Mao Tse-tung is heralded as the outstanding branch member. The Party press has reported the details of Mao Tse-tung's branch life and has stressed that the secretary of the branch could "not have wished for a more dutiful member than Chairman Mao." In 1959, the Party was composed of 1,060,000 branches organized throughout China. The central figure in the branch is its secretary who has three principal and sometimes conflicting responsibilities. First, he must supervise the training and inner-Party activities of the Party members, guiding their performance and disciplining their conduct. Second, he is the last, and perhaps the most important, link in the cadre chain of command; he composes the reports on which later policies are based and directs his own cadres to implement policy measures. Last, he must maintain the Party as a force among the Chinese people and, specifically, within the individual residential or production unit on which the branch is based.

10.   THE ROLE OF THE LAW

George Ginsburgs and Arthur Stahnke

When the Chinese Communists finally consummated their seizure of power in mainland China, one of the first tasks which faced them was that of elaborating a formal institutional structure for the exercise of regular public authority. Indeed, while the new leadership now undoubtedly enjoyed *de facto* control over the country and the mass of the people, it found itself quite destitute of those normal channels of state regulation and administrative management which serve to bestow legitimacy on a claimant to the role of national government and to distinguish a duly constituted, relatively stable political order from an altogether fluid interlude of revolutionary action predicated on *ad hoc* use of organised force under a central direction. The Party soon moved to make up for this grave deficiency by creating, on paper at least, a complex mechanism of state administration to back up its bid for recognition as the official spokesman for the Chinese nation and, concurrently, provide it with the wherewithal to play that role effectively.

In this major undertaking, not all the set objectives proved equally hard to attain. Past experience in Yennan, as well as in the "liberated areas" of Second World War fame, facilitated the work in some sectors where the record of previous experimentation and improvisation furnished a ready pool of relevant and tested solutions for several of the problems at hand. Thus, the process of organisation of local government bodies and lower courts could and did draw from the large fund of precedent established in these matters; likewise, in questions of primary administration, early efforts in that field offered a convenient guideline for the current venture. In other spheres, however, no such aid was forthcoming from some storehouse of experience and the new

SOURCE. Selected from George Ginsburgs and Arthur Stahnke, "The Genesis of the People's Procuratorate in Communist China, 1949–1951," in *The China Quarterly*, No. 20, pp. 1–2, 5, 8–9, 11–15, and 21–26. Reprinted by permission of *The China Quarterly*.

rulers virtually had to start from the ground up, that is, in so far as they were personally familiar with the issues involved. The procuratorate looms as a prime example of such a case, for no comparable administrative device appears on the scene on previous occasions where the Communist Chinese openly maintained supreme jurisdiction over an appreciable extent of territory on a durable basis.

The picture of the genesis of the office in Communist China's government system is interesting, then, not only because the institution still represents one of the least explored of the latter's chief components, but also because, in a broader sense, the history of the process helps shed light on the modalities of operational development and early evolution of an important public organ, literally from its conception, against the general background of the political conditions in the People's Republic of China at the time. In these circumstances, the record of the procuratorate's beginnings and initial progression may well, and, it is here submitted, in fact does, act as a source of illumination of the standard techniques originally implemented elsewhere too by the present Chinese régime in the course of political reconstruction. . . .

The 1951 Statutes

STRUCTURE OF THE OFFICE OF THE PEOPLE'S PROCURATOR-GENERAL

Under the terms of the Provisional Regulations Governing the Organisation of the Office of the People's Procurator-General, as passed at last by the Central People's Government Council, the agency was officially designated as "the highest people's procuratorial organ" in the land and as "responsible for supreme supervision over strict observance of the law by government institutions, civil servants, and the people throughout the country." It was to operate directly under the jurisdiction of the Central People's Government Council and be fully responsible for the exercise of the following functions and powers:

(1) Supervision of government organs of all levels throughout the country, public functionaries, and individuals, to see whether they strictly observe the Common Programme of the People's Political Consultative Conference and the policies, laws and decrees of the People's Government;

(2) Investigation of counter-revolutionary and other criminal cases and instigation of legal proceedings;

(3) Opposition to unwarranted or improper judgments rendered by judicial organs of all levels;

(4) Investigation of illegal measures in the management of prisons and labour reform institutions all over the country;

(5) Handling of petitions for review of cases dropped by lower offices of people's procurators, when such petitions are submitted by people who do not agree with the decision of the lower offices of people's procurators;

(6) Participation as representative of state interests in important civil and administrative law-suits involving the interests of the nation and the working people.

To this the law immediately added, however, that the carrying out of the tasks listed under points 2 and 3 above could "be provisionally entrusted to public security organs in areas where offices of people's procurators of lower levels are not yet established," though still with the provison that, in such circumstances, "these public security organs, when conducting investigations, shall be subject to the leadership of offices of the people's procurators of higher levels."

The personnel of the Office was to include the Procurator-General, two or three Deputy Procurators-General, and eleven to seventeen Councillors, all appointed by the Central People's Government Council. (At the beginning of 1951, when the "Tentative Regulations" were still in force, the staff of the Office reportedly comprised the Procurator-General, his two assistants, and twelve members; in the autumn of that year, after the "Provisional Regulations" had apparently gone into effect, it was said to consist of the Procurator-General, his assistants, and fourteen members.)² The number of Deputy Procurators-General and Councillors could be increased or reduced by the Central People's Government Council at the recommendation of the Procurator-General. The Procurator-General was personally charged with the direction of the affairs of the Office, with the Deputy Procurators-General assisting him in execution of his duties. . . . The Office could also establish a branch office in each administrative region and equivalent unit of local government to execute its functions in such territorial divisions, reportedly "in order to facilitate . . . leadership" of "the lower levels of offices of the people's procurators in the exercise of their powers" and "furnish such leadership on behalf of the Office of the People's Procurator-General to the higher levels of local procuratorial organs."³ Jurisdictionally, "these branches were attached to the administrative committees of the large administrative regions" and, "together with the corresponding branch of the Supreme People's Court, the Department of Civil Administration and the Department of Public Security, the procuratorate was subordinated to the Political and Legal Committee of the given region."⁴ . . .

Directly below the regional headquarters stood the offices of people's procurators of provinces and administrative areas of equivalent status and municipal offices of people's procurators in cities under the jurisdiction of the Central People's Government or any of the administrative regions. Each of these was to be headed by a chief-procurator and one deputy chief-procurator, jointly directing a General Office and the First and Second Divisions (but no Third) which employed a number of investigators, assistant investigators and clerks. The provincial office could, in turn, institute branch offices in the special administrative districts within its jurisdiction, each with its own chief-procurator and deputy chief-procurator, supervising a team of investigators, assistant investigators and clerks. Here, too, a general office could be established, if conditions warranted it.

Next, in order of descent, came *hsien* offices of people's procurators and their municipal counterparts in the smaller urban centres, likewise managed by their respective chief-procurator and his deputy chief-procurator, overseeing the work of a number of investigators, assistant investigators, secretaries and clerks. Once again, a general office could, if so required, be attached thereto. The law further provided that, in sundry national minority autonomous territorial units, "offices of people's procurators corresponding to the level of the various people's governments in these areas shall be set up according to the concrete needs of these areas." . . .

Taken together, then, these various edicts were intended to furnish a comprehensive conceptual framework within which an efficient nationwide network of procuratorial offices was expected to grow in short order and to determine the main lines along which this complex apparatus, once fully established, would discharge its official business. Compared with earlier statutory efforts in this sector, these latest products of the régime's legislative activity covered the subject much more systematically and much more thoroughly and, despite some shortcomings of their own, from a technical standpoint stood infinitely superior to the temporary decrees they now replaced. Most of these improvements, however, fell into the category of stylistic changes—greater care in the formulation of rules, more precise terminology, fewer substantive gaps and textual repetitions and discrepancies, as well as occasionally a deliberate use of different words and expressions.[5] In a material sense, on the other hand, the core contents of the new legislation in the end departed but little from the structural and functional principles hitherto in effect here. . . .

One important modification of prior practice (in terms of organisation) effected at this time and which deserves to be noted revolved around the issue of the choice of the proper patterns of jurisdictional subordination of the individual units of the people's procuratorate within the over-all scheme of State administration. The solution finally endorsed by the "General Regulations" was that of "dual leadership," described by an official spokesman as an arrangement under which "the local offices of the people's procurators of various levels are subject to the leadership of offices of the people's procurators immediately above and, as these local offices are a component part of the people's governments of corresponding levels, to that of the people's government councils at their level."[6] . . .

By contrast, the precept of "lineal leadership" had previously been in force within the procuratorial hierarchy, at least theoretically, since the "Tentative Regulations" of December 1949 had specified that the entire multi-storied edifice of procuratorial offices would operate on the rule of vertical intra-institutional controls alone, each cell taking orders from the one above it, but otherwise functioning free of all restraint from any outside state agency. As was presently conceded that after one year's experience, it was found that the principle was difficult to carry out in practice, and so it was changed to "dual leadership."[7] Indeed, there are many indications that even during that brief interim trial period, the proposed concept of a "single inner channel of command" was never truly tested on any significant scale; instead, for all intents and purposes, the formula of "the independence of local procuratorates from local organs of government temporarily was not applied."[8]

Hence, already at the time the "General Regulations" were first drafted in November 1950, the set-up sanctioned in the original blueprint was revised as still premature and unworkable in the context of existing conditions and, for the next few years, the rule of "dual subordination" elaborated in lieu thereof obtained, until September 1954, whereupon the norm of "lineal leadership" was reinstated. The initial, reluctant switch from a strongly desired organisational form to something that obviously represented a second-best compromise, duly followed after a relatively short spell by a return to the solution preferred from the start, reflects the serious handicaps encountered here by the new régime during this early phase in prosecuting its plans, which forced it once in a while to backtrack and postpone the implementation of projects favoured by it until a later date when circumstances looked more propitious for their consummation. . . .

The adjustment may have been, as claimed, thoroughly "realistic," but there was also a negative dimension to it, for the whole debate over "lineal" versus "dual" subordination held more than academic interests, bearing directly, as it did, on the eminently practical issue of the efficacy of the procuratorate's supervision of the public business of local government bodies, ostensibly one of its principal tasks. True, partisan sources have insisted throughout that, "as is shown by the record of the work of the CPR procuratorate, the temporary organisational subordination of the procuratorate to the local authorities did not prevent the higher procuratorate from protesting against resolutions of lower local government organs, if they contradicted the laws of the Central People's Government."[9] . . .

This way by far the single most important alteration introduced by the 1951 legislation in the precedent established in this field. Possibly another modification, though of lesser significance, was also effected on this occasion, touching on the question of "collegiate direction" within offices of people's procurators, but the available evidence is contradictory. Thus, some authors, analysing the situation before the statutes were revised, claimed then that "the Supreme People's Procuratorate, as well as regional, provincial and army people's procuratorates are collegial organs of supervision. . . ."[10] As against that, however, a few, writing at the same time, maintained that, while the Office of the People's Procurator-General, "just as all the other State organs of China, is a collegial-type institution . . . the lower procuratorates are not collegial and are headed by a single procurator."[11]

In any event, given the rudimentary state of affairs and slow progress in the organisation of the procuratorate at this point, the question could not have represented a very crucial issue in those days. Furthermore, the new edicts soon put an end to the problem by making it clear that henceforth all offices of people's procurators, from top to bottom, would adhere to the rule of "collective policy formulation," a strangely understood concept since in practice decisions so reached always remained subject, of course, to veto by the respective chief-procurator who, if he elected to invoke this right, thereafter was at liberty to pursue his own inclination, under the ever-watchful eye of his official superior, to be sure.

The formal functions of the procuratorate likewise underwent no extensive revision or signal change, barring one exception. As to that, prior to 1951, what skeleton procuratorial machinery was already in existence was not statutorily empowered to conduct criminal investigations on its own. Instead, the situation which then obtained stood as follows: "Preliminary investigation is at the present time a function of the courts, but supervision over it, just as supervision over investigation by the organs of State security, belongs to the procuratorate."[12] With the passage of the new acts, every office of people's procurator acquired in law the independent right, and was enjoined, to initiate investigations of criminal offences which came to its attention and institute legal proceedings against the guilty parties, concentrating especially on episodes of "counter-revolutionary" activity. Indeed, in his "Explanatory Report" on the fresh Regulations, delivered on September 3, Li Liu-ju, one of the country's Deputy Procurators-General, chose to emphasise this last point, letting his audience know that:

> Among the duties of offices of the people's procurators, . . . investigation and prosecution of cases of counter-revolution have been placed above investigation and prosecution of general criminal cases. This is because the Chinese people's war of liberation has achieved only basic victory. It is not yet finally concluded. Moreover, the enemy whom we have overthrown is still actively planning to sabotage the people's régime and the cause of the people's democracy. Therefore, prosecution of cases of counter-revolution is more important than prosecution of ordinary criminal cases today.[13]

That all this so far amounted to no more than pious hope and wishful thinking, however, with no near prospect of becoming reality, is conclusively demonstrated by the acknowledged fact that, despite much talk, "before 1954 the CPR procuratorate did not possess investigation departments" and "all investigation work was conducted by organs of public security and partly by the courts."[14]

Operational Framework

As can be gathered from the above, the 1949–1951 interlude in the life of Communist China's procuratorate was occupied essentially with the preliminary task of defining the institution's formal basis, clarifying its constitutional powers, and outlining its organisational structure. Otherwise, during the first two years of its existence the newly created office transacted very little actual business, in practice playing a minimal role in the momentous revolutionary upheaval directed from above which at this time had already begun to transform the ancient face of the country. While this record of passivity precludes any serious attempt to engage in a meaningful analysis of the procuratorate in early action, the slowness of the agency's growth in itself offers a valuable index to some of the problems encountered by the régime in pursuing this venture.

By the same token, it may be true that in studying this first stage of the procuratorate's evolution in People's China one is confined to a great extent to a textual examination of the relevant legal documents. Yet, the very language of the statutes which gave birth to the institution, the manner of legislatively enunciating its rights, duties, and operational methods, in other words, the whole process of elaboration of the broad juridical framework within which the authorities proposed to have it function thereafter, all these had a direct, and decisive, impact on the future path of the organ's development and on the quality of its performance as an integral component of the administrative tissue of the new order. Hence, despite these limitations, a fairly accurate picture of the total situation nonetheless emerges in the end from a survey of the formal sources supplemented by occasional disclosures of data from the record of the agency's meagre practice.

Needless to say, the original formulas of this assortment of still largely experimental regulations did not remain immutable. Under the pressure of actual experience gained in trying to implement these test rules, many of them soon had to be adjusted and, once in a while, reinterpreted to suit changing conditions, but few, if any, had to be revised outright. Up until September 1954, then, the validity of the substantive contents of these first pieces of legislation in the main stayed unimpaired and so these norms continued for the most part to guide the work of the procuratorate throughout the opening phase of its official career and thereby also succeeded in influencing it even well beyond that point.

Though two years, especially when they happen to be two years of widespread revolutionary turbulence, do not offer much time in which to forge a complex branch of state administration, even in the best of circumstances, still the virtually snail-like pace of the procuratorate's initial progression in Communist China does seem somewhat out of the ordinary and, in this instance, an understanding of the phenomenon must therefore be sought elsewhere than by reference to the sundry difficulties commonly attendant on such projects. Thus, as will be shown below, in the present case several further reasons may be advanced in explanation of this peculiar feature of the institution's history.

The first, and most obvious, possibility that comes to mind in this connection, and one repeatedly cited by the régime itself, is simply the acute shortage of qualified personnel to man a comprehensive and balanced network of procuratorial offices. In itself, the excuse is a valid one, particularly when backed up with appeals to the fact that, as a newly conceived institution, with no true antecedent in the constitutional systems which China had previously known,[15] the procuratorate was bound, logically, to labour under a distinct added disadvantage as compared with most other public organs in the land. Indeed, a great majority of the latter, though reorganised by the current government, nonetheless basically corresponded to some similar agency in the past and could, as a consequence, readily draw upon an accumulation of precedent and inspiration, if they chose to do so, naturally, and perhaps make use, too, of picked elements from the old staff of the departments they had supplanted. No such opportunities lay before the procuratorate.

All this is quite correct, of course, but it paints only half the picture, for it still leaves unexplained why, in the absence of competent cadres, Peking did not at once launch a vigorous training programme to fill the void which it deplored so vocally. The various reasons which could serve to account for this peculiar line of conduct are highly suggestive.

In the first place, it can be cogently argued that while the leadership seized every chance to pay lip service to the idea of the procuratorate as "an important weapon of the people's democratic dictatorship,"[16] this was no more than a formal gesture on its part that did not reflect its genuine feelings on the subject. In effect, the revolutionary government's chief interest in those early years certainly did not focus on legal technicalities, but all of its behaviour emphasised rather the primacy of reliance on administrative means for the achievement of stated purposes. Commenting later on the events of this period, it acknowledged as much, with the revealing observation that, "during this historical stage, a 'detailed and perfect' legal system divorced from actualities could not be and should not have been instituted to bind the hands and feet of the masses." Not surprisingly, in these circumstances even persons on the inside allegedly misread its true intentions, for by its own admission, "not understanding this point, some people gained a wrong impression that procurators' work was not important."[17]

Actually, those who saw it that way were quite right, official contentions to the contrary notwithstanding. Since the procuratorate was, by definition, identified as an organ entrusted with certain tasks of law enforcement and vested with a special role in the dispensation of justice by the courts, the government's avowed neglect of formal legal processes in turn inevitably diminished that agency's stature and practical significance on the public scene. Desirous of complete freedom of action and maximum speed and flexibility in dealing with real or fancied opposition to its exercise of state power, the new leadership simply preferred at the outset to depend on non-judicial methods of suppression and punishment, bound by few rules and even those too vague to offer an obstacle to its wishes, than to have to work through an institution hampered to any degree by procedural restrictions. As long as this type of mentality persisted, the procuratorate was fated to occupy a back seat while various other departments, among them the office of public security, enjoyed undisputed priority of precedence, not only in general, but in its own purported field of safeguarding the law as well.

In the second place, it is suggested that the régime's habit of speaking of the procuratorate as a highly important part of the new state mechanism was more than just a propaganda ploy after all, if considered from a different angle. True, the procuratorate did not deserve the designation at the time it was being so lavishly bestowed upon it, but its constant use would appear to indicate that the authorities firmly expected such a description to fit in the very near future. If so, then their approach to the problem begins to make some sense, since this objective would, in fact, be accomplished best by a slow and careful policy, conditions in the land being what they were. Given an official commitment to building up a special apparatus which would, when completed, be assigned a key role in the management of national affairs, such caution in the choice and training of personnel to carry out a difficult task no longer sounds excessive, indeed was called for.

As already mentioned, the absence in China's previous administrative system of any agency with functions closely resembling those now reserved for the procuratorate made it hard for the latest government to find experienced staff in the currently unemployed ranks of the bureaucracy which had served its predecessor to suit its present purpose. For most other departments, this emergency solution had proved a godsend, especially so in the case of the judiciary which for many years after the political change-over continued to rely heavily on court officials inherited from the Nationalists who, presumably, had succeeded in reorienting themselves intellectually and becoming converted to the Communist outlook, though it remains a moot issue to this day whether the metamorphosis in most instances was more than skin-deep. When it came to the procuratorate, however, there is evidence that the successor regime simply refused to avail itself of this relatively easy way out of the dilemma, namely, by choosing to train and re-educate for its own needs former civil servants familiar with at least some features of the job, preferring instead to work from the ground up and thus, *inter alia,* to make its position doubly secure by also not running the risk of infecting an institution for which it apparently nourished great hopes with the practices of the discredited past. It may have had a very valid point there, as witness the serious trouble it encountered at the start in trying to get the personnel of the reorganised judiciary recruited, as noted, in a not too selective fashion, to perform the way it wanted. Hence, to help keep the procuratorate pure and absolutely loyal to the new order, its cadres would be individually picked and gradually taught their trade from the basics up—a laborious undertaking, to be sure, but one likely to return handsome dividends in the end, or so Peking must have believed.

This brings us to the third, and last, aspect of this particular problem, to wit, the interplay of separate factors which on this occasion allowed the central government to adopt such a leisurely pace and to preserve in its chosen course for several years. What really made it possible for the authorities here to proceed at will was the absence of any marked outside pressure liable to cause them to hurry with the execution of their plans. To begin with, in the field of law proper, conditions were still so rudimentary that no elaborate machinery was required to dispense the simple justice which the régime temporarily deemed adequate for the population's needs. That, in turn, permitted all concerned to move as deliberately as they pleased (within reasonable limits) in organising the procuratorial branch for, in truth, not very much was demanded of the latter as yet in terms of participation in the technical work of the courts, such as it was.

What is more, Peking had at its disposal other channels through which it could act easier and faster, the public security forces again, the various other instruments of administrative control, the Party pyramid, and so forth. Besides lending themselves better to the leadership's purpose because they enjoyed full freedom of initiative whereas the procuratorate laboured under assorted procedural handicaps, they had the added advantage of an early start and so had already managed to grow and accumulate considerable practical experience which now stood them in good stead. To put it differently, in its bid for power every revolutionary movement is bound to concentrate its energies on the development of a few select weapons calculated to further its immediate aims most effectively, normally the ideological élite, an armed auxiliary, etc. Having won, it tends to continue using what lies readily at hand and what it has by then learned more or less how to manipulate, only gradually switching from comparatively familiar tactics to still untried methods. The weight of inertia always favours the old, which also helps explain why it took the procuratorate so long to come into its own. On the other hand, that very same phenomenon must take credit for giving the new government sufficient leeway to go ahead with the proposed business without undue haste such as might, otherwise, have jeopardised the whole venture or adversely affected the quality of the end product.

In short, the régime did not rush with the project because it could not, would not and did not need to. Each of these considerations contributed to the determination of the final outcome of its efforts and the results owed equally to all three.

Notes

1. Text in *People's Daily*, September 5, 1951; CB, No. 183.

2. O. A. Arturov, *Gosudarstvennyi stroi Kitaiskoi Narodnoi Respubliki* (Moscow: Izdatelstvo "Pravda," 1951), p. 24; N. Sudarikov, "Organy yustisii Kitaiskoi Narodnoi Respubliki," *Sotsialisticheskaya Zakonnost,* 1951, No. 10, p. 48.

3. Li Liu-ju, *op. cit., People's Daily,* September 5, 1951; CB, No. 183.

4. A. E. Luney, *op. cit.,* p. 55. According to N. G. Sudarikov, *op. cit.* (note 5), p. 48: "In June 1951, the State Administrative Council, the Supreme People's Court and the Supreme People's Procuratorate adopted the decision on the formation of local political-legal committees in the large administrative regions and provinces."

5. One of these, for instance, involved the substitution of the word "oppose" for "protest" in connection with the procuratorate's action against erroneous decisions by the court, presumably because the term "oppose" from an ideological standpoint sounded more forceful than "protest." This particular revision was noted separately by Li Liu-ju in his "Explanatory Report": "In the original draft regulations, it was provided that offices of the people's procurators may 'protest against any contra-judicial judgment made by the courts.' This is now changed to read: ' . . . Opposition to unwarranted or improper judgments made by judicial organs of various levels.' As the people's judicial organs are entrusted with the task of safeguarding the interests of the State and the people, any illegal or improper judgment or decision they have made must be opposed and the issue brought to higher courts by offices of the people's procurators. . . ."

Where a judgment had become final, this opposition took the form of a "protest" which, prior to 1954, was lodged with the judicial organ responsible for the objectionable ruling, whereas after that date, protests could be submitted to higher judicial instances as well. Be that as it may, before 1954 such protests were rare and all involved the lower courts. As A. E. Lunev, *op. cit.* p. 34, n. 1, notes: "Prior to 1954 in the practice of the courts and the procuratorate of the CPR there were no cases of submission of protests to the Supreme People's Court against sentences which had entered into force. There existed the practice of review of cases in which the sentences had entered into force by the courts which handed down these sentences."

6. Li Liu-ju, *op. cit., People's Daily,* September 5, 1951; CB, No. 183.

7. *Ibid.*

8. A. E. Lunev, *op. cit.,* p. 50.

9. A. E. Lunev, *op. cit.,* p. 50; *idem, Sushchnost Konstitutsii Kitaiskoi Narodnoi Respubliki* (Moscow: Gosyurizdat, 1958); p. 122.

10. O. A. Arturov, *op. cit.,* p. 23.

11. Z. M. Chernilovskii, *Gosudarstvennyi stroi Kitaiskoi Narodnoi Respubliki* (Moscow: Gosyurizdat, 1951), p. 85.

12. *Ibid.* See, also, the description in O. A. Arturov, *op. cit.,* p. 23, of the duties of the procuratorate at the beginning: "They [the offices of the procuratorate] exercise supervision over the activity of the people's police and conduct cases of State prosecution, as well as help with the organisation of social prosecution which was carried out by people's social oganisations."

13. *People's Daily,* September 5, 1951; CB, No. 183.

14. A. E. Lunev, *op. cit.* (note 7), p. 53, n. 1. It was only in the autumn of 1953 that the Supreme People's Procuratorate began creating on a wide scale "experimental-model" offices with investigation departments and in the second half of 1956 that a draft of "Experimental procedures for conducting investigation work by the people's procuratorates of all levels" was completed, according to V. E. Chugunov, *Ugolovnoe sudoproizvodstov Kitaiskoi Narodnoi Respubliki (ocherki)* (Moscow: Gosyurizdat, 1959), pp. 79–80.

15. The procuratorate is occasionally likened to the old censorate, but, if there was in Communist China's administrative system a successor to that institution, the Committee on People's Control would seem to be a better candidate for the job than the procuratorate. See, for example, Siu-Kia-Pei, "La structure administrative en Chine à travers des âges," *Revenue internationale des sciences administratives,* 1952, No. 4, pp. 752–787, at 783–784.

16. *e.g.,* Editorial, "Strengthen and Consolidate the People's Revolutionary Legal System," *People's Daily,* September 5, 1951; Li Liu-ju, *loc. cit.*

17. Editorial, "Strengthen the Procuratorate's Work to Safeguard National Construction," *People's Daily,* May 21, 1954; *Survey of China Mainland Press* (SCMP) (Hong Kong: United States Consulate General), No. 821.

The Process of Control

11. THE CONTROL OF THE MIND

Frederick C. T. Yu

The Propaganda Networks

Until 1951, the Party lacked a permanent, well-planned machinery and program to carry out nationwide propaganda activities. The various campaigns and movements—such as those for signatures to the Stockholm Peace Appeal, for the glorification of "model workers," etc.—as many Communist newspapers freely admit, were temporary movements, suddenly popping up and quickly dying out, creating only a temporary fever of enthusiasm among the Party rank and file and among the people.

In January, 1951, obviously trying to "tighten its unity with the masses," the Party launched the gigantic project of setting up a permanent propaganda system that would radiate into the masses and guide them along the line of orthodox policy. This project was the "nationwide propaganda networks." Their establishment opened a new era in the history of Communist propaganda in China; it enabled the Party to spread new propaganda personnel over the whole country and to advance from theoretical to more practical goals.

On January 1, 1951, the Central Committee of the Party issued an official order: "Decisions on the Establishment of Propaganda Networks for the Whole Party among the Masses of the People." This basic document was presented for study to all Party branches in the country and was followed by a flurry of reports and criticisms in newspapers and magazines, and by group discussions. The first paragraph described the necessity and urgency for more propaganda work among the people. Remarking that propaganda had fallen off in many parts of the country or had ceased completely, it charged that many Party organizations at various levels had overlooked the importance of carrying on propaganda on a permanent basis. The result, according to the document,

SOURCE: Selected from Frederick C. T. Yu, *Mass Persuasion in Communist China,* New York: Frederick A. Praeger, 1964, pp. 78–80, 82–88, and 96–100. Reprinted by permission of Frederick A. Praeger, Inc.

was the rise of reactionary propaganda and harmful rumors now constantly heard among the people. Further, the document criticized Party members for excessive use of administrative commands in their work and for failure to deal with the masses through the methods of persuasion and explanation. In order to rectify such errors, the Party had decided to install "propagandists" in every Party branch and "reporters" to direct Party organs at various levels, and thus to establish a definite nationwide propaganda network.

Under the new arrangement, a "propagandist" was not just a regular worker in the Party's Propaganda Department or the Army's propaganda troupe—who put up posters, prepared wall newspapers, gave street-corner shows, or shouted slogans at mass meetings. A "propagandist" of a "network" was supposed to be constantly carrying on, by simple popular means, propaganda and agitation among the people in his environment. He was supposed to:

1. use simple and popular forms to propagate among and explain to the people in his area current national and international affairs, policies of the Party and government, the people's tasks (especially the most direct and urgent tasks of those whom he is addressing), and "model experiences" of the masses of people in production and other works;

2. refute current reactionary rumors and erroneous ideas among the people;

3. stimulate or agitate people to obtain "model experience" in order to accomplish their tasks in an aggressive manner; and

4. report regularly the conditions among the people to higher Party officials, so that they may decide on adequate propaganda content and methods at different times.

Propagandists are chosen from among members of the Party and the New Democratic Youth Corps (and those model workers or revolutionary activists who volunteer to serve under the guidance of the Party). Party branch secretaries and committee members are also expected to work in this capacity, as are those officials who are in constant contact with the masses of the people: cadres in unions, cooperatives, districts (ch'ü, a subdivision of a country), or villages; school teachers; staff members of mass education centers; and editors of wall newspapers. All appointments of propagandists must be passed on by the propaganda committees of the Party branches and also approved by a higher Party organ. The selection of propaganda material is made by the Party branches.

All propagandists are under the direct supervision of the Party branches. It is repeatedly emphasized in official directives that the success of propaganda depends on the assistance and guidance of Party branches. For instance, in North China and Central-South China, all Party members and cadres in factories, schools, mines, and government agencies are instructed to assist the Party branches in directing the propagandists' work. For this purpose, the Party branches issue working directives, prepare propaganda materials, call meetings of propagandists, and plan, review, and criticize their work. . . .

As an illustration of a typical pattern of operation, the following "propaganda plan," prepared and put into practice jointly by two propagandists for a one-month period, is fairly representative of the work done in small villages, factories, and farms. The two operatives were T'su Ch'ang-cheng and T'su Pi-ch'eng, of a small village in North Kiangsu. Their plans, apparently approved by Party authorities, were given considerable publicity—being published in the Shanghai *Liberation Daily* (May 7, 1951) and in the *Current Affairs Handbook* (No. 19, July 20, 1951), published in Peking:

A. *Objectives and Requirements of Propaganda:*
1. There are 16 families in the section. Each of us will take care of 8 families. We both guarantee that every member of the 16 families will receive constantly the education of the Resist-America Aid-Korea Movement. At the end of half a month, we will compare notes to see which one of us is doing a better job of propaganda.
2. In addition to the fixed objects of propaganda (the 16 families), we will talk to anyone whom we meet. The motto is not to waste one single minute or ignore one single individual. We should change the "conversation on personal affairs" into a "conversation on current affairs" and thus develop the habit of carrying on propaganda at all times and places.
3. The general task of the propaganda in the Resist-America Aid-Korea campaign should be united with the propaganda of the actual tasks carried on in the community. In the patriotic movement of increasing production, we will not only set up our own plans of production but will also mobilize all the people in the community to do the same. We will aim at mobilizing people to plant 40 acres of cotton and 60 trees and to invest in 30 shares of the local co-op; persuading 55 people to sign the Peace Appeal (Stockholm) and vote in the movement for solving the problem of Japan by a united effort (as opposed to the Peace Treaty signed with Japan by the United States and most of the other belligerents at San Francisco); organizing 30 people to participate in the demonstration parade in celebration of May 1; and directing the masses to do a good job in suppressing the counterrevolutionaries.

B. *Content of Propaganda:*
1. To make everyone in the community understand that to oppose America and aid Korea is the only way to protect his home and defend the country; that the actual task of the Resist-America Aid-Korea Movement is to increase production and do a good job in one's own field; that the Chinese and Korean armies will definitely win the war, and that the American devils will eventually be defeated. Meanwhile we should point out the possible difficulties that may be encountered, explain the experiences in China's War of Liberation, and enable the masses to understand correctly the victorious situation at present and not to be disturbed by temporary setbacks.
2. To propagate the ten principles in the speed-up movement in production and organize the masses of the people to participate in the movement through these principles.
3. To propagate current information on the suppression of counterrevolutionaries on the basis of the "Law on the Punishment of Counterrevolutionaries" recently made public by the government.
4. To propagate the advantages of a close relation between co-ops and the people and thus encourage people to purchase shares.

5. To propagate the meaning of signing the World Peace Appeal and voting on the Japanese question, and to explain the reasons for participating in the demonstration parade on May 1.

C. *Source of Material for Propaganda:*

1. To attend the meetings for propagandists punctually, listen carefully to the lectures, and study the propaganda materials.

2. To read newspapers, propaganda handbooks, and any other material handed down from the higher Party organization and to keep constantly in touch with the secretary of the Party branch.

3. To gather reactions from the masses.

4. To maintain constant contact with the *ch'ü* committee of the Party through letters and in person.

D. *Forms and Methods of Propaganda:*

1. To organize four group discussions during this month. At least one of them should be a discussion meeting of women.

2. To conduct individual propaganda or informal conversation at least twice a day and make it a habit to do so.

3. To organize a newspaper-reading group, and read the *Ta Chung Pao* [*The Daily of the Masses,* published in North Kiangsu] every three days. We will take turns in reading newspapers.

4. To put out a "propaganda bulletin board" on current affairs and local news. The board is to be supplied with new material every three days.

5. To grasp every opportunity for propaganda such as working, walking, etc.

6. To make use of the aggressive activists in the masses. It is our plan to make use of Tsu Chang-yu [name of a child] to carry on propaganda among the eighteen children in the community. We are planning to educate and use Siao Chi-yuan [name of a woman] to carry on propaganda among the twelve women in the section.

How successful such propagandists are in winning the people to the cause of the Party cannot be easily ascertained. However, one thing is certain: It did not take the Chinese Communist Party long to establish its "propaganda network" over almost the entire country. According to figures released by the Party in December 1951, there were more than 1,550,000 propagandists in the whole country by October, 1951. The average percentage of propagandists in each factory, farm, or production unit was about 10 per cent of the total. In the Northeast alone, there were 117,823 propagandists in 1950; it was the plan of the area Party authorities to increase the number to 200,000 in 1951. In an electric power plant at Dairen, the number of propagandists was 10 per cent of the total work force; in a mine at Anshan, 6 per cent; in another chemical plant at Mukden, 13 per cent. Within two years, there was hardly any place in China where a person could be free from the persistent persuasion of these propagandists.

The introduction of the propaganda networks changed considerably the social life of peasants, factory workers, and other people on lower social levels. Perhaps never before in their lives had these people been so constantly persuaded to do so many things, attend so many meetings, sign so many pacts—and do so "voluntarily." According to one official report, in two weeks the Party secretary of the City Committee of Peng Chi made 18 reports; the high-ranking cadres in factories and mines made 625 reports to a total audience of 70,000; there were 270 group discussions in which 25,000 people participated; 30 accusation meetings and 15 oral contests were held. In addition, there were evening story-telling meetings, memory meetings (where participants were expected to "recall" sufferings in the "old, feudalistic" days), and farewell meetings to the people joining the armed forces. Then, cadres were organized to conduct interviews in every family in the city. From July 10 to July 20, 1951, in Chaoan, a *hsien* in Kwangtung, there were 8,085 grievance and accusation meetings, including 1,347 mass meetings and 6,738 ones for small groups. Every inhabitant attended an average of at least three such meetings. . . .

The order to establish propaganda networks stipulated that the Party propagandists should meet at least once a month—at most, once a week—to discuss their instructions and the work accomplished. The *hsien,* or county, Party organ was to convene a monthly meeting of propagandists and their representatives. On behalf of the Party's *hsien* committees, the district (*ch'ü*) committees were required constantly to direct the propaganda of the Party branches and to decide on the scope, aims, and methods to be used by each, according to its own conditions. In rural areas, where transportation conditions were poor, district committees followed a system of setting up "instruction relay posts." Selected propagandists representing branch propaganda departments were summoned to receive instructions with regard to propaganda content, methods, and approaches.

These "instruction relay posts" soon spread all over the country. As early as 1951, the Department of Propaganda in the province of Hopei reported that, according to incomplete statistics, there were 710 posts in 29 *hsien*. Besides passing on instructions to Party branches, they also served to educate and train propagandists. In Hopei Province, the heads of all such posts were members of the *ch'ü* committees charged with educational responsibilities. And there, and elsewhere, they not only gave instructions on propaganda to Party branches, but also supervised the "political study" of Party members at a lower level and in turn reported their progress to their superiors.

Realizing that members of Party branches as well as of the *ch'ü* committees were often of low cultural levels, the Central Committee decided that propagandists alone would not be enough to enable the masses to understand fully the Party's policies, especially those designed for special occasions. The Party believed that the directing personnel of the Party's organs at other levels should be available to make systematic reports or lectures on current affairs, policies, tasks, and experiences. For this purpose, "reporters" or "reporting personnel" were installed in Party committees in every province, city, administrative district, *hsien,* or *ch'ü*.

Reporters, as regulated by the Party's Central Committee, "are propagandists of a higher rank and therefore are directing personnel of propagandists.[14] Forming the large army of reporters were secretaries and responsible members of Party committees at all levels, from the *ch'ü* to the province, and Party members holding responsible positions in government agencies. Every "reporter" is required to make a political report at least once every two months before a large gathering of representatives of the masses of people (the workers and peasants). Subject and content must be approved in advance by the secretary of the Party committee to which the reporter belongs. After delivering a speech or completing a speaking tour, the reporter is expected to submit to the secretary of his committee a report both about his talks and about the reactions of the audience; the secretary is responsible for going through these reports and offering any assistance of guidance necessary to guarantee that the reporters' work is always of the approved kind. They are also encouraged to recommend good reports for publication in newspapers.

There is unquestionably a spark of genius in the Party's use of "reporters" and "propagandists." Since most of the propagandists are ordinary Party members, whose words might not be accepted as authoritative, their work, as the Party recognizes, must be reinforced by Party leaders, who are more likely to command the respect of the common people. This function is served by the reporters. On the other hand, since the propagandists work among the people day in and day out, they are expected to create a climate that will make it easier for the reporters to consummate the conquest of people's minds. Furthermore, since both reporters and propagandists are supervised by the Party committees, the Department of Propaganda of the Central Committee is, on paper at least, in a good position to control and direct all propaganda activities.

A word on the principles generally followed by the Party in this field may be useful here. The first principle is that in setting up a propaganda network in any area, all members of the Party committee in the area, especially the Party secretary, must be thoroughly indoctrinated as to the significance of the project before they are presented with definite plans and instructions for carrying it out. The Communist press and propagandists' handbooks frequently repeat that propaganda networks can be established successfully only where the members of the local committee are convinced of its urgency and importance. This is an important point because all responsible leaders of the Party committees are authorized to appoint propagandists, as well as reporters. The Party has admitted that in many areas its leaders are indifferent and simply fill the quota of propagandists set by their superiors, and that in other areas, they simply pass the job on to unions, mass education centers, youth corps, or even entertainment places. The Party cannot afford to allow this laxity because its aim is a centralized control of all propaganda activities, conducted on a permanent basis.

A second principle followed in setting up propaganda networks is that they should be closely connected with production and with the political movements of the people. There are two reasons why propaganda work should be closely associated with production: First, the Party wants to follow the policy that "we do what we propagate," thus making propaganda more timely and stimulating; secondly, it is among producers that the Party can best find "activists" to train for propaganda work. For, according to the Party, "activists" discovered through mass movements are often effective propagandists, once they have received adequate training and indoctrination. "Activists" who are themselves workers know the people in their own labor groups and are familiar with their sentiments and conditions; they can talk the people's language and are accepted more readily than outsiders would be. It is for this same reason that Party branches are given direct supervision over their propagandists.

In the January 1, 1952, issue of *Jen Min Jih Pao,* there appeared an article entitled "The Condition of the Party's Propaganda Networks after One Year of Development, and Objectives of Further Consolidation and Development in the Future." This 2,000-word article reviewed the accomplishments and failures of this gigantic project since it was inaugurated in January, 1950, and it reveals clearly the strength of the huge army of propagandists and reporters in modern Communist China.

According to this article, there were, in December, 1950, already more than 1,920,000 propagandists in the country. The estimated figures for the number of propagandists in each of the six regional administrative areas were as follows:

North China	606,000
Northeast	300,000
East	650,000
Central-South	236,000
Southwest	85,000
Northwest	30,000

Of the provinces, Hopei and Shantung had the largest number of propagandists, each with more than 330,000. In both Hopei and Chahar, the number of propagandists was more than 1 per cent of the total population. In Shantung and Shansi, the number was also close to 1 per cent.

It was the plan of the Party to increase the number of propagandists to 4 or 5 million by the end of 1952. . . .

The System's Operation

The key link in the entire communication system is *Jen Min Jih Pao,* through which the Department of Propaganda operates and to which all papers in the nation turn for guidance and direction. In recent years, the magazine *Hung Chi (Red Flag),* also a mouthpiece of the Party's Central Committee, has been assigned a somewhat similar and equally important function.

What is published in *Jen Min Jih Pao* is reprinted or quoted in Party newspapers at different levels, special newspapers (such as *Worker's Daily* of the All-China Federation of Trade Unions, *Youth Daily* of the Democratic Youth Corps, etc.) and other trade, professional or special-purpose publications. Its reports are carried by the People's Broadcasting Station in Peking, which transmits them to stations in the provinces and other cities, and these stations in turn send the word further down through the radio broadcasting network which makes the message available to listeners either in collective listening meetings or in blackboard or wall newspapers. Eventually its messages are printed as booklets or pamphlets that are made available for *hsueh hsi,* or study groups, for cultural affairs study groups, and for hundreds of other groups or occasions. (It must be noted that the *Jen Min Jih Pao* messages, unless they concern government or party directives or the like, are not always repeated verbatim. In transmitting a message from Peking, the local newspaper, magazine, or radio station normally "integrates" the message with the local situation. This is not a matter of "adding local color to the story," as an American journalist might describe it; it is done not only to relate it to the local situation but also, and mainly, to set the stage for agitation activities.)

Indeed, to read a newspaper in China today is a political obligation. Any news item that is considered important in Peking is required reading in newspaper-reading groups and "collective radio listening groups"; it is discussed at study and indoctrination meetings and may even become part of the people's "thought conclusions" or "work reports." If it is a news story about killing so many sparrows in Town A, one can be sure that the "glory" of Town A will not shine alone: Town B may be "mobilized" to kill twice as many sparrows. And, if this should be the case, there will be special meetings to discuss the methods and operation of sparrow-killing, poems composed, street-corner plays written, slogans coined, and dances planned to popularize the affair. Most certainly there will be criticism and self-criticism meetings. In no time at all, sparrow-killing will be the "central task" of Town B: school children of one class will challenge those in another to a competition; one "work brigade" tries to outdo the record of another; one member of the "propaganda network" labors to outdistance his colleagues. If the "model experience" of sparrow-killing in Town A has inspired truly remarkable activity in Town B, the successes in Town B will not go unnoticed but will be "reflected" in various communiqués to agitate other towns. The contest will continue, to stop only when another "central task" emerges. Tasks vary, but tasks there always are.

It may be helpful at this point to take the case of a truly major movement in order to describe how various kinds of persuasive communications are mobilized. There is no doubt that communization was the major goal of the Chinese Communist Party, even in their early days of revolution. But, remembering the cardinal principle that every campaign or movement requires class consciousness at a specific level, the Communists realized that the nation was not at first "ideologically prepared" for such a drastic move. Even when the People's Republic was proclaimed in 1949, not a whisper was heard about communization. The first years of the Republic were devoted to the Land Reform movement, then the "mutual aid groups," "collective co-ops," the campaign "to combine small co-ops into large co-ops," and the more ambitious program of "collectivization." Finally, the time was ripe for communes.

The movement for people's communes was officially inaugurated in September, 1958. Early in July, 1958, occasional stories began to appear in *Jen Min Jih Pao* suggesting the desirability of having "socialistic families." On July 6, a letter appeared from a housewife, telling the editor of the importance and joy of socialistic families and asking him to give up the idea of "selfish small families." The following day, a long piece appeared on the success of a "public mess hall" in an agricultural co-op. This was followed with another piece advocating "the development of such practices."

On August 11, the paper gave front-page coverage to Mao Tse-tung's inspection tour in Honan, where he had lavishly praised the performance of a "commune" there. "As long as we have a commune like this, there will be more communes," Mao was quoted. (The commune at Hsing-yang in Honan was one of the Communists' major experiments. What was done there was reported and popularized extensively, not only to inspire the nation but also to demonstrate it as a "model" to be followed.) Two days later, Mao was in Shantung and the paper headlined Mao's statement: "We should do well with communes. The advantage: to unite workers, peasants, merchants, intellectuals, and soldiers. Such a system will facilitate political guidance." By the middle of August, when the Politburo was reportedly meeting at Pai Tai Ho, stories suddenly mushroomed in *Jen Min Jih Pao*. There was a long article about a commune in Hsing-yang, Honan (August 18), another about one in Sinkiang (August 16), Chekiang (August 18), and Tientsin (August 19).

Then, on September 1, a front-page story appeared that the Enlarged Conference of the Party's Political Bureau had decided to announce the "great objective of producing 170.7 million tons of steel and of making the people's commune the best form to accelerate the transitional period from socialism to communism." But, the story insisted, "The establishment of people's communes must be made on the basis of the initial consciousness of the masses. It must be done through discussions and indoctrination of the masses as done in the Hundred Flowers movement."

Then came the final official notice, which *Jen Min Jih Pao* front-paged on September 10—"Decisions of the Central Committee of the Chinese Communist Party on the Problem of Establishing People's Communes." (It is significant that the Central Committee's decision was made on August 29, but the official announcement of it not until September 10.)

Weeks before the publication of the official announcement, however, the movement was already being carried out in the nation "with fanfare." One needs only the opening paragraph of an editorial in *Jen Min Jih Pao* of September 3 to see how vigorously persuasive communications were already at work:

"People's communes which symbolize a new period of our socialist movement in the rural area, are now established very swiftly in various areas. . . . The movemest was started as a result of the high level of socialistic consciousness of the masses. After a few early communes obtained their success, many agricultural co-ops began to study such models and thus started the movement. . . . Peasants in many areas have written huge volumes of *Tatzepao* (posters), petitions and letters to express their determination; they requested to establish people's communes."

To be sure that all the propaganda authorities in the nation would carry out their task efficiently, *Jen Min Jih Pao* released on September 11 "Propaganda and Education Directive of the Central Committee of the Chinese Communist Party." The five-point Directive spelled out the meaning of the movement, the propaganda content, the methods to be used, the arguments to be advanced, and the steps to be followed. It emphasized: "From the beginning to the end, this movement must follow the principles of settling contradictions among People; it should make use of confessions, accusations, debates, discussions, *tatzepao*, demonstration meetings, exhibits and all kinds of forms to achieve genuine ideological liberation and to make the movement a REAL, BROAD MOVEMENT OF SELF-EDUCATION."

By this time, the movement had reached its zenith. Before the end of the year, *Jen Min Jih Pao* reported (on December 31), "Agricultural co-ops are already a thing of the past in the rural areas of our country. According to our statistics for November, 99.1 per cent of our peasants have already 26,500 big and fair people's communes which include 126.9 million families. In average, every commune has about 4,756 families."

12.   THE CONTROL OF BEHAVIOR

Franz Michael

The Communist attitude toward law has no connection with either the Chinese traditional attitude or the system introduced from the West. Communist law has neither objectivity nor universality. It is purely an instrument of policy, a tool to intimidate, and a means to introduce Communist measures under the semblance of formal procedure. The Chinese Communist law, like all Chinese Communist measures, is an application in China of a system derived from Communist doctrine and the practice of the Soviet Union.

In the Communist view, the pre-socialist state is but the instrument of the dominant class by which it rules and exploits the suppressed classes. Law is therefore not a guarantee of rights or the protection of a realm of freedom for all, but simply the "will of the dominant class elevated into a statute"[1] and its tool for the suppression of the labouring classes. Since Marx regarded law as a tool of suppression by the dominant class in the "capitalist and other pre-socialist states, his Communist followers now feel free to use their law as a tool of suppression in their "proletarian" state. According to the Communists the "dictatorship of the minority"—the "capitalists"—was broken in the Bolshevik Revolution and replaced by the "dictatorship of the majority"—the "proletariat," represented by its "vanguard," the Communist Party— and the new dominant class must now use the law to enforce its will on the "minority." Law is then a "means of the struggle for socialism."[2] "The dictatorship of the proletariat is authority unlimited by any statutes whatever. But the dictatorship of the proletariat, creating its own laws, makes use of them, demands that they be observed, and punishes breach of them. . . ."[3] Such law is to be used "to guard, secure, and develop social relationships and social orders advantageous and agreeable to the dominant class."[4] It is a method of carrying out the socialist revolution, indeed one of "gigantic

SOURCE: Selected from Franz Michael, "The Role of the Law in Traditional, Nationalist, and Communist China," in *The China Quarterly,* Issue No. 9, pp. 135–140 and 142–148. Reprinted by permission of *The China Quarterly.*

importance—without which the socialist state could not get along until that time when it completely withers away," at which time law will supposedly wither away as well. For the Chinese Communists Mao Tse-tung echoed this Communist doctrine in his essay on "People's Democratic Dictatorship" in 1949, in which he asked the rhetorical question whether the Chinese Communists, who had now taken over, intended to "abolish State Power" and answered: "Yes, we want to but not at the present time. . . . Our present task is to strengthen the People's State apparatus—meaning primarily the People's Army, the People's Police, and the People's Courts."[6] In the meantime Communist "law is entirely and completely direct against exploitation and exploiters. . . . It is invoked to meet the problems of the struggle with foes of socialism and the cause of building a socialist society."[7]

This concept of "law" as defined by the Communists and given by the leading Soviet authority whose works have been translated into Chinese and are studied by the Chinese "legal cadres" as one of the main sources of "Socialist Law," has to be understood in order to appreciate the character of Chinese Communist law. Totally unlike the law of Western tradition or any traditional moral order, Chinese Communist law has even exceeded the Soviet model in its lack of rules of substance and its utter flexibility—the main criteria of this new law which are directly opposed to the principles of law in Western society but are ideal prerequisites for its use as a political tool by the Communists.

When they came to power, one of the first acts of the Chinese Communists was to abolish all existing law, which was "bourgeois," "feudalist" and "semi-colonial" law and therefore utterly reprehensible. The intention of doing away with the whole political and social order was already indicated in January 1949 in the Eight Points of Mao Tse-tung, in which Mao presented the National Government with the Communist demands and showed that the victorious Communists were no longer willing to accept anything but a complete break in the system.[8] Much has been made since by the Communists of this great change from the rotten bourgeois to the great socialist law which came when they threw out the whole of the Six Books of Law promulgated as a result of the painstaking and careful codification policy under the National Government.[9]

The Communists have been, however, in no hurry to fill the resulting void. Today, over twelve years after the establishment of their régime, the Chinese Communists have practically no law of substance. This does not of course mean that there are no courts, that there is no prosecution or criminal punishment of those against whom the Communist authorities take legal action. The organisation of the court system and of the prosecution, and the close control of these agencies by the Party and their co-operation with the police have been well established during these years;[10] and there have of course also been the special laws that established the state structure itself. But a law of substance that provides well-defined norms for human relations does not exist. Leaving aside the Communist Marriage Law, there is no civil law or criminal law worthy of the name. Such settlements of personal conflict as may have to be arranged are handled either by the courts or by arbitration agencies without laws and in the interest of the Communist state and Party. What criminal

prosecution is carried on—and this is the largest area of legal activity—
is handled on the basis of policy directives and sweeping laws against counterrevolution, and has become a major instrument of Communist policy in
destroying the existing society and accomplishing its Communist transformation.

The Marriage Law

The only Communist law that, on the face of it, would fall under our
category of civil law is the Marriage Law promulgated on May 1, 1950, a
few months after the establishment of the Communist régime in September
1949. It is significant that the one social institution which the Communist
state at this stage does not claim to eliminate, that is, the family, was the
one area of human relations singled out for special treatment through legislation.
And much has been made by the Communists in their propaganda about
this Marriage Law that was claimed to have liberated the women from the
shackles of the family—and therefore for work for society.

The claim was that this law abolished the "feudal" marriage relationships
of the past and introduced the principle of equality for women. According
to a pamphlet issued by the Foreign Languages Press in Peking together with
the official translation of the law: "The new Law brings to an end the arbitrary
and compulsory feudal marriage system under which both men and women
had no free choice of marriage partners, these being chosen for them by
their parents—a practice that led to the widespread prevalence of child-mar-
riage," and "China's new Marriage Law paves the way for a wholesome new
system based on 'free choice partners, on monogamy, on equal rights for
both sexes, and on the protection of the legitimate interests of women and
children' . . .''[11]

As far as legal innovations are concerned, this claim is false. Equality for
women, the principle of monogamy, the free choice of marriage partners,
equal grounds for divorce for both partners to the marriage, these and all
the other rules of modern marriage were established through the Nationalist
Family Law, which the Communists had abolished with all the rest.

The actual legal changes introduced by the Communist Marriage Law have
little to do with the modern form of marriage itself, but are significant for
their indication of Communist policy. For one, the legal age for marriage
was changed. Under the Nationalist Law it had been eighteen for the man
and sixteen for the woman. Now it was to be twenty and eighteen (but,
apparently, according to Chinese reckoning), and one may wonder at the
reason for this delay of marriage. The purpose may have been to retain better
control of young people during their most formative years, or else, more important still, to affect the birth rate.

Much more important, however, than this problem of marriage age and
most characteristic of the new law is the role assigned to the authorities in
their control over this most intimate family relationship. Under the former
law, marriage was dependent upon the mutual agreement of the two partners,
but no formal procedure was prescribed and any religious or other rite could
establish a legal marital relationship. Under the Communists, registration and

the issuance of a marriage certificate by the local People's government are essential. In practice this procedure is not the mere orderly formality prescribed by most Western laws and seemingly implied in the text of the Communist law.[12] Actual approval of the marriage in Communist China has been dependent on the filling out of marriage application forms and on an investigation that permits an elaborate check of the parties concerned, and the possibility of either withholding or giving approval according to political or other considerations of the cadres who make the decisions. The application form used in Peking, for instance,[13] shows that "class status" has to be given, that there is government investigation of applicants, and that approval of whatever agency is acquainted with the persons' work or service—government, Army, factory, business, or rural government higher than the village, etc.—is required.

A similar role is played by the government in divorce cases.[14] Divorce is possible on request by both parties or on the request by either party, but the decision, which is in the hands of the local court, is not based on any legal cause. Under Nationalist law causes for divorce included bigamy, adultery, mental illness, malignant disease, cruelty, desertion, and serious criminal conviction. Now the court has no such legal basis for decision, and in practice the granting of divorce depends on the cadre's view whether such divorce will serve the purposes of the Communist state and Party, especially as it affects the person's labour.[15] Conclusion and dissolution of marriage under this law are therefore decisively dependent upon the Communist government cadres, who are to act in the interests of the Communist state.

This use of the Marriage Law for the interests of the state is not accidental. From the beginning the Marriage Law was conceived and described as a drive to reform society in the Communist image. The Marriage Law was actually banded together with the Land Law for the purpose of changing rural society in the Communist pattern. In the words of the Communist pamphlet, issued together with the English translation of the law: "As the agrarian reform sets free hundreds of millions of landless and land-hungry peasants from oppression by the feudal landlords, so the Marriage Law marks the emancipation of the Chinese women from the feudal marriage system under which they were utterly bereft of any rights."[16] The Nationalist Family Law had only gradually affected the customs of rural areas. Now an attempt was made to enforce the principles of the Communist law in the villages. What was enforced, however, was not so much the principle of equality of women and freedom of marriage as a government policy.

Equality of women was not even the problem. The most unequal institution of the traditional Chinese system, concubinage, had long been abolished by the Nationalist Family Law. Under this law an already existing concubinal relationshp was, however, not interfered with if the woman in question did not choose to break it up. The economic security which the already accepted concubine enjoyed as a member of the husband's family was actually protected by the Nationalist law. In the statements that accompanied their law, the Communists also indicated that concubinage practised before the promulgation of their law—which in reality meant before the promulgation of the Nationalist law and therefore affected mainly some rather elderly ladies—would be left alone.[17]

The real issue was the application of the principle of freedom of choice of marriage partners and freedom of divorce for women in rural China. This was a problem of family control, rather than an issue of the authority of men over women. It was this issue of the emancipation of the young generation from family authority which had been the main motive behind the revolt against the traditional social order in the early decades of this century. The Nationalist Family Law had established the freedom of choice of the marriage partner by the parties themselves and the right to divorce. But its application, which had been general in the cities, had been slow in the rural areas. This did not mean that in the old traditional system personal choice had been disregarded as a rule, nor did it mean that divorce for women was impossible. A married woman could leave her husband and could return home, especially if she had the backing of her family. But now under the Communist law the possibility of divorce was to be made easier and divorce was to be encouraged. It was to be encouraged in the form of a drive, and the motive seemed to be the interest of the state in changing society and weakening the family rather than the greater freedom of the individual. The main concern was the control of the individual by the state rather than by the family. The Marriage Law was indeed a political measure to be carried out like other new policies by all the mass organisations used by the Communists for such purposes.

According to the instruction by the Government Council that accompanied the Marriage Law, the law was to be enforced in the form of a drive. "Marriage reform is not merely the task of the courts and local women's associations; every organisation must co-operate in it. There is work to be done in schools, youth organisations, workers' unions, and cultural organisations. The people must be brought together at public accusation meetings to expose those who have failed to live up to the standard of the new law. There must be huge mass trials. The marriage reform is to go hand in hand with land reform. The same technique is to be used for both. . . ."[18]

Criminal Law

The field of criminal law demonstrates even more clearly the different character of law in Communist China, where it has become a tool of the state for carrying through Communist policy. Twelve years after the establishment of the Communist government there is still no ordinary criminal law. All criminal acts are dealt with as political crimes against the Communist state, and the most frequently applied law that deals with crime is the "Regulations of the People's Republic of China for the Punishment of Counterrevolutionaries" approved by the Central People's Government Council on February 20, 1951, and promulgated by Mao Tse-tung personally on February 21, 1951.[19] This law was used in the first stage after its publication as the basis of almost daily mass executions in every city and village, and though this initial period of the destruction of whole groups of the population is over, the executions and severe punishments are still carried out.[20]

Besides this general law, there were special laws and directives issued for major drives. The Land Law of 1950 was directed against the traditional upper group in the Chinese villages. The orders of the Government Administration Council of the Central People's Government in March 1952 dealt with what were called the "three-anti" and "five-anti" movements, in which the government purged many officials of the former National Government and some of its own Party members, and broke the position of the traditional business community.[21]

What characterises these criminal regulations is that, with the exception of some acts of military opposition, sabotage and espionage the crimes of the people attacked remain utterly vague, though they are condemned in vehement language. The punishment is equally vague and varies from short prison sentences or even release of the victim, to life imprisonment and capital punishment according to the gravity of the act as judged by the legal cadres. None of the basic principles of Western criminal law apply. The deed is not clearly defined. The punishment is entirely up to the legal cadre, or rather to his understanding of the purpose of the Party and the Party directives. Acts can be punished by analogy to any offences stated in written rules or regulations, and persons can be prosecuted for acts which became punishable only after they were committed.[22] Punishment depends not only on the act committed but on the social origin of the person accused. If he belongs to "the people," he is to be treated entirely differently from those who are non-people, the "enemies of the people," who can expect no leniency. One of the major principles applied in criminal law is that punishment depends on the co-operation of the accused with the government and its purposes—the principle of "leniency for those who confess; rigour for those who resist; reduction of punishment for those who have merit; rewards for great merit."[23] The victim's confession must tell all the government wants. "Merit" means in practice the denunciation of others. "Great merit" is denunciation of major opponents. If the victim does not admit the crime of which he is accused, this is resistance and will result in a "determined blow" against him. But confession of past mistakes is also used to trap the victim and the confessions have to fit the accusations rather than the reality of the victim's actions. The principle that the accused is regarded as innocent until proven guilty has no place in this system, where the government is not only all-powerful but also all-knowing, and any loyalty to others is a defiance of the only currently valid obligation of a person—that to the state.

Importance of State Policy

For a person used to a Western legal system it is hard to imagine that criminal jurisdiction has been carried out in Communist China on this basis in which all punishment and life or death depend on the legal cadres' application of the government policy. The judge must in fact develop a full understanding of this policy and its intentions if he wants to be successful. To carry out the Party's policy he must become "case hardened," a quality which the Communists develop as part of the training of the legal cadres. The best method is for the judge to keep in constant contact with the respective Party committee for "instruction."[24] If the judges did not fully understand the intent of the Party leaders, it would be said that "the knowledge of the judges is not, in fact, keeping pace with the development of objective factors" as was stated in an article by Tung Pi-wu, criticising the judges for not following closely enough the ever-changing policy of the Party, for "socialist law cannot be detached from the Party and government Policy."[25]

Each new policy requires a new understanding by the legal cadres of the Party's goal. The criminal regulations for prosecution of social enemies under the various drives have been made and enforced for that particular purpose and then forgotten. In executing them the cadres have had to follow the regulations of the government which explain the political purpose and desired outcome in the prosecution of the group under attack. The five-anti drive, for instance, was based on a division of business establishments into "law-abiding," "basically law-abiding," "semi-law-abiding," "serious law-breaking," and "completely law-breaking." When the drive was carried through in Peking, only 10 per cent of the business establishments were found "law-abiding." For the application of punishment Mao Tse-tung prescribed a policy that would provide in general "leniency for past mistakes, severity for new mistakes," "leniency for the majority, severity for the minority," "leniency for those who confessed, severity for those who resist," "leniency for industrialists and severity for merchants," "leniency for ordinary merchants and severity for speculators."[26] Applied only in the vaguest terms and without any possibility of reliance on them, these rules clearly leave no doubt about the political purpose of this "criminal legislation."

The "crimes" denounced in these drives and in the regulations on the suppression of counter-revolutionaries are being defined by the courts "in such a manner that virtually no Chinese on the mainland can be absolutely sure that he has not committed at least one of them, while the Communists themselves are, in the final analysis, the arbiters of the crimes and the motivations of the accused."[27] The punishments for these crimes are determined by the cadres' reading of the Party purposes and of such directives of "leniency" or "severity" as are provided by the leaders, or their own interpretations of the terms "minor case" and "serious case" included in the law itself.[28] On this interpretation, which may change with the change of line, and with new directives against false "boundless magnanimity"[29] or "leftist deviationism," depends the cadres' decision which can for the same "crime" range from no punishment to forced labour in camps or communes, prison sentences of any length, or capital punishment. In an article by a leading Chinese Communist authority, which appeared in the Soviet journal *Sovetskoye Gosudarstvo i Pravo,* this principle is described as a rule for the "party-guidance" in what is called "scientific-legal research work":

> First of all it is necessary to proceed from the political policy of the party, which is the most important weapon in guiding the life of the entire country. . . . The punitive measures, for example, stipulated by the regulations for the punishment of counterrevolutionaries fluctuate from three to five years' imprisonment to a death sentence, including a suspended death sentence. It is possible to correctly discuss punitive measures stipulated by the Regulations only in those cases where the discussions are based on a political policy of the party. Therefore a conscientious study of law and subordination to party leadership is absolutely necessary for every scientist-jurist.[30]

In the words of one of the practitioners of this system: "There is no law to rely on. When the authorities say kill, we kill, when they say release, we release."[31]

The obvious effect of the uncertainty of this system is an atmosphere of terror in which the victim's only hope is to gain mercy by a complete surrender of his inner self to Communist authority. The effect of terror is increased through unusual punishments, such as suspended death sentences combined with forced labour, or the practice of taking the condemned to the execution ground but sparing some of them at the last moment and repeating the procedure. This climate of terror was most effectively created in the prepared dramas, enacted during each drive before the People's Tribunals, involving the audience through the use of terror and hysteria in the condemnation of victims to slaughter. Though the fierceness of the drives has passed, the effect of the terror doubtless lingers on.

Opposition to the System

The ruthlessness of this system and its violation of all legal tradition resulted in opposition to the most extreme practices by some of the Communists themselves. In 1956 and 1957, during the period of the thaw and the hundred flowers, there were some who spoke up in favour of restoring to a certain extent the legal concepts of Western tradition. There was reference to the Soviet example which had preserved more formal procedure than the Chinese system. There were those who thought that the innocence of the accused person could be established and that it was the duty of the lawyer for ·the defence to try to disprove the accusation against his client. The Party's attack against these "rightists," that was not long in coming, declared such views "absurd." The Party's spokesmen were indignant about the idea of defence counsels who "ever spoke up for the accused person" or worse, were "trying to prove the innocence" of the accused.[32] Since the Party was always right, accusation itself indicated guilt and all that was left to the guilty was to confess to the satisfaction of his accusers.

During the time of the thaw and of critical opposition, there was also news of the preparation of a new criminal code.[33] But if a draft of such a law, which might at least have provided some more specific rules concerning criminal action and punishment, was ever completed, it was never made public and the whole policy appears to have been abandoned.

With the reaction against the criticism of the hundred flowers period, the Chinese Communists returned to an approach that implied the complete negation of law, stated once more and even more crudely than before in the pages of the official journal on government and law: "Since the policy of the Party is the soul of the legal system, legal work is merely the implementing and execution of the Party policy . . ." and "The law of our country is a changing law, adapted to the perpetual revolution. . . ." Therefore, "it would be a great mistake to follow a procedure of set, permanent, unchanging rules which would hinder the revolutionary struggle."[34]

The only attempted justification for this system is that the leadership of the Party claims to express in their policy "the line of the masses," a line at which the masses are supposed to arrive with "due guidance." There is today in Communist China indeed "trial without law," a system hard for any Western observer to visualise, since there is neither written law, nor customary law, nor general principles given in law, nor precedent, nor supreme court decisions, nor any combination of these.[35]

All that there is the authority of the Communist Party working through the state agencies in enforcing its policies of destroying the existing society and creating a Communist state. While in traditional China *li,* the moral code backed by law, was the most effective guarantee of the autonomy of the social order, and in Nationalist China law of Western origin played this role, no such purpose exists for law in Communist China. There law is no longer norm but has taken the form of "the drive," a formulated policy with severe sanctions meant not to protect any rights but to enforce the political programme of the Party.

The role of law in Communist China would seem to accord with the Communist concept of state and society. No realm of freedom for the individual or for any social group protected by law or a moral code exists under the present system. That no right or moral autonomy remains is indicated by the Chinese sources I have already quoted. Law is clearly defined in them as a "weapon" of the state to enforce Communist policy, and, since policy changes, "law" has to be elastic and everchanging. The structure through which this "law" is applied can be well established, in fact has to be established, in an orderly fashion. The courts and the system of prosecution have to function smoothly under the direction of Party and State. But law in the sense of norm no longer exists. Law as the protection and expression of the position of the individual and of the manifold complex of human relationships that make up society, is no longer needed Communism professes a different concept of state and society than that existing in the West or in traditional and Nationalist China. The social order is to be reduced to that of a monist Communist power system, the totalitarian state.

In Western tradition, the state is regarded according to different theoretical interpretations by various schools of thought as either a more limited form of grouping or organisation of community than society, or as a special aspect of the social order serving a special purpose. This concept of a limited state has been abandoned by the totalitarian system. The totalitarian extension of the state authority means the destruction of the multiplicity of human relations in society, which to us are ends in themselves. With the elimination of all these autonomous relations it is society itself which is being destroyed in order that it may be replaced by the all-encompassing Communist state order.

The Communists still claim that eventually their state, and with it law, will "wither away." In the latest Soviet Party Draft Programme this claim is not only maintained but the beginning of the process of withering away is even predicted for our time.[36] What this prediction comes down to, however, is that in Communist expectations the process of destroying the social order will soon have gone far enough to enable the Party to execute all policy through an entirely monist system of agencies staffed by like-minded men, the Soviet or Communist man of the future. This monist structure may no longer be called "state," but it would, if realised, be in fact the most totalitarian state imaginable. What is withering away is not the state but society. Indeed Communist totalitarianism may be defined as a programme that aims at the withering away of society. Without the need to protect a multiplicity of human relations in society, there will also be no need for law in our sense. And so, under Communism, law has in effect withered away. The transformation of law in Communist China from a guarantor to a destroyer of the social order demonstrates most clearly the character of this system in which society is to be replaced by the monistic order of the Communist totalitarian state, which, under whatever name, will remain the vehicle of rule of the Communist organisation and its leaders.

Notes

1. Andrei Y. Vyshinsky, *The Law of the Soviet State,* trans. Hugh W. Babb (New York: Macmillan, 1948), p. 14 *et seq.* Vyshinsky gives the authoritative interpretation of Marx and the official Soviet view as presently applied within the Communist *bloc.* This is the theory of "socialist legality" which has replaced earlier theories such as those of Stuchka and Reisner who are now attacked with much venom.

2. *Ibid.,* p. 15.

3. *Ibid.,* p. 48.

4. *Ibid.,* p. 50.

5. *Ibid.,* p. 52.

6. Peking English Language Edition, Third Translation, 1951, pp. 16–17. See *China News Analysis* (CNA), No. 17, Hong Kong, February 4, 1955.

7. Vyshinsky, *op. cit.,* p. 50. Vyshinsky deals also in this authoritative work with "the rights and obligations" of Soviet citizens as given in the Soviet Constitution. Actually the Soviet government is not bound to respect these constitutional rights. In the belief of the Soviet theorist it is the "material guarantees" of the Soviet system—emphasised all the more in Soviet pronouncements the less they mean in reality—that enable each citizen to "realize the rights ceded [*sic*] to him by the state," *ibid.,* p. 89. As discussed by Vyshinsky they turn out to be such rights as participation in free assembly or demonstration when organised by the Communist Party, free speech for Communist policy and under Party direction, and other similar one-sided "freedoms." The principle of this freedom to support Communism was the same as that of the "hundred flowers" period in Communist China.

8. On this evaluation of Mao Tse-tung's eight points in the abortive negotiations with the National Government in 1949, see the article by Chou Hsin-min, "Organisational Questions on the Development of Legal Science in the Chinese People's Republic," *Sovetskoye Gosudarstvo i Pravo,* No. 3, Moscow, February 12, 1961, pp. 64–72. Translated by *Joint Publications Research Service,* No. 4649, May 26, 1961.

9. *Ibid.* The National Government's Law Codes were abolished through the "Directive on the Revocation of the Kuomintang's Complete Book of Six Laws and on the Establishment of Principles and Justice in the Liberated Regions," published by the Central Committee of the Communist Party in February 1949. Article 17 of the Common Programme of the People's Political Consultative Conference of September 29, 1949, repeated the stipulation on abolishing "laws, directives and the judicial system of the Kuomintang reactionary government. . . ."

10. See *Organic Law of the People's Courts* (September 1954). For a short

description of the court system and of the prosecution, see CNA, No. 140, July 20, 1956. A most important part of the Communist legal structure is its elaborate system of prosecution, which is directly under Party control and has taken over a function originally handled by the police. See David Buxbaum, "A Preliminary Study of Chinese Communist Legal Institutions and the Role of the Criminal Law," unpublished manuscript.

11. Quoted in *Current Background* (CB) (Hong Kong: U.S. Consulate-General), No. 136, November 10, 1951.

12. Article 6 of the Marriage Law. For the text see *ibid.*, p. 8 *et seq.*

13. Shiomi Toshitaka *et al.*, "Chūgoku Kon' inhō Kikigaki," *Kazokuseido no Kenkyū*, Vol. 2, p. 217 (1957).

14. Article 17 of the Marriage Law.

15. "Marriage in Communist China," CB, No. 136, November 10, 1951, pp. 16, 24, 33, 37, 40, etc.

16. *Ibid.*, p. 1.

17. See statement by Minister of Justice Shih Liang in *Women of New China*, May 1950, quoted in CB, No. 136, pp. 2–3.

18. *People's Daily (Jen-min Jih-pao)*, September 29, 1951, Cabinet Instructions, September 26, 1951, quoted in CNA, No. 5, September 25, 1953.

19. For the text of the law and a discussion of it, see CB, No. 1, July 24, 1951.

20. In the last two years a number of death sentences have, for instance, been given to people accused of stealing food or looting. See for instance, *Tientsin Jih-pao*, January 20, 1960, trans. in *Survey of the China Mainland Press* (SCMP) (Hong Kong: U.S. Consulate-General), No. 2202, pp. 23–25; or *Ch'ang-chiang Jih-pao*, May 28, 1960, trans. in SCMP, No. 2284, p. 13. See also the case of alleged food poisoning, *People's Daily*, April 7, 1960, trans. in SCMP, No. 2339, pp. 7–8, and *Tzu-yu Chien-hsien*, No. 376, March 28, 1960, p. 15.

21. For documents on the "three-anti" and "five-anti" movements, see CB, No. 168, March 26, 1952.

22. See articles 16 and 18 of the "Regulations of the People's Republic of China for the Punishment of Counter-revolutionaries."

23. CNA, No. 141, July 27, 1956, pp. 5–7.

24. See the case of "A Village Solomon" given in CNA, No. 284, July 10, 1959, pp. 6–7.

25. Essay in *Cheng-Fa Yen-chiu*, April 1959, as quoted in CNA, No. 284.

26. CB, No. 168, p. 13 *et seq.*

27. CB, No. 101, July 24, 1951, p. 3.

28. Articles 4, 6, 7, 8, 9, 10, 13 of the "Regulations of People's Republic of China for Punishment of Counter-revolutionaries."

29. CB, No. 101, p. 3.

30. *Joint Publications Research Service,* No. 4649, p. 10.

31. *Kuang-ming Daily,* January 19, 1958, quoted in CNA, No. 255, November 28, 1958, p. 7.

32. *Joint Publications Research Service,* No. 4649, p. 8; CNA, No. 255, p. 4.

33. At the People's Congress in 1957 it was officially announced that a draft of a criminal code was ready. CNA, No. 187, p. 5 and No. 284, p. 1.

34. Anonymous essay in *Cheng-Fa Yen-chiu,* April 1959, quoted in CNA, No. 284, pp. 2–3.

35. CNA, No. 140, July 20, 1956, p. 2.

36. *New York Times,* August 1, 1961, "Soviet Party's Draft Program of July 30, 1961."

The Military Control

13. THE IDEOLOGY OF MILITARY CONTROL

G. A. KASHIN

In their ideological conflict with the Soviet Union, mainly over the question of the possibility of averting war in our time, the Chinese Communists have proved the more militant party. This is no doubt due in part to Mao Tse-tung's military doctrine, which has remained unchanged since it was formulated in the twenties and thirties and which, judging by Chinese sources, is not considered out of date. The publication of a fourth volume of Mao Tse-tung's selected works in September 1960 was hailed as an event of particular importance. Chinese Minister of Defense Ling Piao wrote a long article stressing the topicality of the questions raised in the book and the continued validity of the answers given. Both *Jen Min Jih Pao* and *Honggi* have devoted much space to the subject.[1]

This spate of propaganda is of particular interest in view of the volume's subject matter. Mao Tse-tung sums up the war against Japan and elaborates plans for the forthcoming struggle with the Kuomintang. He analyzes the various stage of the civil war and points out the strong aspects of the Communist army and the weaknesses of its opponents. He also expounds on the "paper tiger" theme, stating that "the imperialist tiger is a paper tiger in the strategic sense, but a dangerous iron tiger in the tactical sense." This formula represents in condensed form the Chinese Communist leader's entire military doctrine, which is in many ways similar to that of the Soviets but differs in important respects. He agrees that any future war will be a large-scale war, a war of the masses, but he is inclined to think that it will be of incomparably longer duration than is the Soviet view.

Mao Tse-tung's views differ radically from those of Soviet specialists on the importance of the surprise element and certain universal technical factors. He is of the opinion that the factors which are valid for a socialist army are

SOURCE: Selected from G. A. Kashin, "Chinese Military Doctrine," in the *Bulletin* of the Institute for the Study of the USSR, VII (November 1960), pp. 36–44. Reprinted by permission of the Institute for the Study of the USSR.

totally different from those which apply to a capitalist army. Ideological and psychological factors play a far greater role in his military doctrine than they do in the Soviet. Soviet military doctrine recognizes five so-called constantly valid factors contributing to the outcome of a war, factors which were formulated by Stalin as the basic principles of Soviet strategy. These are: stability behind the lines; political morale of the army and civilian population; number and quality of divisions; army equipment; organizational capabilities of commanders (of whatever rank).[2]

In Mao Tse-tung's view, all these are factors of a purely military nature, whereas war is not simply "the continuance of politics by other means," but is itself a form of politics. Consequently, decisive factors can only be of a purely political nature. In his works we read:

> " 'War is the continuance of politics . . .' This means that war is politics: war as such is an act of a political nature, and there has been no war in history which has not been of a political nature."[3] . . .

Purely military considerations must always be subordinated to ideological and political considerations. Mao Tse-tung's doctrine recognizes constantly valid factors too, but in his view they are of another order. An analysis of Mao's writings on "A Protracted War" and "Strategy in the Guerilla War against the Japanese Invaders" as well as all those contained in Volume IV (Chinese edition) of his works enables one to identify these factors and set out Mao's opinion of their relative importance thus:

1. Political morale of the people and the army as well, inasmuch as every socialist army is a part of the people.

2. Time, which inevitably works to the advantage of a socialist army and guarantees it strategical superiority even after a series of tactical defeats.

3. Space, essential to the exploitation of the two foregoing factors.

The formulation of these factors enables one to understand why Mao Tse-tung is so certain of the victory of the socialist camp in the event of a war. Of the three factors, the decisive one is the first; but political morale can only be high, according to Marxist theory, in a socialist state waging a war with the aim, not of enslaving other peoples, but of emancipating all workers and the whole of humanity. From this derives the obstinacy of Chinese ideologists in their campaign against any suggestion that imperialism may be changing its nature. Such a possibility would upset Mao's entire military doctrine and bring it to nought. If imperialism is really able to change its nature and renounce its aggressiveness, it must be in a position to raise the standard of political awareness of its peoples and thus challenge this strategical superiority on which Mao Tse-tung primarily relies. In that event, the determinist factor would be lost from his military doctrine, as so, too, would be the guarantee of eventual victory.

The Chinese leader pushes purely military factors into the background or, to be more exact, he makes them directly dependent upon ideological and political factors. The number and quality of divisions depends on the political morale of the people; the people provides the troops, and therefore the higher its political morale the greater the number of troops it will provide. Thus, the main advantage of a socialist state is its ability to mobilize the people in its entirety to rout the mercenary or semi-mercenary army of the imperialists. Mao Tse-tung believes that the most important military factor is the mobilization of the masses, without which victory is simply impossible. Moreover, he considers that a certain incentive to this end is provided by the enemy himself:

> Even now, after the war has started, political mobilization is still far from universal, and one cannot speak of it as being thorough. The vast majority of the population is made aware of the war by the enemy's artillery fire and aerial bombardment. This is also, in its way, a form of mobilization, but one which the enemy carries out for us. . . . Those who live in isolated regions and do not hear the artillery cannonades are still enjoying a tranquil peace. This situation must be changed; otherwise, we shall not be victorious in this war to the death. In no circumstances must we lose another move to the enemy.[4]

Mao Tse-tung considers that the quantity and quality of armaments may be a decisive problem for the imperialist armies of the West; for the socialist armies of the East it is automatically resolved. Experience of past wars in which the Chinese Communists have engaged would appear to confirm the Chinese leader's views on the subject:

> On the contrary, we must exert all our efforts to make up the lost ground and carry through a comprehensive political mobilization in order to overcome the enemy. Much depends on this. Our inferiority to the enemy in armaments and other equipment is of secondary importance. Political mobilization is the really primary concern. If the entire people is mobilized the enemy will suffer; he will be plunged into the depths of disaster; then conditions will be right for making up our deficiencies in the field of armaments, etc.; we shall have created the prerequisites for overcoming all the difficulties of war.[5]

Mao is resigned to the fact that at the beginning of any war the imperialists will have technical superiority, including tactical superiority; but this was so in the past, in both the war against Japan and the civil war, and in neither case did the enemy know how to use his superiority to achive a strategical victory. In Mao's view they *could* not do so, for here the time factor was of particular importance. Mao Tse-tung is in full agreement with Soviet military specialists that the *Blitzkrieg* is a thing of the past and that any future war, even if atomic weapons be employed, will inevitably last many years, perhaps decades. The goal of socialist armies in the initial stages of a war will be to deprive the enemy of the opportunity to turn a series of tactical successes into a strategical victory. During this initial period, which may last for some years, the armies of socialism and the Chinese armies in particular must work in close operation with the masses, relying on the latter and gradually drawing them into the struggle against the invader.

Here one particularly important factor should be mentioned. Mao Tse-tung envisages any future war in which China participates as being initially a war on Chinese territory. He derives this view from the aggressive and mercantile psychology of imperialism. Ruling Chinese Communist circles always assert that "the Western imperialists have not yet reconciled themselves, and never will reconcile themselves, to the loss of the Chinese market." The position Taiwan occupies in American policy further strengthens this conviction, which means that in the event of a new war the imperialists must perforce invade Chinese territory. All Chinese tactics and strategy for a future world war rest on the assumption that such a war will be waged on Chinese soil, so that the Chinese Communists will be able to utilize all the advantages of China's size and thereby gain time.

This is one reason why the Chinese ideologists cannot concur with Khrushchev's thesis of the possibility of averting wars in our time and the idea deriving from it that imperialism has changed its nature. Mao Tse-tung and other Chinese leaders fully realize that they are not in a position to win a war on foreign soil, especially against an army equipped with all modern technical aids. The practical measures now being adopted in China against a possible war confirm this emphasis upon war on Chinese territory.

On September 6, 1958, the Central Committee of the Chinese Communist Party adopted a resolution on enlisting the entire adult population in the People's Militia. This took place only a few days after the decision to introduce people's communes throughout China, and there can be no doubt that the two measures are linked. There is every reason to assume that the introduction of the people's communes was also partly dictated by military considerations. According to Mao Tse-tung's military doctrine, these communes are to play the part of administrative and industrial units, capable at any time and in any circumstances of supplying the army with arms and ammunition, albeit of a primitive nature. The People's Militia, whose administrative units almost merge locally with those of the people's communes, has come to be armed by the people. Both these organizations help to compensate for deficient quality with the quantity required by Mao's doctrine. As the Chinese news agency *Hsinhua* has stated:

> Intensive training is now being undergone by militiamen throughout the country, with rifles and also with artillery and other weapons. With every eligible member of its 600-million population under arms, China now possesses the strength to defend itself and fight the aggressors.[6]

The fall of 1958 may be regarded as the turning point in Chinese military preparations. Prior to this there is reason to suppose that there were two contending military groups, each with its own views on tactics and strategy. One, which may be termed purely military, was centered around the General Staff of the Chinese People's Liberation Army. The second, which may be called military-political, found its supporters in the headquarters of that same army and had Mao himself as its spiritual leader. The first was for the creation of a, perhaps small, but modern army with all the latest technical equipment. It was inclined to take the view that constantly valid factors are just as applica-

ble to socialist as to bourgeois armies. Like Soviet specialists, it placed organization and equipment first. The second adhered firmly to Mao's military doctrine,
stressing the decisive importance of ideological and political factors. Their
only point of contact was the reliance of both on the Soviet "atomic shield,"
which gave China the opportunity to prepare for a future war without fear
of an imperialist attack.

The conflict ended in August and September 1958 with the victory of the
supporters of Mao Tse-tung's doctrine, which found expression in changes
in the headquarters and General Staff of the People's Liberation Army. Defense
Minister Peng Teh-hwai had to relinquish his post in favor of Marshal Ling
Piao and the former Minister of State Security Lo Juh-ching was appointed
Chief of the General Staff. Informed circles in the West attributed Peng's
retirement partly to his opposition to the plan to use army units on "socialist
construction," and partly to his negative attitude toward expansion of the
People's Militia. The victory of Mao's group was clearly echoed in the Chinese
press. From that moment, preparation of the Chinese army for a possible
war outside China's borders ceased and all efforts of the Party and the General
Staff were concentrated on preparing for a war on Chinese territory. The
journal *Hgueh Si* described the results of the new policy thus:

> Over the past months, under the watchful eye of the Party Central
> Committee and Chairman Mao, a powerful movement to turn the entire
> nation into soldiers has spread to all parts of our country simultaneously
> with the establishment of the people's communes. The movement has
> been launched by our people for the purpose of defending their
> fatherland. . . . Should the imperialist brigands dare to invade our country,
> the whole of the nation will be mobilized to wipe out the enemy resolutely
> and completely. To turn an entire nation into soldiers through the militia
> system has many advantages. It can strengthen the courage and morale
> of the people, demoralize the enemy and embolden the people to despise
> all class enemies at home and abroad. . . . It can build up reserve forces
> with a high degree of political consciousness and military training. It
> can nurture tens of millions of reserve officers. . . . At home it can
> more successfully control landlords, rich peasants, counterrevolutionaires,
> undesirable characters and rightists and strengthen the dictatorship of
> the proletariat.[7]

The military operations conducted in the Taiwan Straits in the summer
of 1958 may be regarded as a practical preparation for the new policy. Detailed
study of the Chinese press shows that the methods used in these operations
aroused much critical comment from the purely military group around the
General Staff, and this opposition has remained vocal ever since. As a result,
the Peking Politburo decided to initiate a major campaign of education within
the army, particularly among the officers. The general press and special military
organs published a number of articles whose theme was that the army is
merely an instrument of the Party and may not assume an independent status.
The same line was followed in an article by Marshal Ling Piao published
on the eve of Army Day 1959. "Our army," he asserted, "does not contain

two opposed and contending classes, bourgeois and working, but the struggle within it between bourgeois and proletarian ideologies is not yet at an end." He enumerated the views which he regarded as the main sign of an adherence to bourgeois ideology:

> Some comrades take the view that modern warfare is different from warfare in the past; that as the weapons and equipment available to our army in the past were inferior in quality we had to emphasize dependence on man and his courage and resourcefulness. They say that modern warfare is a matter of technology, of steel and machinery, in the face of which man has to be relegated to a secondary role. They attach importance only to machinery and want to turn revolutionary soldiers into robots without revolutionary initiative.[8]

He then went on to defend the following two theses, which form the basis of Mao Tse-tung's military doctrine:

First, no war in history has been decided solely by military operations. Any war is of a political nature and therefore military specialists and technicians cannot direct and plan its conduct. Inasmuch as war is primarily a political affair, its direction must be in the hands of the politicians, and that, in modern China, means the Party. The Party is the only force in the country capable of comprehending, planning and synchronizing the action of all the units taking part in the struggle against the enemy. Consequently, the army must realize that it is only a part of the whole and must not infringe upon the leading role of the Party.

Second, the decisive factor in a war is not machines or weapons, but men. During the initial period of a war, deficiencies in quantity or quality of armaments can be compensated for by the enthusiasm of the masses, and subsequently by their industry. Moreover, the enemy may possess any amount of arms and yet, as was shown in the war against Japan and the civil war, they may be taken from him and later used against him. Thus, the enemy provides lines of communication and transport for one's own forces, which enables them to devote more time and energy to other more important questions.

On October 3, 1959, the agency *Hsinhua* published an article by Central Committee member Tu Ping repeating all the views expressed by Ling Piao, but with more direct reference to opposition trends within the army:

> The policy which Chairman Mao set down in the fall of last year for military operations on the Fukien front was a shining example of the subordination of military operations to the political struggle. At first, many foreign military experts could not understand why we were fighting our battle in that way. They said that China's way of fighting was without a parallel in the annals of war and that they had never heard of a war that stopped on even dates and resumed on odd dates, allowing the hostile forces during the ceasefire to replenish their ammunition and supplies. Later on, they learnt that the battle we were fighting was a political battle.[9]

Opposition to Mao Tse-tung's radical views on the political factor and the popular masses in the event of a new war exists not only in the army. The former rector of Peking University, Ma Yin-chu, spoke out against them in his article "My Philosophical Views and Economic Theories," stating that a future war would be a war of brains, not of the masses, and that the victor would be that side which was better equipped technically, better mechanized and armed.[10] In the atomic age, he wrote, quality and not quantity will be the main consideration. Ma Yin-chu regards as China's principal deficiency the disparity between the quantity and the quality of its population. An atomic attack on a primitive, technically undeveloped and undefended China would cause so many casualties that further resistance would be impossible. In his view, China needs, not a social or political revolution, but a cultural one. The main concern of Party and government should be to raise the standard of education of the population and its productivity. For this outburst, Ma Yin-chu was removed from his post as rector and expelled from the Party.

Despite this, Mao Tse-tung's policy has continued unchanged. Even the Soviet revision in 1954–55 of certain Stalinist concepts such as the secondary importance of the surprise factor in modern war has had no effect on it. True, even today Soviet specialists continue to assert that a surprise attack, even with nuclear weapons, cannot by itself decide the outcome of a war, but nevertheless they now assess the significance of such an attack quite differently from before. The appearance of the term "pre-emptive war" in Soviet military doctrine is evidence of this. A preventive attack may, and should, be launched in the event of its becoming apparent that the enemy is preparing for aggressive military action. This term has not established itself in China, and Chinese ideologists and military theoreticians even now regard surprise attack as a quite unimportant factor; indeed, under certain circumstances they consider that it may not furnish even temporary tactical superiority. An analysis of Mao's works and the statements of his supporters indicate that they regard the very primitiveness of China as an advantage in a possible war with the imperialist West. If such a war were to break out in the transitional period before China had been able to build up her own heavy industry and produce her own hydrogen bomb, the absence of large industrial centers would give her two advantages.

First, the lack of suitable industrial targets might well mean that no hydrogen bomb fell on China. The Chinese Communists regard this as quite possible in view of their estimation of the psychology of the Western "imperialists": inasmuch as imperialism will be waging a war for Chinese markets, it will endeavor to avoid destruction. Chinese ideologists frequently point out that during World War II the American air forces refrained from launching destructive attacks on such Chinese ports as Shanghai, Tientsin and Tsingtao, suggesting that this was because they were thinking of the profits they might subsequently amass through exploitation of these ports.

Second, nuclear weapons would be of no tactical or strategical value to the enemy since the People's Liberation Army would depend for its supplies not on large factories, which could be destroyed by nuclear weapons, but on small workshops organized by the people's communes. The decentralization of the country's administration through the people's communes would also play a vital role; the destruction of one commune would have little effect since all the others would continue to function. An actual nuclear attack could not last for long and would necessarily be followed by an occupation of Chinese territory during which the Chinese masses would come into action. On the Chinese side, the war would be conducted in the same manner as that against Japan and the civil war, a fact clearly indicated in Mao's works. Having a high political morale, the people would throw up active elements which would organize a guerrilla movement in the enemy's rear. The first task of each guerilla detachment would be to set up an organization within its appointed area. This would later enable several guerrilla detachments to merge into a regular army formation and quickly establish contact with the main army. The defeat of one or more guerilla detachments or army formations would again have little effect on the overall situation, since the formation of new detachments would continue. An enemy's military victories would thus be turned into psychological defeats. In his article "A Protracted War," which deals with the war against Japan but is regarded in Peking as a textbook for any future war in which China might engage, Mao Tse-tung describes the subsequent course of events:

Extensive development of the guerrilla war in the enemy's rear will doom his garrisons on occupied territory to complete impotence. Although now the enemy is continuing his strategical advance, during which the initiative is in his hands, once this advance is halted he will also lose the initiative. The enemy's lack of manpower will prevent him from continuing his advance indefinitely. That is the first reason why subsequently he will be unable to retain the initiative. The second reason why, having reached certain limits, he will be forced to halt his advance and will not be able to retain the initiative will be our offensive action on an operational scale, the guerrilla war in his rear and a number of other factors. The third reason is the existence of the USSR and changes in the international situation. From this, it can be seen that the enemy's initiative is limited and may be reduced to nought. If China, in its conduct of the war, is in the future able to maintain its policy of carrying out offensive action with regular troops on an operational scale and developing a fierce guerrilla war in the enemy's rear, while in the political field organizing an extensive mobilization of the popular masses, the strategic initiative will gradually pass into our hands.[11]

However naive these plans may appear in the context of modern warfare, there are no signs that others exist in Communist China at the present time. It was by means of this military doctrine that the Chinese Communists won the civil war, as Marshal Ling takes special pains to point out in his analysis of the fourth volume of Mao Tse-tung's works. In the initial period of the war, the marshal says, the Kuomintang armies also possessed overwhelming technical superiority, yet were unable to avoid defeat. He then transfers this lesson from the recent past to the future and asserts that any future war will conform to the same rules.

Apart from its military significance, Mao's doctrine also has a purely propaganda value as a method of compulsion. The people's communes serve both to facilitate the militarization of China and to consolidate the power of Communism. During the initial period of any dictatorship war hysteria is the rule, and Communist China is no exception in this respect. Such hysteria is usually artificially created, and whatever the merits of Mao's military doctrine in the event of a third world war, it is at present serving Communist aims in much the same way as did Stalin's theory of capitalist encirclement. But to ensure its propaganda value some ideological basis is required, and it is this ideological basis that is threatened by Khrushchev's thesis of the possibility of averting war in our time and his policy of peaceful coexistence. . . .

The defense of Mao's doctrine against enemies at home and abroad is absolutely essential, but as time passes it becomes more and more difficult. The Communist bloc cannot afford to support two sharply divergent military doctrines. The growing rift is underlined in an article by Major General Nikolai Talensky, printed recently in the journal *Mezhdunarodnaya zhizn*.[12] The article represents a radical revision of Stanlinist military thought. His revealing assertions include statements that: there is no practical defense against nuclear missile attack; a nuclear war would annihilate whole countries and their populations, killing at least 500–600 million persons; a surprise attack would undoubtedly give the attacker a certain advantage, but would not prevent retaliation; local wars, possible in the past, are no longer so, since such a war would become either the prelude to a world war or the end of all wars; modern technology has rendered Clausewitz' formula totally obsolete.

Talensky's article is but one example of written evidence that Mao Tse-tung's doctrine is not only unacceptable in the Soviet Union, but is regarded there as a direct invitation to suicide. Among Communists "adventurism" is regarded as a most serious charge. By refusing to listen to reason and clinging to his belief in the possibility of victory in a future nuclear war, Mao Tse-tung is coming to be regarded by orthodox Soviet and other—including Chinese—ideologists as an "adventurer" who is threatening to lead the whole Communist bloc along the road to disaster.

As a result, Chinese Communism is finding itself in a vicious circle from which there is no escape. To give in to Soviet revisionism would be to renounce the most powerful ideological and propaganda weapon it now possesses. To continue the struggle would be to strike one blow after another at the unity of the socialist camp. Nevertheless, all the evidence indicates that Mao Tse-tung is intending to do so. In October of this year, a conference of high-ranking officers of the People's Liberation Army took place in Peking at which Marshal Ling Piao made a long speech in which he called for intensified political work in the army and the elimination of opposition to Mao Tse-tung's military doctrine among certain officer circles.[13] Ling Piao left no doubt that this doctrine is recognized by the Peking leadership as the only true military doctrine of our time and there is no question of its revision in any way. Everything indicates that the two most powerful members of the Communist bloc are hopelessly at loggerheads in their views regarding the fundamental problem of the day and there is no hope of the breach being healed in the immediate future. . . .

Notes

1. *Jen Min Jih Pao,* Peking, September 30, 1960; *Honggi,* Peking, 1960, No. 13.

2. J. V. Stalin, *O Velikoi Otechestvennoi voine Sovetskogo Soyuza* (On the Soviet Union's Great Fatherland War), 5th ed., Moscow, 1959, p. 78.

3. Mao Tse-tung, *Izbrannye proizvedeniya* (Selected Works), Translated from the Chinese, Vol. II, Moscow, 1953, p. 263.

4. *Ibid.,* p. 266.

5. *Ibid.*

6. *Hsinhua,* September 18, 1958.

7. *Hgeuh Si,* Peking, January 10, 1959.

8. *Jen Min Jih Pao,* September 30, 1959.

9. *Hsinhua,* October 3, 1959.

10. See *Neue Zürcher Zeitung,* April 21, 1960.

11. Mao Tse-tung, *op. cit.,* p. 290.

12. *Mezhdunarodnaya zhizn,* 1960, No. 10, pp. 31–37.

13. *Peking Review,* October 11, 1960.

14.   THE STRATEGY OF GUERRILLA WARFARE

MAO TSE-TUNG

Without a political goal, guerrilla warfare must fail, as it must if its political objectives do not coincide with the aspirations of the people and their sympathy, cooperation and assistance cannot be gained. The essence of guerrilla warfare is thus revolutionary in character.

On the other hand, in a war of counter-revolutionary nature, there is no place for guerrilla hostilities. Because guerrilla warfare basically derives from the masses and is supported by them, it can neither exist nor flourish if it separates itself from their sympathies and cooperation.

There are those who do not comprehend guerrilla action and who therefore do not understand the distinguishing qualities of a people's guerrilla war who say: "Only regular troops can carry out guerrilla operations." There are others who, because they do not believe in the ultimate success of guerrilla action, mistakenly say: "Guerrilla warfare is an insignificant and highly specialized

SOURCE: Selected from *The New York Times Magazine,* June 4, 1961, pp. 13 and 71–73. Copyright 1961 by The New York Times Company. Reprinted by permission. Digested from Samuel B. Griffith, *Mao's Primer on Guerrilla Warfare.* Copyright 1962 by Marine Corps Association, publisher of the *Marine Corps Gazette.*

type of operation in which there is no place for the masses of the people." There are those who ridicule the masses and undermine resistance by wildly asserting that the people have no understanding of the war of resistance.

The political goal must be clearly and precisely indicated to inhabitants of guerrilla zones and their national consciousness awakened.

There are some militarists who say, "We are not interested in politics but only in the profession of arms." It is vital that these simple-minded militarists be made to realize the relationship between politics and military affairs. Military action is a method used to attain a political goal.

In all armies, obedience of the subordinates to their superiors must be exacted. This is true in the case of guerrilla discipline, but the basis for guerrilla discipline must be the individual conscience. With guerrillas a discipline of compulsion is ineffective.

In any system where discipline is externally imposed, the relationship that exists between officer and man is characterized by indifference of the one to the other. A discipline self-imposed is the primary characteristic of a democratic system in the army.

Further, in such an army the mode of living of the officers and the soldiers must not differ too much and this is particularly true in the case of guerrilla troops. Officers should live under the same conditions as their men, for that is the only way in which they can gain from their men the admiration and confidence so vital in war. It is incorrect to hold to a theory of equality in all things, but there must be equality of existence in accepting the hardships and dangers of war.

There is also a unity of spirit that should exist between troops and local inhabitants. The Eighth Route Army put into practice a code known as "Three Rules and Eight Remarks":

Rules—All actions are subject to command; do not steal from the people; be neither selfish nor unjust.

Remarks—Replace the door when you leave the house; roll up the bedding in which you have slept; be courteous; be honest in your transactions; return what you borrow; replace what you break; do not bathe in the presence of women; do not without authority search the pocketbooks of those you arrest.

Many people think it impossible for guerrillas to exist for long in the enemy's rear. Such a belief reveals lack of comprehension of the relationship that should exist between the people and the troops. The former may be likened to water, and the latter to the fish who inhabit it. How may it be said that these two cannot exist together? It is only undisciplined troops who make the people their enemies and who, like the fish out of its native element, cannot live.

We further our mission of destroying the enemy by propagandizing his troops, by treating his captured soldiers with consideration and by caring for those of his wounded who fall into our hands. If we fail in these respects, we strengthen the solidarity of the enemy.

The primary functions of guerrillas are three: first, to conduct a war on exterior lines, that is, in the rear of the enemy; secondly, to establish bases; lastly, to extend the war areas. Thus guerrilla participation in the war is not merely a matter of purely local guerrilla tactics, but involved strategical considerations.

What is basic guerrilla strategy? Guerrilla strategy must primarily be based on alertness, mobility and attack. It must be adjusted to the enemy situation, the terrain, the existing lines of communication, the relative strength, the weather and the situation of the people.

In guerrilla warfare select the tactic of seeming to come from the east and attacking from the west; avoid the solid, attack the hollow; attack; withdraw; deliver a lightning blow, seek a lightning decision. When guerrillas engage a stronger enemy they withdraw when he advances, harass him when he stops; strike him when he is weary; pursue him when he withdraws. In guerrilla strategy the enemy's rear, flanks and other vulnerable spots are his vital points, and there he must be harassed, attacked, dispersed, exhausted and annihilated.

If we cannot surround whole armies, we can at least partially destroy them; if we cannot kill the [enemy troops] we can capture them. The total effect of many local successes will be to change the relative strengths of the opposing forces.

Guerrillas can . . . gain the initiative if they keep in mind the weak points of the enemy. Because of the enemy's insufficient manpower, guerrillas can operate over vast territories; because he is a foreigner and a barbarian, guerrillas can gain the confidence of millions of their countrymen; because of the stupidity of enemy commanders, guerrillas can make full use of their own cleverness.

The leader must be like the fisherman who, with his nets, is able both to cast them and pull them out in awareness of the depth of the water, the strength of the current, or the presence of any obstructions that may foul them. As the fisherman controls his nets . . . so the guerrilla leader maintains contact with and control over his units.

When the situation is serious the guerrillas must move with the fluidity of water and the ease of the blowing wind.

Ability to fight a war without a rear area is a fundamental characteristic of guerrilla action, but this does not mean that guerrillas can exist and function over a long period of time without the development of base areas. Guerrilla bases may be classified according to their locations as, first, mountain bases; second, plains bases; and last, river, lake and bay bases. The advantages of bases in mountainous areas are evident.

After defeating the enemy in any area we must take advantage of the period he requires for reorganization to press home our attacks. We must not attack an objective we are not certain of winning. We must confine our operations to relatively small areas and destroy the enemy and traitors in those places. When the inhabitants have been inspired, new volunteers accepted, trained, equipped and organized, our operations may be extended to include cities and lines of communication not strongly held. We may at least hold these for temporary (if not for permanent) periods.

All these are our duties in offensive strategy. Their object is to lengthen the period the enemy must remain on the defensive. Then our military activities and our organization work among the masses of the people must be zealously expanded; and with equal zeal the strength of the enemy attacked and diminished.

How are guerrilla units formed?

In [one] case, the guerrilla unit is formed from the people. This is the fundamental type. Upon the arrival of the enemy army to oppress and slaughter the people, their leaders call upon them to resist. They assemble the most valorous elements, arm them with old rifles or bird guns and thus a guerrilla unit begins.

In some places where the local government is not determined or where its officers have all fled, the leaders among the masses call upon the people to resist and they respond. In circumstances of this kind, the duties of leadership usually fall upon the shoulders of young students, teachers, professors, other educators, local soldiery, professional men, artisans and those without a fixed profession who are willing to exert themselves to the last drop of their blood.

There are those who say "I am a farmer" or "I am a student"; "I can discuss literature but not military arts." This is incorrect. There is no profound difference between the farmer and the soldier. You must have courage. You simply leave your farms and become soldiers. That you are farmers is of no difference and if you have education that is so much the better. When you take your arms in hand you become soldiers; when you are organized you become military units. Guerrilla hostilities are the university of war.

[Still another] type of unit is that organized from troops that come over from the enemy. It is continually possible to produce disaffection in their ranks and we must increase our propaganda efforts and foment mutinies among such troops. Immediately after mutiny they must be received into our ranks and organized. In regard to this type of unit, it may be said that political work among them is of the utmost importance.

Guerrilla organizations [can also be] formed from bands of bandits and brigands. Many bandit groups pose as guerrillas and it is only necessary to correct their political beliefs to convert them.

In spite of inescapable differences in the fundamental types of guerrilla bands, it is possible to unite them to form a vast sea of guerrillas.

All the people of both sexes from the ages of 16 to 45 must be organized into . . . self-defense units, the basis of which is voluntary service. As a first step they must procure arms, then both military and political training must be given them. Their responsibilities are: local sentry duties, securing information of the enemy, arresting traitors and preventing the dissemination of enemy propaganda.

When the enemy launches a guerrilla-suppression drive, these units, armed with what weapons there are, are assigned to certain areas to deceive, hinder and harass him. Thus the self-defense units assist the combatant guerrillas.

They have other functions. They furnish stretcher-bearers to carry the wounded, carriers to take food to the troops and comfort missions to provide the troops with tea and porridge. Each member of these groups must have a weapon, even if the weapon is only a knife, a pistol, a lance or a spear.

In regard to the problem of guerrilla equipment it must be understood that guerrillas are lightly armed attack groups that require simple equipment.

Guerrilla bands which originate with the people are furnished with revolvers, pistols, bird guns, spears, big swords, and land mines and mortars of local manufacture. Other elementary weapons are added and as many new-type rifles as are available are distributed. After a period of resistance, it is possible to increase the amount of equipment by capturing it from the enemy. In this respect the transport companies are the easiest to equip for in any successful attack we will capture the enemy's transport.

An armory should be established in each guerrilla district for the manufacture and repair of rifles and for the production of cartridges, hand grenades and bayonets. Guerrillas must not depend too much on an armory. The enemy is the principal source of their supply. For destruction of railway trackage, bridges and stations in enemy-controlled territory, it is necessary to gather together demolition materials. Troops must be trained in the preparation and use of demolitions and a demolition unit must be organized in each regiment.

If Western medicines are not available, local medicines must be made to suffice.

Propaganda materials are very important. Every large guerrilla unit should have a printing press and a mimeograph stone. They must also have paper on which to print propaganda leaflets and notices.

In addition . . . it is necessary to have field glasses, compasses and military maps. An accomplished guerrilla unit will acquire these things.

15. THE STRUCTURE OF MILITARY DECISION-MAKERS

Ralph L. Powell

In the history of the Chinese Communist Party the armed forces have played an unusually important role. The Party came to power through more than twenty years of almost constant revolutionary warfare. In 1938 Mao Tse-tung wrote that, "In China the main form of struggle is war and the main form of organization is the army."[1] There is no national leadership in the world whose senior members have had as much active military service, certainly not as much combat experience, as have the rulers of Communist China. Almost all of the regular members of the Central Committee of the Party once held senior rank in the Chinese Red Army as commanders or commissars.[2] Six of the sixteen or seventeen active members of the Politburo are marshals of the armed forces—the "Peoples Liberation Army" (PLA).[3] The military members of the Party have always played a more influential role than has been true in the Soviet Union. Nevertheless, the influence and independence of the military should not be overestimated. Prior to 1949 it was almost literally true that the Party was in the Army, but it is also true that the Army has always belonged to the Party. In 1938 Mao enunciated a basic rule when

SOURCE: Reprinted from Ralph L. Powell, "The Military Affairs Committee and Party Control of the Military in China," in *Asian Survey*, III, 7 (July 1963), pp. 347–356. Reprinted by permission of *Asian Survey*.

he stated that, "Our principle is that the Party commands the gun, and the gun will never be allowed to command the Party."[4]

Under the Party the armed forces have had exceptionally diversified missions. Aside from traditional military roles, they have been a labor force, a media of mass indoctrination, and a training school, first for administrative cadres and now for technicians valuable to the underdeveloped economy. Finally, they still serve as the major security force and internal bulwark for the Party. Hence, more than most regular military establishments, they are a vast gendarmerie. Naturally, the Party places great emphasis on the control and indoctrination of the armed forces and maintains a complex and penetrating Party apparatus within the PLA to achieve these objectives. This Party machinery inside the armed forces is known in some detail. Under the General Political Department, dominant party committees function at all levels under a system of collective leadership. Both military commanders and political officers are subordinate to their committee. Higher echelon units have political departments, while political officers or commissars are appointed down to the company level. The whole system is further supported by the presence of Party members throughout the rank and file of the PLA.[5]

However, the highest level structure and chain of command by which the Party's leaders seek to preserve "absolute leadership in the armed forces"[6] has been shrouded in some mystery. Constitutional provisions regarding the control and administration of the military establishment are misleading. The military provisions in the national constitution of 1954 read like those in the constitution of a Western democracy and they camouflage the paramount role of the Party.[7] The Party's constitution of 1956 is more enlightening. It states that "the Party must strive to play a correct role as the leader and core in every aspect of the country's life . . ." (General Program). Also that, "The Central Committee guides the work of the central state organs and people's organizations of a national character through leading Party member's groups within them" (Article 34). Still, the 1956 constitution's principal reference to the armed forces is also partially misleading for it states that (Article 35),

The Party organizations in the People's Liberation Army carry on their work in accordance with the instructions of the Central Committee. The General Political Department in the People's Liberation Army, under the direction of the Central Committee, takes charge of the ideological and organizational work of the Party in the army.

In practice, and actually in legal theory, the Party's work in and control over the PLA centers in the Politburo and especially in its Standing Committee, for "when the Central Committee is not in plenary session" (which is most of the time) these latter bodies "exercise the powers and functions of the Central Committee" (Article 37). The communist concept of "democratic centralism" confirms the final authority of the Politburo and its Standing Committee. Thus these small elite bodies are the "ultimate arbiter of military policy."[8] In the field of military affairs the frequent references to the Central

Committee should in most cases actually be interpreted as a reference to the Politburo.

The fact that real power centers in Mao Tse-tung, the Standing Committee and then the remainder of the Politburo, has long been recognized. The serious gap in our knowledge of the political-military power structure relates to the central machinery by which the Politburo directs and coordinates the plans and operations of the Ministry of National Defense, the General Staff, the General Political Department, and other general departments of the PLA, as well as the armed forces themselves. The missing link and key agency in the apparatus is the mysterious Military Affairs Committee "of the Central Committee." (Chung-kung chung-yang chün-shih wei-yuan-hui, which is usually abbreviated in Chinese sources as Chün-wei.)[9]

Very little has been known regarding the Military Affairs Committee (MAC). Some descriptions and charts of the organizations of the Party or the armed forces do not even mention it. Most references to the probable functions or personnel of the Committee have, of necessity, been based on speculation.

The 1945 Constitution of the Communist Party of China (Article 34) mentioned the establishment by the "Central Committee" of a Military Affairs Committee. The MAC, as well as the other departments and committees organized by the Central Committee, was to function under the "direction and supervision of the Politburo, the Central Secretariat and the Chairman of the Central Committee. However, the new Party Constitution of 1956 does not specifically mention any of the central departments or committees. It was not known abroad whether or not the MAC continued to exist, and it was quite widely believed that the actual "control and command" of the armed forces during the period of 1949–1954 rested in the "People's Revolutionary Military Council" (PRMC) of the Central Government.[10] The Council was a relatively small body of considerable influence, for its chairman was Mao Tse-tung and its membership included the majority of the Politburo. Nevertheless, it is not in keeping with basic Party policy to permit real control over a vital institution of the state to exist outside the Party. Furthermore, in 1954 the PRMC was replaced, at least theoretically, by the National Defense Council (NDC). This large body consists of over one hundred members, a considerable number of whom are ex-Nationalist generals. Although the chairman of the government is also chairman of the NDC, and most of the senior communist officers also belong to the Council, it is believed to be an essentially honorific body and a remnant of the concept of a united front government. The NDC rarely meets and is seldom referred to.[11] It is quite apparent that real control over the armed forces does not reside in the NDC.

In 1958 the existence of the MAC was again officially noted, for it was reported that in the spring of 1957 the Military Affairs Committee "of the Central Committee" had resolved to merge two departments of the General Political Department of the PLA.[12] It is possible that the MAC had once been abolished and later reestablished, but it seems more likely that it had continued its unpublicized existence. In recent years sufficient, scattered references to this important committee have appeared to make it possible to present a valuable, but not definite, analysis of the once shadowy MAC.

As of mid-1961 the influential MAC consisted of at least eight Party leaders—six marshals and two senior generals. These were Marshals Lin Piao, Ho Lung, Hsu Hsiang-ch'ien, Lo Jung-huan, Nieh Jung-chen and Yeh Chien-ying, plus Generals Lo Jui-ch'ing and Hsiao Hua.[13] There are no indications that any of these leaders have since been removed from the Committee, but this list probably does not include every regular or standing member.

A major conference of the Committee in mid-1958 was addressed by all of the above marshals except Hsu Hsiang-ch'ien, as well as by Mao Tse-tung, Teng Hsiao-p'ing, and Marshals Chu Te, Ch'en I, Liu Po-ch'eng and P'eng Te-huai.[14] All of the latter group were then members of the Politburo. The fact that these Politburo members and marshals spoke at the Conference led to reasonable speculation that these leaders constituted the membership of the MAC.[15] Some of these latter Politburo members may sit on the MAC, others probably do not.

Owing to his long-standing interest in military matters and the cardinal importance of the armed forces to the Party, Mao Tse-tung may well be the *ex-officio* chairman of the MAC. This would be in accordance with the principle enunciated by the 1945 Party Constitution. However, the reduction in Mao's activities in recent years would indicate that he does not normally take an active part. It is likely that politburo member, Marshal Liu Po-ch'eng, serves on the committee if his age (71) and health permit it. He is a distinguished Party soldier and is less burdened with known functions than are most of the members of the MAC. The venerable Chu Te (77) is almost certainly too elderly to play an active role. He does not even belong to the National Defense Council. The Party's Secretary General, Teng Hsiao-p'ing and the Minister of Foreign Affairs, Marshal Ch'en I were veteran senior officers in the Red Army. In some respects it would seem logical that these leaders would serve on the MAC, but we have no concrete evidence that these overburdened officials are members of the Committee. Like many of the former officers of the armed forces they have switched their major activities to other demanding fields. One has become a specialist in Party matters, the other in foreign affairs. Marshal P'eng Te-huai was purged in September 1959, and it is most unlikely that he now attends meetings of either the Politburo or the MAC.[16]

Marshal Lin Piao is now almost certainly the *de facto* chief of the MAC. He is the only known member who serves on the Standing Committee of the Politburo, and is also the Minister of National Defense and the principal military spokesman of the regime. With one exception, his name has been the only one linked with known references to directives from the MAC.[17]

The membership of the MAC is a very influential group. Even if one excludes all but the known regular participants, the latter include three members of the Politburo and all serve on the Central Committee of the Party. One is a member of the Standing Committee of the Politburo and another is a secretary of the Secretariat. Four are vice premiers and most of the group are also vice chairmen of the honorific National Defense Council.[18]

The membership of the Military Affairs Committee provides an excellent example of the Party's multiple hat policy or the practice of dominating other major institutions of the state by placing Party leaders in controlling positions. In addition to their high Party and government positions, the known members of the MAC occupy most of the key military and military related posts in Communist China. Lin Piao is Minister of National Defense. Lo Jui-ch'ing is Chief of the General Staff and a Vice Minister of National Defense. Lo Jung-huan may again be Director of the powerful General Political Department.[19] Hsiao Hua is a Deputy Director of the General Political Department and may still be Director of the General Cadres or Personnel Department of the PLA.[20] Yeh Chien-ying is President and Commissar of the Academy of Military Sciences. Nieh Jung-chen is chairman of the influential Scientific and Technological Commission, which has jursidiction over both research and development, including that in the field of atomic energy. Ho Lung is chairman of the Physical Culture and Sports Commission, which seeks to improve national physical standards, partly for military purposes. Thus to an amazing degree the supervision of military affairs and of the armed forces is concentrated in the hands of a few of the Party's senior military specialists. In their Party roles as members of the MAC they are in a position to give themselves orders in their governmental military and military related posts.

It would seem logical that within the central machinery of the Party the MAC ranks only slightly below, or possibly on a level with, the Secretariat and that it is senior to all of the other departments and committees "of the Central Committee." Lin Piao is listed above the Secretary General, Teng Hsiao-p'ing, on official party rosters, but the Secretariat includes more Politburo members than are known to serve on the MAC. Of the remaining central organs, only the Control Committee and the Propaganda Department are known to include even one regular or alternate member of the Politburo.

Official references to the MAC and its activities demonstrate that this high-level Party committee outranks and has the authority to control the Ministry of National Defense, the General Staff, the General Political Department and other departments of the PLA, as well as the armed forces. The Ministry of National Defense acts as an implementing agency for the MAC, carries out general orders issued by the Committee and is responsible for the routine administration of the military establishment.[21] The MAC issues instructions to the General Staff Department.[22] As the representative "of the Central Committee" (read Politburo), the MAC directs the work of the General Political Department and of the Party organizations in the PLA.[23] Sometimes the MAC makes decisions or issues instructions that directly apply to all units of the armed forces.[24]

The activities of the MAC are very diversified and cover a wide range of important matters. As the military organ of the Politburo the MAC plays a key role in the formulation and implementation of the Party's major political-military policies and strategy. At an irregular series of meetings and enlarged conferences the MAC has presented and explained important plans and policies to a large number of senior personnel.[25] Available references indicate that generally the MAC operates through the Ministry of National Defense or, more frequently, through the General Political Department, but occasionally the Committee by-passes these agencies and issues important directives to the armed forces in its own name.[26] Despite their very senior rank, members of the MAC have carried out investigations and inspections of the armed forces in the field.[27]

The MAC has taken an interest in all of the roles and missions of the armed forces, not limiting itself to supervising the political indoctrination of the military establishment. In recent years it has launched campaigns to improve both the combat readiness and political reliability of the PLA. In the field of political-military relations the Committee has called for intensive political and ideological education, especially the study of the thought of Mao Tse-tung. All of the armed forces have been directed to raise high "the great red banner" of the political and military works of Mao.[28] The MAC has also stressed the development of revolutionary enthusiasm and the unity of officers and men. Youth work in the armed forces has been emphasized and efforts have been made to create young soldiers who are both red and expert.[29] The very emphasis placed on political campaigns by the MAC and the General Political Department indicate that during the early 1960's the Party leaders have not been fully satisfied with the political "consciousness" and reliability of the armed forces.

In regard to the military missions of the PLA, the MAC has sought within the limitations set by the national economy to increase the combat preparedness of the·armed forces. It has issued training directives, encouraged better maintenance of equipment, promoted the improvement of military techniques, and emphasized military discipline and physical training. In 1957 the Committee called for the integration of the reserves and the militia, while in 1958 it sponsored a review of past developments and future plans for the PLA. Also, the MAC has set forth strategic principles for the armed forces.[30]

No reference has been found that specifically mentions MAC activities regarding the development of atomic weapons or doctrine. However, the majority of the members of the Committee have publicly commented on modern military science and technology or the development of nuclear weapons and the strategy of an atomic war.[31] The MAC probably has much the same responsibility for high level planning and supervision in the atomic field that it has in other areas of military activity.

The MAC has made decisions and issued directives regarding the employment of the PLA as a labor force and as a "builder of socialism." During the "Great Leap," in the fall of 1958, the MAC directed the armed forces to render "prompt and all-out" support to the iron and steel production program of the state. Later, a decision of the Committee required officers and men of the PLA to spend one to two months each year in construction or production projects. After the collapse of the "Great Leap," the MAC encouraged the practice of frugality and economy among the troops.[32]

The influence of the members of the Military Affairs Committee and the high degree to which they dominate key political military positions raises a question regarding the effectiveness of the control by the civilian party leaders over the vital military establishment. However, these civilian leaders are specialists in maintaining power and they have built-in safeguards. Liu Shao-ch'i as the chairman of the government and the legal commander of the armed forces, and Chou En-lai, as Premier and the superior of the Minister of National Defense, have some control over the military establishment. One role of the powerful secretariat may be to counterbalance the MAC. Also, while the MAC supervises the armed forces, none of its members are now known directly to command troops. With the exception of Lo Jui-ch'ing, none of those who serve on the MAC are believed to have had personal command of large bodies of troops since the early or mid-fifties. The Committee could be a threat to the remainder of the Party leadership only if its members united against the Party chieftains. But every member of the Committee has long been a loyal, senior lieutenant of Mao Tse-tung. Certainly the group did not stand together to support Marshal P'eng Te-huai and the former chief of staff, Huang K'o-ch'eng, when the latter were purged in the fall of 1959. The civilian leaders must have great faith in the members of the MAC, otherwise they would almost certainly purge them, as P'eng and Huang were purged. Perhaps the top leaders could not purge the whole MAC, without creating a military revolt, but apparently there is no need to try.

The members of the Military Affairs Committee are veteran Party leaders who have served the Party just as long and just as loyally as have the essentially civilian leaders. The Committee's members are senior Party specialists in military affairs, just as Teng Hsiao-p'ing is now a specialist in Party matters and Chou En-lai is a specialist in government administration. The real power and authority of the members of the MAC results from the fact that they are high Party officials, not from the fact that they are marshals or generals. The distinction that is made in the West between civilian leaders of government and military commanders has little validity in Communist China. In China both groups are basically Party leaders; they merely have different specialties. They operate the government, the mass organizations or the armed forces for the Party.

In the Military Affairs Committee the Politburo has an instrument well suited to control and supervise the military establishment, which is so important to the security of the Party's dictatorship. The members of the Committee are loyal Party veterans. Together they represent a vast amount of combat and administrative experience as commanders and commissars. They constitute the majority of the now almost legendary leaders of the revolutionary Red Army. Most of the senior officers of the PLA have served under them and they have prestige in the military establishment.

Still the MAC has several weaknesses and disadvantages. Its members are an elderly group with an average age of over 62 years. Only Lin Piao, Lo Jui-ch'ing and Hsiao Hua are in their fifties and Lin Piao's health may have again deteriorated. He has not appeared at any important political or military functions since early in 1962, but his name and his directives to the armed forces continue to be mentioned.[33] Nevertheless, within a few years most of the members of the MAC must be replaced by younger men who will command less prestige and loyalty within the PLA.

Most of the extensive experience of the Committee's present members was gained in years of guerilla or semi-conventional warfare. They have long been indoctrinated with Mao's military doctrines, including the concept of the superiority of men over weapons—even atomic weapons. They are masters of revolutionary warfare, but as a group they are less qualified by experience to supervise a vast, modernizing military establishment in the atomic era.

Finally, although these senior Party soldiers are loyal followers of Mao Tse-tung, they will have less reason for a personal loyalty to Mao's successor.

Should there be a struggle for succession, as happened after the deaths of Lenin and Stalin, the military leaders would almost inevitably be involved by the contending factions, who would seek their support. Even if the present influential members of the MAC were still alive and active, it is doubtful that they would be sufficiently united or ambitious to attempt to create a military-Party government, but they would probably have the power to play king maker. Since the military have always had more influence in the Chinese Communist Party than has been true in the Soviet Union, it would be more difficult for a new leader in China to rid himself of his Praetorian Guard than it was for Khrushchev to purge Marshal Zhukov, when the latter became an impediment after he supported Khrushchev's rise to power.

Notes

1. "Problems of War and Strategy," *Selected Works,* Vol. II, (New York: International Publishers, 1954), p. 268.

2. Donald W. Klein, "The Next Generation of Chinese Communist Leaders," *The China Quarterly,* No. 12 (Oct.–Dec. 1962), p. 65.

3. The marshals who serve on the Politburo are, Chu Te, Lin Piao, Lo Jung-huan, Ch'en I, Liu Po-ch'eng and Ho Lung. Marshall P'eng Te-huai was purged in September 1959, although to preserve an appearance of Party unity his name is still officially listed on the Politburo roster.

4. *Selected Works,* Vol. II, p. 272.

5. See S. M. Chiu, "Political Control in the Chinese Communist Army," *Military Review* (Aug. 1961), pp. 25–35; Ellis Joffe, "The Communist Party and the Army," in E. Stuart Kirby, ed., *Contemporary China: 1959–1960,* Vol. IV (Hong Kong: 1961), pp. 62–63; Harold C. Hinton, "Political Aspects of Military Power and Policy in Communist China," in Harry L. Coles, ed., *Total War and Cold War* (Ohio State Univ. Press, 1962), pp. 270–272.

6. Lin Piao, *Hold High the Red Flag of the Party's General Line and Mao Tse-tung's Military Thinking, etc."* (Peking: Foreign Language Press, 1961), p. 22. See also pp. 3, 5, & 9.

7. The chairman of the People's Republic is designated as commander of the armed forces and as chairman of the National Defense Council (Article 42). Under the 1954 constitution, the honorific Defense Council replaced the influential Revolutionary Military Council, but the constitution's references to the Defense Council are limited to outlining procedures for the selection and removal of its members (Articles 27, 28, and 40). No organic law has been published regarding its functions. The State Council or cabinet is delegated the power "to guide the building up of the defense forces" (Article 49) and the Premier is given authority to direct the activities of the Council (Article 50). The Organic Law of the State Council (Sept. 21, 1954) established a Ministry of National Defense (Article 2), but its duties and functions were not outlined.

8. *National Policy Machinery in Communist China,* Subcommittee on National Policy Machinery of the Committee on Government Operations, Senate (Washington, D.C., 1959), p. 13. See also pp. 4–8.

9. The Military Affairs Committee has been referred to in English language sources and translations as the Military Committee, the Military Affairs Commission and as the Military Council.

10. For example see Gene Z. Hanrahan, "The People's Revolutionary Military Council in Communist China," *Far Eastern Survey* 23:5 (May 1954), 77–78;

S. B. Thomas, "Structure and Constitutional Basis of the Chinese Peoples Republic," *The Annals* (Sept. 1951), p. 47; Peter S. H. Tang, *Communist China Today,* 2nd Rev. Ed. (Washington, D.C.), Vol. 1, pp. 211, 215. See also Harold C. Hinton, *Leaders of Communist China* (Santa Monica: Rand, 1956), p. 41.

11. See Joffe, *op. cit.,* pp. 60–61; Hinton, "Political Aspects of Military Power," p. 277; *National Policy Machinery,* p. 14.

12. *Jen-min jih-pao* (People's Daily), March 12, 1958, p. 4. See also *Ibid.,* March 1, 1958, in *Survey of China Mainland Press* (SCMP), American Consulate General, Hong Kong, No. 1729, pp. 1 and 2.

13. *Chieh-fang-chun hua-pao* (Liberation Army Pictorial), June 1961. This edition of the official *Pictorial* provides 7 pictures with captions, showing leaders of the MAC inspecting units of the armed forces. The seven captions provide the names of eight members of the MAC.

14. New China News Agency (NCNA), July 5, 1958, in SCMP, No. 1822, p. 1.

15. Hinton, "Political Aspect of Military Power," p. 277. See also Joffe, *op. cit.,* p. 61.

16. See the interesting but sometimes dubious article by David A. Charles, "The Dismissal of Marshal P'eng Teh-huai," *The China Quarterly,* No. 8 (Oct.–Dec. 1961), pp. 63–76.

17. For example see *Chung-kuo ch'ing-nien pao* (China Youth Daily), Feb. 11, 1961, in SCMP, No. 2459, p. 1; NCNA-Eng, Peking, July 6, 1961, in SCMP No. 2535, p. 2; Urumchi, Domestic radio service in Mandarin, Jan. 18, 1963.

18. Lin Piao, Ho Lung and Lo Jung-huan are members of the Politburo, while Lin Piao serves on its seven-man Standing Committee. Lo Jui-ch'ing was elected to the Secretariat in September 1962. Lin, Ho, Nieh Jung-chen, and Lo Jui-ch'ing are vice premiers.

19. From Jan. 31 to Feb. 9, 1961 the General Political Department (GPD) held a conference on youth work in the armed forces. Among other activities of the conference, the "comrades" present studied directives from the GPD and Marshal Lo Jung-huan. Before the meeting opened Lo issued a directive regarding youth work in the PLA and during the conference Lo was the principal speaker (See *China Youth Daily,* Feb. 11, 1961, in SCMP, No. 2459, pp. 1–2). In Nov. 1961 Lo made the summing up address to an important all-PLA Political Work Conference called by the GPD (NCNA, Nov. 10, 1961, in SCMP, No. 2620, p. 9). In Dec. 1956 General T'an Cheng replaced Lo as director of the GPD. However, there have been no recent references to T'an still holding that post and in September 1962 he was officially removed from the Secretariat, along with the purged General Huang K'o-ch'eng. No reference has yet been found that definitely states that Lo is again director of the GPD.

20. There are some reports that the General Personnel Department was incorporated into the GPD. For example see Chiang I-shan, "The Military Affairs of Communist China," *Communist China 1949–1959,* vol. 1 (Hong Kong: Union Research Institute, 1961), pp. 217, 218.

21. *National Policy Machinery,* p. 14. See NCNA Peking, July 6, 1961, in SCMP, No. 2535, pp. 1–2; *China Youth Daily,* Nov. 30, 1961, in SCMP, No. 2635, pp. 1 and 2. *Cf.* Joffe, *op. cit.* pp. 61–62.

22. NCNA, Peking, Sept. 20, 1958, in SCMP 1868, p. 12.

23. See the Party's 1956 constitution, Article 36, the MAC once demonstrated its authority over the GPD by ordering a reorganization within that department. See *People's Daily,* March 12, 1958, p. 4.

24. *China Youth Daily,* Nov. 18, 1960, in SCMP, No. 2433, p. 2; *Ibid.,* Feb. 11, 1961, in SCMP, No. 2460, p. 6; NCNA, Peking, Feb. 25, 1959, in SCMP, No. 1963, p. 6.

25. NCNA, English, Peking, July 25, 1958, in SCMP No. 1822, p. 1; *Ibid.,* July 6, 1961, in SCMP, No. 2535, p. 2; *China Youth Daily,* Nov. 30, 1961, in SCMP, No. 2635, p. 2; *National Policy Machinery,* p. 13.

26. For examples see NCNA, Peking, Sept. 10, 1958, in SCMP, No. 1868, p. 12; *People's Daily,* May 15, 1962, in SCMP, No. 2753, p. 2; Urumchi, Domestic radio, Mandarin, Jan. 18, 1963.

27. *Chien-fang-chun hau-pao* (PLA Pictorial), June 1961.

28. *People's Daily,* May 15, 1962, in SCMP, No. 2753, p. 2; *China Youth Daily,* Nov. 18, 1960, in SCMP, No. 2433, p. 3.

29. *China Youth Daily,* Nov. 18, 1960 and Feb. 11, 1961, in SCMP, No. 2433, pp. 1–4; No. 2459, pp. 1–2, and No. 2460, p. 6; NCNA, July 6, 1961, in SCMP, 2535, pp. 1–2; *People's Daily,* April 29, 1962, in SCMP, No. 2740, p. 1.

30. NCNA, Peking, July 25, 1958, in SCMP, No. 1822, p. 1; *China Youth Daily,* Nov. 18, 1960 and Feb. 11, 1961, in SCMP, No. 2433, pp. 2–3 and No. 2459, p. 1; NCNA, Peking, July 6, 1961, in SCMP, No. 2535, pp. 1–2; *National Policy Machinery,* p. 14; NCNA, Peking, May 22, 1960, in SCMP, No. 2270, p. 2.

31. See Alice L. Hsieh, *Communist China's Strategy in the Nuclear Era* (Englewood Cliffs, N. J.: Prentice-Hall 1962), pp. 35, 44–45, 81, 99, 112 note, 113, 152 and 177–178. MAC member Nieh Jung-chen is chairman of the Scientific and Technological Commission.

32. NCNA, Peking, Sept. 20, 1958 and Feb. 25, 1959 in SCMP, No. 1868, p. 12 and No. 1963, p. 6; *Hung-ch'i* (Red Flag), No. 15 (Aug. 1, 1959), in *Extracts from Chinese Mainland Magazines* (ECMM), American Consulate General, Hong Kong, No. 182, p. 8; *China Youth Daily,* No. 18, 1960, in SCMP, No. 2433, p. 3.

33. For example see Peking, Domestic radio, Mandarin, March 5, 1963.

Chapter IV
Objectives of Control: The Planned Social Change

A socialist economy is essentially an economy based on state control and planning. Its success or failure, however, depends on the inherent laws of economics rather than ideology. Under the efficient Communist system of control, state planners can conceivably regulate the size of the population as well as its quality and distribution. When a practical problem demands pragmatic actions, the outcome may not always be successful if the best solution runs counter to the ideologically correct one.

John Aird deals mainly with one of such problems, namely, population policy and Communist ideology. Tien, on the other hand, aims to give a careful description of the distribution of population with respect to economic planning. The size of the problem deserves more space than it is given here.

The circularity of Communist thinking is sometimes obvious. Chinese Communists believe that Marxism is basically correct. Hence, close adherence to the essentials of party ideology cannot bring about economic failure. Since economic principles become terribly empirical when statistics are given, Mao's doctrines can neither be seen as revealed truth, nor be socially validated as infallible. Under the circumstances, various trial and error practices must be introduced. Lessons learned from past Soviet experience and from local experiments have to be carefully scrutinized. This may result in a protracted strategy on all frontiers of urban as well as rural economies.

Kenneth Walker and Franz Schurmann give lucid analyses of, and penetrating insight into, the problem of industrial organizations in a Communist economy. Also included in the reading is an official statement on the principles behind urban and rural economic organizations.

Students of Communism often question how economic incentive is provided under such a system. Considerable change has certainly occurred in the Soviet Union in the course of a quarter of a century. Incentive problems usually are related to the state of the economy as well as the economic function of the ideology. The Soviet Union has rapidly been becoming an industrial society in the last decade, and the problems encountered by an industrial society are not met by old answers. In China there still exist some old problems fundamental to traditional Communist ideology. How Peking leaders have been dealing with such basic problems as economic incentives is ably described in the articles by Hoffman and by Nathan.

Problems of Control:
Population Dynamics

16. POPULATION GROWTH AND CONTROL

JOHN S. AIRD

Ten years ago this spring the newly established Communist regime in China began one of the greatest statistical undertakings in Chinese history. For the first time the population of the world's largest country was to be enumerated by modern census methods. When the final census announcement of November 1, 1954 disclosed a figure of 583 million persons on the Mainland as of June 30, 1953, the Chinese Communists boasted that they had succeeded in doing what previous administrations had tried to do and failed: they had finally resolved the age-old question as to the size of the Chinese population. Although some foreign scholars expressed grave doubts, most commentators abroad hailed the census as a great achievement and a further demonstration of the effectiveness of the Chinese Communist administrative system. The prestige of the new regime in the world at large was, on balance, undeniably enhanced. . . .

Sources of Information and Problems of Interpretation

Before we begin to review the circumstances of the 1953 census and the decade since, it is advisable to note certain cautions which must be observed in trying to interpret the current situation in Mainland China. All our information necessarily comes from Mainland sources. Apart from fragments from other Communist bloc countries and the sometimes contradictory reports of visitors to China, most of it comes to us via the publications and news dispatches of the Communist regime. Some of these materials were intended mainly

SOURCE: Selected from John S. Aird, "Population, Planning, and Economic Development," in *Population Bulletin*, XIX, 5 (August 1963), pp. 114–135. Reprinted by permission of the Population Reference Bureau, Inc., Washington, D.C.

for foreign consumption and flavored accordingly. Others were designed for mass audiences at home and may have largely political purposes, not all of which can be divined from here. Still others were addressed to specific segments of the administrative system—technicians, economists, planners, government officials, or Party cadres—and are usually comparatively frank and reliable indicators of how the Communist leaders themselves see their situation. But our information at best flows haltingly, and there are many unfortunate gaps in the source materials. We know nothing of what considerations may be argued in debates within the State Council or the Central Committee. The end result of their deliberations may appear in published directives, but we also know from sudden, unannounced but obviously coordinated administrative actions that at least some executive orders are being delivered through non-public channels.

No standard, universally applicable formula can be devised to compensate automatically for the inevitable biases in our source material. However, as a rule of thumb it is wise to make a deliberate effort to avoid the temptation to take at face value information which suits our inclinations, or to dismiss peremptorily that which does not. It is always advisable to pay particular heed to the source of the information, the circumstances of its release, and the particular group to which it was directed.

Beyond that, patient study of the Mainland scene over time does develop certain faculties of judgment and perspective and a facility in stripping away the dry, dialectical husk of Chinese Communist prose so as to expose the germ of intent within. This does not mean that there will ever be a general consensus among students of contemporary China on all major issues, but on some questions a certain amount of convergence is taking place. Meanwhile, there is something to be said for attempting explicit interpretive syntheses as exploratory devices, which may be re-examined periodically as further information accumulates.

The Socio-Political Context of the 1953 Census

What induced the Chinese Communists to attempt a census in 1953? Their statistical system was rudimentary; trained personnel were lacking, and the administrative apparatus, though capable of acting with great energy, was without experience in the kind of patient, careful work that even simple census-taking requires. Was it really necessary or possible for them to conduct such an operation?

The early years of the Communist regime in China were marked by great confusion and a great show of confidence. The confusion did little to discredit the confidence at that stage, since the revolution was newly instituted and whatever was obviously out of joint in the economy and society of New China could readily be explained as the vestiges of a "feudal" past or the normal turmoil of a great transition, which would presently begin to disappear. Absolute reliance on Marxist-Leninist theory as interpreted and applied to the circumstances of China by Mao Tse-tung gave the Communists, on the one hand, the boldness to attack some of the historic foundations of Chinese Society and, on the other hand, the patience to tolerate with equanimity some delays and disappointments even in their most cherished revolutionary programs. Convinced of the rightness of their cause, they could grant that in some cases they had gone to excess, in others they had been premature, and in still others their work had defects. There was a marked earnestness, almost a modesty, in their admission that they had much to learn, both from other "fraternal" socialist countries and from their own experiences, in perfecting administrative techniques.

About the ultimate attainment of their goals they were persistently optimistic. Their military and political victories were laurels fresh and green, and they enjoyed the profuse admiration of a succession of uncritical visitors from other countries, Communist and non-Communist alike, who were so greatly impressed by the absence of beggary in the streets, theft in the hotels, and spitting on the trains that they extrapolated from these indices an inexorable advance toward great nationhood for China.

The first great social change which the Communists imposed was the "land reform" movement, which was carried forward, mainly during 1949–1952, with as much violence as thoroughness required. In the course of land reform the more depressed sections of the peasantry were given small plots in their own names, and the former landed classes were dispossessed and sometimes executed.

A second major reform was the Marriage Law promulgated in May 1950, which was to end the traditional practice of arranged marriages and to institute a number of improvements in the status of women. The Marriage Law campaign ran at once into serious difficulties of under- and over-enforcement, resulting in a large number of murders and suicides, mainly of women. It has alternately been resumed and allowed to lapse in subsequent years. Otherwise, the period from 1949 through 1952 was generally marked by efforts to consolidate the power of the regime, to crush potential "counterrevolutionary" forces, to establish a centralized administrative system, and to complete the postwar rehabilitation of the economy.

Beginning with 1953, great new developments were scheduled to take place. This year was to mark the start of the first of a series of five-year economic development programs, during which the "socialist transformation" of agriculture, industry, trade, and handicrafts was to be instituted and systematically pushed forward. In preparation for the First Five-Year Plan, the admittedly inadequate statistical department set up in 1950 under the Government Administrative Council, was replaced by the new State Statistical Bureau, which was made responsible for the coordination of all government statistical work. Nationwide elections to select representatives to the local, provincial, and national "people's congresses" were also to be held in 1953. The National People's Congress would have the task of ratifying the new national constitution.

Within the hierarchy itself this year also saw the beginning of several "reform" drives, one against "bureaucratism" in government and another against "commandism" within the Party apparatus. For the people at large a campaign was opened in September to increase production and at the same time to practice strict austerity in consumption of consumer goods. On top of all this it was decided to take a census of the population which would, according to a directive of April 6, 1953, signed by Chou En-lai, provide the basis for the registration of voters for the national elections and supply statistics needed for national planning. All in all, it was a year of great expectations! . . .

Purposes of the 1953 Census

Whatever may be said about the actual level of accuracy of the census data, the abundant press materials from Mainland China suffice to show that without friction, and at considerable cost a tremendous effort was expended by planners, technicians, administrators, and field workers in order to overcome the manifold difficulties of counting the Chinese people. So great administrative resources would hardly have been allocated to it unless the regime regarded it as of considerable importance. What were their reasons?

Some commentators, noting the greater attention to political than to planning purposes in the propaganda accompanying the census and elections, have suggested that the census was primarily a political affair and even that the figures were a political fiction. But neither inference will bear close examination. There is no question that there were political implications in the quasi-judicial procedures for investigation of voter qualifications, involving posted voter lists, public denunciations, and "trials" before "people's tribunals" of those persons who might be disqualified because of past class or political affiliations. Insofar as this ominous procedure was actually carried out, it would have afforded an opportunity to ferret out dissident elements and bring them under closer police and Party surveillance. But neither this objective nor the registration of voters would have required a *de jure* census of the total population by age and sex. Voters had only to be 18 years old or older at the date of the election in order to vote, and could vote wherever they were currently living, regardless of their place of permanent residence. No general census-taking was involved in the voter registrations carried out in connection with local elections in 1956, 1958, 1960, and 1963.

Furthermore, while the elections of 1953–1954 might have accomplished some political purposes, it is clear that the regime itself never intended to permit the National People's Congress to exercise any significant authority. Its function from the outset was mainly to endorse the decisions already handed down by the Party and the government. A few non-Communist deputies who took occasion to criticize the administration or make alternative suggestions during early sessions of the Congress were soon set straight. It is difficult to believe that the regime would have felt the need of a census to establish fair representation in an organ of approbation. As for the emphasis in press propaganda on the importance of the census for the national elections, this may have reflected merely the greater simplicity for propaganda purposes of political explanations compared with the relative complexity of arguments based on the advantages of population data for national planning. Once the elections were over, the political argument seems to have given way largely to the planning argument.

Not only the technical staff and administrators of the regime but also the leaders themselves attached great importance to the idea of a planned economy. The top Party figures may not have had a very lucid conception of the complexities of long-range economic planning or of just how population data were to be used in the process. Mao and his lieutenants have generally shown more aptitude for the subtle arts of political manipulation and ideological homiletics than for the more difficult and uncertain strategies of applied economics. But they had, after all, taken the decision to initiate China's First Five-Year Plan in 1953, and there is little doubt but that they relied on planned development of the economy both for the validation of their political faith and for the restoration of China's national greatness. If the great socialist transformation which was about to get under way required a preliminary national inventory, and if a population census was an essential part of the stock-taking, the importance of the census was established and the great outlay of costs and effort justified. Hence, in the decision to take a census, planning purposes were probably paramount.

Population Policies and Figures Before the Census Period

As for the role of population as a factor in economic development, the attitudes of leadership circles in Communist China seem from the earliest years to have been somewhat ambivalent. Was China's unquestionably large population to be viewed as a resource or as a consumer of resources and thus a liability? In part, the issue seemed to depend upon how large the population was and how fast it was growing. But when the Chinese Communists took control of the Mainland none of these questions could be answered, and the lack of answers aroused both curiosity and concern.

The party leadership were acutely conscious of the historical argument of Marx against Malthus and also of the frequently voiced opinions of many eminent Chinese and Western scholars that China's population problems would always pose a serious threat to her national welfare. In industrial Europe Marx had attacked Malthus and claimed victory, but in the cities and villages of the New China, as in no other part of the world, it was Malthus who challenged Marx. However confident the Party leaders might have been of the ultimate outcome, they could not have ignored the fact that the confrontation was momentous not only for themselves but for the world Communist movement.

But if there was less than complete unanimity among the top leadership about the effects of population growth on the rate of development of a socialist economy, the public posture of the regime was necessarily a rigid one. The prediction of the U.S. State Department's "white paper" in 1948 that overpopulation would remain a problem regardless of what government ruled on the Mainland was denounced by a New China News Agency release of 1949 as "anti-revolutionary." China's large population was "a good thing." Even if it multiplied several times there would be no problem. Since of all things in the world man is the most valuable, the revolution under Communist Party leadership could soon produce an economy of abundance. "All pessimistic statements," the release concluded, "are entirely groundless." Thus warned, those who might have harbored pessimistic thoughts wisely forbore to make them public.

Whether optimistic or otherwise, from 1950 onward there were indications of a considerable interest in government circles in the size and rate of growth of the population. As soon as the administrative machinery of the new regime was set up, the Ministry of Interior and the statistical office under the Government Administrative Council began to collect reports on population from local administrative units. When they had compiled what they received, the figures for most provinces were not much different from the Nationalist figures for 1947. If the traditional local population registers had been consulted for the purpose, they had not in most areas been kept up to date in the meantime; more probably the local official merely sought out whatever totals had last been reported and submitted these as the best available under the circumstances.

Apparently the responsible statisticians and officials in the Ministry of Interior and the statistical office were not satisfied with these figures. It was later reported that they were revised upward six times between 1950 and the end of 1952 and that even then they were considered unreliable and incomplete. Foreign observers have also suspected political motivations behind these revisions. However, there is no sign that the top leadership regarded the order of magnitude of the earliest of these figures as too low for political reasons, much less that they were anxious to have them increased. Quite the contrary, during 1950 both Liu Shao-ch'i and Chou En-lai issued statements endorsing figures under 500 million.

The later revisions, particularly those issued during 1952, showed a sharp increase, until as of the end of the year the total figure for the Mainland released by the Ministry of Interior was just under 570 million, only about 15 million below the subsequently announced census total as of midyear 1953. Some of the revised figures were incorporated in successive editions of the *Atlas of the People's Republic of China* during 1952 and 1953, but, so far as available materials show, virtually no notice was taken during those years of the sudden rise in the reported population totals either in the general press or in New China News Agency dispatches.

If, as the official position on population maintained, a large population was a positive asset for China, or if, as some foreign critics surmised, the regime had inflated the population total for propaganda purposes, the failure to exploit the new figures is hard to explain. It seems more reasonable to suppose that, as Communist officials later claimed, there was basic distrust of these figures on the part of some government statisticians, and it is also likely that the top leadership, despite their doctrinaire position on the advantages of a large population, were in no hurry to greet the first indications of a still larger one. They evidently preferred to await the results of the forthcoming census.

Population Work During Land Reform

If, however, the central authorities made no effort to induce local officials to inflate the reported population figures, why did these figures rise? The official explanation was that during the land reform operations local cadres in charge of the movement had to do some counting of local populations in rural areas in order to allocate appropriately the land taken from large landowners, and that the development of agricultural tax records required further investigations and revisions. In urban areas there was also an attempt by the security police from the first days of the regime to revive urban population registers as a means of controlling population movement and of maintaining political surveillance. These efforts were formally authorized and standardized in July 1951, but the work was not expected to be completed immediately, and during the census planning in early spring 1953 it was admitted that the registration system was still not functioning in some cities.

The population investigations conducted in connection with these administrative activities would have been incidental to the purposes in hand, and therefore probably unstandardized and incomplete. Few details are available on how the work was carried out and by what kind of personnel. The land reform operations, though they followed general instructions from Peking, varied according to local conditions and were not under close central supervision. In later years Hsüeh Mu-ch'iao was to complain that when the State Statistical Bureau attempted to compile agricultural data for this period, they found the land reform records so inadequate as to be totally useless. However, if the land reform population work was, as seems probable, largely an updating of the traditional rural population registers, the results of that part of the effort might have been preserved though other kinds of data and details of methods were lost.

Even unsophisticated methods pursued under the tense conditions which must have prevailed among most sections of the rural population during land reform might have yielded a reasonably close head-count of those who survived the experience and did not flee into the cities. Less may be said about the circumstances or effectiveness of population work done in connection with the reestablishment of tax rolls and the urban registration, but taken all together the meagre evidence suggests that the rising population figures of the precensal period can neither be adequately explained nor summarily dismissed.

The Ministry of Health Surveys of Vital Rates

Of much greater significance as a measure of official interest in population is the series of experimental vital rates surveys conducted in various parts of China from 1950 until near the end of 1954. These were not the by-product of purely administrative efforts. They were initiated under the direction of the Ministry of Health and were expressly intended to supply information on the level of the birth, death, and natural increase rates in China. By the end of 1952 these investigations were being carried out in areas with a total population of about 7.5 million. At that time the Ministry of Health apparently asked the Government Administrative Council for permission to expand the work and presented a draft of proposed vital registration regulations for the Council's endorsement. The Council's decision must have been disappointing for, although the Health Ministry investigations continued, their coverage was not significantly enlarged.

In October 1953 the State Statistical Bureau directed the Health Ministry to reduce the number of both urban and rural experimental districts, and in November 1954 the Bureau finally recommended the termination of the investigations on the grounds that they duplicated the registration work of the public security police in urban areas and of the projected rural registration system then being set up under the Ministry of Interior on the basis of census records. The Bureau argued that people should not be required to register births and deaths both with the health agencies and at the regular registration centers, and that the investigation of cause of death by the local health departments created unnecessary delays in issuing death certificates and burial permits. Toward the end of 1954 the vital rates experimentation of the Ministry of Health was discontinued.

The arguments presented by the State Statistical Bureau were plausible enough and consistent both with the increasing concern of the Bureau over duplication of statistical services among branches of government and also with the proper exercise of the Bureau's authority as the coordinator of government statistical activities. But just a few months later in January 1955 the principal statistical journal of the time carried a signed article in which the writer, after restating the Bureau's case, went on to introduce an altogether different and highly significant argument. Vital statistics as compiled by the health people, he argued, were essentially "bourgeois" and Malthusian, since they dealt with vital phenomena in biological terms rather than as indicators of economic progress, and so inadvertently supported the inclination of certain reactionary circles who would use them to promote Malthusian propaganda. The abolition of the vital rates experiments was thus a blow to these bourgeois elements!

The argument is a curious one, especially since the census announcements which had appeared during 1954 had been accompanied by reports of vital rates investigations on a much larger scale (though apparently less sophisticated) than those of the Ministry of Health. A total sample of over 30 million was supposed to have been the basis for the widely quoted natural increase rate of 2.0 per cent, which was used by contenders on both sides of the population question for several years to come. Moreover, birth, death, and natural increase rates for specified local areas, for particular large cities, and for the country as a whole which were no less Malthusian in their implications, continued to appear through at least 1957, apparently based on data from the Public Security and Interior ministries.

The significance of this argument lies not so much in its peculiar logic as in its implication that some persons within the regime felt that research on population lent itself too readily to a Malthusian viewpoint, and that, unless the propaganda applications could be strictly controlled, it was better not to have such research at all. Apparently this view was strong enough at the close of 1954, shortly after the census results were published, to put an end to the special vital rates surveys.

The Great Debate on Population Policy

The termination of the vital rates surveys coincided with the opening of a great public debate on population policy, in the course of which the anxieties and ambivalence of the leadership over the population question became increasingly apparent. The public debate evidently had its private counterpart within official circles, which had been going on even earlier. The first overt signs of the latter may be read in the great quantities of anti-Malthusian argument which accompanied the census commentaries from August 1954 onward. The first voice raised in public support of a government-sponsored birth control campaign was that of Deputy Shao Li-tzu before the newly convened National People's Congress in September 1954. Soon afterward it became obvious that the anti-Malthusian and pro-contraception arguments together constituted the official stand in the population policy debate. Much ingenious explanation was presented in the press to show that these two elements were not actually contradictory. Yet it was obvious that the official position was no longer that which the regime had held since 1949. What had caused the change?

It cannot be assumed, as has sometimes been suggested, that surprise over the census results drove the Chinese Communists to seek immediately to control population growth. Actually, the Government Administrative Council had already directed the Ministry of Health to "help the masses practice birth control" as early as August 1953, though nothing was heard about this decision at the time. The Ministry had also drawn up "measures" concerning contraception in July 1954. Nevertheless, it is quite possible that the census results added cogency to arguments for a national birth control campaign which had already gained some support among the top leadership on the strength of the evidence from the pre-censal population counts and the vital rates surveys.

In the early stages of the campaign the official line was that birth control was being provided by the government in response to the demands of the people and in the interests of maternal and child health. Economic arguments were presented in individualistic terms: families with too many children could not afford to care for them adequately. The notion that the state might also have an interest in a lower population growth rate was seldom broached before 1956, but in September of that year Chou En-lai told a visting Indian agricultural delegation that India and China were alike troubled by too many people on too little land. At the Eighth Congress of the Chinese Communist Party during the same month Chou declared that "to protect women and children and bring up and educate our younger generation in a way conducive to the health and prosperity of the nation, we agree that a due measure of birth control is desirable."

From this time on other people began to relate population growth to China's economic situation. Mao's famous speech on "contradictions" among the people given in February 1957 had apparently included a strongly worded statement that the Chinese people as a whole should begin to control their fertility, but for some reason in the subsequently published versions of the speech it had been reduced to the cryptic observation that "our country has many people; it is a good thing, but, of course, there are also difficulties." Early in March 1957 Health Minister Li Teh-ch-uan justified the birth control program on grounds that China was "a large, very populous country," and later in the year several authoritative spokesmen on economic matters ascribed to overpopulation a major share of China's economic difficulties.

Of the difficulties there was no lack. There had been bad crop years in 1954, 1956, and 1957, complaints of food shortages were widespread, and an effort to enlist, somewhat belatedly in the spring of 1957, the support of non-Communists in dealing with the country's problems by permitting them a period of free speech had unleashed a flood of hostile attacks on the Party, including suggestions that the government had failed and should be replaced. Certain non-Communist scholars had intimated that the ultimate success of socialism depended upon attainment of a high degree of industrialization, which China might be unable to achieve so long as population growth was uncontrolled; the latter prospect, they pointed out, was a dim one, if the experience of other countries be taken as a guide. During the "great rectification movement" of the midsummer 1957 these and other critics of the Party were denounced and silenced, but the birth control campaign proceeded with, if anything, a rising intensity and an increasing impatience with signs of popular resistance. An unmistakable note of compulsion entered the official propaganda line.

Early in the campaign there had been public assurances that birth control, being intended only for those whose private circumstances made it advantageous, was a purely voluntary affair. But in the later stages the barrage of propaganda, the obligatory discussion meetings, and the uninvited visits of health workers urging couples to use contraceptives seemed to suggest that while birth control was voluntary, volunteering was almost obligatory. When some people complained that the health workers were interfering in their private affairs and that the government was now trying to control even the number of children they could have, they got little sympathy from the authorities. An article in a Peking paper in May 1958 dismissed such complaints with the statement that since birth control had a bearing on the prosperity of the nation, it was not a purely private matter, hence the Party and the government could not help interfering.

Other arguments insisted that the birth control campaign was for the benefit of the people, hence an expression of the will of the people, which no individual had the right to resist. And so in the last months of the campaign public health cadres in Shanghai and Wuhan were pledging themselves to have no more children during the Second Five-Year Plan period and inviting "emulation" by other offices.

The clearly compulsive character of the campaign in its later stages reflected increasing apprehensions within the regime over the pressure of population on economic growth in general and the food supply in particular. The official propaganda line still maintained that under socialism population growth constituted no fundamental problem. But agriculture had not responded to collectivization as expected and food problems persisted. Mao, wearing the mantle of Marx, had encountered Malthus in the paddy fields and found him a more formidable adversary than anticipated.

Population Problems and Food Production

The first response of the leadership to this challenge was to accelerate the collectivization of agriculture, which had begun slowly on a voluntary basis in 1952 but had encountered major popular resistance by 1955. Some peasants wanted to withdraw from the cooperatives. Suddenly during the latter half of 1955 the cooperative movement, which had been scheduled to take place gradually over 15 years, was rushed to completion, and, by the end of 1956, 96 per cent of all peasant households were reported to have joined what were termed "higher" agricultural people's cooperatives, which meant that property and tools were owned in common, peasant labor was centrally managed, and one did not have the option of voluntary withdrawal. Resentment doubtless ran high among the peasants, upon whom some rather menacing methods of persuasion had been used to secure the sharp increase in membership. Convincing arguments have been adduced by foreign scholars to the effect that the forced collectivization drive led to a significant deterioration of the whole agricultural situation. In many areas livestock was slaughtered, sabotage and neglect of collective properties and equipment were widespread, the area under food crops declined, and, following the poor harvest of 1956, hoarding of grain with the connivance of local cadres was suspected.

The peasants were quoted as saying that if the government really cared for the people it should let them have enough to eat; the authorities replied that if the peasants put their own interests ahead of those of the State, they would be abandoning socialism and with it all promise of a better future. Some intellectuals said that the peasants' lot was no better than before "liberation." The Party apologists answered that the grain situation was "tense," but that according to official statistics the peasants were eating better than ever, hence the food difficulties must be largely due to wasteful consumption or were merely the malicious lies of "rightist" elements.

The economic analysts sometimes balanced precariously between these views. T'an Chen-lin, a deputy secretary-general of the Party Central Committee, conceded that with food statistics so inadequate it was hard to show whether or by how much the lot of the peasants *had* been improved. As 1957 was drawing to a close, the reports of the year's harvest were again disappointing; even in the official figures the rate of increase in food production fell well below the officially accepted rate of population growth. From the latter part of 1956 through the first months of 1958, the great debate over population policy was paralleled by another great debate on food problems. . . .

The Nature of the First Five-Year Plan

At the start of the First Five-Year Plan period in 1953 neither plans nor statistics were ready, yet the regime was in haste to get on with its general program of national economic development. In July 1955, a year and a half after the beginning of the period it was supposed to cover, the Plan was finally published. In it the planners explicitly recognized the need for "unified planning," for maintaining a proper balance in rate of development between agriculture and industry, and between heavy industry and light industry, for planning within the limits imposed by the funds available for investment, and for coordinating local development plans with those of the central ministries. They expected that there would be difficulties due to shortages of technical personnel and equipment and that lack of planning experience and incompleteness of statistical data would affect the "accuracy" of the plans. But they were already committed ideologically to the ultimate planning objectives and to the policies which were to attain them; these were not matters for statistical evaluation.

The First Five-Year Plan boldly assigned top priority to the development of heavy industry, and particularly steel production, which was regarded as the key to rapid industrialization. Agriculture, which was to be the source of most of China's investment capital and which, in order to carry the burden of industrialization, would have to fulfill and overfulfill production targets all along the line, was to accomplish these wonders largely on the strength of collectivization, which had reportedly been shown to increase output by 10 to 20 per cent within the first year or two and would sustain uninterrupted growth thereafter. When agriculture faltered, the response was more intensive and more rapid collectivization, but not a change in the basic investment priorities.

By the end of 1957 it was apparent without statistical demonstration that, as far as agriculture was concerned, the First Five-Year Plan was largely a failure. In industry the official statistics registered striking advances in some types of production, though even here not all targets had been fulfilled and industrial production figures, though generally more reliable than those for agriculture, were also subject to exaggeration. While it was possible for the comparatively small state-managed industrial sector, aided by special allocations of material and labor resources and technical assistance from the Soviet Union, to make rapid advances, some of these developments disturbed the balances within the industrial sector.

Without up-to-date and accurate statistics, coordinated development within or between the major sectors of the economy was impossible. Many of the industrial production quotas were met without regard to their effects on other industries requiring the same raw materials, without regard for the relative demand for the products produced, and without much attention to the quality of the products or the economic use of manpower and skills in their production. The production of some types of vehicles and machinery was not supported by a comparable production of spare parts, so that when breakdowns occurred, either the machines were idled or other units had to be dismantled piecemeal to keep others functioning.

Some industries fluctuated between full production and idleness because of unstable supplies. Certain types of heavy industry requiring large amounts of raw materials were expanded until the transport network upon which they depended could not sustain them at full operating capacity. Emergency assignments of transport facilities to rescue industries in distress sometimes interrupted the normal flow of food and consumer goods. Thus, mismanagement, imbalances, and dislocations led to inefficient use of materials, productive facilities, and labor power. Quota fulfillment became so much an end in itself that plans, incentives, and targets were in some cases a contributing cause of economic waste. Corrective action often was taken only after the signs of disruption were already acute. As one Chinese economist remarked, "the Comrades proceed by trial and error."

Where a single, monolithic political system controls absolutely the entire economy and where, in addition, the central authority sets out to transform all sectors of a backward economy by a series of revolutionary strokes not previously proven in a comparable socioeconomic environment, trial and error becomes an especially perilous procedure. The whole economy is risked in the trials and the whole country suffers from the errors. Furthermore, inexperienced planning, coupled with defective statistics, greatly compounds the hazard.

Socialism, Lenin had said, is largely a matter of statistics. But without reliable statistics for evaluation of policy there is a tendency to rely more heavily on ideology for guidance in planning. In Mao's China there seems to have been uncertainty at the highest decision-making levels about the proper relationship between statistics and ideology. Were statistics the test or the proof of the rightness of policy? As statistical evidence began to be employed during the latter part of the First Five-Year Plan period in criticism of the Party's decisions, certain Party leaders began to suspect a fundamental antithesis between statistical objectivity and ideological orthodoxy, and they wanted the subordination of statistics to ideology clearly established. In 1958 this viewpoint was victorious, and the triumph of ideology, first over statistics then over common sense, culminated in the "great leap forward" and the "people's communes," which brought the national economy to the brink of disaster. Neither of these incredible policies can be understood without some conception of the effect of ideology on decision-making in China and on the character of the administrative system.

The Role of Ideology

Ideology is not, of course, inherently antithetical to objectivity. All peoples depend upon ideology in some degree and for certain purposes. It may help to make explicit the prevailing values in a society, establish their relative priorities, adjust internal inconsistencies, and define the relationship of means to ends. But ideology may also invade the cognitive sphere, prescribe its own social, economic, and political reality, and demand simple and unquestioning allegiance. Where such an ideology combines with an authoritarian political structure, there is also the danger that it may invest the leadership with the exclusive right to interpretation and revelation. Where the power of that structure is represented by a single supreme leader, he may acquire first the vestments of hierarchy, then the mantle of prophesy, and finally the aura of infallibility. At this point the contradiction between ideology and reality may so mismatch administrative response with circumstantial challenge as to prejudice national survival.

The role of ideology in Communist China is not actually that simple. In Peking as elsewhere, ideology serves partly to rationalize the power structure and command obedience. The leaders may appear to walk the straight and narrow, but they have been known to shrink back when the path of faith led straight to a precipice. Despite inherent tendencies toward rigidity, a certain element of flexibility enters the system through discretionary considerations of "timeliness" and "appropriateness." The ultimate goals remain unchanged, but the inspired leader may slow or increase the pace of prescribed changes or devise new instrumentalities under the dictates of expediency.

Once questions of timeliness and appropriateness are raised, however, a margin of doubt is opened up between means and ends. In 1956 and 1957 the uncertainty was reflected within the leadership not only in the debates over food and population policy but also in the conviction at the highest levels that agricultural collectivization might have gone too far too fast. In

September 1957 the Party Central Committee announced that large cooperatives had proven unsuited to current conditions in China and that for the next ten years smaller units would prevail.

But too much doubt may undermine the authority of ideology and the power of leadership, as was demonstrated during the brief interval of open criticism of the Party and its programs during the spring of 1957. The "great rectification movement" of mid-1957, which ended the criticism and began to restore ideological certainty to the press, may have foreshadowed the plunge into ideological extremism with the "leap forward" and "people's communes" of 1958. In May 1958, just as birth control was about to become a public duty, Mao and Liu Shao-ch'i declared that poverty and a large population were both positive assets which could generate unprecedented revolutionary fervor and creativity. In August 1958, less than a year after the Party pledge on the stability of small rural cooperatives, the commune "movement" was sweeping the country.

The "Great Leap Forward"

The "leap forward" movement was launched early in 1958 with comparatively limited objectives. In February a warning had been sounded to the statistical cadres that their work lacked political enthusiasm and was not providing sufficient support for production. Through the spring and summer the political pressures on the statisticians mounted until finally they were told point blank that their job was to provide the figures which the Party wanted, and that the objective of statistics was to spur on the masses to higher levels of production.

The net effect of this change in statistical policy quickly undid years of patient work by Hsüeh and the professionals in the State Statistical Bureau and led to the inflated agricultural production figures, which were published as official by the regime in April 1959 and revised downward in August, at a cost of considerable international embarrassment. Yet in December 1959 the statisticians were still being warned that objectivity in statistics was dangerous since it could be used to expose the Party to the ridicule of its enemies.

The Party's decision to transform the statistical system into a magical spinning wheel to convert straw into gold and its willingness to bank on the gold illustrate in the sharpest terms the power of ideology to engender both a profound mistrust of objectivity and a virtual addiction to fantasy. The glittering images of backyard blast furnaces, peasant-made ball bearings, shepherd professors of agriculture, deep plowing, close planting, technological invention by the masses, and a host of other Herculean endeavors proved the power of the masses under Party leadership. Miracles could be accomplished by those who "let politics take command" and who "dared to think, dared to speak, dared to act." Twenty years were as a day. Economic law was overthrown. By act of will, wish became fact.

The belief in the absolute correctness of the Party policy and the infallibility of Chairman Mao's vision and judgment reached new heights. Except for a few brief periods, it had always been the fault of cadres of intermediate and lower rank if the directives of the Party miscarried. When the failure of a program reached such proportions that, statistics or none, the sound of clashing gears could be heard in Peking above the burble of reports about overfulfilled targets, the fault must be found with those responsible for its implementation. The local cadres had misunderstood orders, lacked thoroughness, gone to extremes, failed to take account of local conditions, failed to adhere strictly to their instructions, had not relied on the masses, or had conspired with the masses against the state. However conscientious they might try to be, only by succeeding could they avoid the wrath from above. But with the regime perennially confident of success, counterfeit achievement stood a good chance of getting by in remittances to Peking. With typical bureaucratic solicitude for the humors of the front office, the local cadres found it expedient to see to it that only good news traveled upward. Once in possession of the statistical system during the Leap Forward, they quickly learned to say it with numbers.

The Post-"Leap" Drift in Domestic Policy

In Peking, Mao himself had for the first time made a strong personal identification with specific items of the Party program; the "leap" and the communes were credited to his personal genius. This meant a greater than usual desire to confirm the rightness of official policy and still less freedom to alter the posture in which it was frozen. As the short harvests of the grim post-"leap" years began to compel practical adjustments, the official propaganda progressively lost touch not merely with economic reality but with the actual direction of administrative changes. The communes were extolled while they were actually being dismantled. The "leap" was still being praised as having laid the foundation for great advances in the future while the Party was implicitly admitting the failure of the "leap" by calling for moderation and gradualism. Finally, as industrial expansion stalled and industrial production was being cut back in many sectors, it was discovered that Mao had said all along that agriculture was the foundation of the national economy. As investment priorities were finally being revised to favor agriculture, the Party cadres were advised to "study the writings of Chairman Mao."

How long administrative practice and public posture can continue to face opposite directions it is impossible to say, but this is not the kind of situation in which brilliant new inspirations are received and brave new directions tried. A gray sobriety has enfolded and suffused the once burning aspirations. The day of deliverance, once near, is now afar off. The Party journal talks nostalgically of how in the days of Yenan and the Long March, the Party leaders, by holding fast to the faith, had survived conditions more discouraging than the present, but this is not the happy retrospect with which in former years the Party periodically reviewed its past.

Meanwhile, as major efforts are directed toward producing food for the population, statistical data are scarcer than ever. China's population is still "600 million" (the 1953 census world total of Chinese) or "650 million" (a rounding of the last official total of 647 million for the Mainland as of year-end 1957). Asked by a Western reporter in 1960 about China's rising population growth rate, Chou En-lai replied briefly that it "hovers around"

2 per cent. In the same year Mao reportedly told Viscount Montgomery that the annual increase in population was about 10 million a year, a figure equivalent to a rate of about 1.5 per cent using the official year-end population total for 1957. Among the leaders, only Ch'en Yi has talked of 700 million, which even the official estimates should have passed several years ago, and lesser writers in the Chinese press have generally left this figure strictly alone. This is not the time to call attention to the size of China's population.

Since early 1962 the press has once again taken up the subjects of birth control, vasectomy, and delayed marriage, this time with relatively greater emphasis on delayed marriage than in the campaign of 1956–58. Until recently there was no sign of the energetic publicity, high-level endorsement, and compulsion which marked the former campaign; however, a current news item from Shanghai suggests that the regime may be about to attempt once again a massive assault on the birth rate. Given the statements of Mao and Liu in 1958 on the blessings of a large population, the resumption of a full-scale birth control drive at this time would be a most significant indication of the further erosion of "leap forward" confidence. Meanwhile all eyes anxiously watch the weather and the harvest from year to year.

In foreign policy the voice of China rings out strong and clear in the assertion of a hard ideological position. Communist China's intransigence in international relations toward the West, toward India, and toward other bloc nations conveys a certain impression of strength in a context in which the question of another census of the Mainland would seem to have little relevance. However, a 1963 census might have signified that the regime was at last ready to confront in realistic terms China's basic questions of population and economic development.

However, given the present conditions on the Chinese mainland, a census is probably both impractical and impossible. The Peking *Peoples' Daily,* for June 30, 1963 contains not a word about censuses, past or prospective. In Mainland China, this is not a census year.

17.   INTERNAL POPULATION MIGRATION*

H. YUAN TIEN

Communist China reported a population of 582.6 million in their 1953 census. Because of this huge and still growing population, the focus of concern has

SOURCE: Reprinted from H. Yuan Tien, "The Demographic Significance of Organized Population Transfers in Communist China," in *Demography,* I (November 1964), pp. 220–226. Reprinted by permission of the Population Association of America.

* Part of a research project on Chinese population policies undertaken in Hong Kong during 1961–62 on a grant from the Social Science Research Council.

understandably been upon the need for limiting population growth. This pre-occupation with population numbers has consequently encouraged the belief that Communist China has had no population policy, except during the brief period in 1957–59 when concerted efforts were made to promote birth control.[1] On the contrary, communist China has initiated and implemented a large number of other policy decisions relating to population.

Population growth aside, moreover, decisions must be and have been taken with respect to the ways in which the existing population of 600 million may be accommodated, fed, and gainfully employed. Of obvious importance in the context of the sustenance of existing population is agricultural expansion which, in China, as in many emerging nations, has also been called upon to sustain industrialization. Agricultural expansion means either or both of the two things: (1) to increase the yield per unit of land under cultivation, and (2) to bring additional land into cultivation (land reclamation).

Over 95 per cent of China's population is concentrated on about 40 per cent of the land area of China lying below a hypothetical line drawn from Aihui in Heilung-kiang in the Northeast to T'eng-chung in Yunnan in the Southwest. In terms of agricultural expansion, this "uneven" distribution inspires population transfers from areas of high density (or areas of population surplus) to areas of low density.

The Evolution of the Official Position

Both before and since the turn of the century, possible reclamation of waste-land in China's northeast, northwest, and other border regions has held the attention of many in the country. After the establishment of the Republic in 1912, the first piece of agrarian legislation was, in fact, entitled *"Regulations Concerning the Reclamation of National Wasteland,"* which was first promul-gated by the Peking government in March, 1914. After the Nationalists came into power in 1927, they established a Ministry of Agriculture and Mining in 1928. In the same year, the *First National Program for the Development of Agriculture* was adopted and affirmed the principle of the reclamation of wasteland. At the National Congress on Agricultural Economics and Policy held in Nanking late in 1929, it was resolved that "the Ministry shall establish bureaus in the northwest, northeast, southeast and other places where wastelands may be utilized for agricultural purposes."[2] Relatively little was achieved during the two decades that followed: the Japanese occupation of Manchuria, the Sino-Japanese War, and the Civil War of 1946–49 prevented their implementa-tion.

After 1949, Communist China adopted a similar though much more ambitious program of land reclamation. In the *National Programme for Agricultural Development,* 1956–1967, it was stated that "in the twelve years starting from 1956 the area cultivated by state farms should be increased from the 1955 figure of over *13 million mou to about 100 million mou. Wherever conditions permit, land reclamation should be carried out by organized new settlers."*[3]

Of course, in recent years in Communist China, population shifts (i.e., migra-tion) have not all been government-sponsored. The beginning of the post-1949 population policy in China, in fact, had much to do with the "spontaneous" or "blind" out-migration from rural areas to cities which came to official notice some time in 1952.[4] Given the reported size of the rural population in Communist China, should only 1 per cent of the 500 million rural population change their place of work and residence from the country to the city, it would mean that some 5,000,000 people would require employment and accommodation in the cities annually.[5] In terms of either agricultural development or urban administration, this out-migration posted, in the official view, real threats. Accordingly, measures were formulated to deal with it, and they were to assume the utilization of rural manpower on or near the land rather than permitting out-migration from rural areas to the cities.[6] Along with the reorganization of socio-economic life in the villages, the policy of the retention of rural population was to be realized through the intensive application of manpower in agriculture and in projects of afforestation, irrigation schemes, village road repairs, handicrafts and the expansion of subsidiary occupations and preliminary processing of their products. Thus, the official approach to the population problem was in terms of better organization and effective employment of rural manpower, and is clearly "institutional."[7]

However, two additional problems had also to be faced: (1) the disposition of rural migrants who found their way into the cities, and (2) the natural increase of the urban population itself. To complement the policy of the retention of the rural population, and to meet the two additional problems, a policy of organized population transfers was introduced in the late spring of 1955. The immediate objectives were: (a) the removal to rural areas of rural in-migrants to the cities, and (b) the relocation of a substantial number of urban residents. The latter objective was pursued, not only because of urban congestion, but also because of the need for educated personnel at the village level. Along with the poor and unemployed, graduates of the primary and secondary schools were also mobilized to go to the countryside, and were to be assigned to cultural, educational, accounting and statistical jobs.[8] In order to curb further out-flow from the villages, the following measures were put into effect: a continuous population register, centralized labor hiring procedures, food rationing in the cities, a system of paid annual home leaves for workers who left their spouses and parents in the countryside, and railway checkpoints to turn back unauthorized out-migrants.[9]

The removal of in-migrants from the cities initially meant their return to their villages. Whatever the causes of their out-migration, the re-absorption of the persons sent back from the cities into the village economy presented serious problems. The rural population had itself continued to grow and land available for cultivation and employment opportunities remained limited. Thus, ways had to be found to accommodate and utilize the surplus rural population plus those who were removed from the cities. In 1955 and the following few years, organized population transfers, therefore, involved agricultural settlements in areas of low population density such as Manchuria, Inner Mongolia, Kansu, and Sinkiang.[10]

Policy Implementation and Implications

Innumerable factors help to shape the making of a nation's population policy.[11] In the case of Communist China, agricultural settlement in areas of low population density is not an exception. In one of the discussions of this issue, for instance, it was said that the Northwestern region and other border provinces of China are only sparsely inhabited by minority populations (non-Han Chinese), and are characterized by a low cultural level. After a period of planned migration and land reclamation, it was expected that these areas would become prosperous, and cultural development would then advance at the same pace as in other parts of the country.[12] In fact, between 1949 and 1955, projects were instituted in Sinkiang and other areas to reclaim wasteland and to improve the areas under cultivation. One major difference between the pre-1955 projects and those after 1955 lies in the fact that military personnel were used almost exclusively in the former period. Previously they were part of the forces involved in the pacification of these regions, and their employment in reclamation work was to aid the local population and, at the same time, to become relatively self-sufficient with respect to food and other supplies. While some discharged or demobilized soldiers were included in post-1955 agricultural settlement projects most of the settlers appear to have been *bona fide* civilians.

Land reclamation also was "to increase the production of grain and industrial crops for the state."[13] Apart from political, military, social and economic considerations, moreover, it was also believed to be demographically significant. One of the arguments in favor of land reclamation was the possible adjustment of China's spatially "imbalanced" population distribution.[14]

It is axiomatic that land reclamation and population transfers are necessarily inseparable. However, it should be made clear that the relationship between them is a variable one. Where mechanical means are employed in reclamation work, the number of people needed per unit of land reclaimed would be small; conversely, other things being equal, a greater number of people would be required in the absence of power-driven implements. Here lies the important question of intensive agriculture vs. extensive agriculture. Would it be sound to transfer a large number of people to give each of them a small lot of reclaimed land? Would it be preferable to assign the reclaimed land to large-scale agricultural and allied uses with the aid of extensive mechanical equipment? To answer these and other questions, a closer look at the Chinese experience in land reclamation in recent years is clearly warranted.

In support of the post-1949 reclamation policy, the government repeatedly stated that the vast territory of China consists of 15,000,000,000 *mou* of land, of which 1,600,000,000 *mou* are under cultivation, amounting to a little over 10 per cent of the total land area. According to preliminary estimates, it was also emphasized, China still has some 1,500,000,000 *mou* of arable wasteland, which equals the land area under the plow. Of these, relatively good wastelands are reported to consist of some 440,000,000 *mou*.[15] It was planned that during the First 5-year Plan (1953–1957), a total of some 40,000,000 *mou* were to be reclaimed. During the same period, another 100,000,000 *mou* of wasteland would be surveyed, and the preparations for the reclamation of an additional 40,000,000 to 50,000,000 *mou* of wasteland completed. The latter would pave the way for reclamation projects during the Second 5-year Plan (1958–1962).[16] Thus, at the planned reclamation rate of 40,000,000 *mou* every five years, it would take a total of ten 5-year plans, or 50 years, to reclaim all of what was judged to be relatively good wasteland.

It is, however, difficult to determine the number of persons who could be settled on these 440,000,000 *mou* of relatively good wasteland. Crude calculations indicate that only 1,400,000 settlers could be accepted if each settler were to receive 300 *mou* of reclaimed land. If individual land allotments were reduced to 30 *mou,* of course, the number of potential settlers could be increased to 14,000,000. Should each settler be allowed only 3 *mou* of reclaimed land, which is only slightly higher than the average individual share of land under cultivation in China proper, it would be, on paper, possible to settle a total of 140,000,000 persons in newly-reclaimed areas during the next 50 years. This figure is equivalent to the estimated increase in the population of China during a period of ten years.

In reality, the situation is far more complex as numerous factors affect the outcome of a policy of land reclamation and population transfers. The rapidity with which settlers could be transferred in an orderly way is determined, in large measure, by conditions in the areas of destination. Reports from Communist China of recent experience in this connection clearly illustrate the problem. Apart from the projects involving discharged or demobilized military personnel, population transfers and land reclamation in recent years appear to have been of two principal types: (1) The shift of whole families (households) to areas of low population density, where they are to join existing agricultural cooperatives. Each cooperative is to absorb three, five, or a few more than ten transferred families. These families are to become members of the cooperative and, along with its old members, reclaim and cultivate small lots of wasteland within a short distance of the cooperative. (2) The despatch of selected settlers, in organized groups, to reclamation areas where they are to erect new villages, form new higher agricultural cooperatives, and cultivate comparatively large pieces of reclaimed land made available by the state with the aid of modern farming equipment. Because living conditions in such reclamation areas are invariably primitive, only young settlers are sent at the initial stage to make preparation for production and eventual permanent family settlement.[17]

Consequently, organized population transfers in Communist China in connection with land reclamation did not actually involve a spectacular number of people. For instance, in 1956, for which statistical data are relatively abundant, a total of 725,000 persons were reportedly transferred in China as a whole. However, 292,000 of them were resettled within their respective provinces. In other words, only 433,000 persons were relocated from China proper to the border provinces of Manchuria, Inner Mongolia, Sinkiang, etc.,[18] amounting to only about 3 per cent of the estimated annual net population increase in China.

The 433,000 settlers of 1956 are reported to have reclaimed some 6,520,000 *mou* of wasteland, or 15 *mou* per settler, and to have constructed many new villages. The greater portion of their travel, living and production expenses and the cost of housing construction was borne by the state, and loans from the state made up the remaining smaller part of the resettlement expenditure. According to incomplete statistics for 1956, the total outlay was ¥110,000,000 for the relocation of these 433,000 migrants.[19] The state thus invested about ¥17.00 per *mou* of reclaimed land, or a little over ¥260.00 per settler. Therefore, on the basis of this recent Chinese experience, it would require some 30,000,000 settlers to reclaim all the relatively good wasteland of 440,000,000 *mou*, or a total cost of ¥7,800,000,000 if only settlers were used. This amount is in excess of 25 per cent of Communist China's national budget for 1955.

According to official reports, up to the end of 1956, a total of 454 large state farms were established on newly-reclaimed land, in which 13,620,000 *mou* were under cultivation. As is shown in Table 1, the experience in the establishment of state farms in various parts of the country indicates that the cost of per unit of reclaimed land was much greater than that of the land reclaimed by settlers. Thus, if all the relatively good wasteland of 440,000,000 *mou* could be reclaimed via state farms, it would require a total expenditure of ¥19,800,000,000, exclusive of investment needs for land improvement, transportation, and irrigation schemes.

However, if it should be physically and financially possible to organize the migration of 30,000,000 people, it would take approximately seventy years to accomplish this limited objective as only 433,000 persons were actually transferred in 1956. In the absence of a policy of fertility control, some 980 million people would be added to China's existing population during this period. Even if the implementation of the policy of land reclamation and population transfers could be accelerated to a rate, say, four times more than that of the 1956 record, the utility of the policy would still be likely to be minimal in view of the enormity of the Chinese population problem.

One Chinese writer stated, in 1957, that in the four years 1953–1956, a total of 66,000,000 *mou* of wasteland were reclaimed throughout China. Notwithstanding this achievement, he went on to say, the per capita arable land has actually decreased because of the continuous growth of population. It dropped from 2.85 *mou* per person in 1952 to 2.68 *mou* in 1956, showing an average reduction of nearly 0.2 *mou* per person.[20] However, the decrease in the per capita arable land has not been due to population growth alone. It is also attributable, in part, to large-scale economic development and related projects. These included the construction of new factories, the expansion of transportation and communication facilities, the territorial growth of the cities, housing developments, and the erection of dams and hydro-electric plants. All of these required space; to the extent that they encroached upon arable land, population displacement inevitably followed. According to one official estimate, between 1949 and early 1958, over 20,000,000 *mou* of land were requisitioned by the state in connection with various development projects.[21] This meant that, of the 66,000,000 *mou* of reclaimed wasteland from 1953–1956, almost one-third merely served to replace the amount of land taken out of cultivation. In other words, only 46,000,000 *mou* of arable land were added to the total area under cultivation between 1953 and 1956, or at an average of 11,500,000 *mou* per year. This reported achievement is slightly higher than the rate of reclamation envisaged in the First and Second 5-year Plans. But, as just noted, this rate of reclamation was not sufficient to offset the effect of population growth and the changed pattern of land use in and near the cities.

It also does not seem either sound or desirable to duplicate the pattern of intensive agriculture prevailing in China proper in reclaimed areas. Even though a much greater initial capital investment would be required to reclaim the land with the aid of modern implements, such reclaimed land could probably

TABLE 1. *Average Capital Investment in Land Reclamation*
(State farms only) *

Location	Cost per *mou*†
Heilungkiang, Kwangtung, Kwangsi	¥32
Yangtze Valley	33
Coastal areas	35
North China	53
Kansu, Sinkiang	50–67
Average	45

* Adapted from Chao Hsuch, "On the Question of the Reclamation of Waste-land," *Ta Kung Pao* (Peking), April 29, 1957.

† Exclusive of investment in land improvement and irrigation work outside of the state farms.

be more profitably exploited by large-scale or extensive agricultural enterprises or reserved for uses other than labor-intensive agricultural settlement projects. As Wilbert Moore observed, in a different context, "measures designed to alleviate pressures without changing traditional patterns (or even recreating them) are likely to represent a short-sighted policy."[22] In the demographic context, population transfers in connection with land reclamation work in Communist China in recent years have been of little significance. Whatever their political, military, social and economic returns are, the conclusion is inescapable that the solutions to the Chinese population question must be found in programs other than land reclamation and organized population transfers.

Notes

1. For discussions of this official campaign and recent developments in population control in Communist China, see H. Y. Tien, "Birth Control in Mainland China: Ideology and Politics," *Milbank Memorial Fund Quarterly* 41(3):269–290, July 1963, and "Population Control: Recent Developments in Mainland China," *Asian Survey*, II (5):12–6, July 1962. Also, John S. Aird, "Population Policy in Mainland China," *Population Studies*, XVI (1):38–57, July, 1962.

2. Jefferson D. H. Lamb, *The Development of the Agrarian Movement and Agrarian Legislation in China*, Shanghai, Commercial Press, Lts., 1934, pp. 95–96, 111–12, and 134–35.

3. *National Programme for Agricultural Development*, 1956–1967, Peking, Foreign Languages Press, 1960, p. 16 (Italics added). One *mou* = 0.1647 acre.

4. *People's Daily*, October 23, 1952 and November 26, 1952.

5. In contrast, in Communist China, the increase in the number of employed persons reached an annual average of 1.1 million during the period of the First 5-year Plan (1953–1957). The Second 5-year Plan (1958–1962) called for an increase of an additional 6 to 7 million persons, or at an annual average of 1.4 million. See Wu Ching-chao, "A New Treatise on the Problem of China's Population" *Hsin Chih She* (New Construction), No. 3, March 3, 1957, p. 6.

6. *People's Daily,* October 23, 1952.

7. Mao Tse-tung stated, in 1949, "It is a very good thing that China has a big population. Even if China's population multiplies many times, she is fully capable of finding a solution; the solution is production . . . revolution plus production can solve the problem of feeding the population. . . . Under the leadership of the Communist Party, as long as there are people, every kind of miracle can be performed. We believe that revolution can change everything, and that before long there will arise a new China with a big population and a great wealth of products, where life will be abundant and culture will flourish. All pessimistic views are utterly groundless." *Selected Works of Mao Tse-tung,* Vol. IV, Peking, Foreign Languages Press, 1961, pp. 453–54. Institutional changes included land reform, the introduction of mutual aid teams, producers' cooperatives, higher agricultural cooperatives, and the People's Commune.

8. *Chekiang Daily* (Hangchow), June 30, 1956, and *Yangtze Daily* (Wu-han), November 25, 1956.

9. *New China News Agency* (Peking), July 2, 1955, *Hsin Hua Monthly,* No. 122, 1956, pp. 95–96, and *Tsingtao Daily,* April 24, 1957.

10. Not to be neglected is the fact that the Soviet Union also renewed her reclamation work in the winter of 1954. At the beinning of 1955, Khrushchev vigorously urged Russian youths to go to West Siberia and "to march further eastward from the Altai. How beautiful is the land in the frontier region of Krasnoyarsky," *Tass* despatch from Moscow dated January 7, 1955. However, "there is increasing evidence that Soviet authorities are conscious of the high cost and inefficiency of settling people in remote, inhospitable areas of Siberia. Migration is being encouraged only to the extent that it is economically justified for the development of resources." *The New York Times,* June 6, 1963.

11. In introducing the question of land settlement, Bowman said, ". . . policies grow chiefly out of political, social, and economic conditions and situations." I. Bowman, editor, *Limits of Land Settlement,* Council on Foreign Relations, New York, 1937, p. 5. More penetrating are the remarks of Hope Eldridge; see her *Population Policies: A Survey of Recent Developments,* The International Union for the Scientific Study of Population, 1954, p. 4.

12. *People's Daily,* March 6, 1956.

13. *Proposals of the Eighth National Congress of the Communist Party of China for the Second Five-year Plan for Development of the National Economy,* (1958–1962), Peking, Foreign Languages Press, 1956, p. 21.

14. Ou Yu, "On the Question of Population Transfer and Land Reclamation," *Kung-ming Jih-Pao* (Peking), January 15, 1957.

15. *People's Daily,* March 6, 1956, *Kung-ming Jih-Pao* (Peking), March 3, 1956, and *Nan-fang Jih-Pao* (Canton), December 7, 1955.

16. *Nan-fang Jih-Pao,* December 7, 1955.

17. Ou Yu, *op. cit.*

18. *People's Daily,* December 28, 1956.

19. Chao Hsueh, "On the Question of the Reclamation of Wasteland," *Ta Kung Pao* (Peking), April 29, 1957 ($1.00 = ¥2.355.)

20. *Ibid.*

21. *People's Daily,* Janury, 7, 1958.

22. Wilbert Moore, "Utilization of Human Resources through Industrialization," in Spengler and Duncan, eds., *Demographic Analysis,* The Free Press, 1956, p. 531.

Problems of Control:
Business and Trade

18. THE INTERNATIONAL TRADE

Yuan-li Wu

While Communist China's military infringements of the frontiers of its neighbors to the south and southwest have understandably attracted wide international attention in recent months, another aspect of Chinese Communist strategy in Asia—less spectacular but, in the long run, of much greater consequence—has been receiving far less notice abroad than it deserves. This is Peking's steadily expanding effort to develop trade and other economic ties with the free Asian nations, particularly the underdeveloped countries of southeast Asia with the long-range objective of absorbing them into Communist China's economic and political orbit.

The far-reaching economic and political implications of these "peaceful" activities have not, to be sure, escaped the attention of some of the countries most directly concerned. Thailand's action banning imports from Communist China and Malaya's invocation of an anti-"dumping" law against Chinese goods early this year, though perhaps prompted in the main by immediate economic considerations, nevertheless reflect growing awareness of the broader dangers, present or potential, which Peking's strategy holds for the free Asian nations. Similarly, Burma and Ceylon, as a result of their own unhappy experience in economic dealings with Communist China a few years ago, have become so wary of Chinese motives and trading practices that Peking has found it necessary to tread more softly and to grant financial credits in an effort to repair the damage caused by its earlier overaggressiveness. In contrast to this increasing awareness in a number of Asian countries, however, a full appreciation of the character, purposes, and potential effects of the Chinese Communist

SOURCE: Selected from Yuan-li Wu, "The Weapon of Trade," in *Problems of Communism*, IX (January–February 1960), pp. 31–39.

economic drive in free Asia is still lacking among the general public in the West.

To a certain extent, of course, Communist China's expanding activity in the field of foreign trade is a natural consequence of the growth of the domestic economy. Even though the much-publicized "great leap forward" of 1958 is now acknowledged to have been far more modest than originally claimed,[1] there is no question that the Chinese national economy has grown at a rapid rate since the inception of the first Five-Year Plan (1953–57), and that this has brought a concomitant increase in China's foreign trade capabilities. Nevertheless, the expansion of Communist China's economic relations with the Asian countries has taken certain directions, and involved sacrifices of domestic economic needs and welfare, that cannot readily be explained on purely economic grounds. For another thing, it has been brought about by methods which can hardly be regarded as typical of normal practice in the development of foreign trade. Finally, and most important, Communist China's conduct of its external economic dealings has evidenced a disposition to utilize the augmentation or withholding of trade as a weapon for exerting pressure on the free Asian governments. In short, Chinese Communist strategy *vis-à-vis* free Asia manifests certain distinctive features of economic warfare. It is these elements which will receive particular scrutiny in the present article.

The Meaning of Economic Warfare

Before going on to examine in detail Communist China's economic activities affecting free Asia, it is first necessary to establish a distinction between two somewhat different but closely-interrelated aspects, or levels, of economic warfare, both of which are concurrently manifest in Chinese Communist strategy.

In what may be termed its elementary aspect, economic warfare embraces actions which are relatively short-term in character and, more often than not, are immediately inspired by economic rather than political considerations. As one specific category, it includes any type of arbitrary or abnormal economic action resorted to as a more or less temporary device for the purpose of gaining a foreign trade advantage which the country using it would not be able to obtain under normal trading conditions. The employment of such familiar—but generally condemned—practices as "dumping," "price-cutting," and other forms of "unfair competition" in order to capture a foreign market fall in this category. Another slightly different category embraces actions involving the deliberate acceptance of an abnormal economic sacrifice for the purpose of inducing a foreign country to grant economic or political concessions. The best illustration of this type of action is provided by Peking's extension of financial grants and credits to underdeveloped Asian countries—a clearly abnormal practice in the light of Communist China's own desperate need of capital for domestic industrial development.

In contrast to this limited, short-run aspect, economic warfare also has a much broader, strategic aspect in which it is focused primarily on the achievement of long-range political objectives. Attainment of these objectives normally entails the realization of a simultaneous economic gain, but the latter is not the primary motivation. Simply stated, the end goal of economic warfare in the long-range sense is the absorption into the waging country's economic orbit of another country's economy, not so much for economic reasons *per se* as to permit subjection of the target country to political domination.

A country practicing economic warfare with such long-range political objectives in mind can achieve its aims primarily through measures designed to render the target country's economy so dependent upon its own that the exertion of economic pressure can force political compliance. While it is difficult to state with general validity precisely what degree of economic dependence must be created to obtain this result, there is no question that any substantial increase of the waging country's share in the target country's overall import and/or export trade, or in the latter's total imports and/or exports of certain vital commodities, necessarily results in a corresponding augmentation of the target country's dependence.

This brings out the close interrelationship between the short-term and long-range levels of economic warfare. To the extent that the short-term measures described earlier succeed in expanding the waging country's share in the trade of the target country, they can help to realize longer-range political objectives. On the other hand, it is also possible, as has actually occurred in some areas of Communist China's external economic activity, for the waging country to be so inept in its conduct of short-term economic warfare—either by overplaying its hand or by exerting economic pressure prematurely—as to defeat its own long-run purposes.

It follows from the broad conception of economic warfare just outlined that, contrary to some popularly held notions, its practice need not always entail the sufferance of an economic loss by the practicing country. Certain measures may, indeed, result in temporary loss, but others produce an economic gain even though their primary purpose is political rather than economic. Naturally, a course of action which is profitable from both an economic and an immediate or long-term political standpoint is preferable wherever such an alternative exists. This means that the critical analyst, in trying to determine the motivation behind developments in a country's external economic relations that are both justifiable on normal economic grounds and capable of serving the larger aims of economic warfare, must take into consideration that country's known attitude and past record with respect to the employment of economic pressure for political ends. With these general principles in mind, Communist China's economic activities *vis-à-vis* free Asia in recent years may now be examined.

Trends in Trade

Communist China has succeeded in developing a sizable overall foreign trade program through the conclusion of a network of bilateral inter-governmental trade agreements, further supplemented by annual trade protocols and direct contracts with private foreign commercial groups. In addition to agreements between China and the other Asian Communist countries, Afghanistan, Burma, Cambodia, Ceylon, India, Indonesia, and Pakistan have all entered into governmental trade agreements or contracts with Communist China, while some Chinese trade with Japan has been carried on under extra-governmental agreements with private Japanese groups.[2]

Although Communist China has made public no detailed official reports concerning its trade with individual Asian countries, it is significant that statements by Peking, ever since the Bandung conference of April 1955, have frequently referred to the special category of "Afro-Asian trade." Such a category is new in Chinese Communist foreign trade statistics and is itself indicative of the special importance which the Peking regime—like the rest of the Communist bloc—attaches to the development of economic ties with the Afro-Asian countries, obviously for political reasons. Quantitatively, this group is now second in importance only to the other Communist bloc countries both as a market for Chinese exports and as a supplier of Chinese imports,[3] and its share in China's total trade surpasses that of the non-Communist Western nations by a wide margin. According to official Chinese Communist statistics, only nine per cent of mainland China's total foreign trade during 1953–54 was with the latter group as against 16 per cent with the Afro-Asian countries.

Quite naturally, the bulk of China's trade with the Afro-Asian group as a whole is accounted for by Asia. During 1957, for instance, Burma, Cambodia, Ceylon, India, Indonesia, Japan, Malaya, and Pakistan together took US $212.3 million of exports from Communist China and supplied U.S. $175.3 million of exports to her, as against corresponding figures of $44.1 million and $59.2 million for all the Near Eastern and African countries combined.

Turning specifically to recent trends in Chinese Communist trade with Free Asia, . . . all the individual Asian countries listed, with the exception of India and Pakistan, imported considerably larger amounts of Chinese goods in 1958 than in 1952, the increases ranging from 57.9 per cent in the case of Malaya to 1,726.3 per cent for Indonesia. It should be noted, however, that the 1958 figures for both Burma and Japan showed declines compared to 1956. The reverse side of the picture, *i.e.*, exports to Communist China from the free Asian countries, is more checkered. As the table shows, comparison of the 1958 figures with those for 1952 reveals increases for Burma, Indonesia, Japan, and Malaya, and declines for Ceylon, India, Pakistan, and Hong Kong (see remarks on Hong Kong trade, in note accompanying table). Comparing 1958 with 1956, however, Burma, Ceylon, Japan, India, and Pakistan registered declines, while only Indonesia, Malaya, and Hong Kong registered increases.

Wherever a decline has occurred in trade between Communist China and another Asian country (or Hong Kong), it has been readily traceable to a specific cause or causes. Thus, the decline in exports from Hong Kong to China is explained by the fact that the latter is now bringing directly into its own ports, especially Tientsin and Dairen, foreign imports that formerly were consigned to the Hong Kong entrepôt and then re-exported from there to Communist China. Similarly, the steady decline of Chinese trade with Pakistan is attributable to Communist China's growing self-sufficiency in cotton and jute, while the evident lack of promise in Indian trade with China needs to be understood in conjunction with the sizable expansion of India's trade with Soviet European bloc countries, in turn stimulated by the latter's extension of financial credits to India. The other exceptions to the generally rising trend in Chinese Communist trade with free Asia—Burma, Ceylon, and Japan—will be explained later in this article.

The Chinese Export Drive

Perhaps the dominant feature of Asian trade development in recent years, evidenced quite clearly by the statistics given in Table I, has been the marked expansion of Communist China's exports to most of the free Asian countries. This trend stands out with particular prominence in the period since 1956, when it has to be viewed against the background of concurrently declining exports from several Asian countries to Communist China. It poses two highly pertinent questions. First, to what extent has Communist China already succeeded, through its export drive, in acquiring a large share of the import markets of the Asian countries concerned? Secondly, what does Communist China hope to accomplish by this drive, and what are some of the present effects and potential future effects on the free Asian nations?

An approximate answer to the first question is contained in the figures given in Table II, which appears on this page. From these percentages it can be seen that Communist China's share in the total imports of six out of the nine Asian countries listed (including Hong Kong) rose from very low levels in 1952 to comparatively much higher levels in 1958. The increases were particularly substantial in the cases of Cambodia, Ceylon and Indonesia, where imports from Communist China in 1958 accounted for 6.4, 8.8, and 6.1 per cent, respectively, of total imports. Although these percentages might not seem very impressive, they nevertheless represent the attainment by Com-

TABLE II. *Communist China's Share in Total Import and Export Trade of Free Asian Countries*
(In per cent)

	Imports from Communist China		Exports to Communist China	
	1952	1958	1952	1958
Burma	1.2	0.5	negligible	0.8
Cambodia	–	6.4	–	–
Ceylon	1.9	8.8	8.3	9.9(1957)
India	2.0	0.6	0.8	0.5
Indonesia	1.0	6.1	negligible	2.0
Japan	0.7	1.8	0.1	1.8
Malaya	3.1	4.6	negligible	3.4
Pakistan	0.6	0.3	15.8	negligible
Hong Kong	22.0	30.4	17.9	5.2

SOURCE: For original data, same as in the last table. The percentage figures are computed.

munist China of record shares in the three countries' respective import markets, an accomplishment which can by no means be considered insignificant considering the relatively short period of time in which it was achieved. Moreover while Communist China is still far from dominating the overall import markets of the free Asian countries, it has acquired a much stronger position in certain commodity groups than the overall figures would suggest.

In a developing economy like Communist China's, it is normal for exports to expand with increasing productive capacity. What must be realized, however, is that in China's case the expansion has been pushed much farther than the actual rise in domestic production, related to China's own internal economic needs, would warrant. This is abundantly clear from the fact that cotton textiles and several other consumer items produced by light manufacturing industry have figured prominently in the exports expansion drive at the same time that domestic shortages of these commodities and rationing restrictions on their consumption have steadily intensified.

Moreover, while the increase in exports to a few areas, in particular Hong Kong, may be attributed in part to Communist China's need to earn sterling in order to meet payment deficits incurred in Chinese trade with the Soviet bloc[4] and to build up its foreign currency reserve, the expansion of Chinese exports to such countries as Indonesia and Cambodia cannot be similarly explained in terms of any compelling economic reason. Generally speaking, Communist China does not have a large demand for the raw materials which most Asian countries can supply, nor can Chinese export earnings in non-convertible currencies be used elsewhere. It seems obvious, therefore, that normal and legitimate economic motives, though operative to a varying degree in certain areas of Communist China's external economic activities, do not by themselves provide a wholly adequate explanation of why and how that country's trade with some of the free Asian nations has taken the course indicated by the statistics presented in the accompanying tables. Thus, to find the answer to the second of the two questions posed earlier, one is inevitably led to scrutinize Chinese economic activities affecting free Asia not merely from a strictly economic standpoint but also from the broader standpoint of both short- and long-range economic warfare objectives. China's trade dealings with Burma and Ceylon afford particularly illuminating case studies in this regard.

The Examples of Burma and Ceylon

The case of Burma is edifying, above all, as an example of a fairly obvious attempt by Communist China to make an underdeveloped Asian economy which relies upon a single major export—in this case, rice—economically dependent upon the Chinese market, and hence vulnerable to Chinese Communist economic as well as political pressure. This attempt began in 1955 when Burma's big rice surplus presented a favorable opportunity for Communist China and the Soviet Union to step in with a joint offer to make large annual purchases of Burmese rice. By the terms of the resultant agreement, Communist China committed itself to purchase an annual quota of 150,000 tons of rice from Burma, to be paid for partly by exports of Chinese goods, partly by

Chinese re-exports of goods originating from the Soviet European bloc, and partly in sterling. The arrangement was made highly attractive to Burma by Chinese agreement to a stipulated price for Burmese rice higher than the prevailing world market price.

Actually, however, the transaction proved far less satisfactory from the Burmese standpoint than the original offer had seemed to promise. The reason was that Burma, while exporting the agreed annual amounts of rice to China, had difficulty in finding Chinese export items which it wished to import in part payment. The upshot of this one-sided situation was that China finally offered to meet its obligation under the rice-barter agreement by furnishing Burma with machinery and equipment for a textile mill, together with the necessary technical assistance for setting up the mill.[5] Although the offer appears to have been accepted and implemented, the difficulties experienced by Burma have undoubtedly been an important cause of the steady decline in Sino-Burmese trade since 1956.

In a number of respects, Communist China's trade dealings with Ceylon have displayed the same characteristics as its dealings with Burma. Trade between the two countries, until recently, consisted almost exclusively of an exchange of only two items—rice from China in exchange for Ceylonese rubber. Under a five-year agreement entered into in 1953, China contracted to supply Ceylon with 270,000 tons of rice annually in return for 50,000 tons of rubber, both at stipulated prices which were initially much more favorable to Ceylon than prevailing world market prices.[6] It should be noted that rubber is Ceylon's second largest export next to tea, and its most important export of an industrial raw material; and also that China's contract to buy 50,000 tons annually would make it the dominating export market for Ceylonese rubber.

Again, however, as in the case of Burma, Ceylon's experience under the agreement was not satisfactory. While Ceylonese rubber exports to China were appreciably above the contract level except in 1955 and 1957, China on its side was never able to fill its annual 270,000-ton quota for rice exports to Ceylon despite the fact that, in 1955, it used rice obtained under the agreement with Burma for this purpose.[7] The result was the accumulation of a sizable sterling credit in Ceylon's favor, which in turn provided China with a means of exerting pressure on Ceylon in the 1957 negotiations for renewal of the agreement. As the London *Economist* commented at the time, Ceylon risked losing this credit balance if it rejected China's demand, put forward in the negotiations, that Ceylon favor Chinese goods at the expense of its other trading partners, while on the other hand acceptance of the demand could only mean increased vulnerability to Chinese pressure in the future.[8]

At the time the first agreement was concluded in 1953, Ceylon had been in a much stronger bargaining position vis-à-vis China than had Burma. China had no real need of Burmese rice but, on the contrary, was obliged to turn to Ceylon for the bulk of its natural rubber supply since the latter was the only large source not closed to China by the United Nations embargo imposed as a result of Chinese intervention in the Korean war. In fact, Peking negotiated the 1953 agreement primarily as a countermeasure against the UN embargo, and these circumstances were responsible for the particularly attractive terms obtained by Ceylon. In 1956, however, Malaya dropped out of the embargo, making it again possible for Communist China to buy rubber on the world market.

This weakening of Ceylon's bargaining position was partially offset by the lessons gained through its experience under the 1953–57 agreement with respect to Chinese failure to fulfill contract requirements in matters of specific commodity shipments and delivery schedules. Thus, while Ceylon entered into a new five-year barter agreement with China in 1957, the agreement reduced the annual amounts to be exchanged to 200,000 tons of Chinese rice against 30,000 tons of Ceylonese rubber. More recently, the Chinese yearly quota for its rice shipments has been raised to 230,000 tons, together with the imposition of a 124 million rupee annual ceiling on total Chinese exports to Ceylon.[9]

Although Communist China's share in Ceylon's overall foreign trade is not particularly large, the situation, as mentioned earlier, is quite different when it comes specifically to Ceylonese rubber exports. Under the first Sino-Ceylonese agreement, China took an average of more than half of Ceylon's total annual rubber exports, its share ranging from a low of 33.7 per cent in 1955 to a high of 72.1 per cent in 1954.[10] Even with the reduced scale of exchange stipulated by the second agreement of 1957, 28.4 per cent of Ceylon's total rubber exports in 1958 still went to Communist China.

Meanwhile, China has begun to diversify its export to Ceylon, as evidenced by the fact that the proportion of the total accounted for by rice dropped from 95 per cent during 1954–57 to 80 per cent in 1958. In place of rice, Communist China since 1957 has been pushing the export of cotton textiles to Ceylon even though these are under severe rationing at home; and, starting in 1958 it has expanded its export offerings to include other industrial products such as cement, sewing machines, steel rods, and bars, pneumatic tires, newsprint, and cotton yarn—in many instances offered at lower prices than those of competing items from other countries. This effort to expand industrial exports at the cost of heavy sacrifice to the Chinese consumer—and even, in the case of certain items, at some cost to domestic economic construction—is quite clearly aimed at capturing a bigger share of the overall Ceylonese market at the expense of China's competitors. Among the latter, India and Burma seem to have suffered most from the trade challenge.

Chinese Communist Trade Practices

Price-cutting by Communist China in order to drive out competition and gain control of a foreign export market has been evident in other free Asian countries besides Ceylon. In fact, it is a fairly general phenomenon in China's trade with these countries, and represents one of the chief complaints of traders in Southeast Asia against Chinese Communist trading practices.

In Indonesia, for example, price-cutting contributed substantially to the expansion of Chinese Communist imports into that country—at Japan's expense in respect of manufactured goods, and at Burma's in respect of rice. Thus, China's share of the Indonesian import market for cotton piece-goods rose from 10.9 per cent in 1955 to 23.3 per cent in the first half of 1958, while Japan's fell from 41.8 to 31 per cent over the same period. Hong Kong's share of the same market also rose from 19 to 39.5 per cent in this period, but probably close to one-half of the Hong Kong shipments originated from Communist China. According to an authoritative analysis of the Chinese trade offensive in Indonesia, the gains scored by Chinese piece-goods, both directly imported and through Hong Kong, were due mainly to lower prices.[11] The same article provides further data concerning Chinese Communist price-cutting on other manufactured items imported into Indonesia:

> In 1955, Japan had a monopoly of Indonesian imports from Asia of ferro-concrete, cement, sewing machines, and vehicle tires. By 1958 China had the monopoly of the first of these items and supplied 21 per cent, 27 per cent, and 20 per cent, respectively, of the Asian contribution in the rest. Her prices per kilogram were: ferro-concrete, 1.4 rupiahs to Japan's 1.7; cement, 0.28 rupiahs to Japan's 0.31; sewing machines, 5.1 rupiahs to Japan's 6.5; tires, 12 rupiahs to Japan's 18. In newsprint, Japan's 85 per cent of the Asian supplies fell to 44 per cent, and China's 5 per cent rose to 54 per cent, the Chinese product being 14 per cent cheaper.[12]

Since 1958, Communist China has also expanded its share of the Indonesian import market for rice, evidenced by increased shipments both directly and through Hong Kong. And again the expansion has been achieved by offering Chinese rice at a price slightly below the market price of rice from Burma and Vietnam.

A comparable picture presents itself in Malaya. Until recently Chinese exports to that country consisted of a few traditional food items (fruit, vegetables, fish, and eggs), but these have now been augmented by rice and sugar, as well as by a number of industrial goods, particularly textiles and cement. China began exporting cement to Malaya in earnest in 1956, and already in the following year succeeded in capturing 15 per cent of the Malayan import market for that commodity. The average import price for Chinese cement was St $57.4 per ton, as against St $59.8 for Japanese, and St $72.7 for cement from the United Kingdom.[13]

What is most significant about Chinese Communist price-cutting, however, is not simply that it has become standard practice in China's trade development activities throughout free Asia, but rather the fact that it is carried to such extremes—often, moreover, against competition coming more from other Asian countries than from the West. *The Far Eastern Economic Review* comments as follows on this aspect:

> When China seized a South African rice contract from beneath the noses of the Thais, their quotation was about 25 per cent below the Thai merchants', allowing for the slight difference in quality. . . .

> When Malayan cement was reduced in price to meet the cheaper imported Chinese product, the Chinese promptly reduced their price again. . . . What is less understandable is the extent to which they are willing to undercut, *even more than would seem calculated to gain entry into a new and perhaps suspicious market.*[14] [Author's italics]

Nor is exaggerated price-cutting the only weapon in Communist China's economic warfare arsenal. The devices of "package deals" and bulk contracts, for instance, served China in good stead in its drive to force Indian textile goods out of the Indonesian market.[18] As already noted in connection with the 1957 Sino-Ceylonese barter agreement, Peking often tries to exploit a favorable bargaining situation to extract blanket guarantees of special treatment for Chinese imports. Still other practices of a monopolistic character have been resorted to in Hong Kong, whose geographical position and large Chinese population facilitate Chinese Communist efforts to dominate the local market for certain commodities. For instance, Hong Kong retailers wishing to handle Chinese eggs are required to join a federation whose members are forbidden to sell eggs from other countries. According to a report by the Japan Export Trade Promotion Agency, there have also been Chinese Communist attempts to impose monthly sales quotas on Hong Kong firms acting as agents for Chinese products.[16]

While the methods described above have been effective in some instances, Communist China is, of course, still far from dominating the overall import market of any free Asian country, and as of now the possibility of its achieving such an aim is still somewhat remote, except perhaps in the special case of Hong Kong. In fact, the recent tendencies of some free Asian countries toward restricting their trade with Communist China suggests that the ruthlessness with which the latter has applied economic warfare tactics (of the short-term variety) has boomeranged to the detriment of its long-term politico-economic objectives. To some extent, the desire to remedy this situation underlies Communist China's more recent activities in the area of financial assistance to southeast Asian countries, briefly sketched below.

Financial Aid Maneuvers

Though still on a very modest scale, Communist China's extension of outright financial grants or interest-free credits to several free Asian countries in the face of China's own extreme capital-poor condition affords perhaps the clearest example of action which cannot be justified on economic grounds and must therefore be attributed to broader economic warfare objectives. Closer examination of these grants will serve to illustrate the point more clearly.

Four southeast Asian countries—Cambodia, Nepal, Ceylon, and Burma—have so far been recipients of financial aid from Communist China. Grants were made to Cambodia and Nepal in 1956, the first amounting to 800 million rials (roughly US $11 million) to be spread over a four-year period, and the second totalling 60 million Indian rupees (roughly US $8.8 million) over three years. The Cambodian grant was reportedly to be used partly for the purchase of Chinese industrial equipment (for textile mills and cement, paper, and plywood factories), and partly for a variety of domestic construction projects (farm irrigation, rural electric power plants, roads, hospitals, and schools). The grant to Nepal consisted of one-third cash without conditions attached as to its use, and two-thirds in non-repayable trade credits for the purchase of unspecified types of Chinese machinery. Neither of these grants had any discernible short-term economic justification from the Chinese standpoint and were manifestly calculated to boost Communist China's political prestige and influence in the two countries[17]—and perhaps also to pave the way for later economic penetration.

The Chinese Communist credit granted to Ceylon in 1957, amounting to 75 million Ceylonese rupees (approximately US $12 million), belongs in a slightly different category in that immediate economic considerations also played a part, in addition to the value of the move as a political gesture. The "credit" seems to have been actually tantamount to an outright grant since, according to the best information available, it was interest-free and non-repayable. The ostensible purpose of the grant was to help finance the rehabilitation of Ceylon's rubber plantations, although—as noted earlier—China by this time could again buy rubber on the open market and was no longer so dependent upon Ceylonese rubber supplies. In fact, the major purpose of the credit offer was to induce Ceylon, in conjunction with the negotiations for renewal of the first rice-rubber barter agreement, to grant general free access for Chinese imports into the Ceylonese market. (Simultaneously with the credit agreement, a supplementary trade contract was concluded under which China, in payment for Ceylonese goods, would supply Ceylon with a complete textile plant.)

Very little information is available concerning the reported extension of a 20 million kyat (about US $1.8 million) grant by Communist China to Burma, also in 1957. It is presumably similar to the grants made to Cambodia and Nepal, and very probably is to finance the purchase by Burma of Chinese textile and light manufacturing equipment. The circumstances in which it was extended suggest that one of its chief motivations was Peking's hope of alleviating Burmese antagonism arising out of China's aggressive trade tactics.

Trade as a Political Weapon

If Communist China has, for the most part, tried to conceal its political motives behind some sort of disguise, its blatantly open attempt to exploit the lure of trade as a means of pressuring Japan toward political recognition of the Communist regime exposed those motives to full view. Trade between Communist China and Japan was first resumed in 1952 under a non-governmental agreement entered into, on the Japanese side, by several private trading groups. The third such agreement expired in 1957, and Communist China seized upon the negotiations for its renewal as the occasion for putting forward a series of expanded demands ranging from the conclusion of an inter-governmental payments agreement and further relaxation of Japanese export controls to the establishment of a large permanent Chinese Communist trade mission in Japan and the exemption of its members from finger-printing under the Japanese immigration law. Although the Chinese Communist negotiators finally had to back down and a compromise fourth agreement was signed in March 1958, Peking soon thereafter repudiated it on the principal ground that Japan refused to permit the flying of the Chinese Communist flag over the trade mission headquarters in Tokyo.

From the first resumption of unofficial trade contracts between the two countries, Communist China pressed the line that Japan could reap rich benefits from an expansion of trade with the Chinese mainland and that the only obstacle to such expansion lay in Japan's observance of the United Nations embargo against the Chinese Communist regime. As soon, however, as Japan relaxed its trade controls somewhat, Peking shifted its position and began trying to use the lure of increased trade as a means of driving an opening wedge toward diplomatic recognition. When it failed to make any appreciable dent in the Japanese government's position in the 1957–58 negotiations, it abruptly chose the symbolic issue of the right to fly the flag over the Chinese Communist trade mission as a reason to suspend trade relations.

What conclusions may be drawn, then, from the record of Communist China's overall economic activities affecting free Asia? First of all, the character of these activities, the specific directions they have taken, the methods employed as well as the extreme degree of their application—all combine to make it abundantly clear that what we are witnessing is by no means a normal expansion of Communist China's trade and other economic relations with the free Asian nations, but rather the conscious pursuit of economic warfare in all its forms and with all the long-range political implications of economic imperialism.

As for the effectiveness of the Chinese Communist effort in this area, it would be wrong to place too much stress on the fact that the statistics show China—even where it has been relatively successful—to be still far from achieving the necessary degree of economic dominance over the free Asian countries to permit Peking to enforce political compliance by means of economic pressure. The Chinese effort is, after all, still young, and China's economic capabilities are steadily increasing.

The record does, however, justify one significant conclusion on this score—namely, that Communist China has not thus far been too successful in coordinating and reconciling its practice of economic warfare on the short-term and long-term levels. This is to say, it has in many instances employed such aggressive tactics for the immediate purpose of capturing an Asian market that it has antagonized the country concerned and thus rendered more difficult the realization of its broader political objectives. Again, as illustrated most clearly in the case of Japan, it has sought to use economic pressure for the purpose of extracting political concessions prematurely—that is, before gaining a sufficient economic stranglehold to make this possible.

The setbacks that Communist China has suffered because of these mistakes could temporarily weaken its ability to wage economic warfare, but they could also result in a more astute strategy in the future, In any event, it is vital that the underlying aims and methods of Communist China's "peaceful" economic offensive in free Asia be more fully understood.

Notes

1. A communique issued by the Peking regime on August 26, 1959, announced a decision by the Central Committee Plenum to reduce previously-planned 1959 production targets in the light of serious statistical errors in the assessment of economic progress during 1958. Text reported by New China News Agency, August 27, 1959.

2. For a description of some of the trade agreements and annual contracts, see Robert F. Dernberger, "The International Trade of Communist China,"

in *Three Essays on the International Economics of Communist China,* ed. by C. F. Remer, University of Michigan Press, Ann Arbor, 1958.

3. *Peking Review,* June 1958, p. 14.

4. A number of economists believe that Soviet aid to Communist China has been relatively small, and that China's surplus of imports from the rest of the Soviet European bloc has to be paid for partly through an export surplus in trading with the rest of the world. See study cited in footnote 2.

5. See the author's "The Soviet 'Economic Offensive' in Asia and its Effect on United States-Asian Trade," in *American Trade with Asia and the Far East,* ed. by Robert J. Barr, Marquette University Press, Milwaukee, 1959.

6. For some of the rubber and rice prices agreed to between Ceylon and Communist China, see *Far Eastern Economic Review* (FEER), May 1955, p. 671, and November 1955, p. 659.

7. *FEER,* August 1955, p. 250.

8. *The Economist* (London), Vol. CLXXXIV, No. 5949, August 1957, p. 675.

9. P. H. M. Jones, "Peking's Trade Offensive IV—Ceylon," *FEER,* July 1959, pp. 45–47.

10. *Ibid.*

11. P. H. M. Jones, "Peking's Trade Offensive III—Indonesia," *FEER,* June 1959, pp. 842–44.

12. *Ibid.,* p. 842.

13. Daniel Wolfstone, "Peking's Trade Offensive in South East Asia II—Malaya," *FEER,* May 1959, p. 715.

14. November 1958, pp. 643–44.

15. See note 11 above.

16. Cited in *FEER,* May 1959, p. 669.

17. The 75 million Swiss franc credit extended by Communist China to Egypt in 1956, following the Suez crisis, represents a similar case, although there may have been some provision for repayment in the form of Egyptian long-staple cotton exports to China.

19. THE PRIVATE BUSINESSMEN

George N. Ecklund

The widely-held notion that one of the first moves of Communist regimes in assuming national power is to appropriate the cash registers of private business has been clearly upset in the case of Communist China. Many Chinese merchants remained in business in Mainland China for seven years after the fall of Chiang. When the Communists came to power in October 1949, they

SOURCE: Selected from George N. Ecklund, "Protracted Expropriation of Private Business in Communist China," in *Pacific Affairs,* XXXVI, 3 (Fall 1963), pp. 238–240 and 242–249. Reprinted by permission of *Pacific Affairs.*

chose to put private business to work for them rather than to follow the earlier Russian pattern of confiscation. The Russians, during their period of War Communism from 1917 to 1921, abolished most money transactions in favor of barter exchange and made plans for early nationalization of industry. During the subsequent period of the New Economic Policy in the Soviet Union, a money economy was restored and some elements of private business were allowed to flourish, but the initial hope of the Communists in Russia was for a complete break with capitalism. The initial attitude of the Chinese Communists toward capitalism, on the other hand, appeared much more lenient and restrained. . . .

One of the most pressing economic needs of the Chinese Communists in 1949 was to enlist private businessmen in the reconstruction of China. Nearly half of Chinese industrial output and more than three-quarters of wholesale and retail trade, by value, were in private hands in 1949. With few exceptions, these private businessmen were small operators. For example, of 130,000 privately-owned factories, some 90,000 employed less than 10 persons each and only 5,000 employed more than 50 persons each. Scattered throughout the country were millions of small wholesale and retail merchants, many of whom operated only as peddlers. The Chinese Communist leaders recognized the backwardness of their economy and acknowledged that China would need a rather long period of transition to a socialist state. It was necessary to use private industry and commerce extensively, the Chinese admitted, in order to "increase the supply of manufactured goods, expand the circulation of commodities, provide employment, and train skilled workers and administrative personnel."[1] The Communist objectives, therefore, were to exercise firm control over businessmen but at the same time to gain their cooperation by offering some sort of accommodation with the concept of private profit.

A second element of control during the early 1950's was the curtailment of management prerogatives. It was declared illegal for a businessman to raise wages or to withdraw capital funds on his own initiative. As early as 1950, the government decreed that dividends must not exceed 8 per cent of invested capital. In 1953, all profits-before-taxes of private organizations were subjected to state control and were divided into four categories: (1) the income tax, which carried a rate of 30 per cent for profits above 10,000 yuan; (2) enterprise reserve funds, to be used only for investment in the firm; (3) enterprise reward funds, to be used only for employee welfare; and (4) the dividends to shareholders, limited to 25 per cent of profits-before-taxes.[2]

The regime tightened its grip on the private sector by asking private firms to do business primarily with the government. The government gave orders to private industry for processing jobs and for the manufacture of end-items, and signed contracts with private wholesale and retail firms for purchase and sale at fixed prices. By 1953, the state was purchasing or marketing 62 per cent of the gross output of private factories. Once these agreements with the state were effective, the businessmen were called into frequent conferences with officials and were directed to improve their operations and trim their costs of production. Any delays in deliveries, inferior work, and substitutions of materials brought down "stern criticism" on the businessmen involved. In an apparent effort to curtail management decision-making, it was said that all private businessmen were "educated to depend on workers for improving their business."[3]

The policy of the Chinese Communists to use private enterprise for reconstruction of the economy was clearly revealed in the discriminatory taxes imposed on commerce and industry. Very low rates of commodity taxes and generous deductions from profits taxes applied only to producers and distributors of necessary commodities, such as iron and steel and machinery, whereas producers of non-essential consumer goods were penalized under the tax laws. These tax differentials (consisting of commodity tax rates ranging from 3 to 120 per cent and deductions from profits taxes of up to 40 per cent) would be sufficient in a free market economy to effect some reallocation of resources. In Communist China of the early 1950's, however, the mobility of private capital was very low, primarily because businessmen were uncertain about the final policy of the government toward the private sector. The effect of the new discriminatory taxes was to create a generally favorable outlook in those activities which the Communist wished to encourage and to maintain the production of these essential items by private business at levels comparable to those of the immediate past. On the other hand, high tax rates on non-essential and luxury goods, together with a growing range of items under direct price control, served to limit profits and to reduce production in private firms that were considered by the Communists to be unimportant.

In order to limit the expansion of the private sector as a whole, the regime attempted to drain off as much profit as possible through taxation. Even though favored industries under private operation were granted certain tax concessions, their overall profits were restricted by other features of the tax legislation such as (1) taxing intermediate production processes at the same rates as end-products; (2) applying tax rates to state prices rather than to manufacturers' cost or sales prices (which were lower than state prices); (3) careful auditing by the Communist tax bureaus, which made tax evasion more difficult than in the past; and (4) arbitrary methods of assessing taxes which sometimes proved to be confiscatory. State enterprises, on the other hand, were exempt from the profits tax and had access to state subsidies when necessary, while cooperatives producing light industrial products were taxed under a more favorable rate schedule than private industry and often were granted complete tax exemption for several years.

In spite of the harsh crack-down on profits, the Communists were able to use private industry and commerce extensively during the first three or four years of their regime in China, as is indicated in the table on page 206.

Although the relative share of the private sector in total economic activity decreased from 1949 to 1953, there was a substantial increase in the absolute volume of private industrial production and of retail trade. It may be argued that a large part of this increase in private business was the result of recovery from the war. Nevertheless, the fact that the Communists permitted the value of private industrial production to double, and of private retail trade to increase by 40 per cent, reveals to some extent their high dependence on the private sector during this period.

As early as 1949, the authorities invited private businessmen into a close alliance with the government by forming a new type of business organization known as the "joint public-private enterprise." This was essentially a partnership with the state and represented an irrevocable step toward complete socialization. Although the campaign to form joint public-private enterprises was pushed slowly at first, it became in time the major tool for bringing all private enterprise under state ownership. The statute governing the organization of the new enterprise made it clear that the government would be the dominant partner in the firm. The private businessmen could not assume direct control of the joint organization, but took part in management as ordinary salaried personnel. The government wanted their technical and managerial skills, but only as hired hands. The private owners who contributed all of their assets to these new companies were compensated initially by payments in the form of a percentage of annual profits. This was changed in 1956 to a fixed interest payment of 5 per cent on the private capital involved, all payments being scheduled to cease in 1962.[4]

The Communists at first stressed the need to obtain public support for the new joint enterprises and the voluntary agreement of private owners to enter them. Subtle pressures may have been exerted on private firms to make the change; for example, by holding out offers of cheaper raw materials and more business. The Chinese press reported favorable changes in business operations after private firms were converted to public-private enterprises. A Shanghai foundry reported that its costs were reduced 12 per cent and its output was

TABLE 1. *Private Enterprise in the Chinese Economy, 1949–53*

	Value in Million Yuan*			
	1949	1950	1952	1953
Private industrial production	6,828	7,259	10,526	13,109
Per cent of total industrial production	48.7	S.C.	30.7	29.3
Private wholesale trade		8,026	6,882	8,015
Per cent of total wholesale trade		76.1	36.3	30.3
Private retail trade		10,089	12,149	14,081
Per cent of total retail trade		83.5	57.8	50.3

* Industrial production is valued in 1952 prices. Wholesale and retail trade are in current prices. According to Chinese price indexes, during the period 1950–53 wholesale prices increased 16.6 and retail prices 17.1 per cent.

increased 18 per cent "a few months after conversion." Nine woolen knitting shops had their turnover increased 60 per cent after adopting the new enterprise. In spite of such favorable developments, only 1,000 joint firms had been established by 1954. These joint firms appeared for the most part to be larger industrial companies, which the Chinese authorities said accounted for 13.3 per cent of the combined industrial production of capitalist and joint enterprises.

By the end of 1955, the Communists apparently had lost faith in persuasion and discrimination as methods for controlling private firms and converting them to joint enterprises. Furthermore, the need for coddling the private businessman had passed. As the Communists pointed out, the "high tide in socialist transformation" of commerce and industry became possible in 1956 because (1) agricultural cooperativization had already been successfully achieved, and (2) the production in state-owned industrial enterprises far exceeded the production in private enterprises. Accordingly, a vast campaign was launched in January 1956 to push all private elements of the economy under direct state control. The Communists reported that once the campaign started, capitalists everywhere were anxious to join the movement. In some cases, businessmen may have welcomed the opportunity to leave ventures that had become increasingly unprofitable because of state restrictions. In other cases, pressures were probably applied to make the movement appear a genuine mass campaign. Although no clear evidence is available that businessmen were forced into joint public-private enterprises, descriptive statements in the Chinese press are eloquent testimony of the tactics used.

The Chinese later reported that during 1956 some 112,000 private industrial companies and 1,940,000 private commercial firms had been converted into joint public-private enterprises, cooperative units, or state-owned shops.[16] The precipitous decline in the volume of activity in the private sector during 1956 is illustrated in the following table:[17]

TABLE 2. *Private Enterprise in the Chinese Economy, 1954–56*

	Value in Million Yuan*		
	1954	1955	1956
Private industrial production	10,341	7,266	29
Per cent of total industrial production	19.9	13.3	nil
Private wholesale trade	2,883	1,216	nil
Per cent of total wholesale trade	10.3	4.7	nil
Private retail trade	8,355	5,650	1,150
Per cent of total retail trade	26.5	18.1	2.9

* Industrial production is valued in 1952 prices. Wholesale and retail trade are in current prices. According to Chinese price indexes, wholesale prices were virtually unchanged during this period, whereas retail prices increased 2 per cent.

After this mass conversion to socialist enterprise early in 1956, private businessmen in China had nothing left but memories and an annual interest payment from the state (paid partly in government bonds). Seven years have now passed since private industry and commerce "entered socialism." Have the Communists succeeded in stamping out completely the centuries-old traditions that have made Chinese merchants among the sharpest in the world? In form, yes; in substance, not entirely. The whirlwind campaign for joint public-private enterprises in 1956 slammed the door on capitalist form, in a legal sense, but the subsequent campaign to transform the capitalist man into an honest, working socialist proved to be another matter. The former businessmen have remained a vexing, though relatively quiescent, problem for the Communists for the past seven years. The response to this problem has taken a number of forms. First of all, the government was quick to consolidate the thousands of new public-private enterprises in 1956–57 in order to keep them from reverting to their former status as private firms. Secondly, the capitalists themselves were subjected to a nagging campaign of "thought re-moulding" that was designed, hopefully, to assimilate them with the proletariat. Finally, when the economic difficulties of the past few years made it expedient to tolerate again certain forms of private initiative, particularly in rural areas, the government was careful to control the movement and to rationalize it in terms of the present stage of socialist development in China.

After mass socialization early in 1956, the government found its task of coordinating thousands of small industrial and commercial enterprises vastly increased. As private enterprises, they had been given government orders or had been left to fend for themselves. As joint enterprises, they became the government's direct responsibility. In Shanghai, for example, 84,000 joint pub-lic-private enterprises were formed early in 1956, employing some 600,000 people. To simplify control, Shanghai authorities adopted "management by district" to 20,000 of these enterprises in 1956, designating 2,790 "central fac-tories" which had leadership over the remaining 17,210 "satellite factories."[5] In Tientsin, the reorganization was completed in September 1956, when 5,800 joint public-private enterprises were brought under "unified management" and reduced to 854 primary enterprises with 2,254 branch factories, workshops, and work sections.[6] Similar reports have been noted from other parts of the country. In this way, thousands of small firms were swallowed up by large organizations and lost all hope of regaining any individual initiative.

Efforts to remould the capitalist man after 1955 were cautious and flexible. Businessmen were encouraged to draw up their own plans for self-remoulding. The typical plan consisted of a promise to accept the leadership of the state in management of the joint public-private enterprise, an agreement to contribute personal skills and experience to the firm, a specific project for engaging in physical labor, a course of political study, and a resolution to change bourgeois ways and become more like the workers. This voluntary plan was intended to effect a peaceful reform of the businessman while continuing to draw on his experience. The remoulding campaign apparently reached a zenith in the "heart donation movement" of 1957–58, in which capitalists were urged to donate all of their remaining financial stake in the enterprise, their technical knowledge and their experience to the Party, and to identify themselves com-pletely with the working class.[7]

The campaign to persuade businessmen into the ranks of the proletariat was not entirely successful. The Chinese press reported incidents of illegal capitalism throughout 1956 and 1957. These incidents consisted of black market sales of grain and other consumer goods, as well as underground factories operated for private gain. For example, one former businessman in Kweiyang, Ch'eng Ting-lu, joined the First Iron Tools Producer Cooperative after he lost his own business to the state. He then covertly set up a shop in his home for repairing and making machine parts. Ch'eng stole parts from the cooperative shop, enticed other cooperative members to work for him at night, and had built up a flourishing business when he was discovered by the authorities.[8] The newspaper *Ta Kung Pao* reported in October 1957 that peasant "debates" were held in Hupeh, Shantung, Shensi, Kiangsu, Hunan, and Fukien provinces to discourage peasants from selling grain to speculators and private merchants. It was reported that food grain merchants were "banned" in Chekiang Province in August and in Sinkiang Province in September 1957.[9] . . .

The drive to remould businessmen eventually included members of their immediate families as well. Dependents of former capitalists were urged in 1959 to participate in labor by collecting manure, planting trees, harvesting crops, and building irrigation facilities. "Let all dependents of industrialists and merchants march bravely to the front," admonished *Ta Kung Pao* in March 1959, at the same time complaining that most wives of businessmen were "still sitting on the fence," and were "lingering over the capitalist road and the easy life of exploitation." Li Wei-han, Director of the United Front Work Department of the Chinese Communist Party, admitted in 1960 that although the state had won the fight with capitalism in China on the economic front, through socialization, it was necessary to extend this victory to the political and ideological fronts. "The class struggle," he said, "is still going on and will necessarily continue for a very long time to come. It will not die out while the bourgeoisie still exist."[10] It is symptomatic of this "struggle" with businessmen that as late as July 1962 the Chinese press was still urging industrialists to share with the state their professional experience as technicians and managers by making suggestions for operation of commercial and industrial enterprises.[11] Apparently the capitalists have not yet fully identified themselves with the proletariat, and they must still be prompted to cooperate with the Communist regime.

The door that had been closed so completely to private forms of enterprise in 1956 was opened a crack in 1960 as the Chinese Communists retreated from the Leap Forward and the communes. Supplies of subsidiary foods and other consumer products had fallen so low by November 1960 that peasants were once again permitted to cultivate small private plots, were encouraged to engage in household subsidiary production, and were allowed to sell their extra produce at rural trade fairs. These three elements of private initiative in a socialist state the Communists referred to as "the small freedom under the big collective."[12] Free markets that sprang up in a few large cities in late 1960 apparently were closed several weeks later, but rural trade fairs in the villages have been continued and even expanded, as an incentive to farmers to increase the market supplies of food and miscellaneous handicraft products.

The government has kept a watchful eye over rural trade fairs in order to keep them well within the original conceptual framework. Retail merchandise is classified into (1) first-category goods (such as grain, cotton, and oil-bearing materials) which cannot be sold at rural trade fairs; (2) second-category goods, which can be sold at fairs only after farmers have met their quotas for compulsory sale to the state; and (3) third-category goods (such as vegetables, poultry, and handicrafts) which may be traded freely. Prices are agreed between buyer and seller, but only sales between the producer and final consumer are permitted, thus ruling out transactions by middlemen for profit.[13]

An article in *Ta Kung Pao* in January 1962 summarized the discussions by Chinese economists during 1961 on the topic of rural trade fairs. Some of the achievements of these free markets that were noted in the discussions represent an oblique recognition of the efficacy of private enterprise, at least in rural areas. The fairs, it was said, had promoted production of subsidiary foods and handicraft products by peasants, had increased the flow of materials between town and countryside, had speeded up the circulation of commodities, had relieved state commerce of some of its responsibilities, and had "activated the rural economy."[14] In spite of these favorable comments from the economists, the rural trade fairs also came in for criticism; at a forum held in Anhwei Province in November 1961 it was pointed out that they still gave rise to many problems. Speculative merchants and peddlers were accused of illegal activities such as buying and selling for profit, raising prices, and disrupting the order of the markets. Some farmers were accused of giving up farming for trade and of engaging in long-distance transport and marketing. The remedies for these extra-legal forms of capitalism were said to be greater control by the state. "In short," said *Ta Kung Pao,* "freedom should be allowed boldly where freedom is called for and control should be exercised seriously where control is necessary."[15]

The continued flourishing of rural trade fairs in many parts of China attests to their success in stimulating production of scarce consumer goods, especially foodstuffs. When Peking gave the Chinese farmers a free hand to cultivate private plots in their spare time and to sell their produce in village markets, the response was immediate; there was a substantial increase in the output of vegetables, fruit, and other subsidiary foods, and the composition of the Chinese diet improved perceptibly. The Communists recognized publicly the contribution that a limited private market can make in a time of great scarcity of consumer goods. The Economic Society of Anhwei, for example, concluded that "the holding of [rural] trade fairs was not only necessary at the present stage but would remain so for quite a long period of time to come."[16] Even the large cities experienced some benefit from the private plots, because reports indicated that free markets were reintroduced in such cities as Shanghai during 1962, with prices considerably above those in state markets.[17]

Late in 1962 and early in 1963, the Communist regime seemed more optimistic about the outlook for the Chinese economy than it had been for many months. Concomitant with this rise in confidence, a mass campaign was begun for socialist education in China in order to forestall any further drift toward private enterprise. The effect of this campaign on traders in the rural markets has been to curtail their freedom. Provincial authorities have issued explicit and more stringent regulations on private trade. Perhaps typical of these is the new regulation published in Kwangtung Province in May 1963, which decreed that only certain individuals and organizations will be permitted to engage in trade and that they all must be licensed. Production teams and members of production teams who wish to trade will be required to secure "certificates of self-production and self-marketing," and they will not be permitted to engage in wholesale or resale activities. State farms are forbidden to sell on the free markets, but must sell all of their produce to the supply and marketing cooperatives.[18] This regulation will probably decrease the incentives to cultivate private plots intensively and will reduce the amount of foodstuffs and handicrafts offered for sale on the free markets. Although during the summer of 1963 the regime seemed to be losing the spark of confidence with which it had entered the new year, there has been no let-up in the campaign to restrict the free markets.

The revival of economic freedoms in China since 1960 has at no time gone beyond the stage of small private plots and supervised village markets. The Communist press has been adamant against capitalism at the same time that it has admitted the usefulness of limited free markets in the countryside. There is no hint that the Marxist purists in Peking would permit the resumption of private factories even on a small scale, particularly if this involved the hiring of labor. The most the regime will tolerate is the production of small handicraft items by private families for sale in the rural markets. The people have been warned extensively in the press against speculation in all types of commodities, against exploitation of labor in any form, and against "spontaneous tendencies toward capitalism." There appears to be no chance at present that private businessmen would be permitted to resume operations under any conditions, much less to regain the relative freedom they knew before 1956.

The Chinese Communists have shown clearly in the last decade that they could live with and use private business in the short run, but that they were thoroughly hostile to it in the end. They made effective use of the skills and the capital of private enterprise during the early years of their regime when they were most in need of help to restore and improve industry and commerce in China. They were able to gain the initial support of businessmen by exchanging temporarily their Marxist goal of rapid socialization for a period of tolerance of private profits. It was seven years after their rise to power before the Communist leaders appeared confident enough to turn their backs completely on private businessmen. However, had it not been for the active cooperation of private business during the early part of the decade, the Chinese economy might not have experienced a recovery as rapid as that which occurred during 1950–52 and which set the stage for beginning the First Five-Year Plan in 1953. This willingness to work with the capitalists early in their regime revealed a useful degree of flexibility on the part of the Communists that has characterised their approach to a number of other, though not all, important economic problems.

Notes

1. Ho Kan-chih, *A History of the Modern Chinese Revolution*, Foreign Language Press, Peking, 1960.

2. SCMP, No. 1210, January 18, 1956; No. 1441, January 2, 1957; *Income and Standard of Living, op cit.*

3. Hsuch Mu-chiao, Su Hsing, and Lin Tse-li, *The Socialist Transformation of the National Economy in China*, Foreign Languages Press, Peking, 1960; also SCMP, No. 970, January 18, 1955; No. 820, June 1, 1954; No. 762, March 9, 1954.

4. Kuan Ta-tung, *The Socialist Transformation, op. cit.;* SCMP, No. 884, September 8, 1954.

5. SCMP, No. 1519, April 30, 1957.

6. SCMP, No. 1458, January 25, 1957.

7. Shih Ch'eng-chih, *Urban Commune Experiments in Communist China,* Union Research Institute, Hong Kong, 1962; also SCMP, No. 1834, August 18, 1958.

8. *Ta Kung Pao,* October 21, 1957 (SCMP, No. 1649, November 12, 1957).

9. SCMP, No. 1658, November 25, 1957.

10. SCMP, No. 2349, September 30, 1960.

11. *Ta Kung Pao,* March 15 1959 (SCMP, No. 1982, March 31, 1959).

12. *Ta Kung Pao,* July 5, 1961 (SCMP, No. 2558, August 15, 1961).

13. SCMP, No. 2660, January 17, 1962.

14. *Ta Kung Pao,* January 19, 1962 (SCMP, No. 2675, January 21, 1962).

15. SCMP, No. 2643, December 20, 1961; No. 2660, January 17, 1962.

16. SCMP, No. 2643, December 20, 1961.

17. *South China Morning Post,* Hong Kong, August 1, 1962.

18. *Nan Fang Jih Pao,* Canton, May 15, 1963.

Problems of Control: The Organization of Urban Industry

20. A STATEMENT OF PURPOSE

Po I-po

I. Progress of Socialist Industrialization

One of the great historical tasks of the Chinese people as they carry on socialist construction after the victory of the revolution is to bring about the socialist industrialization of their country.

CHINA'S BACKWARD ECONOMIC LEGACY

Old China left a very backward economic legacy. Industry comprised only a very small part of the entire national economy, and its foundations were very weak. The principal industries were light ones, such as textiles and food products. The very few heavy industries that did exist were of a fragmentary nature; they included a small number of mines and metallurgical plants run by the imperialists to rob China of her resources, and an engineering industry capable only of carrying out repairs and assembly. The overwhelming majority of both light and heavy industries were under the control of the imperialists and comprador-bourgeoisie and so were colonial or semi-colonial in nature. In line with this situation, the geographical distribution of industry was extremely irrational with a handful of coastal cities containing over 70 per cent of all the nation's industry. Because of this state of affairs, China, for more than a century, remained a weak country, her people lived in poverty and

SOURCE: Selected from *Peking Review*, October 11, 1963, pp. 6–12. The article was by the vice-premier of the People's Republic of China and was first published in Spanish in the October issue of *Cuba Socialista*.

she was subjected to aggression and oppression by capitalist and imperialist powers.

During the years of reactionary rule, many Chinese hoped to "save the country by building industry" so as to change the country from a backward agricultural land into an advanced industrial state, but all these hopes remained vain dreams. It was only when the Chinese people, led by the Chinese Communist Party, overthrew the reactionary rule of the Kuomintang, wiped out imperialist influence in China and founded the People's Republic that they were able to realize their ideal of gradually building up their country into a great and powerful socialist industrial state.

The Chinese Communist Party has always attached great importance to the question of the nation's industrialization. In March 1949, on the eve of the nationwide victory of the Chinese revolution, Comrade Mao Tse-tung, speaking at the Second Plenary Session of the Seventh Central Committee of the Chinese Communist Party, called on the people that they should, after the victory of the revolution, "speedily restore and develop production, cope with foreign imperialism, steadily transform China from an agricultural into an industrial country and build China into a great socialist state."[1]

FROM ECONOMIC RESTORATION
TO PLANNED CONSTRUCTION

With the founding of the People's Republic of China in October 1949, we immediately confiscated the bureaucrat-capitalist enterprises run by the reactionary government of Chiang Kai-shek and changed them into state-run socialist enterprises. With regard to enterprises run by imperialist countries in China, we, according to circumstances, either bought them up or took them under government control, gradually transforming them into state-run socialist enterprises. At the same time we carried out the land reform and thoroughly liquidated the feudal system of land ownership which had prevailed in our countryside for thousands of years. By the end of 1952, after something over two years of work we had successfully completed the onerous task of restoring the national economy and healing the wounds of war.

From 1953 to 1957 we carried out our First Five-Year Plan for the development of the national economy. In this period we concentrated our main efforts on large-scale industrial construction which comprised more than 600 key projects, thus laying the initial foundation for socialist industrialization. In 1956 we completed the socialist transformation of agriculture, handicrafts and capitalist industry and commerce, thus winning a decisive victory in the socialist revolution as far as ownership of the means of production was concerned. During the period of our Second Five-Year Plan, 1958–1962, under the guidance of the Party's general line for building socialism, China's industry continued to make great progress while throughout the countryside the agricultural producers' co-operatives were further combined into people's communes.

FOUNDATION OF INDUSTRIALIZATION LAID

With the construction carried out under the two five-year plans, China's industry underwent great changes and the foundation for China's socialist industrialization was laid.

In the past China had no tractor industry or motor vehicle industry, and no industry building ships, aircraft, heavy machines, precision machine tools, precision instruments and meters or chemical synthetic materials. Now all these new industries are being built up. This means that a radical change has taken place in transforming the incomplete state of our industrial departments. We have now built an industrial system of some size.

In the past we were unable to design many important industrial products and had to rely mainly on foreign designs; now we have progressed from copying to independent designing. In the past we could only make small and medium-sized equipment that required relatively simple techniques; now we are able to make some big and precision equipment. In the past, many of our important construction projects were designed with help from fraternal countries who provided the major part or even all of the equipment; now, we are able to design independently and to build with our own technical forces many important construction projects. These include modern coal pits each with an annual output of a million tons; integrated iron and steel works each with an annual productive capacity of 1.5 million tons of steel; chemical fertilizer plants each with an annual productive capacity of 25,000 tons of synthetic ammonia; various heavy-machine building plants; power stations each with a 650,000-kilowatt capacity, and many other types of plants. All this goes to show that we have greatly increased our technical strength for industrial construction and greatly raised our technical level.

With the establishment of these new industrial branches and the increase in her technical strength, China has very considerably raised her level of self-sufficiency in equipment and material needed for socialist construction. During her First Five-Year Plan, China could make about 55 per cent of the machinery and equipment she needed. During the Second Five-Year Plan, this level was raised to about 85 per cent. Our level of self-sufficiency in steel products climbed from about 75 per cent in the First Five-Year Plan period to around 90 per cent in the Second Five-Year Plan period. These facts show that China's socialist industrialization has taken yet another giant step forward along the road of self-reliance in construction.

RATIONAL DISTRIBUTION OF INDUSTRY

There have also been remarkable changes in the geographical distribution of our industry. Our industry was concentrated in the past in a few coastal cities. Nowadays, not only has the industry in these coastal cities been greatly expanded but every province and autonomous region in the country has established modern industry to some extent or other. In the past, our only large-scale iron and steel industrial base was the Anshan Iron and Steel Company, and even this was not fully constructed. Now we have not only thoroughly built up this base but also constructed new iron and steel bases at Wuhan, Pao-tow and elsewhere. In the past our electric power industry was concentrated in a few cities; now all the big, small and medium-sized cities and quite a number of villages too have power stations of various sizes. In the past our textile industry was mainly concentrated in a few coastal cities such as Shanghai, Tientsin and Tsingtao; now many provinces of the country have established up-to-date textile mills. All this means that there has been a general growth of industry throughout our vast country with its many nationalities.

A dozen or so years is just an instant in the long history of our country, but the great achievements we have made in industralization are unprecedented in that history. Even our enemies—the imperialists—cannot but acknowledge China's great achievements in industrial construction. This is the trend of developments: China's weakness is rapidly turning into its opposite—strength. This brings joy and encouragement to our people and elation to our friends throughout the world.

OUR GOALS

Of course, though we have already achieved successes on the road of socialist industrialization, we are still a long way from having reached our goals in this endeavour. The socialist industrialization of our country entails building an independent, comprehensive and modern industrial system and putting the whole of our national economy, agriculture included, on to a modern technical basis in a comparatively short period of time. In other words, we must ensure that the raw and other materials and all kinds of machinery and equipment produced by our heavy industries are able to meet the needs of socialist expanded reproduction, the needs of the technical transformation of all sectors of the national economy and of the modernization of our national defence. We must also see to it that our light industries are able to produce various kinds of consumer goods to satisfy appropriately the requirements of the continuously rising standards of living of the people.

In achieving this aim, of course, all kinds of difficulties may crop up, but no difficulties have ever been able to block our advance. We have an advanced socialist system, over 600 million hard-working and courageous people, the correct leadership of the long-tested Chinese Communist Party headed by Comrade Mao Tse-tung, and rich natural resources; we have all the internal conditions needed for carrying out socialist industrialization. At the same time we also have the support of the fraternal socialist countries and the people of the world. With these favourable conditions, the speed of our socialist industrialization is bound to be faster than that of capitalist industrialization. In the space of only a dozen or so years, we have laid the foundation of socialist industrialization in an economically backward country. We will certainly be able to maintain the same leap-forward speed to carry through the socialist industrialization of our country in a relatively short historical period of time.

II. China's Road to Industrialization

In addition to the favourable conditions mentioned above, one decisive reason why our socialist industrialization can develop fairly rapidly is that we have discovered through our own practice a road suited to our own actual situation for carrying out socialist industrialization with greater, faster, better and more economical results. The principal features of this road are expounded by Comrade Mao Tse-tung in his speech *On the Correct Handling of Contradictions Among the People* as follows:

In discussing our path to industrialization, I am here concerned principally with the relationship between the growth of heavy industry, light industry and agriculture. Heavy industry is the core of China's economic construction. This must be affirmed. But, at the same time, full attention must be paid to the development of agriculture and light industry.

"As China is a great agricultural country, with over 80 per cent of its population in the villages, its industry and agriculture must be developed simultaneously. Only then will industry have raw materials and a market, and only so will it be possible to accumulate fairly large funds for the building up of a powerful heavy industry. Everyone knows that light industry is closely related to agriculture. Without agriculture there can be no light industry. But it is not so clearly understood that agriculture provides heavy industry with an important market. This fact, however, will be more readily appreciated as the gradual progress of technological improvement and modernization of agriculture calls for more and more machinery, fertilizers, water conservancy and electric power projects and transport facilities for the farms, as well as fuel and building materials for the rural consumers. The entire national economy will benefit if we can achieve an even greater growth in our agriculture and thus induce a correspondingly greater development of light industry. . . . With the development of agriculture and light industry, heavy industry will be assured of its market and funds, and thus grow faster. Hence what may seem to be a slower pace of industrialization is actually not so, and indeed the tempo may even be speeded up."[2]

RELATIONS BETWEEN HEAVY INDUSTRY, LIGHT INDUSTRY AND AGRICULTURE

Correct handling of the relationship between the growth of the three most basic branches of production—heavy industry, light industry and agriculture—is of the greatest significance in our socialist industrialization. We have already fully recognized in practice that socialist industrialization cannot be carried out in isolation. It is essential that industry and agriculture should be developed simultaneously and that heavy and light industry should be developed simultaneously; or, in other words, that their development should be mutually coordinated and that they should not get out of step with each other; only in this way can we guarantee the high-speed and balanced advance of socialist industrialization, and ensure that it is well integrated with improving the life of the people. During the past two five-year plans, we constantly educated our cadres to hold resolutely to our road of industrialization and in their practical work guard against and rectify one-sided practice of regarding industry as all-important while neglecting agriculture or of paying attention only to heavy industry while neglecting light industry. This has promoted the sound development of our socialist industrialization.

The question of how to deal correctly with the development of agriculture in the course of socialist industrialization is one that must be solved with the greatest attention in order to uphold our road of socialist industrialization. In a country like ours, with our 500 million peasants, the conditions of the peasantry and of agriculture have a very close connection with the advance of industrialization and the development of socialist construction.

AGRICULTURE—FOUNDATION OF NATIONAL ECONOMY

Our Party's Central Committee has summarized the country's experience in construction and has clearly pointed out that agriculture forms the foundation for the growth of our industry and of the whole national economy. The basic means of subsistence of our population of over 600 million are met mainly by agriculture. Agriculture is also the major base providing raw materials for our light industry and it is the source of some of the subsidiary raw and other materials for heavy industry. Our industrialization is dependent on our internal market, and the countryside forms the major part of this internal market, the biggest in the world. The labour force needed for the growth of industry and for other economic enterprises comes principally from the countryside. The great amount of funds needed for our socialist construction is accumulated within the country, and a large part of it comes directly or indirectly from agriculture. All these are the manifestations of the role of agriculture as the foundation for the development of the national economy; they also constitute the most important conditions for carrying out socialist industrialization in our country. We need to mobilize fully the initiative and creativeness of the broad masses of our peasant allies, and with the support of all branches of the national economy, and the industrial branches in particular, devote great efforts to developing agriculture, greatly increasing the output of agricultural produce and raising agricultural labour productivity. It will then be possible to provide the cities with more and more marketable grains and other nonstaple food, supply more and more cotton and other raw materials to industry, transfer even more labour-power from agriculture to industry and to other branches of the economy, mobilize the vast domestic market to make big demands on industry and absorb vast quantities of heavy and light industrial goods, and amass plenty of funds for industrial construction. The result of all this will not be to slow down but to promote the progress of socialist industrialization and the development of the whole national economy, as well as to facilitate greatly the improvements in the living standards of the people of the whole country and the consolidation of the worker-peasant alliance.

The development of our industry according to the policy of taking agriculture as the foundation of the national economy involves two requirements. One is that the size of the labour force needed for industrial development must be basically proportioned to the amount of marketable grains and other means of subsistence that can be provided by agriculture. The other is that in serving all branches of the national economy, industry must concentrate mainly on serving agriculture. All industry, whether light or heavy, must make the countryside its principal market. Heavy industry in particular must regard supporting the technical reform of agriculture as its foremost task, and must see to it that socialist industrialization and the modernization of agriculture are closely integrated and help each other forward. Practical experience has taught us that our industrialization can advance in the right direction and enjoy unlimited prospects only when it advances along the line of taking agriculture as the foundation of the national economy and adapts itself to the two above-mentioned requirements.

IMPORTANCE OF HEAVY INDUSTRY

Our stress on developing industry according to the policy of taking agriculture as the foundation of the national economy and the carrying out of socialist economic construction centering on heavy industry is not contradictory; the two are a unity. Taking agriculture as the foundation of the national economy does not in the least imply the weakening of the growth of heavy industry; it actually creates even better conditions for heavy industrial development.

The carrying out of socialist industrialization directly entails the gradual building of a powerful industry, the leading branch of the national economy, and, first and foremost, the building of heavy industry which is the principal productive branch of the means of production. This is because only when heavy industry is developed and priority is given to growth of the means of production can social expanded reproduction be realized, can advanced technical equipment be provided for the technical transformation of the entire national economy, including agriculture, and for the strengthening of the national defences. Only under these circumstances can the leading role of industry in the national economy be brought into full play. Unless we make big efforts to build up the machine-building, metallurgical and chemical industries and other heavy industries, we will not be able to obtain the various kinds of machines and the steel products and building materials, electricity and fuel which are needed; we will not be able to equip our agriculture, light industry and transport; our national economy will remain backward for a long time and we will not be able to build up modern national defences.

In an agricultural country such as ours with an extremely weak industrial foundation and standing in the forefront of the fight against the forces of aggression and war headed by U.S. imperialism, the Chinese people urgently demand the development of heavy industry. The Chinese Communist Party is fully aware of this desire of the people, and has consistently given due importance to the development of heavy industry. In industrial construction during the past two five-year plans, we concentrated our main strength on heavy industry. A considerable number of our major construction projects were heavy industrial enterprises. This was absolutely necessary. This is precisely the reason why we succeeded in building the foundations of socialist industrialization in such a relatively short time. It is either a big misunderstanding or a distortion to say that our opposition to one-sided development of heavy industry means neglect of such industry.

ENERGETIC DEVELOPMENT OF LIGHT INDUSTRY

Practice has brought it home to us that energetic promotion and not limitation of the development of light industry in accordance with the possibilities of supplies of raw materials and funds as well as the market demand, is not detrimental but beneficial to socialist industrialization.

As is well known, industry shoulders the task of providing not only the means of labour, but also consumer goods. This is a very heavy task for industry in our country with its large population and economic backwardness. Energetic development of light industry will keep the market brisk, maintain commodity prices stable, satisfy appropriately the needs of the people's livelihood, and link socialist industrialization more closely with the vital interests of the people. This conforms completely with the aims of socialist production.

Moreover, light industry, as an important link, is closely connected with agriculture and heavy industry. The growth of light industry means the production of more and more light industrial goods to exchange for products of agriculture and farm side-occupations, thus promoting agricultural production and supporting industrial construction. Light industry is also an important source of accumulating funds for construction, because its factories are easier to build, need smaller investments, give quicker results and earn larger profits. At the same time, the growth of light industry also demands huge amounts of raw materials, machinery and equipment from the various branches of heavy industry, and this, in turn, promotes the development of heavy industry.

Our experience of industrialization has proved that there is no sound basis to views separating light industry from heavy industry and even opposing one to the other and regarding the energetic and appropriate development of light industry as being detrimental, rather than helpful, to the growth of heavy industry.

SIMULTANEOUS DEVELOPMENT OF NATIONAL AND LOCAL INDUSTRIES

The question of our country's road to industrialization also involves the simultaneous development of national and local industries and of large enterprises as well as small and medium-sized enterprises under the conditions of centralized leadership, overall planning and division of labour and co-operation.

In China, the national industries generally comprise the large enterprises which serve as the backbone in the building of our industrial system; local industries generally comprise the small and medium-sized enterprises which are important and by no means negligible elements in the building of our industrial system. In the course of socialist industrialization, the relations between national and local industries, between large, small and medium-sized enterprises must be correctly handled in regard to systems of management, scale of production and geographical distribution of industry to ensure their planned development, so as to bring about a rapid increase in the productive capacity of industry, improve its geographical distribution, promote the integration of town and countryside, accelerate technical reform in agriculture, and thereby greatly reduce the time it will take to industrialize. In handling these questions it is disadvantageous to our socialist industrialization to put a one-sided emphasis on the development of national industry and large enterprises, or to follow the decentralized method of blindly developing local industry and small enterprises in disregard of the unified state plan.

III. Policy of Self-Reliance

Do we rely mainly on our own efforts or on foreign aid in carrying out our socialist construction and industrialization? We firmly adhere to the policy of self-reliance.

Every socialist country should rely mainly on itself for its construction. This is especially so with China. China has a population of over 650 million and an area of 9,600,000 square kilometres, and is an extremely underdeveloped country economically. It is both inconceivable and utterly impossible for such a country to meet the demands of domestic production and its people's livelihood by depending on imports of large amounts of the means of production and industrial goods for daily use. In our socialist industrialization, it is only by relying on the diligent labour of our people, making full use of our country's rich resources and bringing all our potentialities into play that we can rapidly establish our own powerful industry, build an independent, comprehensive and modern industrial system, create a powerful material and technical foundation for the entire national economy, further consolidate our country and constantly raise the people's living standards. Only in this way can we contribute our maximum strength in fulfilling our internationlist obligations, enhance the might of the entire socialist camp, and oppose imperialism and defend world peace more effectively.

How do we carry out the policy of self-reliance, overcome the difficulties on our road of advance and press ahead with industrialization?

INTERNAL ACCUMULATION OF FUNDS

Large amounts of construction funds are needed for socialist industrialization. The principal source of such funds in China is the internal accumulation provided by the national economy. With the rapid development of agricultural and industrial production, our national income has continually increased. As our national income has steadily increased and the people's standards of living has gradually risen, we have appropriately increased the proportion of funds set aside from the national income for accumulation. In state bodies, enterprises, schools and among the broad masses of the people, we resolutely advocate building up the country industriously and thriftily, practising strict economy and accumulating all the funds that can be saved. We pay full attention to the rational use of funds, to the prevention of waste and to getting more work done with the minimum possible expenditure of money, materials and manpower.

At the same time, we also pay constant attention to adjusting relations between accumulation and consumption in the distribution of the national income, correctly integrating long-range collective interests with immediate individual interests and the development of production with improvement of the people's livelihood.

RAISING THE TECHNICAL LEVEL

To carry out socialist industrialization by our own efforts, it is necessary to achieve a swift rise in the level of our industrial techniques, increase the varieties of products made and gradually raise our level of self-sufficiency in regard to the equipment, raw and other materials needed by our socialist construction. In tackling this problem, we first of all pay attention to the correct handling of the relation between the quantity of industrial goods produced on the one hand and variety and quality on the other hand, so as to combine properly increase in quantity with greater variety and better quality, and check and correct the deviations of putting undue emphasis on quantity while neglecting variety and quality. We adopt various measures and continuously strengthen the work of scientific experiment to increase the varieties of products, improve their quality and rapidly raise our country's technical level.

In order to carry out socialist industrialization by our own efforts, it is also necessary to step up the training of personnel for construction work, and speedily create a strong army of specialists with a high level of socialist consciousness and the ability to master modern science and techniques. To solve this problem we, on the one hand, have energetically developed in a planned way both higher education and secondary specialized education to train various kinds of specialists. On the other hand, we have made big efforts to set up spare-time cultural schools and technical schools so as to achieve a continuous rise in the cultural, technical and vocational levels of workers and employees.

NOT "GOING IT ALONE"

While we have mobilized all positive factors at home for socialist industrialization, we have also endeavoured to obtain, and have actually obtained, the support of the fraternal socialist countries and brothers in other hands. We have learnt from the socialist countries their experience in industrialization, and have endeavoured to strengthen mutual aid and co-operation and mutual support with the socialist countries. Simultaneously we have also studied all the advanced science and techniques of the world and developed trade relations with countries of different social systems on the basis of equality and mutual benefit. This testifies that our policy of self-reliance conforms to the principle of mutual support and assistance based on proletarian internationalism, and does not stand opposed to it; it also conforms to the development of economic relations between countries. The allegations about "going it alone" in separation from the socialist camp and "national closed doors," has nothing to do with our policy of self-reliance.

IV. Party Leadership—Guarantee of Victory

We have consistently strengthened the leadership of the Chinese Communist Party in the course of our socialist industrialization; this is the fundamental guarantee of victory.

The most important aspect of the Party's leadership in economic construction is its unified leadership in the political and ideological fields, in the formulation of policy and in organization. Our Party has not only put forward the policies and line of industrialization, but in order to ensure the correct implementation of the Party's line, has also waged continuous struggles against the Right or "Left" tendencies that deviate from the Party's correct line.

PRODUCTION STRUGGLE LINKED
WITH CLASS STRUGGLE

The socialist industrialization of our country is a great struggle for production which is interlinked with the class struggle. We brought about the socialist transformation of capitalist ownership of the means of production in 1956, and smashed the frenzied attack of the bouregois rightists in 1957. This achieved a basic victory of the socialist revolution on the economic, political and ideological fronts. However, classes and class struggle still exist in our country. The bourgeois elements who do not want to be reformed and the overthrown landlord class are not reconciled to the elimination of their classes, and never give up their attempts to stage a comeback. New capitalist elements are constantly and spontaneously generated in the petty-bourgeois atmosphere. As a result of the corrupting influence of the bourgeoisie and the influence of the atmosphere of the small producers, a very small number of unstable elements within the ranks of our working class have degenerated and become new bourgeois elements. At the same time, imperialism and reactionaries are doing their utmost to spread their influence and even cherish vain hopes of subverting our socialist system. Under these circumstances, class struggle is inevitable.

There is class struggle between the proletariat and the bourgeoisie and struggle between the socialist and capitalist roads throughout the historical period of proletarian revolution and proletarian dictatorship and throughout the historical period of the transition from capitalism to communism. It is most dangerous to forget or overlook the class struggle during socialist construction and the struggle for production. Our Party has therefore never ceased to conduct education in the understanding of classes and class struggle and socialist education among the working class and among all the labouring people, so as to raise their level of class consciousness and socialist initiative, prevent and overcome corruption by bourgeois thinking, and deal resolute blows against the activities of the reactionary classes to stage a comeback.

To ensure the Party's leadership in industrial construction, basic organizations of the Party are established in all our industrial enterprises and are continuously strengthened.

INTEGRATING COLLECTIVE LEADERSHIP WITH INDIVIDUAL RESPONSIBILITY

The Party committee in an enterprise is the core of leadership of all the work of the enterprise. In the production and management work of the enterprise, we have adopted the system whereby the director assumes full responsibility under the leadership of the enterprise's Party committee. This system of leadership requires that all major questions in the enterprise should be discussed and decided collectively by the Party committee, while the director is responsible for carrying out the work of production and management. This system of leadership, on the one hand, inherits the effective and traditional system of leadership of our Party which integrates collective leadership with individual responsibility. On the other hand, this system also suits the nature of modern industrial enterprises which need highly centralized and unified direction. The adoption of this system not only ensures the leadership of the Party committee in production and management, but also brings the roles of the leading members of the management and the management departments into full play. It also ensures that no errors or at least less errors are made by the leading members of enterprises in deciding important problems; it also makes it relatively easier for them to correct errors when these occur.

The leadership of our Party is built on the basis of the mass line, which is the correct method of leadership based on the principle of "from the masses, to the masses" consistently adhered to by our Party during the prolonged revolutionary struggle. This method of leadership has been further developed in the practice of our socialist industrialization.

RELYING ON WORKING CLASS IN ENTERPRISE MANAGEMENT

Our Party manages enterprises by closely relying on the working class. We have established trade union organizations in all enterprises, developed all kinds of activities, encouraged workers and employees to engage in socialist labour emulation, and raised their levels of ideological and political consciousness and their cultural and technical levels. In accordance with the principle of democratic centralism, we have established various kinds of democratic management systems in enterprises, convening regular representative conferences or general meetings of the workers and employees to discuss and solve important problems in enterprises and drawing in the masses to take part in management and supervise the work of management.

The democracy being carried out in our enterprises is democracy under the guidance of centralization; it is opposed to that false slogan and mistaken practice of "workers' self-rule"; our centralization is based on democracy, and is radically different from the practice that relies solely on administrative orders and is divorced from the Party leadership and the masses.

"THREE-IN-ONE" METHOD

In all enterprises we follow the "three-in-one" method of combining the efforts of leading personnel, technicians (including specialized management staff) and the masses of workers so as to bring together leading personnel with the masses, and link technical theoretical knowledge with working practice, and political and ideological work with economic work. This is an important aspect of implementing the mass line.

In practising the "three-in-one" method, leading cadres and administrative cadres participate partly in productive labour while workers participate partly in day-to-day productive management.

In our socialist enterprises, the partial participation of cadres in productive labour is an important question of principle. This concerns the question whether cadres will put themselves among the masses and merge with the masses or sit up on high and be divorced from the masses. Participation in labour enables cadres to maintain their status as ordinary working people, refrain from enjoying special favours and prevent their divorce from the masses; this is a fundamental condition guaranteeing that cadres shall not degenerate. Participation in labour also enables cadres to maintain close links with production, to discover promptly the positive factors of production, clearly discern problems arising in production and solve them together with the masses, thereby preventing the errors of bureaucracy and subjectivism that result from a divorce from reality.

As far as the workers are concerned, their partial participation in day-to-day management of production is conducive to enhancing their sense of responsibility arising from their status as masters of the country, thus bringing their labour initiative into full play and helping them step by step to master the art of managing enterprises. Great numbers of our cadres have been trained and promoted from among the ordinary workers.

It has been proved in practice that the use of the "three-in-one" method is also extremely helpful in creating in our socialist enterprises the new relations between man and man of friendly mutual assistance and unity for a common progress. This cannot but be of far-reaching significance to our country's socialist cause.

Notes

1. *Selected Works of Mao Tse-tung,* Eng. ed., Foreign Languages Press, Peking, 1961, Volume IV, p. 373.

2. Mao Tse-tung, *On the Correct Handling of Contradictions Among the People,* Eng. ed., Foreign Languages Press, Peking, 1960, pp. 67–68.

21. IDEOLOGY AND ECONOMIC PLANNING:

DEVELOPMENTS AND PROBLEMS

KENNETH WALKER

As an introduction it will be helpful to summarize, briefly, the nature of the development problem facing China in 1952, the eve of the First Five Year Plan, 1953–57. Despite the considerable economic progress[1] which had been made by China during the period of postwar reconstruction and monetary stabilization, 1949–52, the overwhelming impression obtained on reading the First Five Year Plan's[2] account of the state of the economy in 1952 and the tasks ahead is that the magnitude of the development problem was immense. But statistics and facts are more desirable here than superlatives. China's machine-building industry was almost entirely limited to repair and assembly work. According to the plan[3] there were no firms producing metallurgical, mining, or electrical equipment, large-scale precision tools, airplanes, lorries, or tractors. The iron and steel industry was minute, with steel output in 1952 only 1.35 million tons[4] (and even this was 50 per cent above the highest

SOURCE: Selected from Kenneth Walker, "Ideology and Economic Discussion in China: Ma Yin-ch'u on Development Strategy and His Critics," in *Economic Development and Cultural Change,* XI (January 1963), pp. 113–117 and 119–133. Reprinted by permission of The University of Chicago Press. Copyright 1963 by The University of Chicago Press.

previously attained output); 1952 output of iron ore was 1.93 million tons, coal 66.49 million tons, chemical fertilizers 181,000 tons, while oil production was a mere 436,000 tons. Electric power generated in 1952 amounted to 7.2 milliard kilowatt hours. Textile and other light industries were better developed, but these, like the heavy industries which existed, were located mainly in the northeast and along the coast. It was estimated that in 1952 the gross value of output of coastal industry accounted for more than 70 per cent of the total gross value of industrial output of China. The proportion of the gross output of China's iron and steel industry produced by the coastal firms was 80 per cent, the same as for light industry. In 1952 the railway network of China was only 24,200 kilometers in length and again was heavily concentrated in the northeast, many parts of China having no railway communications at all. This weakness has been emphasized for many years by economists[5] as one of the crucial factors impeding China's development. The inumerable agricultural problems cannot be listed here in any detail.[6] It is sufficient to record that in 1952 there were approximately 0.188 hectares of cultivated land per head of total population, while the latter was thought to be increasing at a rate of between 2.0 and 2.5 per cent per annum. The area of reclaimable land was not known, but most estimates showed that the possibilities for the near future were far from encouraging. The multiple cropping index was 130; 21.7 per cent of the total cultivated area was irrigated; fertilizer and insecticide supplies were trifling; farm equipment was primitive; crop yields were, not surprisingly, comparatively low. Finally, the problem of water conservation and control must be mentioned as one of the central, long-term tasks. Statistics published by Ping-ti Ho,[7] covering disasters of many centuries, bring out clearly the frequency and enormity of this problem. Figures issued by Peking for the 1950's[8] could be added to Ho's statistics to show that the problem is still acute. Summing up, China's development problem was how to create a modern industrial sector, on the weak base existing in 1952, and how to raise the level of agricultural output high enough to bear the burden of financing such development, in addition to feeding the population of 570–580 million, with its annual increase of over 11 million.

It was, in many ways, a greater problem than that which faced the Soviet Union ready to embark on her First Five Year Plan in 1928. Some similarities exist, however. The Soviet Union, too, had the problem of rural overpopulation;[9] like China she had not yet come to grips with the question of collectivization in agriculture and the allied problem of peasant incentives; there was a shortage of skilled industrial technicians and workers; Soviet industry was highly concentrated in the western regions of the U.S.S.R. Yet even these similarities must not be pressed too far, for they were different in degree. For example, China's area of cultivated land per head in 1952 was no more than 25 per cent of the 1928 Soviet acreage,[10] in addition to which the Soviet Union's reclaimable lands were extensive. The growth rate of the Soviet population was just half that of China. In some years there was a food surplus.[11] Probably the most important difference, however, was that the level of industrialization attained by the Soviet Union in 1928 was considerably greater than China's in 1952. Erlich[12] has pointed out that since the late nineteenth century the capital goods and other industries had been growing rapidly, while a metallurgical industry, using the most modern technology, already existed. The railway network was approximately double the density of the Chinese network. Here, as well as in many branches of Soviet industry, there was considerable excess capacity, providing a valuable breathing space before the investment hump had to be surmounted. This was not the case in China. Finally, in one very important respect China had an advantage over the Soviet Union: the existence of an ally willing to supply technical and economic assistance along with essential imports, on favorable terms. The security enjoyed by China through her alliance with the Soviet Union must, indeed, have had a marked effect on the strategy adopted in the First Five Year Plan period.

The plan brought out three main aims of the Chinese government: (1) to consolidate the political power of the Chinese Communist Party through carrying out a socialist revolution in every sphere of economic activity. (2) To build up a strong national defense. (3) To create, at top speed, the modern industrial basis for large-scale industrialization of China. The keynote was the development of industry, and above all, of heavy industry,[13] while agriculture and light industry were to be developed "in correct proportions." Both in terms of output targets and investment allocations set by the plan the strategy adopted involved a crash program of heavy industrial expansion. The bulk of agricultural capital formation (including water conservation), for example, was to be financed by the peasants themselves, state constructional investment being set at only 7.6 per cent of total state basic investment, while heavy industry was to receive 51.7 per cent.

The Extent of Chinese Discussions of
the Strategy of Chinese Development

. . . It would be interesting to know whether any theoretical discussions took place in China, as in the Soviet Union,[14] among economists or policy makers, prior to the implementation of the plan, concerning the merits of possible alternative policies. Without a great deal of research one cannot assert that no such discussions took place. Since the adoption of the plan, however, it seems likely that they were discouraged, to say the least. The Chinese economic journals were primarily concerned with analyzing very specific problems arising, such as problems of measurement (e.g., the national income), and with explaining particular government policies to the public. Exhortation to do better, to reduce mistakes, and to carry out party policies were the main topics. On the whole, broad questions of policy do not appear to have been discussed. The development strategy adopted was not in question. Attention concentrated on how to improve its implementation. The blooming of the "hundred flowers"[15] in 1957, however, brought to life some expressions of criticism from academic economists on matters of policy. A revealing statement of the position of economics and economists in China at that time was issued as a joint declaration by several famous economists.[16] In a bitterly worded and outspoken document Wu and his co-authors attacked the dogmatism which, they said, had captivated economic discussion during the previous eight years. Explicitly refuting the idea that the writings of Marx and Lenin could provide a set of laws or a complete plan for the economic development of all countries a century after they had been published, the authors went on to criticize the Chinese government for attempting to find such a blueprint in Marx and Lenin. . . .

But this statement did not contain any examination of the state of the Chinese economy, any appraisal of the broad policy questions about which the authors were so concerned, or specific policy prescriptions. Probably the only, and most important, attempt to cover this ground was made by Ma Yin-ch'u,[17] one of China's leading non-party economists, influential elder stateman and president of Peking University. The rest of this article will be devoted to a study of his views and those of some of his critics. . . .

The main theme in Ma's writings was that China should adopt a development strategy which centered upon balanced growth or, in Ma's terminology, "general balance" insofar as this was possible. He was undoubtedly opposed to the zig-zag "great leap forward" approach which had been adopted, involving an all-out concentration on developing a few chosen industries while others were relatively neglected, with its inevitable disproportions and wastes. Writing after the Great Leap Forward of 1958, Ma's views remained unchanged. Cautiously he drew attention[18] to the close correlation between a high speed of growth attempted and the degree of imbalance and dislocation experienced. In reality, he argued, smooth balanced development was impossible to attain completely: development was obtained in moving through the sequence of balance-imbalance to a new balance at a different level.[19] The aim of policy should be to discover the weaknesses which impeded the attainment of balance and to remedy them, thus minimizing fluctuations. An economy in balance over time was represented[20] by Ma as a circle, rotating upwards in a spiral movement (to give it a third dimension of growth). In this metaphor (as far as it is possible to understand it) the circle was composed of a series of links, representing the sectors of an economy, connected to one another as an expression of the sectoral interdependence of real economic life. Sooner or later, Ma argued, the last link will be found to be related to the first in the chain. Thus the circle is completed; the economy is balanced, because all the links are joined. This metaphor was an unnecessarily complicated way of depicting the idea of interdependence, and it is only mentioned here because (not unnaturally) it became one of the main targets of criticism by Ma's opponents. It has been pointed out,[21] however, that the metaphor would be familiar to the Chinese audience, for whom it was intended, and it may have been helpful as a tool of exposition. Policy then, in Ma Yin-ch'u's opinion, should aim to plan for "general balance,"[22] by grasping the "law of planning according to proportional development,"[23] these terms being described as the "most important two principles in political economy"—and of which too few young people in China had heard. In what sense did Ma use these principles?

Behind the camouflage of verbiage surrounding much of the discussion, it is apparent that there existed a fundamental disagreement between Ma and his opponents regarding the use of these terms. It was an expression of their disagreement over economic policy and the political preferences involved. An immediate reaction to the term "general balance" is to equate it with the Western economic concept of balanced growth. Balanced growth, as used in the West, can have at least two distinct meanings: (1) "Simultaneous investment in several industries in conformity with the pattern of consumers' demand and of the different industries' demand for each others' products.'[24] The emphasis is on demand, the market, and on development along a wide front of activity. (2) In China, as in the Soviet Union,[25] it can mean balance between the supply of, and demand for, materials in a very few sectors of the economy, while others are allowed to develop slowly or not at all. Balance here, then, means consistency in an input-output sense, perhaps on a very narrow front of development. It may involve a disregard for market forces and consumer demand, the government being strong enough to dictate the priorities and to control the level of consumption.

Though it was not explicitly stated, it is clear that Ma equated general balance as much with the first as with the second of the above meanings. For Ma, general balance meant more than plan consistency in a narrowly chosen range of activity. He desired that more emphasis should be given to consumer demand, for political and economic reasons, and (as we shall see) greater use of the market mechanism as a means of obtaining the general balance, although he was not arguing for a completely free market economy. Thus Ma's general balance involved the question of the balance between investment and consumption in the national income and the distribution of income between agricultural and industrial workers. Under his scheme, general balance could not exist as long as certain branches of economic activity were badly neglected—for example, as long as the demand for consumer goods greatly exceeded their supply. How much neglect, how great a degree of imbalance Ma was prepared to tolerate before pronouncing that general balance was not being attained, he did not define. It was a question of personal political judgment, but it was certainly behind Ma's plea for general balance. From the goal of general balance, Ma's argument switched to the closely related law of proportional development. Consistency in a plan involves obtaining the correct proportions in an input-output sense. But like the term "general balance," the law of proportional development also involves political as well as economic judgments. Thus the use of these two terms involves some confusion and overlapping in Ma's work. Discussion of the balance between consumption and investment necessitates discussing the correct proportions between the two. What sort of proportion provides the right balance? Ma was trying to argue that general balance was a goal and that the law of proportional development was the instrument for obtaining the goal, but in his writings he was too vague in his use of the terms. It is clear what the law of proportional development means in the input-output sense, namely, that development will be disrupted if the proportions between sectors are planned so as to give rise to shortages of necessary resources. But in its political sense, the precise meaning of the law is hard to find unless it means that incorrect proportions, say, between consumption and investment will sooner or later produce inflation and reduced production because of disincentives. Otherwise all it can mean is that planning necessarily insures that the proportions chosen are correct. Summing up so far, Ma desired general balance in the economy, meaning growth in many sectors, guided by some reference to consumer demand and to a time horizon nearer than the one upon which the government planners were prone to look. The law of proportional development partly involved getting maximum consistency into the plan and partly making political (and economic) judgment about the proportions chosen for magnitudes such as consumption, investment, agricultural and urban income.

Ma's critics, however, did not take this view. They made two major points in answer to him: (1) the law of planning according to proportional development was an objective economic law,[26] a law behind planning[27] providing the priorities[28] to be adopted. (2) To implement the law the method of balance was used. This method insured that the plan could be fulfilled in accordance with the requirements of the law of planning according to proportional development.[29] . . .

The metaphor of links, circles, and spirals received trenchant criticism. It absorbed a large share of attention, probably as a convenient means of diverting the discussion away from some of the real economic policy issues raised by Ma, which were not seriously discussed. Three criticisms made of the metaphor may be mentioned. (1) The circular model was no use for solving problems; in real life, economic relationships were too complex to be portrayed simply as links in a circle.[30] (2) The method was anti-Marx and Lenin, who had provided the only scientific method for analyzing basic proportional relationships, namely, the extended reproduction theory,[31] on which Ma had not put out "a single character."[32] This was added evidence of Ma's vulgar economic and political views. (3) The metaphor smacked of Western economic theory and, in particular, of "Cournot's marginal utility analysis" and "Marshall's idea" of functional relationships. . . .

Most of Ma's writings, however, were concerned not with the foregoing somewhat metaphysical matters, but with examining the problems confronting the economy and especially those involved in the deepening crisis of 1956–57. During the years since 1953 the economy had been far from balanced, in any sense. Many of the dislocations arising were attributed by Ma to weaknesses in planning, which he listed at length. . . .

The name of Ma Yin-ch'u is probably associated more with the question of population than with any other Chinese problem. His views on this issue earned him considerable notoriety and, not surprisingly, the title of Malthusian disciple. As early as 1955 Ma had attempted to bring forward his opinions for discussion at a meeting in Chekiang, but withdrew his speech in view of the reactions of the delegates with whom he first discussed the matter informally. In the "more mature atmosphere" of 1957, however, he was able to publish his views. It must be remembered that the level and growth of China's population were not (and still are not) accurately known. According to the Census of 1953 the population of mainland China stood at 582 million. Some figures have been released by Peking from time to time for subsequent years, but both inside and outside China considerable doubts have been expressed about their accuracy, and many differing figures have been quoted as being the most accurate estimate. A "sample survey"[33] of 30 million people carried out in 1953 revealed a birth rate of 3.7 per cent and a death rate of 1.7 per cent, providing a natural increase rate of 2 per cent. Ma Yin-ch'u quoted figures for certain districts of Shanghai and Chekiang province (where he himself had conducted inquiries). The natural increase rate found for Shanghai was as high as 3.9 per cent, while in Chekiang Ma found a 2.2 per cent per annum rise. Ma was convinced[34] that the 2.0 per cent per annum rise of 1953 was not applicable to 1957–58, in view of developments which must have given rise to lower death rates and higher birth rates. He put[35] the 1957 population at 640 million, which (assuming that the Census figure for 1953 is accepted) implies a rate of growth for 1953–57 of 2.3 per cent per year. Three other Chinese figures do not agree very closely with Ma's estimate. The journal *Statistical Work* published[36] the figure 621 million for the average 1956 population, and assuming that the rates of growth given in this source for the preceding years continued into 1957, then the 1957 population would have been given as 634 million. A 1959 Chinese statistical handbook, however, contained[37] 656 million as the 1957 population figure (excluding overseas Chinese). Mao Tse-tung, in February 1957, stated[38] that China's population was 600 million. He must have been rounding to the nearest 50 million. Leo Orleans[39] has computed the 1957 population at 617 million, while the U.S. Department of Commerce[40] placed it at 662 million (for the mid-year). For our purposes, however, the essential point is that Ma Yin-ch'u considered that China's population level and growth rate were too high and that this queston overshadowed all others. He described the consequences of the population level as follows: "Thus the excessive population is stopping the high speed of our industrialization, making us incapable of advancing with big steps,"[41] an interesting comment, coming just before the Great Leap Forward policy of 1958–59. According to Ma, China's "chief contradiction" was that the population growth and level were too high while capital accumulation was, therefore, too slow.[42]

Briefly, Ma's argument ran as follows. With a large population a high level of productivity for consumption was required—higher, in fact, than a rapid industrialization rate would permit. Thus there was no possibility of increasing the percentage of the national income allocated to accumulation (then standing at 21 per cent), for to do so would be politically "dangerous." In fact the percentage allocated to consumption was bound to rise under these circumstances. The decrease in the rate of investment would reduce the rate of industrialization, putting back the date at which the stage of Communism could be achieved—hardly a popular line of reasoning. A surprising omission was Ma's failure to refer in detail to the age structure of the population with its obvious importance. Perhaps he did not consider that the census data, claiming that 41 per cent of the population was under seventeen years of age, were accurate enough to be used. However, he did refer[43] to the "demands of the young" being frequently misunderstood, pointing out that a young population required greater investment in activity such as housing, involving possible reductions in investment in other sectors which were playing a vital role in the industrialization drive.

On the consumption side Ma's viewpoint was also pessimistic. He indicated that in spite of the reclamation, 1953–56, of 14 million mou of land, the area of arable land per head was declining. Pointing out also that the reclaimable area was not accurately known, he expressed his own skepticism[44] regarding some estimates which suggested an area of 1,500 million mou. Since land reclamation was a lengthy and costly procedure, policy, he agreed, should concentrate on raising the level of agricultural output per mou to maintain food consumption per head. In Ma's view, too many peasants were demanding to retain for home consumption a higher proportion of the total food output. He warned[45] his readers that this retained percentage could not be allowed to rise for a long time, nor could rations be increased in the towns. Indeed, in some areas they would have to be reduced somewhat. Ma criticized the peasants for their lack of "enlightenment" toward the problem of feeding the town population, illustrating the implications of possible minute per capita increases in peasant farm consumption by calculating the total volume of food which would be involved. Full attention should be given to increasing yields, therefore. But the "correct balance" must be found between food crop output and the output of industrial crops. Intense competition for a limited supply of land existed between these claimants, and, as Ma pointed out, if the food crop acreage were to be increased greatly at the expense of industrial crops, this would have grave repercussions on the level of production in the light industries and hence on the supply of consumer goods.

Ma was also preoccupied with the relationship between population and employment, in particular with the problem of technological unemployment. Lenin had argued correctly, said Ma, that the development of socialism inevitably carried with it the spread of mechanization, automation, and electrification, along with the growth of large-scale industry. Capital-intensive industries provided an output per worker 50 times greater than that of agriculture. As the developments in these directions continued in future years, however, Ma wondered what was to happen to the redundant labor force. He presented evidence to show that the problem of technological unemployment was already growing in China. For example, it was associated with the closure of small-scale salt and coal mines, in favor of concentration on larger, more mechanized units. As a further example, Ma pointed out that if all grain storage elevators were mechanized in China, the effect of this alone on the demand for labor would be marked, since the mechanized elevators required only 5 per cent of the labor force of the traditional type. Several times Ma reported[46] that the yearly industrial demand for labor in China was about 1 million, whereas the yearly increase in population was 13 million. Thus, said Ma, 12 million people must be absorbed into the villages every year. Here the argument was too vague. Ma did not make a precise enough distinction between the current and future employment position. It is clearly not correct to equate a 13 million per annum rise in population in 1957 with a net addition to the labor supply of 13 million in that year. Ma nowhere stated that the number of people reaching working age in 1957 actually was, but, assuming 572 million as the 1942 population, a 1.5 per cent per annum rise since 1942, and fourteen years as the school-leaving age, then a very crude estimate of the population (male and female) reaching working age in 1956–57 works out at 8.6 million. Ma repeatedly referred to the problem of how to absorb the 13 million each year as if it were the current problem. He did not state that these 13 million people had to be fed each year, without being able to contribute to production for many years. He must have meant that from about 1965–66 onward there would be an annual problem of finding employment for an additional 13 million (assuming that all women work). If this was Ma's point, it also lacked precision in assuming the current 1956–57 industrial demand for labor of

1 million to be the same in future years. Although substitution of capital for labor might be assumed to continue to rise, thus involving some decrease in the demand for labor, some judgment would also have to be made as to whether this effect would be more than offset by the greater size of the industrial sector. Unfortunately Ma did not make such calculations.

As Ma's opponents were quick to point out, however, Ma and the government were not saying the same thing in their advocacy of birth control. The government claimed that this policy was desirable as a means of improving the health and vigor of women, of lightening their burden, and of setting them free to study and work. It was a policy adopted entirely from choice. For Ma no choice was involved. It was the only solution to the food and employment problems. By limiting births, he argued, it might even be possible to allow consumption as a percentage of the national income to fall a little, thus providing for speedier industrial growth. In the critics' eyes, Ma was unquestionably a disciple of Malthus, and his pessimistic views were entirely groundless. They presented a great many figures relating to total output, the total level of accumulation, etc., to support their claim that "facts testify" to the falsehood of Ma's thesis that the population was slowing down the rate of industrialization. In his 1959 article Ma drew the critics' attention to the relevance of per capita figures. The critics further attacked Ma for failing to understand that socialism was the means of mobilizing peoples' creativeness and activity; that the high population of China and her "brilliant achievements" were cause and effect. All repeated a statement[47] which appears to have been made by Liu Shao-ch'i, that man is primarily a producer and not a consumer. Ma was said to have overlooked this. Like Ma, then, the critics did not consider the details of the population's age structure. Turning to the warnings issued on technological unemployment, they denied that this problem could exist under a planned, socialist economy,[48] explaining away any unemployment problems troubling China as relics from her capitalist and semi-colonial past. Those who wrote in 1958–59 were able to make the point that the Great Leap Forward, resulting in a widespread labor shortage in rural areas, had shown Ma's gloomy forecasts to be invalid. None drew attention to the fact that, at best, a birth control policy can only have marked effects over the long period, and it was strange that Ma should place such emphasis on this, whereas throughout his work he stressed the importance of adopting policies which would produce immediate results.

Inseparable from his employment policy are Ma's views on investment. As well as making a plea for better planning to reduce wastage of scarce capital, Ma desired changes in the way in which the target for basic constructional investment was set and, secondly, in the distribution of investment. Ma considered that the government, in planning the annual target for investment during the years 1953–57, had been alternatively "conservative" and "adventurist." He contrasted the level of state basic constructional investment set for 1955 with that for 1956. In 1955, overcome by "conservative tendencies," the level was set at only 3 per cent above 1954. Since targets for the raw materials industries were not adequately co-ordinated with the investment plan, surplus supplies of steel, pig iron, and cement appeared in 1955, and arrangements were actually made to export them.[49] The investment target for 1956, however, was set at a level 59 per cent above 1955, a policy described by Ma as "adventurist," giving rise in 1956 to an acute shortage of raw materials and other resources. The export contracts made in 1955 were canceled, but this could not alleviate the crisis significantly. Throughout China in 1956 operations were suspended on constructional projects owing to shortages of raw materials, power, skilled labor, and transport facilities (especially railways). Moreover, with a poor harvest the demands of the light industries for agricultural materials were not met, so that they suffered from excess capacity. Commenting on the 1956 crisis, Ma attacked the government for adopting an excessive speed for industrial growth, with the statement "undue haste prevents thoroughness."[50] It was another example, he said, of the failure to grasp the law of proportional development correctly. In 1957, Ma considered that investment should be reduced to put the economy more in balance.[51] Ma's general conclusions on this subject were (a) the target for basic constructional investment should be set realistically, in the intput-output sense; (b) as a proportion of the national income investment should be set in such a way as to "reconcile" the rate of industrialization with changes in people's standard of living. Here Ma left the reader fully aware of his own opinion, that reconciliation involved giving more weight to demands for higher levels of consumption in planning the economy.

Ma also proposed three important changes in the distribution of investment, emphasizing again his preoccupation with the consumer. First, he called for more investment in housing and town public utilities, presenting[52] statistics illustrating the increasing problem of overcrowding and the inadequacy of urban services such as piped water supplies, mains, sewage, and drainage, and transport. Lack of balance existed between industrial growth and the development of these services, he argued, urging that a new "optimum" balance be created.

Second, Ma also favored a rise in the ratio of industrial investment allocated to light industry, in order to bring about a new, "correct"[53] (again, not defined) balance between heavy and light industry. He advocated retaining to priority for heavy industry, but considered that the 1:5.7 ratio for investment adopted[54] on the average in the previous years had neglected the light industries. Several reasons were advanced in favor of this proposed change: (a) it would help to solve the "contradiction between accumulation and consumption," and counter inflationary pressures. (b) It would stimulate "peasant activeness," so strengthening the rural-urban alliance. (c) In the light industries output per unit of investment was usually high. (d) The results of investment were quickly seen. (e) The recoupment period was short. (f) Funds were accumulated more rapidly than in any other branch of industry. (g) Light industrial expansion would encourage agricultural development and stimulate output of the heavy industries, especially the raw materials industries.

Treatment of the peasants was undoubtedly behind this policy toward light industry. It was above all an expression of Ma's political preferences, in spite of the fact that he made as much as possible of the purely economic arguments for the proposed change. Inflation (although suppressed) and marketing dislocations, associated with too rapid increases in purchasing power and with transport breakdowns, were indeed serious problems in 1956. But some of Ma's economic arguments for the change were unconvincing, for example, his insistence that it would be beneficial to heavy industry. The raw materials industries hardly required the stimulus of a higher demand (as Ma recognized) before supply would be increased. Production and supply were limited by physical shortages: additional steel output required new plants which involved more coal and pig iron production. These in turn required more scarce materials before they could be raised. Apart from this, Ma's call for more investment in light industry struck an odd note when considered against the excess capacity in these industries, associated with a shortage of required agricultural materials. Ma must have regarded the excess capacity as a temporary phenomenon, intending the creation of new capacity to be accompanied by a policy which would insure that the required materials were forthcoming.

Third, Ma proposed that investment should be increased in those fields of activity which would give rise to higher agricultural output. Along with the raw materials industries, he regarded agriculture as the economy's weakest link and as the most important. In rural areas he envisaged the widespread development of mass-type water conservation projects to increase drainage, irrigation, and flood control. But these were not intended to absorb large amounts of capital. On the contrary, they were to be as labor-intensive as possible—employment-creating and capital-saving. Ma was critical[55] of large-scale, long-term, multi-purpose water conservation projects such as the three gorges scheme because of their high capital requirements; their long gestation period of up to twenty years, while serious floods could be expected every three to five years; and because the creation of the reservoirs too often involved flooding large areas of highly productive land. All but the most serious floods could be contained, according to Ma, by the small-scale works which, in addition, would help to raise yields in the short run.

It is interesting to note that, unlike some Western economists, Ma did not criticize the government's seemingly inadequate allocation of state investment to agriculture, water conservation, and forestry during the First Five Year Plan period. Like the government, Ma believed that the bulk of capital formation in these activities should be financed locally. He condemned[56] local authorities for their excessive demands for treasury funds which should, he said, be concentrated on increasing the output of chemical fertilizers and agricultural implements, both of which were urgently needed if yields were to be increased.

In advocating the foregoing three increases in investment, Ma did not unfortunately carry the argument further by calculating the magnitude of the increases which were desirable or possible. One cannot help wondering where cuts in investment were to be made as the increases were carried out, or how such cuts could be avoided. He had great faith in the possibilities of increasing production considerably from the existing capacity in many industries, through better management and planning, and criticized the planners for neglecting this matter. It is possible that he considered that even if some investment reduction did accompany the implementation of his policy, production would not suffer. . . .

Finally, from investment we must turn to Ma's views on the role of financial incentives in agriculture. His argument here was that some farm product prices should be raised in order to stimulate production. The events of 1956 had convinced Ma that the peasants were so discontented that they were on the point of refusing to trade on the existing adverse terms. The economic and political implications of such a move were made clear by Ma. Already in 1956, when the free market for produce of the small retained plot on collectives was increased, there were abrupt price rises; peasants withdrew from collectives; large supplies of produce still officially subject to the state marketing schemes found their way into the free market; peasants illegally indulged in trade, while others were "seduced" into selling on the black market.[57] Ma did not indicate how serious these contraventions of the marketing laws were nor how widespread were the withdrawals from collectives, but he certainly considered them indications of deep dissatisfaction among peasants. In his view, the reduction of the price difference between industrial and farm products of 17.25 per cent, 1950–55, was inadequate, and many farm product prices were still "irrational" or "illogical" (again, neither was defined). To encourage increases in supply the price should be raised. This policy, with its effects on income distribution, was consistent with Ma's apparent wish to reduce the gap between the peasants and workers, but paradoxically he indicated that it was not his wish to redistribute income in this way. Thus, to cancel this effect, he actually proposed that, as farm product prices were increased, industrial wages might also rise. Furthermore, he was against raising the price of grain because of its importance in the cost of living. It was the prices of agricultural raw materials (tea, cotton, silk, sugar, oil seeds) which Ma considered too low. The neglect of these crops in recent years was partly attributed by Ma to conditions in the collectives, and he must have had in mind production from the private plot. He claimed, for example, that peasants were reluctant to grow these subsidiary crops because they were likely to be branded as "capitalists" if they did so. Secondly, peasants were said to be afraid that any income derived from the sale of such crops would be forcibly channeled into government bonds or fixed investment in the collective. Thirdly, they were afraid that insufficient time would be allowed for them to give adequate attention to the crops. Ma's solution of raising prices, assuming that these disincentives were widespread, seems to be wide of the mark, for even with higher prices all three deterrents could still continue to operate.

Alongside his proposals to raise some prices, Ma further desired certain marketing reforms. The free market fiasco of 1956 did not prevent his favoring greater freedom for peasants in selling some of their produce, with the proviso that marketing should be strictly supervised and all regulations rigidly enforced. Secondly, he proposed that the monopsonistic powers of the state buying agency, with its history of "squeezing" quality and prices, should be destroyed by the introduction of competitive buying.[58]

Ma showed that he understood at least some of the implications of price policy he was advocating. Thus he recognized that it would raise the peasants' demand for consumer goods, a point used by Ma to bolster his argument for more light industrial investment. This demand would, according to Ma, further encourage peasants to increase the output of raw materials needed by consumer goods industries. Ma also realized that higher prices for farm products implied greater government expenditure, and this, he argued, could result in reductions in expenditure in other fields, if the budget was to be balanced, and assuming an unwillingness on the part of the government to increase taxation. Here the argument was weak. Ma virtually ignored the entire problem of taxation, except to state that taxation policy in agriculture should be geared to increasing the attractiveness of producing more of certain commodities. Lastly, Ma understood the relevance of the income elasticity of demand by peasants for farm products, pointing out that after prices had been raised, higher farm consumption of pork resulted in shortages in the towns. Thus, said Ma, higher prices must be accompanied by strict controls over consumption on the farms. He did not consider what the likely relationship would be between the income elasticity of demand for, and the elasticity of supply of, various farm products. . . .

It is, of course, impossible to estimate what impact Ma Yin-ch'u's work had on policy, but it is worth recording that Ma himself considered that the "Eight Point Charter for Agriculture," adopted in 1959, was his own. Recently a great deal of economic literature published[59] in China has been devoted to the broad question of the relationship between speed of growth and proportional development, much of it reminiscent of Ma's work. Although it is too early to judge with any certainty, some evidence suggests that the Great Leap Forward approach has been abandoned for the time being. More effort is being concentrated on securing balanced development, involving a reduced rate of heavy industrial expansion, with attempts to strengthen the weak links of light industry and, above all, of agriculture. In addition, the merits of adhering to a central, consistently devised plan are being preached.[60] These policy changes have been adopted in the face of the successive harvest failures caused by unprecedented natural disasters, according to the Peking government. It remains to be seen whether the plan for balance in the economy represents a long-term change in development strategy, or a short-term expedient to be discarded for another leap forward when the next two successive bumper harvests have been gathered. Meanwhile, Ma Yin-ch'u's bold analysis is as relevant to the present economic position of China as it was to the China of 1957.

Notes

1. For a detailed survey of this period see Wu Yuan-li, *An Economic Survey of Communist China* (New York, 1956).

2. *Chung-hua jen-min kung-ho-kuo fa-chan kuo-min ching-chi ti-i-ke wu-nien chi-hua, 1953–57* [The First Five Year Plan for the Development of the National Economy of the Chinese Peoples' Republic, 1953–57] (Peking, 1955). Hereafter called *First Five Year Plan*.

3. *Ibid.*, pp. 54–58.

4. Figures for China given in this section unless otherwise stated, are from *Wei-ta ti Shih-nien. Chung-hua jen-min kung-ho-kuo ching-chi ho wen-hua chien-she ch'eng-chiu ti t'ung-chi* [Ten Great Years. Statistics of the Economic and Cultural Achievements of the Chinese Peoples Republic] (Peking, 1959).

5. For example, Colin Clark, *The Conditions of Economic Progress* (London, 1951), p. 328; W. W. Rostow, ed., *The Prospects of Communist China* (Cambridge, 1954), p. 230.; Chang Kia-Ngau, *China's Struggle for Railroad Development* (New York, 1943), p. 297; H. D. Fong, *Industrial Organization in China* (Tientsin, 1937), p. 18.

6. For details see C. M. Li, *Economic Development of Communist China*

(Berkeley and Los Angeles, 1959); K. C. Chao, *Agrarian Policy of the Chinese Communist Party, 1921–1959* (New Delhi, 1960).

7. Ping-ti Ho, *Studies on the Population of China, 1368–1953* (Cambridge, 1959).

8. *Chi-hua Ching-chi* [Planned Economy] (1958) No. 1.

9. Colin Clark, in *A Critique of Russian Statistics* (London, 1939), quotes a source which argues that the 1928 level of agricultural output could be maintained even after a 39 percent fall in the farm labor force.

10. Figures for the U.S.S.R., unless stated otherwise, are from *The U.S.S.R. Economy. A Statistical Abstract* (London: U.S.S.R. Council of Ministers Central Statistical Administration, 1957).

11. A. Nove, *The Soviet Economy* (London, 1961), p. 304.

12. A. Erlich, *The Soviet Industrialization Debate, 1924–1928* (Cambridge, 1960), pp. 161–62.

13. The *First Five Year Plan, op. cit.*, p. 15, refers to the following statement by Mao Tse-tung: "Without industry, no firm national defense, no welfare for the people, and no national power and prosperity." See also *ibid.*: "In adopting an active industrialization policy, namely, a policy of prior development for heavy industry, its aim is a question of providing firm national defense, satisfying peoples' needs, and achieve the material basis for the socialist reform of the national economy."

14. Erlich, *op. cit.;* also G. Grossman, "Scarce Capital and Soviet Doctrine," *Quarterly Journal of Economics,* LXVIII, 3 (August 1953).

15. For a documentary study of this period of free criticism, see R. Macfarquhar, ed., *The Hundred Flowers* (London, 1960).

16. Wu Pao-san, Ch'en Chen-han, Hsü Yü-nan, Lo Chih-ju, Ku Ch'un-fan, Ning Chia-feng, "Wo-men tui tang-ch'ien ching-chi k'o-hsueh kung-tso ti i hsieh i-chien" [Some of Our Thoughts regarding Present Day Work in Economics], *Ching-chi Yen-chiu* [Economic Research], No. 5 (1957). Wu was the author of *China's National Income in 1933* (Shanghai, 1957), and *National Income of China, 1933, 1936, and 1946* (Nanking, 1947). In 1957 he was deputy director of the Chinese Academy of Sciences' Institute of Economics. Ch'en, Hsü, and Lo were teachers at Peking University; Ning was deputy director of a school of the head branch of the People's Bank; Ku was deputy minister of posts and telegraphs. The article, which was not published until October 1957 (that is, four months after the "hundred flowers" period had finished), was accompanied by a great deal of editorial comment in the form of footnotes.

17. Ma Yin-ch'u was born in 1884. He spent the years 1907–14 in the U.S. studying economics. In the interwar years he was a university teacher in China and also a member of the legislative Yuan (1928–47). Critical of the Nationalist government's economic policies, he was imprisoned for a time for his leftist leanings, but in 1949 Chou En-lai invited him to take part in the new Communist regime. After 1949 Ma was a leading non-party economist, holding many important political and academic offices, including the following: membership in the National Peoples' Congress; the Chinese Peoples Political Consultative Standing Committee; the Committee for the promotion of international trade; the standing Committee of the Board of Directors of the Peoples' Bank. He was in turn president of Chekiang and Peking Universities and a member of the Academy of Sciences.

18. *Hsin Chien-she* [New Construction] (November 1959), pp. 23 and 44.

19. Ma, *op. cit.*, p. 105. "Our real existence is developed in the contradictions of balance and imbalance. Our responsibility, then, is that we must adopt, from the standpoint of development, active measures to discover continually new,

weak links and to overcome new imbalances and cause the entire national economy, step by step, to move towards newer and higher levels."

20. *Ibid.,* pp. 7–8.

21. Private communication from John Gray.

22. In Chinese, tsung-ho p'ing-heng.

23. At times Ma used the full form of the law, "the law of planning according to proportional development," but in most places he abbreviatied it in the form, "the law of proportional development." As we shall see, this led to considerable criticism.

24. P. Streeten, "Unbalanced Growth," *Oxford Economic Papers,* No. 2 (1959), 176.

25. For an exposition of its use in the Soviet Union see Nove, *op. cit.,* p. 292.

26. For example, *Collected Essays . . . , op. cit.,* p. 7.

27. *Ibid.,* p. 7. The author refers to general balancing work meeting the requirements of the law. See also p. 41.

28. *Ching-chi Yen-chiu* [Economic Research], No. 5 (1957), 74. The author stated that Marx and Lenin had given a "law" regarding the proportions to be adopted between producer and consumer goods, between consumption and investment.

29. *Collected Essays . . . , op. cit.,* p. 42: "The method of national economic balance serves definite ends—namely—starting out from the requirements of objective economic laws [of which the law of proportional development was said to be one] to realizing, in every period the political and economic tasks proposed by the party, and guaranteeing the development of the national economy at the greatest speed."

30. E.g., *ibid.,* pp. 16 and 20.

31. *Ibid.,* p. 41. "The only scientific basis which studies these basic connections and proportional relationships is Marxist-Leninist extended reproduction theory."

32. This was incorrect; see Ma, *op. cit.,* pp. 49 and 145.

33. *Ibid.,* p. 143.

34. *Ibid.,* pp. 133–34.

35. *Ibid.,* pp. 148 and 158.

36. *T'ung-chi kung-tso* [Statistical Work], No. 11 (1957).

37. *Wei-ta ti shih-nien* [Ten Great Years], *op. cit.,* p. 6.

38. Mao Tse-tung, *Concerning the Correct Handling of the Contradictions among the People* (Peking, 1957), p. 24.

39. Leo Orleans, *Professional Manpower and Education in Communist China* (Washington, 1960), p. 153.

40. U.S. Department of Commerce, Bureau of the Census, *International Population Statistical Reports Series,* No. 15.

41. Ma, *op. cit.,* pp. 148–49. He added, "Some call me Malthusian—I call them dogmatist, anti-Leninist."

42. *Ibid.,* p. 142. "There are still contradictions, and apart from the important ones spoken of by Chairman Mao concerning contradictions among the people, I consider that a high population with a low level of investment is a very serious contradiction." But later, p. 144, "China's greatest contradiction is that population growth is too fast and capital accumulation seems to be too slow."

43. *Ibid.,* p. 160.

44. *Ibid.,* pp. 157–58. He implied that for political reasons much prairie land under the control of the national minorities "fundamentally cannot be reclaimed."

45. *Ibid.,* p. 87. "The Chinese people, under the leadership of the Communist

Party, must bury themselves in production, if all the people are going to get their food rations. Without the guarantee of food, industry will not develop." See pp. 49 and 86–88.

46. For example, *ibid.*, pp. 147–48.

47. *Collected Essays, op. cit.*, pp. 82–83, quote Liu Shao-ch'i's statement: "They only look at man as a consumer; if there are more people then consumption is higher—but they do not primarily look at man as a producer. If there are many people then we can produce even more, accumulate even more. Clearly this is an anti-Marxist-Leninist viewpoint."

48. *Ibid.*, p. 62. "Everyone knows—according to the viewpoint of Marxism and Leninism on the population question—that unemployment and surplus population are the product of capitalists privately owning the means of production." Also, on p. 112, the author states that the "law of relative surplus population" operates under capitalism.

49. Ma, *op. cit.*, pp. 98–99.

50. *Ibid.*, p. 109. Percentage changes over the previous year in basic constructional investment during the First Five Year Plan period were as follows: 1953: +84 per cent; 1954: +13 per cent; 1955: +3 per cent; 1956: +59 per cent; 1957: —7 per cent. From *Wei ta ti shih-nien, op. cit.*

51. Ma, *op. cit.*, pp. 140–41. "This is not blindly withdrawing but returning towards normal development."

52. *Ibid.*, pp. 125–28. Ma's critic, in *Collected Essays, op. cit.*, pp. 29–30, stated that such investment was unprofitable to socialist construction and, therefore, was not required at the present time.

53. Ma, *op. cit.*, p. 96.

54. The yearly ratio of state basic constructional investment allocated to light and heavy industry was as follows: planned 1953–57: 1:7.9; actual average 1953–57. 1:5.7; 1953: 1:4.7; 1954: 1:4.7; 1955: 1:7.1; 1956: 1:6.2; 1957: 1:5.6. From *Wei-ta ti shih-nien, op. cit.*

55. Ma, *op. cit.*, pp. 18–19, 40, 51.

56. *Ibid.*, p. 51. His expression is worth recording: "There are still areas, however, which hold out their hand for state money: they do not see that peasant strength is like drops of water coming together to make a river."

57. *Ibid.*, pp. 103–04.

58. *Ibid.*, pp. 102–03. One critic, *Collected Essays, op. cit.*, p. 34, recorded that he was "astonished" when he read this proposal made by Ma.

59. See, for example, *Wo Kuo ching-chi hsüeh-chieh kuan-yü she-hui chu-i ching-chi fa-chan su-tu ho pi-li wen-ti lun-wen hsüan-chi* [Selected Essays by Chinese Economists on Questions concerning the Speed and Proportions in Socialist Economic Development] (Peking, 1960).

60. Po I-po, in *Hung-ch'i* [Red Flag], p. 25, says: ". . . on the other hand, if one particular aspect [i.e., branch of the economy], one particular unit, departs from the national plan, departs from the requirements of the whole, unilaterally develops its so-called "activeness"—then not only can this fail to benefit the whole, but it will inevitably also fail to benefit that department itself."

22. INDUSTRIAL MANAGEMENT

H. FRANZ SCHURMANN

System Differences in Conflict—The Problem of the Single-Director System

One of the problems in the comparative study of different social systems is that it is easy to suggest contrasts and comparisons but difficult to pin them down methodologically. No two social and political systems are completely alike, even Communist societies, which have many elements of sameness. Yet what do the differences mean? Usually, one can evaluate them only in terms of one's own theoretical approach to the problem. However, system comparison takes on a much more concrete form in instances where two different systems "compete" in a single social setting. In the recent history of Communist China, there are some instances in which "Soviet" and "Chinese Communist" methods of organization competed. We shall examine one in the field of industrial management.

By the time the Chinese Communists had achieved victory, they had built up a powerful Party and a powerful army, the two weapons with which they smashed the poorly organized forces of their opponents. Yet the Communists lacked training and experience in the problems they encountered when they moved from the rural areas into the cities. The remarkable restraint they exhibited during the early days after the "liberation" could not be kept up ad infinitum. It was not only that the cities posed problems that demanded rapid and decisive resolution, but that they were to be the locus of the great process of China's economic transformation. It was in the urban areas that China's new industries were to be built up. It was there that the first steps in the economic revolution were to be taken. Land reform initially involved little more than the distribution of land to the peasants and the liberation of their productive forces. But in the cities, it was a question not of liberating forces, but of organizing new forces for economic reconstruction and development.

When the devastated factories were occupied, the first task was getting them into operation again. The despoiling of Manchuria by the Soviets and the destruction wrought by the Kuomintang presented the Chinese Communists with the massive task of reconstruction. That task was officially completed by the end of 1952, and in 1953 the new First Five-Year Plan was launched. During the "liberation" period, the factories were run by committees appointed

SOURCE: Selected from H. Franz Schurmann, "Organizational Contrasts Between Communist China and the Soviet Union," in Kurt London, ed., *Unity and Contradiction,* New York: Frederick A. Praeger, 1962, pp. 65–81. Reprinted by permission of Frederick A. Praeger, Inc.

by the Communist military administration. Workers were collected, tools and machinery that had been hidden were brought forth, and the wheels of production were again set in motion. Because of the weak organizational base of the Party in the cities, one of its first tasks was building up Party organization there. In the industrial regions, this involved recruiting thousands of workers into the Party. The motivation behind this was not purely ideological, that is, giving proletarian content to proletarian form, but also eminently practical. In a situation that required every available bit of human talent, the workers represented a source of far higher quality that the peasants.[1] Many Party cadres, though good fighters and loyal Communists, were raw country products.

The temptations of city life were too great for many of them; they later expiated their lapses in the great San-Fan purges. As more city people were brought into the Party and military control gave way to civilian administration, leadership in the factories passed into the hands of factory-management committees. These were made up of factory and section directors, military representatives, and top engineers, with the director of the enterprise usually at their head. Organizationally, they were under the jurisdiction of the state ministries, which at that time meant the regional branches of the state apparatus.[2] But the factory directors were often holdovers from the pre-"liberation" period—men of as yet doubtful loyalty. In many ways, the Chinese Communists faced the same problem the Soviets had faced after the Bolshevik Revolution. The Soviets tried to meet the problem through some form of dual economic-political control—double management by economic technicians and Party secretaries. Instead of adopting the system of "two-man management," the Chinese Communists made use of the factory committees to direct and control operations. But the patterns of authority remained unclear. On the one hand, pressure was exerted to diminish the Party's involvement in managerial tasks, as is indicated in a speech by Kao Kang, the first head of the State Planning Commission. On the other hand, the prevailing distrust of the factory directors and other managerial personnel inhibited their authority. The result was considerable confusion in the field of industrial management.[3]

As a consequence, a phenomenon arose that was also widespread in the Soviet Union during the nineteen-twenties: "functional management." Soviet patterns were followed under which "functional staffs" were organized immediately under the factory director. They were concerned with such problems as planning, technology, wages, and finance and accounting. With the decline in the authority of the factory directors and the restraints put on the Party committees, the functional staffs acquired considerable decision-making powers. They were often the only ones who had sufficient knowledge of the details of industrial operations to be technically qualified to make decisions. Yet "functional management" produced the system of "multiheaded leadership," as the Chinese Communists called it, and co-ordination became increasingly difficult.[4]

As early as 1948, the problem of creating an effective system of industrial management posed itself. One solution seemed easy and convenient.[5] Since the Soviet Union had already experienced the same problems, and had presumably solved them in a correct socialist manner, why not follow "advanced Soviet experiences"? It was in regard to the operation of the railroad system in Manchuria that the Chinese Communists first began to talk of the necessity of introducing a more rational, effective, and "socialist" work organization. When they took over the railroads, they faced the necessity not only of putting them back into effective operation, but of co-ordinating Chinese operations and work methods with the Russians, who still ran the railroads under earlier agreements. There was little choice involved; conformity to Soviet methods was necessary. Under the earlier "capitalistic" system, train crews were rotated from locomotive to locomotive, as the need arose. Such a work system often led to accidents and lapses for which no one assumed responsibility. The problem could be solved only by assigning a crew to specified locomotives and making it solely responsible for the operation and maintenance of these locomotives. If anything went wrong, this team and this team alone would have to make good the damage.[6]

The Soviet method, a "system of responsibility" and "work-post responsibility," called for the sphere of responsibility to be closely defined for each work team and each individual. The introduction of this system did not take place solely on the initiative of the Chinese; another factor was the urging of the Soviet Union and specifically of the many Soviet experts who came to China to aid in the reconstruction and construction of industry. Under a 1950 agreement, the Soviet Union promised to supply China with a number of basic industrial units, all of heavy-industry type, which were to form the basis of China's new industrial system. In addition, the Soviet Union agreed to supply technical information and experts to start the new units going and to advise the Chinese on economic and technical problems in developing older industries. The Soviet Union retained operations rights over the Manchurian railways and acquired the right to establish joint Sino-Soviet corporations in Sinkiang, of the sort that had been established in the satellite nations of Eastern Europe.[7]

If Soviet aid was to be decisive in the development of industry, then it was clear that the methods of industrial development to be used would also be based on "advanced Soviet experience." The first Chinese Five-Year Plan, which began in 1953, was drawn up much along the lines of "Soviet experience" and was characterized by intensive, detailed, centralized planning, as in the Soviet case. In 1956, at the Eighth Party Congress, when the change in systems of industrial management was announced, Central Committee member Li Fu-ch'un also announced basic changes in planning: a renunciation of excessive long-term planning in favor of short-term planning, coupled with greater flexibility on lower levels for plan adjustment. But in the first years after the "liberation," the tendency was to follow the Soviet model, and in so doing, the system of industrial management prevalent in the Soviet Union—one-man management—was also introduced.

Under the first stage of the new "system of responsibility," all management and work personnel were given specific, individual responsibility for fulfillment of production tasks and maintenance of equipment in their care. The second stage was the introduction of the "production-sector management system." Under the system of functional management, work organization in many factories had been based on functional rather than ecological criteria. Production teams were organized on the basis of certain specialized tasks, and as the need for their services arose, they would be shifted from place to place. For example, in the steel mills, work teams moved from blast furnace to blast furnace, each time performing their particular technical tasks. The problem of assigning daily work tasks to hundreds of teams and thousands of workers was an immense one.[8] The work teams received their orders from the functional section concerned with their particular technical specialization. After the production-sector management system was introduced—also on the Soviet model—work organization was based on ecological criteria. A certain number of work teams, which included technical specialists, were assigned to a certain defined work area. Whereas earlier, many factories had "hiring halls," so to speak, which every day assigned workers to scores of different tasks throughout the factory, now the problem of allocation of labor was simplified. Most of the specialized production teams were dismantled and their members assigned to the work sectors.[9] The introduction of this system immediately posed the problem of authority.

Thus began the third stage in the introduction of the new kind of management. Since the "system of responsibility" established individual accountability at all levels of organization, it was soon realized that at certain levels a concomitant individual authority would have to be created. The system of functional management had its good aspects, as most mainland publications admitted. Its main weakness lay in the fact that over-all co-ordination was difficult because of the dispersion of authority. "Vested interestism" became a serious problem. The complex and constant problems of adjustment required persons with authority to make decisions rapidly and with enough power to make certain that they were carried out. Undoubtedly on the urging of Soviet advisers, as well as for practical reasons, the single-director system was introduced. Each unit was to be headed by a single individual who held complete authority and bore full responsibility. All enterprises were divided into a number of units, or factories, superimposed vertically. A factory director was put in full charge of the unit and was responsible only to the over-all director, accepting orders from no one else. Each factory was divided into a number of shops, each shop under the sole charge of the shop chief. In turn, each shop was divided into a number of work segments, which, like the shops, were ecological units. Thus, in a steel mill, each blast furnace became the nucleus of a work segment. Each work segment was headed by a work chief or foreman. At his respective unit level, each unit chief held full authority; each was responsible only to his direct superior.[10]

The functional sections—planning, technology, wages—remained, but their authority was rigorously circumscribed. They could no longer issue orders to work supervisors at lower echelons. All "suggestions" from the functional sections had first to be cleared explicitly with the unit chief. Within a rigorously defined framework, however, they could make "technical decisions" and "technical suggestions" to lower echelons. However, such suggestions were not to violate the principle of "single-source decision-making" (*iyüanhua*, the Chinese counterpart of the Russian *edinonachalie*). As before, each unit director had his deputy directors. Yet whereas earlier, deputy directors, who often were "vice-presidents" in charge of the functional sections, had had considerable decision-making powers, now they were ordered to submit unconditionally to the director. They became his advisers, as it was stated. The powers granted the single director were of a very broad nature. He alone was allowed to make the decisions necessary for plan fulfillment, subject only to the restraints that came from higher echelons. As in Russia, criteria of performance were target fulfillment and overfulfillment. Even the work chiefs, the new foremen, acquired quasi-dictatorial powers over the workers in their units.[11]

The production-sector management system and the single-director system permitted a more rational division of labor and specification of tasks, on the one hand, and a more effective concentration of decision-making authority, on the other. These two developments had somewhat contradictory effects. Although the minute specification of tasks for staff members and workers tended to reduce freedom of action, unit directors acquired much greater freedom of action than before. In fact, in the words of later denunciations of the single-director system, these single directors became little despots.[12]

This system of industrial management was more or less directly copied from that of the Soviet Union. It was introduced through the urging of the Soviet experts. It was publicized in the translations of Soviet manuals on plant management. And it was supported by directives from the regime—or at least a segment of the regime. A miniature Soviet system was in the making in China, particularly in the industrial regions, and more particularly in Manchuria. In the Soviet Union, Stalin had personally pushed through the institution of the system of one-man management during the early years of the Soviet First Five-Year Plan. Enough of collegial management, he had said, and away with a system of industrial management that made for an absence of personal responsibility.[13] It was with this policy that a new generation of Soviet technocrats had arisen, many of whom were products of the drive for formation of a "working-class industrial and technical intelligentsia." But despite their loyalty to system and Party, these new men found power in the economic structures they directed, rather than in the Party. An industrial unit in the Soviet Union became a miniature Soviet Union in itself. Just as one personality stood at the head of the great structure of Soviet society, so one director headed the enterprise. The spirit of one-man management also pervaded other Soviet organizations. The case of Comrade Rumyantsev, so well described in Professor Merle Fainsod's book on Smolensk, shows that "little Stalins" began to appear at different levels of Party organization as well.[14] When the Chinese finally denounced the single-director system, they often singled out Party secretaries who had developed excessively "individualistic," "dictatorial," and "arrogant" tendencies.[15]

One crucial result of the full introduction of the system of one-man management in China—which apparently did not come until late in 1953[16]—was the gradual reduction of the Party committees' scope of authority. As in Russia, their functions became more and more explicitly restricted to control and supervision. Kao Kang, early in 1950, had warned: "The secretaries of Communist Party committees (or branches) in enterprises . . . cannot supplant the factory director, they cannot supplant the system of factory-director responsibility." Widely circulated at that time, in several different editions, was a Chinese translation of a Soviet pamphlet on Party functions in factories that made quite clear that control and supervision were the primary functions of the Party committees, not participation in managerial decisions.[17] Economic decisions were to be made by the single director in accordance with directives from higher-echelon ministries. Since the Party committees did not have the competence to judge such decisions, they were simply to make certain that the decisions "worked," that is, that they contributed to target fulfillment. The Party committees were to focus their attention chiefly on "ideological work." They were to organize movements among the workers to assure work discipline and keep an eye on what was going on at the mass level—exactly the function of the Party in the Soviet Union. The factory director, who in most instances was a Party member, became the most powerful individual in the enterprise, far overshadowing the Party secretary. Though technically subordinate in Party committee meetings, in reality the factory director held greater power than the Party secretary and, moreover, was protected from the latter's interference by the principle that the factory director alone could make the relevant economic decisions.

The separation of political and economic authority at the industrial-unit level had even greater repercussions. It threatened the separation of political (Party) and economic (state ministries) apparatuses per se. In the Soviet Union, Stalin had favored such a system of parallel bureaucracies—with Stalin himself holding the reins at the apex. Each could check and observe the other. In fact, the one-man management system necessitated complex systems of control.[18] It was during this period that the Soviet secret police began to develop its functions of economic control and supervision. There is little doubt that a similar process was threatening in China. The tendency toward "parallelization" had gone furthest in Manchuria. In 1949, special branch bureaus of the state apparatus had been set up in the different administrative regions into which China was divided. (One of the most important of these branch bureaus was the one in Manchuria, headed by Kao Kang.) Since the separation of political and economic authority at the unit level became even greater under the single-director system, more and more of the decisive directives for the factory managers came from the state ministries. These ministries had an intermediary apex in the branch bureaus. In one of the most important of these branch bureaus, in Manchuria, the power at the apex was held by Kao Kang.

The process of "parallelization" ran contrary to the basic organizational principles that the Chinese Communists had developed during their years of guerrilla warfare. Mao Tse-tung's phrase "Concentrate the great authority, diffuse the small authority" meant, in practice, that at the apex of any unit, authority should be concentrated in the hands of a collectively deciding body—a Party committee.[19] Initiative is crucial at lower-unit levels, but not if it is of a sort that impinges on ultimate organizational unity. The Chinese Communists had built up their Party as a powerful organizational weapon, one that was to lead rather than simply supervise and control. Successive campaigns of rectification and Party construction had given new strength to the Party, had increased its unity and solidarity. Whatever factionalism existed at the top of the Party at one time had long since ceased to be an important factor. In contrast, Stalin in the late nineteen-twenties dominated a Party over which he had control at the top, but one that had developed into a powerful organization before his assumption of supreme power. Stalin could not trust anything that had not been fashioned completely by his own hands.[20] The secret police, his own creation, was a far more trustworthy instrument. But the Chinese Communist Party, as it existed in the early nineteen-fifties, was the creation of the men of Yenan. It was intolerable to these men, to Mao Tse-tung in particular, that at the moment when the Party had gone through the first post-"liberation" mass-level purge—the San-Fan movement—and had emerged successfully with new cadres, its scope of organizational leadership should contract rather than expand. Furthermore, there was the danger of a growing Soviet organizational foothold. Stalin's basic principle in relations between Communist Parties was that the Soviet Union must have complete control over all Communist Parties, in internal as well as external matters. This meant not simply submission to Stalin's will, but the existence of organizational instruments of control. One must remember that all Communists are Leninists, and as such, always view power in organizational terms. That organizational foothold, the spearhead of Stalin's subversion, was provided in the processes of organizational "parallelization" that began to go on in China at that time. The Soviet advisers in the key industries were the organizational agents. Kao Kang was the principal tool.

To counteract this danger of "parallelization," a countertendency began. The turning point in the process was marked by the Fourth Plenum, in February, 1954, which called for increasing observance of the principle of collective leadership by the Party. Yet at the same time, articles appeared in other organs detailing the full implementation of the single-director system. In the enlarged meeting of the standing committee of the Central Committee in March, 1955, the purge of the Kao Kang–Jao Shu-shih clique was announced. Between these two meetings, a serious internal struggle had gone on. At issue was the great organizational question: parallelization or unity of the apparatus. The struggle was decided in favor of unity. From March, 1955, on, little more is heard of the single-director system, except in a negative way. Obviously, the system could not be scrapped at one blow, for complex webs of organization had already grown up around it. The struggle against it had to be waged piecemeal and with unrelenting energy. Furthermore, the organizational struggle could not be allowed to impede the successful fulfillment of the targets of the First Five-Year Plan. Everywhere, factories were instructed to proceed "according to concrete conditions"—the slogan used when some specific organizational instrument has failed and a transition to something else is being worked through.[21] Attacks on "arrogant" directors began to appear. More and more emphasis was put on the need for constant consultation with the Party committees. Bossism and bureaucratism were attacked.

The single-director system was officially scrapped at the Eighth Party Congress. The director of the industrial department of the Central Committee of the Chinese Communist Party, Li Hsüeh-feng, announced abandonment of the system in favor of a new system called "factory-director responsibility," under the collective leadership of the Party committee. The single-director system, Li Hsüeh-feng stated, had some success, yet it produced some unfortunate side effects:

. . . because there was an erroneous overemphasis on the person responsible for plant administration as the person fully empowered to lead, the functions of the Party organizations in the plant were reduced to assurance [of production-target fulfillment] and control. At times when differences of opinion arose between plant managers and Party committees, the former ignored the resolutions of the Party organization in regard to production management. As a result, plant-management leadership and Party leadership polarized, negating the Party's leadership over management, and putting the Party in a subordinate position. . . . Bureaucratism, capitalistic tendencies, arrogance, self-satisfaction, and arbitrariness began to appear. Splits, alienation, and lack of solidarity began to develop among leadership cadres, between cadres and masses, and between industries.[22]

Under the new system, all major policy questions, which had earlier been decided more or less unilaterally by the factory director or unit chief, were now to be decided by the Party committee collectively. The factory director, as before, retained full personal responsibility for the fulfillment of targets and the execution of decisions. However, he lost all authority to make fundamental policy decisions. It was with the Eighth Party Congress that the system of industrial management based on collective decision-making by the Party committee officially came into being. Factory directors still retained the right to make "draft decisions." Hence, in many instances, direction was still in the hands of managerial personnel, as before. Yet a decisive shift in authority had taken place, from the managers and technocrats to the Party committees. The supreme figure in the factory was now unquestionably the Party secretary The danger of polarization had been eliminated.

The new did not completely change the old. There was no revocation of the production-sector system. In fact, all organizational structuring in the plant, especially that of the Party, continued to follow the ecologically determined units of production. Although the new system represented "centralization" at the top level, it also had certain features of "decentralization." Under the single-director system, the authority of the deputy factory directors and the chiefs of the functional sections had been gravely weakened. Under the new system, much of this authority was restored. Chiefs of the functional sections were given broader leeway to make "technical" decisions. The new principles of industrial management explicitly called for managerial personnel to make decisions of an "everyday" nature, i.e., technical decisions. However, it was not only the factory director who was allowed to make such independent technical decisions; they could also be made by lower-level leadership personnel.[23] In practice, the new principle represented an implementation of Mao Tse-tung's aforementioned slogan "Concentrate the great authority, diffuse the small authority." All policy decisions were to be centralized in the hands of the collectively operating Party committee. All technical decisions were to be made ad hoc, on the spot, by leadership personnel at all levels, particularly at the lower levels.

The dialectic of centralization and decentralization became very important in subsequent years. The Eighth Party Congress called for a renewed emphasis on the "mass line." What this meant in organizational practice was that leadership should be more and more direct. So-called hsiafang (send-them-down) movements became increasingly prominent in the years after the Eighth Party Congress. Although there were all kinds of hsiafang movements, intraorganizationally *hsiafang* meant transfer downward of managerial personnel to the front line of production.[24] Fewer people in the offices and more at the heads of the work teams was the new slogan.

The new system of decision-making was greatly facilitated by the changes in the system of planning announced by Li Fu-ch'un, in a report to the Eighth Party Congress that directly preceded that of Li Hsüeh-feng. The excessively detailed and centralized planning of the First Five-Year Plan was to be scrapped in favor of more emphasis on short-term planning and greater leeway to lower units for adjusting Plan targets. Just as the Soviet-style single-director system was organizationally unadapted to the kind of organizational system the Chinese Communists were developing, so excessively detailed and long-term planning did not work for an economy at so rudimentary a level as China's. But it was precisely the decentralization of planning that made the functions of the Party committees so important—to collect all information on the course of production and periodically to make target and plan revisions. Of course, and this cannot be stressed too strongly, the task of the Party committee was to make certain that target levels were also set as high as possible. The purpose of the mass line was not to lower targets, but to provide the organizational conditions for constantly increasing them.

The full impact of the new system came during the "great leap forward," in 1958. Here all the tendencies initiated by the Eighth Party Congress reached a high point of intensity. On the one hand, Party control of industry reached a degree of totality it had never achieved before. Yet, on the other hand, intraorganization decentralization also reached a high point. More and more, office and staff management was de-emphasized in favor of direct decision-making at the work-team level. And it was at this level that the full frenzy of the mass movements made itself felt. The work team was the nucleus of ideological pressuring. Party members—and most of the work-team leaders were Party members—fired the workers to greater efforts, to constantly increased production. Managerial personnel wailed that the rational ordering of production was being sacrificed in favor of the frenzy of mass movements. Yet the official Party line put down the proponents of routinization and regularization, and ordered the continuation of mass movements in industry. During the campaign against those guilty of "rightist tendencies"—to be differentiated from the anti-rightist campaign—several obstreperous individuals who were suspicious of the excessive rapidity of the "great leap forward" were eliminated from positions of leadership. The new system was seen as the key to rapid development, and no deviation was to be tolerated.[25]

In the three years since the high point of the "great leap forward," intensity has given way more and more to pragmatism. Mass movements have become fewer and fewer. At present, in agriculture, the stress is on practical efforts—*yinti chihyi* (get the best from each area). A period of regularization seems to have set in, but fundamentally the organizational structure that has emerged over the past years has not changed. The communes have become latent; they have not disappeared. Because of the dialectical nature of organization in Communist China, what is manifest today may become latent tomorrow, and vice versa. There is still the powerful instrument of the Party committee, with its absolute and centralized control of decision-making. Yet there are also the work teams, led by dedicated and committed Party members with considerable authority for independent "technical" decision-making. The line between policy and technical decisions is, of course, never completely clear. If the dialectic swings toward centralization, then many decisions that once were "technical" now become "policy." Conversely, if the dialectic swings toward the need for on-the-spot adjustment, for the pragmatic approach, then many former policy decisions become technical decisions. In industry, at the present time, the emphasis is on work-team emulation. Work teams compete collectively against each other to increase production. Considerable leeway has been given the team leaders in the struggle for fulfillment and overfulfillment of targets.[26] In the communes, the production-brigade cadres have now been given widespread powers to do whatever they can to bring in a good 1961 harvest. In neither the factories nor the villages have the organs of centralism disappeared. The Party committee in the factories and in the commune administration—under tight Party control—remains as before. But under the present swing of the dialectic, the emphasis has shifted from the "concentrated great authority" to the "diffused small authority."

In the brief period since the "liberation," system differences have been in actual conflict. The essentially Soviet single-director system was tried and failed. It was replaced by an essentially Chinese system, which has its roots in the period of guerilla struggle. It is not accidental that during the period of emulation of "advanced Soviet experiences," disdain was expressed for the crudities of the village period. Now it is Yenan that evokes fond memories. The Chinese Communists now speak of "attacking production" in the way they attacked objectives during the civil war. Mao Tse-tung's theories of guerilla warfare have their counterpart today in the theories of social and political organization. During the Yenan and civil-war periods, one of the major organizational problems the Chinese Communists faced was maintenance of absolute control from the center coupled with maximal mobility and initiative on the part of individual units. The problem was one of organizationally unifying regular armies, governed by strict "vertical rule," and guerilla armies, enjoying a maximum of "initiative and spontaneity." It was in the context of this and other such "contradictory" problems that the peculiar dialectical thinking that today marks the Chinese leaders arose. The intra-unit situation in the factory is a miniature of what existed militarily during the Yenan period. At the top there is the solidary Party committee, with members from all over the organization, with lines of control and communication going to all these sectors, and with effective authority to make major decisions binding on all. In addition, there are the many individual units, the teams, which operate with considerable independence to reach local, "technical" objectives. They are like the small guerilla bands scrambling over difficult terrain, yet constantly under control from the center.

It is this organizational fact that gives the Chinese Communists the appearance of extraordinary organizational control and co-ordination, of immense concentrated authority and, at the same time, a similarly extraordinary degree of flexibility and ability to adjust. It is an organizational dialectic in contrast to the rigidity of the Soviet system of organization, with its excessive centralized planning (under Stalin), its parallel structures of control, its periodic use of terror to elicit obedience. The Soviet system, as Professor Barrington Moore, Jr., has described it, was one of concentration of power and authority at the top and atomization at the bottom.[27] But this atomization produced a kind of individuation: Individuals managed enterprises. Individuals were rewarded (under Stakhanovism). Individuals were purged in the terror. And it was a single individual who ruled at the top—Stalin. In China, the Communists have rejected the process of individuation. Yet there, too, is a kind of atomization—atomization by groups. Where it was the lone individual who stood at the depths of organization in the Soviet Union, in China it is the small group, the work team, into which the individual has been effectively meshed.

The differences between these two kinds of mass-level atomization are significant. The Soviet type is suited to purposes of control, but poses serious problems for organizational manipulability and eliciting of commitment. In China, the individual is bound to a nuclear group, which can be linked effectively to a larger structure of organization. We know of the effects of group indoctrination in China. There is nothing like it in the U.S.S.R. The locus of this indoctrination is the small nuclear group. There is no real Soviet counterpart to the Chinese *tsot'anhui* (sit-talk meeting). Do we see here a reflection of national differences? Russia was an individuated society although it lacked Western traditions of individualism. China is a society with long traditions of group organization. Yet it is always dangerous to have recourse to national characteristics to explain differences between social systems, if for no other reason than that the study of "national character" and "modal personality" is still nebulous. A more correct deduction can usually be drawn from looking at history.

The histories of the Soviet Union and Communist China are very different. The Chinese Communist Party struggled for twenty-five years against an enemy that held state power. The Bolsheviks acquired state power at one blow. Without state power, bureaucratic rule is impossible. Without state power, reliance on a concentrated instrument of control and repression is impossible. Whereas the Soviets, upon the seizure of state power, could begin to rule through the traditional means of a bureaucracy and an army, the Chinese Communists had to forge means of controlling widely scattered and fragmented areas, and, more importantly, dispersed groups of political and military fighters. Without the invisible organizational ties that linked these groups together, the Yenan Communists would have been precisely what Chiang Kai-shek thought them to be—a motley horde of bandits. Such an organization could not be built by establishing a bureaucracy and assigning individuals to it, or through a regular army with a vertically stratified span of control. The organization could only be built on the basis of tight internal solidarity of the organization's nuclei—the Party cells and the guerilla teams—and unquestioning obedience to the dictates of the center. These two organizational requisites were in fact "contradictory." Sometimes, internal group solidarity became too strong, to the detriment of external obedience, and the groups became guilty of "mountainism"—sticking to their own mountaintops. Or, conversely, the dictates of the center stifled group initiative and provoked internal discontent—the phenomenon of "commandism." A delicate balance had to be maintained. The protracted period of warfare during the Yenan period allowed the Chinese Communists to build a powerful and flexible organizational instrument. The Bolsheviks made a sudden jump from conspiratorial party to rulers of state and society. They claimed to have jumped over capitalism. What they jumped over, in fact, was the long formative experience in open organizational development that the Chinese Communists enjoyed. In the areas they controlled, the Chinese Communists acquired experience for the next stage—development and control of a whole society. The Bolsheviks had no such experience. They seized state power with a Party gripped by conflicting tendencies and factionalism. The democratic tendencies of Western European socialism made for a party that was still "human" rather than "organizational" in appearance, despite Lenin's theories on organization. The turn to bureaucracy in the Soviet Union was a product of the organizational "weakness" of the Bolsheviks rather than a sign of strength. The Chinese Communists, far from the democratic traditions of Western Europe and in a situation that demanded the highest degree of organizational strength, built an effective, Leninist system of organization. . . .

Notes

1. During this early stage, one can often detect notes of contempt for the village era—a contempt that at present has been replaced by nostalgic longing for the guerilla period. Note, for example, the statements of an editorial in the *Tungpei Jen Min Jih Pao,* November 2, 1948, that urged the adoption of "advanced Soviet methods": "Our comrades in industrial work must overcome industrial work habits acquired during long years of work in the villages, and at the same time must prevent themselves from becoming involved in backward and antiquated tendencies of experiences in capitalistic industrial management."

2. Thus, in the Shenyang (Manchuria) Factory No. 53, military control lasted until 1950. From 1950 to 1953, factory-management committees played the major role in the direction of the factory. In 1953, the single-director system was initiated—the introduction of "advanced [Soviet] experiences." Starting in 1954, the Party committees began a counteroffensive to recapture control. See *Jen Min Jih Pao,* July 8, 1956, and February 6, 1950. For a description of the early developments in the Anshan Steel Factory, see Cheng Tsu-yuan, *Anshan Steel Factory in Communist China* (Hong Kong: Union Research Institute, 1955), pp. 25–38.

3. See Merle Fainsod, *How Russia Is Ruled* (Cambridge, Mass.: Harvard University Press, 1953), p. 422. Kao Kang's speech as printed in *Jen Min Jih Pao,* June 5, 1950.

4. Fainsod, *op. cit.,* p. 424. See *Kuomin Chingchi Shihyung Tz'utien,* pp. 2025–26. Liu Che, in an article published in the *Tientsin Takung-pao,* May 13, 1954, discusses the harmfulness of the "functional-management system":

> One of the most important characteristics of the production-sector management system is that it assures the single-director system in leadership, that it does away with multiheaded leadership, and that it assures the concreteness and efficiency of leadership. These words are directly aimed at the functional-management system. Under the functional-management system, there also is a factory director, shop chiefs, and there also are all kinds of functional sections. But all of these functional sections can issue orders and instructions to shop chiefs. The result is that this destroys the single-

director system, and creates multiheaded leadership. Though the factory director can exercise leadership over the shop chiefs, each functional section also represents leadership vis-à-vis the shop chiefs. This is not concentrated, but dispersed leadership.

5. See *Tungpei Jen Min Jih Pao,* November 2, 1948, on "the system of responsibility." Also *Chiehfang Jih Pao,* January 13, 1950.

6. *Tungpei Jen Min Jih Pao,* November 2, 1948.

7. The exact details of these economic arrangements between the U.S.S.R. and Communist China are still not fully known. In July, 1949, Kao Kang, then boss of Manchuria, went to Moscow and signed a one-year trade agreement with the U.S.S.R. Late in 1949, Mao Tse-tung personally led a delegation to Moscow for negotiations that culminated in a number of agreements announced in 1950. These included agreements for the joint operation of the Central Manchurian Railway, joint administration of Dairen and Port Arthur, the establishment of joint-stock companies in Sinkiang for oil, nonferrous and rare metals, and civil aviation. In the same year, the U.S.S.R. agreed to furnish China with an initial fifty industrial units. By 1953, another ninety-one units had been added, making a total of 141. Since then, the U.S.S.R. has made further commitments to supply China with basic industrial units. It is not possible to determine how many are original units and how many are added. For a brief discussion, see *Chung-kung Shih-nien* (Hong Kong: Union Research Institute, 1960), pp. 221–25, 334–36. In any case, it is clear that possibly as early as 1949—certainly no later than 1950—Soviet technicians in large numbers began to enter China, particularly Manchuria, to aid in indusrial reconstruction and construction.

8. See *Jen Min Jih Pao,* February 23, 1954.

9. See *Jen Min Jih Pao,* February 3, 1954.

10. Early in 1954, many articles appeared in mainland China describing the workings of the single-director system; e.g., *Jen Min Jih Pao,* February 23, 1954, and March 10, 1954; *Hsin Hunan-pao,* June 23, 1954; *Shanghai Chiehfang Jih Pao,* May 16, 1954. A thorough article on the subject is the one by Liu Che, "A Discussion of the 'Single-Director System' and the 'Production-Sector Management System,'" *Tientsin Takung-pao,* May 13, 1954. See also *Kuomin Chingchi Shihyung Tz'utien,* pp. 2027–29.

11. See *Tientsin Takung-pao,* May 13, 1954.

12. Thus, for example:

When the single-director system was instituted in industry, some people thought that "henceforth there will be no more democracy." They said that the factory director, the shop chiefs, the work-sector chiefs issuing orders and directing production constituted simply "the usual old bureaucracy." Some said: 'The leadership ducked low during the Three-Anti Movement, but now that the single-director system is being put through, they're strutting about again.' Some go so far as to say that the shop chiefs and the work chiefs have become bosses. 'What was once the boss is today the work-section chief!'" [*Wuchou Kungjen Jih Pao,* August 14, 1954.]

13. Stalin stated, in a speech to a conference of business executives on June 23, 1931: ". . . our combines must substitute one-man management for collegium management . . . Let one president and several vice-presidents remain at the head of a combine. This will be quite enough to take care of its management." (*Problems of Leninism* [Moscow: Foreign Languages Publishing House, 1954], pp. 481.)

14. *Smolensk Under Soviet Rule* (Cambridge, Mass.: Harvard University Press, 1958), pp. 59–60.

15. Denunciations of arrogance and autocratism of certain high Party officials begin to appear after the Fourth Plenum of the Central Committee in February, 1954 (which followed the important Politburo meeting in December, 1953). These obviously reflect the internal Party struggle that was then going on with the Kao-Jao clique. The "errors" that were denounced—vested-interestism, individual arrogance, ignoring of collective leadership, dispersionism, excessive emphasis on "vertical rule"—all these are the "errors" imputed to the Kao-Jao group. All of them are the consequences of a Stalinist system of organization that was beginning to develop in Manchuria at the time, with its parallelization of bureaucracies, one-man management, and complex control systems. See *Jen Min Jih Pao*, February 16, 1954; *Shenyang Tungpei Jih Pao*, March 16, 1954; *Jen Min Jih Pao*, April 23, 1954.

16. At the same time that the single-director system was being fully introduced in many Chinese industries, particularly in Manchuria, the Central Committee launched a counterstruggle to re-establish the authority of the Party committees. But this period—most of 1954—was apparently the period of the struggle against the Kao Kang group.

17. D. Goginava, *Partiinyi Kontrol na Predpriiatii* (Moscow: Gospolitizdat, 1949). See also Kao Kang's speech in *Jen Min Jih Pao*, June 5, 1950.

18. Note Stalin's concern with the problem of control in his report to the Seventeenth Party Congress, in *Problems of Leninism*, pp. 649–52.

19. Mao Tse-tung apparently at one time formulated a set of slogans called "the thirty-two-character principles of leadership." In form, these consist of eight couplets, with four characters in each. I have not been able to find them in any of his published works. An article on principles of industrial management that appeared in the Liaoning journal *Lilun Hsüehhsi*, December 1, 1959, quotes two of the couplets: *tach'üan tulan—hsiaoch'üan fensan*. The idea is that at the top level, all authority should be concentrated, but at lower levels, it can be diffused to allow a certain scope for independent action.

20. Note Richard Lowenthal's observation: "Stalin's greatest personal limitation was his pathological distrust of all forces outside his direct control." (*Encounter* [January, 1961], p. 53.)

21. The present reversion to pragmatism in agriculture is also based on a call for "proceeding according to concrete conditions."

22. *Jen Min Shouts'e 1957* (Peking: Takung Pao Publishers, 1957), p. 111.

23. Thus, an article in the *Ch'ingtao Jih Pao*, December 28, 1956, reported:

The Dairen Steel Factory Party organization . . . first of all changed the shortcoming that all factory business was concentrated in the hands of a small minority. Instead, leading cadres and factory directors, who had acted in a freewheeling manner, now in the broadest way furthered the functions of independent responsibility on the part of the deputy factory directors and the chiefs of the functional sections. Furthermore, they changed the earlier habit of management cadres, of fearing to take responsibility, of always asking for instructions on every matter.

24. Here, too, after several years of *hsiafang*, the dialectic may be swinging again in the other direction. An editorial in the *Jen Min Jih Pao*, February 22, 1961, noted:

In the past, because in many enterprises the [functional] sections' organizational structures were too vast, because "people floated around in affairs," we put through a number of necessary reforms, complying with the principles of efficiency and economy. This was entirely necessary. But if this completely upsets the original functional structure, if we use the method of having leadership cadres direct all kinds of *ad hoc* organized command groups, office, and work teams in order to direct production, then this also is not a good method.

The article called for more stablization, more rational division of labor. It suggested, officially, that this tendency be initiated in other industries. In other words, after three years of "the great leap forward," in which routinization and stabilization were the things to be avoided in favor of *ad hoc* combat teams "attacking production," the pendulum has begun to swing back. There are already a number of "significant signs" that this tendency may grow in the future: the return to the pragmatic and to "operating according to concrete conditions" in agriculture, the call for a renewed emphasis on "hundred flowers blooming and hundred schools contending," and now the call for organizational stabilization in industry. All this has occurred after the Ninth Plenum. In view of the intensity of the Chinese presentation of its theses of authoritarianism, struggle, and discipline in the recent Sino-Soviet dialogue, these changes seem startling.

25. The campaign against "rightist tendencies" that began after the Eighth Plenum, in September, 1959, in contrast to the earlier "antirightist movement," was aimed at intra-Party elements who were in favor of stabilization and routinization, and who were apparently disturbed by the frenzy of the mass movements.

26. See, for example, the literature on the so-called "Communist co-operation pacts," *Peking Review*, January 13, 1961; *Jen Min Jih Pao*, January 9, 1961.

Problems of Control: The Organization of Agriculture

23. THE PURPOSE OF THE RURAL COMMUNE

EIGHTH CENTRAL COMMITTEE OF THE CCP

I

In 1958, a new social organization appeared, fresh as the morning sun, above the broad horizon of east Asia. This was the large-scale people's commune in the rural areas of our country which combines industry, agriculture, trade, education, and military affairs and in which government administration and commune management are integrated. Since their first appearance, the people's communes with their immense vitality have attracted widespread attention.

The movement to set up people's communes has grown very rapidly. Within a few months starting in the summer of 1958, all of the more than 740,000 agricultural producers' cooperatives in the country, in response to the enthusiastic demand of the mass of peasants, reorganized themselves into over 26,000 people's communes. Over 120 million households, or more than 99 per cent of all China's peasant households of various nationalities, have joined the people's communes. This shows that the emergence of the people's communes is not fortuitous; it is the outcome of the economic and political development of our country, the outcome of the socialist rectification campaign conducted by the party, of the party's general line for socialist construction and the great leap forward of socialist construction in 1958.

Although the rural people's communes were established only a short while ago, the mass of the peasants are already conscious of the obvious benefits they have brought them. Labor power and the means of production can, on a larger scale than before, be managed and deployed in a unified way to ensure that they are used still more rationally and effectively, and consequently

SOURCE: Reprinted from the *Resolution of the Eighth Central Committee of the Chinese Communist Party.*

to facilitate the development of production. Under the unified leadership of the commune, industry, agriculture (including farming, forestry, animal husbandry, side-occupations, and fisheries), trade, education, and military affairs have been closely coordinated and developed rapidly. In particular, thousands and tens of thousands of small factories have mushroomed in the rural areas. To meet the pressing demands of the masses, the communes have set up large numbers of community dining rooms, nurseries, kindergartens, "homes of respect for the aged," and other institutions for collective welfare, which have, in particular, completely emancipated women from thousands of years of kitchen drudgery and brought broad smiles to their faces. As the result of the bumper crops, many communes have instituted a system of distribution that combines the wage system with the free supply system; the mass of peasants, both men and women, have begun to receive their wages; and those families which in the past constantly worried about their daily meals and about their firewood, rice, oil, salt, soya sauce, vinegar, and vegetables are now able to "eat without paying." In other words they have the most important and most reliable kind of social insurance. For the peasants, all this is epoch-making news. The living standards of the peasants have been improved and they know from practical experience and the prospects of the development of the communes that they will live still better in the future.

The development of the system of rural people's communes has an even more profound and far-reaching significance. It has shown the people of our country the way to the gradual industrialization of the rural areas, the way to the gradual transition from collective ownership to ownership by the whole people in agriculture, the way to the gradual transition from the socialist principle of "to each according to his work" to the communist principle of "to each according to his needs," the way gradually to lessen and finally to eliminate the differences between town and country, between worker and peasant, and between mental and manual labor, and the way gradually to lessen and finally to eliminate the internal function of the state.

All this has proved the correctness and historic significance of the Resolution on the Establishment of People's Communes in the Rural Areas adopted on the basis of the creativeness of the masses by the Political Bureau of the Central Committee of the Chinese Communist Party at its Peitaiho meeting in August 1958.

People's communes have now become the general rule in all rural areas inhabited by our people of various nationalities (except in Tibet and in certain other areas). Some experiments have also begun in the cities. In the future, urban people's communes, in a form suited to the specific features of cities, will also become instruments for the transformation of old cities and the construction of new socialist cities; they will become the unified organizers of production, exchange, and distribution and of the livelihood and well-being of the people; they will become social organizations which combine industry, agriculture, trade, education, and military affairs, organizations in which government administration and commune management are integrated. There are, however, certain differences between the city and the countryside.

Firstly, city conditions are more complex than those in the country-side.

Secondly, socialist ownership by the whole people is already the main form of ownership in the cities; and the factories, public institutions, and schools, under the leadership of the working class, have already become highly organized in accordance with socialist principles (with the exception of some of the family members of the workers and staffs). Therefore, the transition in cities to people's communes inevitably involves some requirements different from those in the rural areas.

Thirdly, bourgeois ideology is still farily prevalent among many of the capitalists and intellectuals in the cities; they still have misgivings about the establishment of communes—so we should wait a bit for them.

Consequently, we should continue to make experiments and generally should not be in a hurry to set up people's communes on a large scale in the cities. Particularly in the big cities, this work should be postponed except for the necessary preparatory measures. People's communes should be established on a large scale in the cities only after rich experience has been gained and when the sceptics and doubters have been convinced.

The rural people's communes which have already been established have not had time to consolidate their organizations, perfect their working systems, or systematically settle the new questions concerning production, distribution, livelihood and welfare, management and administration which have arisen with the establishment of the communes. This has happened because the communes were only recently set up and most of them, immediately after their establishment, threw themselves into the heavy work of the autumn harvest, ploughing, and sowing and the nationwide campaign for iron and steel. There is as yet insufficient experience in successfully running and developing the people's communes. Different approaches to certain questions are unavoidable. The urgent tasks at present are to quickly achieve a unity of views on the communes among all members of the party and among the people, strengthen the leadership over the communes, check up on and consolidate their organization, define and perfect their working systems, and improve the organization of production and life in the communes. Energetic efforts must be made to strengthen those communes which have already been set up, so that they will be in a position to carry out even more successfully their great mission of promoting the development of the productive forces and the relations of production.

II

The people's commune is the basic unit of the socialist social structure of our country, combining industry, agriculture, trade, education, and military affairs; at the same time it is the basic organization of the socialist state power. Marxist-Leninist theory and the initial experience of the people's communes in our country enable us to foresee now that the people's communes will quicken the tempo of our socialist construction and constitute the best form for realizing, in our country, the following two transitions.

Firstly, the transition from collective ownership to ownership by the whole people in the countryside; and,

Secondly, the transition from socialist to communist society. It can also be foreseen that in the future communist society, the people's commune will remain the basic unit of our social structure.

From now on, the task confronting the people of our country is to develop through such a form of social organization as the people's commune, and on the basis of the general line for socialist construction laid down by the party, the social productive forces at high speed, to advance the industrialization of the country, the industrialization of the communes, and the mechanization and electrification of agriculture, and to effect the gradual transition from socialist collective ownership to socialist ownership by the whole people, thus fully realizing ownership by the whole people in the socialist economy of our country and gradually building our country into a great socialist land with a highly developed modern industry, agriculture, science, and culture. During this process, the elements of communism are bound to increase gradually and these will lay the foundation of material and spiritual conditions for the transition from socialism to communism.

This is a gigantic and extremely complex task. In the light of experience already gained, as conditions now stand in our country, it is possible that socialist ownership by the whole people may be fully realized at a somewhat earlier date, but this will not be very soon. Though the pace at which we are advancing is fairly rapid, it will still take a fairly long time to realize, on a large scale, the industrialization of the communes, the mechanization and electrification of agriculture, and the building of a socialist country with a highly developed modern industry, agriculture, science, and culture. This whole process will take 15, 20, or more years to complete, counting from now.

The imperialists and those who parrot them say that this is too short a time for us to build a highly developed modern industry, agriculture, science and culture, and that we won't be able to achieve our aim. We've got used to such tunes; we needn't pay any attention to them; the facts are bound to batter these people down time and time again. But there will be other people who will say that this time is too long. They are good-hearted people in our own ranks, but they are overeager. They think that the building of a highly developed modern industry and so on, full realization of socialist ownership by the whole people, and even the attainment of communism, are very easy things. They think that ownership in the rural people's communes is even now of the nature of ownership by the whole people and that very soon or even now they can dispense with the socialist principle of "to each according to his work" and adopt the communist principle of "to each according to his needs." Consequently, they cannot understand why the socialist system will have to continue for a very long time. Their view, of course, is a misconception, which must be cleared up.

It should be pointed out that the switch from agricultural producers' co-operatives to people's communes, the transition from socialist collective ownership to socialist ownership by the whole people and the transition from socialism to communism are processes which are interconnected but at the same time distinct from each other.

First of all, the switch from the agricultural producers' cooperatives to the people's communes has expanded and strengthened the existing collective ownership and contains certain elements of ownership by the whole people. But this is not to say that collective ownership in the countryside has been transformed into ownership by the whole people. The whole Chinese countryside has now switched over to people's communes, but a certain time will have to pass before ownership by the whole people is realized throughout the countryside.

True, the establishment of the people's communes has added certain elements of ownership by the whole people to the collectively owned economy. This has happened because the rural people's communes and the basic organizations of state power have been combined into one; because the banks, stores, and some other enterprises owned by the whole people, originally existing in the countryside, have been placed under the management of the communes; because the communes have taken part in establishing certain undertakings in industrial and other construction which are by nature owned by the whole people; because in many countries the county federations of communes, exercising unified leadership over all the people's communes in these counties, have been formed and have the power to deploy a certain portion of the manpower, material, and financial resources of the communes to undertake construction on a county or even bigger scale (this has already started in many areas), and so on. But at the present time the means of production and the products of the rural people's communes are in the main still collectively owned by the communes and differ from those of the state-owned enterprises which belong to the whole people. Both collective ownership and ownership by the whole people are socialist ownership; but the latter is more advanced than the former because the state, representing the whole people, can directly make a unified and rational distribution of the means of production and the products of enterprises owned by the whole people according to the requirements of the national economy as a whole, while this cannot be done by enterprises run under collective ownership, including the existing rural people's communes. To say that ownership by the people's communes as they now exist in the countryside is already ownership by the whole people does not conform to reality.

To gradually promote the transition from collective ownership to ownership by the whole people, every country should set up its federation of communes. In coming years, and on the basis of the energetic development of production and the raising of the people's political understanding, such federations should take suitable steps gradually to increase the proportion of their means of production that is owned by the whole people and the proportion of their products that is subject to unified distribution by the state, and, when conditions mature, should change collective ownership into ownership by the whole people. If timely steps are not taken to promote and complete this change and if the existing collective ownership is kept intact indefinitely with the result that commune members confine their attention to the relatively narrow scope of the interests of their collective, the continuous development of the social productive forces and the continuous development of the people's political understanding will be impeded. This is not appropriate. However, it must be pointed out that collective ownership still plays a positive role today in developing production in the people's communes. How soon the transition from collective ownership to ownership by the whole people will be effected will be determined by the objective factors—the level of development of production and the level of the people's political understanding—and not by mere wishful thinking that it can be done at any time we want it. Thus this transition will be realized, by stages and by groups, on a national scale only after a considerable time. Those who, because they fail to understand this, confuse the establishment of people's communes with the realization of ownership by the whole people, making impetuous attempts to abolish collective ownership in the countryside prematurely, and trying hastily to change over to ownership by the whole people, will not be doing the right thing and therefore cannot succeed.

Furthermore, the change from socialist collective ownership to socialist ownership by the whole people is not the same thing as the change from socialism to communism. Still less is the change from agricultural producers' cooperatives to people's communes the same thing as the change from socialism to communism. The change from socialism to communism will require much more time than the change from socialist collective ownership to socialist ownership by the whole people.

True, the free-supply system adopted by the people's communes contains the first shoots of the communist principle of "to each according to his needs"; the policy carried out by the people's communes of running industry and agriculture simultaneously and combining them has opened up a way to reduce the differences between town and countryside and between worker and peasant, and when the rural people's communes pass over from socialist collective ownership to socialist ownership by the whole people, these communist factors will grow further. All this must be acknowledged. Moreover, with social products becoming plentiful thanks to the continuous advance of industry and agriculture throughout the country; with the proportion of what is supplied gratis under the distribution system of the people's communes gradually growing larger and the standards of free supply being gradually raised; with the consistent raising of the level of the people's political understanding; with the constant progress of education for the whole people; the gradual reduction of the differences between mental and manual labor; and with the gradual diminution of the internal function of the state power, etc., the conditions for the transition to communism will also gradually mature. It is of course not proper to ignore or even impede this course of development and relegate communism to the distant future.

Nevertheless every Marxis must soberly realize that the transition from socialism to communism is a fairly long and complicated process of development and that throughout this entire process society is still socialist in nature. Socialist society and communist society are two stages marked by different degrees of economic development. The socialist principle is "from each according to his ability and to each according to his work"; the communist principle is "from each according to his ability and to each according to his needs." The communist system of distribution is more rational; but it can be put into effect only when there is a great abundance of social products. In the absence of this condition, any negation of the principle of "to each according to his work" will tend to dampen the working enthusiasm of the people and is therefore disadvantageous to the development of production and the increase of social products, and hence to speeding the realization of communism. For this reason, in the income of commune members, the portion constituting the wage paid according to work done must occupy an important place over a long period and will, during a certain period, take first place. In order to encourage the working enthusiasm of commune members and also to facilitate the satisfaction of their complex daily needs, the communes must strive gradually to increase the wages of their members and, for a number of years to come, must increase them at a rate faster than that portion of their income which comes under the heading of free supply. Even after the transition from collective ownership to ownership by the whole people, the people's communes will, during a necessary historical period, retain the system of "to each according to his work" owing to the fact that there is not as yet an abundant enough supply of social products to realize communism. Any premature attempt to negate the principle of "to each according to his work" and replace it with the principle of "to each according to his needs," that is, any attempt to enter communism by overreaching ourselves when conditions are not mature—is undoubtedly a Utopian concept that cannot possibly succeed.

Both the transition from socialist collective ownership to socialist ownership by the whole people and the transition from socialism to communism must depend on a certain level of development of the productive forces. Production relations must be suited to the nature of the productive forces and only when the productive forces develop to a certain stage will certain changes be brought about in production relations—this is a fundamental principle of Marxism. Our comrades must bear in mind that the present level of development of the productive forces in our country is, after all, still very low. Three years of hard battle plus several years of energetic work may bring about a great change in the economic face of the country. But even then there will still be a considerable distance to go to reach the goals of a high degree of industrialization of the entire country and the mechanization and electrification of our country's agriculture; and there will be an even longer distance to go to reach the goals of an enormous abundance of social products, of a great lightening of labor and of a sharp reduction of working hours. Without all these, it is, of course, impossible to talk about entering a higher stage of development in human society—communism. Therefore, since we are devoted to the cause of communism, we must first devote ourselves to developing our productive forces and working energetically to fulfill our plan for socialist industrialization. We should not groundlessly make declarations that the people's communes in the countryside will "realize ownership by the whole people immediately," or even "enter communism immediately," and so on. To do such things is not only an expression of rashness, it will greatly lower the standards of communism in the minds of the people, distort the great ideal of communism and vulgarize it, strengthen the petty-bourgeois trend towards equilitarianism, and adversely affect the development of socialist construction.

On the question of transition from socialism to communism, we must not mark time at the socialist stage, but neither should we drop into the Utopian dream of skipping the socialist stage and jumping over to the communist stage. We are advocates of the Marxist-Leninist theory of uninterrupted revolution; we hold that no "Great Wall" exists or can be allowed to exist between the democratic revolution and the socialist revolution and between socialism and communism. We are at the same time advocates of the Marxist-Lenist theory of the development of revolution by stages; we hold that different stages of development reflect qualitative changes and that these stages, different in quality, should not be confused. The Political Bureau of the Central Committee has pointed out clearly in its August Resolution on the Establishment of People's Communes in the Rural Areas: in the case of the people's communes, "the transition from collective ownership to ownership by the whole people is a process, the completion of which may take less time—three or four years—in some places, and longer—five or six years or even more—elsewhere. Even with the completion of this transition, people's communes, like state-owned industry, are still socialist in character, i.e., the principle of 'from each according to his ability and to each according to his work' prevails. Some years after that, the social product will increase greatly, the communist consciousness and morality of the entire people will be raised to a much higher degree, universal education will be instituted and developed, the differences between worker and peasant, between town and country, between mental and manual labor—the legacies of the old society that have inevitably been carried over into the socialist period—and the remnants of unequal bourgeois rights which are the reflection of these differences—will gradually vanish; and the function of the state will be limited to protecting the country from external aggression; it will play no role internally. At that time Chinese society will enter the era of communism in which the principle of 'from each according to his ability and to each according to his needs' will be practiced." In order to clear up misconceptions about the people's communes and ensure the healthy development of the people's commune movement, extensive and repeated publicity and education based on this Marxist-Leninist point of view must be carried out seriously throughout the party and among all the people of China.

III

The people's communes must plan their production, exchange, consumption, and accumulation. Their plans should be subordinated to the state plans and to the administration of the state. In working out their plans, the people's communes should at the same time fully develop their own characteristic features and their initiative.

Development of production is the key to the consolidation and elevation of the people's communes. The correct policy of the people's communes for the development of production should be to insure the simultaneous development of industry and agriculture and of production for their own use and for exchange, in accordance with the principles of unified state planning, of adaptation to local conditions, and of running the communes industriously and thriftily. In every aspect of production and capital construction, thrift must be observed; careful plans must be worked out; and manpower, material, and financial resources must be used as rationally as possible; production costs must be reduced; expenditures must be cut down and income increased; extravagance and waste among some functionaries of the communes following bumper harvests should be prevented and opposed.

In agricultural production, shallow ploughing, careless cultivation, and "big acreage with small output" should be gradually replaced by deep ploughing, intensive cultivation, and "small acreage with big output." Farming should be carried on as meticulously as gardening, and agricultural production should be mechanized and electrified to bring about a big increase in per *mu* yields and labor productivity and to gradually reduce the area under cultivation and manpower engaged in agriculture. We should strive to reach a yearly average of two to three thousand *jin* or one ton to one and a half tons of grain per capita within a comparatively short period. As the grain problem is solved, the proportion of the total agricultural output occupied by cotton, flax, and jute, silk, soya beans, oil-bearing crops, sugar-bearing crops, tea, tobacco, medicinal, and other industrial crops must be gradually increased. In addition, great attention should be paid to speeding the development of forestry, animal husbandry, farm side lines, and fisheries. In short, as on the industrial front, a great revolution must be carried out on all the fronts of agriculture, forestry, animal husbandry, farm side lines, and fisheries so as to thoroughly transform the face of agriculture.

People in the past often worried about our "overpopulation" and relatively small amount of available arable land. But this idea has been overturned by the facts of our 1958 bumper harvest. Insofar as we succeed in seriously popularizing the rich experience gained in getting high yields through deep ploughing, intensive cultivation, layer-by-layer fertilization, and rational close planting, it will be found that the amount of arable land is not too small but very considerable, and that the question is not so much overpopulation as shortage of manpower. This will be a very big change. In the next several years, local conditions permitting, we should try to reduce the area sown to crops each year to about one-third of what it is at present. Part of the land so saved can be used for fallow rotation, pasturage, and the growing of green manure; the rest can be used for afforestation, reservoirs, and the extensive cultivation of flowers, shrubs, and trees to turn our whole land with its plains, hills, and waters into a garden. By these means:

Firstly, it will be possible to greatly economize the use of water, fertilizer, and manpower, and to considerably increase the fertility of the soil;

Secondly, full use can be made of every mountain, river, forest, and the pasture; and the comprehensive management of agriculture, forestry, animal husbandry, farm side lines, and fisheries can be greatly developed.

Thirdly, our natural environment will be transformed and the whole country beautified.

This is a great ideal that can be realized. People's communes throughout the land should work to realize this aim.

People's communes must go in for industry in a big way. The development of industry by the people's communes will not only accelerate the industrialization of the whole country but also promote the realization of ownership by the whole people in the rural districts, and reduce the differences between town and country. According to the differing conditions in each people's commune, an appropriate part of the labor force should be transferred, step by step, from agriculture to industry so as to develop, according to plan, the production of fertilizer, insecticides, farm implements, and machinery and building materials; the processing and many-sided utilization of agricultural produce; the manufacturing of sugar, textiles, and paper; the expansion of mining, metallurgy, electric power, and other light and heavy industries. Industrial production in the people's communes must be closely linked with agricultural production; it should first of all serve the development of agriculture and the mechanization and electrification of farming; at the same time it should serve to meet the demands of commune members for staple consumer goods, and serve the country's big industries and the socialist market. The principles of adaptation to local conditions and obtaining raw materials locally should be fully taken into consideration; in order to avoid increased costs and waste of labor power, industries should not be set up in places where there are no raw materials or where these have to be brought from very far away. With regard to production techniques, the principle should be carried out of linking handicraft with mechanized industry, and indigenous methods with modern methods of production. All handicraft industries which have good foundations and prospects for expansion must continue to be developed, and gradually carry through the necessary technical transformations. The mechanized industries must also make full use of indigenous methods and iron, steel, machine tools, other raw materials and equipment produced by indigenous methods; they will gradually advance from indigenous to modern, from small to large, and from a low to a high level.

Whether in industry or agriculture, people's communes should develop production for their own use which directly meets their own needs, and they should also develop commodity production on as wide a scale as possible. Every people's commune, according to its own characteristics and under the guidance of the state, should carry out the necessary division of labor in production and exchange of commodities with other people's communes and state-owned enterprises. Only in this way can the economy of our whole society expand at a faster rate, and every commune obtain through exchange the machinery and equipment required for the mechanization and electrification of farming, as well as the consumer goods and ready cash required to meet the needs of commune members and pay them wages, and make it possible to raise wages step by step. To ensure fulfillment of trading plans, an extensive system of contracts should be set up between the state and the communes and among the communes themselves.

It must be stressed that during the course of a necessary historical period, commodity production by the people's communes and the exchange of commodities between the state and communes and among the communes themselves must be greatly developed. Such production and exchange of commodities are different from those under capitalism, because they are conducted in a planned way, on the basis of socialist public ownership and not in an anarchic way on the basis of capitalist private ownership. Continued development of commodity production and continued adherence to the principle of "to each according to his work" are two important questions of principle in expanding the socialist economy. The whole party should have a uniform understanding of them. Some people, attempting to "enter communism" prematurely, have tried to abolish the production and exchange of commodities too early, and to negate at too early a stage the positive roles of commodities, value, money, and prices. This line of thinking is harmful to the development of socialist construction and is therefore incorrect.

IV

The people's communes in rural districts should distribute their own incomes properly on the principle of running the communes industriously and thriftily. To speed up production, the proportion of accumulation should be appropriately increased after production costs, administrative expenses, and taxes have been deducted from the gross income. But on the basis of the development of production, the portion of the income used to meet the individual and collective expenses of commune members (including the portion spent on public welfare, culture, and education) should be increased annually in order to improve the livelihood of the people year by year.

The introduction of a distribution system which combines the wage system and the free-supply system in the part of the commune's income allotted to its members for consumption is a form of socialist distribution created by China's people's communes, and at the present time it represents what the broad mass of members earnestly demand. As stated above, this distribution system includes the first shoots of communism but in essence it is still socialist—based on the principle of "from each according to his ability and to each according to his work."

The proportions of wages and free supplies in the total amount allotted to members should be determined in the light of the varying levels of the development of production in the communes. At present, in fixing the ratio between wages and free supplies, care should be taken as far as possible to avoid reducing the income of households which have relatively few members but are strong in labor power; in general, it should be made possible for more than 90 per cent of the members to increase their income as compared with the previous year while the rest should get no less than in the previous year.

For the present, the scope of free supply should not be too wide. The application of the free-supply system does not seek to make the life of the people uniform. Under the systems of socialism and communism, the needs of the people are on the whole similar while varying according to the individual. Therefore in the future, as well as at present, care should be taken to insure, as far as possible, that members have suitable freedom of choice within the framework of the free-supply system.

Wages must be increased gradually as production expands. For the present, after deducting the items freely supplied, wage scales in the rural areas can be divided into six to eight grades, and the highest grade may be four or more times as much as the lowest grade. But the differences should not be too great; for if they were, they would not conform to the existing differences in laboring skills in the rural areas. Certain differences between the wage levels in different areas are permissible. For the present differences between wage grades in the city are greater than those in the countryside, and this is necessary. In the future, as a result of the tremendous rise in production, everyone will be much better off and whether in city or countryside such differences between wage grades will be unnecessary and will gradually disappear. That will be nearing the era of communism.

The reasons why wage levels in the city are generally higher than those in the countryside are manysided (including the factor of living costs being higher in the city), and this is also a temporary situation which should be explained to the peasants. Some commune members, apart from working in the villages, also receive money sent home by their relatives who are away in cities or elsewhere (such as workers, soldiers, functionaries, and Chinese living abroad). Work should be done to dissuade other members from wrangling about this. In distribution within the commune, members with such receipts should be treated the same as others without discrimination in regard to free supplies and wages, and they should not be urged to make special investments or contributions to the commune. If they rely on family members away from home for the whole of their livelihood, the commune should not interfere, but it may stop supplying them with the usual allotments. Those who leave home for study, apart from those whose needs are covered by the state or can be covered by their own families, should be supported by the county federation of communes according to the standards laid down by the schools.

The more socialism develops and the more abundant social products become, the more abundant too will become the means of livelihood allotted to each individual. Some people think that the switch to communes will call for a redistribution of existing property for personal use. This is a misconception. It should be made known among the masses that the means of livelihood owned by members (including houses, clothing, bedding and furniture) and their deposits in banks and credit cooperatives will remain their own property after they join the commune and will always belong to them. When necessary, the commune may borrow the surplus housing space of members with their consent, but the ownership still belongs to the owners. Members can retain odd trees around their houses, small farm tools, small instruments, small domestic animals, and poultry; they can also continue to engage in some small domestic side-line occupations on the condition that these do not hamper their taking part in collective labor.

Debts incurred before the people's communes were established should not be declared cancelled irrespective of whether these are between individuals, between the commune and its members, or debts contracted by commune members with banks or credit cooperatives. These debts should be repaid where conditions permit and where the conditions do not allow repayment for the time being, they should be held over.

V

The people's commune is the organizer of the production and livelihood of the people and the fundamental purpose of the development of production is to satisfy to the maximum extent the constantly growing material and cultural needs of all members of society. In leading the work of the commune, the party must give all-round attention to the ideological development, production, and livelihood of commune members. It must care for the people and correct the tendency to see only things and not human beings. The greater the working enthusiasm of the masses, the greater the attention the party should pay to their well-being. The more attention the Party pays to the livelihood of the masses, the greater their enthusiasm will be in work. It is wrong to set production and people's livelihood against each other and to imagine that attention to the livelihood of the masses will hamper production. Of course, it is also wrong to put a one-sided and excessive stress on the improvement of the people's livelihood without regard to the raising of their level of political consciousness and the development of production, and not to advocate working hard for long-term interests.

Communists have always held that in a communist society labor will be changed "from a heavy burden into a pleasure" and will become the "primary necessity of life." There is no doubt that the working day will be greatly shortened in future. With the development of mechanization and electrification, we must strive to introduce the six-hour workday within a certain number of years. Our intensive work at the present time is precisely to create conditions for the six-hour workday and even shorter working hours in future. At present, the system of eight hours of actual work and two hours of study should be put into effect in both city and countryside. During the busy farm season or when other work in the rural areas is particularly heavy, working hours may be appropriately extended. But, in any event, eight hours for sleep and four hours for meals and recreation, altogether twelve hours, must be guaranteed every day and this must not be reduced. It is true that there is a labor shortage at present, but the way out must be found in stressing the successful implementation of the reform of tools and improvement of labor organization and not in extending working hours. Special attention must be paid to safety in production and labor conditions must be improved as far as possible in order to reduce to the minimum or completely eliminate work accidents. Adequate rest must be insured to women both during pregnancy and after childbirth and they should also get the necessary rest during menstruation when they should not be asked to do heavy work, to get their feet wet in cold water, or work at night.

Community kitchens should be well run. All commune members must be assured of plenty of good, clean food suited to their national and local habits. The communal eating establishments should have dining rooms, and they should efficiently run their own vegetable gardens, bean-curd mills, bean-noodle mills, and condiment shops; they should raise pigs, sheep, chickens, ducks, and fish. The food should be varied and appetizing. Nutrition specialists should be consulted to make sure that the food contains enough calories and the nutriments needed by the human body. Where necessary and possible, special food should be provided for the aged, children, invalids, pregnant women, and nursing mothers. It is permissible for some commune members to cook at home. Community dining rooms should be managed democratically. Their administrative staffs and cooks should be chosen from among those who are politically reliable. It is best that they be elected democratically.

Nurseries and kindergartens should be run well so that every child can live better and receive a better education in them than at home, and so that the children want to stay there and the parents want to put them there. The parents may decide whether it is necessary for their children to board there, and may take them home at any time. In order to run nurseries and kindergartens well, communes should train a large number of qualified child-care workers and teachers.

The "homes of respect for the aged" should be run well so as to provide better dwelling places for those old people who have no children to take care of them (those who are eligible for the "five guarantees"—food, clothing, fuel, the bringing up of children, and burial).

Communes must ensure the successful running of primary and secondary schools and adult education. Universal primary school education should be instituted in the rural areas throughout the country. Full-time secondary schools and half-time secondary agricultural schools, or other secondary vocational schools, should be well run; and universal secondary education should be intro-duced step by step. Earnest efforts should be made to wipe out illiteracy, organize various kinds of spare-time schools, and conduct political education, cultural classes, and technical education for adults. In reducing the differences between manual and mental labor, the institution of universal education among the working people and the gradual raising of their educational level is an important step which must be carried out conscientiously. The communes, in addition, must also select and send a number of young people to study in senior secondary schools, secondary vocational schools, and institutions of higher learning in the cities so as to train fairly well-educated working personnel for the state and the communes. The principle of combining education with productive labor must be carried out thoroughly in all schools, without excep-tion. Children above the age of nine may take part in some labor to an appropriate extent so as to cultivate the habit of work in childhood and stimu-late their physical and mental development; but full attention must be paid to the health of the children—they must only be given light work for short periods of time, suited to their physical strength and their aptitude.

Ideological and political work among the staffs in community dining rooms, nurseries, kindergartens, "homes of respect for the aged," primary schools, public health centers, clubs, and shops must be strengthened and efforts must be made to give positive guidance to public opinion so that the whole of society and the whole communes regard the successful running of community dining rooms, nurseries, kindergartens, and other collective welfare undertakings and satisfactory work in the personal services as noble work of service to the people. The attitude of the exploiting classes in looking down on work which concerns the daily life and welfare of the masses and work in the personal services, must be criticized and corrected.

The existing old-style houses must be reconstructed step by step; townships and village housing estates with parks and woods must be built by stages and in groups: these will include residential quarters, community dining rooms, nurseries, kindergartens, the "homes of respect for the aged," factories, threshing floors, livestock sheds, shops, post and telecommunications offices, warehouses, schools, hospitals, clubs, cinemas, sports grounds, baths, and public lavatories. The construction plans of townships and village housing estates should be thoroughly discussed by the masses. We stand for the abolition of the irrational patriarchal system inherited from the past and for the development of family life in which there is democracy and unity. This stand has been warmly received by the masses. Therefore, in building residential quarters, attention must be paid to building the houses so that the married couples, the young and the aged of each family can all live together.

There is now a big bunch of fools in the world who are attacking the people's communes with all their might and main and among them is Mr. Dulles of the United States. This Dulles knows nothing about things in our country but likes to pretend to be a China expert and madly opposes the people's communes. What breaks his heart especially is that we have supposedly destroyed the marvellous family system which has been handed down for thousands of years. True, the Chinese people have destroyed a feudal, patriarchal system. This patriarchal system, it must be noted, generally disappeared long ago in capitalist society and that was a progressive step in capitalist society. But we go a step further and establish a democratic, united family and this is generally rare in capitalist society. Only in the future, when the socialist revolution has been carried out and when the capitalist system of exploitation of man by man has been eliminated, will it be possible to establish such families there universally. As to nurseries, kindergartens, and workers' canteens in the factories, these also first appeared in capitalist society. But under capitalism, all such undertakings established by the bourgeoisie are capitalist in nature and are aimed at facilitating the exploitation of men and women laborers by the capitalists. On the other hand, such undertakings run by us are socialist in nature and they facilitate the development of the socialist cause and the emancipation of the individual personality of man. They have truly and completely emancipated the mass of women and enabled the children to receive better education and care. That is why they are warmly welcomed by all the working people, and first of all by the masses of women.

VI

The organizational principle of the people's commune is democratic centralism. This principle must be applied in the management of production, in the distribution of income, in the livelihood and welfare of commune members, and in all other aspects of work.

Unified leadership and management at different levels should be put into effect in the people's commune. The administrative setup of the commune in general can be divided into three levels, namely: the commune administrative committee, the administrative district (or production brigade), and the production team. The administrative district (or production brigade) is in general the unit which manages industry, agriculture, trade, education, and military affairs in a given area and forms an economic accounting unit, with its gains and losses pooled in the commune as a whole. The production team is the basic unit of labor organization. Under the unified leadership of the commune administrative committee, the necessary powers should be given to the administrative district (or production brigade) and the production team over such matters as the organization of production work and capital construction, finances, and welfare, in order to bring their initiative into full play.

The various levels of organizations of the county federation of communes and of the people's commune must learn to make reasonable distributions and deployments of manpower for the different branches of production (agriculture, industry, transport) and for routine production work, shock production tasks, and service work, so as to avoid situations where there is work without men in one place and there are men without work in another. The organization of labor must be constantly improved, the system of responsibility for a given task at a given level must continue to be applied and reinforced in production and other tasks, the system of labor inspection and labor awards must be perfected in order to guarantee effectively the steady improvement of labor efficiency and the quality of work.

There must be both discipline and democracy in the organization of labor in the people's commune. What we describe as getting organized along military lines means getting organized on the pattern of a factory. It means that the organization of labor in the people's commune should be as organized and disciplined as in a factory or the army; this is necessary in large-scale agricultural production. The forces of large-scale agricultural production, like the forces of large-scale industrial production, constitute an industrial army. The modern industrial army was organized by the bourgeoisie, each factory being like a military camp. The discipline for the worker standing before the machine is as rigid as that in the army. The industrial army in socialist society is an industrial army of a single class, the working class, which has got rid of the capitalists who squeezed surplus value out of the workers and which has put into force in the working class a vigorous and lively democratic centralism based on the voluntary principle. We are now applying this system to the rural areas, thus establishing a socialist industrial army for agriculture based on democratic centralism, which is free from exploitation by the landlords and rich peasants and is elevated above the level of small-scale production.

Militia organizations should be set up at corresponding levels of the production organizations in the people's commune. The leading bodies of the militia and production organizations should be separate and, in principle, the commanding officers of the various levels of the militia such as regimental, battalion, and company commanders, should not be concurrently directors of communes and administrative districts (leaders of production brigades) and leaders of production teams. These commanders should take part in the administrative organizations of the same levels in the commune as their members, and they will receive dual leadership: from the administrative organizations of the same level and the superior commanding organizations of the militia. The militia should be equipped with the necessary arms produced by arsenals set up locally. The basic units of the militia should undergo military training according to a set schedule, while the ordinary militiamen should also get appropriate training after work; this is to prepare conditions for turning the whole nation into soldiers. The broad mass of working people in our country greet the militia system warmly, because, in the course of their protracted revolutionary struggle against imperialism, feudalism, and their running dogs, the Kuomintang reactionaries, they came to realize that only by arming themselves would they be able to overcome the armed counterrevolution and become masters of the land of China. After the victory of the revolution, they have come to see further that there are still imperialist pirates abroad who are clamoring every day about wiping out this people's state. Therefore, the whole of our people are determined to continue to arm themselves, and they declare: Be warned, you pirates bent on plundering us; do not dare to make a vain attempt to harm our people engaged in peaceful labor; we are fully prepared! Should the imperialists dare to unleash an aggressive war against our country, then we will turn the whole nation into soldiers; the militia will cooperate with the People's Liberation Army and at any time replenish it to crush the aggressors utterly.

There should be both centralism and democracy in all organizations of the people's communes, including the militia organizations. The people's communes should not only organize the people's production work but the people's livelihood as well. In order to do their work well, the communes must practise a high level of democracy, consult the masses on all matters, faithfully represent their interests, and reflect their will. Therefore, while "organizing along military lines, working as if fighting a battle and living the collective way," the communes must fully implement democratic management. It is absolutely impermissible to use "getting organized along military lines" as a pretext or to make use of the militia system—which is directed against the enemy—to impair, in the least, democratic life in the commune and the milita organizations. The people's commune is the basic organization of our country's state power; only by ensuring democracy in the commune will it be possible to create throughout the country a vigorous and lively political situation in which there are both centralism and democracy, both discipline and freedom, both unity of will and personal ease of mind.

VII

In running a people's commune well the fundamental question is to strengthen the leading role of the party. It is only by strengthening the party's leading role, that the principle of "politics in command" can be realized, that socialist and communist ideological education among the cadres and commune members and the struggle against all kinds of erroneous tendencies can be conducted in a thoroughgoing way and that the party's line and policy can be implemented correctly. There are some people who think that with the emergence of the commune the party can be dispensed with, and that they can practise what they call "merging the party and commune in one." This kind of thinking is wrong.

In its work in the people's commune, the party, besides its task of insuring that the correct line and policy are put into effect, should also pay attention to educating the commune staffs to develop good styles of work—first of all the mass line and a practical and realistic style of work.

Following the 1957–1958 rectification campaign, the party's mass line achieved a new, great victory. The great leap forward in socialist construction and the setting up of people's communes throughout the rural areas are two signal marks of this victory. The mass-line working method of the party is the lifeblood of the people's communes. The setting up and consolidation of the people's communes is impossible without the mass line, without the full faith of the people in the party and in the People's Government, and without an upsurge in the revolutionary zeal of the masses. Therefore, leading functionaries of all levels in the commune must put the mass line thoroughly into practice in every type of work tackled. They must look upon themselves as ordinary working people, and treat the commune members in a comradely way. Kuomintang and bourgeois styles of work which coerce the masses are strictly prohibited. Because of the big leap forward in production and the victory in setting up communes, some cadres are beginning to get dizzy with success; and, unwilling to do the patient work of educating the masses by persuasion, they are exhibiting certain rude attitudes. Though these are individual cases, they should make us keenly vigilant.

In all its work, the party should hold fast to the principle of combining revolutionary zeal with a scientific spirit. The great leap forward in 1958 has won an unprecedented victory for socialist construction in our country. Now even our enemies find it impossible to deny the significance of this victory. But we must never overlook our small weak points because of big achievements. On the contrary, the bigger the achievement, the more we need to remind our cadres to keep coolheaded and not be carried away by the flood of news of victory and become unable or even unwilling to see the weak points in their work. One tendency to which we must pay attention in the present work of socialist construction is exaggeration. This is incompatible with the practical working style of our party, and is harmful to the development of our socialist construction. We must do our economic work in a more thoroughgoing way. Our leading personnel at all levels must be good at differentiating between the reality and the false appearance of things and between demands which are justified and those which are not; in assessing conditions, they must strive to keep close to objective reality. Only by doing so can we work out and carry through our plans on a reliable and solid basis.

VIII

In order to promote the consolidation of the people's communes and ensure an even bigger leap forward in industry and agriculture in 1959, the Communist Party committees of the provinces, municipalities, and autonomous regions should, in accordance with the requirements set forth in this resolution and in close integration with the production tasks of the winter and spring seasons, make full use of the five months from December, 1958, to April, 1959, to carry out, within the people's communes in their areas, educational work, checkup and consolidation, that is the work of checking up on the communes.

In the course of checking up on the communes, it is necessary, in the first place, for leading personnel to make serious self-criticisms and listen with modesty to the masses' opinions, and on this basis, mobilize the masses with great daring to air their views freely and frankly, carry out debates and post up *dazibao* (written opinions in big Chinese characters posted publicly for everybody to read—*Ed.*), to commend good persons and deeds, criticize wrong ideas and bad styles of work, sum up experiences, clarify the line of work, and develop a thoroughgoing socialist and communist ideological education movement.

In the course of checking up on the communes, it is necessary to carry out an overall and thorough inspection of the production plan, distribution, welfare, management, financial work, organization, and leadership in the communes. The organizations of the Communist Party and communes should be carefully checked over at the same time to guarantee that the leading personnel of the Communist Party and communes at various levels are activists, loyal to the interests of the people and to the cause of communism. In addition, the finest people who have been tested in the big leap forward and people's commune movement and are qualified for Communist Party membership, should be enrolled in the party.

Problems related to the style of work of Communist Party members and cadres should be dealt with through party education and frank airing of views by the masses. In dealing with these problems, attention should be paid to safeguarding the zeal and initiative of the cadres and masses, and the principles of "unity—criticism—unity" and "taking warning from the past in order to be more careful in the future" and "treating the illness in order to save the man" must be observed. Those who have committed errors but are willing to correct them should be criticized seriously but treated with leniency. The masses should be mobilized to purge the leadership in the communes of those alien class elements who have smuggled themselves into the leadership and the very few who display a very bad style of work and have never corrected their errors even after being repeatedly admonished.

Complex class struggles not only develop sharply abroad, in the capitalist world, but also exist at home. It is necessary to educate the masses to increase their revolutionary vigilance to prevent disruptive enemy activities. Whether ex-landlords, rich peasants, and counterrevolutionaries and other people formerly deprived of political rights should be accepted as members or probationary members of the communes, or remain to work under the communes' supervision, should be discussed and decided by the masses dealing with each case on its merits in the course of checking up on the communes.

The work of checking up on the communes should first be carried out in one or two communes in each county as an experiment. That is to say help should be given to the comrades in one or two people's communes to get things going well in a fairly short space of time, so as to acquire experience, set examples and then popularize the experience gained generally. Every province, municipality, and autonomous region should organize its inspection team consisting of a thousand, several thousands, or ten thousand people for the checkup, and the first secretaries of the Communist Party at the provincial, regional, and county levels should personally lead the work of checking up on the communes. These inspection teams should compare different special administrative regions, counties, and communes, organize mutual visits, call on-the-spot meetings to develop the good points found and overcome the shortcomings discovered, rouse the drive of the people, and find ways of concretely solving current problems and promptly popularizing successful experience. In short, through these checkups, the work of the people's communes in the country must be generally carried one step forward.

24. URBAN-RURAL RELATIONS

KAO CHENG-SHENG

The nature of relations between town and country depends on the prevailing socio-economic system. Different social systems give rise to different types of urban-rural relations. In all societies based on private ownership of the means of production, these relations are antithetical. This antithesis runs through the entire history of class societies. It becomes unprecedentedly acute under capitalism where the town dominates and ruthlessly exploits the countryside. The growth of capitalist industry, commerce and the credit system results in the expropriation of the peasantry, the bankruptcy of the majority of the agricultural population, the lagging of agriculture far behind industry, and the overall subordination of the countryside to the town.

But "abolition of the antithesis between town and country is not merely possible. It has become a direct necessity of industrial production itself."[1] In order to abolish this antithesis, it is necessary to abolish completely the system of private ownership of the means of production, to abolish the capitalist mode of production.

In old semi-colonial and semi-feudal China, and especially during the period of Kuomintang rule, the antithesis between town and country was more acute than in any other period in China's history. In those days, imperialism, feudalism and bureaucrat capitalism, with the town as their centre and the reactionary Kuomintang regime as their tool, completely dominated and ruthlessly exploited the countryside. They used their monopolist concerns and their control of the market to widen the price "scissors" between industrial and agricultural products to the utmost. They fleeced the peasants through well-organized usury—using banks and credit and loan operations, local money-lenders and landlords. They plundered the rural areas by means of a vast array of taxes and levies, driving millions of peasants to the verge of bankruptcy and completely ruining millions of others.

Great Change in Urban-Rural Relations

Since the founding of the People's Republic the relations between town and country in China have undergone a fundamental change. Under the leadership of the Chinese Communist Party and Chairman Mao Tse-tung, farm collectivization went ahead immediately after completion of the land reform in the rural areas. At the same time, in the cities the socialist transformation

SOURCES Reprinted from Kao Cheng-sheng, "New Type Urban-Rural Relations in China," in *Peking Review*, March 29, 1963, pp. 19–22. [*Peking Review* is the official publication of the Chinese Communist Government. Ed.]

of capitalist industry and commerce was accomplished. In this way, feudal private ownership of land and capitalist private ownership of the means of production were abolished and socialist public ownership of the means of production was firmly established. This uprooted the economic basis of the antithesis between town and country that prevailed in old China. Today, the vital interests of the two friendly classes—the working class and the peasantry—coincide. Their common goal is to build China under the leadership of the Communist Party into a strong socialist state with a modern industry, modern agriculture, modern science and culture and modern national defence. This determines that the vital interests of the cities and the countryside are one and the same. In this way, mutual assistance and co-operation have been formed between the cities and the countryside—a new-type relationship between town and country in the history of human society.

Under China's socialist system, antagonistic contradictions no longer exist between town and country; nonantagonistic contradictions, however, still exist. Comrade Mao Tse-tung said more than 20 years ago: "Economically, in capitalist society where the town under bourgeois rule ruthlessly plunders the countryside and in the Kuomintang-controlled areas in China where the town under the rule of foreign imperialism and the big native comprador bourgeoisie most savagely plunders the countryside, the contradiction between town and country is one of extreme antagonism. But in a socialist country and in our revolutionary bases, such as antagonistic contradiction changes into a non-antagonistic one, and it will disappear in a communist society."[2] At the present time, the following are the main non-antagonistic contradictions between town and country in China:

Industry in general is owned by the entire people whereas collective ownership prevails in agriculture.

Industry on the whole is equipped with modern technology and labour productivity in industry is relatively high whereas agriculture depends primarily on manual operations and animal power, and labour productivity in agriculture is relatively low:

The conditions of material and cultural life in the towns are generally somewhat better than those in the countryside and workers and peasants still form two distinct classes with different economic status.

Why Towns Lead Countryside

The town occupies the leading position in urban-rural relations in China. Under socialism the town leads the countryside. This means that the town transforms the countryside along socialist lines. In the course of the democratic and socialist revolutions, the old towns of China have undergone a fundamental change. They have changed from centres of exploitation into socialist towns and they no longer serve as strongholds for dominating and exploiting the countryside. Instead, they have become centres for leading the countryside politically, economically and culturally. In the first place, the socialist towns are the heart of our nation's political life; they are where the leading organs at various levels of the Communist Party and the state are located. The Communist Party is the leading core of the nation and the peasants can advance victoriously towards socialism only under the leadership of the political power of the working class and its Communist Party.

Secondly, the socialist towns are the focuses of the nation's economic life, the sites of large-scale modern socialist industry. Large-scale modern industry provides the material basis for the technical reform of the national economy, and especially of agriculture. Only under the leadership of large-scale modern industry can agriculture grow rapidly.

Thirdly, the socialist towns are the centres of the nation's cultural life; they are where its scientific and cultural establishments are concentrated. The cutural revolution is a key aspect of socialist construction, and the countryside can overcome its cultural backwardness only with the assistance of the scientific and cultural establishments of the towns. It is therefore clear that politically, economically and culturally the towns are more advanced than the conutryside; they play a leading role in urban-rural relations. Town and countryside are building socialism together with the former leading the latter.

Integration of Industry and Agriculture

Mutual assistance and co-operation between town and country is an important relationship in the period of socialist construction in China. Urban-rural relations are expressed economically in the integration of industry and agriculture. Industry and agriculture are the two basic departments of material production in the national economy. They are interlinked and mutually interdependent. All the marketable grain, most of the manpower and much of the raw materials needed for the growth of industry come from agriculture. On the other hand, the means of production needed for the growth of agriculture and the industrial consumer goods needed by the peasants have to be supplied mainly by industry. The general policy of developing the national economy with agriculture as the foundation and industry the leading factor put forward by Comrade Mao Tse-tung makes a profound statement of the relationship between industry and agriculture both in theory and in practice. Guided by this general policy we are correctly handling the integration of the industry and agriculture and properly arranging urban-rural relations.

Technical reform in agriculture follows in the wake of the further consolidation and development of the collective economy of the rural people's communes. This means not only a steady increase in the quantity of tools and other means of production demanded by agriculture but also a structural change in this demand. Large quantities of small and medium-sized farm tools and implements are needed by agriculture at the present time, but in the near future, agriculture will need increasing quantities of large farm machines. This trend is becoming increasingly evident. The great task of modernizing the farms has become a major item on the agenda of the entire Party and people in building the national economy. In order to meet the needs of technical reform in agriculture all industrial departments are readjusting their work according to the policy of taking agriculture as the foundation of the national economy. The relationship of mutual assistance and co-operation between town and country in China will further develop on the basis of the accelerated integration of industry and agriculture.

Key Links in Urban-Rural Relations

The entire Party and people are turning their attention to agriculture. They are giving top priority to support for agriculture and the collective economy of the people's communes. The key links in reinforcing urban-rural relations today are:

Strengthening the town's aid to the countryside and industry's aid to agriculture;

Further consolidating the collective economy of the people's communes; and

Developing farm production.

At the same time, in developing industry and the town, due consideration must be given to what help the countryside can give. In urban construction and development, in capital construction and industrial production and in developing other undertakings, in planning increases in the number of office staff and other employees and the urban population as a whole, full consideration must be given to the amounts of marketable grain, industrial raw materials and other farm and side-line products that the countryside can supply as well as the manpower that the villages can provide. The growth of industry and urban construction can proceed on a firm footing only when agriculture is taken as the foundation of the national economy, when the rate of industrial growth and the scale of urban construction are determined on the basis of the level of agricultural production, and when proper proportions are maintained between the urban and rural populations.

The integration of industry and agriculture is effected mainly through the economic link between town and country. In China today this link operates in a planned way under the centralized and unified leadership of the Communist Party and the state. This leadership therefore serves as a powerful lever for integrating industry with agriculture.

Economic Link Between Town and Country

Commodity exchange is the basic form of the economic link between town and country in China during the period of socialist construction. There are two forms of socialist public ownership of the means of production in China during the current stage of development, namely, ownership by the whole people and collective ownership. In the case of ownership by the whole people, the means of production are the property of the whole people and products are controlled by the state whereas in the case of collective ownership, the means of production are the property of the collective which also controls their products. These two different forms of ownership must exchange their products through a certain form of economic link. The collective farmer will only part with his farm produce as a commodity in exchange for the industrial goods he needs. Commodity exchange by buying and selling is the only form of economic link acceptable to the collective farmer. Commodity exchange is therefore a most important factor in the economic interchange between town and country in the period of socialist construction in China.

Commodity exchange between town and country under socialism is, however, fundamentally different from that under capitalism. Under capitalism, based as it is on private ownership of the means of production, the bourgeoisie of the towns ruthlessly exploit the peasants of the countryside by "buying cheap and selling dear" and by other means, commercial or otherwise. This gives rise to clashes of economic interests between town and country. In contrast with capitalism, commodity exchange between town and country under socialism is based on public ownership of the means of production. Socialist commerce, in which there is no exploitation of any kind, serves as a bridge linking town and country economically.

Since the founding of the People's Republic, and especially since the great leap forward which began in 1958, under the guidance of the Communist Party's general line for building socialism, tremendous achievements have been made in strengthening the economic links between town and country. In the three years 1958–60, there were big increases compared with the entire First Five-Year Plan (1953–57) in the amounts of both state investments in agriculture and the means of production supplied to agriculture by the state trading organizations. Compared with 1957 the farms by the end of 1960 had far more tractors, irrigation and drainage machines, chemical fertilizers and insecticides, etc. Agriculture was hard hit by natural disasters during those three years. China's peasants, under the leadership of the Communist Party, nevertheless gave tremendous support to the cities and industry, meeting the essential needs of the nation's production and construction and of the urban population.

To exchange industrial goods for farm produce according to the principle of exchange of equal values is an important aspect of the correct handling of the economic intercourse between town and country; and it is in the vital interests of the socialist relationship of mutual assistance and co-operation between town and country. Socialist trade is the bridge for commodity exchange between town and country. It is necessary to set correct price ratios between industrial and agricultural products so that the selling prices of industrial goods and the purchasing prices of farm products can be fixed at proper levels. If the purchasing prices of farm products were set too low and the selling prices of industrial goods too high, the peasants' incomes would be adversely affected and this would naturally affect their enthusiasm in work. This would be detrimental to the growth of agricultural production. If, on the other hand, the purchasing prices of farm products were set too high and the selling prices of industrial goods too low, the state accumulation of capital and the livelihood of the urban population would be adversely affected. This would be detrimental to the growth of industrial production. In either case, harm would have been done to the worker-peasant alliance and to the cause of socialist construction. Only by correctly implementing the price policy of the Communist Party and the state can we facilitate commodity exchange and the interflow of goods between town and country.

Reasonable distribution of industrial and agricultural products is another important element in correctly handling the economic link between town and country. The principle governing this work is that proper attention must be paid to both town and country. This work is done chiefly through the trading departments. When drawing up plans for the distribution of industrial and farm products, these departments should take the needs of both town and country into account so as to bring into full play the enthusiasm which both the workers and peasants have in their work and their initiative in increasing production. In distributing industrial goods, it is necessary in the first place, in order to stimulate the peasants' enthusiasm for production, to invoke the spirit of the town aiding the countryside and follow the principle of priority for the countryside in the case of all the essential industrial consumer goods needed by the peasants. The towns are the political, economic and cultural centres of the nation. To do the work of commodity distribution in the towns well, to ensure that the essential needs of the workers and residents in the towns and the industrial and mining areas are met is also an important guarantee for the smooth progress of socialist construction.

In distributing farm products, it is necessary to observe the principle of paying proper attention to the interests of all three parties—the state, the collective and the individual, to adhere strictly to the policy of the Communist Party and the state concerning the purchase of farm products, to consult the peasants and reasonably determine the proportion of products to be purchased by the state and the proportion to be retained by the peasants, and to stabilize these proportions around certain levels over a certain period of time.

Worker-Peasant Alliance

The relations between town and country in China in the period of socialist construction are manifested politically as the alliance between the working class and the peasantry. The worker-peasant alliance in China has been steadily consolidated and developed during the democratic and socialist revolutions under the leadership of the working class. It has gone through two stages since the founding of the People's Republic and is currently in its third stage of development. During the first stage, the worker-peasant alliance rested on the basis of carrying the land reform to a thorough completion. During the second stage it was built on the basis of socialist farm collectivization. The task of the current—third—stage is to build the alliance on the new economic basis of gradually implementing technical reform in agriculture while further consolidating and developing the collective economy of the people's communes.

Constant consolidation and development of the worker-peasant alliance during the period of socialist construction is the basic guarantee for carrying the cause of socialist construction to victory. Comrade Liu Shao-chi said that "of our over 600 million people, more than 500 million are peasants who constitute a most powerful force both in the revolutionary struggle and construction. Only by relying on this powerful ally and giving full play to the peasants' initiative and creativeness can the working class of our country achieve victory."[3]

Strengthening the Economic Basis of Worker-Peasant Alliance

In order to consolidate and develop the worker-peasant alliance in the period of socialist construction, it is necessary to strengthen the economic basis of this alliance. The worker-peasant alliance is built on the basis of the common interests of the two classes—workers and peasants. It is a class alliance of mutual benefit and mutual assistance of the workers and peasants based on socialist principles. Safeguarding the common interests of the workers and peasants and strengthening the economic basis of the worker-peasant alliance are therefore important conditions for consolidating and developing the worker-peasant alliance in the period of socialist construction. Under the centralized and unified leadership of the Communist Party and the state and guided by the general policy of developing the national economy with agriculture as the foundation and industry the leading factor, we are constantly strengthening the economic links between town and country in a planned way, and properly organizing mutual support between town and country and between industry and agriculture, so that heavy industry is supplying more and more means of production and technical equipment for farm production and the technical reform of agriculture; light industry is providing the peasant masses in the countryside with increasing quantities of consumer goods; while agriculture, in its turn, is supplying the cities and industry with ever greater amounts of marketable grain, industrial raw materials and other farm and side-line products. Only in this way is it possible to consolidate and develop the worker-peasant alliance further on a new economic basis.

Strengthening Working-Class Leadership

In order to consolidate and develop the worker-peasant alliance further, it is also necessary to strengthen the leadership of the working class over the peasantry and give the peasants political and ideological education. Under the leadership of the Communist Party, the over 500 million Chinese peasants overthrew the rule of the feudal landlord class; they have victoriously taken to the broad path of socialism, collectivized the farms and transformed themselves from individual peasants into socialist collective farmers. The mass of peasants actively support farm collectivization because it creates immense possibilities for increasing agricultural production and for the peasant masses to achieve a common prosperity. It is the only road by means of which the peasant masses can liberate themselves and rid themselves of poverty. But, influenced by the system of private ownership which held sway for centuries, it is not possible for the peasants to rid themselves in a short while of the force of habit as petty producers and of their sense of private ownership. The peasant has a dual character. As a toiler, he can take the socialist road; as a private owner, he has a spontaneous capitalistic tendency. It is quite possible for the overwhelming majority of the peasants to advance resolutely along the socialist road under the leadership of the Communist Party. As for the well-to-do middle peasants, however, their force of habit as petty producers is stronger and they have a more deep-seated sense of private ownership, so their spontaneous capitalistic tendency which runs counter to the socialist collective economy will inevitably find expression in one way or another. When an opportunity presents itself, they will try to depart from the socialist road and take the capitalist road.

The class struggle between the proletariat and the bourgeoisie and the struggle between the socialist and capitalist roads will last throughout the entire historical period of the proletarian revolution and the dictatorship of the proletariat, throughout the entire historical period of the transition from capitalism to communism. The education of the peasantry is therefore an important task. Comrade Mao Tse-tung said: "Opposition to selfish, capitalistic spontaneous tendencies, and promotion of the essence of socialism—that is, making the principle of linking the collective interests with the interests of the individual the standard by which all words and deeds are judged—these then are the ideological and political guarantees that the scattered, small-peasant economy will gradually be transformed into a large-scale co-operative economy."[4] Provided we constantly strengthen the political and ideological leadership of the working class over the peasantry, we shall certainly be able to heighten the socialist consciousness of the peasant masses and enhance their enthusiasm for collective production, turn them into truly socialist toilers, consolidate and develop the worker-peasant alliance further, and promote the rapid progress of our socialist construction.

Notes

1. F. Engels, *Anti-Dühring*, Eng. ed., Foreign Languages Publishing House, Moscow, 1954, p. 411.
2. Mao Tse-tung, *On Contradiction*.
3. *Second Session of the Eighth National Congress of the Communist Party of China*, Eng. ed., Foreign Languages Press, Peking, 1958, pp. 46–47.
4. Editor's note to "A Serious Lesson," *Socialist Upsurge in China's Countryside*, Eng. ed., Foreign Languages Press, Peking, 1957, pp. 302–303.

25. THE AGRICULTURAL DILEMMA

Owen L. Dawson

At the same time that China aspires to the role of a model for economic development the nation is fixed on the horns of an age-old agricultural dilemma: how to increase the yield from a limited amount of arable land in order

SOURCE: Reprinted from Owen L. Dawson, "China's Two-Pronged Agricultural Dilemma," in *Current Scene*, III, 20 (June 1, 1965), pp. 2–12.

to feed a steadily growing population. In addition, industry now competes with the people in demands on agriculture.

While the complexities of this Chinese puzzle are well known to observers, the way to any possible solution is cloudy. The level and pace required for increasing food grain production have not been calculated in sufficient detail. Even less well known is China's potential to the two basic determinants for an increased yield—water and fertilizer.

When these two elements are deficient, improved technology can only conserve; it can add little towards increasing crop production. Moreover, even with the utmost conservation and the returning of all available organic fertilizer to the soil there is a slow drain on crop nutrients, making supplements of chemical fertilizer necessary for an increased food grain harvest.

Peking is only too aware of the importance of these two factors in its uphill fight to make the ancient land support the modern China. Water conservancy and chemical fertilizer production receive high priority in economic planning, as evidenced by the facts that the bulk of state capital investment in 1965 will be in water conservancy and that chemical fertilizer production in 1964 was reported 20 per cent higher than in 1963.

Before analyzing China's potential ability to use chemical fertilizer and water to break out of her spiralling struggle, it will be worth while to briefly review the background of agriculture in China.

Early Methods

While China's vast cultivated area is comparable to the United States excluding Alaska and Hawaii, the population is about four times larger. Centuries of mounting population pressure on the land forced exploitation of land resources to extreme limits through use of ingenious agricultural methods. Farming crept into remote valleys and up steep hills and mountains through terracing. Water was led through networks of canals and ditches and carried long distances by people. Mulches were painstakingly devised to conserve all possible moisture. Human and animal excreta, pond mud and every source of plant food available was utilized to a degree that still amazes the Westerner. As some 40 centuries passed, a truly remarkable biological balance was struck.

Losses in agriculture, however, were great and the country's production potential suffered from lack of improved seed, ravages of insect pests and plant diseases, uneconomic crop patterns, crude implements, poor storage facilities, excessive drain on plant residues for fuel and various other handicaps.

It was only in the 1920's and 1930's that governmental agencies and educational institutions, such as the National Agricultural Research Bureau (NARB) and Nanking University began serious agricultural research and study. In those few years great strides were made, but time was too short to effect any massive improvement before the outbreak of war with Japan in 1937 and the later civil war in China. The Nationalist Government won improvements in certain lines of production but fell short in co-ordinating planning for definite production goals and economic objectives.

In 1944, as the war with Japan neared an end, the United States was invited to send a group of top specialists to work with Chinese specialists in drawing up an agricultural programme. This joint Chinese-American Agricultural Mission spent several weeks studying conditions in all parts of China and produced a combined report detailing the chief problems, recommending a forthright agricultural programme and giving a precise outline of the organization needed to carry it out.[1] Setting up the proposed Joint Commission on Rural Reconstruction was delayed to 1948 and little time was left for action before the Communists came to power in 1949.

A five-year programme on food crop promotion, cotton production and industrial development was operating when the Communists took control. Many of the specialists and staff of the established agricultural organizations, such as those from the NARB, the Food Promotion Commission and the National Cotton Improvement Bureau, remained in China under the new regime. Several of these specialists are still there, probably working on similar programmes, but it is unknown whether their advice has been influential or has been disregarded for reasons of political expedience.

Food Grain Statistics

According to John Lossing Buck's calculations in adjusting the NARB's figures to account for unrecorded land, annual food grain production in China from 1931–1937 averaged 168.4 million metric tons (MMT).[2] During the same period, according to my own rough estimate, China's population stood 530 million, a figure lower than Buck's calculation. Checked with consumption surveys, food per capita availability was about 2,400 calories, which seems high but in general agrees with Buck's field survey on land utilization in China.[3] Even if the average figures was above requirements, distribution was very uneven and some areas often suffered from poor crops while food was over-consumed in good crop areas.

The Communists' figures for food grain production in the early years of their regime were much too low and have been readjusted by various researchers. My own suggested series assumes that in 1952 food grain production reached the 1931–1937 level of about 170 MMT, and that the Communists' 1957 figure of 185 MMT was fairly acceptable.[4] The 1958 figure was based on a great statistical error of method or was purposely misconstrued. Figures for that year and after are subject to a wide range of estimates by various writers. This paper estimates 177 MMT average for 1952–1957, 180 MMT in 1963 and 190 to 200 MMT in 1964. These figures are only suggestive and are subject to revision through checks on minimum consumption. Estimates place 1962 production about on a level with 1957. Furthermore, figures for the 1952–1962 period indicate the population increased 23.7 per cent over 1952, while production rose only 12.2 per cent. Food shortages were partially made up by imports but per capita caloric availability apparently was still some 10 per cent below minimum adequate levels.

This apparent deficiency in food grain supply per capita seems too large in view of travellers' observations since 1962 and the fact that no widespread nutritional deficiency has been reported as in 1960. The crop estimates may still be low or the population figures too high.

Attempts to Improve

During the early period of the communist regime some moderate improvements in agricultural production were effected through the agricultural producers' co-operatives. These improvements included more draft animals and better tools, seeds and insecticides. Significant progress was made in water conservancy and farm irrigation works. Certain plans initiated by the Nationalist Government for improving and saving production were carried forward by the Communists. As a result, and due to the generally low level of technology at which the work began, a measure of progress was soon evident. Improvements in early stages were not difficult under more peaceable conditions in rural districts. But as ideology turned its hand to the plough results from technological improvements began to be offset by over-collectivization and poor direction of agriculture, mistakes which culminated in the disastrous Great Leap Forward of 1958.

With the good weather conditions in 1958 China was set for a bumper crop of possibly 220 MMT, but much of it was lost or wasted through mismanagement in the communes. Poor crop years followed from 1959 to 1961.

Peking's leaders came to the late realization that agriculture must receive more support to revive production. But even with increased aid, more perquisites and incentives, such as the use of small individual plots, the basic problem of getting more out of a set amount of cultivated land depends on conservation of water and adequate chemical fertilizer.

Arable Land

Pre-war estimates of the arable area of China were very rough and depended much upon the definition of the term. Certain land could have been brought into cultivation, but would not have paid on the investment unless subsidized substantially by the Government. The individual Chinese farmer was pressing hard on all available land prior to 1949, but appreciable expansion was possible by more irrigation and by extensive farming initially subsidized by the State. There were also areas to be reclaimed along the coast by drainage and renovation of alkali soil and eroded land. Some areas in the hinterland could be cultivated with expansion of communications.

Several geographers and geologists have described the limitations of the arable land in China due to elevation, topography, climate and lack of fertility. One noted expert has pointed out that from the viewpoint of soil conservation, some marginal land cultivated under pressure of overcrowding "may not be considered arable at all. On the other hand, some land which is not considered arable may become good farming land through engineering endeavours."[5] He roughly estimates that 15 per cent of China's land is arable, which would mean about 146 million hectares (based on some 9,736,288 sq. kilometres for 35 provinces excluding Tibet). This compares with about 109 million hectares now under cultivation, leaving about 36 million hectares still available for new cultivation. Wong Wen-hao and Su Chia-yang present a much brighter picture and a higher per cent of arable land.[6] Until a complete agricultural survey is taken and criteria of arability are set up, all estimates will remain rough. How much of the potentially arable land can be opened to cultivation depends in large part on how much investment and emphasis the government gives to this area.

Soviet soil scientists V. A. Kovda has estimated that 30 million hectares of virgin and long fallow lands could be brought into cultivation within 12 to 15 years, but he does not mention poor land which should be removed from cultivation. With due allowance for such uneconomic land which should be taken out of cultivation, it might be possible to increase crop hectares by 10 million in the next 10 years with vast effort and expense in reclaiming saline and waterlogged land and expanding irrigation. At present average yields this reclaimed land could result in a production gain of some 15 MMT of food grain.

To Increase Yields

A large proportion of the cultivated land of China has been cropped for centuries but yields have held up at surprising levels. Soil bank fertility has been annually replenished by many items of organic fertilizer, including animal manure, night soil, pond mud and green manure. Only very small amounts of chemical fertilizer were used in the pre-war years. Some increased yields resulted from improved varieties and better cultural methods but it was generally recognized that large amounts of chemical fertilizer were necessary to sustain such increases.

Communist Chinese plans for increased agricultural production acknowledge the need for a huge expansion in chemical fertilizer production. Minister of Agriculture Liao Lu-yen in 1956 said that the 12-year agriculture plan (1956–67) would require at least 20 MMT of nitrogenous fertilizer—equivalent to about 30 MMT of gross chemical fertilizer—a rough and rather high estimate.

No systematic study had been made of the actual amount of chemical fertilizer needed to increase China's crops. Production of nitrogenous fertilizer in 1956 was only about 0.663 MMT augmented by 0.837 MMT imported. Chemical fertilizer production in 1962 was estimated at 2.12 MMT. In using Peking's chemical fertilizer statistics, however, it should be remembered that recent figures apparently include all types of fertilizers, some of which have low nutrient value, and are not really comparable to earlier statistics which counted only nitrogenous fertilizer.

Since it is evident that large increases in chemical fertilizer are needed to meet the future needs of crop production and that the availability of such supplies is a key factor in agricultural development and thus in the economy as a whole, a detailed analysis of requirements is prerequisite to appraising China's future economic position. Most general estimates are too high and not supportable by statistical analyses.

The important role of organic fertilizer has always been recognized and generally taken for granted, but the definite relation to necessary supplements of chemical fertilizer has not been calculated. Available amounts of plant food nutrients from these organic items must be considered in order to estimate the need for supplemental chemical fertilizer to attain the required increase in yields. Lengthy research into the sources of organic fertilizer in China produced the following table of estimates.

Sources of Gross Organic Fertilizer in China in 1956

	Metric Tons	Per Cent
Animal Manure	815,367	62
Night Soil	156,000	12
Compost	116,000	8.8
Green Manure	30,000	2.3
River and Pond Mud	180,000	13.7
Oil Seed Cakes	6,000	0.4
All Others—ashes, stalks, bones, chimney sweeps, etc.	11,600	0.8
Total	1,314,967	100.0

Needs by 1972

A study was made to determine how much chemical fertilizer is needed to reach a minimum level of 300 kilograms of food grains per capita in the next ten years. That would be equivalent to a daily caloric availability of 1,853 or 2,180 for all food, or slightly above the rate of 2,054 calories in a well balanced diet set by the Chinese Medical Association in 1939.[8] (A safety factor of some 6 per cent was included to offset difficulties of distribution.) This compares with the average caloric availability in 1955–56, but is still 5 per cent short of that officially reported for Japan and Taiwan in 1958.

A normal trend with average weather would suggest 190 MMT of food grain production in 1962, but the actual figure is generally placed at 180 MMT to account for poor weather conditions. In estimating food requirements to 1972–73, however, average weather is assumed for the close of the period and therefore must be assumed for the base period of 1962–63.

At a 2 per cent annual increase from 1962 (assuming 701 million people), population at the close of 1972 would be 882 million.[9] This would indicate an increased requirement of some 74 MMT of food grain over 1962. If 15 MMT could come from increased area, then 59 MMMT would have to come from increased yield. In Japan and Taiwan 40 to 50 per cent of the fertilizer offtake in grain crops is estimated to come from organic fertilizer. Similarly, with an active programme of chemical fertilizer production in China, it is assumed that the source of crop nutrients for increased yields may be supplied in about equal proportions of organic and chemical fertilizer by 1972. This seems to check with increased available supplies of organic fertilizer.

There is also a relationship between increased yield and improved agricultural techniques—including improved varieties, crop rotation, methods of cultivation, harvesting, storing, weed and pest control, water conservation, etc. Estimates show the various factors account for increased yield in the following proportions: organic fertilizer, 40 per cent; chemical fertilizer, 40 per cent; and improved techniques, 20 per cent.

From the 59 MMT of increased yield China will need by the end of 1972, about 24 MMT must come from each chemical and organic fertilizers and 11 MMT from improved techniques. This indicates a requirement of roughly 12 MMT of gross chemical fertilizer in a ratio of about three parts of nitrogen, one part phosphoric acid and one part potash. For other crops such as cotton, fruits and vegetables, some 3 MMT additional gross chemical fertilizer would be needed. In sum, China will need 15 MMT of chemical fertilizer in 1972.

Production Rate

Most recent reports indicate chemical fertilizer production for 1963 was only about 2.8 MMT, compared with 2.1 in 1962. At this rate, the increase in eight years would equal only 5.6 MMT. Eight years are allowed in calculating plant capacity by 1972 as it takes some two years to build extensive units. If this present rate is doubled, it still would not reach the required capacity of 15 MMT. According to a 1963 Peking statement on developing the chemical industry to aid agriculture, chemical fertilizer production is to reach about 8 to 10 MMT in 10 years, or an increase of about 7 MMT.[10]

If the increased production of fertilizer falls short of the requirement by some 7.5 MMT, as my figures indicated before the 1963 statement, gross available food grain per capita would be 265.3 kilograms, based on a 2 per cent increase in population, and 283.3 kilograms if the increase is only 1 per cent. The resulting daily caloric availability would be 1,927 and 2,058 for all food, or about 10 and 5 per cent below a normal requirement. In poor crop years the food grain production might fall short by as much as 5 to 10 per cent, with a commensurate loss in the diet.

These calculations of deficiencies are conservative. A much greater rate in applying improved techniques is assumed than has occurred under the Communists. Ascribing 20 per cent to this factor implies a general adoption of improved methods requiring much greater government support than has been indicated so far and a revival of production incentives set back by mismanagement of the communes.

Difficulties of Development

Entailed in the vast development of the fertilizer industry are problems of sources of supply and distribution. Experimental tests have shown that nitrogen and phosphorus are widely deficient in China. A tremendous development in hydroelectric power to help supply nitrogen would be needed. This could be worked out at considerable expense but supplying the necessary phosphate would be more difficult, even though reports indicate the Communists have found more extensive and accessible sources than the few reported before 1949. Potassium supplies are more adequate and do not present much of a problem.

In addition to the difficulty of assembling the raw materials for a gigantic fertilizer industry, distribution to millions of farms in the vast area of China would be a formidable feat. Such a movement by water, rail and trucks would demand a large part of the present transportation capacity and would require constructing an improved and extended highway network. Distribution to main storage points, then to smaller depots and finally to the millions of farms involved by carts and other means would require a vast organization and would mean attendant losses. Direction of usage on the farms would pose an additional problem.

Already grain imports impose a heavy drain on scarce foreign exchange, making further food grain importation a costly way to attempt making up the impending food deficit. Chemical fertilizer, while expensive, would be much cheaper to import than grain, but might be difficult to obtain in required amounts.

Recent reports put total chemical fertilizer imports from Japan at about 1 MMT for 1964, possibly reaching 2 MMT for 1965. But if China does not increase the pace of domestic fertilizer production more than 0.70 MMT (as in 1963 over 1962) in the next eight years, fertilizer imports must also increase cumulatively by about 0.70 MMT annually.

The implication of importing such large amounts of food grain or fertilizer alongside developing a partial production capacity of chemical fertilizer is enormous. Efforts to transform China into an industrial power could well be disrupted by lack of capital unless increased exports of other products can offset imports of grain or fertilizer.

The Second Problem: Water Conservation

Another indispensable factor requiring huge financial outlays is an adequate supply and regulated use of water for normal crop growth and for effective employment of chemical fertilizer. The problems of irrigation and drainage and the correlative problem of flood control on the whole are more difficult to solve than the question of sufficient chemical fertilizer.

China of the 1930's was already aware of the need to control and efficiently use available water sources and to adapt crops to seasonable supplies. Technical information was collected to utilize the potentials of water conservancy and plans were initiated to carry out several important projects. These included the organization of six Water Conservancy Bureaus under the Ministry of Water Conservancy. The Hwai River project for drainage and irrigation, the Yangtze Gorge project and general plans for controlling the Yellow River were proposed. Many local improvement projects were also begun with the aid of bank loans to co-operatives, and a general study was made of underground water resources in North China. War interrupted these projects. Although they were resumed in 1946, much first had to be done to repair war damage and restore dykes for flood control.

In the first Five-Year Plan (1953–1957) of the Chinese People's Republic these projects were actively resumed and overall studies of requirements of flood prevention, irrigation, hydroelectric power and navigation were outlined. Large-scale projects demanding enormous amounts of labour were called for. A brief sketch of the overall results reported and the possible potentials follows.

Present Supplies

The Chief Soviet Expert at the National Conference on Water Conservancy and Hydroelectric Power held in Peking in early 1959 described the basic limitation on China's water resources for irrigation. According to the figure he cited, China had an annual supply of 2,680 cubic kilometres of water, of which only some 800 cubic kilometers were needed in 1960.[11] But while the total supply was sufficient to meet the potential demand the distribution was very uneven. Statistics of the Yellow River Water Conservancy Commission showed the southern part of the country (line of demarcation not clear) as having 75 per cent of the country's total resources but only 38 per cent of the cultivated land. The North (excluding the Sungari River area because it is relatively well supplied with moisture) was shown with only 7 per cent of the total water resources but 52 per cent of the cultivated area. The Yellow River, the Hwai River Valley, the Hai Ho and the Liao River Valley were thought to be particularly short of moisture. This great cotton and wheat belt is often affected by water shortages, and future development must depend to an important extent on the limited supplies of underground water.

In reviewing general plans drawn up for most of the larger rivers, the Soviet expert pointed out that man-made projects did not sufficiently consider the effect on water equilibrium taking place over the whole basin. And due to poor management, many projects did not play their role in irrigation and flood prevention.

Such comments from an expert revealed the lack of realism in claimed expansion of effective irrigation in 1958, and the great problems to be faced in the efficient use of available water. After the 1959 conference, problems in expanding irrigation were looked into critically. The widespread drought in 1959 and 1960 caused plans to be reviewed again, but definite reports on any revised plans for the country as a whole are not available.

Data on underground water supplies are meagre and conflicting. M. M. Krylov, a Soviet specialist on underground water in China, said in an extensive monograph on the subject:

It is worth mentioning that according to the figures of the Chinese People's Republic, underground water is used for the irrigation of two million hectares of land and is expected to increase to four million by 1967. That would require a colossal volume of water with a discharge half again as much as the annual discharge of the Yellow River. . . .

The solution of the irrigation problem in China depends to a considerable extent on the artificial control of the subsoil waters by a complex system of ameliorative measures. In particular, much work has yet to be done in channelling off the subsoil water in certain areas of China by the construction of a water-catchment and drainage network, afforestation along the irrigation canals, etc., within the complex framework of agrotechnical and hydrotechnical ameliorative operations.[12]

It is apparent that an extensively expanded use of underground water for irrigation entails large-scale planning, including more attention to quantity and quality of water, and not merely installation of pumps. Practical estimates of potential sources of underground water through scientific mapping are meagre.

According to semi-official reports, the area irrigated by wells in the provinces of Honan, Shantung and Hopei increased by five million hectares betweeen 1949 and 1956. But it was admitted that in Hopei as more wells were dug less and less water was obtainable and that only 40 per cent of all the wells were providing an adequate amount of water for the area intended.

The figures quoted by Krylov are much smaller than those quoted above and exemplify the problems of reconciling official and semi-official announcements.

Total Irrigated Area

Various and conflicting estimates also have been given on the per cent and total amount of cultivated land irrigated in China. The actual figures on land irrigated, however, are not so important as the potential which will affect increased production. But as a bench-mark it is worth while to briefly summarize the estimates on irrigated area.

Official Chinese figures claim the "area under irrigation" in 1949 was only 16 million hectares, a figure which seems to have been placed low to make progress look rapid in successive years. In 1952, when food grain production had about regained the 1931–37 level, the figure given for irrigated land was a low 21.3 million.[13] Calculations based on irrigated crops indicate there was under-reporting until 1956. From 1949–1955 the area reported under irrigation was lower than the adjusted pre-war figure of 25 million hectares shown by the *Statistical Monthly* in 1932 and much lower, even up to 1958, than the 40 million hectares indicated by the pre-war land utilization survey.[14]

The best check on officially reported "area under irrigation" is a calculation of irrigated crop areas, which includes the paddy rice area and dry land crops irrigated.

According to Krylov, a recognized authority on irrigation in China, 84 per cent of irrigation water was used on rice.[15] Thus, with a calculated figure on paddy rice we can estimate the total area under irrigation. The communist claim of 32.3 million crop hectares in rice reduced by 3.4 million hectares for double cropping and by 1.9 million hectares of non-irrigated rice gives 27 million hectares of rice irrigated. If other crops use only 50 per cent as much water as rice, the total area irrigated would be 37.3 million hectares. The most competent technical source of information places the 1957 total at 38.3 million hectares which is close to the above calculation.[16] According to other calculations, the figure for 1957 may be somewhat less.

The official figure for 1958 of 66.7 million hectares is completely untenable. From the above estimates it appears that no more than 36 to 40 million hectares are effectively irrigated. The potential increase in food grain production which could be achieved by expanded irrigation thus is difficult to estimate.

In an ordinary year some 6.6 million hectares scattered over the country are subject to flood or waterlogging, according to Peking's expert Ho Chi-feng.[17] This can only be remedied by an extensive system of river control and drainage. Apparently, in the urge to expand irrigation, sufficient attention was not paid to the necessary corollary of adequate drainage.

Expanding Irrigation

Official statements on the potential expansion of irrigated areas are considered broad estimates with details still to be planned. A general summary of estimated increases that might be attained in irrigable area includes:

	(1,000 hectares)
Hwai River Project	8,400[18]
Yellow River	6,600[19]
Hai Ho	2,000[20]
Other irrigation works in North, Northwest and Central China	1,000
	18,000

If two million hectares are added for expanded use of underground water, the impressive result is a potential of 20 million hectares. But much of the underground potential increase would be needed to supplement shortages in river supply. If these estimates could be achieved, the total irrigated area would then be 58 to 61 million hectares, or about 53 per cent of the cultivated area.

This catalogue of projects implies full use of available water in North China. It would take a long time in developing, and detailed schedules are indefinite. Beyond this, to bring further needed water to North China means diverting surplus water from the Yangtze to the Yellow River Basin. This would be a major undertaking in the history of irrigation. The engineering problems are gigantic and it would probably take a few decades before results would be evident. Nevertheless, the potentiality is there according to a pre-war specialist, and over 12 million hectares of the flood plain of North China might benefit by supplementary irrigation.[21]

Outlook

In calculating the chemical fertilizer needed to meet future food grain production demands, allowance was made for reclamation through expanded irrigation and for technological contributions, including more efficient use of water.

Wider use of chemical fertilizer is still economically possible on crops under present conditions for some 50 million hectares but further use depends on having adequate water. Annual progress to date in developing chemical fertilizer production to meet minimum requirements is far below the required schedule and the vast problem of distribution has not been worked out.

Irrigation plans likewise are not progressing to cope with the country's needs. Expanded irrigation affecting some 20 million hectares is possible in the near decades but it entails continued outlay of capital and engineering plans gigantic in scope.

Apparently Peking must look outward for help. Until China can develop adequate sources of chemical fertilizer and regulated water supplies the outlook is gloomy for meeting the required expansion of food grain production. The alternative is large imports of grain and chemical fertilizer. But here China's predicament impinges on another puzzle: how to increase exports, most of which are agricultural products, in order to earn the foreign exchange needed to buy more food and fertilizer.

Notes

1. *Report of the China-United States Agricultural Mission,* Office of Foreign Agricultural Relations, U.S.D.A., May, 1947.

2. John Lossing Buck, "Food Grain Production in Mainland China," in *Food and Agriculture in Red China,* by J. L. Buck, Owen L. Dawson, Yuan-li Wu, to be published this year by the Hoover Institution on War, Revolution, and Peace, Stanford University, 1965. Also see J. L. Buck, "Reliability of Communist China's Data on Food Grain Production," *Current Scene,* Vol. III, No. 14, Hong Kong, March 1, 1965.

3. *Ibid.* Also see John Lossing Buck, *Land Utilization in China,* University of Nanking, 1937.

4. For a different estimate see "Decision For An 'Upsurge,' " *Current Scene,* Vol. III, No. 17, April 15, 1965.

5. T. H. Shen, *Agricultural Resources of China,* Cornell University, New York, 1951.

6. *Ibid.*

7. V. A. Kovda, *Soils and the Natural Environment of China,* Academy of Science, USSR, Moscow, 1959.

8. *Food and Agriculture in Red China, op. cit.* Particularly see the author's study on "Chemical Fertilizer Requirements in Mainland China."

9. U.S. Census Bureau estimates furnished the author.

10. Hsiao Kuei-ch'ang, "Energetically develop the chemical industry in aid of technical transformation of agriculture," *Worker's Daily,* Peking, January 10, 1963.

11. *Water Conservancy Engineering News,* Peking, February 14, 1959.

12. M. M. Krylov, *Brief Review of the Underground Water of Communist China,* Academy of Science of the U.S.S.R., Tashkent, 1958, translated by U.S. Publications Research, Washington, D.C.

13. *Current Scene,* Vol. III, No. 14, *op. cit.,* note 1.

14. *Statistical Monthly,* National Government of China, Nanking, 1932.

15. Krylov, *op. cit.*

16. *Hydro-electricity,* No. 7, Peking, April 11, 1957.

17. Ho Chi-feng at 1957 Conference on Water Conservancy and Electric Power, in *China Water Conservancy,* Peking, September 14, 1957.

18. Outline of the Hwai River Basin Project, in *China Water Conservancy,* April 14, 1959.

19. Teng Tzu-hui, "Multiple-purpose plan for the permanent control of the Yellow River and the exploitation of its water resources," report made at the 2nd session of the First National People's Congress, Peking, July 18, 1955.

20. "Report on the Hai Ho Conservancy," *Geographical Knowledge,* Peking, June, 1958.

21. Shun-ta Hsu, a water conservancy specialist for the National government in mainland China.

Problems of Control:
Economic Motivations

26. INDUSTRIAL WORK INCENTIVES

CHARLES HOFFMAN

Work incentives play an important role in the Chinese Communist Party's economic development strategy, and as general strategy has changed over the years, so have work incentive policies.[1] From 1953 to 1957, primary emphasis was on various material incentives, such as piece-wage rates. During the Great Leap Forward, 1958 to 1960, stress was mainly on non-material incentives, such as honorary prizes. More recently, as agricultural reverses have led the Party to give higher priority to encouragement of the peasants, there has been a switch back to material incentives. This paper deals with the role of labor input in economic development; the ideological and economic bases of incentives; the types of material and nonmaterial systems used; and changing policies during the three periods.

The crying need for underdeveloped countries such as China to transform their abundant labor supply into the capital sinews of industrialization is already well-known. The Nurksean model sees widespread disguised unemployment in agriculture as the main source of capital formation through the re-allocation of labor producing little or nothing to capital construction, the fruits of which would represent net gains to output.[2]

In China, these possibilities are suggested by the uneven and incomplete participation of the labor force in agriculture. Studies undertaken in the 1920s and 1930s reveal that only 35 per cent of all able-bodied men were involved in full-time work with 58 per cent only working part-time. Female labor participation was only 20 per cent of the total able-bodied female population.[3]

The solution to the problem of increasing labor input and re-allocating

SOURCE: Reprinted from Charles Hoffman, "Work Incentives in Communist China's Economic Development Strategy," in *Industrial Relations,* 3 (February 1964), pp. 81–97. Reprinted by permission of *Industrial Relations.*

it to more productive uses hinges, thus, on the effectiveness with which labor can be motivated to put out more effort and to move into alternative activities. Unlike the situation in developed economies, where increased output (capital and otherwise) can be generated by raising labor productivity through mechanization, in an underdeveloped economy such as China, rising output depends mainly on increasing substantially the amount of net brute labor input, male and female.

The work-incentive patterns of Mainland China must be viewed in this context especially when assessing the policies pursued during the Great Leap Forward. For the great potential implicit in the widespread disguised unemployment in the Chinese countryside was the basis upon which that largely unfulfilled design was conceived.

Economic and Ideological Bases of Incentives

While Chinese Communist leaders have made the Leninist claim that labor productivity will rise sharply under socialism, they are fully aware that rapid industrialization places strict limits on consumption.[4] Insisting that "an increase in productivity of labor is of prime importance to the victory of the socialist system" and the continuation of rapid economic development, they have acknowledged that to elevate labor "enthusiasm of the broad masses of workers," it is necessary "first and foremost . . . that wages [be] gradually increased," that "the principle of 'to each according to his work' " be carried out, and that "the wage system of incentive payments" be improved.[5]

Projecting rapid development along classic Soviet lines, Chinese leadership early committed the economy to a very high level of capital investment—22 per cent of national output so that material work incentives had to operate within quite narrow limits. While some room was left for a rise in the level of living, any actual increase in consumption was bound to be modest.[6] Demanding a continuing sharp rise in labor input and productivity, the regime promised only a small portion of the fruits to the workers. They dubbed this policy a "rational low wage system."[7]

For Chinese leaders the goal of communist man is both an ideal to be attained for the multitude in the distant future and a norm of behavior for cadres and elite workers and peasants. The ultimate operation of the communist principle, "from each according to his ability, to each according to his need," as the sole motivating principle, is to await the advance of society to conditions making such a principle workable. In the meantime, while the socialist principle of payment according to work mainly governs work incentives, the rudimentary elements of the communist precept are introduced and fostered.[8]

Nature of Incentive Techniques in Industry and Agriculture

Whatever the basis of incentive techniques—material or nonmaterial—party cadres have always administered the mechanisms with heavy doses of ideological indoctrination. Not only is ideology an integral part of the incentive instrument, but often nonmaterial and material incentives are conjoined.

Material incentives in industry cover a wide range. They range from social insurance payments and similar fringe benefits, special monetary awards, improved working conditions, and payments in kind to the much more important wage systems.

Social insurance for industrial workers, first set up in 1951, covers several risks. Eligible workers are entitled to benefits for injuries and illness, maternity and death. Members of workers' families are also entitled to illness and death payments. A pension system, paying up to 70 per cent of a worker's wages at age 60 for men and 50 for women, includes both workers and their families. They also enjoy the use of communal labor insurance establishments, such as sanatoria, rest homes, homes for the aged, orphanages, homes for the disabled, etc. Extra benefits go to model workers.[9]

Special monetary awards were devised early in the first Five Year Plan to stimulate industrial workers to invent, innovate, and make cost-saving proposals. Cash payments are made both to those who conceive and those who assist in the technological contribution for three to five years for inventions and for one year for technical improvements and cost-saving suggestions.[10]

At the heart of material incentives are the various wage systems which are aimed not only at stimulating greater output but also at motivating workers to develop their skills and move on to more advanced jobs. The evolution in wage payments was from the wage-point system to various multiple wage-grade techniques, the most advanced of which included piece-rate arrangements.

Up to early 1956 the wage-point system was widely used. The wage scale was usually an eight-grade system, ascending on the basis of skill from grade 1 through grade 8 and each grade receiving fixed wage points. The points were the same throughout the country, but their monetary equivalent varied according to the prices of five staple commodities (grain, oil, salt, cotton, and coal) in local areas.[11]

Although this system distributed pay differentials according to skill and performance, the complications of computation probably obscured the relationship between achievement and reward. Thus, the wage-point system was replaced by a scheme of direct wage payments with built-in emphasis on work quota overfulfillment. Broadly, the policy called for 80 per cent of wages to be considered base pay, with the remaining 20 per cent used to spur overfulfillments through piecework or bonus pay. Standard wage scales are set up on a multiple-grade base (usually eight grades but varying) and can be used for time-rate as well as piece-rate payments. The highest payment grade is supposed to be roughly three times that of the lowest grade.[12]

Piecework wages are similarly based on multiple grades. Fulfillment of the grade quota entitles the worker to the standard wage; overfulfillment means payments above the standard, varying according to the degree of overfulfillment and the particular system. Failure to meet quotas calls for wage payments below the standard wage.

Bonuses for specific achievements, such as outstanding production performance, economy in use of materials, high safety levels, and superior product quality, have been employed to awaken worker enthusiasm where piece-rate systems are not in operation. Payment of bonuses usually hinges on output quota fulfillment. Where cost reduction is the goal, 20 to 30 per cent of the cost economized is made available for distribution as bonuses. Individual bonuses are restricted to a maximum of 15 per cent of the standard monthly wage.[13]

While material incentives were being developed in industry, a parallel, if slower, evolution occurred in agriculture. Material incentives were an important feature in cooperatives, though they naturally were shaped by the fact that private ownership and nonlabor income existed until the advent of communes. Thus, the principle of reward according to labor could only be partially applied. In the phased transition from individual peasant ownership to the advanced cooperatives (collectives), material rewards were used both to soften the elimination of the most capitalistic forms and to stimulate production in the new collective units. With the advent of people's communes the problem of motivation was, of course, hotly debated and material incentives were at first downgraded; nevertheless, over time material rewards were developed to spur peasant output.

The pattern of material incentives in agriculture evolved from the more crude type of work-points payments, analogous to wage points in industry, all the way to labor quotas and piecework. Naturally, given the very great number of agricultural units in China, any generalization about techniques used are fraught with peril. Still, the direction of incentive development and the shape of the different techniques employed are clear.

The work-points payments system has had many variants and misapplications, but basically peasants were to receive points according to the quantity and quality of output, with the value of the points set in terms of a staple, such as rice. The awarding of work points was usually made every day on the basis of the total points allotted for each division of the day. The daily evaluation rested on such variables as time put in, quantity and quality of output, basic skill used, attitude toward labor, etc.[14]

Over time the work-points method was transformed into a workday system, with points still being used but presumably in a more systematic fashion. A standard workday or production quota (based on quantity and quality) was set up for various jobs according to skill. Where workers fulfilled the norms for their jobs, the differences in the work points received varied according to the different grades of skill employed.[15]

This graded workday system lent itself readily to piecework payments. Norms set for particular jobs became the basis for paying more or less for the same type of work depending on the number of units produced. Thus, for advanced agricultural producers' cooperatives a piecework method was prescribed.[16]

With the advent of the rural people's communes, a supply-wages system was introduced. Whatever the division between supply (payment in food and other necessities) and wages—and as time elapsed the ratio of 70 per cent supply to 30 per cent wages was reversed—the wages part was usually distributed through a straight graded workday or piecework technique. Obviously, to the extent that the supply part of income (distributed in egalitarian fashion) was great, the material incentive of the wages part was dulled.[17]

Nonmaterial incentives encompass a wide variety of forms; fundamentally, however, all forms involve either emulation or mass participation or a combination of both, as well as heavy doses of ideological indoctrination. The cultivation of nonmaterial stimuli often involves the individual in some group aim, and rewards are meted out both to individuals and groups.

Emulation drives, in which workers and groups vie with one another, aim, through heightening the competitive spirit, at evoking maximum exertion not only by those involved but also by those who are "spectators" in the same or other industrial enterprises. In the process of emulation, workers and groups are supposed to "learn from the advanced, compete with the advanced, catch up with the advanced and help the backward." For broadest impact, the emulation drive is organized on several levels—production group, shift, department, factory, industry, nation—according to the specific aims in view.[18]

Mass participation in a drive to attain certain production ends is another aspect of nonmaterial incentive. The psychology of such campaigns is to arouse interest and action through a keen sense of group participation resulting in a high level of personal sacrifice. Integrating and exploiting such a situation, party cadres are often able through mass persuasion techniques to mount a successful production drive, rationalization movement, or the like.

Mass participation is used widely to deal with problems as well as to commit workers more completely to the plant or unit. Worker groups were often convened to make technical and production decisions during the Great Leap Forward period on increased productivity, reduced absenteeism, innovation, improved quality, etc. Paralleling emulation drives, and often intertwined with them, mass movements have been widely used on large-scale projects in the public eye as well as in narrower situations.[19]

Although emulation and mass participation techniques have some intrinsic motivating power, nonmaterial rewards based on successful individual performance have also been developed. Individuals and groups not only receive titles and honors in emulation contests, but also in their day-to-day activities. Thus titles of "labor hero," "model worker," "outstanding worker" are conferred. Similar honors are bestowed upon groups or teams of workers with widespread publicity, so that they become national heroes. Representatives from among them are sent periodically to conferences of outstanding individuals and groups in Peking; they meet in a festive atmosphere, with nation-wide attention focused on them, and possibly attend a short session with Chairman Mao.

Other advantages which such honored workers enjoy are not as directly linked to performance. Recruitment of new Communist Party members Party and non-Party cadres, and trade union cadres from among model and outstanding workers is a common practice. Advanced workers are sometimes rewarded by being sent to professional and higher technical schools. Some of these elite workers are promoted to jobs ranging as high as plant director.[20]

Work Incentive Policy, 1953–1957

As was suggested earlier, material and nonmaterial incentive schemes have been used with different stresses: in each of three distinct periods emphasis on one or the other has varied. In the first period—roughly that of the first Five Year Plan—material work incentives received primary emphasis. The Party aim of paying according to work done required the use of more refined methods of payment consistent with differences in skill. Piece-rate mechanisms were encouraged to stimulate performance. And yet, while material rewards were employed as the main method, nonmaterial incentives were also cultivated, albeit with less emphasis.

Throughout this period, Party leaders and cadres referred to the many factors limiting worker productivity in industry. The most prominent barriers were: (1) insufficient encouragement to innovate and invent; (2) payments in combinations of money and kind; (3) irrational and egalitarian elements in wage payments; and (4) sharp disparities between increases in labor productivity and increases in wages.

Starting in 1954, regulations were issued on awards for inventions, technical improvements, and labor saving suggestions. In 1955 similar regulations governing scientific groups were put into operation. The focusing of attention on rapid technological advance was a concomitant of the major emphasis placed on heavy industry in the first Five Year Plan and required a more modern incentive system.[21]

The major wage reform of June 1956 superseded the remnants of the wage-point system, where they still existed, by a direct wage system and cost-of-living allowances were abolished. The reform's aim was clearly to connect performance and reward.[22]

Irrational and egalitarian features of the wage system were counted among the main factors deterring industrial workers from maximum exertion. Among the irrational elements were different wage standards for the same type of enterprise, wage differentials unrelated to differences in skill, traditional gratuities and allowances unrelated either to the quantity or quality of performance, bonuses for good attendance, and welfare payments of inconsistent and bizarre nature. Egalitarian features appeared in the form of inconsequential or no wage differentials where work skills and tasks varied markedly.

The wage reform of 1956 attempted to cope with these problems by unifying wage standards and the coefficient of wage grades for each industry, by setting up more consistent differentials by trades and districts, and by eliminating anomalies.[23]

Even successful resolution of the above problems would probably not have boosted morale appreciably, if the general wage level failed to rise in some appreciable degree, especially after repeated party promises. In 1954 and 1955 wages rose very little—2.3 and 0.6 per cent, respectively, while productivity was estimated to have risen 25 per cent. This meager rise in money wages was insufficient for most workers to compensate for price increases. The results did not even approximate the admittedly austere "rational low-wage" policy of the Party, and worker disgruntlement was implied in official comments.[24]

The wage reform of June 1956 put the industrial wage system on a more uniform basis in which wage differentials, bonuses, promotions and other features were coordinated, if imperfectly, toward the end of stimulating both the quantity and quality of output. Wages in general were raised 14.5 per cent above the 1955 levels. In form, the new and modified wage schemes conformed more to the aim of more pay for more work.[25]

The policy of emphasizing material incentives was symbolized in the piece-rate wage system which was seized upon during the first Five Year Plan as a most suitable means of getting workers to overfulfill targets. In both 1956 and 1957, piece-rate systems were developed and extended widely in factories and mines, about 42 per cent of workers being covered by such schemes.[26]

From 1953 to 1957 agricultural incentive policy also emphasized material rewards. However, here the policy was much harder to implement. Furthermore, although incentive problems in agriculture were similar to those in industry, there was a significant additional one—a growing disparity between worker and peasant income.

The introduction of incentive-payment schemes based on output, as agriculture was collectivized step by step, was accompanied by gradual reduction in the amount of compensation paid peasants for use of their land, equipment, and livestock. The suddenly increased pace of collectivization in 1955 and 1956 brought with it rapid elimination of payments to capital. At the same time cadres were under order to put as many peasants as possible on piecework systems.[27]

The introduction of piecework and other incentive systems was impeded by the existence of traditional payment patterns. Egalitarian distribution of grain was directly related to past Party policies, such as the revolutionary supply systems and support of the poorer peasants. In some agricultural producers' cooperatives grain was distributed on grounds unrelated to either work input or output. In many instances cooperatives did not pay for work on capital construction, afforestation, and land reclamation—nor did they make such work part of a voluntary emulative campaign.[28]

Given the very low level of peasant income, the disparity between peasant and worker income was an especially troublesome situation that reached a critical point in 1957. The June 1956 industrial wage reform irritated many peasants who saw a growing gap between their incomes and those of all types of workers, including unskilled workers in rural areas. Party leaders called for readjustments, and new regulations set wages for the least skilled workers on a par with the income of an average peasant doing full-time work in a medium-sized cooperative, with adjustments for the higher cost of living in towns and cities.[29]

Work Incentive Policy, 1957–1960

By the end of 1957, the policy of emphasizing material incentives had run its course and Chinese grand economic strategy veered sharply from the Soviet model to the Great Leap Forward. Material incentives were not abandoned, but for the time being they played a less dominant role; greater reliance was placed on the revolutionary fervor of the masses. It was expected that the success of the Great Leap Forward would raise living levels so high that the movement toward Communism—reflected in the rising prominence of nonmaterial incentives—would be speeded up. Ironically, the failure to increase food production sharply led to nonmaterial incentives being emphasized further, in the beginning, than actual conditions warranted so as to ensure everyone's receiving a bare subsistence.

The swing to non-material incentives did not occur suddenly. In 1956 and

1957, when material incentives were at their peak, there was a marked increase in the number of labor emulation campaigns and more publicity was given to outstanding workers and groups. From late 1957 to the end of 1960, the slogan "politics in command" was operative as the entire economy was harnessed in mass movements and emulations.[30]

In 1958 it became clear that the piece-rate system—symbol par excellence of material incentives—and bonuses were to be restricted drastically, and where continued, their forms and controls were to be modified to take account of both technical imperfections and the tendency to extravagant, undeserved rewards. The constantly raised quotas in many factories during the Great Leap Forward made piece rates mechanisms unworkable. Where the system was not abandoned, it was usually reduced in operational scope, and attention was directed to perfecting its performance through achieving a wage form which combined material stimulation with communist spirit.[31] The new principle regarding bonuses was that they "should be granted with honorary awards as the main thing and with material awards included; they should be granted mainly to collective bodies. . . ."[32]

The positive side of the new incentive policy in industry was the very heavy stress on and expansion in the use of various forms of "socialist and communist competition," in which the motivating forces were primarily nonmaterial. The number of "outstanding" groups and workers doubled in 1958 and 1957. Emulation campaigns were carried out on various levels with great stress placed on developing collectivist attitudes and behavior. Individuals were spurred on with the lure of honorific rewards.[33]

In the people's communes material incentives were diluted as optimistic output goals were not reached and stress was placed on nonmaterial inducements, political indoctrination, and mass involvement. The deemphasis on material incentives was in effect a leveling process. Piecework methods were reduced or operated in an "in kind"—money wages framework which had an averaging effect. Private plots were taken away from the peasants and the rural free markets were abolished. The part- "in kind" part-money-wage distribution system was the negation of the principle of pay according to work. In its extreme form, the supply portion reached as high as 80 to 90 per cent of distribution with the slim remainder distributed as money wages on a basis related to the peasant's output. One commentator expected that under the new system, "one will not set a big store by 'more pay for more work. . . .' This will help one form a habit of performing labour instead of setting a big store by pay. . . . This is the Communist spirit." This was the heroic assumption upon which so much was founded.[34]

Work Incentive Policy, 1960 on

The switch back to material incentives, late in 1960, is related to the worsening conditions in agriculture. The reversal of incentive policy and the operation of a new line stressing material rewards is found in the changes in mechanisms used in industrial plants and in the communes today. Nonmaterial incentives are still in use, though less intensely.

The underscoring of piece-rate systems was a sign of the new policy. Refinements of that mechanism often based payments on team piece-rates—an indication that ideological influence was still at work. When this was not feasible, the unadorned individual piece-rate method was developed. Wage-grade system, bonuses, and other payments were modified in 1961 and 1962 in line with the notion of more pay for more work.[35] By late 1961 the overwhelming proportion of state-operated industrial enterprises was under either the hourly-wage-plus-bonus system or some form of piece-rate mechanism; the straight hourly wage system was seldom used.

The change in incentive policy in the communes appeared abruptly and dramatically late in 1960 with the return of the small private plot to commune members and the reappearance of the rural free market. Other changes reinforced the emphasis on material incentives. First, there was an attack, once again, on egalitarianism. Next, attempts were made to extend the influence of money and to strengthen the relationship between reward and performance; cash payment was to be used more widely, compensation was to be more frequent, and equal pay for equal work was ordered. Payment schemes of a progressive nature, including piece-rates, were once again extended and developed.[36]

Today in Chinese industry and agriculture, the material consideration is again the major one in organizing and motivating the labor force. This reflects the failure of the regime to mobilize effectively the disguised unemployment in the countryside and to raise sharply agricultural and capital output. This strategic aim of the Party will continue to be a policy goal. During the Great Leap Forward there was heavy reliance on the revolutionary fervor of the masses and the ability of basic level cadres to implement agricultural reform programs. In the future it is likely that the Party will move more cautiously; while the peasant and the cadre will still be depended upon (and nonmaterial incentives may be extended once again), they will not be pushed as far and they will probably be aided by increased amounts of capital and consumer goods to spur their efforts.

Notes

1. The author is grateful to the Social Science Research Council—American Council of Learned Societies Joint Committee on Contemporary China for its research grant for 1961–1962 and to the Chairman of the Center for Chinese Studies, University of California, Berkeley, Professor Choh-ming Li, and his staff for their generous assistance. Professors Walter Galenson and Li made helpful suggestions on an earlier draft.

2. Ragnar Nurkse, *Problems of Capital Formation in Underdeveloped Countries* (Oxford: Blackwell, 1953), Chapter II.

3. J. L. Buck, *Land Utilization in China* (New York: Council on Economic and Cultural Affairs, 1956), Chapter X.

4. See Charles Hoffmann, "The Basis of Communist China's Incentive Policy," *Asian Survey*, III (May, 1963), 245–257, on the ideological and economic framework of incentive policy.

5. *First Five Year Plan* . . . 1953–1957 (Peking: Foreign Languages Press,

1956), pp. 170–172, and Liu Shao-Ch'i, "The Political Report of the Central Committee . . . ," *Eighth National Congress of the Communist Party of China,* (Peking: FLP, 1956), I, 54.

6. Li Fu-Ch'un, "Progress of the First Five-Year Plan . . . ," *New China Advances to Socialism* (Peking: FLP, 1956), p. 97; Helen and Yi-Chang Yin, *Economic Statistics of Mainland China* 1949–1957) (Cambridge: Harvard University Press, 1960), p. 17; and *Ten Great Years,* State Statistical Bureau (Peking: FLP, 1960) p. 87.

7. See Mao Tse-Tung, *On the Correct Handling of Contradictions Among the People* (Peking: FLP, 1956), p. 36; "Distribution of Income in People's Communes," *"Chung-kuo ch'ing-nien pao,* January 18, 1961, in *Current Background (CB)* 648 (March 22, 1961), p. 19; and Sung Ping, "Why Is It Necessary to Introduce a Rational Low-Wage System?" *Hsueh-hsi,* No. 23, December 3, 1956, in *Extracts from China Mainland Magazines (ECMM)* 118 (February 10, 1957), pp. 26–31.

8. Chang Ching, "The Question of Distribution According to Labor . . . ," *Hung ch'i,* No. 18, September 16, 1961, in *Selections from China Mainland Magazines (SCMM)* 283 (October 17, 1961), pp. 3–4, and Shen Liao-Cin, "Politics is the Life-Line of All Economic Activities, *Kuang-ming jih-pao,* June 6, 1960, p. 6, in *U.S. Joint Publications Research Service (JPRS)* 5223 (August 8, 1960), pp. 17–18.

9. See *Ten Great Years,* p. 218; *Labour Laws and Regulations of the People's Republic of China* (Peking: FLP, 1956), pp. 31–53; and Chao Kuo-Chün, *Economic Planning and Organization in Mainland China* (Cambridge: Harvard University Press, 1960), II, 100–103.

10. *Labour Laws and Regulations . . . ,* pp. 54–64.

11. Leon Lavallee, and others, *Economic de la Chine Socialiste* (Geneva: Librairie Rousseau, 1957), pp. 415–416.

12. See *Lao-tung (LT),* Nos. 7, 8, 10, April 3, 18, and May 18, 1957 in *JPRS* 754 (October 14, 1958), pp. 16–23.

13. Ibid., No. 5, March 3, 1957, in *JPRS* 754, *loc. cit.* On piece-rate problems, see Sun Shang-Ch'ing, "On the Nature and Destiny of our Current Piece-Rat Wage System," *Ching-chi yen chiu,* No. 4, April 17, 1959, in *ECMM* 180 (August 17, 1959), pp. 35–40.

14. Robert Carin, *China's Land Problem Series: Agricultural Co-operativization Movement* (Hongkong, 1960) II, 22–29, 241–259.

15. *Decisions on Agricultural Co-operation* (Peking: FLP, 1956), pp. 22–25 (hereafter *Decisions . . .*), and *Model Regulations for an Agricultural Producers' Cooperative* (Peking: FLP, 1956), pp. 33–39. (hereafter *Model Regulations . . .*).

16. *Model Regulations . . . , loc. cit.,* and *Model Regulations for Advanced Agricultural Producers' Co-operatives* (Peking: FLP, 1956), pp. 18–22.

17. See Peter Schran, *The Structure of Income in Communist China* (Ph.D. Dissertation, University of California, Berkeley, 1961), pp. 21 ff., and Miao Yueh-Sheng, "An Investigation of Conditions of Distribution of Income in a People's Commune in Honan," *Tung-chi kung-tso,* No. 21, November 14, 1958, in *ECMM* 155 (January 23, 1959) pp. 36–39 and Fu Wen-Yeh, "What Is the Basic Work-Day System?" *Kung-jen jih-pao (KJJP),* December 1, 1961, in *SCMP* 2655 (January 10, 1962), pp. 16–17.

18. *National Conference of Outstanding Groups in Industry, Communications and Transport, Capital Construction, Finance and Trade* (Peking: FLP, 1960), pp. 32–37, and "Developing Collectivistic Thought . . . Carry Out Comprehen-

sive Cooperation, Competition and Mutual Assistance . . . ," *KJJP*, November 27, 1960, in *JPRS* 8101 (April 15, 1961), pp. 155–160.

19. For examples of mass participation, see "Exploit Labor Potentialities by Consulting Masses," *Jen-min jih-pao* (*JMJP*), April 11, 1961, p. 1, in *JPRS* 9491 (June 26, 1961), pp. 42–44; "Fushun Coal Miners Develop Mass Movement for High Output," *KJJP*, February 28, 1961, p. 1, in *JPRS* 8227 (May 1, 1961), pp. 32–34; and "Mass Movement and Enterprise Control Experiences . . . in Tientsin," *Chung-kuo fang-chih*, February 10, 1960, p. 26, in *JPRS* 6866 (March 8, 961), p. 192.

20. Liu Chien-Kuo, "Contest Between Red Banner Sections and 'Six-Good' Workers," *KJJP*, May 27, 1961, p. 2, in *JPRS* 4936 (August 31, 1961) pp. 1–5. Money prizes were also given the three award classes. For examples of honors, see Liang Ya-Shen, "Tientsin . . . [Factory] Becomes an Advanced Unit," *KJJP*, December 2, 1960, p. 2, in *JPRS* 8101 (April 15, 1961), pp. 115–116; "Depend on Activists . . ," *KJJP*, February 16, 1962 in *Survey of China Mainland Press* (*SCMP*) 2693 (March 3, 1962), pp. 14–16; and "Peking Working Women's Contribution in Past Year," *New China News Agency* (*NCNA*), March 5, 1961, in *SCMP* 2454 (March 13, 1961), p. 14.

21. See *NCNA Daily News Report* 1686 (April 16, 1954), p. 115, and *NCNA,* September 1, 1955, in *SCMP* 1122 (September 2, 1956), pp. 10–11; Leo Orelans, *Professional Manpower and Education in Communist China* (Washington, D.C.: National Science Foundation, 1961), pp. 122–123; and *Labour Laws and Regulations . . . ,* pp. 54–64.

22. See *NCNA,* April 14, 1956, in *SCMP* 1275 (April 25, 1956), p. 18; Tso Chun-T'ai, ". . . Reform of the Wage System," *Cheng-chih hsueh-hsi,* No. 6, June 13, 1956, in *ECMM* 47 (August 13, 1956), pp. 8–11; and Ma Wen-Jui, "Report to the Third Session of the First National People's Congress . . . ," June 29, 1956, in *CB* 405 (July 26, 1956), pp. 1–9.

23. Tso Chun-T'ai, *loc. cit.;* Ma Wen-Jui, *loc. cit.; NCNA,* April 14, 1956, *loc. cit.;* and Peter Schran, *op. cit.,* pp. 249–252.

24. *Ta Kung-pao* (Tientsin; *TKP*), May 22, 1956, in *SCMP* 1314. See also, Chou En-Lai, "Report on the Proposals for the Second Five Year Plan . . . ," *Eighth National Congress of the Communist Party of China,* I, 285 ff.

25. Chin Li, "Certain Problems Concerning Betterment of the Current Wage Grading System," *LT,* No. 3, March 6, 1956, in *ECMM* 35 (May 14, 1956), p. 32, and Ma Wen-Jui, *loc. cit.*

26. July 6, 1956, in *SCMP* 1331 (July 18, 1956), pp. 4–6, and Sun Shang-Ch'ing, *loc. cit.*

27. See *Socialist Upsurge in China's Countryside* (Peking: FLP, 1957), pp. 98–100; Government of India, Ministry of Food and Agriculture, *Report of the Indian Delegation to China on Agricultural Planning and Techniques* (Delhi: 1956), p. 117; and Union Research Institute, *Communist China 1949–1959* (Hongkong, 1961), I, 160–161.

28. *Socialist Upsurge . . . ,* p. 88, and Robert Carin, *op. cit.,* II, 421–423, 500–502.

29. See Teng Tse-Hui's report in *New China Advances to Socialism,* pp. 130–131; Mao Tse-Tung, *op. cit.,* p. 38; P. Schran, *op. cit.,* p. 246; and Chao Kuo-Chün, *op. cit.,* II, 108–109.

30. See *Ten Great Years,* p. 186.

31. *Ts'ai-ching yen-chiu,* No. 8, November 15, 1958, in *JPRS* 1337 (March 12, 1959), pp. 1–2, and Liu Ch'eng-Jui, and others, "Contradiction in the Piece-Wage System . . . , "*Chiao-hsueh yü yen-chiu,* No. 9, September 4, 1958, in

ECMM 153 (January 12, 1959), pp. 10–17. See also, Sun Shang-Ch'ing, *loc. cit.;* "A Study of the System of Piece-Wage Incentive Awards," *LT,* No. 23, December 23, 1959, pp. 22–24, in *JPRS* 2640 (June 1, 1960) pp. 9–16; and *JMJP,* September 25, 1958, in *SCMP* 1875 (October 15, 1958), pp. 30–31.

32. Liu Ch'eng-Jui, and others, *loc. cit.*

33. *Ten Great Years,* p. 186, and Li Po, "Keen Competition and Close Co-operation," *HC,* No. 8, September 16, 1958, pp. 39–40, in *JPRS* 9181 (May 9, 1961), pp. 13–18.

34. "Resolution . . . on . . . People's Communes . . . ," *People's Communes in China* (Peking: FLP, 1958), pp. 6, 8; "Draft Regulations of the Weihsing People's Commune," in *Contemporary China* (Hongkong: Hongkong University Press, 1960), III, 237, 243–244; and HuSheng, "Let us Begin . . . with the Supply System," *Hsueh-shu yueh-kan,* No. 11, 1958, in R. Carin *op. cit.,* III, 167–168.

35. See Ch'en Han-Ch'uan, "Strengthening of the Piece-Work System," *TKP* (Peking) August 23, 1961, p. 1, in *JPRS* 10720 (October 25, 1961), pp. 90–94; Chou Yen-Pin, "Wages . . . in Industrial Enterprises Must be . . . According to Work Done," *Chung-kuo ch'ing-nien pao,* November 8, 1961, in *SCMP* 2633 (December 6, 1961), pp. 8–13; and Lin Fang, "A Discussion on the Forms of Wages," *JMJP,* October 28, 1961, p. 7, in *JPRS* 11969 (January 15, 1962), pp. 20–24.

36. Ch'en Yi-Yen, "Acknowledgement of Difference Versus Egalitarian Distribution," *Nan-fang jih pao* (Canton), December 21, 1960, in *SCMP* 2415 (January 12, 1961), p. 10; "Same Pay for Same Work . . . ," *Chung-kuo fu-nu,* No. 11, 1961, in *SCMM* 291 (December 11, 1961), pp. 13–15; and "Wages by Piece-Work in Rural Communes," *JMJP,* August 4, 1961, p. 7, in *JPRS* 10353 (October 6, 1961), pp. 43–48.

37. The author has benefitted from the paper, "Rural Income and the Great Leap Forward," delivered by Professor Peter Schran at the Sixteenth Annual Meeting of the Association for Asian Studies, March 20–22, 1964, Washington, D.C.

27. AGRICULTURAL SPLITTISM

Andrew Nathan

The traditional economic relationship between farmer and government in China was the simple one of taxation: some quantity of produce was taken away and the rest was left for the producer to consume or sell. The reorganization of agriculture under Communist rule has changed this, however, and the farmer now gets most of his income in the form of wages. The piece-work wage system currently in use was not easily arrived at; on the contrary, each stage

SOURCE: Reprinted from Andrew Nathan, "China's Work-Point System: A Study in Agricultural Splittism," in *Current Scene,* II, 31 (April 15, 1964), pp. 1–14.

of the reorganization process leading from lower-stage co-operatives to communes has been accompanied by a different wage system. Peking has experimented with piece rates, graded time rates, ungraded time rates, bonuses and free supply in its search for the optimal system.

The optimal system must provide a convenient and workable way to measure labour in order to effect "the socialist principle of distribution according to labour." At the same time, it should offer incentives, either material or ideological, for the labourer. And it must be adapted to whatever form of collective entity in which it is being used—lower co-operative, higher co-operative, or commune—and to the special demands of agricultural rather than industrial labour.

Refugee farmers from the southern counties of Kwangtung Province have described these successive wage systems in some detail. This article examines these systems and the problems which seem to have influenced their evolution. Practice in other areas of China may have been somewhat different from that described by the Kwangtung farmers, but the general problems and experiences were probably the same.[1]

The Reason Why

Under the lower-stage co-operatives, where land was worked collectively but ownership was retained by the individual peasant, a simple ungraded time wage was combined with an allowance based on the amount of land owned. Under the higher-stage cooperatives, where collectively used land was owned by the co-operative, a piece work system was introduced. When the communes were formed in the abortive Great Leap Forward, a system of graded or ungraded time wages with bonuses, in combination with a system of free supply, was inaugurated. When Peking retrenched after the failure of the Leap Forward, the communes returned to the piece rate. In each case, wages were expressed in terms of work points rather than dollars and cents, and converted to money terms on pay day (after each rice harvest).

The Chinese communists view wages as one of several categories of "distribution" of a harvest. Some produce is remitted to higher levels under various headings, some is retained by the collective for seed grain, emergency funds and production capital, and the rest is distributed as wages.[2] The State determines the relationship among the components of distribution—it may decide to procure the maximum of grain to support industry and foreign trade, or it may decide to encourage the farmers with a relatively large allowance in wages. In practice, of course, it tries to strike a balance acceptable to all its interests, and with due regard to the quantity of the harvest.

The use of work points rather than absolute money terms to express wages ingeniously preserves Peking's control over the allocation of the harvest. If wages were expressed in money terms, the State would be committed to a certain expenditure in farmer's wages; but with work points, the money value is only known after State procurement. Then the total number of points earned on the team is divided into the total value to be distributed to arrive at the value of each work point. Meanwhile, the farmer has competed with others to get more points only in order to get a higher proportion of the distribution ultimately allotted by the State. The State holds all the cards. The peasant, his labour already given, waits on the State's convenience.

Whatever the specific wage system in use, the basic procedure is the same. Men are organized into teams to work common land. Either the time worked or the amount of work done is recorded in work points and after the harvest distribution of grain and money is made in proportion to the work points earned by each labourer. At times when wages have been paid monthly, they have been considered as advances out of the final post-harvest reckonings. During the period when rice was supplied "free" in the dining halls it also amounted to an advance in wages, although it was at first not dependent upon work points. All this will be shown more fully below.

Work Points and Mutual Aid

The work point actually made its first post-"liberation" rural appearance in the mutual aid teams.[3] At that stage, work points were used to keep track of the work put in by Farmer A on the plot of Farmer B, so that the latter could reciprocate fairly accurately, in accordance with the principle of "exchanging work for work." Points were based solely on time, and did not differentiate between types of work (ploughing, weeding, harvesting) or qualities of labour (the labour of an active young man versus that of a less strong elder); a day's labour was a day's labour. Since there were no wages at this stage—the farmer's income was still what was left after taxes—work points related only to labour exchange, not to income, and strictly speaking this stage falls outside the purview of the present article. Dissatisfaction with this system, however, may have been one of the reasons for the switch to-the lower co-operative. Clearly, larger families with more available labour could never hope to receive a full measure of reciprocal labour from their less prolific neighbours under the mutual aid system, and the only incentive for them to labour on the land of others would be wages.

First Appearance of Wages

The lower co-operatives were used on a large scale in 1955, on the principle of collective labour on privately owned land. Farmers who joined the cooperative were now organized into teams, and their work on each other's fields was directed by a captain. Part of the peasant's income was still based on the land he owned, but now a part was also based upon labour. The income from land-ownership in this arrangement was based on a fixed per-*mow** formula, theoretically allocated by the co-operative from its total income (rather than being a flexible quantity retained by the cultivator after fixed State procurement; flexibility was in the wage portion of income). For example, one farmer from Kwangtung said that his income per *mow* consisted of a basic allowance of 50 *catties*† (unhusked rice), plus 10 *catties* to cover the cost of seed, and 8 to cover the cost of fertilizer—altogether 68 *catties* for each

---

* 1 *mow* = 0.1647 acre.
† 1 *catty* = 1.1 lbs.

mow he owned. This could, if desired, be translated into cash at a fixed rate (i.e., sold to the State at a fixed price). In the case of other crops, a similar formula as followed. Practice as to the communal use of livestock and tools varied; where they were "cooperativized," they were considered to be capital and the co-operative paid the owner for their use.

When wages were first introduced on the co-operatives, the system for deciding the relative amounts each person would get was fairly simple. Rough distinctions were introduced based on the condition of the labourer. The regime appears to have been groping at that time for a system of "inflexible allocation and flexible appraisal" based upon grades of labourers.[4] All team members were supposed to be classified into "labour grades" by democratic discussion and common agreement, on the basis of their physical ability to work, their industry and their skill.[5] There have usually been from three to five such grades among able-bodied male workers, an equal or smaller number of grades for females and some provision for the elderly. The day's labour of a person of each grade had a work point value based upon his grade classification: e.g., 10 points for first grade male, 9 for second grade male and first grade female, etc. Because labour grades are theoretically subject to frequent and regular revision, they are supposed to have an incentive effect. But because this incentive effect is a step removed from the actual day's labour, "inflexible allocation" was to be tempered with "flexible appraisal," i.e., the docking of loafers and extra rewards for those who put in extra good work, on the basis of group discussion and agreement.

In practice, peasants were reluctant to scrutinize and judge each other's work, and since this was the first time wage grades were used in the countryside, they were sometimes inept at establishing them. One farmer reported that on his co-operative there were only two grades: able-bodied workers got ten points per day, and aged or infirm persons got five. An egregious loafer might be docked a half-day's worth of work points, but beyond this the intended incentive value of the system was destroyed. On the other hand, there were probably co-operatives in which the system of inflexible allocation and flexible appraisal was carried out generally according to plan.

Appearance of Piece Rates

Kwangtung farmers have reported that the actual procedures of payment at this time were close to the traditional practice of the farmer keeping his own produce. Rice produced on the farmer's land, less State procurement, would be retained by the farmer after the harvests, some to be eaten and the rest to be sold at a fixed price to the State. Once annually, at the end of the autumn harvest, everyone's proper income would be calculated according to fixed per-*mow* allocations and work points earned. Those families which had had too much during the year would owe the co-operative, and those who had not received their full share would be paid. Many grain-rich families anticipated this reckoning by sharing out grain during the year to families to whom it would be owed anyway that winter.

"Higher collectives" were started in 1956 and 1957 on the principle of collective ownership of collectively used land. There was no more landbased income and farmers had to rely almost entirely on wages (some other income might come from livestock and private plots). It must therefore have been necessary, from an incentive point of view, to find a system that could more accurately measure labour and realize "the socialist principle of pay according to labour." At the same time, now that the farmer had had experience with collective labour, a more complex system seemed administratively feasible.

Farmers say that cadres came to the villages in 1957 and explained the principle of pay according to labour. They also explained the use of labour grades and piece rates. Labour grades, of course, had already been established in most villages but piece rates had not been used before. Therefore meetings were held at the co-operative (or village) level in which the farmers considered all the farm jobs one by one, discussed them and established pieces rates—in terms of work points—for each. For example, they decided that ploughing paddy should be worth 10 points per *mow*, harrowing 9 points per *mow*, collection of nightsoil 10 points per hundred *catties*, and so forth. The system thus evolved was withdrawn temporarily during the Great Leap Forward and was restored after the Leap Forward had been abandoned. During the first year or two of the communes the "system of supply and the system of basic wages plus bonuses" was used.

Supply-Wage-Bonus

It is not clear that the central government actually intended a universal switch to the supply-wage-bonus system after the communes were established in August, 1958. The Resolution of the Central Committee on the subject, published by *NCNA* on September 1, 1958, was conservative:

> After the establishment of the People's Communes, there is no need hastily to change the original system of distribution. . . . Where conditions are not yet ripe, for the time being we may continue to adopt such systems as originally practised. . . . The distribution system, whether it be the wage system or remuneration according to labour days, is still "to each according to his labour."[6]

Retrospective Chinese communist accounts also tend to pass over the Great Leap Forward wage system as a small deviation in the continuing progress of the piece work system and hardly worth mentioning. But whether on the initiative of the central authorities or that of local cadres, the new system had come into force "in all rural People's Communes"[7] by January 1, 1959. At the time, it was stated that the piece rate system, in addition to being unwieldy and giving opportunities for dishonesty, would dampen the aroused activism of the workers by letting their minds dwell too much on material considerations.[8] (The same thing was said in industries where piece rates had been in use.[9]) It was apparently felt that if a less exact way of measuring and rewarding labour were used, the way would be cleared for non-material incentives, such as patriotism and emulation, to drive the workers to supernormal exertions. Also, the introduction of a system of "free" supply—at first unlimited in quantity—implies that the regime thought the problem of insufficient grain had been solved.

"Eight Guarantees"—for Sale

The "system of supply" referred to the assumption by the commune of the duty of fulfilling some basic needs of its members "free." This varied from grain alone, provided by the dining hall and to which the individual in some cases had to add his own meat and condiments, to the "seven things," or the "eight guarantees" (food, clothes, room, education, funerals, medicine, movies, haircuts).[10] The farmers say the more ambitious programmes such as the "eight guarantees" (the slogan varied locally) quickly faded away into nothing, with the listed items available at a price as usual or not available at all.

The associated "system of basic wages plus bonuses" utilized the wage-grade system. Work points were awarded, in slightly different ways in different communes,[11] to the different labour grades on a time basis—sometimes with a wide variation in the number of points awarded, and sometimes with so small a variation as to amount to no more than a way of keeping attendance. Wages were paid by the month (under the other systems described in this article they were usually paid semi-annually). These, and mess hall rations, amounted to allowances in advance from the semiannual reckonings which took place at the harvests, but were meant to give the impression (and were so reported in the press) of a proto-communist society in which one's income was guaranteed by the state and in which the "rudiments" of the "communist principle of to each according to his need" had been introduced.[12]

The "bonus" was to provide some material incentive. Twenty per cent of wage income was to be distributed as bonuses monthly to 40 to 60 per cent of the commune members, at the discretion of the cadres.[13]

The withdrawal of the supply-wage-bonus system followed the rapid realization that it caused more problems than it solved. According to Kwangtung farmers, while the communal dining halls lasted, the "supply" system continued. The dining halls usually lasted for about a year although, judging from press reports, they managed to survive for two or more years in many places.

However, the supply, far from being infinite, was quickly rationed. Explained the People's Daily:

"Members of the commune misunderstood the significance of the provision of free rice and thought no restraint necessary in rice consumption."[14]

After this, the concept of labour grades was applied to help determine rations. Women's rations were sometimes also subdivided into a few grades. The rations of children (below 16, 17 or 18 depending on the commune) were set simply according to age and the same was true of those who had reached retirement age (usually 60 for men, 56 for women). The grain problem had not been solved after all.

An Opportunity Not to Work

Not only the lack of supplies but the lack of incentive in the new system soon became apparent. "Some people" took the supply system as an opportunity not to work.[15] It was soon emphasised that this "rudiment of communism" was only a rudiment. Again, *People's Daily* explained:

> We should actively protect and support the growth of this rudiment. But . . . as stated in the resolution of the Sixth Plenum (of the Eighth Central Committee of the CCP) during a considerably long period to come, the wage portion will be the principle portion.[16]

In accordance with the voluntary principle of the mess halls, it was recognized that workers who did not wish to participate were entitled to a ration from the mess hall administration which they could cook at home. This underlined the fact that "free supply" was not really free but only collectively administered rations. The story of the decline and rearguard propaganda defence of the mess halls is a long one in itself.

Originally, a ratio of 50:50 was considered permissible between supply and wage in a commune member's income.[17] Shortly thereafter the ratio of 60:40 was stated to be best.[18] Then the ratio of 30:70 was being mentioned and was soon ensconced in a slogan as "the ratio of three to seven."[19] At the end of 1960 the *People's Daily* stated that in the supply system "all people (except old people, children or those unfit for work) must earn specified work points in order to enjoy the food rations supplied,"[20] a statement which effectively crushed the "rudiment of communism" supposedly represented by the supply system.

Return of the Piece Rate

During 1961 the press recorded the resumption of the piece rate in many communes, lauding the experience of the former higher co-operatives.[21] By July 1961, the newspapers reported that it was "enforced in all areas."[22] Farmers from Kwangtung Province said that the dining halls were closed and the piece rate system was resumed as early as the end of 1959. Some press accounts, however, imply that the "basic working day system" or graded time rates were used as late as 1962 in places.[23]

In any case it is very likely that by 1963 the old piece rate system was in use everywhere,[24] including the communes which had not had time to try it out before the Leap Forward.

As stated above, farmers from Kwangtung recalled that the piece rate system was first evolved, under cadres' directions, in village meetings in 1957 when the farm jobs were taken one by one and discussed.

To show how the piece rate system was applied to the growing of rice, the harvesting process used in southern Kwangtung is a useful example. The rice plants are cut off low on the stalk near the ground, then cut in half. The top half, with the grain, is carried to the threshing ground where it is threshed on a round stone turned by a bullock. The grain is laid on the ground and raked back and forth in the sun to dry, then carried to a wind machine which separates the chaff, and then to a storehouse. The top half of the stalk is dried on the threshing ground and then built into houseshaped haystacks. The bottom half is burned on the field in the first season but collected and used for fuel after the autumn harvest when it is considered of better quality.

To cut the stalks on the field and bring the top half to the square is worth three points per 100 *catties* (about 110 lbs.) of stalks. The man in charge of the threshing machine weighs it and records the points, giving the record to the team accountant later.

Threshing is worth 1.2 points per 100 *catties* of the stalks originally brought and weighed.

Disposing of the stalks on the square for drying is worth 0.4 points per 100 *catties* of the original weighing.

Making the stalks into haystacks is worth 0.2 points per 100 *catties* of the original weighing.

Drying the grain in the sun is worth 0.8 points per 100 *catties* of grain as finally weighed in the storehouse.

Carrying the grain to the wind machine and to the storehouse is worth 0.2 points per 100 *catties* of grain as finally weighed. At the storehouse the grain is weighed by the storehouse keeper who gives the record to the team accountant later on.

Burning the stalks of the first harvest on the field is worth 4 points per *mow*.

"There are more than a hundred varieties of crops and several thousand varieties of work" on the co-operative (or commune).[25] Rice culture involves ploughing, transplanting, cultivating and irrigating as well as harvesting. Ploughing must include at least a first ploughing and a harrowing. Transplanting includes the original planting of the seedlings in a corner of the field and their subsequent transfer to the paddy. Furthermore, many communes raise vegetables, sugar cane, silk worms, fish or livestock. In other words, a great complexity of jobs must be distinguished and each one given its appropriate work-point reward, expressed in terms of the appropriate piece.

Fight Equality

Many jobs are done by the group. Harvesting, as described above, is done by a team of four. It is therefore necessary that the workers split up the points of the team among them; they tend to divide the points equally rather than undergo the bother and conflict of arguing over them. Cadres have been instructed to fight this tendency for it destroys the immediate incentive effect of the piece rate. The proper procedure is "piece work done by the group and assessing and recording work points earned by individuals."[26]

A few other examples given by farmers are illuminating. Keeping a bullock, which includes housing and feeding it, is paid in some communes at 10 points per day. However, the *Southern Daily* once reported an exceptionally "advanced" commune where the concept of the "unbreakable rice bowl" for cattle tenders was challenged by attaching piece rates per *catty* to the grass cut for the cattle and the manure collected.[27] Otherwise, cattle-tending amounts to a time rate. Mending river dikes with clay was rewarded in one commune at 15 points per 100 cubic feet of clay delivered at the dike.

Among the jobs frequently regulated by area are planting and cultivating vegetables, sugar cane and rice, and collecting and spreading nightsoil. Nightsoil gathering is also frequently regulated by weight, as are harvesting of crops, fishing and gathering of grass, leaves or wood. Time rates are supposed to be used as little as possible but may extend to almost any kind of maintenance work—carpentry, ditch-digging, widening of fish ponds—or any other kind of simple hard labour for which other piece units have not been or cannot be established.

No Revolutionary Change

As a rule, jobs are rated so that the average daily wage of a reasonably talented and sincere worker will be 10 points per day. This is about what it would have been under the time rates used in the lower co-operatives and in some of the communes during the Leap Forward. Therefore, as different as the piece work system was in conception, it meant no revolutionary change in the farmer's mental calculations of income. These still centre on the final accounts for the year which are determined after the second (winter) rice harvest. Salary and ration advances are given either at the end of the first harvest (June or July) or monthly. In December when the total value to be distributed is known, the value of 10 work points or a day's work (usually from JMP 0.20 to JMP 0.80,* although *NCNA* reported one commune where in 1962 the value of 10 work points reached JMP 2.00†[28]) is established. From this, a man's total income for the year may be known and, after deduction of what he has already been paid, the December payment is determined.

Rice rations and ration coupons form an important part of income in addition to cash. Usually a monthly basic rice ration is set for the different classes of labourers (say 20–30 *catties* of unhusked rice). The ration for children and old people is based on age. One variation on this is to set a basic semiannual ration for all persons (say, 24 *catties* in June, 36 in December) and then add to this another 19 *catties* or so per 100 work points earned. Rice rations may be kept at home or in a central storehouse whence they can be drawn on the strength of a ration booklet at intervals convenient to the householder. These rations are paid for at an "official price," which is lower than the so-called "high price" at which extra rice may be purchased on the free market, and therefore must be considered as a part of income. The cost of the rice ration is deducted before the payment of salary at the two harvests.

Cadres Are Different

In addition ration coupons are issued monthly for other staples such as sugar, salt, oil and cloth, and sometimes for matches, kerosene, tobacco, etc.

---

* 6½d. to 2s. 2d. sterling or U.S.$0.08 to U.S.$0.33, approximately.
† 5s. 6d. sterling or U.S.$0.84 approximately.

They must also be purchased but at lower than the market price. The ration is constant at any given time and place no matter what the labour status of the peasant (although cadre rations are sometimes different).

Thus, as a typical example, a single farmer earned 3,200 work points during the year. In July he received JMP 20.00* after deduction of rice costs, and 132 *catties* of rice, a 6-month portion of a monthly ration of 22 *catties* given to the second labour class. In December the value of the work point was fixed; he got another 132 *catties* of rice plus JMP 50.00† net. Ration coupons were issued monthly.

It should be noted that a certain amount of other income can come to the farmer, including produce grown on the private plot and the proceeds of sales of pigs, chickens, eggs and ration tickets (the sale of the latter is illegal but sometimes practised).

Wage grades still serve a function, which varies from one commune to the next, in the piece-rate system. In some communes, farmers say wage grades apply whenever the time rate is used—say for road-building, maintenance work or even for cultivation of the crop. In other communes, only a worker of the first grade is eligible for certain harder, more technical and more remunerative jobs, such as ploughing or transplanting, while women and old men, in grade three, are assigned to cattle tending or simple cultivation.

The function of enforcement is usually vested in the team captain, with the assistance of the assistant captain, or in a specially elected official called the *k'uai-chi* (most nearly but inexactly translated "accountant"). If possible, a formal standard is established, for example, that rice plants shall be transplanted at distances of 4 (5, 8, depending on the current theory) inches from each other. In this case the enthusiastic *k'uai-chi* can walk around with a marked bamboo pole which he lays on the field for measuring. More commonly, a basic and understood standard must be invoked. The standard rule seems to be that if a job is done 80 per cent up to standard, the full measure of points may be given. If the job is one where imperfect execution will harm production (e.g. transplanting), an imperfect job must be destroyed and the work done over before any points at all will be given. In other cases, a proportion of the full award may be given for a sub-standard job.

Another official called the *chi-fen-yuan* ("work point recorder") keeps the record of work points. Farmers say the *ch'u-na* ("bursar") handles money and the *pao kuan* ("storekeeper") receives and disburses grains.

In one commune at least, the piece rates established in 1957 have never had to be revised and only one was later added to the list; labour grades, however, are reconsidered each month in this commune. The more typical case is probably that of the suburban Peking commune reported to have established 1,192 "quotas" by 1957 (a quota in this context is another word for a "piece"; for example, in the formula "10 points per *mow*," one *mow* is the piece or quota); of these, 204 were revised because they were irrational to begin with; 41 were revised because the farming methods or operational techniques they covered had been changed; 226 were revised as frequently

* £2 15s. 0d. sterling or U.S.$8.40 approximately.
† £6 17s. 6d. sterling or U.S.$21.00 approximately.

as necessitated by circumstances, such as the weather, distance of fields, thickness of the crop.[29]

Piece Rate Problems

These figures underline the major difficulty of the piece rate system for agricultural labour—its incredible complexity and difficulty of administration. The work point value of each of several thousand jobs must accurately reflect its difficulty and the labour involved in order to avoid giving over-incentives to some jobs and under-incentives to others. A very careful and honest job of recording is essential—and there are about 60 adult workers on the production team to be accounted for. Someone must also inspect work to be sure that the designated "quota" is not only quantitatively filled but also qualitatively acceptable.

Such difficulties are reflected in the fairly frequent articles which have called for rational and consistent work point levels for all jobs,[30] criticized the system for its complexity,[31] called for honesty and efficiency in its administration,[32] attacked "neglecting quality while running after quantity,"[33] and criticized "egalitarianism" such as the division of earned work points equally among members of a group doing the same job.[34] On the other hand, in communes sufficiently "advanced" to overcome these difficulties, the piece rate system is lauded by the Chinese communists as the scientific way of implementing the principle of payment according to labour.[35] Because, they say, it more closely defines and records labour, it has more incentive value than a time rate.

Experience with wages based on time rates in the lower co-operatives gave cadres and farmers some practice in working the "socialist principle of pay according to labour." When, at the stage of the higher co-operatives, wages became far and away the largest portion of income, the piece rate was introduced for its superior ability to measure labour and provide incentive. But the piece rate did not suit the revolutionary atmosphere which accompanied the founding of the communes and the beginning of the Great Leap Forward in August, 1958; it gave way to a system which contained the "rudiments of communism" in the concept of free supply and deemphasised material incentive in order to permit non-material incentives to work. When free supply did not work and non-material incentives failed to inspire the peasant, piece rates were reinstated.

Doctrinal Dichotomy

Peking appears to be experiencing a certain ideological embarrassment over the need to resort to material incentives in a society being groomed as a model for communism. Doctrinally, material incentives are "bourgeois," "individualistic," a capitalist device and have no place in a communist society where patriotism, emulation, the inspiration of Chairman Mao's writings, the love for the proletariat should spur the peasant to greater production. Not long ago, a Peking paper reflected this embarrassment when it considered whether the "principle of material interest" is a function of the "not very high level of consciousness of the people during the stage of socialism" or a principle that will prove common to both socialist and communist society.[36]

Notes

1. I am deeply indebted to Dr. Ezra Vogel of the Harvard East Asian Research Centre for the opportunity and the encouragement to work on this article and for his innumerable valuable suggestions.

2. Li Pai-kuan, "On distribution of income in the higher agricultural producers' cooperatives," *New Construction (Hsin Chienshe)*, No. 7, Peking, July 4, 1957.

3. Hsieh Chi-huang, "On 'Appraisal of work for the allocation of work points,' " *Ta Kung Pao*, Peking, September 22, 1961; Fan Ching-kuo, "Assess work and record work points properly," *Liberation Journal (Chieh-fang)*, No. 7, Shanghai, June 5, 1962.

4. Hsieh Chi-huang, *op. cit.*

5. "A Production Brigade in Honan takes differences in skill into consideration when determining basic wage points," *People's Daily (Jen-min Jih-pao)* Peking, March 4, 1962.

6. "Resolution of the Central Committee of the CCP on the Establishment of People's Communes in the Rural Areas," *NCNA*, September 1, 1958.

7. Wang Lu, "The way the peasants look at the system of remuneration according to labour," *Red Flag (Hung-ch'i)*, No. 22, Peking, November 16, 1960.

8. Chao Kuang, "The system of ration supply plus basic wages—distribution system of the Weihsing People's Commune, Suip'ing," *People's Daily*, Peking, September 20, 1958; Chang Shu-chih, "Introducing a people's commune," *Financial and Economic Research Journal (Ts'ai Ching Yen-chiu)*, No. 6, Peking, September 15, 1958.

9. Chao Te-huan, Jen Chung-teh and Ma Yu-t'ien, "How do we raise the masses to cancel the piece wage system?" *Daily Worker (Kung-jen Jih-pao)*, Peking, August 29, 1958; Hsueh Chin and Yin Chen, "They don't want piece wages," *China Youth (Chung-kuo Ch'ing-nien)*, No. 19, Peking, October 1, 1958.

10. Chao Kuang, *op. cit.*

11. Within the "system of supply and the system of basic wages plus bonuses" the wage and bonus component, while always a time rather than a piece rate, took many slightly different forms. See, for example, "Distribute according to labour, more pay for more work," *Current Events (Shih-shih Shou-ts'e)* No. 6, Peking, March 21, 1959, where five such systems are briefly described: fixed grades and variable wages, basic working days, basic wages based on basic working days, recording work points and determining grades, work-point recording—award for overfulfilling target. As described in the text, the supply portion of the system also took various forms.

12. Chang Yu-san, "An investigation of the supply-wage system in a people's commune in Shansi," *Red Flag*, No. 10, Peking, October 16, 1958;

Cheng Ssu, "The supply system is a touchstone," *China Youth*, No. 21, Peking, October 1958;

Hsu Li-ch'un, "We have already reached the stage of communism," *Red Flag*, No. 12, Peking, November, 12, 1958;

Li Chia-ch'i, "Problem on the distribution of consumption fund in the people's communes," *New Construction*, No. 11, Peking, November 3, 1958.

13. Chao Kuang, *op. cit.;*
Li Ch'i-hsiang, "Several problems concerning the adoption of the wage system," *Journal of Political Study (Cheng-chih Hsueh-hsi)*, No. 9, Peking, 1958.

14. Ts'ao Shou-shan, "Meal coupon system introduced in Hopei commune," *People's Daily*, Peking, March 7, 1959.

15. "Fixed grades and flexible wages introduced in Hupeh," *People's Daily*, Peking, March 9, 1959.

16. "Thorough implementation of the principle of 'to each according to his labour' in the people's communes," *Red Flag*, No. 6, Peking, March 16, 1959.

17. Chao Kuang, *op. cit.*

18. Chao Ke, "Onward courageously under the Red Flag of the People's Communes," *Tientsin Daily*, Tientsin, March 18, 1960.

19. "The ratio of three to seven," *Southern Daily (Nan-fang Jih-pao)*, Canton, November 12, 1960;
Chin Ming, "How people's communes finance work serves distribution," *Red Flag*, No. 22, Peking, November 16, 1960.

20. "Carry out comprehensively the Party's policy on distribution after the autumn harvest," *People's Daily*, Peking, December 12, 1960.

21. Investigaton Team of Lukouch'iao People's Commune, "How a production team in Peking suburbs enforces quota control and assesses work and awards wage points," *People's Daily*, Peking, May 22, 1961;
"Hsinlou production team improves method of calculating rewards and implements the principle of pay according to work done," *Southern Daily*, Canton, May 18, 1961;
"More pay must be given for more labour," *People's Daily*, Peking, July 5, 1961.

22. Ch'eng Sheng and Hsu Chien, "The presence of labour quotas does not mean that everything is alright," *Southern Daily*, Canton, May 5, 1961.

23. Fu Wen-yeh, "What is the basic working-day system?" *Daily Worker*, Peking, December 1, 1961;
"The problem of basic labour wages," *People's Daily*, Peking, April 3, 1962.

24. "More on the problem of basic labour wages," *People's Daily*, Peking, April 15, 1962;
Ts'ai Yuan-yuan and Teng Tse-hui, "A tentative discussion on methods of calculating pay for labour in rural people's communes—the system of recording work on a piece basis," *Kwang-ming Daily*, Peking, May 20, 1963;
Ch'eng Sheng and Hsu Chien, *op. cit.*

25. Liu Cheng, "Administration of norms in agricultural labour and estimating the work and recording the share," *Economic Research Journal (Ching-chi Yen-chiu)*, No. 8, Peking, August 17, 1961.

26. Ch'eng Sheng and Hsu Chien, *op. cit.;* Ch'in Tzu-ying, "Honestly make a good job of assessing work performance and recording work points," *People's Daily*, Peking, June 28, 1961;
Investigation Team of Lukouch'iao People's Commune, *op. cit.*

27. The Rural Work Section, CCP Kaochow *Hsien* Committee, "What should be reasonable remuneration for labour for cattle tenders?" *Southern Daily*, Canton, May 15, 1962.

28. Ho Chen-lu and Li Hui-chao, "The origin of the evaluation of a work-day at 2 *yuan*," *Southern Daily*, Canton, December 21, 1962.

29. Investigation Team of Lukouch'iao People's Commune, *op. cit.*

30. "Make a good job of the preliminary distribution of summer harvests," *People's Daily*, Peking, May 20, 1956;

Ch'eng Sheng and Hsu Chien, *op. cit.;*
Fan Ching-kuo, *op. cit.*

31. Chao Kuang, *op. cit.;*
"More on the problem of basic labour wages," *op. cit.*

32. *ibid.;*
Ch'eng Sheng and Hsu Chien, *op. cit.;*
Ch'in Tzu-ying, *op. cit.;*
Fan Ching-kuo, *op. cit.*

33. Correspondence Group of CCP Hsiyang *Hsien,* Shansi, "Introduction of piece-work rates leads to greater attention to quality of farm work," *People's Daily,* Peking, May 26, 1962;
also see CCP Heilungkiang Provincial Committee, "How the 'pay for labour according to output' system is enforced in Heilungkiang co-operatives," *People's Daily,* Peking, August 5, 1958;
Investigation Team of Lukouch'iao People's Commune, *op. cit.*

34. Ch'eng Sheng and Hsu Chien, *op. cit.;*
Ch'in Tzu-ying, *op. cit.;*
Investigation Team of Lukouch'iao People's Commune, *op. cit.*

35. "The ratio of three to seven," *op. cit.;*
Chin Ming, *op. cit.*

36. "Concerning the question of socialist distribution according to work," *Ta Kung Pao,* Peking, December 15, 1961.

Chapter V
The Institutional Consequences of Control

William Ogburn believed that technology is the prime cause of institutional changes. Back in the early days of automobiles and airplanes, Ogburn's thesis was amazingly accurate. His early works anticipated by nearly half a century the need for a presidential committee to deal with the effects of technology and science on American society. The Marxists, too, believe in the economic determinism of human history. The difference, however, lies in the passion of Communist ideology.

Perhaps the role of ideology in social change in China is too obvious to mention. The more interesting question is: what has happened there after nearly two decades of Communist-sponsored programs.

This section deals with various institutional consequences of Communist party control. Interesting questions include: what has happened to the many minor parties that existed before the revolution? If they are still allowed to function, what precisely are their functions—manifest or latent? What has happened to trade unions now that the proletariat has seized political power? If strong unionism is a function of strong capitalism, have trade unions ceased to exist, having achieved the goal for which they are formed? George P. Jan gives a clear and concise description of the state of minor political parties in China, while the official Communist party spokesman, the *Peking Review*, presents the main function of trade unions in a socialist society.

Leaders of a Communist country often pride themselves on the enormous progress made in health, education, and welfare. Since it has been a historical truism that Communism does not take place in economically more advanced countries, there always seems to be a great need to improve the health, welfare, and literacy in countries where Communism has been politically successful.

The gains in literacy on or throughout mainland China have been remarkable, considering the high fertility rate and the inherent difficulty of the written language. In order to reduce the illiterate portion of the population, it was first necessary to simplify the complicated ideography and to devise new teaching techniques. Beyond the literacy program, the regime faces enormous problems in secondary and higher education. Leo Orleans and R. D. Baredsen show how leaders in Peking deal with these problems, including the financing of this expensive task. For those who are curious about the state of the teaching profession, Theodore Chen's study, originally written for the U.S. Department of Health, Education, and Welfare, is most illuminating.

Little, however, has been said about family and youth. Among several available sources, Professor Yang's work gives concise answers to some general questions. Professor Vogel's painstaking work on the subject, which is still in preparation, promises to reveal more facts about family life in China. Professors Irene Taeuber and Leo Orleans have also done some work on this subject, but it is not *directly* related to the family. Denis Lazure makes some interesting observations on the Chinese personality from the viewpoint of a psychiatrist. Much more work on these subjects is needed.

For those who are interested in the concept of Communist morality and basic values, an interesting account which originally appeared in the *China News Analysis,* published in Hong Kong, may be worth noting. Corresponding to the familiar question, "Is God Dead?" it may be asked, "Is Confucius Dead?" by many who feel that perhaps Confucius is still the symbolic expression of a brilliant cultural heritage. Joseph Levenson may have the right, if not the complete, answer.

The Political Groups

28. MINOR PARTIES AND THEIR POLITICAL ROLES

GEORGE P. JAN

One of the characteristics of the Communist regime on the mainland of China thirteen years after its establishment is its continued tolerance of the existence of minor parties. This policy of the Communist party of China (hereafter C.P.C.) raises some interesting questions. Why does the C.P.C. continue to tolerate the existence of these minor parties? To what extent can these minor parties exert influence on the policies of Communist China? What are these parties and who are their leaders? What is their legal status in Communist China?

At the beginning of the People's Republic of China in 1949, there were 11 minor parties in the "coalition government."[1] One of them, the Chinese People's National Salvation Association, dissolved itself "honorably" on December 18, 1949, because it considered that its mission had been accomplished.[2] Two other minor parties, the Association of the Comrades of San Min Chu I and the Kuomintang Association for Promoting Democracy, were subsequently merged with the Kuomintang Revolutionary Committee and suspended their separate activities. Therefore, today there are only eight minor parties in Communist China.[3]

The elements of these minor parties are extremely complex. There are overlappings in their party membership. One individual often belongs to more than one minor party. In general, members of these minor parties can be classified into four major categories. The first category consists of leftist intellectuals. Their cooperation with the Communists is motivated by their patriotic sentiment and idealistic convictions. They were dissatisfied with the Kuomintang one-party rule and the unjust political, social and economic conditions in China. They believed that the Communist party could correct the evils of China. Most of them were not Communists although many of them had illusions

SOURCE: Selected from George P. Jan, "Minor Parties in Communist China," in *Current History*, September 1962, pp. 174–177 and 183. Reprinted by permission of Current History, Inc.

about the Communist party. To this very day few of them are Communist party members. In this category, there are many outstanding Chinese scholars in various fields. Many leaders in the minor political parties belong to this category, especially members of the China Democratic League.

The second category consists of the Kuomintang (the Chinese Nationalist Party) members who are opposed to Chiang Kaishek. Most of them are frustrated former Kuomintang officials and generals. Most of them, at one time or another, occupied high positions in the Kuomintang government. But they lost favor with Chiang Kai-shek or turned against him. This category includes most of the members of the Kuomintang Revolutionary Committee.

The third category consists of persons who are relatively unknown in Chinese politics. They are neither established scholars nor onetime high-ranking Kuomintang officials, but are for the most part opportunists trying to get government jobs through the bargaining power of the minor parties. This category includes many of the rank and file members of all the minor parties.

The fourth category consists of Communists who disguised themselves as non-Communists and penetrated into minor parties before 1949, such as Chou Hsin-min of the China Democratic League.[4] After 1949, the C.P.C. openly encouraged the Communists to join the Democratic League. In the last analysis, although all these minor parties are pro-Communist, not very many of their members are card-bearing Communists.[5] Even the official analysis of the Nationalist government on Taiwan did not classify most of their members as Communists.[6]

The original political platforms of these minor parties were not Communistic in orientation. For instance, the policy of the China Democratic League before 1949 resembled, in many ways, the concept of a multi-party parliamentary system.[7] While all the minor parties have their constitutions and platforms, in reality, they are organized on the basis more of personal following than specific principles. They rely on cooperation between well-known leaders and their respective personal followings. Because they hated the Kuomintang one-party rule, these parties allied themselves with the C.P.C. to oppose the Kuomintang. In 1949, they joined hands with the C.P.C. under a coalition government and thus established the People's Republic of China, generally referred to as Communist China. By now, for all practical purposes, the minor parties no longer have independent principles and policies contrary to those of the C.P.C. The best evidence of prove this point is the "Joint Message of Greetings to Chairman Mao" signed by six minor parties in 1960. In this message, the minor parties pledged to Mao that they would lean to socialism, listen to him and follow the C.P.C.[8]

The membership of these minor parties is unknown to outsiders. The only organizations that know their exact membership are perhaps the parties themselves and the C.P.C. However, it is safe to say that their membership cannot be large. Another interesting aspect about the minor parties is their financial support. There is evidence to indicate that they receive subsidy from the Communist government.[9] This gives the C.P.C. another means of controlling these parties.

The most active year of the minor parties under communism was 1949 when the Chinese People's Political Consultative Conference (hereafter

C.P.P.C.C.) held its first session. Under the category of party delegates in the C.P.P.C.C., there were 14 "democratic parties." Two of these were official Communist organizations, the Communist Party of China and the China New Democracy Youth Corps. Eleven of these were pro-Communist parties but not official Communist organizations. The "independents" were pro-Communist leaders claiming to be non-partisan independents.[10]

In the C.P.P.C.C. the Communist party refused to have more delegates than the Kuomintang Revolutionary Committee and the Democratic League.[11] Superficially it appeared that the latter two parties had equal representation with the Communist party. However, a close examination of the membership revealed the hypocritical gesture of the Communists. In the C.P.P.C.C. of 1949, 165 delegates were labeled as party delegates, 116 as regional delegates, 71 as military delegates, 235 as delegates from civic organization and 75 as special delegates. There were 662 delegates altogether including alternates.[12] Although the Communist party had equal representation with the Kuomintang Revolutionary Committee and the China Democratic League under the category of party delegates, the regional delegates and the military delegates were all Communists, and so were most of the delegates from civic organizations. The special delegates were mostly former Kuomintang officials who surrendered to the Communists and pro-Communist "independent leaders." The reality was that about two-thirds of the delegates in the C.P.P.C.C. were Communists, placing the C.P.P.C.C. under the effective control of the Communist party.

In the government established in 1949 under the Common Program adopted by the C.P.P.C.C., Mao Tse-tung was elected Chairman of the Central People's Government Council. Of the six Vice Chairmen of the same Council three were non-Communists. Of the 55 members of the same Council about 22 were non-Communists. The Premier of the Government Administrative Council was Chou En-lai. He was assisted by four Vice Premiers of whom two were non-Communists. Of the sixteen members of the Government Administrative Council nine were non-Communists. Of the thirty ministers and commissioners in the central government nine were non-Communists. The minor parties also occupied a number of subministry positions. Shen Chun-ju, a leader of the Democratic League, was even given the position of the President of the Supreme People's Court, roughly the counter-part of the Chief Justice of the United States.[13]

However, the minor parties felt the pressure of the C.P.C. not long after the first session of the C.P.P.C.C. In 1950, the C.P.C. ordered all the minor parties to revise their party programs.[14] They had to pledge support of the policies of the C.P.C. against the interest of their own classes. The C.P.C. forbade the minor parties to try to build up a large following. In 1951, the C.P.C. specified the groups from which each minor party might recruit members.[15]

For instance, in December, 1950, the Central Committee of the China Democratic League adopted a resolution concerning the development of the League's organization. In this resolution, the League decided that it should recruit members from bourgeois intellectuals, cultural and educational workers. It decided that it would not develop its organization in the People's Liberation Army including security forces, military organizations, military schools and military enterprises, nor intelligence agencies, revolutionary universities,[16] agencies dealing with diplomatic affairs, nor among minority nationalities. It also decided not to develop its organization in small cities and rural areas, and only to develop its organization in large cities which were political, economic and cultural centers.

These decisions were obviously made under the pressure of the C.P.C. for they seriously limited the area of activities of the Democratic League. This meant that the activities of the League were excluded not only from many government agencies, but also from rural areas, small cities and minority nationalities. This was a change from the League's policy before 1949 when it insisted on sharing political power in the central government as well as in local governments under a coalition government.[17]

The adoption of the constitution in 1954 further reduced the influence of the minor parties in the Communist government. Under the "Constitutional Government" of Communist China, the C.P.P.C.C. was reduced to a consultative institution according to Article 13 of the Common Program. It is no longer the legislature of the national government. The National People's Congress, the new national legislature, is not elected on a party basis. Of the 1226 deputies to the National People's Congress (hereafter N.P.C.) in 1954 the overwhelming majority were Communists. Of the 65 members of the Presidium of the N.P.C. in 1954, the majority were Communist deputies.[18] The N.P.C. also adopted the committee system to handle legislative bills. A close examination shows that in all the committees in 1954, the majority were Communists.

In the constitutional government of 1954, the minor party leaders were given some ten ministerial positions plus a number of subministry posts. Superficially, it seemed that the minor parties maintained roughly the same strength in the central government as they had done before 1954. Nevertheless, there were some major changes in the constitutional government in comparison with the government established under the Common Program in 1949. For instance, the number of deputy chiefs of state, the vice chairmen of the Central People's Government Council, was reduced from six to one. Therefore, all the five former non-Communist deputy chiefs of state were dropped. Although the position of deputy chief of state is more a position of prestige than influence, the Communists felt the need in 1949 to share this prestige with the minor parties. This made the government look more like a coalition government.

In 1954, the Communists apparently felt that they no longer needed to share this prestige with the minor parties. Tung Pi-wu, an old-time Communist leader, replaced Shen Chun-ju as the President of the Supreme People's Court. All the Vice Premiers were Communists, as compared to two non-Communist Vice Premiers out of a total of four Vice Premiers before 1954. Of the 15 Vice Chairmen of the National Defense Committee only 4 were former Kuomintang Generals; all the rest were Communists. Through further collectivization of the rural areas after 1954, the activity of minor parties at the local level became increasingly difficult.

By 1958, when the people's communes were introduced, the activity of minor parties in the countryside was virtually impossible. By the end of 1958, Communist China organized all the peasants into communes. Later, the Communists established many communes in smaller cities and a limited number of communes in large cities. Nowhere in the commune organization was the role of minor parties mentioned; the C.P.C. is the only party organization in the communes.

After the rectification and anti-rightist campaigns of 1957, the rightists were subdued. In the Second National People's Congress beginning in 1959 the strength of minor parties was further reduced. Of the 62 members of the Standing Committee of the N.P.C. only about a dozen or so were non-Communists. In the central government in 1959, of the 30 ministries and 32 commissions and agencies under the direct supervision of the Premier only about 10 were headed by non-Communists. In the central government today headed by Liu Shao-chi, all important positions above ministry level are headed by Communists with only a few exceptions.

It is true some of the minor party leaders were given positions in the Communist government. But do they have real power and influence? The position of the minor party leaders who participate in the government can be evaluated from a report submitted to the Standing Committee of the N.P.C. in 1956 by Li Wei-han, Director of the United Front Work Department of the C.P.C. Central Committee. In his report, Li pointed out that some Communist officials did not respect the authority of the non-Communist officials in the government, nor did they cooperate with non-Communist officials.[19]

It is safe to say that members of the minor parties who work in the Communist government do not have real political power concerning decision-making or even day-to-day routine administration. Although some of them are appointed as heads of ministries or commissions, actual power is in the hands of the vice ministers or deputy commissioners. The minor party leaders who head ministries or commissions or lower level government agencies are only figureheads.

The minor parties do not perform the function of opposition nor can they supervise the C.P.C. by criticism. A few minor party leaders who were naive enough to criticize the C.P.C. during the "Hundred Flowers Bloom" period in 1957 were ruthlessly purged. The participation of the minor parties in the Communist government is obviously not in the tradition of the multi-party parliamentary system that is practiced in the West.

The participation of minor parties in the Communist government is a false pretense of shared authority, a masked exercise of Communist one-party totalitarian dictatorship.

What will be the future of the minor parties in Communist China? The Communists have assured them that the united front will be continued beyond the attainment of socialism; as long as the C.P.C. exists, the minor parties will continue to exist.[20] But how sincere is this Communist assurance? The fate of the minor parties depends upon the policy of the C.P.C. The period of massacre is over in Communist China unless serious situations call for it. There is no indication that the Communists want to liquidate these parties by force. On the contrary, the C.P.C. has adopted a long range policy designed to reform these parties step by step. This is the so-called "soft-breeze-and-light-

328 The Political Groups

drizzle" policy.[21] This means that the minor parties will be transformed into socialist parties slowly and gently like a soft breeze and light drizzle. The process of transformation will be long, but it will be steady.

Notes

1. *Parties Collaborating with the Communists* (Fu Ni Tang Pai) (Taipei, Taiwan: Investigation Bureau, Ministry of Interior, the Republic of China, 1950), p. 1.

2. *Materials for the Study of the Great Charters of the People* (Jen Min Ta Hsien Chang Hsueh Hsi Tze Liao) (Tien Tsin, China: Lien Ho Tu Shu Chu Pan Sho, 1950), p. 171.

3. *People's Handbook* (Jen Min Shou Tso) (Peking: Hsin Hua Shu Tien, 1959), pp. 263–264.

4. Chu, Chu-yang, *How the Chinese Communist Party Treated the Democratic Parties* (Chung Kung Zen Yang Tui Tai Min Chu Tang Pai) (Kowloon: Yiu Lien Chu Pan Sho, 1952), p. 49.

5. *The Bright Road for Intellectuals* (Chi Shih Fen Tze Te Kuang Ming Tao Lu) (Canton, China: Kuang Ming Chu Pan Sho, 1952), p. 42. This is an official publication of the China Democratic League.

6. See *Parties Collaborating with the Communists.* The nature and composition of the minor parties in Communist China were analyzed at some length in this official publication of Nationalist China.

7. *Political Report of the Plenary Session of the Second Central Committee of the China Democratic League* (Min Chu Tung Meng Erh Chung Chuan Hui Cheng Chi Pao Kao) (Shanghai: Headquarters of the China Democratic League, 1947), p. 2.

8. *Current Background* (Hong Kong: American Consulate General, 1960), No. 639, p. 67.

9. *The Nature and Function of the China Democratic League* (Chung Kuo Min Chu Tung Men Te Hsing Chi Yu Jen Wu) (Canton, China: Kuang Ming Chu Pan Sho, 1950), p. 11. This is an official publication of the China Democratic League. Government subsidy is provided in Item 3 of Chapter 8 of the Constitution of the China Democratic League.

10. *Documents on the Establishment of the People's Republic of China* (Chung Hua Jen Min Kung Ho Kuo Kai Kuo Wen Hsien) (Hong Kong: Hsin Min Chu Chu Pan Sho, 1949), pp. 14–19.

11. *Materials for the Study of the Great Charters of the People,* p. 14.

12. *Documents on the Establishment of the People's Republic of China,* p. 13.

13. This analysis is based on the writer's examination of the name lists of the high-ranking government officials in the Central Chinese Government. See *Documents of the People's Political Consultative Conference* (Jen Min Cheng Hsieh Wen Chien) (Peking: Hsin Hua Shu Tien, 1950), on various pages.

14. Chu, Chu-yang, pp. 49–50.

15. Harold C. Hinton, " 'Democratic Parties': End of An Experiment?" *Problems of Communism,* No. 3, Vol. 7, 1958, p. 42.

16. These are special universities for the training of career revolutionaries for the Communist regime.

17. *Political Report of the Plenary Session of the Second Central Committee of the China Democratic League,* p. 26.

18. *Documents of the First Plenary Session of the First National People's Congress of the People's Republic of China* (Chung Hua Jen Min Kung Ho Kuo Ti Yi Chieh Chuan Kuo Jen Min Tai Piao Ta Hui Ti Yi Tse Hui Yi Wen Chien) (Peking: Jen Min Chu Pan Sho, 1954), p. 146.

19. *Documents of the Third Plenary Session of the First National People's Congress of the People's Republic of China* (Chung Hua Jen Min Kung Ho Kuo Ti Yi Chieh Chuan Kuo Jen Min Tai Piao Ta Hui Ti San Tse Hui Yi Wen Chien) (Peking: Jen Min Chu Pan Sho, 1956), p. 296.

20. *The People's Daily* (Jenmin Jihpao), September, 1956, p. 1.

21. *Current Background*, No. 639, 1960, p. 3.

29.   TRADE UNIONS IN COMMUNIST CHINA

PEKING REVIEW

May 1, International Labor Day, 1965 marked the 40th anniversary of the All-China Federation of Trade Unions. The following is a brief account of the history of the Trade Union Movement as given by the *Peking Review,* a government weekly publication in English.

China's trade unions were formed and developed under the direct leadership of the Chinese Communist Party.

Soon after its foundation in 1921, the Communist Party set up the Chinese Trade Union Secretariat to lead the working class movement. The secretariat was in fact the earliest national leading body of China's trade unions. The First All-China Labour Congress held in Canton in 1922 by the representatives of 270,000 members recognized it as the liaison centre for trade unions throughout the country. The All-China Federation of Trade Unions (A.C.F.T.U.) was formally set up at the Second All-China Labour Congress held in Canton in 1925 were 540,000 members were represented.

Early Role

From the beginning, the Chinese trade union movement played an important part in the Chinese people's democratic revolution led by the Chinese Communist Party. The first wave of strikes took place between January 1922 and February 1923. In a little over a year more than 100 strikes were called in the major cities and industrial centres. These included the well-known Hongkong seamen's strike which began in January and ended victoriously in March 1922; the successful Anyuan coalminers' strike in September 1922; and the February 7 strike of Peking-Hankow railway workers in 1923 which shook the whole country. During this wave of strikes trade union organizations sprang up one after another. Soon after its founding, the A.C.F.T.U. led the great

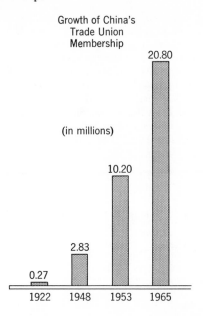

Growth of China's
Trade Union
Membership

(in millions)

20.80

10.20

2.83

0.27

1922   1948   1953   1965

"May 30" strike of 1925 against the Japanese and British imperialists, and the Canton-Hongkong strike which lasted 16 months from June 1925 to October 1926. These strikes gave a powerful impetus to the Chinese people's struggle against imperialism.

In 1927, Chiang Kai-shek collaborated with the imperialists and the domestic feudal forces, betrayed the revolution, and began massacring workers and peasants and brutally suppressing the working-class movement. The A.C.F.T.U. was forced to go underground.

In the long years from 1927 to 1949, the Chinese people fought against the imperialists and the Kuomintang reactionaries in order to overthrow the rule of imperialism, feudalism and bureaucrat-capitalism. During that period, the Chinese working-class movement and trade unions led by the Communist Party were active in two different areas: in the enemy-controlled areas they co-ordinated their work with the armed struggle in the countryside, carried out both legal and illegal, open and secret, economic and political struggles to win over the bulk of the working class, build up their strength and make preparations for the final decisive battle. In the revolutionary base areas they rallied and educated the workers to raise their level of class consciousness and labour enthusiasm and strengthen labour discipline so as to ensure the fulfillment of production tasks, develop industry, consolidate and expand the revolutionary base areas, and give substantial support to the fighting front.

During the War of Resistance Against Japan (1937–45), the trade unions organized the broad masses of workers to carry out with other sections of the population anti-Japanese activities. After Japan's surrender, the trade unions waged struggles against the U.S. imperialists and the Chiang Kai-shek clique and took an active part in the patriotic democratic movement of the Chinese people.

In 1948, on the eve of liberation, the Sixth All-China Labour Congress was held in Harbin and the A.C.F.T.U. resumed open activities. In response to the call of the congress, workers in the liberated areas launched a vigorous campaign to boost production; those in Kuomintang-controlled areas waged patriotic anti-U.S. struggles together with people of other strata and protected their factories and mines from Kuomintang sabotage in anticipation of liberation.

With the founding of the People's Republic of China, the Chinese working class became the leading class of the state, and the workers masters in their own house. This created most favourable conditions for developing the working-class movement and trade union work. The A.C.F.T.U. rallied all sections of workers and became the broadest mass organization of the working class. When the Seventh All-China Congress of Trade Unions was held in 1953, the federation had 10,200,000 members; the number rose to 16,300,000 at the time of the eighth congress in 1957. Today, the federation boasts more than 20 million members. Its organizations at all levels are active in many fields and play an important part in China's socialist revolution and socialist construction.

Nature and Tasks Under Socialism

China's trade unions are mass organizations of the working class led by the Communist Party. They are the Party's assistant in mass work and a link through which the Party keeps in touch with the masses, a social pillar of the people's democratic state power, and a school of communism for the workers.

In the period of the socialist revolution and socialist construction, the central task of the trade unions is to educate the workers in the spirit of communism, encourage them to work hard to boost production, and, on the basis of production growth, work to improve their material and cultural life.

The prime task of the trade unions at the present time is to continue to hold high the banner of Mao Tse-tung's thinking, take class struggle as the key and build their work around production and construction. It is to go to the grass-roots and mobilize the workers to take an active part in the socialist education movement, help revolutionize their ideology further, and develop and deepen the movement to "compare with the advanced, learn from and catch up with them, and help the less advanced"—a movement to increase production and practise economy. The aim to bring about a new upsurge in production, fulfil and overfulfil the 1965 state plan, and prepare for the implementation of the Third Five-Year Plan which is scheduled to begin in 1966.

Political and Ideological Work. Trade union work in China is work dealing with man. First place is given to political and ideological work. Workers and their families are educated in socialism and especially in the class struggle. The purpose is to acquaint them with the situation in the class struggle both at home and abroad and the Party's principles and policies, continuously raise their level of class consciousness, and in this way bring their initiative and creativeness into play to fulfil the tasks in production and construction assigned to them by the state.

The trade unions help the workers study the works of Comrade Mao Tse-tung by the method of "studying to find a solution to a particular problem on hand, integrating study with application, studying and currently applying what has been learnt."

In every field of work, the trade unions adhere to the principle of the "four firsts." This means: giving first place to man in handling the relationship between man and material things; giving first place to political work in handling the relationship between political and other work; giving first place to ideological work in handling the relationship between ideological and routine tasks in political work; and giving first place to living ideas in handling the relationship between ideas in books and living ideas in ideological work. This principle is applied in work to help boost production, in welfare work, and activities among the workers' families, and in carrying out other tasks of the trade unions. In this way, the trade unions closely integrate their political and ideological work with their routine work. Attention is focused on ideological work at the basic level—the work teams and shifts.

Work to Help Boost Production. All trade union work is designed to help enhance the workers' political conciousness and boost production. The trade unions undertake to organize enterprises and workers to take part in the movement to "compare, learn, catch up and help" so as to enable more enterprises and workers to achieve the goal of "five goods." For enterprises, this means good political work, fulfillment of production plans, efficient management, good living arrangements for workers, and a good working style of cadres. For individual workers it means a high level of political consciousness, competent fulfilment of tasks, strict observance of labour discipline, persistence in studies, and unity and mutual help with others.

The trade unions actively assist the managements in mobilizing the workers to take part in the technical revolution and the introduction of technical innovations. Trade union organizations help to organize extensive technical co-operation among workers and get the workers, technical personnel and leading cadres to co-operate closely to solve key problems in production. Efforts are made to spread experience that has been tested and proved in practice. Trade unions also help to organize inter-plant emulation and co-operation.

Welfare Work. The trade unions work constantly to improve the material and cultural lives of the workers and to educate them correctly to link their immediate interests with the long-term interests of the working class, and to combine their personal interests properly with those of the collective.

The administration of the labour insurance fund is entrusted to the trade unions by the state. China's workers today enjoy the benefits of a very comprehensive system of labour insurance with all the expenses borne by the managements. The system gives wide assistance in relation to childbirth, old age, sickness, injury, disablement and death. Workers who may have financial difficulties are helped out with grants from trade union funds.

There are more than 2,800 sanatoria, rest homes and overnight sanatoria with a total of 90,000 beds run by the trade unions, factories, mines and other enterprises.

The trade unions assist the managements in running collective welfare establishments such as workers' housing estates, canteens, medical and health centres, public baths, nurseries and kindergartens. This is done by organizing the workers to take part in the democratic management of these undertakings.

Educational Work. In co-operation with the managements and other departments concerned, the trade unions organize workers' spare-time education to extend general knowledge and raise technical levels. In many large and medium-sized enterprises, a comprehensive spare-time educational system has been established, ranging from literacy classes to spare-time study at the university level.

The trade unions help to organize workers' recreational activities as a means to educate them in socialism and enrich their cultural life.

International Activities. True to the spirit of proletarian internationalism, China's trade unions actively support the revolutionary struggles of workers in other countries and strive to strengthen workers' unity throughout the world. Together with workers the world over and progressive mankind, China's trade unions wage struggles against imperialism headed by the United States, and for world peace, national liberation, people's democracy and socialism.

Structure and Organizational Principles

China's trade unions are organized on both an industrial and regional basis. This means that all members of the same enterprise, government office, or educational institution, irrespective of their specific jobs, are organized in the same primary trade union. These primary organizations at places of work are the foundation of China's trade unions. Today, there are 160,000 of them. The bigger primary organizations may set up workshop or department committees to guide the activities of the trade union groups under them.

Industrial unions are organized on national and provincial levels. There are today 16 national trade union committees (see box on p. 23). The number of provincial industrial unions in a province (or autonomous region, or municipality directly under the central authority such as Peking and Shanghai) depends on the distribution of industry in that province and the actual needs of trade union work.

There are also provincial, autonomous regional, municipal and county trade union councils not organized on an industrial, but on a regional basis. These give unified leadership to all trade union organizations in their respective areas, including the local industrial unions at the same level. There are today 21 provincial, two municipal (Peking and Shanghai) and five autonomous regional trade union councils, the last of which—for the Tibet region—was set up last December. Its formation reflects the rapid growth of industry and a working class in Tibet.

The primary trade unions are led in the first place by the local trade union councils as indicated above. But they are also led by the corresponding industrial trade union committee at a higher level where there is one. Both local trade union councils and national industrial unions are led by the A.C.F.T.U. which is the national leading body of China's trade union movement. Trade union organizations at all levels are led by the Communist Party committee at the same level.

The executive committee of the A.C.F.T.U. is elected at the national trade union congress. When the committee is not in session, the presidium of the A.C.F.T.U. is responsible for carrying out the decisions of the national congress and the executive committee and gives leadership to trade union work throughout the country. Guided by the presidium, the secretariat has charge of A.C.F.T.U.'s day-to-day work.

The A.C.F.T.U. has under it a general office and departments for production, education, propaganda, sports and physical culture, workers' living conditions, labour insurance, organization, women workers, international liaison, and other work. It also runs a training school for cadres and publishes the newspaper *Gongren Ribao* (Workers' Daily).

The basic organizational principle of China's trade unions is democratic centralism—centralism based on democracy and democracy under centralized guidance. Its main content is:

1. The leading bodies of the trade unions at all levels are democratically elected.

2. The leading bodies of the trade unions at all levels observe the principle of integrating collective leadership with personal responsibility. All matters of importance are discussed and decided upon collectively.

3. The trade unions at all levels carry on their work in accordance with the Constitution of the Trade Unions and decisions of trade union organizations. They submit reports on their work at regular intervals to the membership and give heed to criticisms and opinions voiced by members or lower organizations.

4. Every member must carry out trade union decisions. The minority abides by the decisions of the majority, and the lower trade union organizations abide by the decisions of the higher bodies.

This principle of democratic centralism makes it possible correctly to handle the relationship between unions and their members, among members, and between higher and lower trade union bodies. It enables the leaders to follow the mass line in every field of work, thus bringing the trade union organizations closer to their membership, and bringing the initiative of trade unions at all levels and of their members into full play to accomplish trade union tasks successfully.

Education

30. AN OVER-VIEW OF CHINA'S EDUCATION

Leo Orleans

China's constitution states that "citizens of the People's Republic of China have a right to education." In their attempt to make this right a reality, the Communists had to overcome most of the problems that had faced the previous regimes. The difficulties in attaining their goals are reflected in the often unsystematic and haphazard nature of the numerous educational reforms. Such success as they achieved was primarily the result of comprehensive centralized control over the population, the willingness to spend the necessary funds for the expansion of educational facilities and also the willingness to sacrifice quality in order to provide at least some education for the great masses of the population. Under the direction of the Ministry of Education and, of course, the indomitable leadership of the Communist Party, the educational system has undergone a number of major reorganizations and reorientations which have affected not only the administration and curriculums but the basic principles of education as well.

The basic educational reform of the new regime was adopted by the Administrative Council of the Chinese People's Republic on August 10, 1951. It provided for the types of schools, the length of the various courses, age limits, and requirements; however, for the most part, the system retained the structure that the Nationalists had given it. Most of the difference was in the approach and in the philosophy. Ch'ien Chun-jui, Vice Minister of Education, summarized it as follows:

1. It clearly and completely guarantees to all the people in the country, first of all the workers and peasants, an opportunity to receive education.
2. It establishes the appropriate position and system of technical schools,

SOURCE: Selected from Leo Orleans, *Professional Manpower and Education in Communist China* (National Science Foundation Publication NSF 61-3), Washington, D.C.: The United States Government Printing Office, 1960, pp. 11–14 and 31–45.

specialized schools and colleges, and special courses in order to meet the need for training large numbers of persons for national reconstruction.

3. It guarantees to all young and old-type intellectual elements an opportunity to receive revolutionary political training and to all working cadres an opportunity to receive further education.

4. It correctly integrates uniformity of policy and objectives on the one hand with flexibility of method and procedure on the other.[1]

The influence of the Soviet Union on the Chinese education system is undeniable. Although the attempt has been to learn from Soviet experience and try to adapt this experience to the peculiar conditions and needs of China, there have been numerous complaints of blind imitation of things Russian, although usually these criticisms have been quite specific and have not extended to the system as a whole. One of the more frequent expressions of resentment in connection with education refers to the wholesale translation of Soviet textbooks, many of which are obsolete, and many of whose methods and examples are quite foreign to the Chinese student. During the single year of 1953, 277 translations of Soviet textbooks were published for use in Chinese schools. The demand for Soviet technical and scientific literature has been even greater; between 1949 and 1955, about 2,000 titles were translated into Chinese.[2] The total number of Russian books translated into Chinese is considerably larger: between 1950 and 1957, 190 million copies of 12,400 books were printed and distributed.[3]

The Party maintains rigid control not only over the educational system, as such, but over every school through Party representatives who have more authority than any of the professional educators. These representatives must approve the curriculum, all student activities, all promotions and graduations, appointment of teachers, and every other phase of school activity.

The political and practical education of youth is given an emphasis equal to that of the basic subject matter studied. Ideological indoctrination and orientation permeate every lesson. Time is set aside daily for group meetings and political discussions. . . .

Utilizing this concept of education, the Communists are able to report figures implying that perhaps a quarter of the population of China is attending some type of "educational" course. Although this total by no means implies that one-fourth of the Chinese people have experienced some type of formal education in the Western sense, the Communist Chinese have in fact made great progress in expanding the educational system of the country.

Two ministries under the State Council were established to take charge of education. The Ministry of Education was inaugurated in October 1949 and the Ministry of Higher Education was set up in November 1952. The latter was abolished in February 1958, leaving the Ministry of Education as the highest government authority for the control of all levels and types of education. The Ministry issues directives in respect to the administration and organization of schools, curriculums, textbooks, and methodology to education bureaus and educational and cultural offices in provinces, municipalities, and special districts. These bureaus and offices are nominally under the control of People's Committees at their corresponding levels, but actually they are under the leadership and close surveillance of individual members of the Communist Party. . . .

Although central direction and control persists, the recent trend has been more and more toward decentralization, giving local administrative organs and even individual schools (still under Party leadership) some authority in planning, organizing, financing, and maintaining the schools, depending upon local conditions and needs. . . .

Primary Schools

The development of primary schools in China has been rapid, particularly during the early years of the Communist regime. The highest growth occurred between 1950–51 and 1952–53, when the primary school enrollment increased by over 75 per cent. On the other hand, during the next 4 years, enrollment increased by only 2 million. Between 1955–56 and 1956–57 there was a 10 million jump in the number of children in school; there was a very slight increase in 1957–58; then there was the 22 million "leap forward" in 1958–59 enrollment (Table 1).

Although there is usually variation in reported proportions of school-age children in school in any one year, the trend cannot be disputed, as evidenced by two sources: 50.7 per cent in 1953, 61.3 per cent in 1956, 85 per cent

TABLE 1. *Primary Schools, 1948–60*
[In thousands]

School year	Entrants	Enrollment	Graduates
1948–49	–	–	[1]2,387
1949–50	–	[1]24,391	[1]2,829
1950–51	–	[1]28,924	[1]4,232
1951–52	–	[1]43,154	[1]5,942
1952–53	–	[1]51,100	[1]9,945
1953–54	–	[1]51,664	[1]10,136
1954–55	–	[1]51,218	[1]10,254
1955–56	[2]17,500	[1]53,126	[1]12,287
1956–57	–	[1]63,464	[1]12,307
1957–58	[3]16,169	[1]64,279	[1]16,225
1958–59	[4]20,170	[1]86,400	–
1959–60	–	[5]90,000	–

Blanks indicate figures are not available.

[1] *Ten Great Years* (Peking: State Statistical Bureau, 1960).
[2] *New China News Agency*, Sept. 1, 1955.
[3] *New China News Agency*, July 1, 1957.
[4] *Ibid*, Feb. 13, 1958.
[5] *Ibid*, Jan. 22, 1960.

Structure of Educational System (circa 1960)

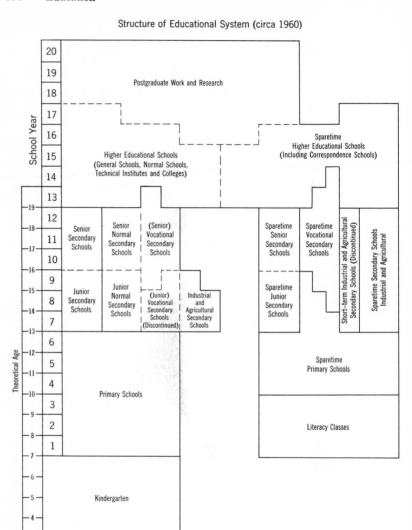

in 1957 and 1958, and 87 per cent in 1959 and 1960.[4] Although none of the reports is specific in what is meant by school-age children, they obviously refer to children of primary school age, or roughly between 7 and 12 years of age. The quoted percentages seem to be more or less consistent with estimated age distribution of China's population . . . however, this consistency ignores one important fact: Because of the large number of overaged children attending primary schools, the actual number of pupils who are between 7 and 12 constitute a much smaller proportion of the total number of "school-age" children than reports would indicate. As the years go by, the increase in the participation rate will be much less rapid for two reasons: (1) There is a normal slowing up as the proportion in school approaches the school-age population, and (2) the increase in school attendance of children 7 through 12 will to some extent be counteracted by the decrease in the number of overaged children. In any case, it is unlikely that the announced target to achieve universal primary education by the mid-1960's will be attained.

A word of caution about the statistics in the number of graduates from primary schools, as presented in Table 1: Both the magnitude of the figures and the discrepancy between them and other reports point to the probability that there is an element of double counting. Since the majority of children, particularly in rural areas, have not been going beyond the lower primary school, they were counted as primary school graduates after completing 3 or 4 years of school. Those who went on to senior primary school were counted again after completing the second 3 years of primary school. This may be illustrated by comparing the enrollment with the graduates after subtracting the number of entrants for the current year. Thus, by subtracting 17,500,000 entrants from the 53,126,000 enrolled in 1955–56, a figure of 35,626,000 is obtained, which represents an impossibly high 3:1 ratio between enrollment and graduates for a 6-year school.

Other figures in different sources reporting the number of primary school graduates seem more realistic and probably represent the actual number of graduates from the full 6-year elementary schools. (From late 1951 to late 1953, primary schools consisted of only five grades.) For example, it was reported that during the period 1952–53 through 1955–56 there were 13,370,000 graduates[5] as opposed to a total of 42,622,000 derived from Table 1. Another report states that for the inclusive period 1949–50 through 1956–57,[6] there were 22 million primary school graduates, versus 67,932,000 in table 1. In both instances there is a reasonably stable relationship between the two figures: 31.2 per cent and 32.9 per cent. This relationship suggests that perhaps the differences have a basis and that the higher totals include anyone who had completed at least 3 years of primary school.

Prior to 1952 there was little standardization in the texts used in primary schools, and every province and many individual schools had their own books, depending on what was available. Starting with 1952, there was an attempt to standardize textbooks, but in all probability there is still a considerable variety of books used in millions of primary classes throughout China.

Because of the special difficulties in learning the Chinese characters, the primary school curriculums assign half of the study time in grades 1 to 4 and one-third in grades 5 to 6 to the study of language (see appendix table B-1). Ideally, during the 6 years in primary school the children should master 4,000 characters. An hour a day is also devoted to arithmetic. Both political training and practical extracurricular activities also form an integral part of the curriculum. Particular emphasis on production was introduced in 1958. It would seem reasonable to assume that because of the nature of agricultural work, the children in the rural areas are expected to contribute somewhat greater time to work than do their counterparts in the cities, whose usefulness in factories and other urban enterprises would be much more limited.

Secondary Schools

The secondary schools in China are divided into the general and the specialized secondary schools. The general (sometimes translated as "ordinary") secondary schools are essentially academic in character and consist of 3-year junior and 3-year senior schools, or a total of 6 years. The specialized secondary schools are subdivided into two types: The normal or teachers' schools and the vocational schools. Theoretically, both are divided into the lower and higher levels of 3 years each. Actually, the structure is not that precise: Depending on the particular course and school, the term of study may fluctuate anywhere from 2 to 6 years. . . .

SECONDARY GENERAL SCHOOLS

The secondary general schools supply the overwhelming majority of students who go on into higher education. . . .

The development of these schools has been more rapid than that of the specialized secondary schools—either the normal (or teachers' schools) or the vocational schools. The sharp increase in the enrollment between 1957 and 1958 may be attributed to the creation of the so-called agricultural middle schools "and other industrial schools" (falling within the secondary general-school category) on the communes. Although this type of school would more appropriately fall under the vocational heading, enrollment statistics suggest that in most instances they are included in the secondary general schools. In 1958 these schools had 2 million students,[7] comprising 70 per cent of the total increase over the previous year. No further breakdown of this figure is available; however, the increase has been especially apparent at the junior secondary level, where in a single year the number of students increased by 3 million. Undoubtedly the "middle schools" in the communes are limited to the first three grades and the overwhelming majority of the senior secondary general schools are still located in the urban areas.

Although the secondary general schools now number 20,000,[8] those on the communes are in no way comparable to those in the cities. The rural schools "closely combine theory and practice" and "carry out extensive research on their own farms." A sample investigation of secondary agricultural schools in Kiangsu Province in 1959 showed that they were "inadequate and inferior in their material equipment and teaching staffs as compared to the secondary general full-time schools."[9] Of course the article then goes on to state that "under the leadership of the Party, with the support of the masses and the strenuous efforts of the teachers and students," the schools are constantly improving. The same article mentions one interesting reaction to agricultural schools: "What is the use for farmers to study farming?" The obvious answer, according to the Communist, is increased production and the fact that the students learn more than just farming. For example, one secondary agricultural school has opened six special courses: ". . . agricultural techniques, tool manufacturing, animal husbandry, veterinary medicine, civil engineering, gardening, and silkworm raising."[10] It would appear safe to assume that a completed primary education is not necessarily a prerequisite for these schools. It is even safer to assert that these schools confuse the educational statistics even further. . . .

Students in secondary general schools have been spending approximately 30 hours per week in classwork. Since 1958 an increasing amount of their time has been spent in production; however, it is difficult to determine precisely to what extent these extracurricular activities have limited classwork. It seems probable that much of the productive work expected of students in the cities is contributed outside of the school hours, except as it may relate to specific courses. Because of the nature of agriculture, the contribution of the students in rural schools is probably more seasonal and more intensive than in the urban areas. In October 1958 students from over 20,000 secondary schools were asserted to be running "170,000 small factories, producing over 4,000 simple machines and 1,700,000 tons of organic and chemical fertilizer. They have more than 16,000 experimental farms and are getting good harvests."[11] This is very impressive until one stops to consider that the figures imply that every school has an average of over eight "small factories"; that each school built an average of one-fifth of a "simple machine," which need not be anything more than an agricultural implement; and that probably all of the fertilizer was organic and not chemical.

As for the regular curriculum in secondary general schools, about 40 per cent of the total class time is devoted to Chinese language and literature, history, and political education. About 26 per cent of the time is allotted to mathematics and physics, and 17 per cent to geography, biology, and chemistry. The remaining hours are devoted to physical education, music, and art. One obvious gap in many of the schools is the absence of training in foreign languages. Until recently, students went to special language schools, and only a limited number of secondary schools provided language courses in the regular curriculum. In 1959, however, Yang Hsiu-feng, Minister of Education, quoted Chou En-lai as stating that "foreign language courses should be required throughout high school."[12] Undoubtedly the number of city schools offering language courses will increase in the future. . . .

NORMAL (OR TEACHERS') SCHOOLS

Like the secondary general schools, normal schools are theoretically divided into 3-year junior and 3-year senior schools. Actually, the length of the courses does not seem to be that precise—some courses may run anywhere from 2 to 4 years at each level. Entrants to the junior level must have completed the 6-year primary school, while entrants to the senior normal schools must have graduated from either the general or the normal junior secondary school. Theoretically, graduates from both levels of the normal school are required to serve in primary schools for a specified number of years, after which time the graduates of senior normal schools may then be promoted to teach in the junior level of the secondary general schools. Actually, because of the shortage of teachers, many go on to teach in the secondary general school system, upon graduation, without the primary school experience. Presumably to avoid the possibility of teenagers' teaching students who are virtually the same age, the Ministry of Education decreed in 1955 that candidates for normal schools must be at least 15 years old and not more than 30.[13] A further comment on the quality of normal-school students (future teachers), is the fact that the most promising students are channeled into the secondary general schools. Thus, the normal schools find themselves with average and below-average students as well as with reputations as second-rate schools; this, in turn, prompts fresh graduates from primary schools to seek admittance to the schools with the greater prestige—the general schools.

The curriculums in normal schools are very similar to the ones in secondary general schools, except that there are courses in educational techniques and time is allotted for practice teaching. To some extent the curriculums vary with the type of normal school. In 1954, for example, the following distribution of some 369,000 students and 791 schools was reported: 357 senior normal schools training teachers for junior secondary and junior normal schools, with 111,291 students; 7 schools training kindergarten teachers, with 6,755 students; 427 junior normal schools for future primary school teachers, with 251,132 students.[14] The same source stated that among these students there were 95,266 women, or only 25.8 per cent of the enrollment in secondary normal schools.

Despite the acute need for more and more teachers, normal-school education has been developing at a relatively slow pace. It was not until 1958–59 that enrollment in these schools doubled. Although data are reported on the total number of graduates from specialized schools, it is not broken down between secondary normal and secondary vocational schools. . . .

It is anticipated that the shortage of qualified teachers will persist for at least a decade in the cities and even longer in the countryside; therefore enrollment in secondary normal schools may be expected to increase for some time to come. Despite the need and the increase in absolute numbers, the proportion of normal-school students to the total number in specialized schools has been declining steadily from 66 per cent in 1949–50 to 41 per cent in 1955–56. It is estimated that in 1958–59 this decline was arrested and that enrollment in normal schools was 42 per cent of the total specialized-school enrollment. . . .

VOCATIONAL SCHOOLS

There is perhaps more confusion in the data dealing with secondary vocational education than with any other type of training. There is a strong impression that this confusion is not limited to persons outside China—that the Chinese themselves are bogged down in the fluid and ambiguous system that was set up and frequently revised for the training of middle-level technical specialists.

The often vague terminology and imprecise categories make it necessary to depend on a close familiarity with quantitative data to seek the proper interpretation of the material. For example, the Chinese term "chuan-yeh" is used to signify both types of specialized schools (normal and vocational) and vocational schools as such. This confusion is magnified in translation. The broad category of specialized schools, the vocational schools, and the industrial (or engineering) courses of vocational schools are interchangeably translated as "vocational," "technical," "trade," or "specialized" schools.

Originally, the vocational schools were set up in two 3-year levels, like the other secondary schools. This does not seem to be the case at present, and the earlier distinction between lower and higher vocational schools has been abandoned. Even when the distinction was apparently in effect, separate data on enrollment in the two levels was rare, while at present it seems to be nonexistent. One source did give such a breakdown for 1954,[15] showing the following enrollment for junior and senior vocational schools respectively: 1950–51, 22,651 and 75,172; 1951–52, 38,912 and 124,028; 1952–53, 77,109 and 213,337; 1953–54, 56,282 and 243,712. The initial reaction is that the figures were inadvertently reversed, since the enrollment in the senior classes is from three to four times greater than in the junior classes. The text, however, suggests that these figures are presented correctly for in 1953, in the process of reorganizing secondary vocational schools, a policy was adopted of "gradual retrenchment and cessation of student recruitment for the junior vocational schools." The numbers in the junior level did in fact decrease, but this did not affect the enrollment at the senior level, which kept increasing. The most direct evidence of the abandonment of the two-level system is in the reports of the established length of study for the various specialties in vocational schools:

The secondary vocational schools, which train technicians of intermediate grade in more than 200 professions, will enroll graduates of junior secondary schools. Schooling period for courses of industry is 3 to 4 years; for courses of agriculture, forestry, public health, and other professions, 3 years; and for courses of accounting and economic planning, 2½ years.[16]

In other words, entrants must have already completed 3 years of the secondary school before starting on a 2½- to 4-year course in a vocational school. Even this does not seem to be universal, however, for in some instances primary graduates may go into "certain" vocational courses.

Another difficulty is in the fact that there is a considerable amount of overlapping between on-the-job training, spare-time education, and certain vocational schools. This is especially true of industrial and technical training which during the past few years has become so closely integrated with industrial enterprises. To a lesser extent, this condition exists in all other types of vocational schools.

At present most of the vocational schools are of three types. The first is established directly by one or more industrial enterprises and is supposed to improve the cultural-technical level of the workers in the given enterprises. The second type is attached to a particular plant or enterprise—that is, an existing school is given to a particular enterprise, which administers it, facilitating the organization and training of workers and employees for its specific requirements. The third type of vocational school is still more or less independent but maintains a semiformal relationship with one or more enterprises because of the requirement for all students to participate in production. The makeup of the student body is to some extent revealed in the following announcement:

In order to fulfill the student-enrollment quota in the secondary vocational schools this year, the Ministry of Higher Education appealed to all places to strive to augment the sources of students and to mobilize junior secondary school graduates from the past few years to submit their applications. It also appealed to all factories, mining enterprises, government organs and people's organizations to encourage their young workers having a cultural level equivalent to junior secondary school to enter secondary vocational schools.[17]

The confusion has been intensified by the fact that most of the workers attend some type of school, while all the students participate in some form of productive activity in the enterprise associated with or running the school. It is therefore difficult to compare the enrollment in spare-time vocational training with data given for vocational schools. . . .

The extent to which the State depends on vocational schools versus on-the-job training may be gleaned from the fact that during the 3 years 1954–56, the enterprises under the Ministry of Textile Industry trained 37,656 persons on the production line and 8,250 workers in vocational schools.[18] Although this example may not be typical, it is nevertheless indicative of the emphasis.

Despite this confusion of concepts and numbers, it is clear that, realizing the shortage of intermediate technical personnel, the Communists have tried to emphasize secondary vocational education. The reported enrollment in these schools has grown from 77,100 in 1949–50 to 337,000 in 1956–57 and at present is probably approaching 1 million. Nevertheless, considering the need, the progress has not been impressive: Over a 10-year period the secondary vocational schools had graduated only an estimated 740,000. During this 10-year period there was a major shift in emphasis in the field of training in vocational schools: In 1949–50, only 27.8 per cent of the students were taking training in technical and industrial courses; in 1955–56 the percentage had reached 55.8; and in 1957–58 it increased to 58.9. It is estimated that by 1957–58, roughly 300,000 graduated from technical and industrial courses of secondary vocational schools, or about half of the total number of graduates from vocational schools.

Notes

1. *Jen-min Chiao-yu* [People's Education], November 1951.

2. Pin Min, *Istoriya Kitaysko-Sovetskoy Druzhby* [History of Sino-Soviet Friendship] (Moskva: 1959), p. 341.

3. *Shih-chieh Chih-shih* [World Knowledge], No. 3, Feb 5, 1958.

4. *New China News Agency,* Sept. 19, 1959; *Hung-ch'i* [Red Flag], No. 3, Feb. 1, 1960.

5. *New China News Agency,* Sept. 24, 1956.

6. *Chiao-shih Pao* [Teachers' Biweekly], Oct. 1, 1957; translated by U.S. Joint Publications Research Service, in Rept. No. 753, Oct. 16, 1958: *Education in Communist China.*

7. *Ten Great Years* (Peking: State Statistical Bureau, 1960).

8. *New China News Agency,* Feb. 11, 1960.

9. *Hung-ch'i* [Red Flag], No. 9, May 1, 1959.

10. *Ibid.*

11. *Fu-tao yuan* [Instructor], No. 10, Oct. 12, 1959; translated by U.S. Joint Publications Research Service, in Rept. No. 1165-D, Feb. 12, 1960.

12. *Hsin-hua Pan-yueh-k'an* [New China Semimonthly Journal], No. 11, June 10, 1959.

13. *Jen-min Jih-pao* [People's Daily], June 17, 1955.

14. *Jen-min Chiao-yu* [People's Education], October 1954.

15. *Jen-min Chiao-yu* [People's Education], October 1954.

16. *New China News Agency,* June 15, 1956.

17. *Ibid.,* June 17, 1957.

18. *Wo-kuo Kang-t'ieh, Tien-li, Mei-t'an, Chi-hsieh, Fang-chih, Tsao-chih Kung-yeh Ti Chin Hsi* [Pas and Present of China's Iron and Steel, Electric-Power, Coal, Machine-Building, Textile, and Paper Industries] (Peiping. July 1958).

31. THE INNOVATION OF HALF-WORK AND

HALF-STUDY SCHOOLS

Robert D. Baredsen

The Agricultural Middle Schools

In expanding secondary schools in rural areas, initial efforts naturally had to be concentrated at the junior, or lower, secondary level. The reasons why a special type of junior middle school was deemed necessary in these areas were primarily economic. On the one hand, the regime felt it was unable to support a general academic-type junior middle school education for the great numbers of primary school graduates then emerging into the countryside. On the other hand, it saw a great need for a vast number of young people who possessed a minimal ninth-grade general education and who had in addition some knowledge of modern scientific agricultural methods and the ability to handle farm tools and machines. Furthermore, the relevant age group from 13 to 16 was not yet adjudged to be physically mature and capable of carrying a full load in the workaday world. Therefore, it was considered feasible and advisable to allow this group to continue its education to a point enabling it to play a more useful role in society, provided that this schooling would not involve large expenditures of public funds. A corollary of this view was that education for older rural youth at the senior middle level would generally be available only on a spare-time basis, since young people over 16 were needed for full-time employment. . . .

The need for "junior agricultural technical personnel" in the communes was seen as being very urgent. Lu Ting-i, in his February 1960 article in *Jen-min*

SOURCE: Selected from Robert D. Baredsen, *Half Work, Half Study Schools in Communist China* (U.S. Department of Health, Education, and Welfare Publication), Washington, D.C.: The U.S. Government Printing Office, 1964, pp. 3–5, 8–19, 24–26, and 28–35.

Chiao-yü, stated that China would need 1,840,000 agricultural machine operators and 440,000 "technical farming cadres" in order to complete the task of mechanization and modernization of agriculture. These were the people who would be counted upon to drive the tractors and combines, maintain the electric motors powering irrigation equipment, perform skilled tasks in local fertilizer and insecticide factories, act as surveyors, veterinary assistants, and bookkeepers, and do similar lower-level technical work in commune farms and factories.

ORIGIN AND EARLY GROWTH

It is difficult for an outside observer to ascertain with assurance just when the type of institution referred to in recent years as the "agricultural middle school" first appeared on the Chinese scene. There are a few retrospective references in available materials to schools of a similar nature in existence in 1956 and 1957, but the genesis of the idea is usually credited in mainland sources to the authorities in Kiangsu province, where the first agricultural middle schools were reportedly established in March 1958. . . . The pace of frenzied activity can best be traced through the record of what happened in Kiangsu, where the course of the movement is best documented. Starting from a base of two such schools in mid-March, Kiangsu was reported to have established more than 2,000 by the end of the month. . . .

The national rate of growth of the agricultural middle schools during the following year and a half is difficult to trace, as reports for the latter part of 1958 and early 1959 are not available in sufficient numbers to establish a pattern. It would appear that during the hectic several months after the mass campaign to establish communes began in the late summer of 1958, the agricultural middle schools were revamped and adapted to the new organizational framework in rural areas. A domestic news release suggested as much when it later reported that the schools had been "comprehensively overhauled, consolidated, and improved" in the wake of the communization movement.[1] In the spring of 1959 there was again a flurry of publicity tied to the first anniversary of the official founding of these schools. By the latter part of 1959 and early 1960, the situation had apparently become sufficiently stabilized so that new statistics on the schools and their enrollment could be released. . . .

However, the emerging role of the agricultural middle school in expanding the opportunity for middle school education, as seen in the spring of 1960, was a major one. For example, a Kiangsu delegate, speaking to the National People's Congress in April, reported that his province alone planned to have 1,450,000 students enrolled in agricultural middle schools by 1967. The attainment of such a level of participation on a national scale would enable the regime to approximate its goal of universalizing junior middle school education, since there will probably be between 40 and 50 million young people in the relevant 13–16 age bracket at that time.[2]

CHARACTERISTICS OF THE SCHOOLS

Keeping in mind the role that the agricultural middle schools were playing in the total educational picture in 1960 and the importance ascribed to their future development, one may turn to a more detailed examination of the nature of this new type of institution and the kind of educational experience it offered to the boys and girls in rural areas.

First of all, it must be remembered that the agricultural middle school of this period was a *part-time* school. It was thus distinguished from the other two types of educational institutions in Communist China considered from the point of view of the daily proportion of the student's time spent in classes: The ordinary junior middle school was a *full-time* school; and many *spare-time* (i.e., after a normal working day) schools and classes at all levels were run by communes and factories. The agricultural middle school was often referred to in mainland sources as "half school, half farm," since its students normally devoted half their time to classes and the other half to productive labor, usually of an agricultural nature, the proceeds from which were used to finance the operation of the schools.

The size of these early agricultural middle schools seems to have varied considerably. The national statistics indicated that the average enrollment was about 100 students per school, but enrollment as high as over 600 was cited in the sources. In Kiangsu the recommended enrollment was between 200 and 500 per school, with 300 considered an ideal number, but the actual reported enrollment in the spring of 1960 averaged well below 200 per institution. . . .

Little data is available on the physical facilities assigned to the schools for classroom work. Early schools were apparently operated in temples, pagodas, and temporarily unused buildings and rooms. The *Jen-min Jih-pao* of April 7, 1958, described the classrooms as having a bare minimum of furnishings, with tables and benches brought in by the students from home or borrowed temporarily from offices. An article in *Hung Ch'i* on May 16, 1960, looking back in retrospect on the early days of the movement in Kiangsu, said that "some of the [schools] were started . . . without fixed premises. The teachers taught . . . in the open, and doors were temporarily used as blackboards with the students squatting and using their knees as desks." Items describing the situation at a later date referred in some cases to new permanent classroom buildings, but offered no details. In view of the considerably greater attention given to describing the installations available for productive labor, this information left the impression that classroom facilities were rather limited.

It is not clear from available data to what extent the students lived on the school premises. Probably where housing existed, this practice was generally followed, but there are very few references to dormitories in the source materials. One article concerning the situation in Kiangsu in 1959 took up the question of whether or not the schools should be boarding schools, and concluded that this point was a controversial one after a year's experience. The author stated that the living-in system had some clear advantages where suitable facilities existed, but cautioned against large boarding institutions.[3]

Teaching Staff. More important than the physical facilities, in determining the total educational environment, is the teaching staff. In numbers, the teaching force available for agricultural middle schools in these early years was relatively small. For example, the February 2, 1960, item in *Jen-min Jih-pao,* which gave the national figure of over 20,000 agricultural middle schools with over 2 million students, said that there were 60,000 instructors in these schools—an average of less than 3 teachers for each 3-year school and one teacher for each 36 students. The reported ratio for Kiangsu and Szechwan (the only areas where provincial-level figures for total teachers are available) was approximately the same as the national ratio.

Teachers were drawn from several sources. When available, graduates of ordinary senior middle schools were used. Otherwise, the recourse was to ordinary junior middle school graduates, primary school teachers, government functionaries who had been sent to the countryside for work experience, local Communist Party leaders, and even experienced peasants. The principle behind teacher recruitment was that "every knowledgeable person can teach" and that formal teaching qualifications were not necessary. As a result of this approach and the general shortage of teaching personnel throughout the country, the agricultural middle schools were staffed largely with people who, at the time of their appointment, admittedly had had neither teacher training nor teaching experience.

The nature of this group posed persistent problems, and necessitated special training measures which will be discussed later. The problems were apparently not overcome after 2 years of experience with the new schools. A report on the situation in the Szechwan schools delivered to the National People's Congress in April 1960 stated that only slightly over half of the teachers in that province had had a senior middle school level education, and that inadequate political training and lack of teaching experience were prevalent shortcomings. A speech to the same convocation by a delegate from Liaoning acknowledged that the teachers in that province's schools were "not very good," and cited the difficulties experienced by a fresh graduate of an ordinary junior middle school assigned to teach in an agricultural middle school. According to an article in *Hung Ch'i* in May 1960, teachers in the early days of the Kiangsu schools were often poor: The author cited the case of a female teacher of agriculture who knew nothing of agricultural production, and of a teacher of agricultural mechanization who could not operate a tractor or identify parts of the machine. The article claimed that conditions in 1960 were much improved, and that 87 per cent of the teachers in the province at that time had a senior middle school or better level of education.[4]

Time Allotments for Study and Labor. Such, then, was the educational environment into which a student of an agricultural middle school entered. But how did he spend his time while he was enrolled? As indicated previously, the student spent about half his time in classroom study and half in productive labor. Apparently the majority of the schools used a split day, and a minority used alternate days for study and work. Other arrangements, such as alternate-week systems and a system with study in mornings and evenings and work in between, were apparently tried and rejected because of poor academic results or the overburdening of the student.[5] The half-day or alternate-day system was a general practice, but was subject to alteration according to the farm calendar. A joint report to the National People's Congress in April 1960 by three Fukien delegates stated that the principle which governed division of time in that province was "less study during the busy farming season, more during slack farming season, occasional study during the busiest season . . . and all-day study on rainy days."⁶ A Szechwan delegate told the same meeting that the work-study schedule in his province varied from month to month and that in busy seasons, teachers went to the fields to conduct brief review lessons or introduce new material. Schools in Kiangsu were reportedly in session for 11 months of the year, with either the equivalent of 5 months given to study and 6 months to labor, or 5 months for labor and 6 months for study. In Hopei, on the other hand, schools were apparently in session for virtually the full 12 months, with their overall time divided equally between study and labor.

The Kiangsu schools were variously reported to spend 20 or 23 hours per week in classroom study, and one Anhwei school was described as having 24 lesson periods per week. The schools presumably operated on the 6-day week basis which is the usual system for middle schools in Communist China. No weekly hours were reported for other provinces, but Szechwan schools were said to provide 900 "lesson-hours" per year, a figure which would average out to about 18¾ hours per week for an 11-month (48-week) year, and less for a longer school session.⁷

Curriculum and Academic Standards. The curriculum in agricultural middle schools consisted of a limited number of subjects. There were four basic courses: Chinese language, mathematics, politics, and a course in agriculture which was most commonly referred to as "basic agricultural knowledge." Language and mathematics were cited as the two major courses in the curriculum.

No specific information on the coverage of the language course at this period is available, other than the general statement that it corresponded to that offered in ordinary junior middle schools. Since most accounts did not mention "literature" specifically, however, they left the impression that the course coverage was actually narrower than the scope of the course in Chinese taught in ordinary middle schools. It was not completely clear whether mathematics as taught in the typical agricultural middle school in Kiangsu included algebra and geometry, but presumably it did; a spokesman from Szechwan listed these subjects as well as arithmetic in the curriculum generally in use in his province. The course on politics included material presenting the regime's official explanation and interpretation of such subjects as important domestic and international current political topics, the program for agricultural development, and Mao Tse-tung's political thought. The coverage of the "basic agricultural knowledge" course was not well defined in the sources, but it apparently included such things as basic techniques of crop cultivation, irrigation methods, and fertilizer application. One source stated that the teaching materials for this course were derived from those used in ordinary junior middle school botany and zoology, and gave special emphasis to the regime's "8-point charter" for agriculture (a set of guidelines regarding close planting, deep plowing, fertilization, etc.).⁸ Perhaps the best way to indicate what was included in the basic agricultural course is to cite some of the courses added to the original four in some schools. Most prominently mentioned among these was a course on agricultural machinery, indicating that this topic was not included in the basic agriculture course. Other special courses which were added to the curriculum in some areas included animal husbandry, gardening, and sericulture. It was claimed that some of the schools taught physics and chemistry to students in the second or third year of the 3-year course, but it was clear just how widely these courses were offered.

There is unfortunately little indication of the way in which the 20-odd hours of weekly classroom work were divided among the various subjects. The writer found only one such schedule in the available data, and it pertained to a single agricultural middle school in Anhwei. The schedule covered a class week consisting of 24 "lessons" (presumably equal to class hours), and was divided as follows:[9]

	Lessons per week
Language	6
Mathematics	6
Politics	2
Biology	3
Chemistry	2
Cotton cultivation	2
Animal husbandry	2
Physical education	1
Total	24

Since it was not made clear for which of the 3 years this plan was designed, and since the plan does not include a basic agriculture course as such, and does include a course in biology which is not mentioned in other sources, it is impossible to generalize from this one example. It may be indicative, however, of a lack of standardization in the curriculum pattern of such schools.

What standards were achieved in the academic courses in the agricultural middle schools, and how did the record of performance of their students compare with that of students in the ordinary junior middle schools? The general claim repeated frequently in mainland press and periodical articles about the agricultural middle schools was that their students achieved standards comparable to those of students in the ordinary junior middle schools in the "main subjects" in their curriculum. But careful scrutiny of the claims reveals that they were often considerably qualified, so that this evaluation would apply only to some of the students, or some of the schools, in a given area. A typical example of the resulting vagueness is a statement in a joint article by three officials from Kiangsu in the November 17, 1959, issue of the *Jen-min Jih-pao*. Discussing the schools in Kiangsu, the article said that "the standard of *several* subjects taught in the agricultural middle schools is not lower than that taught in the regular middle schools *in general*, while results achieved by students of *a number of* agricultural middle schools are even better than those achieved by the students of regular middle schools" (italics supplied).

As for achievements in specific subjects, there were several claims of equivalence or near-equivalence to ordinary middle school standards in language and mathematics, and one or two claims of comparable performance in tests on politics, but these claims were balanced by provincial reports which conveyed a different impression. A Kiangsu delegate to the National People's Congress in April 1960 stated that only about half of the Kaingsu schools covered in a survey equalled or surpassed the standards of local ordinary full-time middle schools in language and mathematics. A joint report to the same meeting by three Fukien delegates stated that in less than one-fourth of the agricultural middle schools in Fukien did the quality of language and mathematics teaching match that in ordinary schools. Tests in three areas in Hopei, reported in the *Jen-min Jih-pao* on August 10, 1960, showed that only 50 per cent of the agricultural schools there had attained the standard of ordinary full-time schools in "cultural studies." It may be noted, also, that whereas there was frequent mention of admirable standards in language and mathematics, standards in physics and chemistry were almost never specifically cited.

Perhaps the best evidence of actual nation-wide standards in these new schools was contained in an editorial in the *Jen-min Jih-pao* published March 16, 1960, on the occasion of the second anniversary of the founding of the schools. Although praising the schools and calling for greater numbers of them on a national scale, the editorial said that since they were half-day schools, they "should naturally be regarded as different from the ordinary full-time middle schools in the standards of such fundamental subjects as cultural and scientific subjects." The editorial added that they "may be able to catch up" with ordinary schools in such "principal subjects" as "language, mathematics, etc." This evaluation was in line with that voiced by a Liaoning delegate to the National People's Congress the following month. He told the meeting that "generally speaking, the students of agricultural middle schools are still somewhat behind the students of full-time middle schools in book knowledge, but their knowledge of productive labor far exceeds that of the latter."[10]

It is clear from the available data that in the period from 1958 to 1960 the agricultural middle schools in general offered a substantially watered-down course of study compared to that obtainable in the ordinary junior middle schools. It may well be true, as claimed, that by offering only a limited number of basic courses, the schools provided as many annual hours of instruction in these courses as are offered in the ordinary schools. But it also is evident that the complete absence of the usual junior middle school courses in history and geography, and the indicated lower standard in physics and chemistry where these science courses were offered, sufficed to draw a clear line of distinction between graduates of these new schools and the ordinary schools.

Productive Labor Activities. The foregoing material has provided a brief outline of the way in which the student in an agricultural middle school spent that half of his time which was devoted to classroom study. It now remains to consider his use of the other half of his time—that devoted to productive labor. The picture derived from numerous accounts indicates that the student's labor was performed in a variety of enterprises in "production bases" made available to the schools through the local communes. The production bases were of two kinds: agricultural and industrial. Schools had their own crop farms, part of which were experimental plots. They also often had livestock and poultry farms, orchards, and tree nurseries. In some cases they had vegetable gardens, tea plantations, aviaries, and stocked fish ponds. The factories run by the schools were generally small, many of them in the nature of handicraft workshops. The two most commonly mentioned types of small plants were those producing local types of fertilizer (both chemical and bacterial) and insecticides. Other shops engaged in the processing of economic crops such as soy beans. The *Jen-min Jih-pao* of March 16, 1960, stated that the principal undertakings of productive enterprises run by the schools should be cultivating high-yield economic crops and making handicraft products of the types produced by rural people as sideline occupations.

No national figures were released for acreage of farmland cultivated or the number of workshops operated by agricultural middle schools; however, provincial-level figures for three provinces were reported. In Kiangsu, the 2,174 schools were said to be cultivating 115,400 *mou* (a *mou* equals about one-sixth of an acre) and operating 1,466 handicraft workshops and factories in April 1960. In Fukien at the same time, 560 schools were tilling 16,500 *mou* and running 330 "factories and farms." In August 1959, 930 schools in Liaoning were cultivating 4,532 *mou* and operating 1,016 factories. These figures indicated a rather wide variance in the scope of productive enterprises in the three areas and suggest that in many schools the students were confined to agricultural labor or work in enterprises not run directly by the schools.

The production plans of the schools were incorporated into the overall plan of the commune, and the commune assisted the schools in obtaining draft animals and large agricultural tools, making arrangements for the supply of raw materials for the workshops, and organizing the marketing of products. Divisions of labor within the schools was reportedly based on age and sex, with the older students specializing in agricultural labor and the younger ones in handicraft production. The boys were commonly assigned to heavier work, and the girls undertook lighter tasks such as feeding animals and poultry.

There is little information available on the type and volume of products produced by the school workshops. One account of a school in Anhwei reported that it had trial-manufactured 98 kinds of insecticides and 177 different kinds of chemical and bacterial fertilizers, and that over a period of 2 years it had produced over 4 million catties (a catty is slightly heavier than a pound) of insecticides and 37 million catties of fertilizer for market.[11]

Part of the staff of the school was charged with the special responsibility for supervising productive work. For example, one Kiangsu school with 303 students was reported in the spring of 1959 to have 7 "experienced peasants" and "technical workers" in charge of production, in addition to the 11 teachers on its staff.

Financial Self-sufficiency. A description of the productive enterprises of the agricultural middle schools leads logically into a discussion of their finances, since at this period the schools were designed to be virtually self-sufficient through their own production activities. The proudest boast concerning these schools had to do with the economy of their operation.

In discussing the economic advantages of the agricultural middle schools, the regime released some interesting figures on the comparative costs of educating a youth in agricultural middle schools and ordinary junior middle schools. The figures used in the discussion were based on statistics collected in the model province of Kiangsu. Three somewhat different versions of these figures are available in the data, but perhaps the most authoritative is the one included in a detailed report to the National People's Congress in April 1960 by a Kiangsu delegate. The figures, on a per student per year basis, were as follows:[12]

	Cost to state (yuan)	Cost to family (yuan)
Ordinary junior middle school	187	108
Agricultural middle school	13	38

The figure for the cost to the state of ordinary middle school study was roughly confirmed by another source, which reported that it cost the state about 500 *yuan* to put a junior middle school student through his 3-year course.[13]

It is not completely clear what was meant by "cost to the state" in the case of agricultural middle schools. This expenditure may have been actually charged to the communes, but it is possible that the provincial or lower-level governmental subdivisions still played a small role directly in the financing of the schools. In any case, it is apparent that the expense borne by the authorities in running the agricultural schools was but a small fraction of the cost of supporting ordinary junior middle schools. The reduction in the financial burden on parents was not so great, but was still equal to two-thirds of the cost of supporting a student in the ordinary schools.

Any expense involved in the initial steps in establishing the schools, such as making available school buildings and farmland, was usually borne by the communes out of their welfare fund. From that point on, the school was expected to strive as quickly as possible to earn enough to pay its teachers' salaries and its students' tuition, to provide operational funds, and to supply the students with food, books, and other needed school supplies.

The extent to which self-sufficiency was actually achieved by these schools is difficult to determine. There were glowing accounts of individual schools or groups of schools which paid all their expenses and returned a profit to the communes, and there were frequent statements that "many" agricultural schools were "wholly or partially" self-supporting. Few hard statistics were released, however, and those which did become available indicated that the goal of self-sufficiency proved to be elusive. The case of Kiangsu is again illustrative: In May 1959, after one year's experience with these schools, a Kiangsu official wrote in *Hung Ch'i* that all the agricultural middle schools in his province should be entirely self-sufficient within 2 years—i.e., by the spring of 1961. About a year later, in July 1960, an enthusiastic NCNA English-language news release stated flatly that most of the schools in Kiangsu were already able to cover all their expenditures. But Kiangsu delegate Kuan Wen-hui's speech to the National People's Congress a few months earlier suggests that this report was premature. In this speech (in April 1960) Kuan stated that at that time only 19 per cent of the Kiangsu schools were "wholly self-supporting," another 18.6 per cent were "to a large extent self-supporting," and 31.8 per cent were "partly self-supporting." The implication left was that the remaining 30.6 per cent were still wholly dependent on outside sources. In the same speech it was reported that the plan now called upon the schools in Kiangsu to "strive for self-support, partly or wholly" within "2 years or a little longer," indicating that full independence was not seen as attainable before 1962 or later.

Reports concerning Fukien in the spring of 1960 suggested a similar situation. Of the 560 agricultural middle schools there, 55 were reported to be able to pay their teachers' salaries fully, and another 61 to be self-sufficient in food. Individual cases of schools which had paid for teachers' wages, food, and other expenses were cited, but the impression conveyed was that only a relatively small minority of the schools were able to pay the major part of their expenses.[14]

The best available example of the way in which a typical agricultural middle school sought to balance its budget was given in an article in *Hung Ch'i* on May 1, 1959. It concerned a school in Kiangsu, and presented the school's balance sheet of receipts and expenditures in 1958 as follows:[15]

Receipts:

Source	Amount (yuan)
Agricultural products	13,824.40
Silkworm rearing	400.00
Wool	76.00
Pig rearing	280.00
Rabbit rearing	11.00
Manufacturing of straw ropes	25.00
Manufacturing of rush mats	300.00
Manufacturing of fertilizer and insecticides	1,100.00
Total	16,016.40
Expenditures (not itemized)	18,792.00

For 1959, the same school planned to attain complete self-sufficiency by earning a total of 30,890 *yuan* through cultivating 135 *mou* of wheat, 121 *mou* of paddy rice, and 5 *mou* of soy beans, and by growing vegetables and ramie, raising pigs, sheep, chickens, and fish, and making rush mats.[16] Expenses contemplated for 1959 were as follows:

Item	Amount (yuan)
Yearly boarding charges (calculated at 6 *yuan* per capita per month)	22,608
Wages and salaries of teachers and staff	5,160
School operating expenses	1,100
Books and stationery	1,212
Total	30,080

Research and Experimental Work. In addition to producing goods for market to achieve self-sufficiency, the agricultural middle schools, like all middle schools and colleges in Communist China, were supposed to give substance to the tripartite combinations of learning, labor, and research by engaging in various types of experimental work. The schools were generally reported to be devoting at least a part of their agricultural acreage to experimental plots, and there were numerous reports of their achievements in attaining high yields. A number of schools were reported to conduct experimental work in meteorology (weather forecasting) and water conservation. Some schools apparently also did research on fertilizer, insecticides, and soil analysis, and their students designed (as well as trial-manufactured) new types of farm implements and machinery. In regard to this latter category of investigation, one report stated that upper-classmen in Kiangsu agricultural middle schools had "created" 10 kinds of modern agricultural tools, including a mowing machine, a fodder mixing appliance, an insecticide sprinkler, and rice and wheat threshing machines.[17] As has been noted previously, another account stated that students in one school in Anhwei had trial-manufactured 98 different kinds of insecticides and 177 kinds of chemical and bacterial fertilizers.

This kind of activity was considered to be very important. After 2 years of experience with the schools, the regime emphasized their role as "strongholds for scientific research for the people's communes" and exhorted them to do more in this field.[18] In carrying out experimental work, the schools were urged to focus on problems confronted in current production and to seek solutions through native methods appropriate to local conditions.

Communist Party Leadership. The importance attached to the agricultural middle schools is apparent in the particularly intimate role which Communist Party functionaries played in the daily life of the schools. From the days of their inception, reports from all areas stressed that the secretaries of the Party Committees in the communes commonly acted as heads of the schools. They or other high-ranking local Party functionaries usually were reported to teach the political courses in the schools. An unsigned article in the *Jen-min Jih-pao* on Februray 2, 1960, stated that throughout the country, Party committees at all levels actively supported the schools, included discussions of their work on the agenda of their daily meetings, and inspected them regularly. An editorial in the same paper on March 16, 1960, emphasized strengthened leadership by commune Party committees as the basic guarantee of the success of the schools, and stressed the familiar dictum that "politics must be in command" and the ideological and political consciousness of both students and teachers must be brought to a high level. Due attention was paid to the fostering of membership in the Young Pioneers and Communist Youth League (for students) and the Communist Party (for teachers). . . .

Most of the advantages seen by the regime in the 1958–60 period in the institution of the agricultural middle schools have been mentioned earlier in this study. To summarize briefly, the Chinese Communist leadership viewed these schools as a means to satisfy growing popular demands for post-primary education. It also saw them as a way to train large numbers of rural youths to serve the communes in a variety of lower-level technical and administrative jobs requiring a rudimentary form of junior middle school education plus

vocational training in crop-cultivation agriculture and other related rural occupations. It placed high value upon the form of the schools because they
were at least potentially able to be self-supporting. They were also able to
function with fewer teachers than ordinary middle schools and to utilize local
sources of teaching personnel. It was also claimed that the integral combination
of education and labor in these half-day schools provided the student with
an ideal environment in which to see more clearly the relationship between
theory and practice and, through opportunities to apply his learning directly
and immediately to practical work, to digest and better understand the things
he was taught in class. The research and experimental work performed by
the schools was considered to be especially valuable because it was closely
geared to current local problems and its results were directly popularized
among the local rural people through the students who lived and worked
among them.

One final advantage of the schools was seen in the political sphere. The
student body was given political instruction and was then used as an organized
young activist group in the furtherance of the various centrally inspired mass
movements through which policy is implemented in Communist China. One
account, for example, noted that because of their active role in the campaign to establish the communes in 1958, the Kiangsu schools "were
praised as 'political propaganda stations,' while their students were called
'propagandists.' "[19]

Although the agricultural middle schools were highly praised and their allegedly great advantages were frequently cited in the available mainland sources
of the period, these same sources also made it clear that the establishment
of the schools elicited criticism from some quarters and resulted in a number
of admittedly difficult problems. Among the difficulties mentioned as encountered by the new schools in their early days were shortages of competent
teachers, lack of needed school facilities and equipment, shortages of funds,
inadequate provision of production facilities, and poor arrangements for the
division of time between study and labor. As a result of these problems, there
was apparently considerable early skepticism about these schools on the part
of the masses and some cadres, and these doubts were reflected in low
enrollments and, in some cases at least, a serious rate of dropouts. . . .

Probably the most persistent single problem faced by the regime in attempting
to consolidate the schools was the recruiting of sufficient teachers with adequate
preparation. The existence of this problem was not surprising, since there
is abundant evidence of a chronic shortage of qualified teachers in the schools
at all levels in Communist China.[20] But the frequent references to the problem
and accounts of a variety of stopgap measures taken to deal with it show
that it was particularly serious in the agricultural middle schools. Reference
has been made earlier in this study to the calibre of teaching personnel and
their level of qualifications. The problem arising out of the recruitment of
such people was recognized by the regime. A Kiangsu official, writing in *Hung
Ch'i* on May 16, 1960, stated that at the beginning, when the agricultural
schools had no full-time teachers and therefore borrowed instructors from
the ordinary schools, the policy question arose as to whether it was better
to train teachers first, or to set up the school first. It was decided to establish

a school, obtain a staff, and then train it. This training was given through correspondence courses, short-term special vacation courses organized by normal schools and normal colleges, and in some cases by sending outstanding teachers to attend normal schools. The aid of teachers in the ordinary schools was solicited, and teachers in the agricultural schools visited their classes and learned from them. . . .

Although all evidence indicates that the agricultural middle schools were highly evaluated and approvingly publicized by the regime in the spring and summer of 1960, the onset of the fall of the year marked the beginning of a prolonged period during which virtually no news of the schools appeared in Chinese Communist sources. Throughout the fall and into the spring of 1961 there was no indication in available materials that these new institutions were discussed at any appreciable length in the mass media. Up until March 1961 the absence of such accounts was not particularly noteworthy, as gaps of several months had occurred between earlier flurries of publicity on the subject. But when the third anniversary of the officially celebrated founding of the schools passed in March 1961 without notice, the contrast with earlier anniversaries was rather striking. Logically, the third anniversary should have been an especially auspicious one, since it marked the approach of the close of the third year in the life of the new 3-year schools and thus the potential occasion for the first large-scale emergence of their graduates. . . .

The long period of virtual silence on the agricultural middle schools was finally broken in the middle of 1961, and during the latter half of the year scattered reports concerning the status of schools in various parts of the country gradually began to appear once again in mainland publications. By the spring of 1962 reports had become available in sufficient number to enable one to reconstruct in general outline, if not in detail, the picture of what had been happening to these institutions during the preceding year and a half.

The new material released in late 1961 and 1962 did nothing to update the statistical data available on the status of agricultural middle schools in the nation as a whole. No new national figures were offered for either numbers of schools or total enrollment. Nor were there any reports on the number of agricultural middle school graduates in the whole country in 1961 or 1962, despite the fact that under normal conditions these figures could logically have been expected to be rather impressive. . . .

New total enrollment figures were given for only one province (Kirin), and they could not be compared with any available earlier data. The only enrollment comparison that could be made involved the outskirts of Shanghai, and it indicated that enrollment (as well as numbers of schools) had sharply declined in that area; the decline in enrollment between 1959 and 1961 was from 27,000 to 16,000.

With regard to graduates, most of the new reports were confined to giving cumulative figures for the total number of graduates that had emerged from the schools in various areas since their founding. Such cumulative figures covering the situation in several provinces through 1961 were released. The total graduates accounted for in these reports was between 225 and 230 thousand, a substantial figure considering the small number of provinces represented, but still a far cry from the much larger national figures that could logically have been anticipated that year. No new figures for graduates at either national or provincial level became available in 1962.

Thus the statistical data released in late 1961 and 1962 leaves a clouded but essentially unimpressive quantitative picture of the number of agricultural middle schools, their enrollment, and recent graduates.

ADOPTION OF A MODIFIED SYSTEM

New Schedule for Annual School Session. The new material published in the 1961–62 period makes it quite clear, however, that in a gradual process which apparently began in the autumn of 1960 and culminated sometime in 1961 in most areas, the system under which the schools operated was modified to a considerable degree. According to the data of the 1958–60 period, most of the schools at that time were run nearly all year round on a split-day basis, with students studying for half of the day and then working in the school's own farms or factories for the other half of the day. In the new more flexible pattern which came to be generally adopted in 1961, some of the schools were reported to be operating on the split-day (or alternate-day) basis and others were run on a spare-time basis, but most were on a still different schedule. The new system, of which there were a number of variations, provided essentially for the schools to operate on a full-day basis in the slack season of the agricultural year, and then to close down during the busy season. The length of the schooling period apparently varied from as little as 4 to as many as 7 months, but generally was of about 5 months' duration. In most parts of the country, school was in session more or less continuously, except for a vacation break around Chinese New Years in January or February, from early November until the end of March or sometime in April. During the balance of the year, the students generally returned to their homes and worked in the commune's fields with other peasants. While working in the communes, the students were expected to do regular self-study and participate in small group study sessions in their spare time; the teachers traveled around an assigned area and gave periodical individual tutoring and group guidance during the labor months. Under this system, during the working period the students were supposed to study by themselves for about an hour a day and to meet three or four times a month in groups for several hours of group discussion or instruction.

Judging from the several accounts of schedules for the study months, it would appear that the schools which are in session for 5 months of the year have about 120 days of classes during this period, allowing for a 1- or 2-week vacation at Chinese New Years and for Sundays off. This is roughly comparable to, but slightly less than, the approximately 130 days (in terms of full-day equivalents) which were obtained under the former split-day system. During the approximately 20 weeks in which students are attending classes, they have about 5 hours per day (or 30 hours per week) of classroom work, amounting to a total of about 600 hours for the school year. Students in regular full-time junior middle schools, on the other hand, have about 1,000 hours of class-time in their much longer (37 to 40 weeks) school year. The indicated relationship between class hours for regular and agricultural junior middle schools is roughly confirmed by an article in the *Kuang-ming Jih-pao* which stated explicitly that the total study time in agricultural middle schools in Kiangsu was only about one-half of that in regular junior middle schools, on an annual basis.[21]

Reasons for the Change. The rationale behind the change in the system under which the agricultural middle schools were operated was indicated in several items in mainland publications. The primary reason for the move was clearly the need to have more labor power available for use during the busy season in the agricultural calendar. This was a reflection of the regime's over-riding concern, from 1960 on, with the mobilization of all resources to bolster lagging agricultural production. But a question of pedagogical efficiency was also cited as one of the justifications for the change. It was acknowledged that the former year-round split-day or alternate-day system provided the advantages of a built-in continuous interplay of theory and practice. Yet the constant shifting from study to labor had resulted in special problems: the teachers had insufficient time to prepare their lessons, and the students were unable to "consolidate" their learning. Under the new system, the opportunity to immediately apply knowledge to concrete problems was sacrificed to some extent, but lessons were related to everyday life by a strong "practical" orientation. Furthermore, during the prolonged period of labor the teachers could have time to develop their teaching materials, and the students were able to review and digest their lessons in organized and supervised spare-time study. The basic economic and pedagogical rationale behind the change was best summarized in an article in the authoritative *Jen-min Jih-pao* at the end of 1961, which stated:

> When the agricultural middle schools were first established, the method of dividing a day into half for labor and half for study, and the method of labor and study on alternate days, were adopted. Later it was found that such methods could not enable the students to provide full support to agriculture during busy seasons, nor to devote their full energy to study during slack farm seasons. But after the present method has been adopted, we have been able to meet more satisfactorily the needs of agricultural production, and the time for study has been more concentrated, to the satisfaction of students, teachers, and parents.[22]

Another aspect of the economic advantages seen in the new system had to do with the financing of the operation of the schools. Under the new system the schools were largely financed by tuition fees paid by the students out of their earnings as laborers on the communes during the busy season. It was claimed that in most cases these earnings were sufficient to pay the tuition and have something left over to bolster the finances of the student's family.

The tortuous path actually followed by one of the schools in arriving at the new system was outlined in a revealing item published in a leading mainland newspaper in December 1961.[23] This item traced the vicissitudes through which the school passed from the time of its founding, and the record is worthy of discussion in some detail. When first established in the latter part of 1957, the school reportedly got off on the wrong foot. It had no fixed "production base" (school farm or factory) in which its students could work, and at the same time it overambitiously attempted to emulate a regular middle school in its curriculum. The unhappy result was that both study and productive labor activities were admittedly "confused." In early 1958, the school was given a substantial amount of land and it was "demanded" that it become self-supporting. It eventually became largely self-sufficient, but the ensuing "excessive pursuit of economic profit" subjected the students to a heavy burden of labor, and resulted in an acknowledged "failure to accomplish the tasks of education." The school "almost turned itself into a production team, arousing the uneasiness of some teachers and students to such an extent that some students even asked permission to leave the school." Faced with this unsatisfactory situation, the Party officials in the province in which the school was located decided to switch to the "5 and 7" system (5 months study in the slack season, 7 months labor in the communes). Under the new system, all of the productive activities operated by the school were returned to the jurisdiction of the communes and their sub-units, and the students worked in the fields like other peasants to earn the money to cover their tuition expenses.

Other Significant Aspects of the Revised System. As indicated in the foregoing, the single most significant change in the system was that the student's time for study, although still described as approximately "half-time" on an annual basis, was concentrated in about 5 months of full-time schoolwork rather than being spread virtually throughout the year on a half-day or alternate-day basis. The time for labor was similarly concentrated in the approximately 7 months remaining in the year. Involved in this basic change, however, was the virtual abandonment of one of the most fundamental features of the agricultural middle school in its original (1958–60) form. This was the self-sufficiency feature—the principle that these schools were designed to be self-supporting on the basis of the income to be produced by students and teachers working in farms and factories established and run by the schools. In the new material available in 1961 and 1962, there were a few references to schools having farm acreage or experimental fields, but there were no references whatsoever to the operation of any factories or workshops, and claims of partial or complete self-sufficiency were conspicuous by their almost total absence. The new system of financing was based upon tuition payments made by the students out of their earnings during the labor season. These tuition payments accounted for the bulk of the cost of operating the schools. They were supplemented by appropriations by the commune and, in some cases, government subsidies. There is some evidence that the earlier system of financing the schools with the income from their own productive enterprises had not worked out satisfactorily. . . .

The curriculum in the agricultural middle schools under the new system remained basically concentrated on the four subject areas included in the early period: language, mathematics, agriculture, and politics. The main difference between accounts of the curriculum published during the two periods was that the later material explicitly and strongly emphasized the "practical" bias observed in the teaching of all courses. For example, it stressed that language courses paid special attention to training students to handle common everyday writing such as letters, reports, records, notices, and labor contracts.

It mentioned that instruction in bookkeeping, "accounting," and "statistics" had been introduced in new added courses or covered in language or mathematics courses. Mathematics courses were widely reported to include instruction in the use of the abacus and the calculation of areas and volume. Courses in physics and chemistry were quite frequently mentioned, but in nearly half of the reports there were indications that the course content was narrower than that covered in the regular full-time junior middle schools and was focussed on practical applications of these sciences, such as the working of agricultural machines and the manufacture of chemical fertilizers.

The net effect of the new material, when considered in comparison with that of the 1958–60 period, was to make it more explicit that the courses were different from those of similar title offered in the regular schools at that level, and also to suggest that the schools had become more a vehicle for producing people to handle the paper work in the communes and production teams, rather than the mechanical and technical jobs. This impression was strengthened by the 1961 and 1962 accounts of how recent graduates of the schools were being used in various parts of the country. These accounts mentioned assignments as accountants, bookkeepers, "statisticians," and work-point recorders much more frequently than assignments as machine operators, mechanical maintenance men, and general agricultural "technicians." They also mentioned prominently that many graduates had been given administrative posts as heads of production teams or secretaries of Party or Youth League branches, or were serving as school teachers.

There were few indications of the relative proportion of time given to the various courses in the curriculum, but such reports as became available suggested that from one-half to three-fourths of the class time was devoted to instruction in language and mathematics, and one-fourth or less to courses on agriculture. One account concerning a school in Shansi province stated that during the whole 3-year course the students spent just slightly over two-thirds of their time on "cultural" courses (mainly language and mathematics, but also simplified courses in chemistry and physics; no other "cultural" subjects were mentioned), one-fourth of their time on "technical" courses in agriculture, and between 6 and 7 per cent on political courses.[24] The proportion of time devoted to language and mathematics is more typical of the pattern in Chinese primary schools than that in regular junior middle schools; in the latter considerably less than one-half of the total time is given to these two subjects. The earlier claims that a student in the agricultural middle schools receives as many total hours of instruction in language and mathematics as a student in the regular full-time junior middle schools were repeated in the 1961–62 data, but must be measured against the indications that the material covered was not at the same level of sophistication. The evidence of different course content is strengthened by several references in available material to new textbooks which had been, or needed to be, compiled for use in the agricultural schools.

Material published in the 1961–62 period indicated that some of the agricultural middle schools had classes at the senior middle level. There was no real evidence that the idea of continuing these schools at the higher level was being implemented very widely, however. The senior schools in Kiangsu, where this extension of the idea was first tried out in 1959, were still described as experimental in the spring of 1962.

Notes

1. *Hung Ch'i,* No. 7/1959 (Apr. 1, 1959); in *Extracts From China Mainland Magazine* No. 168, p. 18.

2. Lu Ting-i, in an open letter released at the time of the first anniversary of the founding of the agricultural middle schools, said that there were then about 37 million in the 13–16 age bracket. He added that only a little over 7 million of them could be accommodated in ordinary full-time junior middle schools. NCNA, Mar. 22, 1959; *SCMP* No. 1985 (Apr. 3, 1959), p. 27.

3. *Hung Ch'i,* No. 7/1959 (Apr. 1, 1959); in *ECMM* No. 168 (May 18, 1959), p. 22–23.

4. *Hung Ch'i,* No. 10/1960 (May 16, 1960); in *SCMM* No. 215 (June 27, 1960), p. 15.

5. See *Hung Ch'i,* No. 7/1959 (Apr. 1, 1959); in *ECMM* No. 168 (May 18, 1959), p. 21–22.

6. *Jen-min Jih-pao,* Apr. 16, 1960; in *Union Research Service* (Hong Kong: Union News Agency), Vol. 19, No. 17 (May 27, 1960), p. 250.

7. *Ibid.,* p. 255.

8. *Ibid.*

9. *Hung Ch'i,* No. 13/1960 (July 1, 1960); in *SCMM* No. 221 (Aug. 8, 1960), p. 42.

10. *Jen-min Jih-pao,* Apr. 12, 1960; in U.S. Joint Publications Research Service report No. 6491 (Dec. 29, 1960), p. 93.

11. *Hung Ch'i,* No. 13/1960 (July 1, 1960); in *SCMM* No. 221 (Aug. 8, 1960), pp. 39–41.

12. NCNA, Apr. 7, 1960; in *SCMP* No. 2240 (Apr. 19, 1960), p. 15. The other two versions of these figures differ mainly in the cost to the state of the agricultural middle schools, which is variously cited as 10 and 18.20 *yuan.* One U.S. dollar equals roughly 2 to 2½ *yuan.*

13. *Jen-min Jih-pao,* Nov. 27, 1959; in *SCMP* No. 2156 (Dec. 15, 1959), p. 40.

14. *Jen-min Jih-pao,* Apr. 16, 1960; in *Union Research Service,* vol. 19, No. 17 (May 27, 1960), pp. 251–52.

15. *Hung Ch'i,* No. 9/1959 (May 1, 1959); in *ECMM* No. 179 (Aug. 5, 1959), pp. 22–23.

16. The breakdown of income among these several sources was not given.

17. *Kuang-ming Jih-pao,* July 23, 1960; in *SCMP* No. 2336 (Sept. 13, 1960), p. 8.

18. *Jen-min Jih-pao,* May 18, 1960; in *SCMP* No. 2275 (June 13, 1960), pp. 11–12.

19. *Jen-min Jih-pao,* Nov. 27, 1959; in *SCMP* No. 2156 (Dec. 15, 1959), p. 41.

20. In this connection, see Theodore H. E. Chen, *Teacher Training in Communist China,* Studies in Comparative Education series, OE-14058. Washington: U.S. Government Printing Office, 1960.

21. *Kuang-ming Jih-pao,* Mar. 12, 1962; in *SCMP* No. 2710 (Apr. 2, 1962), p. 15.

22. *Jen-min Jih-pao,* Dec. 18, 1961; in *SCMP* No. 2652 (Jan. 5, 1962), p. 18.

23. *Kuang-ming Jih-pao,* Dec 14, 1961; in *Union Research Service,* vol. 27, No. 17 (May 29, 1962), pp. 297–98.

24. *Jen-min Jih-pao,* Jan. 6, 1962; in *SCMP* No. 2660 (Jan. 17, 1962), p. 15.

32. HIGHER EDUCATION

Leo Orleans

Higher Education

GENERAL NATURE OF THE SYSTEM AND THE PROBLEMS

In May 1950 the first conference dealing with problems of higher education was called, and the basic program for the reorganization of the existing system was discussed and outlined. Because of the shortage of technicians and specialists, one of the first reforms undertaken by the new regime was to convert gradually from a general system of university education to specialized institutes and to reduce the curriculums from 4–5 years to 3–4 years. In 1955, however, a decree again changed the length of study in many fields to 5 years, although some special institutes continued to have 2-year, 3-year, or 4-year curriculums. In the field of medicine the change to 5 years was introduced in 1954.

When the Communists took over control of the Chinese mainland, the country had slightly over 200 institutions of higher learning. In 1957–58 there were approximately 236 universities and institutes of higher education. The figure is approximate because the Communists themselves are undecided as to the exact number, different sources listing figures that vary from 5 to 10 or more schools. This is also true of the more detailed breakdown of such institutions. One representative distribution lists them as follows: 17 general universities, 10 polytechnical universities, 40 engineering institutes, 31 agricultural and forestry institutes, 37 medical colleges, 5 institutes of finance and economics, 5 institutes of law and political science, 8 language institutes, 57 teachers' (normal) colleges, 17 institutes of fine arts, 6 physical-training institutes, and 3 others.[1] Although many of the new universities and institutes have been established in the interior provinces of China, they still predominate in the large cities of the coastal provinces. Peking is undoubtedly the educational center of the country, with 50 institutions of higher education enrolling 121,000 students.[2]

The "leap forward" in higher education resulted in the usual distortion and

source: Selected from Leo Orleans, *Professional Manpower and Education in Communist China* (National Science Foundation Publication NSF 61-3), Washington, D.C.: U.S. Government Printing Office, 1960, pp. 57–66 and 77–80.

confusion of statistics, and the latest reports inform us that the "number of universities and colleges trebled during 1958 and 1959, the 2 successive years of the big leap forward, bringing the total up to 840."[3] It is clear that the latter figure includes not only the bona fide institutions of higher education but also some of the more advanced "red and expert universities" and spare-time universities in industrial enterprises that have been set up as part of the peasant- and worker-education program. (See ch. II for a description of "red and expert universities.") The care that must be exercised in utilizing these statistics is apparent from the following quotation which illustrates an instance in which "red and expert universities" were obviously included:

> Here we will cite the example of Kaifeng, Honan Province. Between July 1 and 14 [1958], 162 agricultural cooperatives in 22 townships [hsien] founded 256 colleges and 695 research institutes with 3,266 departments attended by 201,700 students.[4]

Despite the loose definition of higher institutions, the data on enrollment and on the number of entrants and graduates usually excludes the "red and expert universities" but does include the spare-time students. Unless specifically stated to the contrary, everything that follows on higher education excludes the "red and expert universities."

Only the universities provide the student with a general education somewhat comparable to that attained by a student in the West, and even there the tendency is toward overspecialization. The institutes, for the most part, turn out narrow specialists whose courses outside their particular field seldom include more than those required to make them "red" as well as "expert" in one particular specialty (see ch. V). This is also true of normal colleges, which are supposed to train teachers for secondary schools. The so-called "multiplicity of courses" has been eliminated; probably partly due to this reduction of requirements, the number of 2-year normal colleges has been greatly expanded. In these pseudoinstitutions of higher education, many of the courses were combined, as for example biology and chemistry, and history and political science. In 1954 more than 75 per cent of the normal-college graduates were the product of the 2-year system.[5]

It is interesting to note a few of the problems dealing with the system of integration of work and study as it pertains specifically to higher education. There it met considerably more opposition than at any other level. (The general aspects of the work-study policy are discussed in ch. II.) This opposition is not surprising because, according to the Communists, the majority of students in higher education during the earlier period of the regime had been brought up in "bourgeois and petty bourgeois families and their bourgeois viewpoint" had not been "completely transformed." These "rightists" students and teachers continue to maintain that "it is better to read more books than to participate in labor" and that they "could not learn anything from the peasants."

Although student objection to productive labor was quite widespread, the integration of study and work was carried out more smoothly in the fields where there was some natural relationship between theory and practical training and where students could be assigned work which had either direct or at least marginal relationship with their studies—such fields as engineering, agriculture, and medicine. The transition was more difficult among students in such fields as arts, history, and philosophy. . . .

It is also clear that productive labor which is the result of brain and not brawn may not be substituted in the work-study program: Only physical labor, which throws students in direct contact with the masses, is considered beneficial in creating the new well-rounded Chinese intellectual. . . .

The national policy of "walking on two legs" also has a special meaning for higher education. Although quality education cannot be provided for all, there are certain key institutions that attempt to give exceptionally qualified students the best education available in China. One such institution is the University of Science and Technology, which was established in 1958 in the western suburbs of Peking. It is reported that this new type of university differs from most of the existing polytechnical institutions in that its chief purpose is to train research workers in the most advanced branches of science. The Chinese Academy of Sciences and the Ministry of Education assume joint responsibility in guiding its work, and Kuo Mo-jo, who heads the Academy, is its president.

The new university has 13 departments: Nuclear physics and nuclear engineering, technical physics, applied geophysics, chemical physics, radio electronics, radioactive and radiative chemistry, thermal dynamic engineering, high polymer chemistry and physics, applied mathematics and computing technique, dynamics, geochemistry and rare elements, biophysics and automation. The teaching staff comes mainly from top-level research workers of the Academy of Sciences. Enrollment during the 1958–59 school year was 1,600.[6]

However, the principle of combining work with study holds for this university as well. The professors and students of the university set up "five factories, an electronic computer plant, an electronics instrument plant, etc.—even before the academic year began."[7]

There are few detailed discussions of the curriculums in institutions of higher education. Furthermore, there have been several radical reorganizations of approaches and methods of instruction and also little uniformity between various institutions. The brief description below (based on the Northeastern Polytechnical Institute of Shenyang) seems to be more or less typical of the current setup in higher technical institutions.[8] The curriculum consists of four component parts, inseparable from each other: Political and ideological training of the students; technical (special) studies; productive work; and military training and physical education.

The curriculum for political and ideological training includes such subjects as the course and policy of the Party, the history of the Chinese revolution, the history of the international Communist movement, and political economy and philosophy. During a period of nine semesters, 560 to 600 hours are set aside for these subjects. Compulsory attendance at political lectures and participation in discussion groups is not included in this time. . . .

The study of technical and scientific subjects is closely coordinated with productive work. For example, physics is no longer taught as a distinct and integrated subject. Instead, a student majoring in electrical engineering will study electricity; one majoring in mechanical engineering will study only those aspects of physics which are directly pertinent to his field, etc. Similarly, analytical chemistry is combined with technical analysis, and physical chemistry with electrochemistry. New theoretical courses have been devised for each specialty. Also, that part of the material which can be assimilated by the student during the course of his productive work is not included in the lectures. During a 12-hour workday, the student spends 4 hours in production at adjoining plants, 4 hours in independent work (discussion of lectures, homework, etc.), and 4 hours in academic studies. An average of 1 hour per day is set aside for physical education and military training.

A significant change has also been made in conducting examinations. The evaluation of a student's knowledge in a given discipline is determined on the basis of the opinions of the party organization, instructors, and students, taking into account the ability of the student to solve specific production problems, the level of his theoretical knowledge, and the political consciousness of the student. Following a written examination, the students form themselves into groups to discuss the answers of their fellow students and to make evaluations. Then an evaluation is made by the instructor.

ENTRANTS

The annual quotas for enrollment in the institutions of higher learning are set by the state. All such institutions must participate in the plan of "unified enrollment" and are not allowed to enroll students on their own:

> The unified enrollment for institutes of higher learning is handled by the national, regional, provincial, and municipal enrollment committees and offices for the examination areas set up by the departments of education, public health, and personnel; and the institutes of higher learning under the leadership of the Party committees and governments.[9]

New entrants are assigned to fields of study according to a detailed plan provided by the Ministry of Education. For example, for the 1954–55 school year, 37.42 per cent of the entrants were to go into engineering, 6.34 per cent into science, and 2.17 per cent into finance and economics.[10]

Every province and municipality has an enrollment-work committee which is composed of the presidents of all institutes of higher learning in the area and which is subordinate to the regional department of education. This committee is responsible for administering entrance examinations and for registration, selection, and placement of the successful candidates. There are 77 cities in China which hold college entrance examinations (7 in the north, 10 in the northeast, 18 in the east, 26 in the central-south, 10 in the southwest, 4 in the northwest, and 2 in Inner Mongolia).

Presumably to strengthen and unify leadership in the college enrollment work throughout the nation, the National Committee of College Enrollment was inaugurated in Peking on March 19, 1956. The committee consists of 30 members who are the responsible persons of the relevant departments of the Central Government and some higher institutes of Peking.[11]

All the young people who want to sit for entrance examinations for the institutions of higher education must first pass a physical examination at the medical center in their locality or neighboring locality. They may then register at nearby designated places for entrance examinations to quality for admission to institutes of higher learning. Although candidates theoretically have a choice of schools and specializations, they must "indicate their desire to subordinate themselves to planned distribution." . . . Planned distribution was said to have been abolished in 1957 and selection by students to have been established entirely on a voluntary basis.[12] By 1958 it was reported that students did have a choice of schools and specializations and that planned distribution had accounted for only 17 per cent of the total enrollment back in 1955 and only 6.3 per cent in 1956. Other statements make the above report seem most unlikely. The explanation may lie in the phrase "planned distribution on a voluntary basis"; probably all students or prospective students "volunteer" to permit the state to decide their fate.

On July 2, 1957, "political quality"—to be measured primarily in terms of "knowledge of and performance during the rectification and antirightist campaigns"—formally became the primary consideration in the selection of candidates for higher education. The new regulation of the Ministry of Education also authorized exemptions from matriculation examinations and "priority considerations" for applicants of worker or peasant origin who demonstrated their political and labor capabilities and could satisfy certain minimal academic requirements. Defending the new system, the Party newspaper stated editorially that although such applicants might be inferior in "book knowledge," their greater experience in class struggle and production work would actually raise the standard of new students.[13]

In case several candidates have similar qualifications and grades on the entrance examinations, first consideration is given to workers, peasants, and current-year graduates from secondary schools. Next in order of priority are demobilized servicemen, employees who have participated in revolutionary work for 3 years, and then children of martyrs and national minority students, together with overseas Chinese and students from Hong Kong and Macao.

A continuing problem with regard to recruitment for higher education is the shortage of qualified applicants as a result of the inadequate number of graduates from senior secondary schools. The following excerpt well states the problem:

"In order to supply all kinds of higher construction personnel needed by the state, higher institutions have been greatly extended since the liberation. But the sources of students are extremely wanting. Apart from mobilizing senior secondary school students to apply for admission into higher institutions every year, we had on many occasions to mobilize and send people holding working posts to sit for the matriculation examinations and to expand sources of students in other ways. This year, in view of the demand of the situation of the nationwide leap forward, higher institutions have to enroll a greater number of students. Because the sources of students are still lacking, it is required that all those senior secondary school students due for graduation this year [1958] who are able to study further, actively apply for admission into higher institutions."[14]

In the summer of 1956, 41 per cent of 351,000 applicants were that year's secondary school graduates; 22 per cent were workers in government departments, factories and mines, and other enterprises. The residual is unspecified. Also, 65,800 primary-school teachers were to take part in entrance examinations for teachers' colleges.[15] The last statement is of dubious validity, since the great majority of primary-school teachers do not have a completed secondary education. Although teaching experience may possibly be substituted for formal education, special courses would still have to be set up to suit the average level of achievement attained by these primary-school teachers.

Lengthy discussions have taken place to resolve many of the problems involved in recruiting college students. In the process of increasing the number of entrants, not enough care has been taken to insure the quality:

> The very fact that there were large numbers of students leaving their schools in the middle of their courses of studies has proved that accepting unqualified students by force of circumstances could only lead to the incurrence of heavy wastage in manpower and material to the country and cause the students to suffer.[16]

Another point under discussion is the large number of persons failing the entrance examinations, particularly among candidates already on the job who had left school several years earlier and wish to return to school. For example, in 1955, "three quarters of the cadres on active duty failed in their examinations."[17]

Although the number of entrants into the institutions of higher education has increased from 35,000 in 1950 to a planned 270,000 in 1959 (see table 1), the trend has not been consistently upward. The greatest drop occurred between 1956 and 1957, when the number of entrants into universities and institutes decreased from 165,000 to 107,000. This drop was explained or accounted for by the statement that the plan for admitting new students followed the development of production and the country's needs: Sometimes more students were needed and sometimes fewer. Also, it was during this period that much of the discussion occurred about the quality of students in higher education. Accepting the smaller number of entrants was perhaps designed to improve the quality of these students. Despite this drop, the number of entrants into higher institutions still exceeded the number of graduates from the higher secondary schools (general, normal, and vocational) in the spring of the same year. . . .

One curious fact about the social background of the college students: Whereas peasants and workers constitute the overwhelming proportion of the total population of China, it is proclaimed with pride that the proportion of students of worker and peasant origin in higher education had increased from 20.46 per cent in 1952–53 to 29.20 per cent in 1955–56, and to 36.42 per cent in 1957–58.[18] This means that despite the pressures on the intellectual, the capitalist businessman, and the like, the sons and daughters of these "reactionaries" still constitute the great majority of the students in higher education after some 8 years of the Communist regime. . . .

ADVANCED STUDIES

The present situation with regard to advanced degrees in China is somewhat vague. Although the plan to award advanced degrees in Chinese universities was announced in 1956, it is believed that this plan was never put into effect and that no higher academic degrees have been awarded. There appears to have been no mention of graduate students since 1957. There are students who complete a 4- or 5-year university curriculum and remain to do additional research and often act as instructors. In all probability they are the same individuals who are referred to as graduate students. . . .

Perhaps the most competent graduate study-research program was instituted by the Academy of Sciences in 1955 (see section on the Academy in ch. VI). Upon completion of the 4-year graduate program either at the Academy or at a university the student earned the title of "fu-po-shih" [associate doctor]. According to regulations issued by the Ministry of Higher Education, candidates for the title of associate doctor must be under the age of 40, graduates of polytechnical colleges or universities, with 2 years of experience in scientific or technical work. Exceptions may be made under the last two requirements for exceptionally qualified candidates, but all applicants must pass the entrance examination.[19]

The Communists also continued the previous practice of sending students abroad for study, the difference being that since 1950 the overwhelming majority of the students have gone to the Soviet Union for their training. A special examination is held by the Ministry of Higher Education to insure the quality of students going abroad. A sample of the reports dealing with their number reveals the difficulty in making a reasonable estimate for this group. It was reported that between 1949–50 and 1954–55, 5,000 students were sent out of the country for study.[20] Another report states that from 1953–54 through 1956–57, 7,099 persons went abroad to study, while 801 returned.[21] Four months later one Chinese journal stated that "between 1950 and 1957 the Soviet Union gave us great help in connection with higher education and trained over 7,000 teachers and over 6,000 students and postgraduates."[22] Still later, the Communists reported that between 1950 and 1959 the mainland regime sent 14,000 students to the Soviet Union and that 8,500 of that number had returned to China.[23] While presenting these seemingly contradictory figures, a few points of possible agreement must be mentioned. The 5,000 sent between 1949–50 and 1954–55 and the 7,000 sent between 1953–54 and 1956–57 seem fairly compatible with the 14,000 sent abroad between 1950 and 1959; the 6,000 trained students (obviously returned) between 1950 and 1957, and the 8,500 returned students between 1950 and 1959 are also in fair agreement. . . .

Another difficulty arises in trying to determine what proportion of the students sent abroad were undergraduates and what proportion were sent abroad only after graduating from a higher institution. Referring to 1955, an announcement stated that 80 per cent of the students returning from abroad were postgraduates and 20 per cent were undergraduates.[24] This does not seem to be a representative distribution, especially since it includes only returning students, and refers to persons who left China in 1951 or 1952 and probably completed their undergraduate work prior to 1949. It would be surprising if graduate students constituted more than a third of the total number of students who went abroad to study during the past 10 years. This same report gives the following distribution of the student returning from the Soviet Union in 1955: "Thirty of these students took up the study of engineering, while the other took up specialized courses on communications and transportation, architecture, medicine, finance, and economics. . . . In addition to taking up the study of foreign languages, they usually took up courses lasting from 3 to 4 years." It must be noted here that one of the major obstacles to successful study in the Soviet Union is, of course, the language barrier.

In view of the foggy data and the vague concept, it is difficult to determine precisely the level of educational attainment of persons that are reported to have earned postgraduate degrees. Most probably anyone who remained at the university for an additional period of time to participate in further study or research is included. Undoubtedly, anyone who had done any postgraduate work abroad, or possibly simply studied abroad, is considered to have earned a higher degree. In any case, Communist China has managed to produce only a few really highly qualified scholars, and the postgraduate studies can in no way be equated with advanced study engaged in by students in the West.

Probably the advanced-degree level of competence is now being achieved by a limited number of persons working at the various institutes of the Academy of Sciences and at some of the better universities with more advanced personnel and facilities. The University of Science and Technology, opened in Peking in 1958, may be one such institution. Most of the students in the field of science and engineering probably attain competence through work and research in the laboratories, industrial plants and other establishments and not as a result of a formal system of education that awards higher degrees.

Notes

1. *Student's Directory of Higher Education* (Peking: Ministry of Higher Education, 1958).
2. *New China News Agency,* Oct. 29, 1959.
3. *Ibid.,* Jan 27, 1960.
4. *College Students of New China* (Peking: 1958).
5. *Jen-min Chiao-yu* [People's Education], Oct. 1954.
6. *Peking Review,* Sept. 30, 1958.
7. *Ibid.*
8. *Izvestiya Vysshikh Uchebnykh Zavedeniy, Tsvetnaya Metallurgiya* [Bulletin of the Higher Educational Institutions, Nonferrous Metallurgy], No. 5 (Moskva: 1959).
9. *Cheng-ming* [Contend], No. 2, Feb. 10, 1958.
10. *New China News Agency,* May 20, 1954.
11. *Ibid.,* March 19, 1956.
12. *Cheng-ming* [Contend], No. 2, Feb. 10, 1958.
13. *Jen-min Jih-pao* [People's Daily], July 3, 1957.
14. *New China News Agency,* Apr. 7, 1958.
15. *Ibid.,* July 13, 1956.
16. *Kuang-ming Jih-pao* [Kuang-ming Daily], Aug. 16, 1955.
17. *Jen-min Jih-pao* [People's Daily], Mar. 17, 1956.
18. *Peking Review,* May 20, 1958.
19. *An-shan Jih-pao* [An-shan Daily], July 20, 1956.

20. *New China News Agency,* July 8, 1955.
21. *Jen-min Chiao-yu* [People's Education], Oct. 9, 1957.
22. *Shih-chieh Chih-shih* [World Knowledge], No. 3, Feb. 5, 1958.
23. *Jen-min Jih-pao* [People's Daily], Oct. 4, 1959.
24. *New China News Agency,* Aug. 4, 1955.

33. THE TEACHING PROFESSION

THEODORE HSI-EN CHEN

Much effort is expended in Communist China to extol the "glory" of the teaching profession and the contributions of teachers to national life. Nevertheless there are indications that the professional status of teachers is not high and the morale of the teaching personnel is often very low. As a matter of fact, the abundance of laudatory and exhortatory oratory may be in itself an indication of low morale and of widespread dissatisfaction on the part of those engaged in teaching.

The curriculum of teacher-training institutions consists of political subjects, academic subjects, "professional" subjects, and practice teaching. In practice, political education is considered the most essential part of teacher education; academic study ranks next. "Professional" subjects consist usually of a course in education, a course in psychology, and courses in methods of teaching. Even these have very pronounced political overtones and constantly stress the importance of the Marxist viewpoint. In the case of short-term courses and spare-time teacher education, these "professional subjects" and practice teaching are most likely to be dropped. Some short-term programs concentrate on political indoctrination alone, while others are mainly concerned with academic study to remedy the limited schooling the teachers have had, but the latter would not completely disregard political indoctrination, because, as we have noted, no Communist education on any form can be separated from politics.

Much is said about the "professional spirit" of teachers. A large part of this talk is directed toward rectifying the current reluctance of qualified persons to enter teaching and the tendency of teachers to look for the first chance to leave teaching for more desirable work. State policy demands of the student a complete sacrifice of his personal interests and ambitions and an unquestioned readiness to accept any assignment of the state to any job in the service of "people's education." It severely condemns any form of individualism as a "bourgeois" shortcoming. The devotion it calls for is no different from the

SOURCE. Selected from *Teacher Training in Communist China* (Publication of the Office of Education, U.S. Department of Health, Education, and Welfare), Mimeographed, pp. 31–42.

devotion the government and the Party expect of any worker in any field as long as the work is considered important by the state.

There is little stablity in the teaching ranks. There is no provision for tenure. Salaries are low, and living conditions are rarely satisfactory. A delegate to the national conference of the Union of Educational Workers in 1956 gave three reasons why teachers were unhappy with their lot: (1) their political status was low; (2) their salaries and living conditions were inadequate; and (3) they were kept so busy that they had no time for rest and some had developed nervous disorders.[1] Since 1956, in an effort to win over the "higher intellectuals," the living and working conditions of the university professors have been noticeably improved, but few of the ameliorative measures have benefited teachers of the lower schools. In 1956, the Ministry of Education announced a 32.88 per cent increase of salaries of elementary school teachers, but even after the increase the salaries were still very inadequate. According to the officially announced wage scale, the minimum salary for elementary school teachers should be about 20 *yuan*,[2] but many teachers actually get much less. Some school teachers get as low as 4 *yuan* a month, and 10 *yuan* is not considered unusual.[3]

Salaries depend on academic qualifications. The wage scale provides for 11 gradations within each bracket. For a person who has had 3 years of junior normal school or other secondary school of comparable level, the prescribed minimum is 20 *yuan* per month and the maximum is 26 *yuan*.[4] One who has had 2 years of normal school (or senior secondary school) get 24–31 *yuan,* a graduate of the 2-year higher normal course gets 34–44 *yuan*, while completion of 4 years of higher education (including higher normal college or university) would command a salary of 40–52 *yuan*.[5] Thus, even the best qualified secondary teacher could get no more than the equivalent of about U.S. $22.00, and the majority of his colleagues get much less.

With the meager salaries, elementary school teachers have a hard time maintaining themselves even on a subsistence level. They have to cook their own meals with the limited rations they can get, and they live under conditions which must be considered detrimental to health, not to say professional morale or pride. In an editorial calling attention to the grave housing problems of teachers, the *Chiao Shih Pao* (a semiweekly newspaper for teachers) stated that many teachers were either unable to find housing or could not afford to pay the rent.[6] After loud complaints during the so-called "hundred flowers" period of 1956, when the expression of diverse opinions was actively encouraged by the regime, the authorities released some houses for the use of teachers, but a reporter visiting these homes found that many were only tiny and poorly ventilated rooms, and one of them was an erstwhile garage "in which a car would rust."[7]

Theoretically, educational authorities are supposed to establish welfare funds which may be drawn upon to relieve needy teachers, especially in times of family sickness, but few teachers have benefited. Deductions are made from teachers' salaries to build up welfare funds, but too often the funds are allowed to accumulate indefinitely without use, or misappropriated for other uses.[8] Or, applications for relief are too often considered on the basis of the "attitude" of the applicant, which leaves the whole matter to the arbitrary whim of the Party cadres. A directive of the Ministry of Education on this matter cited cases of dire need which were denied help from the welfare funds. In one case, a teacher with a family of six persons had no change of clothes and had to wear the same clothes day and night without washing them, and yet his application for aid was denied because of his "poor relations with the masses."[9] Politics, again, became the dominating factor.

Political Control

Teacher morale is adversely affected not only by low salaries and inadequate living conditions, but also by psychological factors, chief among which is the stifling political control to which all teachers are subjected. The teacher does not have the opportunity of independent judgment or decisions based on purely professional considerations. He is first of all a servant of the Party and state or at best a functionary to carry out the decisions and policies handed to him by the Party and state. Political control is exercised in many ways. In the first place, there is the unrelenting demand that teachers must engage continuously in political "study." They submit to this "study" and to "thought reform" regularly in their schools and also in more intensive sessions at centralized locations.[10] In these "study" sessions, the teachers are constantly being told that they are products of bourgeois society and their thinking has been poisoned by "bourgeois ideology." It is necessary for them to make a complete break with the past and start anew as dedicated servants of proletarian society. The confessions, the self-denunciations, the acceptance of the new ideology, and the required pledges of new loyalties are harrowing and humiliating experiences which are anything but conducive to the development of a true professional spirit.

In addition, the Communists put teachers under the authority of domineering cadres whose academic standing could not measure up to the standards of the pupils. These cadres freely and flauntingly exercise the power vested in them by the Party they represent: They lecture the teachers on their ideological inadequacy; they pose as authorities on the Marxist-Leninist cliches which they require the teachers to repeat; they pass judgment on the progress of each teacher in his "thought reform"; their reports to the Party organization determine to a large extent the official evaluation given to the work of each individual teacher. Teachers have been dismissed as a result of the unfavorable reports of cadres.

The cadres are especially harsh on the elementary school teachers. Teachers are not permitted to eat in the school dining rooms, which are reserved for the Party cadres and their families. The cadres scold and discipline the teachers in the presence of the students. In one school, teachers arriving late at a meeting convened by the cadres were made to stand at attention to listen to the cadres' reports.[11] So widespread was teachers dissatisfaction in 1956 that the official Party organ had to take notice and to demand a rectification of the deplorable situation. The *Jen Min Jih Pao* said in an editorial:

We have recently received letters from readers calling attention to discriminatory practices against teachers in many areas, providing concrete evidence of the unreasonable treatment of elementary school teachers. There are cadres, especially those in the rural districts, who despise the work of elementary school teachers and treat them with rudeness and unreasonableness, sometimes belaboring them with ridicule and sarcasm, or even accusing them of ideological deviations. They insult the personality of the elementary school teachers and interfere with their personal freedom. In some places cadres treat elementary school teachers as their personal valets to be sent on errands at their beck and call. In other places, there is discrimination against teachers in the supply of grain, vegetables and meat, so that teachers receive reduced rations or are intentionally given inferior products.[12]

Teachers must of course accept the guidance of the cadres in their political "study" and their "thought reform." Carelessness may invite the charge of "bourgeois ideology" or other specific ideological deviations. Once charged with ideological deviaton, teachers can expect nothing but long and continued harassment, nerve-wracking inquisition in the form of "criticism and self-criticism," and treatment as virtual outcasts. But in other aspects of their work, teachers also have to be constantly mindful of the authority of the "Party leadership" in the school. "Disobedience to the leadership" is a major offense that all must endeavor to avoid. To be safe, teachers must tread the narrow path specified by the "leadership" or the Party organization. They carefully prepare their teaching outlines and submit them for the approval of the "leadership." Even in their personal activities outside the school they follow the dictates of the "leadership."

While secondary school and university professors are not treated with as much scorn as teachers of the elementary schools, they are by no means free from the domination of the overbearing cadres. The cadres do not hesitate to tell the higher intellectuals how they should "reform" themselves in order to serve the Party; they even have the temerity to direct the academic and scientific studies of the intellectuals on the ground that no intellectual activity can be divorced from politics, and those who are politically and ideologically sound have the right to dictate the direction of classroom teaching and scientific research. Many complaints were voiced in the "hundred flowers" season of 1956–57. A college professor of economics gave vent to his frustration as follows:

> Since Liberation, the responsible representatives of Party and state in the universities have come to evaluate a professor's lectures not in terms of his "creativity" or his ability for independent research, but according to his willingness to submit to "discipline." "Discipline" means that the professor lectures in class exactly according to the outline of lecture notes previously approved by the "leadership"; he is not allowed to use any lecture material not previously approved. . .
>
> At present, what keeps us professors most busy are the meetings and the writing of lecture notes. Especially time-consuming is the search for "authority." Every word and every bit of content must be based on "authority." The best authority is of course the words of Marx, Lenin, or some prominent official of Party or government.[13]

A well-known socialist described the harmful effects of the political domination of education as follows:

In the early stage of educational reform, teachers went through a period of great tension. Because it was necessary to learn from the Soviet Union, they had to prepare new teaching materials. Furthermore, as a result of the thought-reform movement, they had to discard what they had studied, but they were not able to establish a new system to take the place of the old. The task of rushing to produce Russian or translated syllabi kept them extremely busy. . . .

Books from England and America would merely take up room on the shelves, so they were sold as scrap paper. There was no time to study Russian and so the teachers had to be satisfied with the small translated editions they could buy. When they wrote articles or lectured in class, all they needed to do was to cite passages from the words of the approved authorities, and to pick out a few British and American scholars to criticize and revile. This was not difficult to do, and it was exactly what many scholars did.[14]

Teachers are supposed to obey the Party and the state on all matters. When the government proposed to combine departments and institutions in the "reform" of higher education in 1951–52, any professor who dared raise a voice of dissent was condemned as "reactionary" and as unable to shed the "individualism" and "particularism" characteristic of "bourgeois thinking." The "progressive" teacher is one who readily accepts the plans and policies of the state and works energetically for their fulfillment. To raise questions on even purely academic grounds is to betray one's "bourgeois ideology."

Teachers at all levels have complained that political activities take up too much of their time. There is no end to the meetings they must attend and the activities they must engage in. Failure to participate invites the criticism of "alienation from the group." In many schools, teachers are required to read the daily newspapers "collectively."[15] Teachers are kept busy 10 to 15 hours a day and are still unable to devote enough time to academic work, for political and other nonacademic activities frequently take as much as 40 per cent of their time.[16] Teachers have been assigned to clerical chores in government offices and to various tasks in construction projects and propaganda campaigns that bear no direct relation to their teaching. They have been asked to help in the local post office, to sell books and newspapers for the state-owned bookstore, to collect savings for the bank, even to deliver letters, to take care of the granary, etc.[17] During the Aid-Korea Resist-America campaign of 1950–51, more than 90 per cent of the element teachers in Shanghai formed propaganda teams to go out on the streets and harangue the populace.[18]

Another frequently heard complaint is that the high and mighty cadres and Party representatives hold themselves aloof and have built up a wide chasm between themselves and the teachers. They discuss questions of school policy among themselves without consulting the teachers and administrators. Important directives from the Party or the government are sent to them and discussed by them before they are made known to the teachers and the titular administrators. Professors of the well-known Tsinghua University reported that Party members on the campus were so haughty that they even refused to return the greeting of non-Communist teachers and students.[19] Those who desire to enter the inner circle find that the door is not open. In spite of recent efforts on the part of the Communists to induce China's "higher intellectuals" to join the Party, most teachers, especially those of the lower schools, find that "admission into the Party is more difficult than entering heaven." They remain outsiders who can only accept without question the decisions handed down to them.[20]

Political control over teachers is also exercised through the students. In the name of democracy, expressed in student participation in school affairs, the Communists make use of the students as a fulcrum for applying pressure on the teachers. Under "the leadership of the Party" the students demand that the teachers should take up political "study," purge their teaching of "bourgeois ideology," engage in labor, and prove themselves worthy of their new tasks. In the "thought reform" of teachers, the students were vociferous in demanding confessions and recantations from their teachers. During the mass movements for ideological reform in the early 1950's[21] students scrutinized the record of individual teachers and exposed their offenses. This role of the students as overseers has inevitably complicated the relations between teachers and students and further degraded the position of the teacher. As Professor Ch'ien Wei-ch'ang of Tsinghua University pointed out, teachers have to be extremely cautious when the students can find fault with whatever they say and charge them with serious offenses in public denunciation meetings. How could one really teach, he asked, when the students could turn around any time to wage a "struggle" against the teacher?[22]

Teachers Organizations

The Communists have promoted teachers organizations as a form of "mass organizations." These are not professional organizations rising out of the initiative or felt need of teachers. They are, rather, organizations sponsored and directed by the Party and state and charged with the duty of keeping their members in line and "mobilizing" them to support the programs of the Party and state. Even before coming to power in 1949, the Communists had sponsored organizations of "democratic professors" and of "progressive elements" from among the teachers. After 1949 there appeared various teachers organizations such as the Federation of Workers in Higher Education in Shanghai, the Federation of Teachers and Staff Members of Secondary and Elementary Schools in Peking, and the like. These groups were subsequently merged under the overall national organization known as the All-China Union of Educational workers.

The Union of Educational Workers is not only an organization of teachers. Its membership includes teachers, staff members, janitors, laborers, school police, and all persons in the employ of educational institutions of all kinds. The initiative for the organization came from the All-China Federation of Trade Unions, which convened a conference of delegates of educational workers from various parts of the country in August 1950. Three hundred twenty-nine delegates attended the conference, which gave birth to the Union of Educational Workers.[23]

To have one organization for all "educational workers" instead of separate organizations for teachers and to make it a part of the labor movement are in line with the Communist insistence that intellectuals must identify themselves with the working class. At the same time, the teachers are deprived of the opportunity of a truly professional organization specifically concerned with the problems of teachers.

One of the leading lights of the Union of Educational Workers is Wu Yu-chang, chairman of its National Committee. In this opening address at the inauguration conference of 1950, he said: "The aim of the Union of Educational Workers, like other trade unions, is to protect the interests of the working class and to guarantee the fulfillment of the production plans of the state."[24] Kuo Mo-jo, then chairman of the Committee on Education and Culture of the central government, said that the birth of the Union meant for teachers a "class transformation" because teachers of bourgeois and petty bourgeois background were not transforming themselves into members of the working class.[25] Another speaker at the conference stressed the importance of having the teachers "reform themselves in order to establish a new philosophy of serving the workers, peasants, and soldiers."[26] The conference adopted a constitution which spelled out the functions and the scope of activities of the Union.

The constitution[27] provides that the Union must be under the direct supervision of the All-China Federation of Trade Unions and that the organization must follow the principle of democratic centralism, with lower levels subordinate to the higher (provincial and national) levels and the minority pledged to obey the majority. The duties of members are listed as follows: (1) To observe labor discipline, (2) to engage in political, cultural, and professional study in order to raise the level of political consciousness and professional work, (3) to carry out the resolutions of the Union and take active part in its work and social activities, (4) to unite with and educate nonmembers, and (5) to pay monthly dues.

It is thus clear that the Union is designed to serve as an instrument for "reforming" and disciplining the teachers or, in other words, as an instrument of control. The political objectives have been predominant since the beginning. At the inauguration conference, it was declared that the Union must take an active part in the campaign for mass signatures in support of the Communist-sponsored World Peace Movement. The Union is affiliated with the World Federation of Teachers Unions (Federation Internationale Syndicale de l'Enseignment) and observes November 20 as the "International Day of the Teachers' Charter" in conformity with the decision of the conference held in Moscow in August 1957.[28] The Union played an active role in the Aid-Korea Resist-America campaign and in all patriotic campaigns initiated by the Party or state. It urged its members to learn from the Soviet Union and encourage Chinese school children to exchange correspondence with Soviet school children.[29]

Inasmuch as the Union of Educational Workers is a part of the trade union movement and its constitution is inspired by the constitution of the national trade union organization, it may be helpful to refer briefly to the constitution of the All-China Federation of Trade Unions, as revised and adopted in 1957.[30] The preamble of the constitution states:

Under the leadership of the working class, the interests of the state are identical with the common interests of the entire people and also with the fundamental interests of our working class. The trade unions should educate the workers and recognize the unity of interests between the state and the individual and, when these two conflict, realize that individual interests should be subordinated to state interests.

In order to do its work, declared the *Workers' Daily,* a trade union must be completely under the leadership of the Party.[31] The prescribed duties of all trade union members are similar in tone and spirit to those of members of the Union of Educational Workers. They are stated in its constitution as follows:

1. To observe the policies, laws, and decrees of the state and work discipline; to fulfill enthusiastically their tasks in national construction;
2. To safeguard the socialist system and protect public property; to fight against all antisocialist views and acts, the destruction of public property, violations of law and social and work discipline, and all acts of corruption and waste;
3. To engage assiduously in political, cultural, technical and professional studies so as to raise their level of class consciousness and ability;
4. To foster class fraternity, unity, and mutual help;
5. To abide by the constitution of the trade unions, implement trade union decisions, and pay membership dues punctually.

At the second National Congress of the Union of Educational Workers held in August 1956, it was reported that the membership of the Union had reached 1,351,134, constituting more than 60 per cent of the total number of "educational and scientific workers" in the country. It was proposed that a drive be launched to increase the percentage to 80 or 90 per cent in the following year.[32] The Union of Educational Workers, editorialized the *Jen Min Jih Pao*,[33] should help educational and scientific workers to further their self-education, strengthen spare-time study, and elevate their ideological and cultural level. Self-education is, in large part, political and ideological in nature. In other words, a constant objective of the Union is to "mobilize" teachers and other educational workers to engage in "thought reform" in order to purge themselves of bourgeois ideas and bourgeois attitudes and to implant firmly the "workers' viewpoint," which is the Communist viewpoint. As stated in the resolutions of the second congress of the Union, one of the most important functions of the Union is to serve as a "school for Communism" to produce loyal and faithful workers to carry out the educational program of the Party and state.[34]

In 1958, the National Committee of the Union called upon local organizations to launch an intensive campaign of ideological "self-education" in order to make the educational workers more "Red" and more "expert."[35] Meetings were held in which teachers pledged to wage an uncompromising struggle against anti-Party and antisocialist views and actions, to undertake serious study of Marxism-Leninism, to engage actively in physical labor and learn its discipline, to learn humbly from the workers and peasants, to stamp out bourgeois thinking in a thorough way, and to carry out faithfully the educational policies of Mao Tse-tung. In "oath ceremonies" teachers shouted, "We give our hearts to the Party, we give our knowledge to the people, and we shall speed up our ideological reform." The Unions in different places also launched "thought reform emulation campaigns" to stimulate greater effort to raise the "level of socialist consciousness."[36]

Notes

1. *Chiao Shih Pao,* August 14, 1956.
2. At the official rate of exchange, the *yuan* equals about 42 cents in U.S. currency.
3. See Wu Yen-yin's speech on teachers' salaries, *Kuang Ming Jih Pao,* August 16, 1956.
4. As will be seen (pp. 46–48), many teachers are below this academic level.
5. See salary scale in *Fa Kuei Hui Pien,* Vol. 6, p. 478.
6. *Chiao Shih Pao,* July 20, 1956.
7. *Ibid.,* August 3, 1956.
8. Such abuses were admitted in a Ministry of Education directive regarding teachers' welfare funds. See *Fa Kuei Hui Pien,* Vol. 4, pp. 463–467.
9. *Ibid.,* p. 464.
10. For more information on the "thought reform" of teachers, the reader is referred to the author's *Thought Reform of Chinese Intellectuals* (New York: Oxford University Press, 1960).
11. "Pu Neng Che Yang Tui-tai Hsiao-hsueh Chiao-shih" (Elementary school teachers should not be treated this way). *Kung Jen Jih Pao* (Workers Daily, Peking) July 14, 1956. Other complaints about the harsh treatment of teachers are made in the same paper, September 11, 1956, and in *Nan Fang Jih Pao* (Southern Daily, Canton), September 7, 1956.
12. *Jen Min Jih Pao,* October 5, 1956.
13. Wu Ta-k'un, "Jan Chiao-shau Men Tu Li Chiang K'e," *Jen Min Jih Pao,* August 19, 1956.
14. Fei Hsiao-t'ung, "Chih Shih Fen Tzu Ti Tsao ch'un T'ien Ch'i," *Jen Min Jih Pao,* March 24, 1957.
15. The *Chiao Shih Pao* reported on July 20, 1956, that authorities in Kirin province had adopted ameliorative measures to relieve the teachers, and one of them was to discontinue the collective reading of newspapers.
16. *Jen Min Chiao Yu,* February 5, 1953, p. 40.
17. *Jen Min Jih Pao,* September 11, 1956.
18. *Jen Min Chiao Yu,* September 1, 1951, p. 39.
19. *Jen Min Jih Pao,* May 15, 1957.
20. *Kiangsi Jih Pao,* June 24, 1956, also July 6 and 8, 1956.
21. These campaigns were directed against various evils attributed to bourgeois mentality and ideology.
22. Interview recorded in *Jen Min Jih Pao,* May 17, 1957.
23. *Jen Min Shou Ts'e,* 1951 (People's Handbook, published by *Ta Kung Pao,* Shanghai, 1951), p. 83.
24. *Chung Kuo Chiao Yu Kung Tso Che Shou T'se* (Handbook of Chinese Educational Workers, published by Kung Jen Ch'u Pan She, 1951), p. 2.
25. *Ibid.,* pp. 5–8.

26. *Ibid.*, p. 18.

27. Text of constitution in *Ibid.*, pp. 26–40.

28. *Survey of China Mainland Press* 1658:46, November 25, 1957.

29. See report on the Preparatory Committee for the Conference of Educational Workers' Delegates in *Kuang Ming Jih Pao,* October 11, 1959.

30. *Eighth All-China Congress of the Trade Unions* (Peking: Foreign Languages Press, 1958), pp. 106–125.

31. *Kung Jen Jih Pao* editorial, reprinted in *Chiao Shih Pao,* July 4, 1958.

32. Report of Wu Yu-chang at the Conference, *Jen Min Jih Pao,* September 4, 1956.

33. *Ibid.*, August 16, 1956.

34. *Survey of China Mainland Press* 1358:16, August 27, 1956.

35. *Chiao Shih Pao,* April 8, 1958.

36. *Loc. cit.*

Health and Welfare

34. DOCTORS AND PATIENTS

Marie Sieh

The Doctor

A doctor's working day extends officially from 8 A.M. to 6 P.M. but he seldom completes his work within this time and his working hours are variable and always long.

In a small urban hospital four to eight doctors usually look after eighty to a hundred beds. Each doctor treats a variety of complaints instead of specializing as he would in larger hospitals. Wards may have two or three nurses each though these figures vary from hospital to hospital. A large city hospital in Canton or Shanghai is divided into two main departments of Surgery and Internal Medicine, with various specialty sections in each. Doctors are assigned to specific sections. Nurses work on three shifts, a larger number during the day and a skeleton staff by night. Interns are on twenty-four hour call.

When a physician reaches the rank of visiting doctor his work load eases and he finally has more time to devote to research and study. As a visiting doctor he takes out-patient work at most twice a week to deal with more serious cases referred by the junior doctors. He has less routine though far more responsibility for ward patients. His duties are limited to the daily rounds and serious cases and to checking and controlling the work of those under him. He himself is responsible to the chief of department who also limits his medical activities to the morning rounds and referred cases.

Each morning the official rounds are made by a group composed of interns, junior doctors, Chief Resident, visiting doctors and the department chiefs, followed by the nurses and sometimes the matron. The hospital chief makes spot checks, going unexpectedly to each ward and out-patient clinic at least

SOURCE: Selected from Marie Sieh, "Medicine in China: Wealth for the State, Parts I and II," in *Current Scene,* October 1964, pp. 2–7, and November 1964, pp. 2–14.

once a month. In larger hospitals the prelude to these visits may be a lecture by the Chief on a certain type of sickness and the visits will most certainly be the time for discussion and for questions from any member of the staff.

From Specialist to One-Man-Band

The routine of a doctor's day varies according to size of hospital and area. For example, a surgeon in a small four-doctor hospital (in which all doctors will most likely be surgeons) has ward patients to care for and operations to perform in addition to half-day outpatient clinic (both internal and surgery). In such a situation all may operate and finish before out-patient clinic or two may do the clinic and leave all operations to the other two. In a large hospital with many doctors, surgeons take only surgical out-patient clinic. In some large hospitals a junior resident takes two sessions of out-patient clinic each day for three months and has no ward duties. At the other end of the scale, the doctor who operates a commune hospital does everything that comes his way, whether he is a "middle doctor"[1] (a graduate of a two to three year course) or fully trained.

Any free time during the day is generally taken up with paper work, medical history charts for all patients seen during the day and orders for night duty staff and nurses. Senior doctors, with more free time, are encouraged to read medical journals and write articles on rare cases. Generally the hard-pressed doctors are too tired in the evenings to do more than wash their personal clothing, clean their rooms and fall asleep, provided they are not required to attend the one, two or more per week political meetings scheduled to absorb the precious evening hours. Except for these meetings, they seldom go out and, if not too tired, will try to read medical journals in bed.

In most city hospitals of around five hundred beds, one floor is devoted to library facilities where most reputable medical journals from all the Western countries can be found in the original as well as Chinese journals. Many of the important articles will have been translated into Chinese but doctors who can read a foreign language prefer the original. While any hospital doctor may avail himself of these facilities, the library is not open to students. In theory, students neither know enough nor have enough time to benefit from such material. There is however one special research journal which is for senior doctors only and must be read behind closed doors in a special room, the contents to be divulged to no one outside the circulation list, perhaps because the research is not yet complete.

Many doctors with relatives abroad and a knowledge of foreign languages request new medical books to be posted to them. They can make extra money by translating articles and demonstrating new techniques in any free time they can find.

Herbalists and "Middle Doctors"

In 1958, the Party's Central Committee, as part of its drive to de-emphasize Western learning and technology, decreed that traditional Chinese medicine was to occupy a place equal to or superior to Western medicine. This was consistent with Peking's policy to give first place to whatever springs from the masses—and to devalue the intellectuals.[2] As a consequence, schools have been set up to teach herbal medicine, medical students training in Western medicine also attend lectures on acupuncture and herb medicine, and the Chinese traditional doctor of today is usually a regular graduate of a standardized course in Chinese traditional medicine. He has equal official status, if hardly equal training, with physicians trained in Western medicine.

To further alleviate trained personnel shortages, there is a category called "middle doctors," who undergo a two-year practical course in basic medical knowledge and, if assigned to larger hospitals, serve one year as an assistant to gain practical experience. They are then assigned as assistants to regular doctors or sent to set up clinics in the country areas where, since no other form of care is available, their duties are varied. While they are supposed to be limited to work as assistants until they acquire greater knowledge and can treat patients without supervision, in actual practice they are accorded the same title as regular doctors (who are referred to officially as "higher educated").

After a long lapse, the medical course for Western trained doctors once again takes six years and includes a year of internship. One college in Peking has started an eight-year course, the first students being graduated this year. This is to be the primary research and post graduate training centre.

Not all students who hope to take a medical course are admitted to colleges, but those chosen must have signified medicine as their first preference (unlike other courses where students are assigned regardless of their desire). In this way, there is at least the initial interest of each student. Those who fail courses in their first or second year are either given a chance to take the test again or are re-routed to another job, according to the extent of their failure. Students who fail courses in the final year are not allowed to become doctors but are shunted to other types of medical work, perhaps to public health, X-ray or laboratory jobs, where they are not responsible for diagnosis but do work of a technical nature.

Grades and Politics

Each year the number of medical school applicants exceeds the places available in medical colleges and, though grades from middle school play an important part in acceptance, academic qualifications are closely linked with political reliability. In the early years students from upper-class backgrounds outnumbered the lower-class "political progressives" by 70:30 whereas today the situation is reversed and students from "worker backgrounds" number around 80 per cent of the total of medical students. This however does not give too clear a picture because many children of "intellectuals" are also included in the "worker class" category and children of the capitalist class are dwindling in numbers. Some student refugees believe that medical school selection is now based more on ability than on demonstrated political zeal though of course all must at least give lip service to ideology.

Each province has one medical college and the main centres such as Canton,

Shanghai and Peking have at least one more. All except one provide six-year medical courses.

The curriculum in all colleges is theoretically the same but the quality of teaching varies with the quality of teaching staff. While all professors are either doctors trained in the West or locally educated Western-medicine doctors of proven skill, the most expert are concentrated in the larger cities. The reason for this is probably that, as the experts are also used as consultants in the large hospitals, their particular knowledge can be utilized where specialist hospitals are to be found.

Details vary but a typical medical course would consist of the following:

Year I	Year II	Year III	Year IV
Physics*	Chemistry*	Physical diagnosis	Physical diagnosis
Chemistry	Biology*	Clinical diagnosis	Clinical diagnosis
Laboratory	Laboratory	Statistics	Statistics
Chinese language	Calculus	Two mornings in	Two mornings in
Anatomy	Anatomy	hospital examining	hospital examin-
		patients†	ing patients
			Lectures in college
		Lectures on cases	on cases
		examined	examined
			Lectures on public
			health and X-ray

* In every case where chemistry and physics are mentioned the classroom course is two to three hours and half day in laboratory for each course per week. Biology is four hours class, half day laboratory.

† In Year III hospital mornings are spent in obstetrics and pediatrics departments.

Every week there is a half day political training course which is vital in the final examinations. Another important course is sports which occupies two hours a week.

Some colleges report a course in psychology, others do not have this. A course in skin diseases is also elective. They are spread over the third and fourth years. Each lecture takes two to three hours per course. Laboratory and hospital work take half a day each per subject. Free class periods may be spent in reading or checking over notes either in a classroom or in dormitory. School lasts eight hours per day but this always includes one or two free periods. In the early 1950s the students also studied Russian but refugees report that these courses were stopped in the mid-fifties.

An average student day would be as follows:

7.00 A.M.: get up, wash face

7.15–30: exercises outdoors (compulsory)

7.30–8.00: breakfast
8.00–12.00: lessons
12.00–1.00 or 2.00 P.M. (winter and summer variation): lunch and rest or sleep in summer (compulsory)
1.00–5.00 (or 2.00–6.00 in summer): lessons or practice in laboratory or hospital
5.00–6.00: free time (compulsory exercises within this period)
6.00: dinner
7.00–9.00: evening revision class, political meetings
10.00: lights out (compulsory)

Professors lecture from their own notes and assign certain parts of reference books for students to read outside class hours but do not test on any until the end of the year. Assistants go over lessons in the evening with small groups. If any student fails he has to sit again for the examination during summer vacation. If he fails a second time he is expelled from the course. He must go up with the class or leave college. Repeating a year is impossible because each class is fixed from the first to the final year and no one may enter another class.

The choice of reference books is a matter for the individual professor. Such books as Pathology (Boyd), Physical Diagnosis (Cabot & Adams), Surgery (Christopher), Obstetrics (Eastman & Hellman), Textbook of Medicine (Cecil & Loeb) are generally used, and are available in pirated English editions, popular with those who have a knowledge of English, or in Chinese translations. Students grumble that often the translations are not too accurate or are too difficult to understand and, if they can read English at all, prefer to work harder to study the original. All lectures are in Chinese, however, and students have no chance to speak in English.

Manual Labour = Good Thoughts

Before the completion of their four/five years' study in college and one year internship, all students are required to do two months manual labour in the country. Without this they cannot graduate and their performance at this labour is a deciding factor as to whether they pass or not. Good, willing labour means good thoughts and political conformity. Recent news indicates that all university students from 1964 onwards will be required to undergo two years compulsory country labour before assignment, but whether this applies equally to doctors is not yet known.

Summer vacations have also been abolished from 1964. The time is to be spent in labour so students away from home will have little chance to revisit their families once they enter university. Students can go home, if it is near by, only on Saturday afternoon but must return to college by 8.00 A.M. on Monday at the latest. The college gate is locked at exactly 8.00 A.M. to ensure that no unauthorized persons stray into the college. Each student must wear a badge and gatemen check every one on entry.

In the required one year of internship, eight months are spent in surgery (two months in women's wards, two months in men's, one month each in children's operations, chest, osteopathy, half a month in harelip and cleft palate operations and half a month in urogenital); four months are given to gynaecology, obstetrics, pediatrics, ear, nose and throat, etc. Sensitive students who faint when first faced with a corpse to dissect are brought back to try again and, if they still show signs of agitation after several classes, they are asked to help in the preparation of the corpse.

Bodies for anatomy classes are either unclaimed accident cases or are purchased from those families so poor that they are willing to sell the body for desperately needed money. The purchase price for a corpse is generally 200–300 yuan.[3] Corpse-stealing is also prevalent. Families who will not give permission but are too poor to pay for cremation expenses are asked if they wish the hospital to make arrangements. The arrangements made by the hospital are for mass cremation and it is fairly easy to filch one or two good specimens.

A student must graduate with a good mark from each department of the hospital during internship in order to obtain an assignment as a doctor. Those who show good academic but weak practical skill are retained as assistants to the professors in medical school and aid in the preparation of lectures and demonstrations. To be a professor requires, in addition to a good school record, proven skill in the practical line over a considerable period of years.

In early years only about 30 per cent of the medical students were Party or Youth League members but membership has now risen to about 50 per cent in each medical college. Whether the student is or is not a Party or League member may be crucial in his chances of future research or promotion.

First Assignments

On graduation all students attend a large meeting in their college where volunteers for the less desirable rural areas are always called for. The Youth Leaguers and Party Members are of course always the first to volunteer, thus proving their loyalty to the Party. Not all who volunteer in this way are sent to such areas as a result of this ritual but those with less academic skill are certainly accepted.

There are never enough volunteers to fulfil all rural requirements and many other graduates are sent although they may not have volunteered. They are picked at random from the group left after the specialized cases have been assigned to the cities or to research centres. The term "specialized cases" refers to those students with aged or ailing parents, those in poor health, or only children. Although they must always request permission to stay in their home areas, it is usually granted. However, true "progressives," even if they can claim this exception, usually insist on volunteering for rural or frontier assignments.

The college authorities inform a graduate of the area to which he is to be sent; the nature of assignment is left to the hospitals concerned on the basis of their needs. As a result no graduate can plan to specialize in any given field; whether or not he gets the assignment he wants is a matter of luck. There is no doubt that this causes great dissatisfaction; a young, fragile girl hoping to become a pediatrician finds herself assigned to surgery or a budding young surgeon applauded for his skill in medical school ends up in radiology.

Salary for a graduate on first assignment is 42–48 yuan per month,[4] the difference depending on the area. Canton commands the highest, Shanghai next, Peking third and the rest of the country is on an equal scale. Food costs are borne by the individual and the amount spent varies with the particular circumstances. Most people eat in the hospital for convenience but there is no fixed rule; those who are married cook at home, at least on some occasions. Average expenditure for food is approximately one third of the salary but living quarters are either free or, for married couples, available at minimal cost.

Hospital Etiquette

In urban hospitals there must be at least two doctors on operations and any major operation requires a senior doctor to be present in addition, either to teach or observe. Two nurses are also in attendance. In rural hospitals a doctor may have to do everything on his own with an untrained helper who does not even understand what the instruments are for.

Fear of criticism permeates all actions. For instances, a doctor is responsible for the nurse attending to his case. Should he find her guilty of an error or omission he may discipline her, provided it is done with the utmost courtesy. No show of temper or impolite phrasing may enter into it and, if he wishes to avoid possible trouble, he can report the fault to the head nurse instead of rebuking the nurse himself. This is seldom done except in cases of repeated disobedience or error when the doctor may take this step to protect himself from future denunciation. On the other hand, if an experienced nurse sees a doctor committing what she believes to be an error, she may correct him and point out the mistake. By no word or expression may the doctor indicate his annoyance without risking the ritual criticism. He can either explain to the nurse that her knowledge is insufficient or do as she suggests if she is right.

Even a junior may point out errors to a senior, if he is sure that the senior is committing an error. If two people do not agree, a third must be brought in to settle the dispute but under no conditions may they make a personal issue out of it or resort to argument or pulling of rank. Pointing out errors is supported to show one's zeal and cooperation.

The Malingerers

Because of this ever-present danger of criticism, it is difficult for doctors to deal with the shammers who feign illness and demand absence notes. Doctors have to be constantly on the alert to avoid criticism from the patient and still devote enough time to helping others in greater need. If examination discloses no symptoms after all necessary tests have been made (they must be done regardless of whether the doctor personally suspects a patient or not), the doctors resort to various devices such as offering to give the malingerer a harmless but very painful injection guaranteed to cure him or suggesting that, if the sickness is as bad as the patient says, absence of symptoms would indicate neuroses and offering to recommend him to the mental hospital. A person pretending illness generally backs off at this.

Prior to the Leap Forward, a patient requesting an absence note for the first time generally received it without too close scrutiny in order to save the doctor's time. A second request would be refused and after thorough examination a patient would either be admitted to the wards or cautioned for shamming. A threat to report to his factory manager generally was sufficient to stop any argument.

During the exhausting Leap Forward, however, the enormous number of patients visiting doctors caused great concern among the authorities. Many came just to snatch a few hours off, with the added dividend of an absence note if they carried out the deception cleverly. The frustrated doctors dared not antagonize the patient for fear of resultant criticism nor be too lenient in issuing absence notes even for the genuinely sick because they might find themselves in trouble with hospital authorities for sabotaging the drive for maximum productivity.

Regulations were rigid: to be excused from production temporarily, a person had either to have a temperature of 39° C, or be an emergency case admitted to hospital or, by the nature of his complaint, be unable to work (e.g. eye injury, injury to hand). Doctors who tried to explain to their administrative officers that many sicknesses were not accompanied by high temperatures or that a certain man was in great pain and could not possibly walk to work on his injured leg would be informed that, although the patient could not walk he could be carried and this injury did not prevent him from doing useful work with his hands.

One doctor who issued several absence notes was sharply criticized: "You have given thirty hours leave to each of five people. One man produces a thousand screws per hour. Do you realize that you have deprived our country of 150,000 screws?"

In some hospitals doctors dealing with patients under these tense conditions suggested that Youth Leaguers and Party members take over the responsibility for issuing leave slips and leave the wards entirely to them. The beleaguered physicians reasoned that they were not sufficiently eloquent to deal with these workers and their inadequate excuses would reflect badly on the hospital.

The Patient

For patients in hospital there is little to fill the bed-ridden hours. Libraries and radio earphones are not available. Some patients spend their time making cut-outs or weaving straw baskets as gifts for the doctors; others read newspapers which family members bring in; some do bits of sewing or just chat. Lights are so dim (to save electricity) that after dark they cannot read or sew, even in large city hospitals.

The only necessities a patient provides are his washing bowl, tooth-brush, face towel and hot water flask for the drinking water delivered by the hospital workers early each morning. There are no particular restrictions and patients may stay in bed or get up and walk around. The sojourn in hospital is so short that few feel well enough to spend much time out of bed and most Chinese gratefully accept the chance to rest.

Patients going to hospital only for a previously prescribed injection pay a registration fee. They do not see the doctor but go straight to the pharmacy to purchase the required medicine and then carry this to the injection room. All medicine prescribed must be available in the hospital pharmacy; if a desired medicine is out of stock a substitute is recommended to the prescribing doctor. Patients may, if they wish, buy from an outside pharmacy but these pharmacies have less complete stocks than hospitals—and the prices are higher—so few patients take the trouble.

Because foreign exchange is desperately scarce, medicines formerly imported are now being produced in China. Often they are not up to standard but are still used. Where China cannot produce the required medicine in sufficient quantity, a substitute is sought, either a Chinese traditional medicine, a cheaper imported Western medicine, or some approximation which can be locally produced. Hospitals reserve a quantity of effective Western medicines to be used only on the more severe cases and when substitutes have no effect. The patient has no choice in the matter. If a substitute can be used, even though the cure may take a little longer, the expensive medicine is denied him. The types of medicine in short supply vary and often doctors have to be versatile. One woman doctor reported a case of dysentery which persisted despite the use of medicines. Certain medicines which might cure the disease could not be given because of palpitations in a weakened heart. The doctor then remembered old stories she had heard about the efficacy of raw onions and tried this peasant remedy. The cure was slower but it worked.

Medical Coverage

The extent of medical care to which each industrial worker is entitled varies from factory to factory. Some people are fully covered, others only partly, and some are entitled to coverage for both themselves and their immediate family dependents. Workers pay monthly medical dues based on their wages. Officially the rate is supposed to be one per cent but it seems to vary and some workers earning 30 yuan[5] reported paying 2 yuan dues.

Each factory or organization has a contract with a specific hospital and workers are covered only at this hospital. A small factory can choose the nearest hospital regardless of size but a large factory with a greater number of workers may have to go further afield.

First aid stations appear to exist in a large number of factories. These stations offer only the simplest facilities, treating cuts and bruises, coughs and colds, giving injections. Where a factory has a clinic on the premises, patients generally cannot go to hospital for a minor ailment or an injection unless recommended by the clinic doctor because production time would be lost and production time is the whole point of medical care.

Unemployed persons must pay their own medical fees but in recent years charges have been fairly modest and relatives usually help, if necessary. Students have school hospitals but, if the school doctor is unable to deal with the sickness, they are allowed to go to the hospital of their choice where all medical charges except registration are the responsibility of their school or college.

Registration fees are 20 cents for the first visit, 10 cents thereafter. Fees for operations range from 10–20 yuan for minor operations to 20–30 yuan for most major surgery. Worker patients pay only for their food.

Blood from the Poor

Blood transfusions are not included in operating charges and must be paid for as an extra. The cost of blood in China is extremely high because there are no free blood donors. Most Chinese have a traditional horror of giving their blood and only the poor who are in urgent need of additional income sell their blood. Paid donors receive 45–50 yuan per 400 cc. Large hospitals may have a blood bank but smaller ones rely on a list of donors whom they may call when the need arises. These donors receive regular medical examinations. When a worker is involved in an accident and requires a transfusion, his factory colleagues may be asked to help. Youth League and Party members set the pace so that others will volunteer blood. When an unidentified accident victim (who may not be a worker) is brought to the hospital, the medical staff may donate blood if no one else comes forward. These donors are then allowed extra rations.

Because short stays are insisted upon, a certain amount of convalescent leave may be granted to a worker on the doctor's recommendation. How much pay an urban worker on sick leave receives varies with position and length of time in a job. The Party member, always the privileged caste in the new hierarchy, receives full pay for any length of sickness. A woman worker on maternity leave gets fifty-six days leave with full pay. Some refugees have reported that a worker with more than eight years service will receive full pay for an indefinite period. Workers from other areas report getting full pay for one month, then 50–60 per cent for up to six months, when the amount is either reduced again or the worker is dismissed. Dismissal will depend on political standing and length of service. There seems to be no fixed standard.

Charity by Committee

For those people who are too poor to pay for hospitalization and cannot raise the money from friends or relatives, the Lane Committee may be approached for help. The amount of help extended (after thorough investigation of the patient's background) will be limited and the decision as to whether to help or not will be based mainly on the type and degree of sickness. The Lane Committee never pays the cost of blood transfusions.

Whether the Lane Committee will advance the necessary money depends primarily on the financial condition of the supplicant. First, friends and relatives will be approached for help. If they are able but unwilling to help, the Lane Committee will probably drop the case. If it is an emergency and delay will endanger the life of the patient, hospitalization will be authorized immediately and it will be up to the Lane Committee to put pressure on relatives to pay. Generally however, Chinese families, no matter how poor, still help out in cases of real need. Because the family system stubbornly persists in China in spite of all efforts to eliminate it, there are relatively few real charity cases.

A chronic ailment that is bound to be terminal (such as advanced cancer) is not hospitalized because little can be done in hospital and treatment can prolong but not save the life. Health for production is the criterion and a terminal case is not going to produce "wealth for the state." Due to shortage of bed space and medical staff, hospitalization is usually limited to cases of a contagious nature or emergencies and turnover is rapid.

The Party Member

In theory every citizen is eligible for the same facilities and medical care, but the leaders or high Party members are sent to specialized hospitals where better accommodation is available. For these privileged members of the Communist aristocracy, private physicians and private rooms are customary.

Apart from the chosen few, private rooms are no longer available except for those who must have absolute quiet or for patients who, by the nature of their sickness, require day and night treatment which would disturb the ward routine. Generally only the larger or specialized hospitals have facilities for such special treatment. For an urban patient who can get such care, however, charges are the same as they would be in the ward.

Private nurses are available in large cities such as Shanghai and Peking but only for those with both financial ability to pay and a critical illness which requires more care than the hospital staff is able to provide. This service is provided by nurses wishing to make extra money during their periods of annual leave. The nurses register at several hospitals and when required they are hired at a fee of 8–10 yuan a day, payable to the nurse. Workers' organizations provide nurses for their members in cases of certified necessity.

In large hospitals boasting interns, the intern often takes over special-nursing duty. In smaller hospitals lacking interns, ward patients help out as best they can.

There are no facilities whatsoever for home visits in the cities except in maternity cases. For expectant mothers who do not wish to go to hospital, midwives are available from the maternity and child care centres scattered throughout the country. These midwives have undergone a three to six month training course and are employed by the maternity centre on salary. All charges are paid by the patient direct to the centre. In the countryside, far from centres or hospitals, peasants have to rely on the old-style midwives who, after the Communist conquest, were given a seven-day course in basic hygiene. These midwives charge 2 or 3 yuan for their services and work entirely on their own in the old tradition of private enterprise.

By Litter and Wheelbarrow

In large cities ambulances are available but are rarely used except in very serious cases. Such use requires approval from the chief of the hospital. These vehicles are actually hospital cars which double as ambulances when the need arises. Factories of any size generally have their own cars or lorries which can be pressed into service to carry injured workers to hospital.

Outside large cities, the lame, the halt and the sick have to find their own way to hospital. There is no ambulance service at all and patients arrange transportation by bus, pedicab, wheelbarrow, bicycle, luggage rack, piggy-back or homemade litter carried on two poles by neighbours or relatives.

In theory, all areas, no matter how remote, will eventually offer some facilities for medical care when and if enough personnel have been trained. Medical facilities are now divided into area (specialized), provincial, municipal, district, county, commune, mental, pediatric and tuberculosis hospitals, plus maternity homes. This does not include sanatoria. In addition public health, preventive treatment and sanitary clinics, staffed by graduates of three to six month courses, are supposed to be available in the countryside. The mental hospitals are situated only in cities but treatment is mainly limited to insulin and electric shock treatments. Very few drugs are used. The few psychiatrists in China are confined to this type of hospital and are not available in any general hospital or for symptoms which in the West would call for a psychiatrist.

The degree of medical care available depends on the nature of both the sickness and the area. For example, a paying patient in a city has many hospitals to choose from and a worker suffering a major illness is sure of being transferred to a better hospital. In the countryside, however, patients, no matter whether peasant or unemployed, are very limited in choice for a minor sickness although they do have the possibility of transferring to a larger city hospital for a major sickness.

A large area, provincial or municipal hospital may have as many as five hundred beds but these are only in the main centres. A smaller district hospital will have only eighty to a hundred beds (although in some cities this number may be higher), a county hospital about twenty to fifty beds and a commune hospital (where it exists) will have twenty to thirty beds.

Commune Medicine

The few commune hospitals actually in existence in the mid-fifties were generally abandoned after the collapse of the Great Leap Forward because the faltering communes could no longer support them. The country people now go either to the traditional Chinese doctors who practise in all villages or to county hospitals.

During the Leap Forward, individual cadres in communes often refused to let ailing peasants go to hospital because absentees might impede the frantic drive to meet quotas but the sick are now usually urged to see a doctor.

Some peasants refuse to go to doctors trained in Western medicine because of their superstitions and dislike of Western methods of examination though such superstitious attitudes are severely castigated and pressure may be applied by cadres. Village pharmacies sell Western-type remedies of a more common nature which require no prescription and many people prefer to buy these rather than trek over the mountain roads to hospital. Most Chinese traditional doctors in the villages now give penicillin injections.

Communes are supposed to pay medical care fees for their workers from the commune profits. However, during the Leap Forward there were numerous cases of communes sending people to hospital and then refusing to pay for the medical care. Many county hospitals lost money and faced accounting difficulties, but they continued to give treatment whether or not the commune could or would pay. The hospitals reported their losses to the Ministry of Health which finally made them up.

County and commune hospitals in remote areas may be staffed by a graduate of a regular medical course, assisted by one or two "middle doctors" and a few untrained nurses whom he is responsible for teaching. More often they have no regular medical graduate at all. On the other hand the majority of the staff in urban hospitals are regular medical graduates with experienced Western-trained doctors in charge and 80 per cent of the nurses are fully trained.

Indentured Doctors

Communes hospitals close to large cities are usually in a better position because they are often staffed with highly skilled doctors who have been sent to these agrarian St. Helenas as a punishment ("reform through labour") and their performance there is the determining factor in their eventual return. To supplement these politically indentured professionals, many doctors are sent from city hospitals to county or commune hospitals once a year for two weeks at a time as part of their annual (but not corrective) labour. However, there are generally sufficient numbers of offenders in the former category to ensure a steady supply for those communes adjacent to urban centres.

Doctors' country labour differs in no way from labour done by other workers and can range from ploughing and planting to gathering of harvests. In some areas doctors toil on the mountain sides cutting trees, in others they may construct highways, but most work in the fields. Helping the local farmer to raise his crops, the doctors tend to raise a crop of blisters at the same time. In the case of a surgeon who may be on duty within hours of returning to his hospital, this misuse of his hands results not only in bitterness at his wasted time and effort but in considerable pain and difficulty. No doctor may be excused from duty for such a minor disablement nor may he be excused from criticism should his blistered hands cause him to make a slip during the operation.

The main purpose of commune hospitals is to attend to minor cases and ensure some sort of minimum medical care for the great majority but lack of adequate medical facilities in country areas means that many peasants prefer to disregard aches and pains as long as they can stay on their feet. Superstition engenders reluctance and the inconvenience of distant medical facilities is also a deterrent to peasants in need of care. For the sick, the tiresome and lengthy journey for a minor complaint does not seem worth the scant medical care they receive at their destination. As one patient put it, "I took two hours to walk there and two to return. I waited in queue nearly all morning, yet the doctor examined me for no more than five minutes and told me to return the next day—I would have been better off resting at home."

Rotation and Rusty Sterilizers

Other peasants, feeling ill, have come willy-nilly to the hospitals without advance notice or real need for hospitalization. In many areas this created chaos. Long queues of patients appeared on litters or bedrolls outside hospitals in the early hours of the morning. No bed space was available in the hospital. After a number of these traffic jams, Peking decided that doctors should be sent out in rotation to the nearby country areas to offer temporary clinics in different hamlets at regular periods. This puts considerable strain on the other doctors who have to take over their hospital work but it has helped to alleviate the distress of the peasants and has allowed hospitals to reserve bed space for cases recommended by the doctors.

Although in theory each commune was supposed to have a hospital after 1958, there are still many areas where there are either no hospital facilities or where facilities are so poor as to be almost useless. In one part of Kwangtung province, a medical graduate on first assignment found himself in an old building with neither light nor power. A sterilizing machine assigned to him was rusted by the time the power line came in two and a half years later, the X-ray equipment had still not arrived, yet he was expected to operate.

In areas around Chungking doctors report old equipment and no means of cooling the operating-theatres. Even fans are unavailable and most operations have to be left until late evening in the hot summer days.

In country areas doctors often find themselves hampered by the head of the hospital, a non-medical man without any education who holds his position because he is a loyal old Party member from Yenan days. He will often go round demanding to know why the doctors should continue wasting medicine and care on a patient who apparently cannot recover. The doctor's authority is superior in medical matters—if he is brave enough to assert it. Officially the non-medical man's job is administrative and political but without other support the doctor may often find himself in a quandary, afraid to exercise his authority lest the Party man should retaliate by accusing him of a political error.

Notes

1. See *Current Scene,* Vol. III, No. 5, p. 3.
2. See *Current Scene,* Vol. II, No. 33.
3. Equivalent to £27 10s. 0d.–£41 5s 0d. or U.S. $84.00–$126.00.
4. Equivalent to £5 15s. 6d.–£6 12s. 0d. or U.S. $17.64–$20.16.
5. 1 yuan = £0 2s. 9d. or U.S. $0.42.

35. HEALTH TRENDS SINCE THE

"GREAT LEAP FORWARD"

ROBERT M. WORTH

Introduction

Judging from official reports from Mainland China and from the accounts of Western visitors in China (1), the authorities there have promoted a great amount of public health activity directed with considerable success toward solving some of the vast health problems they inherited when they took control of China in 1949. From 1949 to 1952 these efforts were focused mainly on vaccination, retraining of midwives and accelerating the rate of training of health workers of all types. Beginning in 1952 there was a nation-wide "patriotic health movement" energized by massive propaganda concerning United States "bacteriological warfare" in Northeast China, and directed toward improved environmental sanitation and control of flies and mosquitoes. Concomittantly there have been long-range campaigns to control kala-azar, schistosomiasis, hookworm, malaria and filariasis. These campaigns have been characterized by direct involvement of the people themselves, rather than by having things done for them by "experts." Since the "Great Leap Forward" of 1958 there has been considerable emphasis on extending preventive and curative services into the rural communes and on expanding the "free" medical services available to industrial workers and other favored groups.

Official reports may be susceptible to overoptimism, and visitors may well be limited in their observations by the wishes of their hosts. Therefore, other sources of data would be helpful in coming to some conclusion about the validity of these potentially biased claims. This paper reports two other sources of information about recent health conditions in China. First, a series of observations on 80 young children was made shortly after their arrival in Macau from neighboring rural districts of China, and compared with observations made concurrently on 120 children of the same age in Hong Kong. Second, a series of interviews was held with 9 doctors who migrated from China to Hong Kong in 1952. In spite of the inescapable fact that refugee children are not a random sample of Chinese village children, and the fact that refugee doctors may have certain vested interests in the kinds of things they report, some useful inferences may still be drawn.

SOURCE: Selected from Robert M. Worth, "Health Trends in China Since the 'Great Leap Forward,'" in *The American Journal of Hygiene,* 78 (November 1963), pp. 349–357. Reprinted by permission of *The American Journal of Epidemiology.*

Sampling Methods and Laboratory Procedures

People coming out of China into Hong Kong or Macau may be divided into 3 main categories:

1. Wealthy people fleeing the communists (mostly during 1949 to 1951), accompanied by artisans and others who served them, coming with capital or urban skills, or both.
2. "Wealthy farmers" and rural landlords fleeing the communist land redistribution program (mostly during 1951 to 1954), accompanied by some village artisans, without capital and with little or no urban skills.
3. "Middle" or "poor" farmers coming in search of food in 1959 to 1962.

The children in this study represent the people of the third group who came out of southern Kwangtung Province villages as a result of a shortage of food at home. Many of these people had relatives already in Hong Kong from whom they may have received food parcels and upon whom they depended to tide them over until they could find employment in Hong Kong. Unrestricted immigration has not been permitted by the Hong Kong government for several years; so upon arrival in Hong Kong illegal immigrants disappear into the population and are not available for observation. Macau, 35 miles west of Hong Kong, still accepts immigrants from China with or without exit permits. Hence in recent years Macau has become the "staging area for the assault on Hong Kong," where the opportunities for employment are much better than in Macau. When the escapees from China arrive in Macau they virtually all register immediately with the Catholic relief organization for food and housing while they wait for relatives in Hong Kong to make arrangements with the "snakeheads," or Hong Kong immigrant smugglers. The people in charge of the Catholic refugee center in Macau were kind enough to request cooperation of all children who met the following criteria:

1. Age 5, 6, or 7 years (by the European system of counting);
2. Arrived in Macau during the previous 48 hours from Kwangtung Province;
3. Were of Cantonese ancestry (not Hakka or other cultural subgroup);
4. Whose father was a farmer or laborer in a rural village in nearby Kwangtung.

During the first 5 months of 1962 approximately 100 children who met these criteria appeared at the center and were sent to a Catholic dispensary for tests. Of this number, 80 actually showed up for the tests. Physical examinations were not done to avoid potential difficulty with local authorities.

For the comparison group of children living under observable conditions and of similar cultural and genetic background, consideration was limited to the one large coastal plain in the New Territories of Hong Kong where climate and traditional agricultural practices are analogous to those in adjacent areas of southern Kwangtung. The main "Cantonese" group of farmers settled this southern Kwangtung region about 600 years ago, and spread into what is now British territory during the few centuries thereafter. The border was created only 64 years ago, and during most of the time since then there has been a relatively free flow of population across it. Of the 7 clusters of small villages under consideration in the New Territories, two were excluded because they had access to fresh water piped down from nearby hills. Two of the remaining 5 clusters of villages were chosen by lot for the study. They were on flat land and obtained their water supply from shallow dug wells, protected only by a flat concrete pavement around the mouth of the well. The chosen villages had a combined population of 1,401 (1961 census), with a total land area of about 8.6 acres, excluding the surrounding fields and grazing areas. The occupants of these villages are virtually all tenant farmers who pay one half of their rice crop for land rental. Refuse, chickens, dogs, cats and human feces were seen in the spaces between buildings, and many pig pens were adjacent to dwellings. Human and pig feces were collected in pits adjacent to the houses and then carried to the fields for fertilizer. These villages appeared very much like the villages known to the author some 30 years ago in central China, except for the following important differences:

1. Almost all the children aged 7 through 12 years were in school, and most of them were wearing slippers or shoes around the villages;

2. About half the children had been delivered in a government maternity home (this was largely determined by the nearness of the home);

3. At least once a year a mobile team comes to each village to offer smallpox, diphtheria, and cholera immunization.

The authorities in these villages were kind enough to try to persuade the villagers to cooperate in the examination of all children who met the following criteria:

1. Age 5, 6, or 7 years (by the European system of counting);
2. Were born and lived exclusively in the native village (no visits to China);
3. Were of Cantonese ancestry (not Hakka or other cultural subgroup);
4. Whose fathers were farmers or laborers in the selected villages.

Approximately 130 children met these criteria, and of these, 120 actually showed up for examination.

The laboratory examinations used in this study were based on the following premises:

1. Young children who spent their entire lives in a specific environment will reflect the health conditions of that environment:

2. When working across language and cultural barriers objective measurements are likely to be more reliable than question-and-answer data;

3. Infectious disease transmission patterns can be conveniently tested by considering representative diseases in the 3 main categories: respiratory transmission, fecal-oral transmission, and transmission through extra-human cycles;

4. Since protein is probably the most critical item in the Chinese low-income diet, relative nutritional standards can be estimated by measures of protein nutrition.

Five types of information were sought:

1. Indices of usage of preventive health services (proportion with vaccination scars);

2. Indices of prevalence of infectious diseases transmitted by the respiratory route (by examining one blood specimen from each child to find the proportion with mumps HAI titers of 1 in 8 or higher,[3] and by observing tuberculin positive rates[4]);

3. Indices of prevalence of infectious diseases transmitted by the fecal-oral route (by examining one fecal specimen from each child[5] to ascertain the prevalence of helminth ova, and by examining one plasma specimen from each child to find the porportion with *Salmonella* group D titers of 1 in 80 or more[6]);

4. Indices of prevalence of infectious diseases transmitted through an extra-human cycle (by examining one fecal specimen from each child[5] to ascertain the prevalence of hookworm ova, and by examining one thick blood smear from each child to obtain malaria parasitic indices[7]);

5. Indices of nutritional status (by microhematocrit determination in each child to find the mean values for the group,[8] by total plasma protein determination in every second boy to find mean values,[9] and by determining the urine urea N: creatinine ratios in every second boy to find mean values.[10]

The specimen collections, tests and statistical analyses were carried out as described in the preceding paper in this journal (5). The recently arrived immigrant group in Macau were, of course, different boys in the spring, fall and winter of 1962, but the comparisons were all made with the same group of Hong Kong village children, who underwent additional testing in the fall for plasma proteins and in the winter for urine examinations. The results are presented in table 1.

Discussion

The lack of a physical examination of the children under study from China may be partly made up for from the observations of a physician in Macau who has personally examined hundreds of these recently arrived people. An interview with him revealed the occasional finding of a palpably enlarged liver and the rare observation of edema. The edema tended to disappear rather quickly on a noraml diet, but liver enlargement may persist for months after arrival in Macau.

With regard to the use of preventive medical services, both groups had a high percentage with vaccination scars. This rather adequate protection against smallpox can evidently be gained by a once-a-year visit of a mobile team to the villages, judging from the Hong Kong experience.

With regard to the respiratory transmission of disease, mumps was used as an index of intimate contact between children. The proportion of young children from Chinese villages who had presumably had mumps was significantly higher (at the 5 per cent level of confidence) than those in the Hong Kong villages, although their ages were the same. The "mumps positive" rate of 68 per cent in the children from China was virtually the same as the

TABLE 1. *Comparison of Children, Aged 5 to 7 Years in 1962, from Kwangtung Villages and Hong Kong Villages*

	(Column 1) Kwangtung villagers (within 2 days of arrival in Macau)	(Column 2) Hong Kong villagers	Comparison between columns 1 and 2
Size of sample	80	120	
Preventive medical services			
% with vaccination scar	90	85	$Z = 1.0*$
Diseases transmitted by respiratory route			
% with mumps HAI titer of 1:8 or more	68	53	$Z = 2.1†$
% with positive tuberculin test	32	32	
Diseases transmitted by fecal-oral route			
% with helminth ova (predominantly *Ascaris* and *Trichuris*)	98	82	$Z = 3.4‡$
% with more than one helminth species	77	48	
% with *Salmonella* group Do titer of 1:80 or more	4	4	
Diseases transmitted by extra-human cycle			
% with hookworm ova	10	8	$x^2 = 0.086*$
% with malaria parasites	5	0	
Nutritional data			
mean microhematocrit males	39.1	38.2	$t = 1.26*$
females	38.1	38.9	
mean total plasma protein (gm./100 ml) males	7.23	7.35	
sample size	28	32	
mean urca N/creatinine ratio in single fasting urine specimen males	6.32	6.05	

* Difference not significant at 1% confidence level.
† Difference significant at 5% but not at 1% confidence level.
‡ Difference significant at 1% confidence level.

rate found positive in two groups of urban Hong Kong children living in a very crowded environment (5). This may be taken as indirect evidence of the truth of the accounts of the formation of nurseries and kindergartens in rural communes to care for the children while the mothers are working. This would be a reasonable explanation for the observation of an increased rate of child-to-child transmission of respiratory disease. The lack of difference of tuberculin-positive rates may also be taken as indirect evidence of the exaggeration of accounts of commune life, in which the children were purportedly removed from contact with their parents and grandparents to be brought up in boarding schools. This presumably would have tended to reduce the amount of contact between young children and the tuberculous adults in the village, and should have been reflected in a lower tuberculin-positive rate than that found in their counterparts living in bosom of their families in "old style" villages in Hong Kong.

With regard to the fecal-oral transmission of the disease, one does not see evidence of any lasting or revolutionary effects on village sanitation of the "patriotic health movement" of 1952–53 in China, which involved mobile health education exhibits featuring captured American pilots (or movies of them) "confessing" their attempts to spread plague, cholera, etc., in North Korea and China. There has been no such campaign in the Hong Kong villages, yet the Hong Kong children studied were no worse off than their counterparts from China with regard to evidence of previous *Salmonella* group D infection, and they were somewhat better off with regard to the ordinary intestinal helminths of the village (predominantly *Ascaris* and *Trichuris*).

With regard to diseases transmitted through an extra-human cycle, fewer useful indices were found than had been hoped for. Both Hong Kong and the Kwangtung districts near Macau from which the refugee children came are outside the endemic *Schistosoma japonicum* areas and therefore this study could not give a clue as to the effectiveness of the anti-schistosomiasis campaign in Kwangtung. The prevalence of *Clonorchis sincnsis* ova would have been a useful index, but it was found that these ova are very rarely present in young children even in a population where the parasite is common among adults (5). There is plenty of promiscuous defecation by children in Hong Kong villages, and there has been no antihookworm campaign there, but evidently the habit of wearing shoes or slippers most of the time has been sufficient to hold hookworm prevalence down to the moderate figure of 8 per cent in this survey, a figure equivalent to that found in the children of the same age from Chinese villages. One may therefore postulate that the long-range control of hookworm in the Chinese village may owe more to fundamental social changes, such as the introduction of schooling (and perhaps shoes) at an early age, rather than to the short-range antihookworm campaign of 10 years ago. No clear statement can be made about malaria, except to say that it has not been eradicated in Kwangtung. The authorities there have never claimed eradication of this disease. There are hilly districts in Hong Kong where one can get a 10 per cent *Plasmodium vivax* parasitic index in young school children, and there are flat-land brackish water areas (such as the district chosen for the Hong Kong sampling) where one gets a parasitic index of 0 per cent, even though there is no rural malaria control program in that district. These differences have more to do with the bionomics of the vector species of mosquitoes than with human attempts at malaria control.

With regard to nutritional indices, one should bear in mind that the families most likely to escape to Macau are those with Hong Kong relatives waiting to assist them with the illegal voyage on to Hong Kong, and these are the same families most likely to have been receiving food parcels from their Hong Kong relatives. None of the 3 nutritional indices showed any difference between the children from China and the Hong Kong village children, and the two indices for which there are accepted standards (microhematocrit and total plasma proteins) fall well within normal limits for American children of the same age (6). The more sensitive index of protein nutrition (urea N: creatinine ratio) has no accepted standard as yet, but showed values similar to those found in low income rural children in Guatemala whose protein intake is known to be marginal (7). One may therefore tentatively infer a marginal protein intake in both the groups of children in this study.

Interviews with Doctors from China. From about 1955 through 1962 quite a number of doctors from China have come into Hong Kong. No one knows their exact number, but local gossip places it somewhere in the neighborhood of 200 to 300, with almost half of them having come out after 1960. It is the impression of the author that a very large proportion of these grew up either in Hong Kong (and who went to China for their medical education), Canton or Shanghai. Furthermore, most of those who are not natives of Hong Kong already have relatives there. Most of those who came to Hong Kong in 1962 had permits from the Chinese authorities to go to Hong Kong to visit their relatives, and they have simply overstayed their time. It was the privilege of the author to meet socially 9 of these doctors who came out of China in 1962. All were natives of the 3 cities listed above; all came out with permission of the Chinese authorities, and all had at least moderately wealthy relatives in Hong Kong. Five of them stated that the main force which caused them to leave China was that they were urban people and the Chinese authorities wanted them to work for at least 5 years in impoverished rural districts. The other 4 stated that the simply wished to be with their families again. Two had spent time working in rural districts; the others were all from large cities, but had been sent to rural districts periodically for brief visits by the authorities. These people had worked in northeast, eastern-central and southern parts of China. Each one was interviewed independently for over an hour and there was virtually no contradiction in the reports given. In fact, there was a remarkable degree of independent unanimity.

Apparently the people of China cooperated willingly with the government in its health efforts until the "Great Leap Forward" from the summer of 1958 to the summer of 1959. Two things then happened simultaneously. The people became exhausted and apathetic from the excessive work demanded of them, and the crop failures of 1959 and later gave rise to a severe, prolonged shortage of food, particularly during the winters of 1959–1960 and 1960–1961. The government's reaction to this food shortage was to institute rigid nationwide food rationing. The amount of the food ration varied according to the degrees of heavy labor and age, but averaged about 25 to 30 pounds of grain or substitute (mostly sweet potato substitute), 4 ounces of oil, and 4 ounces of sugar per month per adult, or about 1,800 calories per day. Small amounts of vegetables were available in season. Soybean curd, beansprouts, or fish were rarely available. Meats were available only on special days, and then in very small quantity. Few famine deaths occurred, but weaness and lassitude became widespread, and resistance to infectious diseases was noticeably diminished.

Low protein edema became common in adults and children. Amenorrhea became very common, especially in younger women. Malnourished "marasmus" children were seen occasionally on pediatric wards, but classical kwashiorkor was very rare. A diffuse, anicteric liver enlargement appeared late in 1959 and became very common in both adults and children. It took months to regress, did not respond to the soy-bean supplements which cured edema promptly, and occasionally progressed to cirrhosis and death, especially among infants. Several liver biopsies on such people were reported as showing "fatty infiltration" or "cloudy swelling." Some of the doctors estimated that about 50 per cent of the city people were affected by this liver enlargement and more than that in the country people.

Typhoid fever, malaria, and tuberculous meningitis of infants had all but disappeared by 1958, but began to increase again as chronic malnutrition was experienced. Prostitution had been suppressed (and with it venereal diseases), but began to reappear in 1960 due to hunger. Theft also began to reappear as an urban phenomenon. The food situation has begun to improve very slightly since the spring of 1962.

Although the official claims of "virtual eradication" of schistosomiasis and hookworm are exaggerated, there has been real progress on the control of these diseases, and also on the control of malaria in urban areas, largely through the medium of public education and local responsibility. Almost all urban babies are born in hospitals or maternity homes, and these are all given BCG and are vaccinated within the first 3 days of life.

Summary

Chinese medical literature and the reports of Western visitors to China both tell of great progress in combatting the vast health problems faced by that country. Attempts were made to test the validity of these potentially biased reports through observations made on 80 young children escaping from rural districts in Kwangtung Province and by interviewing doctors who left China during 1962. Laboratory observations on the children from China were compared with the same measurements made at the same time on 120 children of the same age living in observable villages in Hong Kong. The two groups of children did not differ with regard to 3 indices of nutritional status (both showing evidence of marginal protein intake), to percentages with vaccination scars, percentages with Salmonella group D agglutination titers, percentages with positive tuberculin tests, or percentages with hookworm ova. The children from China were found to have a slightly higher percentage excreting helminth ova and a higher percentage with mumps HAI titers. Keeping in mind that the refugees are not a random sample of the population from which they came, these data show that the children from China are at no special advantage with regard to health, and at no special disadvantage, except perhaps in that they are apparently in closer respiratory contact with other children at an early age, presumably due to attendance at commune nurseries.

Separate interviews with 9 doctors who arrived in Hong Kong in 1962 from northeast, eastern central, and southern China reveal a unanimity of opinion on the following points:

1. Willing, effective public cooperation on health programs from 1949 to 1958, and a genuine fall of incidence of many infectious and parasitic diseases;

2. A state of exhaustion and increasing apathy during and after the "Great Leap Forward" in 1958–1959;

3. A severe food shortage during 1959–1962, with strict rationing which limited the number of famine deaths but resulted in: (2) diffuse, anicteric liver enlargement in 50 per cent or more of the people, (b) amenorrhea in many women, (c) a rise in incidence of many infectious diseases formerly under control, and (d) a return of certain social phenomena formerly under control (prostitution and theft);

4. A slight improvement in food supplies in 1962.

Notes

1. This investigation was supported by Public Health Research Grant AI 04189-02 from the ICMRT Program, Office of International Research, National Institutes of Health, U.S. Public Health Service.

2. Research Fellow, Hooper Foundation, University of California Medical Center, San Francisco; Honorary Research Fellow, University of Hong Kong Medical Faculty, Department of Preventive and Social Medicine.

Present address: Department of Public Health, University of Hawaii, Honolulu 14, Hawaii.

Acknowledgement is made of the assistance of the University of Hong Kong through the kindness of its Vice-Chancellor, Sir Lindsay Ride. Acknowledgment is also made of the assistance of Dr. D. J. M. Mackenzie, Director of the Medical and Health Department, Mr. O. Donohue, Director of the Education Department, and of the Hon. C. G. M. Morrison, Commissioner of Resettlement, Hong Kong Government.

3. Performed with "Microtiter Kit" (Cooke Engineering Co., Alexandria, Va.) with eluates of blood-soaked filter paper discs which had been dried overnight and stored at −20 C for 1 to 6 months prior to testing (2).

4. According to Chinese literature and discussion with Chinese doctors, BCG immunization is still limited to the cities and therefore it is presumed that none of the village children from China had had BCG. None of those in Hong Kong had had it either since they were born before BCG immunization of infacts was extended to their district and they first went to school after the last visit of the BCG team to their schools. Tuberculin testing was done in all children with the same "Sterneedle" multiple puncture gun and the same lot of Connought tuberculin material.

5. Feces concentrated by HCl-sodium sulfate-Triton NE-ether method (3), and one drop (about 0.02 ml) was examined on the same day. At least 20 per cent of the Hong Kong fecal specimens were collected under observation and these did not differ from those collected at home. All of the Macau specimens were collected under observation and are of guaranteed authenticity.

6. 0.02 ml of heparinized plasma was mixed on a ringed slide with 0.03 ml. of *Salmonella* group D O bacterial antigem (Lederle) for agglutination at a titer of roughly 1 in 80 (4).

7. Standard think smear was stained with Giemsa and read independently by the author and an experienced malaria technician.

8. Approximately 0.03 ml of blood was drawn into a heparinized microhemato-

crit tube, centrifuged at 7,000 r.p.m. for 5 minutes and read in an I.E.C. micro-hematocrit reader.

9. 0.02 ml of plasma was tested by Biuret reaction in Unicam colorimeter (green filter).

10. A single fasting voided specimen was tested for creatinine by the alkaline picrate method and for urea nitrogen by the diacetyl monoxime method.

References

1. Worth, R. M. Health in rural China: from village to commune. Amer. Jour. Hyg., 1963, 77:228–239.

2. Worth, R. M. The filter disc blood collection method adapted for a mumps HAI survey. Manuscript in preparation.

3. Hunter, C. W., Hodges, E. P., Jahnes, W. G., Diamond, L. S., and Ingalls, J. W. Studies on schistosomiasis. II. Summary of further studies on methods of recovering eggs of S. japonicum from stools. Bull. U.S. Army Med. Dept., 1948, S:128–131.

4. Worth, R. M. A simple micro-agglutination method for studying group D salmonellosis. Manuscript in preparation.

5. Worth, R. M. Urbanization and squatter resettlement as related to child health in Hong Kong. Amer. Jour. Hyg., 1963, 78.

6. Silver, H. K., Kempe, C. H., and Bruyn, H. H. Handbook of Pediatrics. Fourth edition. Los Altos: Lange Medical Publications, 1961.

7. Arroyave, G. The estimation of relative nutrient intake and nutritional status by biochemical methods: proteins. Amer. Jour. Clin. Nutrition, 1962, 11:447–461.

Family and Youth

36. MARRIAGE AND DIVORCE

C. K. YANG

The basic points of the Marriage Law had been developed in the family revolution in the pre-Communist period, and many of them, such as the prohibition of concubinage and other forms of polygamy, are found in the Nationalist marriage law. Instead of breaking any new ground, the Communist marriage law represents the continued advancement of the family revolution in two major respects, the extension of the new marriage concept to a larger proportion of the population and the use of political power to achieve institutionalization of the new marriage system. It is obvious that the form of marriage defined by the new law is unacceptable to the traditional mind. In the urban upper and upper-middle classes, from which the intelligentsia mostly stem, the long process of family revolution has broken down much of the resistance of the older generation, but resistance to the new form of marriage remains strong among the working class and the peasantry, where the voice for freedom of marriage has not been widely raised. It is in the latter segment of the population that the greatest change is being brought about by Communist propaganda, indoctrination, and enforcement of the new Marriage Law. . . . Political power, with many forms of social and economic pressure at its command, is thrown directly into the conflict on the side of the new marriage system against the old one. The development of the new family institution, hitherto mainly part of a spontaneous process of social change, is now being aided by the leverage of political power and law.

One means of using political and legal power to gain popular acceptance of the new form of marriage, especially among the multitudes of workers

SOURCE: Selected from C. K. Yang, *The Chinese Family in the Communist Revolution*, Cambridge, Mass.: The M.I.T. Press, 1959, pp. 32–35, 67–71, 73, and 83–85. Reprinted by permission of The M.I.T. Press, Cambridge, Mass.

The notes for this selection have been deleted as all original source materials were from Chinese newspapers. *Ed.*

and peasants, is the new legal requirement of the registration of all new marriages. Couples intending to get married come before the Communist official in charge of marriage registration for the locality. He asks the couple whether the intended marriage is taking place with the consent of both parties, whether duress from any third party has been exerted, whether polygamy or concubinage is involved. If the answers agree with the legal provisions, and if the results of an investigation check with the answers, a marriage certificate is issued and the couple is legally married. In the cities, medical examination is required in addition to the above procedure.

Although marriage registration is stipulated in the Marriage Law as promulgated in 1950, the Communist government issued a supplementary Rules for Marriage Registration in 1955 to insure universal enforcement. This legal document introduces to new features. The first is the addition of marriage registration as one of the functions of the large number of lower-level government agencies such as the neighborhood offices in the cities and the People's Committees of village districts and towns in the rural areas, thus vastly increasing the accessibility of the registration facilities to the common people. Secondly, the registering officials are required to explain to the registrants the stipulations of the marriage law so as to acquaint them with their own legal rights and obligations before proceeding with interrogations and examination of the case for approval or disapproval of the registration. The measure has the merit of informing the common people of the contents of the new law as a vital step in its effective enforcement, which is in contrast to the conditions under the Nationalist government, when the majority of the population were ignorant of the existence of a new marriage law.

There is no systematic quantitative data on the extent of the success of these means in establishing the new form of marriage. Fragmentary figures in reports from various parts of the country show that a beginning of the new system is being made in rural communities which had not been generally influenced by the family revolution in the pre-Communist period. In 178 villages of Huailai county of Chahar Province, in the period of ten months following the promulgation of the Marriage Law on May 1, 1950, there were altogether some 400 marriages, of which some 300 were based on the free will of the contracted parties "plus the agreement of the parents on both sides." In other words, about 75 per cent of all the marriages in the stated period followed the new form, although the expression of agreement of the parents on such marriages shows that some influence of the old tradition still exists among these new marriages. Again, in two rural subdistricts of Hailien county of Shantung Province, in an unspecified period of 1951, there were 290 traditional "selling-and-buying" marriages as against 227 marriages based on the free choice of partners and love. There are fragmentary figures which do not provide any comparison with the number of traditional marriages in the same locality in the same period. Thus, it is stated that in the rural county of Yaoyang in Hopei Province 120 couples were married according to the provisions of the new law. In the rural town of Pochen of Shantung Province, within the period of a year following the promulgation of the Marriage Law, 488 young men and women married of their own free will and for love, and many of them won parental consent only after a "bitter struggle." All these localities are a part of North China. Statistics on other regions are available only in a few instances. A report covering seven counties in Chiahsing Special District of Chekiang Province, four counties of the Hsuanch'eng Special District in the southern part of Anhwei Province, and Jukao county in the northern part of Kiangsu, a total of twelve counties, shows that "34 per cent of all women who were married [time unspecified] did so of their free will." Such is the reported picture of the East China Region. In the Central-South Region "according to incomplete statistics, during the period from January to April, 1951, 23,600 new couples registered their marriage with the government."

There are questions of accuracy and comparability regarding the above figures, particularly the percentages in the twelve rural counties of the East China Region. Nevertheless, they indicate that the idea of the new form of marriage is being widely disseminated among the conservative rural population. The new marriages in the hitherto isolated countryside, although few in number, are becoming fermenting agents, causing local youth to react against the repressive traditional family and to challenge its authority.

In terms of individual situations, these statistical figures represent an increasing number of cases of struggle by young peasants and workers for the freedom of marriage. Typical among the peasants is the case of Li Ta-kuei, a peasant girl in Hsiawan village of Luchiang county, Anhwei Province. She was betrothed to a maternal cousin against her wish. The engagement was so unpleasant to her that she once attempted suicide as a means of forcing its cancellation. When the propaganda corps of the Marriage Law came to the village to explain the new legal stipulations on marriage, she became emboldened. After some struggle with the family, she went to the subdistrict government and obtained a legal cancellation of the betrothal. Finally she married a young peasant with whom she had fallen in love.

Among the urban workers the enforcement of the new Marriage Law yields similar cases of struggle between the young and the older generation. Typical is the experience of Yen Ts'ai-nü, a nineteen-year-old girl who worked in a Shanghai cotton mill. Her father and grandmother, in accordance with the old custom, betrothed her to a worker in a grocery store. Her first knowledge of the betrothal came when relatives arrived for the ceremonial feast. She was very angry and demanded that the betrothal be nullified. Her father and grandmother beat her for protesting. When she could not stand the mistreatment any longer, she went to the family of her deceased mother for support and appealed to the Association of Family Women (an affiliated organization of the Democratic Women's League) requesting assistance in the cancellation of the betrothal. The father and grandmother heard of this and rushed to the maternal relatives to raise trouble. The ensuing quarrel stirred up the whole neighborhood, and the case was taken to the people's court. The court ruled that the betrothal should be canceled.

There are, however, less tortuous circumstances by which new marriage has come to the workers. Tai Yu-lan (woman) and Chao Ch'uan-yung were both workers in Cotton Mill Number 1 in Tientsin. They had been in love with each other for some time, but owing to the traditional stigma placed upon free choice of partners and love, had not dared talk about getting married. After they learned of the new Marriage Law in May 1950, they became engaged, and in March of 1951 they were married by the legal formality of registering with the local government.

The preceding cases illustrate the re-enactment of social conflicts centering upon the marriage problem, a familiar scene among the modern urban intellectuals in the pre-Communist period, now being extended to the peasants and workers. But such cases may not represent a universal picture of the marriages reported as being in conformity with the new law. Thus, in the 178 villages in Chahar Province all the 300 new marriages were reported to be based on the free will of the partners as well as the consent of their parents, but it is hard to judge the relative weight between free will and parental consent. The latter in some instances might mean actual parental arrangement and verbal profession of free will by the boy and girl before the local official, an act of formality under previous instruction from the parents. On the other hand, there were many instances even in the pre-Communist period when a couple were married on the basis of love but, after going through the new simple form of marriage, again went through the full ceremony of the traditional marriage in order to appease the family and to gain institutional recognition from the local community. . . .

Freedom of Divorce in the Communist Law

A strong demand for the right of divorce formed an important part of the family revolution. After half a century of agitation and struggle, the right of divorce for both men and women had gained acceptance at least among the new intelligentsia in the Republican period. To the newly educated generation the demand was altogether reasonable since the basic premise of marriage itself had already shifted and marriage was no longer considered a bond tying a woman to a family for life but the result of love between two individuals. If the two indivduals could not get along together, the new generation saw no reason for the continuation of their suffering. Gone from the young minds was the once dominant consideration of marriage as a means for the perpetuation of the family, and ancestral lineage was no longer a matter of grave concern.

By 1930 the Nationalist government had translated the demands of the young into law permitting divorce. Although the new law retained many favorable considerations for the perpetuation of the ancestral lineage, and no effort was made by the Nationalist government to acquaint the common people with their new legal right, for the educated young who knew about the new law a legal instrument was available to facilitate a divorce should they choose to go to court. New urban developments meanwhile had opened increasing fields of employment for women, which reduced the economic difficulties of a divorce. Divorce and remarriage of divorcees became fairly common among the new intelligentsia in the cities, but the new conception of divorce, while threatening the organization of a small number of urban families in the upper and middle classes, left the families of the peasantry and the urban working class almost untouched. Such was the picture under Republican China.

When the Communists came to power in 1949, they inherited this development, and the new concept of divorce was fully written into Communist law.

In fact, the subject of divorce received more elaborate attention than any other subject in the Marriage Law, taking up nine out of a total of twenty-five articles. These nine articles set forth the right of divorce for either of the matrimonial parties and seek to guard the economic interests of the divorced wife and the children, but the husband's parents and the family in general are excluded from any legal attention. As it was consideration for the solidarity of the patriarchal family as the dominant factor in traditional marriages which had formerly ruled out divorce, so it is consideration for the married individuals as the dominant factor in new marriages that now justifies divorce. Hence: "Divorce should be granted when husband and wife both desire it. In the event of either the husband or the wife insisting upon divorce, it may be granted only when mediation by the people's subdistrict government and the subdistrict judicial organ has failed to bring about a reconciliation" (Marriage Law, Article 17).

Divorce is facilitated for the wife by the new legal stipulations concerning the custody of and responsibility for the children, the settlement of family property, and support for the divorced wife. Custody of the children shall be decided "in accordance with the interests of the children" (Marriage Law, Article 20), which in the actual operation of the law means most frequently the granting of custody to the wife; and "after divorce, if the mother is given custody of a child, the father shall be responsible for the whole or part of the necessary cost of the maintenance and education of the child" (Article 21). The father's responsibility may be discharged by payment "made in cash, in kind, or by tilling the land allocated to the child" (Article 21). "In case of divorce, the wife shall retain such property as belonged to her prior to her marriage. The disposal of other family properties shall be subject to agreement between the two parties. In the case where an agreement cannot be reached, the people's court shall render a decision after taking into consideration the actual state of the family property, the interests of the wife and the child or children, and the principle of benefiting production" (Article 23). It may be mentioned here that since Communist land reform the wife's share of the family property may be written in her own name and may even be registered in a separate deed, thus assuring her a fair share in case of a divorce. "After divorce, if one party has not remarried and has difficulties in maintenance, the other party should render assistance" (Article 25). The "other party" which has to render assistance means the husband in most cases. Later, the socialization of urban business and collectivization of agricultural land minimized the importance of property settlement in divorce.

The Consequence of Increased Family Instability

With political support for the assertion of individual rights against family "oppression," and with propaganda on the new concept of marriage and divorce penetrating into the working class and the peasantry, the influence of the family revolution has spread from a minority of the urban intelligentsia to a much larger segment of the population. There are visible signs that the stability of a larger number of families has begun to waver and that divorces are on the increase. The Minister of Justice of the Communist Central Government, Shih Liang, a woman, reviewed the situation seventeen months after the promulgation of the Marriage Law in May 1950:

Statistics from different localities show that after the promulgation of the Marriage Law the number of matrimonial suits received by judicial organs of different levels increased appreciably. In twenty-one large and medium-size cities, including Peking, the number of matrimonial suits received were 9,300 for the months from January to April 1950, and it was 17,763 for the months from May to August of the same year. In other words, there was an increase of 91 per cent in the four months following the promulgation of the Marriage Law in comparison with the preceding four months. In ten county-seat towns in Hopei, P'ingyuan, and other provinces the number of matrimonial suits received was 986 for the months from January to April 1950, and it was 1,982 for the months from May to August of the same year. The increase here has been 101 per cent. In Hupei Province the average number of matrimonial suits dealt with by each people's court was 13.7 for February of 1915, and it was 23.9 for July of the same year, showing a considerable increase.

Some two years later, in March 1953, the municipal court of Canton handled about eight hundred matrimonial cases as compared to one thousand-odd cases of labor-capital conflict. Domestic disharmony came to rank with labor-capital struggle as the two numerically largest items of litigation during the early Communist rule. Such was the situation in the major urban centers.

It is noteworthy that the rural communities, which remained so long in the tight grip of traditional conservatism, are also sharing in the increase in matrimonial suits which reflect growing family instability. The beginning of serious rural reaction to the new concept of divorce is shown in Ch'en Shao-yü's statement made in April 1950, just before the promulgation of the Marriage Law: "According to statistics from the eight cities of Peking, Shanghai, Tientsin, Harbin, Sian, Kalgan, Shichiachuang, and Paoting, from 71 rural counties in the old liberated areas of North China, from some places in the old Shensi-Kansu-Ninghsia border area, and from eight rural counties of Shansi Province 17.4 to 46.9 per cent of all urban civil litigation cases are matrimonial cases, and 33.3 to 99.0 per cent of all rural litigation cases are matrimonial cases." "In the Central-South Region the 32,881 matrimonial cases constitute over 60 per cent of all civil suits received by the People's Courts during the months from January to May 1951." Matrimonial cases accounted for 90 per cent of the 700 civil cases handled during the months from January to the end of August 1952 by the People's Court of the rural county of Laipin, Kwangsi Province of the Central-South Region.

While these reports do not present the contents or nature of the matrimonial suits, they do give a general indication of growing family instability as the new agitation of the family revolution has made it increasingly difficult for the traditional family institution to maintain role harmony among members who have become exposed to the idea of individual liberty as against family restriction. This is particularly true of the role of the wife, as a very high proportion of the matrimonial cases are brought to court by women (see the discussion on women's status in Chapter VI). Where the traditional family institution is operating effectively, family conflicts are very seldom brought to court for settlement, sometimes not even when human life is involved. Among the increasing number of matrimonial cases, divorce suits constitute a high percentage. Of the 32,881 matrimonial cases of the Central-South Region in 1950, 29,972, or 90 per cent, were divorce suits. A year later "divorce suits constituted from 46.44 to 84.32 per cent of all urban matrimonial cases, and from 54.1 to over 90 per cent of all rural matrimonial cases according to statistics from the four cities of Peking, Shanghai, Tientsin, and Harbin, from seventy-one counties in the old liberated areas of North China, and from some places in the old Shensi-Kansu-Ninghsia border area."

The trend of the high proportion of divorce cases apparently persisted at least until 1953. In the month of March in that year 80 per cent of all cases received by the municipal court of Canton were divorce suits, and the percentage may have been higher in the subsequent months owing to the launching of the "enlarged propaganda campaign on the Marriage Law" to acquaint more people with their new rights in marriage and divorce. The Communist authorities have published little further statistical information on marriage and divorce since 1953, possibly because of fear of the socially disturbing nature of the figures; but a hint of the general continuation of this trend is seen in the report made in July 1957 by Tung Pi-wei, Communist judicial leader, that domestic conflicts still constituted an increasing and prominent proportion among all cases handled by Communist courts throughout the nation.

Only a few facts are mentioned in the official reports regarding the contents of the divorce figures. First, there is the almost overwhelming proportion of divorce suits brought by women as compared to those brought by men, especially in the rural communities, where conservation is strong and the suffering of women under the traditional institution has been deep. For example, in 1950 in the cities of Shang-hai, Peking, and Tientsin, 546 of the 800 divorce suits, or about 68 per cent, were brought by women, 176, or about 22 per cent, by men, and 78, or about 10 per cent, by both husband and wife. In the provincial town of Nanchang, in Kiangsi, from January to October 1951, it was stated that 84.3 per cent of all divorce cases received by the municipal people's court were brought by women. Of the 21,433 divorce cases in 32 cities and 34 rural county-seat towns mentioned in the *Jen-min Jih-pao* (People's Daily) of September 29, 1951, 76.6 per cent were brought by women. The 1951 edition of the *Hun-yin Fa Chi Ch'i Yu-kuan Wen-chien*. (The Marriage Law and Its Related Documents, p. 72) listed 763 divorce cases in three rural counties in Shansi Province; of this total, 705 cases, or 92.4 per cent, were initiated by women. Among 29,972 divorce cases in 1951 in the Central-South Region, including both urban and rural areas, "The vast majority of them were brought by women who have suffered the severest oppression from the unreasonable institution of traditional marriage."

Without specifying time or locality, Ch'en Shao-yü, who led the drafting of the Marriage Law, gave an analysis of the age composition of the parties involved in divorce suits. According to him, "About 50 per cent of them were between the ages of 25 and 45, about 40 per cent youths under 25, and about 10 per cent were very young people married before their maturity

and old couples." Teng Yung-ch'ao, wife of Premier Chou En-lai and a leading
figure in the Democratic Women's League, which was vitally concerned with
the drafting and enforcement of the Marriage Law, surveyed the statistical
information possessed by the government on marital conditions and stated
that the "vast majority of those demanding divorce were young and middle-aged
laboring people." . . .

These fragmentary divorce figures are given in such a form that they cannot
be compared to figures for periods preceding the Communist regime; therefore
there is no statistical evidence whether or not this is a new phenomenon
created by Communist rule. In the Nationalist period divorces were notably
on the increase, especially after 1930, but they were largely limited to the
big cities where the sanctity of the traditional marriage institution had been
seriously undermined. The traditional kinship system, including the institution
of marriage, had been strongly maintained in the countryside, and divorce
in the modern sense was still repulsive to the peasantry. The sharp resistance
to the injection of the divorce idea into rural communities even under Communist rule, to be considered later, attests to the newness of the divorce factor
in the rural social situation. Hence, while it is not known how many urban
divorces mentioned above represent a consequence of Communist reform, it
may be taken with some degree of certainty that rural divorces constitute
a new phenomenon in the hitherto vast redoubt of the traditional institutions.

Even in cities considerable legal expense was entailed under the Nationalist
government to obtain a legal divorce, something only the upper and middle
classes could afford, and only an educated few were acquainted with the
law. But the use of lawyers is no longer part of the Communist legal system,
and the people's court has abolished court fees. The propaganda campaigns
on the Marriage Law are introducing legal knowledge to the common people.
Hence the poor and even the illiterate can use the court to settle matrimonial
disputes and to obtain divorces. The many cases of legal divorce among the
urban working class is a new phenomenon, then, and some increase in urban
legal divorces since the establishment of the Communist regime seems quite
possible. . . .

Social Resistance against Divorce

It is important to note that even under communism strong social resistance
against divorce survives, particularly in rural communities, which not only
precludes the possibility of rapid spreading of indiscriminate divorce but also
limits legitimate divorces. . . .

To the many people who feared that marriage by free choice of partner
and romantic love would lead to promiscuity, the idea of freedom of divorce
and political support for it was an even more unthinkable evil. Local sentiment
in many places ran strongly against the Marriage Law for its sponsoring freedom
of divorce and regarded it as a step that would "plunge the family and social
relations into general chaos," that would "break up the family," that would
"wipe out moral obligations." In East China "the people regarded freedom
of divorce as a step that would lead men to 'lose both person [wife] and

wealth,' and regarded the right of 'child brides' to cancel their marriage contracts as being against moral conscience."

Significance of Freedom of Marriage and Divorce

Since freedom of marriage and divorce may be viewed as the most significant factors in the disorganization of the traditional Chinese family system and the development of a new one to supersede it, it seems worthwhile to summarize their effects.

First, the generational composition of the family has been affected. With marriage focused on the couple to the exclusion of interference by parental and family authority, the husband-wife relationship becomes the center of the new family, and the married son's parents occupy only a peripheral position. The traditional arrangement of the parents-children relationship taking precedent over the husband-wife relation is now reversed. In the husband-wife-centered family the married son's parents are no longer *ipso facto* members holding a controlling position. Should conflict arise between the parents and the daughter-in-law, the parents' position is no longer protected by institutional authority or law, and they may have to leave the son's family. Even in the 1920's, when freedom of marriage first became a strong demand by the young urban intellectuals, modern women had already raised the question of setting up separate households from the parents-in-law, and many of them succeeded in doing so. In such cases a two-generation family replaces the traditional three-generation system.

Even if the parents continue to live with the married son's family, they no longer enjoy a controlling position in the family. Should they have several married sons, they no longer possess the authority to hold them together in a closely organized unit or integrate them into a single household. They can live only with one of the married sons at a time. Thus their continued living with the married sons no longer has the same significance as before, for the traditional primary importance of the parents in the family is now being superseded by the primacy of the husband-wife relation. The parents in the new family are an adjunct, not a controlling authority; their continued presence depends a great deal on the pleasure of the daughter-in-law. This new situation nullifies the ability of the traditional family to expand into a large, multi-generational structure.

Second, the size of the family has been affected. While the average of four to six persons per family for the majority of the population will remain unless altered by a change in birth rates, the size of the middle and upper classes will be reduced, for the old large family composed of parents and married sons, so common in the wealthier classes, is no longer possible when marriage is no longer an affair designed for family expansion. As the generational composition of the family changes, there is a corresponding reduction in size.

Third, the solidarity of the family organization has been affected in various ways. The relation between parents and married sons and daughters-in-law is weakened by the modern affirmation of the husband-wife relation as the closest tie. The solidarity of the traditional family, based on the primacy of the parents-children relation, is thus diminished. The new conjugal family gains solidarity by a closer husband-wife relation not morally subjected to alienation by parental interference, but this new solidarity has the effect of restricting the strong family tie to the small circle of the married couple and their unmarried children.

The new right of remarriage for widows, with the related privilege of taking children and property to their new home, has obvious disorganizing effects on the solidarity of the traditional family, which treated a widow as a member permanently related to the family as a whole and not to the husband alone. The new marriage would be similarly centered on the husband-wife relation and not on her relation to the new parents-in-law.

The new trend against institutionalized polygamy affects various aspects of the family differently. The discontinuation of polygamy means the loss of its formal function in helping to insure continuity to the ancestral lineage and a large membership to the traditional family. On the other hand, the informal function of providing men with romantic experience or additional sexual pleasure has always been a disruptive influence on domestic harmony. Thus the abandonment of polygamy would increase the solidarity of the family organization. The suppression of open prostitution as institutionally condoned behavior has a similar effect.

Fourth, by emphasizing the couple's mutual interest, modern marriage by free choice of partners assigns no importance to the continuation of the family lineage. Belief in the necessity of continuing the family lineage made marriage a religious act in ancestor worship which, among other functions, served to expand the membership of the kinship system and to generate solidarity among them by translating biological relatedness from common descent into a social bond. The longer the family lineage continued, the larger the number of descendants. But a large number of descendants from a distant ancestor would not know each other or recognize any social ties and obligations among themselves if ancestor worship did not translate biological relatedness into a living social bond. The traditional identification of marriage with the sacred function of perpetuating the ancestral lineage had the purpose of insuring both size and solidarity for the kinship organization. Now that the main purpose of modern marriage is to fulfill only the romantic or other requirements of the couple, the result is the weakening of the relationship between the couple and other kinship members, especially collateral relatives, thus reducing the organized kinship circle to a small group of lineal male descendants and their wives. . . .

The reduction in size and solidarity of the family and its extended kinship organization is of major significance. A small family without support from a large kinship organization cannot perform the multiplicity of socio-economic functions and retain its traditional position as the core of the Chinese social system.

37. THE DECLINE OF IMPORTANCE OF AGE

C. K. YANG

The practical value of age as a major basis for the great respect of the age hierarchy began to be challenged with the impact of revolutionary currents early in this century. The dominant note of the modern times has been the acquisition of Western knowledge and technological skills and the development of new institutions to implement Western-inspired ideas in an effort to save China in the struggle for national existence; and these could not be acquired simply by experience in the traditional social environment. The only means of acquiring them were through learning and training in schools and through new sources of information; and the required method of developing them, in China as elsewhere, was through science, not empiricism enriched by age.

In the acquisition of new knowledge, new skills, and new ideas the young (those from families capable of affording a modern education) had a distinct advantage over the old. The young had plasticity of mind, eagerness for the new and the adventurous, fewer obstacles in the consciousness of vested interests and entrenched traditional social relationships. Above all, rigid repression of the young by the hierarchy of age gave them an eagerness to alter their old status by acquiring new knowledge and skills and by promoting the adoption of new institutions. Hence, the modern educated young Chinese formed a nucleus from which new influences germinated and gradually developed into leading forces in political, economic, and social trends. The young were no longer bowing to the old at every turn, and age was no longer always a mark of personal prestige and social authority.

Over the past half century every political revolution and social development has acted as a new force in expanding the number and influence of the modern educated young. In the course of its limited success in encouraging revolutionary ideas championed by the young the Republican revolution of 1911 put a larger number of young elements into prominent political positions than there ever had been under the old imperial government. In the turbulent years of 1917 to 1919 the young were presented to the nation as a distinctive age group under the term "new youth" by the rising crescendo of the youth movement, culminating in the May 4th Movement of 1919, which placed the educated young in a position of new importance in political and cultural fields. Led by the historic periodical, *Hsin Ch'ing-nien* (The New Youth), tons of literature in the form of magazines, press articles, and pamphlets poured forth on

SOURCE: Selected from C. K. Yang, *The Chinese Family in the Communist Revolution*, Cambridge, Mass.: The M.I.T. Press, 1959, pp. 94–104. Reprinted by permission of The M.I.T. Press, Cambridge, Mass.

The notes of the original work have been deleted. *Ed.*

the subject of the new youth and its problems, forcing the new age group to the nation's attention. Political and economic crises of the period, the necessity of new means for their solution, together with the impotent traditionalism of the old and the general illiteracy of the common people, created a new role for the modern educated youth and led them to demand revision of the subordinate status of the young. For the first time a powerful social and political movement put up a young group in opposition to the old and the institutions the latter stood for.

When the Second Revolution swept the country in the mid-1920's, the exaltation of the young was carried to new heights. The revolutionary regime based in Canton was marked by the youthfulness of the personnel that staffed it. Every branch of the new political machine that baffled and at times frustrated the old was led and manned mainly by young men and colored by the outlook of youth. The occasional presence of an old man over sixty in their midst was a spectacle, for here was "an old dog that had learned new tricks." When the seat of political power, the center of formal social control, was captured by the young, the sanctity of the age hierarchy could not be expected to remain intact.

In the cultural field the "Renaissance" of the May 4th Movement was a product of the young, and by the mid-1920's it had made deep inroads into the educational system of the country, particularly in the storm center of the South. The quantity of "New Culture" publications in all fields had by that time distinctly pushed Confucian classical works to the side, at least in the cities. The new literature, particularly in works of fiction, clearly steered away from the traditional motif of fairy tales and from Confucian themes and drew its inspiration from Western ideas that concerned the special problems of the young. Its undisputed literary dominance together with its modern theme of romantic love led the educated young and indirectly the younger generation in general, toward an outlook of life and love which retained little respect for the age hierarchy and frequently held little consideration at all for the old.

In the economic field accelerated industrial development after World War I gave increasingly responsible positions to the young, who alone commanded modern technical qualifications. Technical dreams of the young set the blueprints for the nation's economic development. The "old master's" prestige declined with the diminishing importance of the traditional crafts under the crushing superiority of modern technology. The old master still held sway in the vast pre-industrial sector of the country's economic structure, but his technical competence no longer commanded the moral respect to the educated young, and his outmoded technical role could no longer support the age hierarchy in that modernized segment of the population which was leading to the trend of economic development. The social and economic plight of the growing army of unemployed old craft masters was hardly conducive to the effective maintenance of age as a criterion of technical competence.

The older generation watched in bewilderment the making and unmaking of governments, the waging of the unending civil wars, the ever-rising prestige of new commodities and new economic organizations, the unfamiliar events that occupied increasing space in the newspapers and in the people's daily conversations, the untraditional ways of training and educating the young—all these changes staged by a group that had hitherto been in an inferior position in the age hierarchy forced society to grant more consideration to the young. In the family, if the young still paid a measure of respect to parents and senior members in the age hierarchy, it was done with a tinge of begrudging formality and seldom with the spontaneous sincerity and voluntary devotion formerly developed by filial piety and veneration of age.

The vital change of attitude toward age was limited largely to the modern educated young, the new youth, but the new youth were an articulate group playing a strategic role in the shaping of social trends. The facilities of modern education were rapidly expanding, with its middle and primary levels steadily extending to members of the lower middle class, and the mass education movement which started after the May 4th Movement of 1919 served as another vehicle for the diffusion of the new attitude into a small part of the working class and the peasantry. Largely centered in urban areas, the change affected also the young elements of the richer portion of the rural population as they took to the cities for better educational facilities, where their attitude toward the traditional age hierarchy was altered by absorbing new ideas and by insulation from the immediate pressure of parents and senior kinsmen at home.

When the great upheaval of the 1920's settled down to a divided course in the 1930's, with the Kuomintang dominating the nation and the Communist Party setting up red areas in the South, the traditional Chinese attitude toward the age hierarchy had already been substantially diluted. The two decades that followed saw the continued extension of the new influence to growing numbers of the young, aided by the increased absence of the young of all social classes from home in a period of increasing population mobility, which freed the younger generation from the immediate pressure of the age hierarchy in the kinship system. In the early 1930's such mobility was mainly a consequence of the accelerated development of urbanism, which set many of the young on the move away from home for jobs or educational opportunities. After 1937 the Japanese invasion drove millions far from their local communities, and the young were left free to develop the new attitude toward age with a minimum of immediate interference from older kinsmen. Thus, long before 1949 the ground had been prepared for the developments under communism.

Status of the Young under the Communist Regime

The triumph of the Communist revolution carried the exaltation of the young to a new height. If youth furnished the vital force of China's previous revolutions, it certainly did so even more emphatically with the Communist revolution. Its radical ideological departure from tradition first found acceptance only in the more plastic young minds, and the Communists possessed great skill in organizing the young for the service of the revolution.

The elevation of the status of the young under the Communist regime has been, first of all, a highly organized movement, not a spontaneous development. Secondly, that movement has spread from the hitherto confined circle of upper- and middle-class young intelligentsia to the numerically large group of young workers and peasants. For some three decades before Communist accession to power youth organizations had had a steady growth, but they were comparatively small in membership and poorly integrated. Under the Communist regime youth organizations have been vastly expanded in membership, centrally directed, and well-disciplined.

The New Democratic Youth League is an example. According to statistics of September 1951, its national membership had reached 5,180,000—twenty-seven times the membership figure of 190,000 of April 1949. There were 24,200 branches in various parts of the country. Classification of the membership was as follows: workers, 33.88 per cent; peasants, 51.18 per cent; students, 11.44 per cent; others, 2.5 per cent. Females accounted for about 30 per cent of the total. By 1957 the League membership had leaped to 23,000,000, "accounting for 19.17 per cent of the total number of young people in China."

It is notable that students who monopolized the youth movement in the pre-Communist period now comprise only a little over one-tenth of the membership of the most important organization of the young under the Communist regime. In this respect, the Democratic Women's League, with its vast network of affiliated organizations, also has a fast expanding membership, the majority of whom are now women peasants and workers, not intellectuals. Above all, the Chinese Communist Party itself, which has experienced a phenomenal growth in membership since 1949, is dominated numerically by the young, who are drawn mainly from the peasantry and the workers, only a minority coming from the urban intelligentsia.

Youth organizations and other organizations containing a majority of young members serve a variety of purposes, among which is the conscious and unconscious function of advancing the power and status of the young. In this sense, these organizations have the significance of representing a formally organized struggle, aided by political power, to alter the status of the young in the traditional age hierarchy.

Organized struggle for status by the young is actively advanced by the publication of literature on the subject of youth in unprecedented quantity. Let us consider the publishing activities of the New Democratic Youth League in 1951 alone: "For the purpose of propaganda and education, the Youth League publishes 61 newspapers and periodicals for its general membership throughout the nation. The Youth Publication Company under the Central Committee of the Youth League, which was established in 1950, has published 14 categories and 260 kinds of book series and periodicals, which total 8,800,000 copies. *Chung-kuo Ch'ing-nien pao* (Chinese Youth), the daily newspaper serving as the official organ of the Central Committee of the Youth League, will be published on April 27 of this year [1951]. (*Chung-kuo Ch'ing-nien Shuang-chou-k'an* (Chinese Youth Biweekly), also an organ of the Youth League's Central Committee, is among the most widely circulated periodicals in the country."

If the youthfulness of the personnel of the Southern revolutionary regime in the mid-1920's had the effect of elevating the status of the young, the same is even more true of the present Communist regime. Although the top leaders of this regime are generally older than their counterparts in the mid-

1920's, Mao Tse-tung and the majority of the leading party figures started their political career in close connection with youth organizations. The three decades of struggle for power advanced their age, but it did not lessen their identification with the cause of youth.

As for the middle- and lower-ranking party members who form the lower echelon of the Communist regime, the average age level is lower than that of corresponding personnel in any previous Chinese government. A government announcement on the recruitment of young men and women for training to be junior officers in police work listed an age limit of eighteen to twenty-three. Similar age limits for other types of political work can be seen in other recruiting announcements. Young men in their twenties and thirties head local government departments that concern the vital interests of tens of thousands of people. In urban neighborhood and village indoctrination and propaganda meetings it is the young leaders who do the talking and lay down the line, and it is the older people who have to do the listening and following. In enforcing policies, be it a bond sales campaign, suppression of counterrevolutionaries, mass trial of landlords and local bullies and the redistribution of land, the Five-Anti movement against businessmen committing bribery, evasion of taxes, theft of state property, cheating on state contracts and theft of confidential state economic information, or a score of other major and minor movements that have disorganized the traditional pattern of life under Communist rule, it is the young leaders, ranging in age from the teens to the thirties, who have been running the show.

The amount of political power and responsibility vested in the hands of young local leaders is certainly without precedent in China's history; and it is shared by young men and women belonging to public organizations which are regularly mobilized to participate in current movements and to help enforce government policies. Members of the Youth League, the Democratic Women's League, the student union, and many other organizations work side by side with party officers in carrying out major government policies.

The young have come to possess not only coercive power but also social prestige under the new standards set up by the regime. To the young go the large proportion of awards for "model workers," "model farmers," winners in production emulations; they are the recipients of many other honors symbolizing new values that are foreign to the old generation. The leading "model workers" held up as examples of production efficiency for the rest of the workers, from Ma Heng-chang in mining to Nan Chien-hsiu in the textile industry, the counterparts of Stakhanovites in the Soviet Union, are young men and women, most of them in their twenties. The influence of youth begins to invade even the old empirical field of agriculture wherever improvements of agricultural methods are being vigorously introduced:

In the patriotic production movement in the villages, members of the Youth League are vigorous shock brigades. They not only participate in agricultural production but also actively propagandize the agricultural policy of the People's Government among the people. They lead in organizing mutual-aid teams, in popularizing new agricultural methods. For example,

Kuo Yu-lan in Heilungkiang Province and Wang Ching-mei in Hopei Province, both female members of the Youth League, have won the title of model agricultural workers. They both have popularized seed-selection, the soaking of seeds before sowing, and other new agricultural methods in their own communities, and the yields from their fields are higher than the average of other farmers. In the irrigation project of controlling the Huai River, members of the Youth League inhabiting the banks of the river mobilized large numbers of young people to participate in the work. Last winter [1951], in the northern part of Anhwei Province alone, one-third of the 600,000 labor conscripts were young people. Among these young workers were 16,000 members of the Youth League who formed the leading force of the labor conscripts. In the county of Pu-yang, Youth League members accounted for 30 per cent of the model irrigation workers.

If it was the young technical men of the modern bourgeois intelligentsia who dimmed the prestige of the traditional "old craft masters" in the pre-Communist period, now the progressive young workers and peasants are doing the same thing on a more extensive scale. In traditional days a brilliant and successful young man might be held up as an example for members of his own generation, but never for his senior members in the age hierarchy or the old masters of the trade, who might regard him with benign approval but always considered him immature, with more to learn from older people. Now in every factory, every neighborhood, and in the villages young models of production and revolutionary conduct are glorified with fanfare and honored with material rewards. Ended is the sanctity of the time-honored rule that the old teach and the young learn, the old lead and the young follow. A student leader told his professor in 1951: "You and your generation are too beset with considerations and worries for decisive action, so we young ones should lead in changing the nation's way of life."

Change of Status of the Old in the Family

It is clear that the traditional older generation with its conservatism is regarded as an obstacle to progress. Even though there is no substantiation to rumors of summary gross mistreatment of all old people as an age group, such rumors reflect the general decline in status and power of the older generation. This change has inevitable effects on the status of the older generation within the family organization.

The political struggle in which the young are playing a leading part is carried into the family. From the time the Communists took control of the nation, and through the successive crises of the suppression of counter-revolutionaries, the Five-Anti and the Three-Anti movements, and the "thought reform" of the intellectuals, every progressive young person has been increasingly under group pressure to disregard kinship ties and the prestige of age and ferret out dissenters and recalcitrants for correction and, at times, even for elimination. Since parents and uncles and elder brothers have been openly accused or secretly reported by junior members in the age hierarchy for offenses leading to police surveillance, fines, labor correction, imprisonment, or even death, the progressive young person is as much feared at home as in public. It is common to find older people suddenly stop talking about public matters, particularly political affairs, as soon as a progressive young family member comes home, especially if he comes home from school, where ideological indoctrination has been vigorously carried on. While the exact proportion of progressives among the young will remain unknown for some time, there is little doubt of the widespread effect of the new ideology on young minds and the rapid extension of this effect from the bourgeois intelligentsia to the much wider circle of young workers and peasants, as seen in the membership growth of the Youth League. Sharp is the contrast between this situation and the traditional order when family mores were in complete harmony with the nation's political ideology, when a successful and prominent son paid homage to his socially humble parents and other senior kinsmen.

Communist law and political principles no longer provide any support for the superiority and rights of an individual over another based on age. On the contrary, they tend to limit traditional authority and the rights of the old over the young. The prohibition of mistreatment of children limits what the parents can do with the young. Elaborate legal stipulations on the protection of children's interests in the family have the same effect. The single legal requirement of children is that they must support the parents and must not mistreat or abandon them. In stipulations of the Marriage Law responsibilities of parents are much heavier than their rights over children—a reversal of the requirements of traditional filial piety which compelled almost one-sided devotion by the children.

There are no stipulations in Communist law governing the relationship of the older generation to the young aside from that of parents to children. However, since the parent-child relationship is stronger than the relationship between other members in the age hierarchy, when the parents' position is greatly weakened the position of other senior members in the family over the young deteriorates more rapidly. For a young progressive the traditional authority of an uncle or an aunt carries little weight, and that of more distant seniors in the age hierarchy means even less. Published documents show more political accusations by the young against other relatives than against parents.

If the older generation finds no protection for their traditional status from politics and law in the revolution, it finds the safeguards also weak in other directions. Wherever modern economic development prevails, older people are finding it difficult to retain positions of leadership in family production. The replacement of numerous family businesses in trade and industry by state enterprises and the development of collectivized agriculture have had serious effects in this respect. The tendency of increasing economic qualifications and rights of the younger family member and the growing system of free education lessen the dependence of the young and reduce the economic authority of the older generation as a factor in maintaining its traditional status in the age hierarchy.

The development of centers of activity outside the home for the young adds another difficulty to the maintenance of the age hierarchy as a system of family status and authority, both because of the lack of time to teach the traditional ideas to the young at home and because of the conflicting ideology being instilled into the minds of the young in outside centers of activity. The development of modern schools during the past half century and the rapid growth of membership of youth organizations under the Communist regime are examples of this development. Under the Communists young men and women are recruited in large numbers as paid workers or volunteers for a great variety of public activities which take them away from home part time or full time at an age from the early teens to the twenties, an age in which they would have remained very close to home in the traditional system. The following is illustrative of the increasing separation of the young from family influence.

In Feng Ch'i village near the city of Canton over forty young men and women, led by some twenty Youth League members, cultivated an acre of "tabooed" land [land that the villagers would not till for superstitious fear of bringing misfortune]. They sold the rice yielded from it, bought lumber with the money, built a house, and called it "The Home of Youth." They used the house for ideological classes, meetings, and activities. It has become the youth center in the village.

The establishment of a center of organized activities exclusively for the young as an age group in the rural community is a new phenomenon, for all activity of the young except school was traditionally centered in the home. It is interesting to note the name of the center, "The Home of Youth," still using the word "home" which has a connotation of strong social affinity for the Chinese. At this "home" the older generation can no longer exercise discipline and control over the young.

With the superiority of age being seriously undermined, with the young tending to move out of the range of family education and discipline, with the legal support of filial piety gone, with the basic concept of the marriage of the children being changed, the welfare and security of the old becomes a weighty consideration in this transitional period. True, Communist law requires children to support their parents. In Shanghai, for example, an old woman abandoned by her son obtained support from him by order of the "people's court." But the law does not prosecute such cases unless brought to court. In spite of increased accessibility to the law, there is a question whether every neglected or abandoned parent will bring the case to court in a situation where rule by law is still unfamiliar to common people. There is little doubt that such legal support is incomparably weaker than the guarantee provided by the traditional family for the welfare and security of the old.

The spectacular rise of the young and the decline of the old in power and prestige are plainly products of that stage of revolution which needs plastic young minds to accept the novel ideology, to practice the new standards, and to effect a drastic break with the traditional past. As the revolutionary situation settles down to an established order, with its new institutions and tradition sufficiently developed, age as a factor affecting the status and authority of individuals will undoubtedly resume some degree of importance, and accumulated knowledge and experience through age will again bear weight in the social evaluation of an individual. But it is doubtful whether age will ever resume the former traditional importance which summarily subjected the young to an inferior position in disregard of his other qualifications. The development of industrialization, which emphasizes technical competence, not age, and the popularization of science, which discounts empiricism, are both major goals of the present Communist revolution. Should the revolution successfully set up its institutions and traditions, these two factors among others will preclude a full return to the former Chinese consideration for age.

38.   FROM GENERATION TO GENERATION

Denis Lazure

During my recent trip of five weeks in China, I made a special point, in my capacity as a child psychiatrist, of observing the family structure and the relationships between parents and children. I was also interested in exploring the attitudes of young people, their problems and aspirations, and in gaining some insight into the type of character which the new Chinese leaders have been trying to form in their youth over the last 12 years and hopefully into the type of adult character which will emerge from this system.

The numerous visits which I made to such places as schools, nursery schools, "crèches," hospitals, public parks, "Pioneer Palaces," private homes, and institutions for delinquent children, enabled me to see Chinese youth from many angles and to gather much valuable information in the course of many conversations with the children, their parents, and their educators.

In order to obtain material of greater "depth" as well as to objectify to some extent my impressions, I obtained permission in Shanghai and Canton to examine 15 school children of both sexes, aged 10 to 16 years, by means of a psychiatric interview and the *thematic apperception test* (T.A.T.).

Although the subjects of this study were probably not typical of the "average" school children of this age because most of them were members of the specially selected group known as "Young Pioneers," it may be supposed that they represent in their comportment and character the "ideal type" of the new regime.

Each adolescent was examined individually by the author, with an interpreter serving as intermediary. The psychiatric interviews were on the classical model; they generally began on a rather superficial level, but I had the impression that these boys and girls were able to deal with serious material more readily

source: Selected from Denis Lazure, "The Family and Youth in New China: Psychiatric Observations," in *The Canadian Medical Association Journal,* 86, 179 (January 1962), pp. 179–182. Reprinted by permission of The Canadian Medical Association and the author.

than young people of North America. Almost all co-operated with genuine enthusiasm in the interview and on the test.

The following questions were asked systematically of each subject, though not always in the same order:

1. What is the most favourable thing that someone could say about you?
2. What is the best act you could perform?
3. The worst act?
4. Of which sex is your best friend?
5. What is your earliest memory?
   From what age does it date?
6. Tell me one of your recent dreams.
7. What are your major worries, anxieties?
8. What makes you angry most often?
9. What makes you sad?
10. What occupation do you plan to choose?

The most frequent answers to these questions were as follows:

1. As to the most favourable comment someone could make, typical replies were: "She does her best for the mother-country"; "he is a good student and a good worker"; "he is selflessly devoted to the cause"; "he appreciates criticism in order that he may improve himself." Thus, these adolescents seem to place particular value on patriotism, diligence in their studies and in their work in general, altruism, and accepting constructive criticism.

2. As to the best act one could perform, the following answers were typical: "Help an old person carry his packages"; "help reconcile children who are fighting"; "return a lost article to the Police"; "contribute to the success of the Agricultural Plan by growing a garden."

Respect and care for the aged, maintenance of interpersonal harmony, honesty and collaboration with the plans of the Party are the dominant themes.

3. The third question, dealing with the worst act possible, brought a unanimous response from the subjects. With apparent sincerity and conviction, they all replied: "It is impossible for a Pioneer or for a good student to commit a bad act."

This more or less unconscious denial of all unacceptable behaviour is a good illustration of the wave of moralism which so astonishes most Western visitors to China.

4. In the choice of their best friend, the subjects did not feel that the sex made any difference, with the exception of two subjects whose best friends were of the same sex. The following answer given by a boy of 16 years is typical: "My best friends are both boys and girls; we study and work together in harmony like brothers and sisters." (This type of answer throws some light on the almost total absence of "dating" among adolescents which will be discussed later.)

5. The question about their earliest memories brought answers which were interesting from several points of view. In the first place, there is a significant difference between the sexes in the age of the first memory. For the girls, the first memory was placed at the age of 3 years whereas for the boys it

was at the age of 4 in all cases, except for one boy who could remember nothing before the age of 5. Operating on the assumption that the choice of an event from early childhood is a more or less reliable index of the affective climate of that period as well as of the subject's present state, the writer found it useful to classify these memories in three categories according to the predominant affect: happy, sad, and neutral. For example, the memory. "When I was three years old, Mammy took me to Hantchow to play" would be classified as a "happy" one. This classification reveals a striking difference between the sexes: While all the boys without exception give a "happy" memory, this is true for only 20% of the girls, who give predominantly "neutral" memories instead. In interpreting this finding, one may wonder whether it reflects the relatively privileged position of the male child in the traditional Chinese family or whether it may be attributed, on the other hand, to the devaluation of emotional life which is a striking characteristic of the modern Chinese woman.

6. Dreams are very rare for 60% of the subjects; 20% claim to dream frequently, and the remaining 20% dream with moderate frequency. Of all the dreams reported, only one had a manifest content with a pleasure-seeking theme, and even this one ended in punishment. A boy of 16 reported a dream in which he was playing, "but the next morning, I was too tired and got up too late for school. I was very sad." All the other dreams reflect a strong concern and anxiety about success in one's studies and vocation. They point out the moral that one cannot hope to succeed without hard work. A good example is this dream reported by a 15-year-old boy: "I performed so well my work as a locomotive driver that my commune chose me as delegate to the Model Workers' Congress in Peking and at that meeting I was introduced to Chairman Mao, who shook my hand." "After I had this dream," the adolescent added, "I redoubled my efforts in my studies." Aside from the type of dream dealing with realistic concerns, the subjects unanimously denied having any nightmares.

7. To the question "What are your main worries?" all subjects replied that they had none. A typical answer is this one given by a girl of 13: "I have no fear or worry. I know that Chairman Mao and the Party are concerned with my welfare and can protect me against any danger even against an attack by the American imperialists."

8. The most frequent source of anger for these adolescents (66% of them) is the disapproved conduct of a younger sibling (such behaviour, for example, as teasing, laziness, lying, or disobedience). Among the other frequent causes of anger, 22% claimed having this feeling when they returned home to find the parents had gone out and, lastly, a minority admitted being angered by bothersome tricks of their playmates. One cannot help but notice the frequency and intensity of aggressive attitudes toward younger siblings. On the one hand, the adolescent projects on to his younger brothers and sisters a good part of the forbidden impulses and behaviour (laziness, disobedience, etc.) which he so vehemently denies in himself, and, on the other hand, no doubt he reacts with jealousy to the privileged treatment which is accorded to preschool-aged children in the Chinese family. One wonders whether the adolescent is not thus displacing the aggression which he unconsciously feels toward the parents for favouring the younger children and being absent from the home.

9. Of the whole group of subjects, only one was able to admit to having feelings of sadness. It was a girl of 13 who stated: "I feel sad when one of the leaders of our country or of another socialist country dies. Thus I felt sad at the death of Stalin and of Wilhelm Pieck because those men were our true comrades." A more typical answer was the one given by a boy of 14: "In New China everybody treats me well. I have no reason to be unhappy. Maybe I was before the Liberation . . ." With minor variations, this response was repeated by the entire group.

10. The question concerning future occupations elicited a remarkable diversity of choices. The vocations of scientist and specialized worker were of equal popularity at the head of the list. They were followed by teaching, military service, professional athletics, dancing, and agriculture, all more or less equally preferred.

Analysis of the T.A.T. Responses (Murray's Thematic Apperception Test)

I am indebted to my wife, a psychologist, for the interpretation of the T.A.T. responses. The following characteristics were noted:

1. The subjects were overly preoccupied with sociopolitical themes in contrast to their denial of intrapsychic conflicts. They lacked contact with their deeper impulses, relying excessively on outer rather than inner stimuli (the "outer-directed" personality of David Riesman).

2. Hostility is not expressed directly towards the immediate environment. By the mechanism of displacement and projection, it is directed toward the "capitalists" or American "imperialists" who are always seen by the subjects as symbols of aggression and cruelty. Thus, to the T.A.T. card 18 GF, a boy told the following story: "The mother looks sad. It seems that the girl who works in a factory is exploited by her capitalist boss who beat her or else paid some gangsters to beat her, she is exhausted and her mother is comforting her."

There also seems to be a remarkable capacity in these subjects to sublimate their aggressive impulses in hard work for personal improvement and for the advancement of the country. On one card in particular (3 BM), the theme of suicide frequently appears (hostility turned inward on oneself), but it is always specified that the scene does not take place in China but rather in a capitalist country.

3. The fear of failure is associated with high ambition.

4. There is marked blocking in the area of sexuality.

5. Attitudes of dependence and submission are expressed toward authority figures and rationalized as moral acts. Rarely are rebellious attitudes expressed, and, in such a case, these feelings are projected on a young child who is not yet "enlightened" as to his proper conduct.

One of the adolescent girls describes a mother-child scene as follows: "It is a young schoolgirl whose mother is trying to help her learn her lesson, but she is spoiled and disobedient and will not listen to her mother's advice. The mother, however, will keep on trying to explain it to her."

6. Parental figures are consistently perceived as affectionate and supportive, in marked contrast to the T.A.T.'s of North American adolescents.

Clinical Observations

Among the subjects of this study as well as among the adolescents and children observed more briefly during my visit, the symptoms I noticed most frequently were psychogenic facial tics and nail-biting. This would seem to indicate a state of excessive tension and anxiety, as these are generally considered neurotic traits. I was also particularly struck, as mentioned above, by the prevalence of sibling rivalry, especially as directed toward younger brothers and sisters.

On the other hand, certain symptoms which are very frequent among North American children, such as enuresis, nightmares, stuttering, and juvenile delinquency, seemed very rare.

All of the psychiatrists, psychologists, and educators questioned maintained that there were practically no mental defectives, and it seems that the Chinese do not feel a need for special classes or institutions for these cases. My informants stated that the rare cases of intellectual retardation were able to catch up with their classmates because of the special attention given by the teachers and sometimes by the brighter students.

At the modern psychiatric hospital at Shanghai, the director informed me that the 20-bed section originally set apart for children was now used for adults because there were not sufficient children to fill it.

All the psychiatrists I talked to denied having ever seen a case of infantile psychosis in China, although they had read in the literature that such a syndrome is not unusual in Europe and America.

The Chinese adolescent, unlike his Occidental counterpart, does not seem to go through a phase of more or less open revolt against his parents or parental figures in general. The notion, prevalent at least in North America, that adolescence is the period "par excellence" of confusion and intrapsychic disturbance, is strongly rejected by teachers, psychologists and doctors in China, who attribute this lack of conflict to the unlimited security and opportunities for youth to fulfil its aspirations in that country.

Comments and Conclusion

The most significant conclusion from this necessarily somewhat superficial study of present-day Chinese youth seems to be that their leaders have very effectively accomplished the revolution of transferring the emotional investment formerly reserved for the family to society as a whole and to the role which the individual will play in building his society. The sense of family and their relationships with their parents seem to occupy but little place in the psychic life of these young people. The family as an institution has certainly lost importance in all socialist countries based on the Russian model, but this is even more true in China, particularly since the establishment of the communes in 1958. Nearly 90% of the population now lives in these communes, which had as one of their principal purposes the "liberation" (according to the slogan)

of Chinese women from the "drudgery" of household tasks. The consequent
mass exodus of women to the factories and the fields does not, however,
seem to me to be the principal factor in the weakening of family ties, in
spite of the contrary opinion which is sometimes expressed.

We must take into consideration the fact that, now that she is freed from
the tasks of cooking meals and running the house, the mother is able to
devote her time entirely to her children when she arrives home from work.
I was particularly impressed to see, for example, that even very young children
accompany their parents in the evening on trips to the local park or movie
theatre. It seems quite possible that these few hours of close contact in a
relaxed atmosphere make up, to a large extent, for the absence of the mother
during the day.

The preschoool-aged child is treated with extreme indulgence by adults, but
as soon as he reaches school age, he must assume heavy responsibilities: first
of all, to succeed in an intensely competitive academic situation; secondly,
to become a "model child" and thus earn a conveted membership in the
Young Pioneers; and finally, to become equally skilled in manual work, because
he must devote, following a principle sacred to the new Chinese leaders, several
hours each week to physical labour. I had the impression that, almost without
transition, the child is encountered with these heavy demands and that this
must create in him considerable anxiety as well as a chronic fear of failure.

As for the adolescent, when compared to his Western counterpart, he lives
a life of great austerity. Dating, cigarettes and alcohol have been eliminated
from his life, not by law but by persuasion. During his few hours of leisure
he generally takes part in sports, but even here he is more concerned with
improving himself, with beating a record, than with simply enjoying himself.

The Chinese adolescent looks toward adult life with great confidence. Success
in his mind is not associated with a few stereotyped occupations as is often
the case in Western societies. The State has succeeded in giving prestige to
the most humble occupations by means of propaganda and such concrete measures as salary: thus the truck driver has an income comparable to that of
the medical school graduate.

As in any society where the emancipation of women is still a recent phenomenon, one sees in China an aggressive determination on the part of the
women to prove their equality, if not their superiority, to men. Even more
than the young man, the modern Chinese woman rejects disdainfully the idea
of "romantic love" (which, it must be admitted, she knew little of in traditional
China). One's mate is chosen, according to the new ideal, for his qualifications
as a model worker and for the degree of his political consciousness.

It is perhaps in these countries, China and the United States, that the
adolescent of today experiences the strongest pressure toward conformity. For
the American teen-ager, the norms of the peer-groups are all-compelling, while
the young Chinese wants at any price to be identified with the norms of
the Five-Year Plan and the Party slogans.

Thus, when all the adolescents examined seriously maintain that they have
no problems and no worries, we cannot take their statements at face value.
It would be ridiculous to believe that their society has achieved such a utopia;
it is more realistic to presume that the State has been highly successful in

creating an image of happy youth and that the young people, in their desire to conform, have accepted that illusion.

The Chinese have an unlimited faith in the power of education, of persuasion—patiently served up in various forms (radio, TV, movies, periodicals, and slogans) to obtain "correct thought." For the local criminal as well as for the foreign prisoner or the unruly child, it is "explanation" which has replaced physical punishment, and it would be dangerous to underestimate the extraordinary talent which the Chinese possess for this task. From his earliest years, the Chinese child is educated to feel gratitude and affection for Chairman Mao, who is the source of all that is good, while it is "explained" to him that the American capitalists are responsible for all that is bad. Such a policy tends to fix the individual in an infantile mode of thought which encourages the projection of blame on to others and develops fanaticism.

In my own opinion, it is precisely this systematic use of "persuasion" which has contributed more than any other factor to the weakening of emotional ties to the family; a method which has managed to present the Party leaders, not as obstacles between the child and his parents, but rather as infinitely wise and generous beings who stand above the family and who only naturally must take precedence in the child's mind.

Summary

The author reports on observations made on a recent five-week visit to New China. The general establishment of rural and urban communes since 1958, while affecting the structure of the home, does not appear to threaten the sense of belonging to the family. The commune has brought radical changes in social living; for instance, 80% of women who are physically fit work outside their homes. Because they are "reformed through work," adult criminals or juvenile delinquents are extremely rare.

As early as three months, the child is placed in the communal "crèche." The pre-schooler is indulged by adults while the school-aged child must work very hard on the academic level in addition to giving to the State several hours of manual work. The child and the teenager appear to be more concerned with sociopolitical themes than with conflicts which would exist in their relationships with their parents. Dating among adolescents is non-existent.

In this type of society, there should be little variation in the frequency of psychotic conditions, but probably a marked decrease of psychoneuroses, character disorders and antisocial behaviour. The existence of mental deficiency is denied by the official authorities.

In conclusion, there is a fairly remarkable civic pride but at the same time a stereotyped attitude in thought and behaviour. The State does not place itself between the child and his parents, but rather above the latter. Understandably, such a society has assigned to each individual a definite role: and this structure, at least at this phase, appears to be a favourable factor in the mental health of the Chinese.

Values and Ethics

39. THE PLACE OF CONFUCIANISM

JOSEPH R. LEVENSON

In Chinese Communist fashions, Confucius seems to be "in" this year. Earlier, certainly in the nineteen-twenties, revolutionaries were quite ready to see him out, and even now, in the first decade or so of the People's Republic, there are plenty of people with little patience for the sage of the old intelligence. Indeed, "despise the old" and "preserve the national heritage" have been chasing each other down the nineteen-fifties and incipient sixties, and contemporary historians, in this area, should perhaps not dwell too seriously on trends *pro* and *anti,* so foreshortened, if discernible at all, in the foreground of our age. What seems historically significant is the range, not the petty successions, of recent Communist options in evaluating Confucius. For all the possibilities are equally modern, all plausible and consistent within a new Chinese view—an essentially anti-Confucian view informing even the pro-Confucius minds.

In the early years of the 1911 Republic, embattled radical iconoclasts, out to destroy Confucius, and romantic conservatives, bent on preserving him, had been equally untraditional.[1] Now, in the People's Republic of 1949, successor-radicals, with that battle behind them and those foes crushed, may bring the romantic note into their own strain and celebrate Confucian anniversaries in the name of the national heritage. But the Communists who wish Confucius happy birthday only swell the chorus that sounds him down to burial in history.

Imperishability of the Confucian Spirit?

A grand old question: is Confucianism a religion? Certainly the problem of Confucianism is rather different from the problem of Buddhism in the

SOURCE: Selected from Joseph R. Levenson, "The Place of Confucius in Communist China," in *The China Quarterly,* 12 (October/November 1962), pp. 1–18. Reprinted by permission of *The China Quarterly.*

Communist era; there is no organised Confucian body whose state can be statistically assessed.[2] Actually, when there had been some sort of effort, before the First World War, to conceive of it as a church, Confucianism was at its nadir, and no Communist policy about that Confucianism need or can be scrutinised. Other questions claim attention. First, is there Confucianism *in* Communism? Second (and more important here), what of Confucius himself, his current reputation and its meaning?

There are those, with a taste for paradox, who feel that the new régime is "in spirit," in real content, whatever the surface forms of revolution, Confucian forever. This implies an interpretation of continuity in terms not of process but reality; past is related to present not by sequence but by the persistence of essentials. From this point of view it is enough to remark that (give or take a few degrees) both Communist and Confucian China have been institutionally bureaucratic and despotic, intellectually dogmatic and canonical, psychologically restrictive and demanding. And for those who balk at forcing Confucianism and Communism to match, there is still the "Legalist" label for Mao's China. The principle of "sinological determinism" might thereby still be defended, a Chinese ideal type still preserved against corrosive historical thinking; and, with Mao a Ch'in Shih Huang-ti, Confucianism would still be implicitly there, an alternative or a partner, as in the days of that Legalist "First Emperor" or of later dynastic autocrats.

If, in such a timeless, noumenal version of continuity, China were "always China," the place of Confucius in Communist China would be pre-ordained, and empirical inquiry gratuitous or fussily misleading. Yet, if only out of piety to history (or, less grandly, in defence of his occupation), a historian has to assume the authenticity of phenomenal change, and, in this instance, contemplate not the ideal of a ghostly Confucius in the mere flesh of a modern Communist, but the idea of Confucius in the minds of men who publish under Communist aegis. One of them, Lo Ken-tse (editor of Volumes IV, 1933, and VI, 1938, of *Ku Shih Pien, (Symposium on Ancient History)*, the famous collection of modern critiques of Classical historical orthodoxy), makes a point in discussing Confucius that could seem to assimilate Confucianism to Marxism. What lies behind the appearance?

In some observations about Confucius on poetry, Lo remarks that Confucius had basically philosophical, not literary, interests. Knowing that poetry had a lyrical, expressive character, he wanted to impose on it standards of moral orthodoxy, because he valued poetry from a utilitarian not an aesthetic point of view. Lo speaks of Confucius' practice of *tuan chang ch'üi* ("cutting off the stanza and selecting the principle"), a proceeding traditionally related to the way the *Chung-yung (Doctrine of the Mean)*, for example, cites the *Shih-ching (Book of Poetry)*: to extract moral dicta. Literature was a tool for him, and rhetorical considerations *per se* played no part. That is why, though his doctrine of "seizing the word" had a great influence on the development of literary criticism, its purport was not "revise words" but "rectify names."[3]

Now, surely not only Lo's ancient subject but his contemporary patrons have a utilitarian not an "aesthetic" conception of literature. Mao as well as Confucius has viewed literature as the carrier of an ethos. Long ago, in the nineteen-twenties, it could seem like a throwback to the Confucian doctrine of "literature to convey the *tao,*" when the "Creation Society," a body of writers imbued at first with a Western-tinged aetheticism, turned toward Marxist commitment.[4] Yet, in the "Creation" affair, the later commitment was quite as remote from Confucian premises as the earlier; indeed, it was the exhaustion of Confucianism, premises and all, which had rendered "art for art's sake"— though a radical slogan against a vital Confucianism—seemingly superfluous, and exposed it, in Communist eyes, as counter-revolutionary for a post-Confucian age.[5] Lo Ken-tse, some thirty years later, is just as far from simply engrossing a Confucian motif in a Marxist one. Rather, when he speaks of Confucius "imposing standards" on the *Shih-ching,* Lo (rather late in the critical day) means to release the poems from their Confucian blanket and to reveal them, by restoring their natural, poetic quality, as truly "popular." He wants to save a Classic by redeeming it from Confucian associations, thus permitting it to qualify for a Communist accolade.

The Dwindling Share of Confucian Matter in Intellectual Life

But why should Communists care about such a salvage job? Would not revolutionaries (once we take them seriously as such) be expected to cancel the old intellectual currency, instead of converting it? At least from a quantitative standpoint, certainly, the old concerns of Confucian scholarship get relatively meagre attention. In 1958 Kuo Mo-jo, in a briskly modern, no-nonsense mood, said that ancient studies had only a slight claim on available Chinese energies.[6]

Even so, a considerable programme of annotation, translation into modern Chinese, and publication of Classics and other early literature was reported for the next two years.[7] But with the development of a paper shortage (undoubtedly real since spring, 1961, and already blamed in 1960 for the serious cut in publications export), the ancient texts were the first to go.[8] And this is not surprising, since Shanghai publishers—typically, we may suppose—were proclaiming in 1960 the necessity of "learning about science and technology," "catching up with science and technology," and "overtaking science and technology."[9] These are the twins, not classical arts and letters, that the Communists especially foster in the educational system.

Intellectual training, then, once a Confucian preserve, is now pervaded by a spirit quite alien to the Confucian. Science and technology are there, on the one hand; and on the other, especially since 1958, some sort of material production and physical labour has been injected into the curriculum, with the avowed aim of domesticating the intellectuals, destroying any lingering Confucian assumptions about the "higher life" and its natural claim to prestige.[10]

Confucian Matter De-Confucianised
MILESTONES TO THE PRESENT

In a society where an anti-classical education sets the tone, what can the Classics be used for? In contemporary China, where Confucian scholars are invisible, scholars in Confucianism still do find employment. Their principal aim is not to extol antiquity, but to illustrate a theory of process.[11]

Accordingly, the Classics retain no scriptural authority; far from providing criteria for historical assessments, they themselves are examined for significance in history. The authority they had is an object of historical study, instead of its premise.

Historical revisionism, whereby a Confucianist's villain becomes a Communist's hero, is widespread nowadays, but where the Classics are concerned it is the pattern rather than the praise-and-blame which is markedly revised. True, Kuo Mo-jo can stand an old judgment on its head and rehabilitate Chou Hsin of Yin, whom the *Shu-ching* (*Book of History*) made the classic example of the "bad last emperor." But when Kuo says that the latter was really competent, that he struck blows for the Chinese people's expansion and unification,"[12] Kuo is fitting him into the annals of Chinese progress; and it is this orientation to progress, more than the bleaching of a blackened name, which puts Kuo in the un-Confucian stream. In Communist use of the Classics for making historical points, Marxist process is the governing idea, not, however revalued, a moralistic absolute.

Thus, history teachers should use the Classics in illustrating stages, *e.g.*, "For the waning of primitive communism and the coming of slave society, cite the *Li-yün* section of the *Li-chi* (*Book of Rites*), from 'Ta tao chih hsing yeh' to 'Shih wei hsiao-k'ang'" (*Li-chi* VII A, 2–3; Legge, "When the Grand Course was pursued, a public and common spirit ruled all under the sky. . . .").[13] This passage was dear to nineteenth-century innovators and egalitarians, T'ai-p'ing rebels and K'ang Yu-wei's Reformers.[14] But these groups (though generally far apart in their attitudes toward the Classics) used the *Li-chi* for the validity that a Classic might lend; while Communists cite the same text as illustrative, not exemplary—to corroborate a theory, not authenticate a value.

As a matter of fact, some Communists see not only their modern predecessors' *Li-yün* citations, but the *Li-yün* itself, as a falling back on authority. For the *Li-yün* attributes the "Grand Course" passage to Confucius, though it really dates from some two centuries after his time.[15] There are harsh words for one Comrade Jen Chüan, who seems to accept the attribution uncritically.[16] And yet, while inviting this attack from a critic who denies that Confucius had any intention of "abolishing distinctions," Jen Chüan is really not in the business of praising Confucius by raising him out of his time, taking him as a validator of socialism, or socialism as validator of him. Jen Chüan suggests that Confucius (like K'ang Yu-wei, who revered this *ta-t'ung* side of him) had a vague *kung-hsiang* (fantasy) socialism, impracticable in his day. Therefore, lacking a clear road ahead to his goal, he looked back to primitive communism. When, "Ta tao chih hsing yeh. . . ."[17]—or, back to the *Li-yün* as reflector of primitive communism, a superseded stage.

And so for the next progressive transition, from slave society to feudalism: this is said to be reflected textually in the sequence of *I-ching* (*Book of Changes*) to *I-chuan* (*Commentary on Changes*—possibly included among the "Ten Wings," appendices to the *I-ching*). For these texts are equated, respectively, with an early Chou religious idealism (*T'ien-tao*, "Way of Heaven") and a "Warring States" materialistic naturalism.[18]

And as materialism is a higher stage of thought than idealism, and naturalism higher than religion, so the "Warring States" advance of the doctrines of Confucius towards victory was advance indeed, in the historical sense of the word. For as a pair of authors interprets the *Lun-yü* (*Analects*), Confucius' concept of *jen* (human kindness) was both anti-aristocratic and anti-religious. *Jen*, the special mark of the *chün-tzu*, undercut the nobles by substituting individual quality for blood line in distinguishing *chün-tzu* from *hsiao-jen*, the "princely man" from the "small." And inasmuch as *jen* implied "esteeming wisdom," this was progressive, too, in its humanist agnosticism, that strain in Confucius that Feuerbach praised, when he marked the advance of capitalism on European feudalism, reflected in the attrition of religion.[19]

Other authors, too, appreciate the *Lun-yü* for the humanism and materialism they sometimes strain to find. One, for example, sees the message of *Lun-yü*, III, xii ("One should sacrifice to a spirit as though that spirit were present") as, "Gods and ancestral spirits exist only in the mind." Passages indicating Confucius' preference for non-speculative direct perception, and for enriching the people before teaching them, are cited as materialist, in different senses of the word. And so is Confucius' scepticism about knowing the "Way of Heaven" (see *Lun-yü* V, xii)—a Way referred to often, superstitiously, by men recorded in the *Ch'un ch'iu* (*The Spring and Autumn Annals*), but materialistically doubted in the *Tso-chuan* (the main classical "commentary" appended to the *Annals*), Ch'ao-kung 18: "The Way of Heaven is far, the way of man is near. . . ."[20]

As the *Lun-yü* and *Tso-chuan* contribute humanism to the march of progress, so the *Shih-ching* (which we have seen already as "popular") is said to begin a great tradition of realism, reflecting the creativity which burgeoning feudal society so abundantly released.[21] We know well enough, from modern invective, that feudalism *per se* wins no Communist admiration. It is the progressive stage, not the entity, that is praiseworthy; and a Classic is used for documenting, and praised for projecting, this progress.

Accordingly, possible Communist respect for Confucian Classics, as creative expressions of social revolution, does not usually carry over to Confucian classical scholarship. It may be said occasionally that there is much to be learned from one of its practitioners, as in recent praise of Chia I (200–168 B.C.), a Han official who made a famous critique of Ch'in rule by power alone. Such praise, far from implying Communist self-identification was the past through a Confucian fellow-feeling, reflects more likely a stung reaction to allegations of "Legalism"—the hostile way of identifying the Party with the past. And what is Chia I's virtue? It is nothing absolute, but relative to process. In what he was, he had to be imperfect: he could not escape limitations of time and place. His merit lies in where he was going.

His lifetime (so the argument runs) coincided with a great change in feudal society, and Chia I, seeking to construct a program for a new feudal government, represented the interest of a newly rising commoner landlord class. (He had a realistic viewpoint (good), and he paid special attention (very good) to Ch'in and contemporary (early Han) history—*i.e.*, for his own day, modern history.[22] Thus, the Communist favour goes to modern times, and, among men and events of the past, to the modernising forces.

For the most part, then, Confucian scholarship after classical times themselves is seen as the main line of Chinese feudal culture, the support of feudal monarchy, and feudal society (as distinct from the feudalisation of slave society) has no intrinsic virtue. Han Wu-ti (regn. 134–86 B.C.) winnowed the *Ju* (Confucianists) from out of the "Hundred Schools" for special honour, and established their texts as authoritative. Thus the Classics became the preserve of the feudal land-holding, bureaucratic literati. And one of the aims of classical study now (runs the argument) is to show how classical study then could serve the feudal interests.[23] The Sung *li-hsüeh* neo-Confucianism—to cite an impressive school of classical scholarship—constrained thought, imposed rote, blocked science; and the "Han-chien (Chinese traitor) Tseng Kuo-fan" (1811–72) was a great patron of *li-hsüeh,* not by chance.[24]

In short, the contemporary approach to the Classics is neither *necessarily* to damn them as feudal (some do), nor to praise them (in the Confucian vein) as timeless. They are subject to scrutiny from a mental world beyond them; they do not govern the mental world (as once they did) themselves. As a Communist *Mencius* study-group expressed it: *They* (traditional intellectuals) used *Mencius* as a vehicle—Chu Hsi (1130–1200) did it to carry his neo-Confucianism, Tai Chen (1724–77) did it to correct Chu Hsi, K'ang Yu-wei (1858–1927) did it as a "modern-text" Confucian Reformer, all of them summoning up antiquity to sanction innovation. But *we* use the tool of Marxism-Leninism for an analytic critique.[25]

This means, of course, that a Marxist commentary on Mencius conveys Marxism. In this it may seem to be doing, *mutatis mutandis,* just what Chu Hsi, Tai Chen and K'ang Yu-wei did. Yet, while such Sung and Ch'ing commentators may not, indeed, have been doing what they claimed, expounding Mencius or Confucius "authentically," still they assumed that only if they did so would their own views be valid. However individual their interpretations, however eccentric they seemed to outsiders, these earlier scholars had to establish—for their own satisfaction as much as for anyone else's—that classical Confucian authority was being duly upheld. But Marxists scout Confucian authority, considering it a specimen to be analysed (not idolised) and put in its place in history—a place in the flux of the past, not an eternal place of ever-present judgment.

That is why a Communist reversal of older radical textual critiques is comprehensible. It may seem extraordinary that a contemporary scholar in Communist China should take up the traditional Confucian line on the *Tso-chuan:* that it really was compiled by Tso Chiu-ming as a commentary on the *Ch'un-ch'iu* (which was Confucius' own).[26] Yet, despite appearances, decades of "doubting antiquity" have not gone quite for nothing. For the main point of Confucius, said to be "rectification of names," is seen as completely feudal and only feudal. And Confucius, while commendably materialistic in some ways, and incomparably important in planting history in Chinese education, was a step behind Ssu-ma Ch'ien, the "Grand Historian" of the Former Han; while Confucius did not (as so often advertised) see history as an irredeemable fall from sage-antiquity, he did see an eternity of oscillation (in the Mencius phrase, "now order, now chaos") while Ssu-ma Ch'ien had a sense of historical progress.

We have, then, in this account of Confucius, another avowal of progress (indeed, to see progress *is* progress), not a triumphant return of an old unfaded perennial. If progress goes through Confucius (as evinced in his *Spring and Autumn*, not the first of its name, but first to deal with "the Empire" and not just a single state), it also goes beyond him. And therefore, without identity, a Communist may now agree with orthodox Confucianists on the link of *Tso-chuan* to *Ch'un-ch'iu*, because they agree on the error of the *Kung-yang* school, which had to deny the link in order to make its specious case for Confucius as the ultimate progressive. This is same stand, different standpoints; different effects from the same description. For progress matters in Communist theory, while it mattered precious little in the orthodox Confucian. In the present day, when the thrill of iconoclasm in the field of Classics has worn off—because icons no longer sacred tempt fewer men to break them—old conventional combinations (like the *Ch'un-ch'iu* and the *Tso-chuan* respectably together) are no witness at all to renascence of Confucius.

Thus, praise of Confucius (*e.g.,* for seeing the true relation between "ideol ogy" and "reality"[27]) tends to be patronising, no reverent expression of discipleship. Confucius cannot guarantee this truth; he simply decorates the discussion. One points up a thesis, perhaps, by referring to the Classics, but legitimacy flows back from Marx (Lenin, Mao), not forward from Confucius. "Ideology" and "reality," in our example, are *wen* and *tao,* luminous classical terms—but here, metaphorical, used clearly in the expectation that no one will misunderstand. And nothing so marks the relegation of values to the past, to historical significance, as the metaphorical drift, whereby originally literal statements of content become rhetorical allusions.

Confucian Matter De-Confucianised

GRAVESTONES FROM THE PAST

On this showing, when writers in Communist China display some admiration of Confucius, they are not reproducing the traditional admiration. Therefore, when other contemporary writers sound unregenerately, untraditionally anti-Confucian, this is no sign of Party schizophrenia. For this is the kind of controversy that a Marxist world can contain. If one wants to put a reactionary construction on Confucius' work (holding that he feared the future and was generally "anti-people"),[28] this taste in interpretation clashes, to be sure, with the "progressive" taste, but the tasters, all the same, have a common assumption: that history moves regularly through progressive stages, no matter which stage one sees as dear to Confucius, or to which he seems appropriate. The controversy is tame, like the more general one about when slave society ends the feudal begins. Within a framework of agreement on the historical reality of these societies in China, in that order, there can be several ideas about their boundaries.

But even if one acknowledges that the relatively pro-Confucius wing of Communist opinion is safely Communist enough, not Confucian, why did it come into being? Why does it differ not only from traditional conservatism but from traditional (earlier twentieth-century) radicalism? The fact that it can co-exist with Communist hostility to Confucius does not explain how it came to exist at all. It is challenging, surely, that after all the vitriolic treatment of Confucius so usual in the "Renaissance," the "New Tide," all the early radical intellectual groupings, we can find a scholar in mainland China, vintage 1958, with this fine antique allusion: "The Great Pheasant gives a cry, dawn comes to the world." Confucius, here no wretched feudal crow, is the "Great Pheasant," and it is his galvanising of scholarship and his diffusion of it in new milieus, non-aristocratic, that give rise to the "Hundred Schools." "This has great significance in the history of Chinese thought and Chinese education. Thereafter, literate men took Confucius as their great ancestral teacher. . . ."[29]

The big difference between early days and now for the Communists and Confucius is the difference between social and national associations. In Communist eyes originally, Confucius was simply the idol of the rulers of the old society; if those feudal rulers (or their abortively revolutionary bourgeois successors), for their part, claimed that Confucius embodied the "national essence," this was only a reactionary fiction, designed to avert the class struggle which would sweep the old away. Thus, Confucius, in trouble enough just for his traditional distinction, was further compromised by traditionalistic efforts to revive him.

For at first, in the new Republic after 1911, the old elementary education in Confucian *hsiu-shen tu-ching* (moral culture and classical reading) had fallen into abeyance, and the texts of Confucian learning were left to the universities, where a spirit of detachment—knowledge *of*, not knowledge *in*, judgment, not immersion—was expected to prevail. However, in 1915 Yüan Shih-k'ai, appealing to conservatives with his monarchical movement, put the old formula back in the lower schools. In 1923, *hsiu-shen* slipped once more, supplanted by a blandly modern "citizenship and hygiene," and *tu-ching* vanished, too, as the literary language, with its Confucian aura, yielded to the colloquial in the primary and high schools.[30] But when Chiang Kai-shek turned to the old pieties, with his *"San-min chu-i* (Three People's Principles) education" for an anti-Communist China's destiny, Confucius again turned up in school. Ch'en Li-fu's directives in January 1942 had agriculture as the basis of national life, *Ch'un-ch'iu* and *Li-chi* as the heart of instructions in ethics.[31] (And twenty years later, on Formosa, Confucius was still being enlisted against the "alien revolution.")[32]

What the Communists made of this should be easy to imagine. Confucius needed only the curse of Japanese sponsorship to make his exposure complete. Reactionary "sellers of the nation," the indictment ran, "revived the old, revered Confucius." And the predatory buyers, the Japanese fascists, pumped their own gas of "Confucius and the Kingly Way" into occupied China.[33]

This made two things clear. First, Confucius must be anathema to Communists as long as he seems identified with a contemporary Chinese class cause or a Japanese foreign cause: to the Communists, by no means always distinguishable. But second, Communists, preempting the *national* cause, can nationalise Confucius, freeing him of current social associations, taking him out of history from now on—by putting him back into it (in another sense), packing him away in the past as *historically* significant!

For the very fact that their enemies, foreign and domestic, *used* Confucius meant that the defence of Confucius was not their genuine end; and if these enemies, exactly like the Communists, were really concerned with present interests, their used Confucius was just as dead as a Communist might wish him. A dead man, superseded as a target, could be measured for a monument. Publicity for a "people's tradition" against a "gentry" (Confucian) tradition[34] is not inconsistent with a restoration of Confucius. Once, during the days of the Paris Commune, Jacob Burckhardt rushed to believe a rumour of something he rather expected, the burning of the Louvre and all its contents[35]; to Burckhardt, the treasures of art and culture seemed destined for ruin in the dawning age of destruction of authority. What should they do, revolutionaries from the lower depths, but destroy the products of the old high culture, symbols of their own subservience?

But Burckhardt might have remembered the first French Revolutionaries' preservation of the Bayeux Tapestry as a national treasure, even though, as a relic of the grandeur of nobles, it had been threatened, like its associates, with destruction.[36] And Burckhardt (in a heroic feat of clairvoyance and broadening of sympathies) might have applied the lesson in envisioning the fate of Confucius: "the people," without abandoning hostility to bearers of the "other culture," can conceive of themselves as capturing it. Confucius need not be shattered; he can be preserved, embalmed, deprived of life in a glass case instead of in a cultural holocaust. He can be restored, in short, not as an authentically resurgent Confucianism (or an immanently Confucian Communism) might restore him, but as a museum-keeper restores, his loving attention to "period" proclaiming the banishment of his object from any living culture. What could be more aggressive than that (new masses *vs.* old elite), and yet more soporific? Revolutionaries, in a *metaphorical* way, kissing off into the past instead of blowing up in the present, commit the destruction which Burckhardt half-literally expected. As the Communists claim to stand for the whole nation, the ancient mentor of a high, once mighty part is quietly taken over, and given his quietus. Nobody raises his voice in a National Gallery—on either side of the exhibition frames.

Under the new dispensation, then, Confucius can have all the class-associations anyone envisages, as long as they are ascribed to him *for his own day only*. Make him "slave" or "feudal," but only for late Chou. He can then belong to the modern nation by being in its history, or (to say the same thing) by being *now* de-classed: *i.e.*, out of historical action. Thus, "the feudalist system which set up his name as a symbol has gone for good; but the name of Confucius himself is, and always will be, respected and cherished by the Chinese people."[37] And another writer, in the same business of extricating Confucius from the past for present admiration, consigns him to the past, too, as a matter of practical influence: "I myself am not a Confucianist, and I think, to speak frankly, that what he taught belongs now irrevocably to history."[38] A biographer censures Yen Fu (1849–1921) for using Confucius after World War I as a stick for beating Western civilisation. To a Communist, this is using the ante-historical concept of "Chinese essence" to damn modernisation, and he says that Confucius' teaching had the form of the feudal consciousness, which was not for modern China, not for the modern world. But the critic is attacking Yen Fu, a late antagonist, not Confucius, a late, late one. He agrees that the thought of Confucius, *in history*, had a great position and applicability.[39]

To accept literal Confucian influence is wrong; he must be dead to the present. Therefore, even the generally favoured Hung Hsiu-ch'üan, the T'ai-p'ing ruler, may be scored off for "traditional feudal superstition" implanted by his youthful Confucian training.[40] But to acknowledge some national Confucian ancestry, over a gulf of time unbridgeable to influence, is all right. For this means continuity, or life to the culture. Thus, an alphabetic script-reformer would preserve against obliteration Confucius and the culture which he dominated, though this culture was enshrined in the script that is marked for discard.[41] And the historian, Ch'en Po-ta, avowing that "today's China is an extension of historical China," refers to a Mao statement of 1938: "As we are believers in the Marxist approach to history, we must not cut off our whole historical past. We must make a summing up from Confucius down to Sun Yat-sen and inherit this precious legacy."[42]

"Broaden the modern, narrow the old," Ch'en continues, as he makes it clear that a line is thrown back to the past not for the sake of the past, but for the present. (Recall the praise of the past's Chia I for attention to his own present.) The tie is for continuity, not constraint. What, to Ch'en, distinguishes the Communist zeal for the modern from that of earlier iconoclasts, with their capitalist world-view and their slogans on the order of, Break through the web!" or Break down the Confucianists' shop!"? What these men lack, with their capitalist-reformist mentalities, is scientific detachment regarding ancient thought and culture. Some of their fellows try superficially to harmonise the old and the new; they themselves go to extremes, and cut off the old from the new absolutely. A new scholarship is needed, and the Communists will supply it: neither Classical, nor Sung neo-Confucian, nor Ch'ing empirical, nor late-Ch'ing reformist. It must be a scholarship fulfilling each earlier type, transcending the accomplishments of all the preceding Chinese.[43]

Fulfilment—neither dismissal nor resuscitation. For the former would leave an impression of China de-nationalised, the victim of "cultural imperialism," and the latter would leave her unmodernised, a relic of feudalism. The great aim is to be modern *and* Chinese, that combination so desperately sought through a century of reformist and revolutionary exasperation at a seemingly immobile China and an all-too-kinetic West. Thus, for all the Communists' hostility to the reactionary use of Confucius, there is an equal animus against what they see as the liberal, bourgeois, pro-Western abuse of Confucius. Ku Chieh-kang, in a new preface (1954) to a 1935 book on Han dynasty scholarship, censures himself for his old unmitigated rejection of the Confucian thought of those days—an error stemming from his failing in historical materialism.[44] And another writer, not bearing the culpability as his own but spreading it around, indicts the Chinese bourgeoisie for an overweening reverence for Western culture and disparagement of China's, though Mao had ordained that "today's China is the extension of historical China."[45]

Confucius, then, redeemed from both the class aberration (feudal) of idolisation and the class aberration (bourgeois) of destruction, may be kept as a national monument, unworshipped, yet also unshattered. In effect, the disdain of a modern pro-Western bourgeoisie for Confucius cancels out, for the dialecticians, a feudal class's pre-modern devotion. The Communists, driving history to a classless synthetic fulfilment, retire Confucius honourably into the silence of the museum. In a concrete way, this is evident in the very making of museums in Communist China.

For the Confucian temple at Sian is restored, to house a historical museum. The temple and tomb (and environs) of Confucius at Ch'ü-fu are repainted, regilded and preserved.[46] In April 1962, during the traditional "Ch'ing-ming" spring festival for worshipping at graves, streams of visitors were drawn there, in a market-fair atmosphere, officially contrived, along the route of procession from the "Confucian grove" to the temple.[47] (The *K'ung-lin,* "Confucian grove," had once been proposed as the Mecca and Jerusalem of Confucianism as a religion.)[48] And such acts of piety (consistent with, not confounded by, a "feudal" identification)[49] convey the Communists' sense of synthesis in arresting physical ruin. Products of the old society, which might be (and, earlier, were) deemed proper objects of iconoclasm, provocative symbols of a social type which Communists ought to attack, nevertheless had suffered neglect and depredation, not loving care, from the society which the Communists succeeded.[50] This neglect, combined with foreign plundering, comes to the fore as a cultural crime of the old society, overshadowing the inequities of the even older society which made the relics in the first place. If anything, it was the pre-Communist neglect which consigned these things to history, which stamped them *non-contemporary.* When the Marxist historicism of the current society relativises its "restored" Confucius to a remote stage of society— and preserves him for the present through the Museum's trick of dissociating art from any life at all—it only confirms the action (or inaction: the working of neglect) of the society just before this one. In a satirical fantasy from that Kuomintang era, the 1930s, the novelist Lao She, now thoroughly acceptable to the Communists, mordantly pictured two things, perceived as a combination: conservative spirit in clinging to a moribund culture, and material failure to conserve. For the museum in "Cat City" is empty, its possessions all sold to foreigners.[51]

Any comtemporary assault against Confucius, then, while still a sort of ritual exercise (at the moment, in abeyance) for some writers in Communist China, is ideologically superflous. The Communists know they have living men to assail, non-Communists as modern and post-Confucian as themselves, not the stuffed men from a costume past (whose clothes they are stealing anyway, to display as their "national heritage"). The stake today is title to the prestige of science. Science, as we have suggested, sets up values alien to the Confucian, and a Confucian challenge on this issue could only be remote. But a non-Communist anti-traditionalism cannot be stripped of a claim on that title so easily. An attack on a biologist for basing himself on Darwin instead of Michurin[52] is a more typical accusation of "rightism" than an attack on grounds of Sinocentric narrowness. The Confucian literatus, who might have been narrow in that way, is so faint a memory that no one gets credit now in the Communist heaven, as a new man, just by being a Western-trained scientist. The latter is now the old man (the Confucianist is the dead man), and the "post-bourgeois" scientist is the new.

Scientists have tended lately to be less harassed by ideologues in a technologically hungry China, but the demand for "red and expert," the redder the better, has long been heard in the land,[53] and will doubtless be heard

442   Values and Ethics

again. The question has been raised of possible affinity between this point of view and the Confucian preference for the highly indoctrinated universal man over the specialist.[54] If the affinity existed, then the Confucian spirit might well be thought, in a sense, imperishable. Yet, the "red and expert" formula may better be taken, perhaps, to prove the opposite: scientific expertise, specialised knowledge, far from being inferior to the general, is indispensable. It is this very indispensability that makes it such an important thing to capture; it must not be seen as independent, or anything but derived from the Marxist point of view. The Communists have to own science—or *they* will appear not indispensable.

A Chinese world in which science has to be owned, to be captured, is the very world in which Confucius can only be captured, cannot be free and dominant. Where science is all-pervasive (even seeping into the rhetoric applied to the social system), Confucius is under lock and key and glass. It is the curators, not the creators, who look to Confucius now. No longer a present incitement to traditionalists (these having been crushed), Confucius is ready for history.

But not for "the dustbin of history"—the museum, in every sense (and to one in particular) is not that by any other name. The museum where Confucius is posed may be a storehouse of value and inspiration. And "museumified" is not "mummified." Still, the "museumified" Confucius does not speak; no longer involved in the handing down of judgments, he is therefore not much involved in clamorous class struggle. One is neither quartering Botticelli nor taking his as the last word for a contemporary jury, when one hangs him on the wall, far from the social context of his patronage. The critics, by and large, call him masterly. They also call him *quattrocento*. Confucius, too, is wise today for many revolutionaries, and may grow wiser as his patrons grow deader. But Confucius is also *Chou*.

The first wave of revolution in the twentieth century had virtually destroyed him, and seemed to destroy with him a precious continuity, a historical identity. Many schools have tried to put these together again. The Communists have their own part in the search for time lost, and their own intellectual expedient: to bring it back, bring him back, by pushing him back in history. It has been a long peregrination, from the Confucian *tao*, K'ung's Way, to the past recaptured.

Notes

1. For this bond of "anti-traditional" and "traditionalistic" as both non-traditional, see Joseph R. Levenson, "The Suggestiveness of Vestiges: Confucianism and Monarchy at the Last," in David S. Nivison and Arthur F. Wright, ed., *Confucianism in Action* (Stanford Un. Press, 1959), pp. 244–267.

2. *Cf.* Holmes Welch, "Buddhism under the Communists," *The China Quarterly*, No. 6 (April-June 1961), pp. 1–14.

3. Lo Ken-tse, *Chung-kuo Wen-hsüeh P'i-p'ing Shih* (*History of Chinese Literary Criticism*) (Shanghai: Ku-tien Wen-hsüeh Ch'u-pan-she, 1957), pp. 39, 48–49.

4. Chow Tse-tsung, *The May Fourth Movement: Intellectual Revolution in Modern China* (Harvard Un. Press., 1960), pp. 284–287, 309–310.

5. *Cf.* Joseph R. Levenson, "The Day Confucius Died" (review article), *The Journal of Asian Studies,* XX, No. 2 (February 1961), p. 225.

6. Kuo Mo-jo, "Kuan-yü 'hou-chin po ku' wen-t'i" (On the "broaden the new, narrow the old" question), *People's Daily (Jen-min Jih-pao),* June 11, 1958, p. 7.

7. *Daily Report: Foreign Radio Broadcasts,* No. 248 (December 22, 1960), BBB 10–11.

8. CCS report (July 1961).

9. *Weekly Report on Communist China,* No. 28 (June 3, 1960), p. 26.

10. Leo A. Orleans, *Professional Manpower and Education in Communist China* (Washington: National Science Foundation, 1961), p. 18.

11. For description and analysis of the use of Classics as sources in Communist periodisation of history, see Levenson, "History under Chairman Mao," *Soviet Survey,* No. 24 (April–June, 1958), pp. 32–34; Levenson, "Ill Wind in the Well-field: the Erosion of the Confucian Ground of Controversy," in Arthur F. Wright, ed., *The Confucian Persuasion* (Stanford Un. Press, 1960), pp. 268–270, 285–287; Albert Feuerwerker, "China's History in Marxian Dress," *American Historical Review,* LXVI, No. 2 (January 1961), pp. 336–340; Albert Feuerwerker and S. Cheng, *Chinese Communist Studies of Modern Chinese History* (Harvard Un. Press, 1961), pp. 2–9, 21–26, 209–213.

12. Kuo Mo-jo, "Kuan-yü mu-ch'ien li-shih yen-chiu chung ti chi-ke wen-t'i," ("Several problems concerning present-day historical research"), *Hsin Chien-she,* April 1959, p. 5.

13. Wang Chih-chiu and Sung Kuo-chu, *Chung-hsüeh Li-shih Chiao-shih Shou-ts'e (Handbook for History Teachers in Middle Schools)* (Shanghai: Shanghai Chiao-yü Ch'u-pan-she, 1958), p. 56.

14. As noted with context of "primitive communism," in Feng Yu-lan, "K'ang Yu-wei ti ssu-hsiang" ("The thought of K'ang Yu-wei"), in *Chung-kuo Chin-tai Ssu-hsiang Shih Lun-wen Chi (Collection of Essays on Modern Chinese Intellectual History)* (Shanghai: Shanghai Jen-min Ch'u-pan-she, 1958), p. 120.

15. Chinese Academy of Sciences, philosophical research department, history of Chinese philosophy section, ed., *Chung-kuo Ta-t'ung Ssu-hsiang Tzu-liao (Materials in Chinese Utopian Thought)* (Peking: Chung-hua Shu-chü, 1959), p. 1. For an indorsement of this position, see Ku Ti, "K'ung-tzu ho 'ta-t'ung' ssu-hsiang" ("Confucius and utopian thought"), *Kuang-ming Jih-pao* (hereafter KMJP), May 24, 1961, p. 2.

16. Ku Ti, 2, referring to Jen Chüan, "K'ung-tzu Li-yün 'ta-t'ung' ssu-hsiang" ("Confucius' *Li-yün* utopian thought"), KMJP, May 12, 1961, p. 4. Ku Ti maintains that Confucius was unconnected with *ta-t'ung* ("Great Harmony") utopianism. His article insists that in the *Lun-yü (Analects),* in large part a reliable source for Confucius' thought, there is no shred of *ta-t'ung* doctrine; and Ku Ti declines to accept the two *Lun-yü* extracts in the Academy of Science volume [note 15] as specimens of *ta-t'ung,* on the ground that the *Lun-yü* has non-utopian class-distinction (*viz.,* between *jen* and *min*) built into it.

17. Jen Chüan, p. 4.

18. Wang Ming, "*I-ching* ho *I-chuan* ti ssu-hsiang t'i-hsi wen-t'i" ("The Problem of *I-ching* and *I-chuan* systems of thought"), KMJP, June 23, 1961, p. 4.

19. Kuan Feng and Lin Yü-shih, "Lun K'ung-tzu ti 'jen' ho 'li' " ("A discourse on Confucius' *jen* and *li*"), *People's Daily* (July 23, 1961), p. 5; for *jen* as humanistic base of *li,* liberating thought from an original superstitious theology, see also Chi Wen-fu, *Ch'un-ch'iu Chan-kuo Ssu-hsiang Shih-hua (Historical Discourses on the Thought of the "Spring and Autumn" and "Warring States"*

Periods) (Peking: Chung-kuo Ch'ing-nien Ch'u-pan-she, 1958), pp. 20–22, and "Chung-nan ti-ch'ü shih-hsüeh-chieh tsai Kuang-chou chü-hsing hsüeh-shu t'ao-lun-hui" ("The historical society of the Chung-nan region holds a scholarly discussion meeting in Canton"), KMJP, May 19, 1961, p. 2.

20. Chang Tai-nien, *Chung-kuo wei-wu-chü-i ssu-hsiang chien-shih* (*A Brief History of Chinese Materialist Thought*) (Peking: Chung-kuo Ch'iang-nien Ch'u-pan-she, 1957), pp. 20, 22. For a more cautious discussion, locating Confucius between materialism and idealism, since he professed neither belief nor disbelief in "Heaven's decree" or "spirits," *cf.* Kuo Shao-yü, *Chung-kuo Ku-tien Wen-hsüeh Li-lun P'i-p'ing Shih* (*A Critical History of Classical Chinese Literary Doctrines* (Peking: Jen-min Wen-hsüeh Ch'u-pan-she, 1959), p. 28.

21. Jen-min Wen-hsüeh Ch'u-pan-she Pien-chi-pu, ed., *Shih-ching Yen-chiu Lun-wen Chi* (*Collection of Research Papers on the Shih-ching*) (Peking: Jen-min Ch'u-pan-she, 1959), p. 1; Yu Kuan-ying, "China's Earliest Anthology of Poetry," *Chinese Literature*, No. 3, 1962, pp. 109, 111; *cf.* Kuo Shao-yü, p. 16, for Confucius recognising the *Shih-ching's* realism.

22. "T'an-t'ao Chia I ssu-hsiang ho *Hsin-shu* chen-wei wen-t'i" ("An inquiry into Chia I's thought and the question of the authenticity of the *Hsin-shu*"), *People's Daily*, October 5, 1961, p. 7.

23. Chou Yü-t'ung and T'ang Chih-chün, "Wang Mang kai-chih yü ching hsüeh chung ti chin-ku-wen hsüeh wen-t'i" ("Wang Mang's reform and the problem of modern and ancient texts in classical scholarship"), KMJP, May 16, 1961, p. 2; Chou Yü-t'ung and T'ang Chih-chün, "T'an-t'ao Chung-kuo ching-hsüeh wen-t'i" ("An inquiry into the problem of Chinese classical scholarship"), *People's Daily*, May 31, 1961, p. 7.

24. Hsü Lun, *Shen-mo Shih Feng-chien She-hui* (*What Is Feudal Society?*) (Shanghai: Shanghai Jen-min Ch'u-pan-she, 1954), p. 69.

25. Lanchow University Department of Chinese Literature, Mencius-annotation subsection, *Meng-tzu I-chu* (*Menicus: Translation and Commentary*) (Peking: Chung-hua Shu-chü, 1960), p. 13; and similarly, "Chung-kuo Jen-min Ta-hsüeh che-hsüeh-hsi t'ao-lun Meng-tzu p'ing-chiai wen-t'i" ("The Philosophy Department of the Chinese People's University discusses the problem of evaluating Mencius"), KMJP, July 28, 1961, p. 1.

26. For this reference, and others in this paragraph and the next, see Shu Shih-cheng, "K'ung-tzu Ch'un-ch'iu" ("Confucius' *Spring and Autumn*"), *Li-shih Yen-chiu*, No. 1 (1962), pp. 47–50, 55, 57.

27. Tai Shih-chien, "Wen yü tao" (*"Wen* and *tao"*), *People's Daily*, January 21, 1962, p. 5.

28. Examples: For Confucius (a) loving the old, specifically to inculcate conservatism, *cf.* Chu Tung-jun, ed., *Tso-chuan Hsüan* (*Selections from the Tso-chuan*) (Shanghai: Shanghai Ku-tien Wen-hsüeh Ch'u-pan-she, 1956), p. 8. (b) On the side of a declining class of masters of slaves, or a tool (with Classics) of reactionary feudal class against the people, *cf.* "Chung-nan ti-ch'ü shih-hsüeh-chieh . . ." (note 19, above), p. 2; "Of Confucius, Fung Yu-lan and Others," *China News Analysis*, No. 398 (November 24, 1961), pp. 3, 5, 7; *Communist China Digest*, No. 17 (June 6, 1960), p. 83; Jen-Chi-yü, "Ho Ch'i Hu Li-yüan ti kai-liang-chu-i ssu-hsiang" ("The reformist thought of Ho Ch'i and Hu Li-yüan"), *Chung-kuo Chin-tai Ssu-hsiang Shih Lun-wen chi* (Collected Essays on the History of Modern Chinese Thought) (Shanghai: Shanghai Jen-min Ch'u-pan-she, 1958), p. 86. (c) As an idealist and a religionist, fostering anti-materialist, anti-scientific thought, upholding traditional superstition through the doctrine of the "Will of Heaven," with its implication that the fate of society

is determined from outside society, *cf.* Ch'en Po-ta, "P'i-p'an ti chi-ch'eng ho hsin ti t'an so" ("A critical inquiry into heritage and novelty"), *Red Flag* (*Hung Ch'i*), No. 13, 1959, p. 44; Kuo Shao-yü, p. 19; Kuan Feng and Lin Yü-shih, "Lun K'ung-tzu" ("On Confucius"), *Che-hsüeh Yen-chiu* (*Philosophical Research*), No. 4, July 25, 1961, pp. 54–56 (some points in this article and others is similar vein summarised in "Of Confucius, Fung Yu-lan and Others," p. 5). Feng Yuan-chun, *A Short History of Classical Chinese Literature* (Peking: Foreign Languages Press, 1958), p. 39; A. A. Petrov (Li Shih, tr.) *Wang Ch'ung—Chung-kuo Ku-tai ti Wei-wu-chu-i-che ho Ch'i-meng Ssu-hsiang-chia* (*Wang Ch'ung—An Ancient Chinese Materialist and Enlightened Thinker*) (Peking: K'o-hsüeh Ch'u-pan-she, 1956), pp. iii, 73–75. (d) As a reformist, basically conservative, seeking to harmonise class-contradictions and prevent the rising of the poor against the governing class, *cf.* Ho-nan Ta-hsüeh Li-shih-hsi, ed., *Chung-kuo T'ung-shih Tzu-liao Hsüan-chi* (*Compilation of Materials for a General History of China*) (Kaifeng; Honan Un., 1953), p. 40; Kuan Feng and Lin Yü-shih, "Lun K'ung-tzu," pp. 46–47; Kuan Feng and Lin Yü-shih, "Lun K'ung-tzu ti 'jen' ho 'li,' " p. 5.

It is significant that in many of these references (*e.g.*, the last, with which compare purport of note 19), criticism of Confucius is combined with respect: both idealist *and* materialist elements, conservative *and* progressive, etc., are often noted. *Cf.* "Review of Reviews," *China News Analysis*, No. 410 (March 2, 1962), p. 3, for summary of yet another article on Confucius and *jen* and *li*, with Confucius being granted at least a relative merit while at the same time his limitations (as a member of the dominant class) are noted.

29. Chi Wen-fu, 16–17. *Cf.* also Tu Shou-su, *Hsien-Ch'in Chu Tzu Ssu-hsiang* (*The Thought of the Pre-Ch'in Philosophers*) (Sheng-huo Shu-tien), p. 6, and Chang Tai-nien, p. 20, for Confucius as more than the progenitor of the *Ju* school—as the first spokesman for open, public instruction in the history of Chinese education. For an account of others' emphasis on Confucius as a pioneer non-discriminatory educator, characterised by the spirit of study and eagerness for knowledge, *cf.* "Of Confucius, Fung Yu-lan and Others," pp. 2–3; and for a more grudging respect for Confucius as mildly progressive in his own day, an opinion clinched by reference to his disciples "propagating knowledge," *cf.* Feng Yuan-chun, pp. 26–27.

30. Chiao-yü pu, ed., *Ti-erh-tz'u Chung-kuo Chiao-yü Nien-chien* (*The Second Chinese Educational Yearbook*) (Shanghai: Commercial Press, 1948), pp. 205–206, 209.

31. *Ibid.*, pp. 5, 8, 12, 355.

32. *Cf. Shih-chieh Jih-pao* (*The Chinese World*), San Francisco, April 14, 1962, p. 1, for Chiang Kai-shek blessing a commemorative effort of the "Confucius-Mencius Society" and urging everyone to study the Sages, restore the Chinese ethic, and thereby sweep the Communists aside.

33. Wu Yü-chang, *Chung-kuo Li-shih Chiao-ch'eng Hsü-lun* (*Introduction to the Teaching Pattern for Chinese history*) (Shanghai: Hsin-hua Shu-tien, 1950), p. 1 (preface), p. 8. For another suggestion, from the outside, of an appropriate link between the pro-Confucian and anti-national causes (or the anti-Confucian and anti-fascist), *cf.* Ezra Pound, *Impact: Essays on Ignorance and the Decline of American Civilization* (Chicago: Regnery, 1960), p. 139: "Lady Hosie's introduction in a recent reprint tells us that the Four Classics have been relegated to University study and are no longer the main preoccupation of Chinese schools. She dates the essay 1937, which year brought the natural consequences of unusual idiocy in the form of Japanese invasion. If China had

got to this point, naturally there would be an invasion, and quite naturally some Chinese would, as they do, hold the view that such an invasion is to be welcomed."

34. For reference to Mao and Lenin on these "two cultures," *cf.* Miu Yüeh, "Chiang-shou Chung-kuo li-shih tui-yü wen-hua pu-fen ju-ho ch'u-li" ("How to handle the cultural portions in lecturing on Chinese history"), KMJP, May 30, 1961, pp. 2–3.

35. Alexander Dru, ed., *The Letters of Jacob Burckhardt* (New York: Pantheon, 1955), p. 24.

36. Frank Rede Fowke, *The Bayeux Tapestry: a History and Description* (London: Bell, 1913), pp. 6–7.

37. "Of Confucius, Fung Yu-lan and Others," p. 2.

38. *Ibid.*, p. 5.

39. Wang Shih, *Yen Fu Chuan (Biography of Yen Fu)* (Shanghai: Shanghai Jen-min Ch'u-pan-she, 1957), p. 96.

40. "Ho-nan shih-hsüeh-chieh t'ao-lun Hung Hsiu-ch'üan ti ssu-hsiang yü Ju-chia ti kian-hsi wen-t'i" ("The Historical Society of Honan discusses the thought of Hung Hsiu-ch'üan and the problem of its relationship to Confucianism"), KMJP, June 1, 1961, p. 1.

41. Ni Xaishu [Ni Hai-shu], *"Lunjy" Syanji ["Lun-yü" Hsüan-i] (Selected Translations from the Lun-yü)* (Shanghai: Dungfang Shudian [Tung-fang Shu-tien], 1954), pp. 1–2.

42. Ch'en Po-ta, p. 37. For Mao's remarks, *cf.* "The Role of the Chinese Communist Party in the National War," *Selected Works of Mao Tse-tung* (London: Lawrence & Wishart, 1954), II, pp. 259–260. For another reference to Mao in this vein ("learn from the people—and learn from the ancients"), *cf.* Tang Shu-shih, "A Brief Discussion on Comrade Mao Tse-tung's Contribution to Marxist Literary Style," translated in *Communist China Digest*, No. 17, June 6, 1960, pp. 84–85.

43. Ch'en Po-ta, pp. 37–38.

44. Ku Chieh-kang, *Ch'in Han ti Fang-shih yü Ju-sheng (Taoists and Confucianists of the Ch'in and Han Periods)* (Shanghai: Ch'ün-lien Ch'u-pan-she, 1955), p. 15.

45. Li Shu, "Mao Tse-tung t'ung-chih ti 'Kai-tsao wo-men ti hsüeh-hsi' ho Chung-kuo li-shih k'o-hsüeh ("Comrade Mao Tse-tung's 'Reform our learning' and Chinese historical science"), *People's Daily*, June 8, 1961, p. 7.

46. Joseph Needham, "An Archaeological Study-tour in China, 1958," *Antiquity*, XXXIII, No. 130, June 1959, pp. 116–117.

47. *People's Daily*, April 8, 1962, p. 2; *Hua-chiao Jih-pao (China Daily News)*, New York, April 16, 1962, p. 1; *Shih-chieh Jih-pao*, April 24, 1962, p. 1. The latter account cites Hong Kong speculation to the effect that, with a shortage of seeds for spring plowing, Mao prefers to divert attention to the Confucian associations of spring. (This does not seem to be a very powerful analysis.)

48. Ch'en Huan-chang, *K'ung-chiao Lun (On the Confucian Religion)* (Shanghai, 1912), p. 27.

49. *Cf. Glimpses of China* (Peking: Foreign Language Press, 1958): "Confucius (551–469 B.C.) was a famous thinker of ancient China. His teachings held sway in feudal society. Temples dedicated to him were built in various places. The on in Chufu, his native town, is the largest and houses a large number of precious cultural objects and relics."

50. For impressions of this neglect of monuments, see K. M. Panikkar, *In Two Chinas: Memoirs of a Diplomat* (London: Allen and Unwin, 1955), pp. 34, 99–100.

51. Cyril Birch, "Lao She: the Humourist in His Humour," *The China Quarterly*, No. 8, October–December, 1961, pp. 48–49.

52. Roderick MacFarquhar, *The Hundred Flowers Campaign and the Chinese Intellectuals* (New York: Praeger, 1960), p. 90.

53. *Cf.* Franklin W. Houn, *To Change a Nation: Propaganda and Indoctrination in Communist China* (Glencoe, Ill.: Free Press, 1961), p. 7.

54. Mary C. Wright, "The Pre-Revolutionary Intellectuals of China and Russia," *The China Quarterly*, No. 6, April–June, 1961, p. 179.

40. ON MORALITY

CHINA NEWS ANALYSIS

India is immersed in metaphysical speculation, while in China people are fascinated by moral questions, by conscience, moral goodness, and a question that may appear excessively abstruse, the goodness or evil of human nature; these have for thousands of years been the centre of discussion and are familiar to every educated person. Indeed there is no one in China who would not follow with interest a discussion on conscience and morality.

In this country therefore the moral foundations of communist behaviour should be clearly explained, and it is on this vital question that Professor Fung Yu-lan of Peking University threw a bomb-shell when he spoke three years ago, in 1961, of ultilitarianism and argued, with proofs from the works of Mao, that communist morality is utilitarian. In the traditional Chinese conception, to aim at *li*, utility, is immoral. Comrade Lo Ko tried manfully to show that Mao could not possibly mean that. We dealt with this in our 423rd issue eighteen months ago and here we shall follow up the discussion which was prolonged.

It is a discussion not confined to the home front. The question of morality is one element in the ideological confrontation of Peking and Moscow. In the new look at Marxism published in the 1958 Russian textbook *Foundation of Marxist Philosophy* by F. W. Konstantinov though it is stated that "our morality is completely subordinated to the interest of the class struggle of the proletariat," the book adds that the real class interest represents the interest of the whole people; the class-character of the proletariate expresses what has been and is truly and universally human. The 22nd USSR Party Congress went further and laid down a 12-point Moral Code in which respect for man and family, honesty and truthfulness, were enumerated together with the collective spirit and fidelity to communism—but class and class struggle were not mentioned and according to the new Party Programme "communist morality includes the fundamental, universal human norms of morality."

SOURCE: Selected from *China News Analysis*, February 21, 1964, pp. 1–7.

It is with this in mind that one should study writings on ethics and morality in China, where at present everything centres on class and class-struggle.

Essays on Ethics

At the end of 1962 a People's Daily article summarised these discussions in that year:

Fung Yu-lan wrote that the purpose of Ethics is the study of what morality is, what is the meaning of Good; while according to Lo Ko the purpose of ethics is not to explain but to reform the world, realizing true goodness, true communist morality, in class-struggle. *Shih Liang-jen* postulated the study of the falsehood of feudal and bourgeois morality in order to understand the communist code.

Another discussion arose from another assertion of Fung Yu-lan in the role of motivation and the effect of the human act. Prof. Fung said that in dialectical materialism the effect is dominant, the interest of the class determining good and evil. An article by *Chiang Fa-Tseng* and *Li Kuang-Yao* reproached Prof. Fung with omitting to emphasise class interest. The class character of morality was insisted on in other articles also.[1]

Utilitarianism

The question whether Marxist ethics is utilitarian or not is still unresolved. It is a question of the exegesis of some words of Mao. In his 1942 Yenan speech on art and literature he distinguished feudal and bourgeois utilitarianism from his own which is the utilitarianism of the proletariate, of 'over 90 per cent of the population.' This was a statement which was used with effect by Prof. Fung.

In October 1962 an essay by *Li Chih-hsi* explained that the Confucianist school was wrong in opposing the idea of usefulness and preaching a morality deduced from law of nature, *t'ien-li,* "heavenly reason," and from the nature of man, *jen-hsing,* inculcating filial piety and obedience—obviously in order to reinforce the power of the ruling class. The ethics of Kant emphasised the idea of duty, for the same end.

In modern times the bourgeois class, Bentham for example, spoke of utilitarianism but only from the point of view of the individual. (The author quotes from a 1959 Chinese edition of Bentham.) The utilitarianism of the proletariate is different, and considers, as comrade Mao Tse Tung said, the utility of the broad labouring masses.[2]

An answer to this came four months later from Li Kuang-yao. He said that it would be most regrettable, as Lo Ko had said, to adopt the term "utilitarianism." He had also, like Lo Ko, to explain away the words of Mao. Li Kuang-yao made a subtle distinction: Marxist canons use the word utility in two senses. One is the sense understood by tthe bourgeois class and the other the general meaning of usefulness to a class. Comrade Li Chih-hsi omitted this distinction. He was right in criticising bourgeois utilitarianism but he did not point out that, although his words can be applied to ethics, comrade Mao Tse Tung in Yenan was speaking of art and literature and not of ethics.

Therefore one can speak in general of utilitarianism but in the science of ethics one should not call morality utilitarian.[3]

Li Chih-hsi replied modestly and triumphantly. Indeed, he said, his previous essay was not carefully composed and he is grateful for the corrections; but the essence of his essay could not have been wrong for it is the teaching of Chairman Mao. *"One cannot eliminate the idea of utilitarianism and thus deny the statement of Chairman Mao."* Did not Chairman Mao say, "there is nothing in this world apart from utilitarianism"? The distinction made by comrade Li Kuang-yao is meaningless. Yes, the concept of utilitarianism came from the bourgeois class, but it was used in earlier ages too and in Chinese history there is the example of Mo Ti who spoke of *li,* usefulness. Chairman Mao said rightly that all materialism is utilitarian. Comrade Li Kuang-yao did not understand Chairman Mao who spoke of usefulness to the great majority of the people explaining thus the development of the idea of utility.

At the end comrade Li Chih-hsi considerately adds that he does not mean that comrade Li Kuang-yao intended to deny the contribution of Chairman Mao to the science of ethics.[4]

As the whole question discussed is not what ethics is but what Mao meant in 1942, the easiest solution would be, one would think, to put the question directly to the oracle, Chairman Mao himself. But the god remains silent.

Chinese Morality

Another controversy revolved round the question not what ethics is but what its content is or should be. It was a controversy with comrade Wu Han, well known to our readers, a historian of considerable authority and vice-mayor of Peking.[a]

HSÜ CH'I-HSIEN

Prof. Wu Han published in 1962 in *Front,* the Party paper of Peking city, two short articles on morality. Intellectual reactions nowadays are slow in China and the first answer appeared in August 1963. It was by *Hsü Ch'i-hsien* who wrote that he agreed with Wu Han that morality is not unchangeable and that it accepts elements selectively from the ancient cultural heritage. But he disagrees on other points. Comrade Wu Han wrote that in history the class ethics is the ethics of the ruling class. But then does not the class that is ruled possess ethics? There is the famous description in *Shih Chi* (the first historical book of China) of the *yu hsia,* the noble brigands[b] who

---

[a] One might get the impression, from our frequent quotations from the writings of Prof. Fung Yu-lan and comrade Wu Han, that there are few such scholars in China. In fact public controversies involve few persons, the few who have a wide culture and who are in a position to express themselves fairly freely in print. But there are many, a great number indeed, who have withdrawn into silence, men whose writings, printed ten years ago, no longer appear.

[b] The term is translated by Burton Watson, the recent translator of the Shih Chi, as "wandering knights." The accuracy of this translation was questioned in an article in the Pacific Affairs by the eminent scholar Ping-ti Ho, but the criticism was not convincing.

were faithful to their word, consequently in their actions kept their promises, and indifferent to danger, were ready to sacrifice their lives.

Comrade Wu Han said in those articles that one could inherit from the time of feudalism *chung* faithfulness, *hsiao*, filial piety, honesty, hard work and courage; and from the bourgeois class its prudent calculation and its ability to make money. This to comrade Hsü appears untenable. Everybody knows, he says, that the feudalist landlords were idle exploiters. As Chairman Mao said, "they possess the land and do not work. . . ." No, the feudalist *chung* and *hsiao* should not be accepted, nor the so-called virtues of the bourgeois class—and then he explains at length how ugly and repulsive these moral qualities are.[5]

WU HAN

This was more than Prof. Wu Han could stand. He wrote an answer. He did not question the naiveté of the fundamental position which divides the morality of society into that of the rulers and the ruled, so obviously an artificial figment of the imagination in a country like China with its Confucianist, Buddhist, Moslem and Christian population and moral principles. Perhaps comrade Wu Han personally believes in such a simplification of complex facts. Perhaps he does not. But as a historian he was not ready to accept the rest.

He answered under the headline *The Third Time on Morality*. The sub-heading was menacing precisely because it was stiffly polite. He did not write as is usual, "Answers to Hsü Ch'i-shen," he wrote *"Respectful answer to comrade Hsü Ch'i-hsien."* Excessive politeness in China verges on the insulting.

He began by saying that when he published his first short article on morality some young comrades expressed their disagreement; that is why he wrote the second. But then his thesis had been put up for discussion at some scholarly meetings and many were opposed to it. Today I happened to read the article of comrade Hsü Ch'i-shen. I very much approve of it and I want to express my gratitude. I propose however a few minor points so that the question can be more deeply discussed.

He said that his critic was perfectly right. It was a slip to write on the ruling class alone. In those two short articles he had no room to deal with every aspect of the question. But, on the other hand, one should not say that in the history of feudalism everyone in the ruling class was wicked and that there was not one single good man among them, when in fact there were quite a number of persons who sympathized with the ordinary folk and were ready to stand up in defence of their interests. To illustrate he enumerated a number of such persons beginning with Yüeh Fei, the legendary figure in Chinese history. These are the type of men of whom Chairman Mao wrote "the Chinese people is famous not only for its hard and enduring labour but also for its passionate love for freedom and for its rich tradition of revolution"; "during the thousands of years of the history of the Chinese people a great many national heroes and revolutionary leaders have appeared."

He agrees fully with the idea that in accepting the historical heritage some moral qualities of the ruled should be accepted. Here he quotes from Kalinin who wrote in his book on communist education that at the beginning of the history of mankind morality arose from living conditions to become gradually the norm of conduct. And so it is, says Wu Han. There are the ideas of democracy and freedom which originated with the bourgeois class but were ennobled in a different sense, under socialism. And there are the national heroes and revolutionary leaders mentioned above who have shown real faithfulness and courage and lived a simple life. To say, as comrade Hsü does, that these moral qualities have nothing to do with present day patriotism is perhaps an error.[6]

[This article certainly does not show Prof. Wu Han at his best. It is part of a futile discussion about a futile subject revolving in a vicious circle hemmed in on all sides by some words of Mao, shackles imposed upon intellectual work which paralyse thinking and lead even intellectual people into writing pointless articles about the morality of rulers and ruled, etc.]

SHACKLES

The word "shackles" was mentioned in a different sense in an essay by Chiang Fatseng on *Moral Ideals*. He quoted the words of the Bulgarian Dimitrov that a good communist remembers the shackles which heroic comrades suffering for their convictions have on their hands. The moral ideal is not that served up by the philosophers of the Sung dynasty, Reason and Mind; nor is it the Taoist teaching of Lao Tzu and Chuang Tzu, passivity, *wu-wei*, denial of difference between life and death, good and evil, being and not being [moral concepts which are still common in China]. We do not deny the existence of particular individuals whose moral behaviour was outstanding like Yüeh Fei [a reference to the article of Wu Han], but the real science of ethics is built up by the heroes of communism, by persons like Liu Hu-lan and Lei Feng—modern propaganda figures in Party literature. Their example inspires faith in morality, forms the idea of morality which thus becomes a scientific concept, obviously different from those of mathematics or biology, but truly a guiding principle. The study of model heroes is the best education to morality.[7]

LI CHIH-HSI

The controversy with Wu Han continued. His statement about the heroic figures in Chinese history provoked a long essay from Li Chih-hsi who evidently was determined at any price to find some fault in Wu Han, some slip in his Marxism. To state, wrote Li Chih-hsi, that the ruling class and the ruled have a mutual influence, that in some way one permeates the other, is entirely untenable because in that case where would be the class antagonism between rulers and ruled. *"It is known by all that in the theory of historical materialism morality is determined by the material living conditions of society, is a reflection of class interest, an ideological weapon of class struggle for maintaining the interests of a certain class."* Therefore the moralities of the two classes are irreconcilable, though this does not mean that single individuals of one class may not accept the moral ideas of the other class.

Wu Han seems to state a contradiction when on the one hand he says that morality is changeable and on the other that the *chung*, faithfulness, hard labour and courage, these virtues persist and can be accepted. He quotes another example, that of democracy and freedom, which, transformed, had been accepted from the bourgeois times. Where they really accepted, asks Li Chih-hsi. Should one not say that only the words, the terms, were accepted and not the content? That there is no question here of heritage of a previous morality? In fact *"democracy and freedom are two empty terms and concepts."* It seems that one cannot say that the proletariate had accepted any moral concept from the previous ruling classes. To speak otherwise is to fall into the error of "abstract inheritance" [the term coined and defended by Fung Yu-lan, *cf.* CNA, No. 241, p. 6].

But one may say that individual outstanding persons in the ruling class were under the influence of the class they ruled and there is the example of Yüeh Fei who resisted the Chin invaders in a truly patriotic manner and this at that time was the defence of the people, of the ruled.

The article ends with polite words to Wu Han saying that all this is only a question put to the author [Wu Han] by a reader; it may be a question which was not considered by the author; it is a question open to all for discussion.[8]

CAUTION

The next long essay was by *Chiang Feng*. It is a good example of how cautiously a writer has to express his thoughts, defending them from every angle against the eventual attack.

Chiang Feng mentioned that the question brought up by Wu Han had been discussed a few years ago and ever since there have been two opinions, one which says that the morality of the past must be rejected entirely and the other which speaks of heritage. His own opinion is that the morality of the ruling, i.e., the exploiting, classes cannot be accepted at all, but he makes a distinction, a subtle one: The fundamental principle of their morality must be totally rejected but certain particular moral tenets enunciated by some outstanding single individuals may and should be accepted.

This is the thesis of Chiang Feng. He explains carefully what he wanted to say. The *chung hsiao chieh yi* (loyalty, filial piety, moderation, justice) of the feudalist times [which in communist conception began B.C. and ended in the middle of the 19th century] must be totally rejected as it was evolved during the time of slavery and is a slave morality which demands subjection to emperor, to the ministers, to father, to elder brothers, to husband. This idea of filial piety with all its extensions carefully elaborated later in the Sung and Ming times is unacceptable. But the individual moral tenets of individual thinkers or historical persons can be inherited with due selection.

This he explains carefully: The ruling class in the historical period has a certain vitality at the beginning of its ascendency to power and at a time *"when the fundamental contradiction with the interests of the people is not yet evident and when, at the time of the opposition to the former ruling class, it had a common interest with the people"*—[cf. the theory of Fung Yu-lan, CNA, No. 395, p. 6 in which he wrote that this was a fraud and people who cooperated with the rising class were oppressed later].

The author did not explain what kind of rising power Meng Tzu and Hsün Tzu belonged to. But he quoted a saying (taking it from Wu Han) from

Meng Tzu and another from Hsün Tzu, which he said are acceptable moral tenets. Meng Tzu spoke of the spirit of the *ta chang fu* ("the outstanding man") (*"whom wealth and position cannot corrupt, poverty and humble position cannot cause to waver, whose dignity is unshakable."*) And there is the *te ts'ao* ("moral principle") of Hsün Tzu, expressing a similar thought: a person whom *"power cannot corrupt, the masses cannot change, whom nothing in the world can move; neither life nor death can change him."*

Chiang Feng adds cautiously that of course these ideas of Meng Tzu and Hsün Tzu reflect feudalist class ideals and that as such they could not be accepted. But as the ideal of a new revolutionary class fighting against slavery, expressing fortitude in face of danger, this was a progressive thought, though the full realization of the principles can be seen only in the proletariate and in our revolutionary martyrs and communist warriors.

No, our revolutionary warriors should not be compared with the *ta chung fu* because their courage has a different content and their class interest and purpose are different; but the spirit of constancy and heroism are comparable and it is in this sense that ancient things can serve as a mirror.

Then Chiang Feng speaks of Yüeh Fei, whose class position, what class he belonged to, has not yet been finally decided. Undoubtedly he had an admirable spirit, a national spirit and the character of the people of which his *chung* was the expression.

Some explain that such persons in past history in reality belonged to the ruled, exploited, classes, but Chiang Feng does not think so. He believes that the patriotism of Yüeh Fei was that of the landlords. Could one say that Yüeh Fei did not belong to the landlord class? Or could we say that the ideal of Meng Tzu, the *ta chang fu,* was taken from the labouring people?

Some say [see above] that the only thing common between past and present is the use of terms, nomenclature only, and there is no question of continuity in ethical principles. Chiang Feng disagrees. He does not believe that everything in the past must be rejected. He says modestly that "for the time being I could not work this out," and he feels confirmed by the words of Mao, which he quotes, that not all should be absolutely rejected and that "ancient things should serve as a mirror."[9]

PA-KU

Wang Tzu-sung had an original thought when, joining this discussion about the acceptance or non-acceptance of traditional morality he wrote about the famous novel *All Are Brothers.* But he looked at this old and popular book through the distorting lenses of Marxist spectacles. This book, the story of noble brigands, is called here the story of a revolutionary army. Popular stories, Wang says, were written down and then given a feudalist twist by educated people and that is why phrases like "fidelity to the prince" occur in the novel. But on the whole it shows the oppressed labouring class . . . and thus he goes on in this odd description of that wonderfully entertaining book which is favourite reading of Chairman Mao.* The article does not spare words

---

* At present youth is being discouraged from reading the old popular novels. (Nanfang Daily, Canton, September 15 and 19, 1963).

in explaining what in the book reflects the morality of the rulers and what that of the class ruled, and the whole is seasoned with words of comrade Mao Tse Tung—a mechanical stereotyped way of writing much worse than the *pa-ku* literature under the Manchu dynasty, essays with set formulas and hackneyed developments.*[10]

A ROUGH THEORY

To quite one more article on Wu Han, there is a rude and primitive essay by *Kao Chung-t'ien* which says that there must be no question of heritage of feudal or bourgeois moral principles. The false bourgeois moral ideas of democracy and freedom were overthrown not by discussion but by fighting. To speak of *chung*, faithfulness, loyalty, one can speak only of that of the poor and lower middle peasants of today who after learning to love Chairman Mao, are most faithful to socialism.

What comrade Wu Han says about outstanding individuals in the ruling classes means only that they have accepted the morality of the labouring people.

It may be true as comrade Wu Han said that history should not be completely given up but the rejection of the morality of the old ruling classes does not mean the denial of history since the morality of the proletariate is the continuation of the morality of earlier labouring people. At present the vestiges of corrupt feudal morality are still with us and it will take a long period of tenacious struggle to extirpate them.[11]

Kao Chung-t'ien is a rough fellow—and thus there passes before our eyes an interesting array of Party members from cultured Wu Han to this boorish Kao Chung-t'ien, comrades who profess the Marxist faith but whose temperament and cultural background, whose fundamental ideas about culture, even Marxist culture, are utterly different. The CCP is not as monolithic as it may appear. If some event were to shake the persons in the highest leadership there are two possibilities: One may expect the rule of those who are less subtle and more fanatical than the present leaders; but with more reason one may expect the rise of those Party members who do not renounce their Chinese identity, men who have brains. The question of traditional Chinese morality is certainly not a negligible factor in the political future of China.

The discussion about morality has not yet ended and will probably never end. The Kuang Ming Daily received 50 more essays which the editor was unwilling to publish,[12] but the discussion continued in the pages of Philosophical Research. In the last issue of that journal in 1963 the leading article was by *Shih Liang-jen*. It reflected the present atmosphere when politics again dominate scholarship. It is ridiculous, it said, to go back in the study of morality to ancient times, *"to search for gold in a pile of rubbish,"* to speculate

* Such are the serious essays which nowadays feed the minds of the readers. We have rarely reported them as fully as now because instinctively one looks for essays which have some significance and some originality. But it is useful to see even in brief summary the distortion of values and false perspectives to which readers are now exposed and how narrow the little world in which they are constrained to live.

about the abstract meaning of morality: Morality is the product of the proletariate, the product of production, the product of class struggle.[13]

Questions and Answers

COMMUNIST MORALITY

The Canton Nanfang Daily answered a question, What is it that is called communist morality? The answer was: *"It is the behaviour based on communism demanded of man by the proletariate. It contains many things, collectivism, patriotism, love of labour, protection of public wealth as well as a communist attitude towards family, woman, old people and children, etc."*

Comrade *Liu Shao-ch'i* stated it well when he wrote that *"this type of morality is not based upon the protection of the interests of exploiters, be they individuals or a minority, it is based on the interests of the proletariate, of the wide number of labouring people, it is based on the final liberation of the whole of mankind, delivery of the world from the evil of capitalism, building it upon the foundation of the interests of a happy and a beautiful communist world and upon the scientific communist theory of Marxism-Leninism"* [—as clumsy a sentence in Chinese as it is in English].

That is why we say that the interest of the Party is above everything, and that for the interest of the Party one should sacrifice all personal interests. This is the highest expression of communist morality[14]—and indeed the essence of communist ethics.

A PERNICKETY YOUNG MAN

A young man wrote and asked the Chinese Youth Daily: *"Comrade Liu Shao-ch'i in his Formation of a Communist said: "as we communists see it, it is undeserving and worthless to make a sacrifice for any single person or for a minority."* However newspapers often publish stories about persons who sacrifice their lives in order to save a person as of persons drowned when they had dived into a river to save a child. Are such acts not sacrifices in order to save an individual?"

An embarrassing question. The paper answered: Such heroic acts indeed save one person but that one person is a member of the socialist construction of our country, is a comrade-in-arms, is a brother. To save such a person is a sacred duty. What Liu Shao-ch'i wrote in the book was directed at those individuals or groups who belong to the exploiting class, people who are not worth saving.[15]

Notes

1. People's Daily (PD), Peking, December 27, 1962, p. 5
2. Kuang Ming Daily, (KM), Peking, October 5, 1962
3. KM, February 22, 1963
4. KM, June 28, 1963
5. KM, August 15, 1963
6. KM, August 19, 1963

7. KM, August 23, 1963
8. KM, September 21, 1963
9. KM, October 6, 1963
10. KM, October 15, 1963
11. KM, October 7, 1963
12. KM, November 1, 1963
13. Philosophical Research No. 6, 1963, pp. 1–13
14. Nanfang Daily, Canton, April 20, 1963
15. Chinese Youth Daily, Peking, August 20, 1963

Literature and Arts

41. THE MORALITY OF CREATIVITY

LI SHU-CHIH

Modern revisionists in the field of art and literature use a whole battery of arguments to support what they describe as the "central principle" in aesthetics—"writing honestly." Brandishing this "principle," they denounce as "dishonest" works of art and literature which describe the people's revolutionary struggles, faith in the revolution, and communist ideals. They use this "principle," too, to justify their approval of works which indiscriminately wax eloquent about bourgeois humanism, bourgeois pacifism and the bourgeois "ideal" of a life of creature comforts and indulgence in the trivialities of home life. Only such works, they say, are "honestly" written, and any work that is "honestly" written must be a good work.

The Theory of "Writing Honestly"

It is well worth our while to make a close examination of what is at the bottom of this theory of "writing honestly."

Generally speaking, all works of art and literature should grow out of true feelings and real emotions. It is the duty of the writer to reflect life and the age faithfully, writing only what he honestly believes to be true according to his own observations, experience and analysis. He is not supposed to write with false feeling or anything in which he himself has no faith and by which he himself is not moved. As an old saying goes, he must be "genuinely moved within before giving expression to his emotion in words"; he must not "fake feeling for literary purposes." This is all common sense. As for the revolutionary writer, he loathes and despises all the more literary works that ring false. It is said that "Indignation creates the poet." As a powerful sentiment, indigna-

SOURCE: Selected from "In the Field of Art and Literature Modern Revisionists Follow in the Footsteps of the Declining Bourgeoisie," in *Hongii* (Red Flag), 1962. Translated by the Editors of *Peking Review*, February 6, 1963, pp. 11–15.

tion, like passionate love, is indispensable to a writer if he wishes to produce works that are truly moving.

However, to ask for true feeling and real emotion in a writer is one thing; but what such true feelings and real emotions add up to and whether they are good or bad is quite another thing.

All writers make a distinction according to their class outlook between right and wrong, good and bad, the beautiful and the ugly, and decide what they like and what they oppose. All such issues involve questions of a class nature.

Gorky once said: "The writer is the eye, the ear and the voice of his class. He may not be conscious of this. . . . Nevertheless he is . . . the sense-organ of his class." All writers write in accordance with the stand, viewpoints, thoughts and feelings of their class, upholding them and fighting for them. Their honesty, too, has a class nature. Thus, viewing things from the proletarian stand and point of view, proletarian writers faithfully express the thoughts and feelings of the proletariat, whereas bourgeois writers propagate bourgeois ideas and sentiments from their bourgeois standpoint. In this sense, there is no common "honesty" in the abstract, but only a writer's own concrete honesty.

The claims insistently advanced by certain bourgeois political commentators that Leo Tolstoi was the "common conscience" and a "great conscience" were long ago exposed by Lenin as "empty phrases" and as "lies deliberately broadcast by the liberals." No less then can be said of the attempt to laud "honesty in writing" in the abstract and set it up as a criterion for evaluating literature. A counter-revolutionary work produced by a counter-revolutionary writer may well be the result of his "writing honestly." But why should the revolutionary people and revolutionary writers just for that reason consider it a good work? The argument that any honestly written work is automatically a good work will not bear questioning. In judging a literary work to determine whether it is good or bad, there must be a political, a class criterion.

Revisionists Cover Up Their Class Nature

Why have modern revisionist writers come to play around with this lie that anything honestly written is a good work? It should be noted that the "honesty" they advocate is in essence the "honesty" of the bourgeoisie. If we discard examination of the class content of this "honesty" and accept the thesis that as long as it is honest it is good, then there would of course be grounds for what they advocate. Modern revisionists always try to concel the class nature of their ideology by trying to make out that it is of "the whole people," "of all mankind." They do this precisely because they know that their bourgeois ideas and standpoint are incompatible with the interests of the revolutionary people. In order to propagate bourgeois humanism and pacifism in literature, they claim that the misfortune of death, love between inseparable lovers, and even lovers who are class enemies, and so on and so forth are the "eternal themes" of literature—themes that are close to the hearts of, and stir all readers. In order actually to publicize the ideas of bourgeois liberalism, they argue that "men are by nature inclined to freedom." In order to advocate "individual happiness" as the supreme goal in life to which all else must be sacrificed they make great play in literature with the melancholy, the exasperation, the loneliness and despair of men in the course of their pursuit of such "individual happiness," and present these feelings as "characteristically human" and supremely worthy of our sympathy, denouncing every "obstacle" to the attainment of this "individual happiness" as a bitter "cruelty." In order to negate the existence of classes and the class struggle, they urge that what is important in our social life is not the class struggle but the struggle between the "animal" in a man and his "human nature." From this they go on to demand that we should pay more attention to describing universal "human nature" and that we should not get "over-involved in the class struggle." They want to market their baggage of bourgeois decadence and degeneration in a big way so they argue volubly that to eschew in literary works bold descriptions of relations between the sexes and of the beauty of the human body is to neglect major questions of human nature. It is not difficult to see that what they are trying to do is to pass off their decadent bourgeois trash as something pertaining to "all mankind," that is, as something transcending classes. What is sure is that in the depths of their hearts, there are a host of bourgeois things striving to break loose from all restraints so that they can come out into the open and dominate the stage. That is why modern revisionist writers are so enthusiastic in publicizing "honesty in writing," which they wish to use to cover up the bourgeois nature of their ideology. This is undoubtedly one of the "high" aims of this theory of "writing honestly."

"By the Yardstick of a Knave"

By calling things bourgeois "honest" and then asserting that this bourgeois "honesty" is the honesty of "all mankind," modern revisionists claim that they themselves are "honest" and at the same time revile as dishonest those writers who firmly adhere to the proletarian standpoint. This, as the old Chinese saying has it, is "to measure the mind of an upright man by the yardstick of a knave." This is exactly the way modern revisionists treat writers who uphold the proletarian standpoint; they judge such writers' proletarian minds according to their own bourgeois hearts; they denounce as dishonest anything that does not suit their own ideas and standpoint. Thus, when a proletarian writer warmly praises some advanced phenomenon or revolutionary heroes of the new, proletarian age or sharply criticizes some decadent phenomenon, the protagonists of "honest writing," basing their judgment on their own negative and scabrous sentiments, assert that this writing is not honest, that the writer is not speaking from the heart but is pretending. According to them, only those writers are honest who, like themselves, depict and lavish their sympathy on fallen women, rogues, nihilists and all sorts of queer characters who stand outside the mainstream of social history. When a proletarian writer, drawing on the logic of the people's life and the logic of the characters of his heroes and heroines, gives a vivid portrayal of lofty communist sentiments, the advocates of "honest writing" again proceeding from their empty, debased and degenerated outlook say: This is not honest because the writer has put on the "coloured spectacles" of the "doctrinaire," and so fails to write what is really in his heart. According to them, only people like themselves who unreservedly publicize individualism, liberalism, and what they call "liberty, equality and fraternity" are honest. It is clear that these means have been adopted by modern revisionists to strangle the development of proletarian literature and to drag proletarian writers onto the wrong path. They say to proletarian writers: Do you want to achieve "honesty in writing"? Then discard those Marxist "coloured spectacles" of yours! Marxist ideas are not the "words of your heart." If you don't forsake Marxist ideas and express "what is in your heart," you will inevitably fall into the abyss of "hypocritical writing." This is another of the "high" aims of the modern revisionists in advertising "writing honestly."

Proletarian Literature—The Most Honest Literature

The revolutionary literature of the proletariat is the most honest literature in the world today. Unlike the exploiting classes, the proletariat openly admits that its ideology (including its art and literature) has its class nature and Communist Party character, and expresses the fundamental interests of the proletariat. The proletariat is best able to reveal the truth and the true essence of life; because the interests of the proletariat accord with the trend of social development and with the fundamental interests of the broad masses of the labouring people, it has no need to cover up the class nature of its ideology. As an instrument for waging the class struggle, as a means for educating and rallying the people and for striking at and defeating the enemy, the revolutionary art and literature of the proletariat is very clearly tendentious. Revolutionary writers, in their works, are also clear-cut, strong and firm in their attitude—clearly showing what they like and what they hate, what they approve of and what they fight against. The honesty of the revolutionary writer lies in this firm and clear-cut Party character and tendentiousness that must never be obscured for a moment. This is precisely that principle of Party character in literature which Lenin instilled into us in his *Party Organization and Party Literature*. The modern revisionists are playing their little game with this talk about "honesty in writing" precisely because they want to attack this Party character of proletarian revolutionary art and literature; they want to transform proletariant art and literature into bourgeois art and literature.

Integrating Revolutionary Tendentiousness with Artistic Truth

The revolutionary art and literature of the proletariat calls for the integration of revolutionary tendentiousness with artistic truth. As Comrade Mao Tse-tung has pointed out, we oppose works with wrong political viewpoints but at the same time we also oppose the tendency to produce works that only have correct political views but lack artistic merit, that is, works written in the so-called "slogan-style." The revolutionary writer works hard to pen a true account of our social life, broadly and deeply conceived, to create typical characters who are the embodiment of both common and individual characteristics and to expound his clear-cut social ideals from the proletarian standpoint describing what he loves and what he hates, what he approves of and what he censures; by these means he will be the better able to stir the hearts of his readers, set them thinking about life's problems, move them, raise their level of consciousness, and inspire them to action—to struggle against the reactionary classes and irrational social systems and to fight for the realization of the great revolutionary ideals, and evoke in them an ardent love for what is true, good and beautiful, and an intense hatred for what is false, evil and ugly. There is no doubt that the revolutionary writer, by persistent effort, can succeed in expressing powerful and clear-cut revolutionary ideas and feelings in ever more perfect artistic form. To achieve this, we must admit, necessitates a long process of arduous work and in this process the writer is bound to meet with many difficulties.

Quite possibly such a writer is confronted with the difficulty of not being sufficiently acquainted with the new things and the new people about which he wishes to write and as a result his work is not sufficiently true to life; his characterization is not sufficiently vivid, and he falls short of creating flesh-and-blood types. The modern revisionists, as we know, are quick to take advantage of this difficulty of the revolutionary writer and condemn his not so successful attempts to portray new heroes and advanced things as being dishonest. But this is not a question of honesty or dishonesty. That a work is not sufficiently true to life may be due to the writer's need for more experience in life, or lack of depth in observation and thought, or to the immaturity of his literary technique.

As to the creation of typical characters in literature, this is an even more difficult matter. The history of literature shows that quite often the successful creation of a typical character may involve the labour of several generations of writers. At the start, many writers may undertake to depict a certain typical social character, doing this from various angles, gradually improving their treatment, passing from the crude to the fine, from the shallow to the deep, and from the simple to the richly complex. This done, a basis is provided for a later writer who, giving full play to his literary talents, finally succeeds in producing the typical character that his predecessors sought to create.

Revolutionary Writers' Difficult Task

The task of the proletarian revolutionary writer is to produce in his works types of the new people of the new society, people who have not been known previously in history and in literature. To bring such an entirely new and pioneering task to fruition naturally requires a great deal of effort. It certainly cannot be said that if a writer fails to produce such types convincingly it is due to the fact that he is not honest. Nor, on the other hand, can it be said that as long as the writer is honest, he is automatically able to produce such typical characters. The reason is clear. If the difficulty lies in the fact that the writer in question is not sufficiently familiar with the new things, then what he should do is to go out into the thick of life and of the people. Lenin once said to Gorky that writers should go to the countryside and to the factories "to directly observe the new in the life of workers and peasants, that is, nine-tenths of the population of Russia," and to understand how they "build life anew." But the modern revisionists are trying to lead writers in the contrary direction. They advertise "honesty in writing" so as to drag writers onto the path of seeking "honesty of the inner-most soul." If a writer acts in accordance with what modern revisionists tell him, he will become more and more divorced from reality, more and more withdrawn into his own individual inner world, and be headed for a dead end so far as creativity is concerned. The "honesty in writing" advocated by the modern revisionists is therefore extremely harmful to writers.

The Honesty of Revolutionary Writers

Revolutionary writers should realize that real honesty for them means to extol the new people with whole-hearted enthusiasm and describe their struggles, to write on revolutionary themes, to depict the main current of real life under socialism, and to portray the progressive forces of our time. They should never lose their bearings because of difficulties arising in their creative work due to the fact that they do not have a rich enough experience of life or for the time being lack literary skill. The proletariat's revolutionary literature has invariably grown and gradually gained strength because the writers of the proletariat have steadfastly taken a revolutionary stand while learning and practising constantly and diligently, engaging in creative work to the best of their ability, actively and eagerly enriching their experience of life, and improving their literary skill. When proletarian literature made its debut, the bourgeoisie heaped abuse on it, and called it "puerile," "hypocritical" and so on. Proletarian literature could never have built up the powerful tradition it has today if our forerunners, in face of this abuse, had abandoned their efforts to portray proletarian heroes and express proletarian ideas and feelings, and, in order to "write honestly," had surrendered to bourgeois literature which with its far longer history had achieved more artistic refinement as the result of a long period of cultivation, and followed the beaten path of portraying bourgeois heroes and bourgeois ideas and sentiments. Today, we should stride forward steadfast in the struggle just as did our great precursors in the history of proletarian literature.

Revolutionary writers do not rest satisfied with a superficial portrayal of life. Starting out from real life, by means of artistic imagery and artistic synthesis, they depict the truth of life in a concentrated and more forceful manner so that the life projected in their works is on a more exalted plane and more deeply packed with meaning than ordinary everyday life. And this again is attacked as being "dishonest." This attack obviously comes from those who have fallen back on the stand of bourgeois objectivism and naturalism. As a matter of fact, to distil from life what is universally significant and typify this so as to reflect the essence of life in literary works is not to depart from real life but to depict it in a more profound way. But it is precisely the approach advocated by modern revisionists that is calculated to deceive the masses. They are zealously pushing the sort of literature that records the trivial details of daily life and lacks a clear theme or key figure or plot, the kind of literature which, with its philistine descriptions of superficial trivialities obscure the main currents and distorts the truth of life.

Revisionists Seek to Negate Ideological Remoulding

In the ranks of revolutionary writers there are still some people who are going through the process of ideological remoulding, of changing their class stand. They have reached a certain level of revolutionary consciousness and feeling, but at the same time their innermost soul is still petty bourgeois. On many occasions, proletarian and bourgeois ideas still fight a sharp seesaw battle in their minds. They have not yet completely proletarianized their ideas and sentiments. That is to say, the conflict between old and new ideas is still going on in their minds. In writing about new things, therefore, they are all the more likely to encounter difficulties. And modern revisionists take advantage of these very difficulties to check their progress. At a time when these writers are energetically studying Marxism, trying to discard their old, non-proletarian ideas and acquire new, proletarian ones, modern revisionists tell them: "You can't give answers to problems by going according to the old class categories!" You must free yourself from "dogmas" and project "your own philosophy of life!" Modern revisionists tell them that the new ideas are "false" and it is not worth one's while to write about them or expend energy in chasing after them; while, on the contrary, the old ideas are "honest," so it would be better to follow the old ways and write about these old ideas "honestly." Obviously, this theory of "writing honestly" is motivated by the vicious aim of negating ideological remoulding and pulling these writers back.

Modern revisionists publicize the need to free oneself from the "fetters" of dogmas even more frenziedly in the field of art and literature than they do in politics. Having freed themselves from these "fetters" what do they then describe as being in tune with their "own philosophy of life"? As we indicated earlier in this article, some of them declare that their only ideal and faith is that everyone should live and have a good time, increase and multiply and concentrate on creature comforts. They have indeed freed themselves from the "fetters" of Marxist "dogma" and "courageously" stated their "own philosophy of life," which, in fact, is nothing but the philosophy of bourgeois philistinism. For them, "honesty" in literature can only be achieved by shaking off Marxism which, they think, necessarily entails formulism and abstract generalization in writing.

Revolutionary Literature Rejects Formulism

The revolutionary literature of the proletariat is firmly opposed to formulism and abstract generalizations. Marx and Engels long ago advocated writing like Shakespeare did in his time and letting the writer's tendentiousness emerge from the scenes, plot and characterization in his work. Comrade Mao Tse-tung has always taught us that revolutionary writers must study Marxism—living Marxism that has a practical bearing on the life and struggle of the people—and not Marxist catchwords. He has taught us that revolutionary writers must study Marxism to remould their ideology and sentiments, to make Marxism a part of their own flesh and blood, to perceive the world, society and art and literature from the Marxist stand and viewpoint and by using the Marxist method, and that they must not turn their literary works into Marxist discourses.

He has said that revolutionary writers must temper themselves in the flames of the people's struggle and go to the only source, the broadest and richest source to observe, study and analyse various persons, various classes and various communities, and all the vivid patterns of life and struggle. Guided by the Marxist world outlook, revolutionary writers must gradually form their own opinions, sentiments and view of truth on the basis of their own observations, analyses and experience. Only then can they undertake creative work. They must never get out of touch with social life or with the people or approach creative work in a mechanical way by using preconceived formulas.

By its brilliant achievements proletarian literature has long ago proved irrefutably that it is the most honest of all literatures and is faithful to reality. The honesty advocated by revolutionary proletarian writers lies in mirroring reality, the objective truth and the struggle of the people in making history, in praising socialism and communism, and in expressing the revolutionary will and ideals of the people. Taking a proletarian stand and observing life with the Marxist world outlook as his guide can only help a writer to reveal life's truths courageously, to portray vividly the greatest and noblest revolutionary sentiments of the proletariat in art, to depict the will and aspirations of the people, and to reflect the struggle of the people as they make history. The allegation that the Marxist world outlook is incompatible with honesty in art is an absurdity fabricated by the enemies of Marxism.

Where Revisionist Literary Theory Leads to

Finally, it may be worthwhile to discuss whether the literary theory of modern revisionists can serve writers as a guide to writing honestly. Modern revisionists don't, in actual fact, want socialism; they want capitalism, but they pretend to side with socialism. They are bent on imitating the decadent and declining culture of imperialism, but they want to give the impression that they have not departed from the proletarian stand. They have in fact discarded as "dogma" the revolutionary principles of Marxism-Leninism, but they still want people to believe that their "theory" represents a development of Marxism-Leninism. For this reason, they cannot help but stammer, stutter and talk falteringly. In most cases they cannot and dare not speak their mind out fully. They describe their imitation of reactionary and decadent imperialist literature as the pursuit of a "modern international style"; they describe as a "reform" and a "quest" their abandonment of the fine traditions of revolutionary literature; they dig up out of the dog-eared literary theories of the bourgeoisie the view that "a book bares its writer's soul, it is his means of self-expression" and, proclaiming this view as their own invention, use it to defend their decadence. We are justified, therefore, in saying that modern revisionist literary theory is a theory of the most dishonest kind. It can only create confusion among writers. Writers who have been caught by it are reduced to ravings which they cannot even understand themselves. If they are really honest, the modern revisionist literary theorists should discard their disguise and frankly admit that their theory is just an echo of modern bourgeois theories, that the "honesty" they advocate is exactly what is advocated by modern bourgeois literary theorists—simply self-expression, a baring of the soul, an escape from reality, a distortion of the truth, vilification of socialism, the lauding of capitalism and a portrayal of individualistic, liberalistic and nihilistic "complex souls," "melancholy states of mind" and "frenzied passions." The literary theory of modern revisionism is in essence the subjective-idealist literary theory of the declining bourgeoisie.

The Mire of Reactionary Subjective-Idealist Literary Theory

It would be well for those who have been befuddled by modern revisionist ideas in art and literature to take a look at the reactionary literary thought of the imperialist bourgeoisie. There they will find the "pinnacle" reached by those who have endeavoured to shake off the fetters of all "dogmas" and to glorify in every way the "honesty" of the soul. Some literary "theorists" of the Freudian school, for example, have developed the following argument according to their own logic: an honest literary work is determined by the honesty of the writer's soul; honesty of soul, in its turn, is determined by a welling forth of the subconscious; all reasoning is a fetter on the subconscious and an honest depiction of the world is possible only when the subconscious is not directly affected by conscious thinking. They therefore claim that in order to write honestly, one must describe the world as one feels it as it were, in one's dreams. But even then, to carry the logic further, the dream is still affected by reason, so that the mental state best fitted for artistic creation should be that of a sick man in a coma. But even so, limited consciousness is still present in a state of coma, so in order to shake off the fetters of thought and consciousness completely, the artist should really describe the world as perceived by the mentally deranged. When the artist reaches such a state, his "honesty" is complete, he is free from all fetters of "dogma" and is thus in a position to create miracles of "beauty" at will! The theory of "writing honest'y" advertised by modern revisionists is imbued with the same spirit as the literary theories of the reactionary bourgeoisie. If subjective-idealist literary theory is carried to its logical conclusion, one must inevitably land in the mire of complete reaction such as we have just described. This is well worth pondering over.

It is now quite clear what it is modern revisionists are peddling with this idea of "writing honestly." It is obvious that they raise this cry about "writing honestly" and oppose "hypocrisy" not because they want to solve the common sense problem that genuine feeling is necessary for vivid and effective writing. What they want to do is to prepare the way to discard Marxism and to publicize revisionism. At the same time they try to brand revolutionary Marxist writers as "hypocritical" in the hope that this will force these writers, for fear of being branded "hypocritical," to discard the great ideological weapon of Marxism and join them in "honestly" extolling revisionism. But this is sheer wishful thinking. The broad masses of the people and proletarian writers will never be misled by this.

42. FICTION IN COMMUNIST CHINA

HOWARD L. BOORMAN

Well before they gained military control of the mainland, the Chinese Communists had already solicited substantial support, either active or passive, from the authors. By 1949, the majority had tacitly indicated their agreement with the general Communist political program; after 1949, almost all the well-known writers remained on the mainland of China. Such a beginning appeared auspicious for the authors. The literary front could lay retroactive claim to a varied and substantial body of writing which had been produced, despite discouraging conditions of military conflict, political censorship and economic insecurity, during the three decades since the May Fourth movement. The literati looked forward to reaping the benefits which the well-known Communist attention to "cultural work" seemed to promise.

Anticipation was better than realization. The new Communist authorities at Peking, for their part already equipped with a well-defined set of objectives, began at once to reorient the course of literary development which had emerged during the 1919–1949 period. Thus it was that the establishment of the People's Republic of China formally ended one literary period and ushered in another. The new era has been marked by an emphasis upon "people's literature," an emphasis embodying new and rigorous standards applicable to all writers, non-Communist and Communist alike. The relation between literature and politics since 1949, therefore, may best be understood within the framework of Peking's general policy intentions.

Essentially, Peking aims at a nation-wide program of accelerated modernization. This program requires, specifically, a unified system of total control over the nation, a thoroughgoing reorientation in the traditional values and attitudes of the Chinese people, and a radical change in the structure of Chinese society. It demands the employment of advanced technological methods to build China into a modern industrial nation capable of supporting a strong military force.

In pursuit of these ambitious goals, Peking has initially confronted the problem of purposeful stimulation of the minds and energies of that quarter of the earth's population living within the borders of the People's Republic of China. To that end, Peking must strive to overcome widespread illiteracy in order to bring literature to the common people. Simultaneously, it must utilize literature as a key channel to reach those who can read in order to mobilize maximum public support for its national programs. Thus the Party seeks, first of all, expository works which preach a simple social moral attuned

SOURCE: Selected from Howard L. Boorman, *Literature and Politics in Contemporary China*, New York: Institute of Asian Studies, St. John's University Press, 1960, pp. 113–123. Reprinted by permission of St. John's University Press.

to its immediate purposes. Given this aim, literature has no valid autonomous role, for its basic rules require that it accept without challenge the premises underlying the Communist system and that it find fruition within the new, chaste confines prescribed.

As the general function of writing is defined in accordance with Communist presuppositions regarding its social role, so the specific position of the writer is delineated. The author is not permitted to be a detached observer of the nuances of life or of the triumphs or tragedies of its actors. For him there is no private recording of the realities of his age. On the contrary, he must participate actively, though mechanically, in the pursuit of definite goals, and he must observe positive obligations both to the Communist Party and to the people of Mao Tse-tung's China. He must give unconditional and enthusiastic support to the dictates of the Party line, and he must encourage his readers to break with their "bourgeois" past and to help in building the "new society" which the Party sets as its major objective. Working within these prescribed limitations, he becomes a political pamphleteer for the state.

Peking has thus prohibited—or at least seriously inhibited—the production of literature as defined in the non-totalitarian world. Consciously and without conscience, the Chinese Communists utilize the novel, the story, the poem and the play as advertising maneuvers in the sale to the Chinese people of whatever the regime currently desires in consumption. State policy dictates the need, be it agricultural collectivization, anti-Americanism, or exposure of "rightist elements." A campaign is outlined. Themes are prescribed. Production targets are set. Progress is reviewed.

If the morality plays which flow from the pens of Peking's hucksters appear more melodramatic than meaningful to non-Communist eyes, the assumptions which undergird them are nevertheless solidly rooted in a positive set of assumptions. Reinterpreting and refashioning the classical standards of Chinese civilization—equilibrium and stability—Mao and his colleagues move toward radical transformation of both man and society. With the conviction of the chosen, they combine faith and works in a creed which holds that all things are destined to be possible for the "New China."

A dominant literary theme, therefore, is the sharp contrast between the social order prior to Communist control—by definition "old" and, therefore, "evil"—and the "new"—which is, *ipso facto,* "good." The old must be relentlessly exposed and condemned; the new must be ceaselessly praised. The parables depicting this theme find various settings—farm, factory and battlefield predominating—but the lessons are similar. Simple virtue, once crushed by political oppression and economic exploitation under the direct rule of the Kuomintang and the indirect influence of "American imperialism," rises triumphant, with the helping hand of Communism, to smite erstwhile enemies. The heroes are new types in Chinese fiction: the common man, striving to realize the revolution in his immediate *milieu,* or the Communist cadre, selflessly devoted to the common good. The villains are stereotyped: cruel landlords, corrupt capitalists, selfish "idealists," dishonest officials.

Since the primary purpose of Chinese Communist literature is the political education of the masses, the correlation between fiction and political drives is manifest. During the early years (1949–51) of the regime, the land reform

program, aimed both at mobilizing rural support and at disrupting the traditional social-economic system in rural China, furnished the backdrop for many
stories of land-hungry peasants delivered from the exploitation of rapacious
landlords. More recently, Peking's drive toward agricultural collectivization,
aimed at gaining maximum control of farm output for the purposes of the
state, has spawned a new set of tales depicting the advantages of cooperative
rural endeavor. In another sector of Chinese life, the growing program of
industrialization provides background for stories of workers intent upon meeting
production targets and surpassing quotas. Aspects of the social upheaval are
manifest in stories of the earnest and emancipated Chinese woman, free from
the restraints of the old male-dominated family system, now capable both of
free choice in marriage and of contributing to the reservoir of Chinese woman-
power available to aid the "New China." And, from 1950–53, the Korean
war provided an important source of nationalistic themes: the heroic exploits
of the Chinese "Volunteers" fighting American "imperialists" beyond the Yalu
and the patriotic efforts of civilians on the home front to support the war
effort to the limit.

The peculiar nature of literature in Communist China necessitates consideration not only of the major themes contained in its products but also of the
political policing of writers and writing. The organization of literary control
involves the Communist Party, the government and the major professional
association of writers established under Communist supervision.

The key element in the direction of literature on a nation-wide basis is
the central apparatus of the Communist Party itself. Drawing upon past experience in the mobilization of literature for political purposes, the Party has
in recent years refined its methods of surveillance. Since 1949, the Party, operating on the premise that it has sharper instincts in literary matters than the
writers themselves, has provided all basic directives in the literary field, while
the Party's central organization, specifically the Propaganda Department of
the Central Committee, has consistently been the ultimate source of ideological
orthodoxy and the final arbiter of its transmutation into "literature."

In the national government structure, the most important channel through
which the Party operates in the literary realm is the Ministry of Culture,
in fact headed by the veteran cooperating non-Communist novelist Mao Tun
(Shen Yen-ping, 1896–   ). This ministry has broad administrative authority
in the cultural field (including literature) and is the top level in a nation-wide
pyramidal network of subordinate bureaus which provide direction of provincial
and local cultural affairs.

Still another national apparatus facilitating Party direction of cultural life
is the All-China Federation of Literary and Art Circles. The Federation, organized under Communist auspices in the summer of 1949 (even before the
organization of the Central People's Government itself), is one of the most
important of the many "people's organizations" which the Communists have
sponsored to assist in the extension of controls throughout China without the
necessity of using the apparatus of the Party itself. The Federation is headed
by Kuo Mo-jo (1893–   ), with Mao Tun and Chou Yang (of the Propaganda
Department of the Party) as vice-chairmen. Established in 1949 and reorganized
in 1953, the Federation has primary responsibility for coordination of the

activities of national organizations in several fields: literature, drama, art, music, film, dance and others.

The literary subdivision of the Federation of Literary and Art Circles is the Union of Chinese Writers, headed by Mao Tun. Established in 1949, the Writers' Union is the principal professional organization in the literary field through which the Party transmits its mandates. Its monthly publication *Jen-min wen-hsueh* (People's Literature), is designed to disseminate current writing and criticism throughout the country and has the largest circulation of any literary journal in Communist China.

The organization of writing on a national basis is, however, only one aspect of a more fundamental issue. Organization is the means used to attain the Party's desired end: complete control over those who do the writing. At one level, the spur to conformity has been pressed within the framework of "thought reform" (*ssu-hsiang kai-tsao*), which has been so prominent a part of the Chinese Communist program of brute persuasion. Through careful exploitation of this new variety of psychological warfare, the Party has touched virtually every intellectual on the mainland of China. This nation-wide indoctrination program, keyed to Chinese requirements and aimed at a higher degree of saturation than superficially similar programs in other parts of the Communist bloc, has been a major element in Peking's efforts to control both the writer and his product.

At another level, the Party has gone beyond the general "thought reform" program to launch specific attacks against writers accused of being lax in political reliability or lethargic in production of the approved varieties of literature. The primary instrument employed in these campaigns has been public criticism by the Party. The primary purpose has been to force the writers thus stigmatized to recognize and accept the strict guidance of the Party in literary as well as in political matters.

This series of campaigns aimed at reaffirming the primacy and purity of Party leadership has encompassed both non-Communist and Communist writers, including some veteran Party members.[2] The roots of the recent attacks extend back to the period during the Japanese war when the Communists, confronted with expanding membership and with extended geographical lines of control, embarked upon a thoroughgoing program of tightening intra-Party discipline along strict Leninist lines. Both at Yenan during the early 1940's and in the Communist-occupied areas of Manchuria after 1945, the Party authorities dealt abruptly and harshly with Communist writers who ventured overt criticism of official policies.

During recent years, since their victory on the mainland of China, Communist attacks on the writers have been intensified. One major campaign, launched in the autumn of 1954, focused upon Yu P'ing-po (1899–   ), leading non-Communist scholar of Chinese literature and professor at Peking University, for "ideological errors" in the assessment of the classic eighteenth-century novel, *Hung Lou Meng* (Dream of the Red Chamber). The Communists first criticized Yu, an acknowledged authority on the great novel, for his failure to use Marxist categories of analysis and to grant adequate recognition to the Party line delineating the "social realism" of the work. Having condemned Yu P'ing-po for his failure to focus attention upon the social and historical background of the *Hung Lou Meng,* the Communists generalized their attack, censuring Yu's continued reliance upon "bourgeois idealist" concepts stemming from Hu Shih, major intellectual leader of the May Fourth period and modern China's most prominent non-Marxist savant.

Late in 1954, the Party attacked Feng Hsueh-feng, an erstwhile associate of Lu Hsun, who had become Communist vice-chairman of the Chinese Writers Union and editor of *Wen Yi Pao* (Literary Gazette). Accused of having manifested excessive "individualism" in opposition to the "collectivist spirit" required by Peking, Feng was belabored with general censure for his "revolt against the principles of Marxism-Leninism" and his "anti-Party conduct" and with specific criticism for his "dictatorial conduct" as editor of *Wen Yi Pao,* the principal organ of the Federation of Literary and Art Circles.

Another major victim of the drive toward tighter ideological control was Hu Feng, leftist writer who had been an associate of Lu Hsun and close to the Communists for twenty years. After the establishment of the Communist regime at Peking in 1949, Hu Feng became increasingly critical of the Party's attempts to dominate all literary activity in China. This smouldering resentment erupted in a general statement, "Views on the Literary Question," which Hu Feng boldly submitted to the Central Committee of the Party in mid-1954. In reply to this overt criticism of the sterility of literature under its rigid rule, Peking launched a massive attack. The Communists declared Hu Feng guilty of "bourgeois reactionary" thinking and arrested both Hu and other members of his "clique" on charges of "counter-revolutionary" activities.

Peking's manipulation of the Hu Feng case during 1955 demonstrated the manner in which the Chinese Communists utilize controversy over "cultural" policies to support their larger political maneuvers. Clearly the political aspects of the Hu Feng case overshadowed the literary. The immediate eradication of deviant ideological trends was required by the long-range demands of political mobilization. The drive to expand control over the writers was but a single aspect of the larger social engineering program: the creation of a new type of Chinese society constructed according to Communist specifications.

A period of liberalization in ideological controls came during 1956–57, an interlude introduced by Peking's announcement (in classical Chinese phrasing) that the regime would "let all flowers bloom, let diverse schools of thought contend." The apparent relaxation in Communist policies brought forth a brief and abortive spasm of protest from frustrated Chinese writers and intellectuals. A short story, "A New Young Man Arrives at the Organization Department," published in the September, 1956 issue of *Jen-min wen-hsueh* (People's Literature), provides, for example, a perceptive account of the growing disillusionment experienced by an enthusiastic young Party worker in the face of bureaucracy, lethargy and indifference. Yet the period of relaxation was too brief to permit significant literary production.

This interlude of criticism was soon brought to an end in 1957 through a nation-wide drive against "rightist elements" aimed not only at the writers but also at virtually all other strata of Chinese society. The most dramatic case affecting the Chinese literary world during this period was that of Ting Ling, prominent Chinese Communist authoress and Stalin Prize winner, who was attacked for leading an "anti-Party conspiracy" within the Communist ranks. Chou Yang, the most influential literary arbiter in Peking, summarized the official line denouncing the errant behavior of Ting Ling and an associate, Ch'en Ch'i-hsia:

> Instead of remoulding themselves in the spirit of collectivism, they want to remould the Party and the revolution according to their individualist outlook.[3]

The mass of verbiage publicly pressuring the Chinese writer to political purity leaves many questions obscure. One essential fact does, however, emerge clearly. The Communist authorities in Peking unequivocally affirm the principles first enunciated by Mao Tse-tung at Yenan in 1942: first, that literature must be subordinate to politics; second, that the Communist Party must direct the course of contemporary Chinese literature; and, third, that the primary purpose of literature in Communist China must be to educate the common people—peasants, workers and soldiers—in the policies of the Party.

Thus Peking officially—and paternally—spells out the author's role. Working alone, the writer is a craftsman and must constantly struggle to overcome his individualism and his egocentrism. As one of the most important contributors to the development of the "new socialist soul" in China, he must constantly cleanse his spirit, study Marxism-Leninism, maintain contact with the life of the common people, and accept Party leadership.

Literature and Politics in Contemporary China

"Socialist realism" and "Party-mindedness"—the major principles underlying Soviet fiction—have weathered transplanting to become the ground rules governing creative writing in Communist China. Indeed the Communists in Peking have moved far more rapidly in imposing controls in the literary realm than did the Communists in Moscow during the first decade of their rule after 1917. Since 1949, Peking has governed literary activity under a set of precise and internally consistent premises. Some critical discussion has been possible over how expression is to be manipulated, but no questioning of fundamental Party dogma is tolerated.

Within the Communist design, no genuine criticism of the *status quo* as determined by the Party leadership is possible. Subject to the semantic oversimplification which the totalitarian outlook produces, the authorities in Peking proceed from the orthodox Communist assumption that individual thought and feelings have their genesis in the "objective reality of the class struggle and the national struggle." Conditioned by proper proletarian stimuli, the writer should move unerringly through the Marxist maze to expound his inspiration in Politburo-patterned platitudes.

The Communist victory in China has thus wrought drastic changes both in the personal position of the Chinese writer and in his social situation. Prior to 1949 (and despite the Kuomintang censorship so sharply condemned by the Communists), a *bona fide* literature of social protest—a literature which served as a sort of national conscience—could and did exist in China. It might seem that the authors of that literature—the writers who had been opposed to the Kuomintang and sympathetic, either politically or psychologically, with the Communists—would have required little coercion to find fulfillment in the new Marxist order. But facile transition has proved impossible. The creativity of which these authors were master—creativity which stemmed in part from the conflicts surrounding them in Nationalist China and thrived in part on the ferment and frustration of the Republican period—has progressively withered in the pursuit of "progress" under Mao Tse-tung. The most interesting and evocative works of recent Chinese fiction, still read in Communist China today, are by authors who learned their craft in the pre-Communist period. Since 1949, the literary garden which the Communists have been attempting to nurture synthetically has produced numerous political pamphlets but nothing like the vigorous literary crops of the pre-1949 period.

England's most prominent contemporary novelist discussing, in lectures many years ago at Cambridge, certain aspects of the novel, struck the mark. In 1927, Mr. E. M. Forster observed:

A mirror does not develop because an historical pageant passes in front of it. It only develops when it gets a fresh coat of quicksilver—in other words, when it acquires new sensitiveness; and the novel's success lies in its own sensitiveness, not in the success of its subject matter.[4]

The observation is one which no writer of fiction may ignore—and one which no contemporary author in Communist China can afford to heed.

In the non-Communist tradition, creative literature must be an individual expression of experience, real or imagined, and the relationship between the writer and his product must of necessity be one of integrity, spontaneity and sincerity. Fiction conveys many levels of meaning and emotion, some intended by the author, other unintentional. For the writer working on a large scale, the purpose of creation is inherently a complex vision, frequently implicit rather than explicit, of man and of human life. As an artist, he communicates, through his selection of personalities and problems, his unique verity of intuition and his individual aesthetic or intellectual standards. Inevitably he must scorn political expediencies and shun the demands of organized groups committed to transient programs of social action. Like Robert Frost, he must pick the road "less traveled by" and follow it independently to its end. Where political authority presumes to stipulate either the scope or the mode of expression, the literary result is constrained by either moral or imaginative lassitude.

These observations on the function of fiction may be acceptable in the West. In essence, however, they embody value judgments on the role of literature—*judgments with which the Chinese Communist Party is in total disagreement.* It is possible to debate the validity of the Western and the Communist literary theories. Failing the opportunity for such debate, however, it is at least necessary for the Western reader to acknowledge:

First, that the literary standards set by the Communist regime in Peking are the only standards now existing in China;

Second, that Peking's standards are fundamentally opposed to those held in the non-Communist world;

Third, that the authorities in Peking are committed in practice as well as in theory to *their* estimates of the social role of literature in the People's Republic of China—estimates which decisively proclaim the supremacy of politics over prose.

Secure in his bourgeois bias, the non-Communist observer may well conclude that the government at Peking, through its proletarian prejudices and preconceptions, has doomed the Chinese literary field to stunted growth. He may feel that analysis of the voluminous product now officially defined as "Chinese literature" will be of scant help, to political or social understanding since it is inherently a literature unlikely, except by omission or oversight, to reveal the real experiences of real Chinese living in Communist China.

Yet the links between literature and the social processes are complex and elusive. For the Western student, an understanding of these links is far less easily achieved in the exploration of a non-European culture such as contemporary China than in the assessment, for example, of the manners and moods of nineteenth-century England through the fiction of Thackeray, Dickens, Trollope and George Eliot. Even in the case of China, however, much may be learned with initiative and patience.

Perhaps the major requirement is perspective, for reflection may suggest the need for a re-evaluation of the relation between artistic creativity and political activity, between literature and politics. The grand design of the Chinese Communists is to channel all the productive energies of their proud land into a single, all-embracing dream: the "New China." The vision of social change, while itself a major feat in an ancient, tradition-bound civilization, is actually not novel in modern China. But the implementation of radical change on a national basis under decisive and dedicated direction is new Comrade Mao Tse-tung has blended implementation with imagination and thereby confounded Mr. Forster's tidy image. Perhaps the actual "historical pageant"—the positive process of constructing a new Communist society in Asia—is itself a more daring and comprehensive work of the imagination than any mirroring work of literature which can be produced in contemporary China.

Notes

1. Of the principal literary figures, only Lao She, who was abroad at the time, was absent. He returned to China slightly later, toward the end of 1949, and has remained in Peking since. Lao She is chiefly known in the United States as the author of *Rickshaw Boy*, published in an adapted English translation in 1945.

2. On the recent developments in the literary field in Communist China *see* Shau-wing Chan, "Literature in Communist China," *Problems of Communism*, VII, 1 (January–February 1958), pp. 44–51, and Cyril Birch, "The Dragon and the Pen," *Soviet Survey*, London, special China issue, No. 24 (April–June 1958), pp. 22–26.

3. Chou Yang, *A Great Debate on the Literary Front*, Peking: Foreign Languages Press, 1958, p. 13.

4. E. M. Forster, *Aspects of the Novel*, New York: Harcourt, Brace, 1927, p. 38.

Recommended Readings

General and Institutional History of China

Biggerstaff, Knight. *The Earliest Modern Government Schools in China* (Ithaca: Cornell University Press, 1961).

Boode, Derk. "Feudalism in China" (In Rushton Coulborn (ed.), *Feudalism in History,* Princeton, N.J.: Princeton University Press, 1956), pp. 49–92.

Callis, Helmut G. *China: Confucian and Communist* (New York: Holt, 1959).

Chang, Chung-li. *The Chinese Gentry. Studies on Their Role in Nineteenth-Century Chinese Society* (Seattle: University of Washington Press, 1955).

Chien, Tuan-sheng. *The Government and Politics of China* (Cambridge, Mass.: Harvard University Press, 1950).

Ch'u, T'ung-tsu. *Local Government in China under the Ch'ing* (Cambridge, Mass.: Harvard University Press, 1962).

Clubb, O. Edmund. *Twentieth Century China* (New York: Columbia University Press, 1964).

Creel, H. G. *Chinese Thought from Confucius to Mao Tse-tung* (Chicago: University of Chicago Press, 1953).

Cressey, George B. "Changing the Map of China," *Economic Geography* (January, 1955).

Cressey, George B. *China's Geographic Foundations: A Survey of the Land and Its People* (New York: McGraw-Hill, 1934).

Cressey, George B. *Land of the Five Hundred Millions: A Geography of China* (New York: McGraw-Hill, 1955).

de Bary, W. T. (ed.) *Sources of the Chinese Tradition* (New York: Columbia University Press, 1959).

Eberhard, Wolfram. *Conquerors and Rulers, Social Forces in Medieval China* (Leiden: Brill, 1952).

Fairbank, John K. (ed.) *Chinese Thought and Institutions* (Chicago: University of Chicago Press, 1957).

Fairbank, John K. *The United States and China* (New York: The Viking Press, 1962).

Fairbank, J. K., and Teng, S. Y. *China's Response to the West* (Cambridge, Mass.: Harvard University Press, 1954).

Fairbank, J. K., and Teng, S. Y. "On the Ch'ing Tributary System," *Harvard Journal of Asiatic Studies* (June, 1941).

Feuerwerker, Albert. *China's Early Industrialization: Sheng Hsuan-huai and Mandarin Enterprise* (Cambridge, Mass.: Harvard University Press, 1958).

Feuerwerker, Albert. "China's History in Marxian Dress," *The American Historical Review* (January, 1961).

Fitzgerald, C. P. *The Birth of Communist China* (London: Penguin Books, 1964).

Fitzgerald, C. P. *China: A Short Cultural History* (New York: Praeger, 1954).

Fitzgerald, C. P. "The Historical and Philosophical Background of Communist China," *Political Quarterly* (July–September, 1964), pp. 23–35 of this book.

Franke, Wolfgang. *The Reform and Abolition of the Traditional Chinese Examination System* (Cambridge, Mass.: Harvard University Press, 1960).

Ho, Kan-chih, *A History of the Modern Chinese Revolution* (Peking: Foreign Languages Press, 1959).

Hsiao, Kung-chuan. *Rural China: Imperial Control in the Nineteenth Century* (Seattle: University of Washington Press, 1960).

Hsü, Immanuel C. Y. *China's Entrance into the Family of Nations: The Diplomatic Phase, 1858–1880* (Cambridge, Mass.: Harvard University Press, 1960).

Hu, Chang-tu, and others. *China: Its People, Its Society, Its Culture* (London: Mayflower, 1960).

Kracke, E. A., Jr. *Civil Service in Early Sung China, 960–1067* (Cambridge, Mass.: Harvard University Press, 1953).

Langer, W. L. *The Diplomacy of Imperialism* (New York: Knopf, 1950).

Latourette, Kenneth Scott. *The Chinese: Their History and Culture* (New York: Macmillan, 1946).

Levenson, Joseph R. *Confucian China and Its Modern Fate: The Problem of Intellectual Continuity* (Berkeley: University of California Press, 1958).

Levenson, Joseph R. *Liang Ch'i-ch'ao and the Mind of Modern China* (Cambridge, Mass.: Harvard University Press, 1953).

Li, Chien-nung. *The Political History of China 1840–1928* (New York: Van Nostrand, 1956).

MacNair, Harley F. *China* (Berkeley; University of California Press, 1946).

Marsh, Robert M. *The Mandarins: The Circulation of Elites in China* (New York: The Free Press of Glencoe, 1961).

Michael, Franz. *The Origin of Manchu Rule in China, Frontier and Bureaucracy as Interacting Forces in the Chinese Empire* (Baltimore: Johns Hopkins Press, 1942).

Schurmann, Herbert Franz. *Economic Structure of the Yuan Dynasty* (Cambridge, Mass.: Harvard University Press, 1956).

Sheng, Hu. *Imperialism and Chinese Politics* (Peking: Foreign Languages Press, 1957).

Ware, James R. *The Sayings of Confucius* (New York: Mentor Books, 1955).

Weber, Max. *The Religion of China: Confucianism and Taoism* (New York: The Free Press of Glencoe, 1951).

Welch, Holmes. *The Parting of the Way: Lao Tzu and the Taoist Movement* (Boston, Mass.: Beacon Press, 1957).

Wilbur, C. Martin. *Slavery in China during the Former Han Dynasty 206 B.C.–A.D. 25* (Chicago: Field Museum of Natural History, 1943).

Wittfogel, Karl August. *Oriental Despotism: A Comparative Study of Total Power* (New Haven: Yale University Press, 1957).

Wittfogel, Karl August, and Feng, Chia-sheng. *History of Chinese Society: Liao (907–1125)* (Philadelphia: American Philosophical Society, 1949).

Wright, Arthur F. (ed.) *Studies in Chinese Thought* (Chicago: University of Chicago Press, 1953).

Wright, Mary C. *The Last Stand of Chinese Conservatism. The T'ung-chih Restoration, 1862–874* (Stanford: Stanford University Press, 1957).

The Rise of Communism in China

Black Cyril E. "Political Modernization in Russia and China," (in Kurt London (ed.), *Unity and Contradiction: Major Aspects of Sino-Soviet Relations,* Praeger, 1962), pp. 3–18.

Bowie, R. R., and Fairbank, J. K. (eds.) *Communist China, 1955–1959: Policy Documents with Analysis* (Cambridge, Mass.: Harvard University Press, 1962).

Brandt, Conrad. *Stalin's Failure in China* (Cambridge, Mass.: Harvard University Press, 1958).

Brandt, Conrad, Schwartz, Benjamin, and Fairbank, John K. *A Documentary History of Chinese Communism* (Cambridge, Mass.: Harvard University Press, 1952).

Chiang, Molin. *Tides from the West* (New Haven: Yale University Press, 1947).

Ch'iao-mu, Hu. *Thirty Years of the Communist Party of China* (Peking: Foreign Languages Press, 1951).

Francis, John de. *Nationalism and Language Reform in China* (Princeton: Princeton University Press, 1950).

Hsiao, Tso-liang. *Power Relations within the Chinese Communist Movement, 1930–1934: A Study of Documents* (Seattle: University of Washington Press, 1961).

Hsueh, Chun-tu. *The Chinese Communist Movement, 1921–1937* (Stanford: Stanford University Press, 1960).

Hsueh, Chun-tu. *The Chinese Communist Movement, 1937–1949* (Stanford: Stanford University Press, 1962).

Johnson, Chalmers Ashby. *Peasant Nationalism and Communist Power: The Emergence of Revolutionary China, 1937–1945* (Stanford: Stanford University Press, 1962).

Kiang, Wen-han. *The Chinese Student Movement* (New York: King's Crown Press, 1948).

Liu, F. F. *A Military History of Modern China 1924–1949* (Princeton: Princeton University Press, 1956).

North, Robert C. *Kuomin-tang and Chinese Communist Elites* (Stanford: Stanford University Press, 1952).

Powell, Ralph L. *The Rise of Chinese Military Power 1895–1912* (Princeton: Princeton University Press, 1955).

Schwartz, Benjamin I. *Chinese Communism and the Rise of Mao* (Cambridge, Mass.: Harvard University Press, 1951).

Snow, Edgar. *The Other Side of the River: Red China Today* (New York: Random House, 1962).

Wilbur, C. Martin, and How, Julie Lien-ying (eds.). *Documents in Communism, Nationalism, and Soviet Advisers in China, 1918–1927* (New York: Columbia University Press, 1956).

Communism in China (General)

Barnett, A. Doak. *China on the Eve of Communist Takeover* (New York: Praeger, 1963).

Barnett, A. Doak. *Communist China: The Early Years, 1949–55* (New York: Praeger, 1964).

Center for International Affairs and the East Asian Research Center, Harvard University with a foreword by Robert R. Bowle and John K. Fairbank. *Communist China, 1955–1959; Policy Documents with Analysis* (Cambridge, Mass.: Harvard University Press, 1962.)

Chang, C. M. "Five Years of Communist Rule in China," *Foreign Affairs* (October, 1954).

Creel, H. G. *Chinese Thought from Confucius to Mao Tse-tung* (Chicago: University of Chicago Press, 1953).

Klatt, Werner (ed.). *The Chinese Model. A Political, Economic and Social Survey* (Hong Kong: Hong Kong University Press, 1965).

Lindsay, Michael. "Changes in Chinese Communist Thought, 1937–1960" (in *Symposium on Economic and Social Problems of the Far East,* University of Hong Kong, 1961, Proceedings, 1962).

Michael, Franz. "Chinese Communism, Past and Present," *Problems of Communism* (July–August, 1963).

Mits, F. T. "Developments in Mainland China," *Current Scene* (July 1, 1965).

Pentony, Devere E. (ed.). *China: The Emerging Red Giant. Communist Foreign Policies* (San Francisco: Chandler Publishing Company, 1962).

Rostow, W. W., Hatch, R. W., Kierman, F. A., Jr., and Eckstein, A. *The Prospects for Communist China* (New York: John Wiley, 1954).

Tang, Peter S. H. *Communist China Today* (Washington, D.C.: Research Institute on the Sino-Soviet Bloc, 1961).

Tang, Peter S. H. *Communist China Today: Domestic and Foreign Policies* (New York: Praeger 1957).

U.S. Senate, "Nature of Communism in Occupied China: A Documentary for the Record of the Subcommittee to Investigate the Administration of Internal Security Acts and Other Internal Security Laws" (Washington, D.C.: U.S. Government Printing Office, 1957).

Walker, Richard L. *China under Communism: The First Five Years* (New Haven: Yale University Press, 1955).

Wint, Guy. *Communist China's Crusade* (New York: Praeger, 1958).

Population and Economic Planning

Barendsen, Robert D. *Half-Work, Half-Study Schools in Communist China. Recent Experiments with Self-Supporting Educational Institutions* (Washington, D.C.: U.S. Department of Health, Education, and Welfare, 1964).

Chandrasekhar, S. *China's Population* (Hong Kong: Hong Kong University Press, 1959).

Emerson, John Philip. "Manpower Absorption in the Non-agricultural Branches of the Economy of Communist China, 1953–58," *The China Quarterly* (July–September, 1961).

Gould, Sidney H. (ed.). *Sciences in Communist China* (Washington, D.C.: American Association for the Advancement of Science, 1961).

Ho, Ping-ti. *Studies on the Population of China, 1368–1953* (Cambridge, Mass.: Harvard University Press, 1959).

Jackson, W. A. Douglas. "The Chinese Population Problem," *Current History* (September, 1962).

Kirby, E. S. "Peiping's Growing Dilemma—Population," *Problems of Communism* (March–April, 1958).

Orleans, Leo A. *Professional Manpower and Education in Communist China*

(Washington, D.C.: National Science Foundation, U.S. Government Printing Office, 1960).

Taeuber, Irene B., and Orleans, Leo A. "Mainland China" (in Bernard Berelson et al. (eds.), *Family Planning and Population Programs. A Review of World Developments,* University of Chicago Press, 1965), pp. 31–54.

Mao and Maoism

Cohen, Arthur A. *The Communism of Mao Tse-tung* (Chicago: University of Chicago Press, 1964).

Cohen, Arthur A. "How Original Is Maoism?" *Problems of Communism* (November–December, 1961).

Elegant, Robert S. *China's Red Masters: Political Biographies of the Chinese Communist Leaders* (New York: Twayne, 1951).

Inoki, Masamichi. "Leninism and Mao Tse-tung's Ideology" (in Kurt London (ed.), *Unity and Contradictions: Major Aspects of Sino-Soviet Relations,* Praeger, 1962), pp. 103–121.

Lewis, John Wilson (ed.). *Major Doctrines of Communist China* (New York: Norton, 1964.

Mao, Tse-tung. *Selected Works,* 5 vols. (New York. International Publishers, published in various years).

Onoe, Masao. "Factors Binding the U.S.S.R. and Communist China" (in Kurt London (ed.), *Unity and Contradictions: Major Aspects of Sino-Soviet Relations,* New York: Praeger, 1962), pp. 142–158.

Rigby, T. H. "The Embourgeoisement of the Soviet Union and the Proletarinization of Communist China" (in Kurt London (ed.), *Unity and Contradiction: Major Aspects of Sino-Soviet Relations,* New York: Praeger, 1962), pp. 19–38.

Schram, Stuart R. *The Political Thought of Mao Tse-tung* (New York: Praeger, 1963).

Schwartz, Benjamin. "The Legend of the 'Legend of Maoism'," *The China Quarterly* (April–June, 1960).

Schwartz, Benjamin. "Mao Tse-tung and Communist Theory," *The New Leader* (April 4, 1960).

Schwartz, Benjamin. "A Marxist Controversy on China," *Far Eastern Quarterly* (February, 1954).

Snow, Edgar. *Red Star over China* (New York: Grove Press, 1961).

The Party

Chang, J. Chester. "Problems of Chinese Communist Leadership as Seen in the Secret Military Papers," *Asian Survey* (June, 1964).

Chao, Kuo-chün. "Leadership in the Chinese Communist Party," *Annals of the American Academy of Political and Social Science* (January, 1959).

Chen, A. S. "The Ideal Local Party Secretary and the 'Model' Man," *The China Quarterly* (January–March, 1964).

"Chinese Communist Party Membership Statistics," *Current Background* (November 19, 1956).

Dai, Shen-yu. "Party Rule in Communist China," *Current History* (September, 1962).

Keesing, Donald B. *Use of Top-level Personnel by the Chinese Communist Gov-*

ernment, 1949–1953 (Center for International Studies, Massachusetts Institute of Technology, 1954).

Klein, Donald W. "The 'Next Generation' of Chinese Communist Leaders," *The China Quarterly* (October–December, 1962).

Klein, Donald W. "Peking's Leaders: A Study in Isolation," *The China Quarterly* (July–September, 1961).

Klein, Donald W. "Succession and the Elite in Peking," *Journal of International Affairs,* No. 1 (1964).

Lewis, John Wilson. "The Leadership Doctrine of the Chinese Communist Party: The Lesson of the People's Commune," *Asian Survey* (October, 1963), pp. 179–188.

Lewis, John Wilson. *Leadership in Communist China* (Ithaca. Cornell University Press, 1963).

MacFarquhar, R. "Communist China's Intra-party Dispute," *Pacific Affairs,* 31 (1958).

Newton, Wyndham. "Communist China's Hierarchy Undergoes Change," *Far Eastern Economic Review* (May 7, 1959).

Pringsheim, Klaus H. "The Functions of the Chinese Communist Youth Leagues (1920–1949)," *The China Quarterly* (October–December, 1962).

U.S. Senate, "Staffing the Party" (in *Staffing Procedures and Problems in Communist China,* Government Printing Office, 1963), pp. 155–178.

Whiting, Allen S. "Political Dynamics: The Communist Party of China" (in Ward and Macridis (eds.), *Modern Political Systems: Asia,* Englewood Cliffs, N.J.: Prentice-Hall, Inc., 1963), pp. 129–155.

Yang, Hsien-chien. "Collective Leadership Is the Highest Principle of Party Leadership," *Current Background* (April 17, 1956).

The Urban Economy: Past and Present

Barnett, A. D. "The Economic Development of Communist China" (in *Communist China and Asia,* Harper & Row, Publishers, 1960), pp. 374–396.

Chen, T. H. "The Liquidation of Private Business in Communist China," *Far Eastern Survey* (June, 1955).

Cheng, Chu-yuan. *Communist China's Economy, 1949–1962: Structural Changes and Crises* (South Orange, N.J.: Seton Hall University Press, 1963).

Eckstein, Alexander. *Communist China's National Income* (New York: The Free Press of Glencoe, 1961).

Eckstein, Alexander. "Conditions and Prospects for Economic Growth in Communist China," *World Politics,* 7 (1954–55).

Eckstein, Alexander. *The National Income of Communist China* (New York: The Free Press of Glencoe, 1962).

Fried, Morton H. "Ideology, Social Organization and Economic Development in China," *East Asian Institute.*

Hollister, William W. "Capital Formation in Communist China," *The China Quarterly* (January–March, 1964).

Hollister, William W. *China's Gross National Product and Social Accounts, 1950–1957* (New York: The Free Press of Glencoe, 1958).

Hooton, G. L. V. "The Problem of Working Capital in Communist China," *Far Eastern Economic Review* (November 15, 1955).

Hsia, Ronald. "The Development of Mainland China's Steel Industry since 1958," *The China Quarterly* (July–September, 1961).

Hsu, Li chun. "The Relations between Industry and Agriculture and Heavy and Light Industry," *Peking Review* (May 19, 1959).

Hughes, T. J. and Luard, D. E. T. *Economic Development of Communist China, 1949–1958* (New York: Oxford University Press, 1962).

Klein, Sidney, "China's Industrialization. Critical Sectors," *Current Scene* (May 20, 1962).

Kuo-chün, Chao. *Economic Organization and Planning in Mainland China: A Documentary Study (1949–1957)* (Cambridge, Mass.: Harvard University Press, 1958).

Li, Cho-ming. *Economic Development of Communist China. An Appraisal of the First Five Years of Industrialization* (Berkeley: University of California Press, 1959).

Li, Choh-ming (ed.). *Industrial Development in Communist China* (New York: Praeger, 1964).

Li, Choh-ming. *The Statistical System of Communist China* (Berkeley: University of California Press, 1962).

Liu, Ta-chung, and Yeh-Kung-chia. *The Economy of the Chinese Mainland: National Income and Economic Development, 1933–1959* (Princeton: Princeton University Press, 1965).

Luard, D. E. "The Urban Communes," *The China Quarterly* (July–September, 1960).

Ngau, Chang Kia. *The Inflationary Spiral: The Experience in China, 1939–1950* (New York: John Wiley, 1958).

Orleans, Leo A. "The Recent Growth of China's Urban Population," *Geographical Review* (January, 1959).

Perkins, Dwight H. *Market Control and Planning in Communist China* (Cambridge, Mass.: Harvard University Press, 1966).

Schurmann, H. F. "Organizational Contrasts Between Communist China and the Soviet Union" (in Kurt London, (Ed.), *Unity and Contradiction: Major Aspects of Sino-Soviet Relations,* Praeger, 1962), pp. 65–102.

Tsao, Chu-ju. "Banking in New China," *Peking Review* (January 12, 1960).

Wu, Y. L. "Chinese Industrialization at the Crossroads," *Current History* (September, 1961).

Wu, Yuan-li. *The Economy of Communist China. An Introduction* (New York: Praeger, 1965).

The Rural Economy: Past and Present

Barnett, A. D. "China's Road to Collectivisation," *Journal of Farm Economics* (May, 1953).

Bonwit, R. "Communist China's 'Leap Forward,' " *Pacific Affairs* (June, 1958).

Buck, John Lossing. *Land Utilization in China* (Chicago: University of Chicago Press, 1937).

Cheng, Chu-yuan. "The Changing Pattern of Rural Communes in Communist China," *Asian Survey* (November, 1961).

Chou, Ya-lun. "Chinese Agrarian Reform and Bolshevik Land Policy," *Pacific Affairs* (March, 1952).

Crook, David, and Crook, Isabel. *Revolution in a Chinese Village* (New York: Humanities Press, 1959).

Donnithorne, A. "Background to the People's Communes: Changes in China's Economic Organization in 1958," *Pacific Affairs* (December, 1959).

Donnithorne, A. "The Organization of Rural Trade in China Since 1958," *The China Quarterly* (October–December, 1961).

Dutt, G. "Some Problems of China's Rural Communes," *The China Quarterly* (October–December, 1963).

Fei, Hsiao-t'ung. *Peasant Life in China: A Field Study of Country Life in the Yangtze Valley* (New York: Dutton, 1939).

Fei, Hsiao-t'ung, and Chang, Chih-i. *Earthbound China, A Study of Rural Economy in Yunnan* (Chicago: University of Chicago Press, 1945).

Fei, Hsiao-t'ung, and Chang, Chih-i. "Peasantry and Gentry, and Interpretation of Chinese Social Structure and Its Changes," *The American Journal of Sociology* (July, 1946).

Klein, Sidney. "The Land Reform Policies of the Chinese Communist Party, 1928–1958: A Brief Economic Analysis," *Agricultural History*, 35 (1961).

Kuo-chün, Chao. *Agrarian Policies of Mainland China: A Documentary Study (1949–1956)* (Cambridge, Mass.: Harvard University Press, 1957).

Kuo-chün, Chao. *Agrarian Policy of the Chinese Communist Party, 1921–1959* (Bombay: Asia Publishing House, 1960).

Kuo-chün, Chao. "Agricultural Advances in China," *Current History* (December, 1960).

Kuo-chün, Chao. "The Organization and Functions of the People's Communes," *Contemporary China,* 3 (1960).

Meissner, Boris. "The People's Commune: A Manifestation of Sino-Soviet Differences" (In Kurt London (ed.), *Unity and Contradiction: Major Aspects of Sino-Soviet Relations,* Praeger, 1962), pp. 122–141.

Myrdal, Jan. *Report from a Chinese Village* (London: Heinemann, 1965).

Orleans, Leo A. "Problems of Manpower Absorption in Rural China," *The China Quarterly* (July–September, 1961).

Osgood, Cornelius. *Village Life in Old China. A Community Study of Kao Yao Yünnan* (New York: The Ronald Press Company, 1963).

Rovenholt, A. "Chinese Communes: Big Risks for Big Gains," *Foreign Affairs* (July, 1959).

Schiller, Otto. "The Agrarian Systems in the Soviet Union and Communist China: A Comparison" (in Kurt London (ed.), *Unity and Contradiction: Major Aspects of Sino-Soviet Relations,* Praeger, 1962), pp. 331–352.

Schurmann, H. F. "The Communes: A One-Year Balance Sheet," *Problems of Communism* (September–October, 1959).

Shen, T. H. *Agricultural Resources of China* (Ithaca: Cornell University Press, 1951).

Skinner, G. William. "Marketing and Social Structure in Rural China, Part I," *The Journal of Asian Studies* (November, 1964).

Skinner, G. William. "Marketing and Social Structure in Rural China, Part II," *The Journal of Asian Studies* (February, 1965).

Skinner, G. William. "Marketing and Social Structure in Rural China, Part III," *The Journal of Asian Studies* (May, 1965).

Skinner, G. William. "Peasant Organization in Rural China," *Annals of the American Academy of Political and Social Science* (September, 1952).

Tawney, R. H. *Land and Labor in China* (New York: Harcourt, Brace & World, 1932).

Wu, Yuan-li. "The Communes in a Changing China," *Current History* (December, 1959), pp. 445–453.

Wu, Yuan-li. "Farm Crisis in Red China," *Current History* (September, 1962).

Yang, C. K. *A Chinese Village in Early Communist Transition* (Cambridge, Mass.: Harvard University Press, 1959).
Yang, Martin. *A Chinese Village: Taitou, Shan-tung Province* (New York: Columbia University Press, 1945).

The Legal System

Barnett, A. D. "Political Power in Communist China," *Journal of International Affairs,* No. 2 (1957).
Buxbaum, David C. "Preliminary Trends in the Development of the Legal Institutions of Communist China and the Nature of the Criminal Law," *International and Comparative Law Quarterly* (January, 1962), pp. 340–371.
Chang, Ting-ch'eng. "Report on Procuratorial Work since 1956," *Current Background* (July 12, 1957).
Chang, Ting-ch'eng. "The Work of People's Procurates," *Current Background* (May 4, 1959).
Chang, Yu-nan. "The Chinese Communist State System under the Constitution of 1954," *Journal of Politics* (April, 1956).
Chao, Kuo-chün. "How Communist Power Is Organized in China," *Foreign Affairs* (October, 1955).
Chao, Kuo-chün. "Mass Organization in Mainland China," *American Political Science Review* (September, 1954).
Chao, Kuo-chün. "The National Constitution of Communist China," *Far Eastern Survey* (October, 1954).
Current Background "Administrative Areas of Communist China," (October 29, 1958).
Current Background, "China, Laws, Statutes, Etc. Draft Conscription Law of the People's Republic of China" (February 18, 1955).
Dai, S. Y. "Government and Law in Communist China," *Current History* (September, 1961).
Houn, F. W. "Communist China's New Constitution," *The Western Political Quarterly* (March, 1955), pp. 213–251.
Houn, F. W. "Communist China's New Constitution," *World Affairs Interpreter* (Winter, 1955).
Hsia, Tao-t'ai. "The Constitution of Red China," *American Journal of Comparative Law* (Summer, 1955).
Jo, Ch'uan. "The Party's Control of the Judiciary in China," *Soviet Survey* (April–June, 1958).
Kao, Ko-lin. "Work of the Supreme People's Court since 1955," *Current Background* (May 4, 1959).
Ku-Tun-jou. "The Evolution of the Chinese Hsien Government," *Chinese Culture,* 2, No. 3 (1959).
Lee, Luke T. "Chinese Communist Law: Its Background and Development," *Michigan Law Review* (February, 1962), pp. 308–340.
Leng, Shao-chuan. "The Lawyer in Communist China," *Journal of the International Commission of Jurists* (Summer, 1962).
Steiner, H. Arthur. "Constitutionalism in Communist China," *American Political Science Review* (June, 1955), pp. 191–213.
Tung, Pi-wu. "Judicial Work in China in the Past Year," *Current Background* (July 3, 1956).
Tung, Pi-wu. "The Legal System of China," *Current Background* (October 16, 1956).

Tung, Pi-wu. "Report on Work of the Supreme People's Court," *Current Background* (July 12, 1957).

Tung, Pi-wu. "The Work of the People's Courts in the Past Year," (in *New China Advances to Socialism*, Peking: Foreign Languages Press, 1956).

Thought Reform and Education

Abe, Munemitsu. "Spare-Time Education in Communist China," *The China Quarterly* (October–December, 1961).

Barendsen, Robert D. "The Agricultural Middle School in Communist China," *The China Quarterly* (October–December, 1961).

Barendsen, Robert D. *Planned Reforms in the Primary and Secondary School System in Communist China* (Washington, D.C.: U.S. Department of Health, Education, and Welfare, 1960).

Boorman, Howard L. "Literature and Politics in Contemporary China: An Essay in Interpretation *Thought Patterns*, Vol. 7 (1960).

Chao, Chung. *The Communist Program for Literature and Art in China* (Hong Kong: The Union Research Institute, 1955).

Chen, Hsi-en. *Thought Reform of the Chinese Intellectuals* (Hong Kong: Hong Kong University Press, 1960).

Chen, S. H. "Multiplicity in Uniformity: Poetry and the Great Leap Forward," *The China Quarterly* (July–September, 1960).

Chen, Theodore H. E. "The Marxist Remolding of Chinese Society," *American Journal of Sociology* (January, 1953).

Chen, Theodore H. E. *Thought Reform of the Chinese Intellectuals* (Hong Kong: Hong Kong University Press, 1960).

Cheng, J. Chester. *Basic Principles Underlying the Chinese Communist Approach to Education* (Washington, D.C.: U.S. Department of Health, Education, and Welfare, 1961).

Goldman, Merle. "Hu Feng's Conflict with the Communist Literary Authorities," *The China Quarterly* (October–December, 1962).

Houn, Franklin W. *To Change a Nation. Propaganda and Indoctrination in Communist China* (New York: The Free Press of Glencoe, 1961).

Hu, Chang-tu (ed.). *Chinese Education under Communism* (New York: Teachers College, Columbia University, 1962).

Hu, Chang-tu. "Communist Education: Theory and Practice," *The China Quarterly* (April–June, 1962).

Hunter, Edward. *Brainwashing. The Story of Men Who Defied It* (New York: Farrar, Straus and Cudahy, 1956).

Jan, George P. "Mass Education in the Chinese Communes," *Asian Survey* (October, (1964), pp. 499–513.

Kierman, Frank A. *The Chinese Intelligentsia and the Communists* (Cambridge, Mass.: Center for International Studies, Massachusetts Institute of Technology, 1954).

Kun, Joseph C. "Higher Education: Some Problems of Selection and Enrollment," *The China Quarterly* (October–December, 1961).

Lifton, Robert J. "Brainwashing in Perspective: A Psychiatrist Interprets Peking's 'Thought Reform'," *New Republic* (May 13, 1957).

Lifton, Robert J. "Thought Reform of Chinese Intellectuals: A Psychiatric Evaluation," *Journal of Asian Studies* (November, 1956).

Lifton, Robert J. "Thought Reform of Chinese Intellectuals: A Psychiatric Evaluation," *Journal of Social Issues* 13, No. 3 (1957).

Lifton, Robert Jay. *Thought Reform and the Psychology of Totalism. A Study of "Brainwashing" in China* (New York: W. W. Norton, 1961).

Moore, Barrington, Jr. *Political Power and Social Theory* (Cambridge, Mass.: Harvard University Press, 1958).

Mu, Fu-Sheng. *The Wilting of the Hundred Flowers. The Chinese Intelligentsia Under Mao* (New York: Praeger, 1962).

Orleans, Leo A. *Professional Manpower and Education in Communist China* (Washington, D.C.: National Science Foundation, 1960).

Wang, Y. C. "The Intelligentsia in Changing China," *Foreign Affairs* (January, 1958).

Winance, Eleutherius, O. S. B. *The Communist Persuasion. A Personal Experience of Brainwashing* (New York: P. J. Kenedy & Sons, 1959).

Yu, Frederick T. C. *Mass Persuasion in Communist China* (New York: Praeger, 1964).

The Military Organization

Cheng, Chu-yuan. "Progress of Nuclear Weapons in Communist China," *Military Review* (May, 1965), pp. 543–550.

Chiu, S. M. "Political Control in the Chinese Communist Army," *Military Review* (August, 1963).

Grittings, John. "China's Militia," *The China Quarterly* (April–June, 1964).

Grittings, John. "Political Control of the Chinese Army," *World Today* (August, 1963).

Hsieh, Alice Langley. "Communist China and Nuclear Warfare," *The China Quarterly* (April–June, 1960).

Jan, George P. "Red China's Militia," *Military Review* (March, 1965), pp. 535–542.

Joffe, Ellis. "Contradictions in the Chinese Army," *Far Eastern Economic Review* (July 11, 1963).

Joffe, Ellis. *Party and Army: Professionalism and Political Control in the Chinese Officer Corps, 1949–1964* (Cambridge, Mass.: Harvard University, East Asian Research Center, 1965).

Kashin, A. "The Atom and China," *Asian Review* (April, 1962).

Mao Tse-tung. *Selected Military Writings of Mao Tse-tung* (Peking: Foreign Language Press, 1963).

O'Ballance, Edgar. *The Red Army of China: A Short History* (New York: Praeger, 1963).

Powell, Ralph L. "Everyone a Soldier: The Communist Chinese Militia," *Foreign Affairs* (October, 1960).

Powell, Ralph L. "The Military Affairs Committee and Party Control of the Military in China," *Asian Survey* (July, 1963).

The Chinese Family: Past and Present

Chandrasekhar, S. "Mao's War with the Chinese Family," *The New York Times Magazine* (May 17, 1963).

Fried, Morton, H. *Fabric of Chinese Society: A Study of the Social Life of a Chinese County Seat* (New York: Praeger, 1953).

Hsu, Francis L. K. *Under the Ancestors' Shadow: Chinese Culture and Personality* (New York: Columbia University Press, 1948).

Lang, Olga. *Chinese Family and Society* (New Haven: Yale University Press, 1946).

Levy, Marion J. *The Family Revolution in Modern China* (Cambridge, Mass.: Harvard University Press, 1949).

Lin, Yüeh-hua. *The Golden Wing: A Sociological Study of Chinese Familism* (London: Kegan Paul, Trench, Trubner, 1948).

van der Valk, M. H. *Conservatism in Modern Chinese Family Law* (Leiden: Brill, 1956).

The Value System: Past and Present

Levenson, Joseph R. *Confucian China and Its Modern Fate* (Berkeley: University of California Press, 1958).

Levenson, Joseph R. "The Intellectual Revolution in China," *University of Toronto Quarterly*, 30, 3 (1961).

Mivison, David. "Communist Ethics and Chinese Tradition," *Journal of Asian Studies* (November, 1956).

Needham, Joseph. "The Past in China's Present: A Cultural and Social Background for Contemporary China," *Pacific Viewpoint* (September, 1963).

Nivison, David S., and Wright, Arthur F. (eds.). *Confucianism in Action* (Stanford, Stanford University Press, 1959).

North, Robert C. "Soviet and Chinese Goal Values: A Study in Communism as a Behavior System" (in Kurt London (ed.), *Unity and Contradiction: Major Aspects of Sino-Soviet Relations,* Praeger, 1962), pp. 39–64.

Vogel, Ezra F. "From Friendship to Comradeship: The Change in Personal Relations in Communist China" *The China Quarterly* (January–March, 1965).

Wright, Arthur F. (ed.). *The Confucian Persuasion* (Stanford, California: Stanford University Press, 1960).

Wright, Mary C. "Modern China in Transition, 1900–1950," *Annals of the American Academy of Political and Social Science* (January, 1959), pp. 13–22.

China's Foreign Policy

Barnett, A. Doak (ed.). *Communist Strategies in Asia* (New York: Praeger, (1963).

Benz, Ernst. *Buddhism or Communism: Which Holds the Future of Asia?* (New York: Doubleday & Company, Inc., 1965).

Boyd, R. G. *Communist China's Foreign Policy* (New York: Praeger, 1962).

Dutt, Vidya Prakash. *China and the World. An Analysis of Communist China's Foreign Policy* (New York: Praeger, 1966).

Halperin, Morton H. *China and the Bomb* (New York: Praeger, 1965).

Hinton, Harold C. *Communist China in World Politics* (Boston, Mass.: Houghton Mifflin Company, 1966).

Hoeffding, Oleg. "Sino-Soviet Economic Relations in Recent Years" (In Kurt London (ed.), *Unity and Contradiction: Major Aspects of Sino-Soviet Relations,* Praeger, 1962), pp. 295–312.

Sherwani, Latif Ahmed. "Sino-Soviet Aid Programs in Asia" (In Kurt London (ed.), *Unity and Contradiction: Major Aspects of Sino-Soviet Relations,* Praeger, 1962), pp. 316–330.

Index